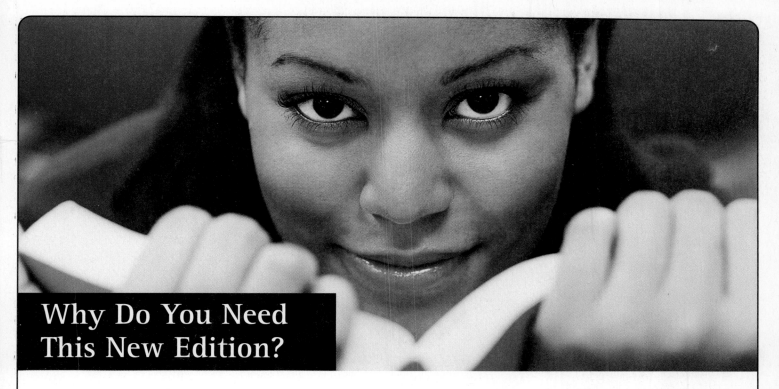

Why Do You Need This New Edition?

If you're wondering why you should buy this new edition of *Breaking Through: College Reading*, here are 5 good reasons!

1 A new feature, "The Reading Workshop," provides numerous tips and strategies to help you think, talk, and write about books and other materials that you read for pleasure.

2 A new reading selection in the casebook, "What Is Beauty?" gets you thinking about concepts of beauty both in the United States and abroad and the steps some people take to achieve what they consider to be ⌐eauty.

3 New readings get you thinking about such areas as how to deal with criminals with mental illness, how cancer has been interpreted and treated from ancient times to today, how diversity is presented in school textbooks and curriculum, and the story behind the red carpet that is used at award ceremonies.

4 New or expanded coverage of previewing textbooks; organizational patterns; main ideas; following directions; and purpose, tone, and critical reading give you even more practice with key reading skills.

5 A new MyReadingLab feature at the end of every chapter sends you to MyReadingLab for additional online practice on key reading skills.

H.S.I. / LEAD

D1456374

PEARSON

Breaking Through

College Reading

NINTH EDITION

Brenda D. Smith

Professor Emerita, Georgia State University

LeeAnn Morris

San Jacinto College

Longman

New York   San Francisco   Boston
London   Toronto   Sydney   Tokyo   Singapore   Madrid
Mexico City   Munich   Paris   Cape Town   Hong Kong   Montreal

To my Mother and in Memory of my Father
—B.D.S.

To my precious family
—L.M.

Acquisitions Editor: Kate Edwards
Development Editor: Janice Wiggins-Clarke
Senior Supplements Editor: Donna Campion
Marketing Manager: Thomas DeMarco
Production Manager: Ellen MacElree
Project Coordination, Text Design, and Electronic Page Makeup: Nesbitt Graphics, Inc.
Cover Design Manager: Wendy Ann Fredericks
Cover Designer: Bernadette Skok
Cover Photo: Corbis/Art Life Images
Photo Researcher: Linda Sykes
Senior Manufacturing Buyer: Dennis J. Para
Printer and Binder: Courier/Kendallville
Cover Printer: Coral Graphics Services Inc.

For permission to use copyrighted material, grateful acknowledgment is made to the copyright holders on pp. 586–587, which are hereby made part of this copyright page.

Library of Congress Cataloging-in-Publication Data

Smith, Brenda D., 1944-
 Breaking through : college reading / Brenda D. Smith, LeeAnn Morris. —
9th ed.
    p. cm.
 Includes bibliographical references and index.
 Includes index.
 ISBN-13: 978-0-205-63933-5 (student ed.)
 ISBN-13: 978-0-205-63964-9 (instructor's ed.)
 ISBN-10: 0-205-63933-X (student ed.)
 ISBN-10: 0-205-63964-X (instructor's ed.)
 1. Reading (Higher education) 2. Study skills. I. Morris, LeeAnn. II.
Title.
 LB2395.3.S62 2009
 428.4071'1—dc22

2008053492

Copyright © 2010 by Pearson Education, Inc.

Longman
is an imprint of

ISBN 13: 978-0-205-63933-5; ISBN 10: 0-205-63933-X (Student Edition)
ISBN 13: 978-0-205-63964-9; ISBN 10: 0-205-63964-X (Instructor's Edition)

www.pearsonhighered.com   1 2 3 4 5 6 7 8 9 10–CRK–12 11 10 09

Contents

Chapter 8   Efficient Reading 359

Preface

The Goals and New Features of the Ninth Edition

The ninth edition of *Breaking Through* is designed to continue and further develop the focus of previous editions—guiding students to be independent readers who can understand, digest, and retain the material in freshmen college texts. Further goals are to motivate and equip students to achieve their academic and career goals and to build and use background knowledge. The methods used in the text emphasize strategic learning in both individual and collaborative settings. The ninth edition offers instruction in effective reading techniques; extensive practice; interesting independent, partner, and group activities; and engaging reading selections from a variety of academic disciplines—all of which stimulate interaction with the text.

This edition of *Breaking Through* presents several new features. **The Reading Workshop** encourages students to read for pleasure. This feature is designed as a flexible tool that professors may use in conjunction with a book read in common by the whole class, a few books read in common by groups of students, or with individual, self-selected books. The workshop activities make use of the powerful connection between reading and writing by prompting students to think and write about their pleasure reading in a **Reading Workshop Journal**. Additional writing suggestions appear in Appendix 5. The underlying purposes of the Reading Workshop are to develop background knowledge, fluency, enjoyment, and, ultimately, lifelong readers.

The **beauty casebook has been refreshed with a new reading selection** that illustrates concepts of beauty outside the United States. The casebook fosters a more in-depth exploration of the question "What is beauty?" Students begin the casebook by responding to an inventory that assesses their current beliefs about the topic. They go on to read material from three different perspectives in diverse academic sources to expand their thinking on the topic of beauty. The casebook ends with a second inventory that causes students to reflect on how their views may have grown or changed.

In addition, the ninth edition contains **four new, longer reading selections** that represent a broad spectrum of academic disciplines. There is also new or expanded coverage of previewing textbooks (Chapter 1); main ideas (Chapter 4); organizational patterns (Chapter 5); following directions (Chapter 5); and purpose, tone, and critical reading (Chapter 11).

Also new in the **Instructor's Edition** of *Breaking Through* is the addition of **grade-level equivalencies (GLEs) for the longer reading selections**. The GLEs appear in the Instructor's Edition within the Table of Contents and also at the beginning of each longer reading selection. This feature is intended as another tool to assist instructors in matching readings with students' skill levels. While GLEs are based on style features, such as sentence and word length, the elements of readers' interest, background knowledge, and the depth of the concepts in the readings are also very important comprehension factors. GLEs were determined using the Raygor Readability Estimate.

The **MyReadingLab** icon at the end of Chapters 1 through 11 alerts students to the online material at the MyReadingLab Web site. Brief notes direct students to the area of the site, particularly in the Reading Skills section, that offers skill practice related to the topic of that chapter. The Web site offers extensive skill development activities in reading, vocabulary, and study skills, as well as useful research tools.

Organization of the Text

The ninth edition of *Breaking Through* opens with a chapter on motivation, attitude, and action. Success starts with a vision and is built on determination, perseverance, and activity. Chapter 1 also offers a collection of student success strategies, including previewing a textbook. Chapter 2 moves to theories of reading and the strategies used by successful readers. To control the process, readers must understand it. Reading is thinking and interacting with the printed page in three stages: before, during, and after the process. Chapter 3 is devoted to vocabulary. It introduces context clues, word parts, analogies, and the use of the dictionary, thesaurus, and glossaries. Explanations and exercises are included.

Understanding the main idea—the most important reading comprehension skill—begins with models and practice exercises in Chapter 4 and extends into Chapter 5 with attention to supporting details, organizational patterns, and the beginning stages of notetaking. Chapter 6 explains annotating, notetaking, outlining, and mapping.

Chapter 7 offers advice on multiple-choice and true-false test-taking, as well as essay responses. Heightened awareness and insight into expectations can give students a winning edge and help improve test scores. The efficient reading discussion in Chapter 8 presents techniques for rate improvement and provides exercises to assess student reading rates.

Chapter 9 recognizes college students as analytical reasoners and problem solvers, with exercises provided to help students develop and refine analytical reasoning skills. Chapter 10, on implied meaning, and Chapter 11, on critical reading, focus on unstated attitudes and assumptions. These chapters are designed to help students become more aware of suggested meaning and to be more critical of what they read. Success in college depends on being able to transfer reading skills to daily textbook assignments.

The reading casebook, entitled "What Is Beauty?" follows a different organizational plan. It contains three readings but fewer questions than other, longer reading selections. The focus of the casebook is on reading on a single topic for personal discovery and growth. The casebook follows Chapter 5.

Book-Specific Ancillary Materials

For Instructors

Annotated Instructor's Edition (AIE) (0-205-63964-X)
An exact replica of the student text, with answers provided on the write-in lines in the text.

Instructor's Manual (0-205-63965-8)
Offers teaching tips, sample syllabi, and other teaching resources.

Printed Test Bank for *Breaking Through*, Ninth Edition (0-205-63966-6)
Offers a series of skill and reading quizzes for each chapter; formatted for ease of copying and distribution.

The Pearson Developmental English Package

Pearson is pleased to offer a variety of support materials to help make teaching reading easier on teachers and to help students excel in their coursework. Many of our student supplements are available at no additional cost or at a greatly reduced price when packaged with *Breaking Through: College Reading,* Ninth Edition. Contact your local Pearson sales representative for more information on pricing and how to create a package.

Acknowledgments

We would like to thank our acquisitions editor, Kate Edwards, for her unflinching support. Our development editor, Janice Wiggins-Clarke, has been organized, and attentive; we appreciate her hard work and incisive decisions. She has worked tirelessly to produce a quality ninth edition. Finally, we would like to acknowledge the reviewers of the ninth edition and their contributions:

Jane Anderson
Northland Community and Technical College

Diana Lerma
Palo Alto College

Angela Blakenship
Arkansas Northeastern College

Jerolynn Roberson
Miami Dade College

Acquanetta Bracy
Alabama State University

Margaret Shaw
Nassau Community College

Gretchen Crupp
Yuba College

Marjorie Sussman
Miami Dade College

Patricia Davis
Houston Community College, Southwest

Michael Taylor
Orange Coast College

Lisa Hoonan-Trujillo
Green River Community College

Brenda D. Smith
LeeAnn Morris

1 Student Success

- Are you a winner?
- Do you think about what you *can* do or what you *cannot*?
- Do you set high standards?
- Do you plan for success?
- How can you manage time efficiently?
- What are the behaviors of success?
- How can fellow students be learning resources?
- What student responsibilities determine success in college?

Everyday Reading Skills: Searching the Internet

Think Success

Are you mentally ready to go to college? Do you have a desire to achieve? Have you set goals for yourself, and are you ready to plan for achieving those goals? College life and college work are fun, but they require extra effort. Begin by cultivating an attitude for success.

Most of this book focuses on strategies for reading college texts. Before you concentrate on the books, however, take a look at yourself and your dreams. You are now shaping your future. To become a winner and reap the rewards, you must first think like a winner. Studies show that not only do college graduates enjoy more social and self-esteem benefits, but they also earn more than those with only high school diplomas. In 2006 the median annual income for full-time year-round workers with bachelor's degrees was $60,910 for men and $45,410 for women; the income for workers with only high school degrees was $37,030 and $26,740 respectively.[1]

This chapter will help you shape your thinking and behaviors by presenting the thoughts and describing the actions of successful people. Working on yourself can be as important as working on the books.

Set Goals

Entering college is a major turning point in life. College offers freedom, variety, and increased responsibility. Success in college requires a commitment of time, money, and energy. College is an investment in the future that requires a sacrifice in the present.

Build a team of caring people to support you as you go after your goals. Begin with your instructor. Respond thoughtfully to the Personal Feedback sections that appear throughout this text and hand them in to your instructor. Share your dreams, enthusiasm, and anxieties in order to build a learning partnership and strengthen your determination. This partnership will be only as strong as each of you allows it to be. Your instructor is not a mind reader, so reveal who you really are. Move beyond the academic and respond to questions regarding your habits, responsibilities, joys, and stresses. Your instructor wants to know you as a person and wants to help you be successful.

For the first Personal Feedback section, think about your feelings as you begin your college career, and then respond to the questions.

Create a Positive Attitude

Your dreams are your goals. Hold them in a corner of your mind as you go through college. You might even write them on a banner over your desk or on the cover of a notebook. On rough days, think of the dreams and picture the excitement of achieving your goals. Imagine your graduation celebration and think about those who will join in the fun. Allow your dreams to renew your enthusiasm and keep you focused on your goals. Let motivation overshadow your anxieties. Program your mind to think of success. Don't worry about why something *cannot* be done. Instead, think about how it *can* be accomplished. What you think of yourself determines what you will become.

Seek Excellence

All of us would like to do well. Some people, however, set higher goals and eventually achieve more than others. What explains the difference? In his book *CEO*

---

[1]National Center for Education Statistics, U.S. Department of Education Institute of Education Sciences. *Digest of Education Statistics, 2007*, Table 371. http://nces.ed.gov/programs/digest/d07/tables/dt07_371.asp

Personal *Feedback* **1**   Name _____

1. What three dreams and/or influences motivated you to come to college?

   (a) _____

   (b) _____

   (c) _____

2. In five years what do you hope to be doing both professionally and personally?

   (a) Professionally: _____

   _____

   (b) Personally: _____

   _____

3. Explain three anxieties that you have as you begin college.

   (a) _____

   (b) _____

   (c) _____

   Tear out and submit to your instructor.

of Self: You're in Charge!, Herman Cain suggests that having a dream is one of the first steps to achieving success.

Reading 1

SUCCESS STARTS SOMEWHERE

Born into a hardworking Georgia family, Herman Cain was encouraged to receive a college education by his parents. With their support Cain became an accomplished businessman, speaker, and writer. By empowering and nurturing the employees of a floundering company, Godfather's Pizza, Cain was able to recreate its vision of success. In fact, Cain made a career of inspiring others to pursue excellence in their own lives.

I have felt in charge of my life since I was sixteen years old. I did not call myself CEO of SELF then, but that was how I felt, because it was then that I set for myself my first major goal in life—earning $20,000 a year in salary. I did not know how or when I would achieve such a goal, but that became my dream. I had heard or read somewhere that you needed an annual income of ten thousand dollars a year to qualify for an American Express charge card. I did not want to just qualify, I wanted to more than qualify. And I thought $20,000 a year in income would provide a very comfortable lifestyle, one where I would not have to work three jobs like my Dad to live comfortably.

I can still remember driving home from my part-time job working in my father's small neighborhood grocery store when I got what then seemed like this very wild idea of earning $20,000 a year. At the time I formulated this extremely bold dream, I also had no idea what profession I wanted to pursue, because there was not a lot of talk in our house about what we should be when we grew up. We did talk about being able to get a good job to make a lot of money, and $20,000 was a whole lot of money to a sixteen-year-old in 1961.

Both Mom and Dad encouraged my brother and me to go to school and to get a good education, because the more education we got, they told us, the better the job. Both Mom and Dad were able to get only a limited amount of formal education when they were growing up. Mom had gotten through the eighth grade before she left her father's small farm in Georgia, and Dad made it through a small town high school in Tennessee.

Our high school teachers stressed getting a good education if we wanted to be successful, and they also encouraged us to pursue college and a professional career. At the time, the whole idea of going to college and becoming a professional "anything" seemed so unachievable, since no one in my family had ever gone beyond high school, and since segregation and discrimination "red lights" were still legal. How could I believe I could become an engineer or corporate vice president?

Charles S. Johnson was my homeroom teacher and mathematics teacher for all five years of high school. He encouraged me to go to college and to major in mathematics, and he told me that I could decide later what profession I might pursue. Mr. Johnson also told me that I could be whatever I wanted to be, but that I might have to *work a little harder, and work a little longer,* to get there. My high school band teacher, Mr. Lloyd Terry, also constantly encouraged me—as well as the others in the band—to be the best because we had the ability to be the best. He wasn't just referring to our instrument playing, but to all of our aspirations.

Mr. Johnson, Mr. Terry, and my dad also suggested that college would help me make a lot of money, so college was definitely part of my game plan, and Dad and Mr. Johnson and Mr. Terry were definitely influential members of my board of SELF, Inc.

I applied to, and was accepted by, several historically black colleges, and was even offered scholarships to most of them, because of my rank as salutatorian of my graduating class (second highest grades). I certainly was not offered the scholarships based on my standardized test scores, because they were consistently mediocre, as were the scores of most of my classmates.

In my case, I believe this was mostly due to poor reading habits while growing up. My parents never read to us as children, and they never insisted that we read books outside of schoolwork, so my reading skills at the time always lagged behind where they should have been ("speed bump"). Fortunately, when I entered Morehouse College, I was required to take a semester-long reading course to get my reading skills closer to where a college freshman's should be. Fifty percent of the entering freshmen had to take this course, which definitely helped. Yet, I believe I didn't really catch up to my reading level even then, which is why I struggled in all my college courses except for math and science.

Morehouse awarded me a first-year tuition scholarship, which could be renewed if I maintained a B average or better in my classes. The scholarship was not renewed at the end of my freshman year, which was another little "speed bump" I had to deal with. Although I was disappointed, I never felt defeated because I knew I had worked as hard as I could. But to help pay the tuition from then on, I worked various part-time jobs, during school and during summers, and Mom and Dad helped with the rest.

At the time I began college, I was not familiar with Morehouse's reputation as a great institution of higher learning, nor had I ever heard of Dr. Benjamin E. Mays, its president. For every young man who attended Morehouse, he was a demanding educator, an inspiring leader, and an even more inspiring member of their personal boards of directors. Consider his charge to us: "There is an air of expectancy at Morehouse College. It is expected that the student who enters here will do well. It is also expected that once a man bears the insignia of a Morehouse graduate, he will do exceptionally well. We expect nothing less."

My high school teacher, Mr. Johnson, was a Morehouse graduate, as was Willie Harding, a friend at church. Both of them had encouraged me to go to "The House," as it was affectionately called by people who knew of its reputation.

My decision to attend Morehouse was one of the best decisions I ever made, not just because of the great education I received there, but also because of the great inspiration it provided me from three different sources: the fact that it was all male and all black, the fact that so many of its graduates had done so many great things following graduation, and the fact that its president was Dr. Mays. He not only had high expectations of his graduates but he instilled in me and many others one of the larger truths I've followed throughout my life: *"It's not a calamity to die with dreams unfulfilled, but it is a calamity to have no dreams."*

Later in my life, I would learn that this is, and should be, the mantra for the true CEO of SELF.

Before deciding to attend Morehouse, I had also applied to the University of Georgia (UGA) and Georgia Institute of Technology (Georgia Tech), both of which denied me admission. In 1963, when I graduated from high school and started college, these two state-funded institutions had been desegregated for only two years. The number of black students they admitted was still being kept to a minimum. Although I am not sure if I would have attended either school had I been admitted, I would have liked having that choice.

Poor reading skills, an inability to keep my scholarship in college, and the disadvantages of discrimination created a bumpy start for this future CEO, but they were not enough to defeat my determination and perseverance. I could have chosen to drop out of college when I lost my scholarship, and I could have chosen to use discrimination as an excuse to settle for the first job that came my way.

As CEO of SELF, I chose to graduate from Morehouse College, which gave me the opportunity to choose from twenty-five great job offers. I chose to stay focused on my dream.

—From *CEO of Self: You're in Charge!* by Herman Cain

exercise 1

Think and Write. Answer the following questions.

1. Explain what is meant by the sentence "It's not a calamity to die with dreams unfulfilled, but it is a calamity to have no dreams." _____

_____

_____

2. What do you see as the intended meaning when Cain refers to himself as the "CEO of SELF"? _____

_____

_____

Plan for Success

A business maxim known as Parkinson's Law states that work expands to fill the time available for its completion. Have you ever had all Saturday to finish an assignment and found that it did in fact take all day, whereas if you had planned to finish it in four hours, you probably could have done so?

Personal *Feedback* **2**   **Name** _____

1. Identify three people on your personal support team.

   (a) _____

   (b) _____

   (c) _____

2. Define the word *mentor*. Describe one of your mentors.

   Mentor: _____

   Who? _____

3. What are three things you want to learn from this reading course?

   (a) _____

   (b) _____

   (c) _____

4. What grade do you realistically seek in this course?

   Grade: _____

   Explain: _____

5. List four responsibilities you have as a college student who wants to be a high achiever with excellent grades.

   (a) _____

   (b) _____

   (c) _____

   (d) _____

6. Name one of your high school teachers whom you thought was an excellent instructor.

   _____

7. What do you expect from a college instructor? List four responsibilities of a good instructor.

   (a) _____

   (b) _____

   (c) _____

   (d) _____

Tear out and submit to your instructor.

Time is limited, and everyone has only twenty-four hours in a day, even the president of the United States. Does the president get more done than you do? The key to success is to plan and use the minutes and hours wisely. Establish a routine and stick to it. Plan for both work and play.

Reading 2
MAKING THE MOST OF PRIORITIES

Alan Lakein, the Harvard graduate who invented time management consulting, works with businesspeople all over the country. His book, How to Get Control of Your Time and Your Life, *has sold over 3 million copies and is used as a textbook in business courses. He offers the following daily method of planning for achievement.*

The main secret of getting more done every day took me several months of research to discover. When I first started delving into better time use, I asked successful people what the secret of their success was. I recall an early discussion with a vice-president of Standard Oil Company of California who said, "Oh, I just keep a To Do List." I passed over that quickly, little suspecting at the time the importance of what he said. I happened to travel the next day to a large city to give a time management seminar. While I was there I had lunch with a businessman who practically owned the town. He was chairman of the gas and light company, president of five manufacturing companies, and had his hand in a dozen other enterprises. By all standards he was a business success. I asked him the same question of how he managed to get more done and he said, "Oh, that's easy—I keep a To Do List."

ONLY A DAILY LIST WILL DO

People at the top and people at the bottom both know about To Do Lists, but one difference between them is that the people at the top use a To Do List every single day to make better use of their time; people at the bottom know about this tool but don't use it effectively. One of the real secrets of getting more done is to make a To Do List every day, keep it visible, and use it as a guide to action as you go through the day.

Because the To Do List is such a fundamental time-planning tool, let's take a closer look at it. The basics of the list itself are simple: Head a piece of paper "To Do," then list those items on which you want to work; cross off items as they are completed and add others as they occur to you; rewrite the list at the end of the day or when it becomes hard to read.

Some people try to keep To Do Lists in their heads, but in my experience this is rarely as effective. Why clutter your mind with things that can be written down? It's much better to leave your mind free for creative pursuits.

WHAT BELONGS ON THE LIST

Are you going to write down everything you have to do, including routine activities? Are you only going to write down exceptional events? Are you going to put down everything you *might* do today or only whatever you decided you *will* do today? There are many alternatives, and different people have different solutions. I recommend that you do not list routine items but do list everything that has high priority today and might not get done without special attention.

Don't forget to put the A-activities for your long-term goals on your To Do List. Although it may appear strange to see "begin learning French" or "find new friends" in the same list with "bring home a quart of milk" or "buy birthday card," you want to do them in the same day. If you use your To Do List as a guide when deciding what to work on next, then you need the long-term projects represented, too, so you won't forget them at decision time and consequently not do them.

Depending on your responsibilities, you might, if you try hard enough, get all the items on your To Do List completed by the end of each day. If so, by all means try. But probably you can predict in advance that there is no way to do them all. When there are too many things to do, conscious choice as to what (and what not) to do is better than letting the decision be determined by chance.

I cannot emphasize strongly enough: You must *set priorities*. Some people do as many items as possible on their lists. They get a very high percentage of tasks done, but their effectiveness is low because the tasks they've done are mostly of C-priority. Others like to start at the top of the list and go right down it, again with little regard to what's important. The best way is to take your list and label each item according to ABC priority, delegate as much as you can, and then polish off the list accordingly.

—How to Get Control of Your Time and Your Life
by Alan Lakein

exercise 2 Answer the following questions and make a To Do List.

1. What does the author believe is the difference between the To Do Lists of people at the top and those of people at the bottom? _____
_____
_____

2. Prior to reading this passage, what method have you used to keep up with things you need to remember to do? _____
_____

3. What kinds of things does the author say belong on a To Do List? _____
_____

4. How can you indicate levels of priority on your To Do List? _____
_____

5. Why do you think a student would feel that it is not necessary to keep a daily To Do List? _____
_____

6. Make your own To Do List today. In the left margin, indicate priorities with an A, B, or C. Keep your list in a notepad, your assignment book, or a PDA (personal digital assistant), so that it is always handy. Remember to cross off each item as you complete it.

Example
A	(1)	Pay rent
B	(2)	Change oil in car
A	(3)	Call Maria
C	(4)	Buy dictionary
B	(5)	Get breakfast foods

To Do List

_____ (1) _____

_____ (2) _____

_____ (3) _____

_____ (4) _____

_____ (5) _____

_____ (6) _____

_____ (7) _____

Think and Write

What did Ben Franklin mean by "Employ thy time well if thou meanest to gain leisure"?

_____

_____

Plan Your Week

Organize yourself every week. Project your schedule for next week and put it on the following time chart. Be specific about each item and note what you anticipate studying when listing a study time. Be realistic about your activities and plan recreation and work time.

The majority of your activities will remain routine. For example, your class hours are probably the same each week. Put them on the chart first. If you have a job, plug in your work hours. If you work while attending college, you will have even fewer minutes to waste, and thus you must become a superefficient time manager. Put in your mealtimes and your bedtime. If you can't live without a favorite television show, plug that in as well. Be honest with yourself and never pretend that you are going to be studying and then not live up to your expectations.

Lay out your life the way you would like to live it for the week, then stick to the plan. At the beginning of each week, adjust your plan for any changes that you foresee. Use your weekly schedule as a goal.

Reader's _Tip_ Time Savers

Using time wisely becomes a habit. Analyze your current activities according to the following principles of time management to gain greater control of yourself and your environment.

1. Plan. Keep an appointment book by the day and hour. Write a daily To Do List. Use a notepad or a PDA (personal digital assistant).
2. Start with the most critical activity of the day and work your way down to the least important one.
3. Ask yourself, "What is the best use of my time right now?"
4. Don't do what doesn't need doing.
5. Concentrate completely on one thing at a time.
6. Block out big chunks of time for large projects.
7. Make use of five-, ten-, and fifteen-minute segments of time.
8. Keep phone calls short or avoid them.
9. Listen well for clear instructions.
10. Learn to say No! to yourself and others.
11. Limit your online, TV, video game, and text messaging time.
12. Strive for excellence, but realize that perfection may not be worth the cost.

WEEKLY TIME CHART

Time	Sunday	Monday	Tuesday	Wednesday	Thursday	Friday	Saturday
8–9							
9–10							
10–11							
11–12							
12–1							
1–2							
2–3							
3–4							
4–5							
5–6							
6–7							
7–8							
8–9							
9–10							
10–11							
11–12							

Tear out and submit to your instructor.

Study the Syllabus

On the first day of class almost every professor distributes a syllabus that outlines the goals, objectives, and assignments for the entire course. The syllabus includes examination dates and an explanation of the grading system. Depending on the professor, the syllabus may be a general overview or a more detailed schedule of each class session. Keep your syllabus for quick reference; it is your guide to the professor's plan for your learning. Sophisticated students do not use class time to ask questions about test dates or details that they could find by looking at the syllabus.

exercise 3   Review the following history syllabus and answer the questions.

United States History Syllabus

Class: 9–10 daily   10-Week Quarter: 1/4–3/12
Dr. J. A. Johnson   Office Hrs.: 10–12 daily
Office: 422G   Phone: 562-3367
                             E-mail: jaj@gsu.edu

Required Texts
(1) *A People and a Nation* by Norton et al.
(2) One paperback book on immigration selected from the list for a report.

Course Content
This course is a survey of United States history from the early explorations to the present. The purpose is to give you an understanding of the major forces and events that have interacted to make modern America.

Method of Training
Thematic lectures will be presented in class. You are expected to read and master the factual material in the text as well as take careful notes in class. Tests will cover both class lectures and textbook readings.

Grading
Grades will be determined in the following manner:

> Tests (3 tests at 20% each)
> Final Exam (20%)
> Written Report (20%)

Each test will include multiple-choice and identification items and two essay questions.

Important Dates
> Test 1: 1/22   Final Exam: 3/18
> Test 2: 2/11   Written Report: 3/10
> Test 3: 3/3   Makeup Test (with permission): 3/16

Written Report
Your written report on immigration should answer one of the three designated questions and reflect your reading of a book from the list. Each book is approximately 200 pages long. Your report should be at least six typed pages. More information to follow.

Assignments

Week 1: Ch. 1 (pp. 1–27), Ch. 2 (pp. 28–49), Ch. 3 (pp. 50–68)
Week 2: Ch. 4 (pp. 69–86), Ch. 5 (pp. 87–103), Ch. 6 (pp. 104–122)
Week 3: Ch. 7 (pp. 123–139), Ch. 8 (pp. 140–159), Ch. 9 (pp. 160–176), Ch. 10 (pp. 177–194)

Test 1: Chaps. 1–10

Week 4: Ch. 11 (pp. 195–216), Ch. 12 (pp. 217–236), Ch. 13 (pp. 237–253)
Week 5: Ch. 14 (pp. 254–272), Ch. 15 (pp. 273–288), Ch. 16 (pp. 289–304), Ch. 17 (pp. 305–320)
Week 6: Ch. 18 (pp. 321–344), Ch. 19 (pp. 345–358), Ch. 20 (pp. 359–375)

Test 2: Chaps. 11–20

Week 7: Ch. 21 (pp. 376–391), Ch. 22 (pp. 392–410), Ch. 23 (pp. 411–428)
Week 8: Ch. 24 (pp. 429–450), Ch. 25 (pp. 451–466), Ch. 26 (pp. 467–484), Ch. 27 (pp. 486–504)
Week 9: Ch. 28 (pp. 505–520), Ch. 29 (pp. 521–533), Ch. 30 (pp. 534–553)

Test 3: Chaps. 21–28

Week 10: Ch. 31 (pp. 554–569), Ch. 32 (pp. 570–586), Ch. 33 (pp. 587–599)

Final Exam: Chaps. 1–33

1. What is the stated purpose of this history course? _____

_____

_____

2. How will your grade be determined? _____

_____

3. How many pages do you have to read during the first week? _____ Second
week? _____ Third week? _____

4. On average, how many pages should you read each day for the first week?

_____

5. Will you have any pop quizzes? _____

6. Does the final exam count more than the individual tests? _____

_____

7. What questions might you ask about the tests? _____

_____

8. Do you have questions that are not answered by this syllabus?

_____

9. Have you saved your professor's and two classmates' numbers in your cell
phone? _____

Reader's *Tip* Making a Learning Schedule

Use your assignment calendar to devise a learning schedule. Mark important dates for this class.

- Enter all test dates and due dates for papers and projects.
- Divide large textbook reading assignments into manageable units and record as daily and weekly goals. Leave several days for study and review before tests.
- Record dates for completing extra library and Internet readings.
- Analyze assigned projects and create daily or weekly goals. Record start dates and interim small-step goals.
- Designate dates for completing the first draft of written reports.
- Use your calendar of expected achievements to stay on schedule in each of your classes.

Use a Calendar to Decode a Syllabus

Students who just glance at the course syllabus might think there is no immediate assignment because the first test is four weeks away. Wrong! These students will find themselves falling behind by the second class session because of their "slow start" or "no start" strategy. Avoid this pitfall. As soon as the course begins, use your calendar along with the syllabus to divide your work according to the days and weeks of the course.

Be cautious of unlimited freedom; it could become the freedom to fail. Some professors make short-term goal setting entirely the student's responsibility. For example, some courses have only a midterm and a final. Period. No interim goals are provided. Thus students must take control and design their own detailed learning plans.

Act Successful

Brenda Smith

Successful people share certain observable characteristics. Study those characteristics and adopt the accompanying successful behaviors. Watching other students reveals behaviors that lead to success—or failure.

College Professor "Takes" American History

In order to prepare for a course to assist students in learning history, I "took" American History 113. I put the word *took* in quotation marks because I skipped the hard part; I did not study or take the exams. I did, however, attend class, take notes, observe, and learn.

Since the university operated on the quarter system at that time, classes met for ten weeks with an extra week for exams. My particular class met on Tuesdays and Thursdays from 10:50 to 1:05, which meant the class lasted for two hours and fifteen minutes. I attended all but one class.

I had an excellent professor who seemed concerned that students learn and make good grades. In fact, after the first class, I would have been astonished if any student could fail. To my amazement, the professor distributed a list of ten questions from which he would choose the two essay questions on the first exam. After talking with students in other classes, I learned that this was not unusual; many professors distributed lists of possible exam questions.

Personal *Feedback* 3

Name _____

1. When did you receive the syllabus for this reading course? Where is it now?
   _____

2. When is your next test, and how much does it count toward your final grade?
   _____

3. What material does your next major exam cover? Will the questions be multiple choice or essay?
   _____
   _____

4. Is there a penalty for turning work in late?
   _____

5. What is the purpose of this course?
   _____

6. What questions do you have about how your final grade will be determined?
   _____
   _____

7. What questions do you have about the syllabus or the course?
   _____
   _____

Tear out and submit to your instructor.

As the course progressed, I noticed that some students were their own worst enemies. I could see opportunities for learning that students were ignoring. I began taking notes on student behaviors, as well as my regular notes on the history lectures. From my observations of the entire course, I formed opinions about why some students make A's and others barely pass or even fail. For example, I observed that many students skipped class or came late; some took very sketchy lecture notes; students rarely talked to each other; and many students did not seem to have grasped clearly defined expectations. Although my observations were made only in a history course, after talking to other students and professors, I believe that the behaviors necessary for success apply to most college courses. I wanted to say to some individuals, "You are shooting yourself in the foot." Some of the suggestions outlined below are simple and obvious, yet many students ignored them.

Attend Class

"I missed the last class. Did we do anything?" Does this sound familiar? Although the class lasted almost two and a half hours and covered too much to repeat, some students seem unconvinced that an absence puts them at a disadvantage. In my history class, the professor used the exam questions as a guide in organizing his lectures. I was astounded at how many students skipped classes. Even though 40 students were registered for the course, no more than 33 ever showed up at any one session. At the session following the midterm exam, only 17 students were present. I asked myself, "Why would a student pay for a course, yet not take advantage of the instruction?" Professors cannot teach students who are not there.

Assume some of the responsibility for your class sessions. If your interest is not sufficiently stimulated, move beyond blaming it all on the professor. Ask questions and participate in class discussions. Arrive prepared so class sessions will be more meaningful. Talk with other students. Suggest ideas to the professor. Every class period can be significant if you, the professor, and other class members participate in making it meaningful.

Be on Time for Class

Be in your seat for the "business announcements." Professors usually begin with important reminders about test questions, assignments, or papers, and then give an overview of what will be discussed in class that day. If you come late, you arrive for the details and miss the "big picture." You put yourself at a disadvantage and must scramble to catch up. In my history class, sometimes as many as seven students arrived late, strolling into class with sodas and snacks, suggesting they did not make a prompt arrival their first priority.

Be Aware of Essential Class Sessions

Class sessions vary from vital to crucial. Always strive for a solid beginning, a "fast start" rather than a shaky one. At the first class meeting students usually ask questions to clarify the syllabus, and the professor responds with important, unwritten details that can help you improve your grades. For example, does your history professor expect you to memorize dates, to understand the causes and effects of social change, or to critique historical interpretations? Goals such as these will be explained on the first day.

Students who do not attend the last class before an exam put themselves at an extreme disadvantage. By this time, the professor has usually written the exam and feels pressured to cover anything that he or she will ask on the test that has not been previously discussed in class. Student questions usually prompt a brief but extremely helpful review, pinpointing essential areas of study. Hearing the professor comment, "That's not really important," helps you eliminate study areas and save time. In addition, be sure you have studied enough before this session so that you know which things you need to clarify.

Never miss an exam unless you are on your death bed! The exam makeup may be in a noisy study area or scheduled two weeks later. This could mean you receive academic feedback too late to use it to improve. "Makeup" is just what the word implies, trying to move from behind to regain a position. Unfortunately, I observed that some students did not start studying or take the course seriously until after the first exam. Be sure to be in class when exams are returned. Listen to the professor's description of a good answer. Learn from the professor's responses to other students. Find out what you did right, what you did wrong, and exactly what is expected. Also, find out who made the best grades and ask those students how they studied. The exam and subsequent discussions help you understand expectations and set your future learning goals.

Be Equipped for Success

Be prepared, organized, and ready to learn. Some students arrive on the first day of class without paper and end up writing lecture notes on the back of the syllabus. Every college student should always have at hand the equipment listed in Exercise 4.

exercise 4

Put a check mark next to each item of equipment that you have with you.

_____ Assignment calendar with large daily spaces *or* personal digital assistant

_____ Three-ring binder for organizing papers

_____ Spiral notebook or laptop for lecture notes

_____ Three-ring hole punch for putting handouts in binder

_____ Notebook paper

_____ Notebook dividers (at least five) or flags for organizing by topic

_____ Some sort of container in which to keep the following:

_____ pencil _____ regular pen

_____ erasable pen _____ highlighter

_____ correction fluid or tape _____ small pencil sharpener

_____ small stapler _____ small "Post-it" notes

_____ small paper clips

Preview Your Textbook

Understand how your textbook is organized so you can use it to your best advantage. Quickly flip through the book to absorb some of its features. Do you see pictures, graphs, text boxes, exercises or other special features? Now glance at the title page. Who is the author, and what are the author's credentials? Examine the table of contents. Do you see any features that are repeated in most or all chapters? Get an idea of the topics that are covered. Look at the end of the table of contents. Are there special sections that may be of use to you? Is there an answer key? An index? A glossary? Do this with every textbook you have.

exercise 5

Read the table of contents of this text and glance through the chapters. Notice the format of the chapters and selectively scan the subheadings. Preview the text to answer the following questions:

1. How many major chapters are in this book? _____

2. Other than the obvious differences of topics covered, how does the organizational format of Chapter 3 differ from the format of Chapter 4?

   _____

   _____

   _____

3. What is My Reading Lab? _____

   _____

4. What is the Reading Workshop? _____

_____

5. What is the purpose of Summary Points? _____

_____

6. In which chapter would you find information on drawing conclusions?

_____

7. In Chapter 4, Main Idea, what other words are sometimes used to mean the same as *main idea*? _____

_____

8. Name five college subjects represented in the longer selections at the end of the chapters. _____

9. In which chapter would you learn more about patterns of organization?

_____

10. What is the purpose of Appendix 1? _____

_____

11. In which chapter would you find hints on time management? _____

Mark Your Text

Get the most from your books and use them as learning tools. Read your textbooks with a pen or highlighter in hand and mark information that you will most likely need to know later. A well-marked textbook is a treasure that you may want to keep as a reference for later courses.

Don't miss an opportunity to learn by being reluctant to mark in your text. Marking your text actively involves you in reading and studying. The small amount of money that you receive in a textbook resale may not be worth what you have lost in active involvement. Some books, such as this one, are workbooks. Use this book to practice, to give and get feedback, and to keep a record of your progress.

Communicate with Your Instructor

Don't be an anonymous student. Let your professor know who you are. Get your money's worth and more. Make a special effort to speak to your professor about assignments you found interesting or something you did not understand. Overcome your fear and seek help when you need it. Contrary to popular opinion, good students are more likely to seek help than weak ones. Visit during office hours, call, or send an e-mail when you have a question or concern. Professors want their students to be successful.

Review Your Lecture Notes

Review your lecture notes within twenty-four hours after each class session. Recite to yourself what the professor said. Identify gaps of knowledge and seek clarification. This kind of review reinforces your learning and reminds you of what the professor thinks is important. Unfortunately, most students wait until test time to review notes, thus missing these easy opportunities to solidify learning. Your notebook is a valuable resource; use it.

Network with Other Students

Use the other students in the classroom as learning resources. For the first four weeks of my history class, almost none of the students spoke to each other. I was amazed. Even when I arrived five or ten minutes early to observe behavior, no one spoke. Most stared straight ahead, some read the history text, and some read the newspaper. After the first exam, however, students started to compare scores and to talk about correct answers.

Put fellow students on your learning team. Research shows that students who are part of a study group are less likely to drop out of school. Study groups teach students to collaborate and to form academic bonds. Networking is important for all students, including older, returning students who may initially feel out of the mainstream.

Begin your team building on the first day of class. In each course, ask for the name, telephone number, and e-mail address of at least two other students. Write this information in your text or lecture notebook so you won't lose it. Better yet, enter it into your cell phone right away. These names and numbers are insurance policies. If you are absent or unclear about an assignment, call a classmate for clarification, homework, and lecture notes. Students *can* help other students. Begin your network right now with two people. Don't be bashful.

Classmate _____ Phone _____ E-mail _____

Classmate _____ Phone _____ E-mail _____

Collaborate to Divide Work

Find a "study buddy" to share the work. In my history class, only two essay questions would be chosen for the exam from the list of ten distributed on the first day. The professor expected answers to include information from the lectures as well as details from the history text. To be thoroughly prepared for the exam, each student should have a written study outline answering each of the ten questions. Such an assignment presents an obvious opportunity to cut work in half. Why not get a study buddy and each prepare five possible essay answers and share? Seize every opportunity to collaborate and divide work efficiently. Of course, it is then each person's responsibility to study and learn the information.

Look at an "A" Paper

When exams are returned, always find out the correct answers. For essay responses, always ask to see an "A" paper. Ask the professor or a top-scoring student to allow you "an opportunity to read an excellent paper." Who would deny such a request? Analyze the "A" paper to determine how you can improve. Ask yourself, "What is this student doing that I'm not doing?" Even if you made an "A," read another paper. Maybe your next exam response will earn an "A+." In my history class, I noticed that the good students sought examples, but the weak students slipped out of the room without seeking any help or insight from others.

Use Technology to Communicate

Communicate without wasting time. Do you really need to meet face to face to study together? Conflicting class and work schedules make getting study groups together difficult. Cell phones, fax machines, e-mail, class bulletin boards, and chat rooms can eliminate some of those barriers. Outlines, lecture notes, and math problems can be discussed and sent back and forth rapidly.

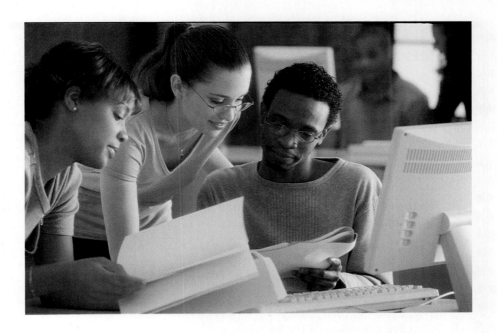

Consider a Tape Recorder

If you need audio reinforcement, try using a tape recorder. Do not use the recorder as an excuse to postpone the organizing and priority setting involved in notetaking. Instead, use the audio replay as another sensory tool for learning. The tiny digital recorders now available make this option fairly convenient. One history student said she listened to the replays while driving her car or fixing dinner.

Pass the First Test

Always overprepare for the first exam. Success on the first exam builds confidence, allays fears, and saves you from desperately trying to come from behind.

Watch Videos or DVDs

Visual learning is powerful. Find videos or DVDs on subjects covered in your text. Use the college library, the public library, and well-stocked video stores. If you are studying the Great Depression, check out newsreel clips or watch *The Grapes of Wrath*, a movie drama set in that period based on the classic novel by John Steinbeck. For an introductory psychology course, check the college library for a movie about Sigmund Freud or theories of personality.

Predict Exam Questions

Predict both essay questions and multiple-choice items for exams. Not all professors provide possible essay questions and study guides. On your own you can review your textbook's table of contents and turn major headings and chapter titles into possible essay questions. Consider subheadings and bold-face print a ripe source of multiple-choice items. Review lecture notes for any indication the professor has given about areas of special importance. Ask previous students about the professor's exams. The format and questions of a major exam should not come as a total shock to you. Predict and be prepared.

Personal *Feedback* 4

Name _____

1. What procrastination tactics do you use to delay homework?
   _____

2. Describe a personal intention that you regret not putting in action.
   _____

3. What specific activities do you think academic winners do that academic losers do not want to do? _____
   _____

4. Why might speaking up in class be considered risk taking? _____
   _____

5. What are the rewards for speaking up in class? _____
   _____

6. Describe a situation in which you have sought help individually from a college instructor. _____
   _____

Tear out and submit to your instructor.

Reading 3

BOUNCING BACK FROM FAILURE

It is a very rare person who achieves a dream without meeting problems and disappointments along the way. Even the people we consider the most successful have made mistakes, suffered setbacks, and felt discouraged. What makes some people keep going after a failure? In this article you will find five good suggestions and the inspirational story of a person who overcame many obstacles on the way to success. What can you use in your life?

There's an old Japanese proverb that counsels: "Fall seven times, stand up eight." But how do you get back up when you've fallen flat on your face? Below you'll find 5 tips to help you gather the pieces and pull yourself back together after you've failed.

1. Always expect success. However, you need to get rid of the notion of the "overnight success" or the "get-rich-quick-scheme." People who appear to be overnight successes have actually spent a lot of time before-hand honing their skill. Success requires a lot of preparation and a prolonged effort. Unfortunately, there are a lot of people who feel like failures when something doesn't work immediately and they just give up. If you don't succeed right away this doesn't mean that you've failed. Recognize that setbacks are simply part of the process, and that hard work and perseverance are two of the most important ingredients of success. If you've failed in the short run it simply means you need to take a longer term view of success.

2. Do not identify yourself with your failures. You are not your actions. To say that you have failed many times is not the same thing as saying that you are a failure. Whatever happens, keep referring to yourself, in your conversations with others and in your self-talk, as someone who has the full capacity to succeed.

3. Create a "fame wall." Hang your diplomas or certificates on this wall. You can also add framed photographs of yourself with your friends and family having fun or sharing a close moment. Anything that gives you a sense of accomplishment can go up on the wall. In times of failure, refer to your wall. It will serve to remind you that you have succeeded in the past and that you will succeed again in the future

4. Collect stories of failure about people who have gone on to become successful so that you can use them as inspiration when you're down. For example, consider the following life story.

This person:

At age 22—Failed in business;
At age 23—Was defeated for the State Legislature:
At age 24—Again failed in business;
At age 25—Was elected to the State Legislature;
At age 26—His sweetheart died;
At age 27—He suffered a nervous breakdown;
At age 29—Was defeated for the office of speaker;
At age 31—Was defeated for elector;
At age 34—Was defeated for Congress;
At age 37—Was elected to Congress;
At age 39—Was defeated for Congress;
At age 46—Was defeated for the Senate;
At age 47—Was defeated for Vice-President;
At age 49—Was defeated for the Senate;
At age 51—Was elected President of the United States.
This person was Abraham Lincoln.

Personal *Feedback* 5

Name _____

1. Consider the obstacles that might get in the way of your success in college. Write them in the chart below. (Lack of motivation or interest, the distraction of friends, lack of transportation, family responsibilities, illness, unhealthy habits, a difficult class, procrastination are some common examples.)

2. Share at least part of your list with a classmate and listen as he or she suggests possible solutions. Write them in the chart below.

3. Switch roles and offer suggestions to your partner.

Obstacles I might face	Possible solutions
_____	_____
	_____
	_____
_____	_____
	_____
	_____
_____	_____

4. Now, make a plan. What will you do if the obstacle comes your way? Be specific. How will you get to class if the car breaks down? How will you keep up in class if you are ill? What will you say when your friends want to go out and you have an exam the next day? Who might help you if your child is sick? Where can you get help with a tough class?

Obstacle	The plan
_____	_____
_____	_____
_____	_____

Tear out and submit to your instructor.

5. Keep things in perspective; do not over-generalize. The fact that you've failed at something does not mean that your life is over. It does not mean that your reputation is forever ruined and that you'll never get another chance. Don't make the situation bigger or more pervasive than it really is. Instead, remember the famous line:
"And this too shall pass . . ."

— *5 Tips for Overcoming Failure* by Marelisa Fábrega

exercise 6   **Think and Write.** Answer the following questions.

1. How have you responded to past failures and disappointments?

   _____

   _____

2. Select two of the tips in this article and explain how you might apply them to your life. _____

   _____

   _____

Summary *Points*

➤ **How can you mentally prepare for college success?**
Think like a winner. Formulate a dream that you turn into reality. Create the self-image of a star. Believe in your possibilities, and feel "born to win."

➤ **How can you use a To Do List as a planning tool?**
List daily goals, set priorities, check off your accomplishments, and relist items that were not achieved.

➤ **How do you use a calendar to decode your syllabus?**
Use your daily planning calendar to list your test dates, papers, and projects. Divide weekly homework into manageable units and list as daily and weekly learning goals. Decode your syllabus on the first day and keep it for quick reference.

➤ **How can you make class time more beneficial and meaningful?**
Arrive on time and participate in class. Take responsibility and contribute to class discussions.

➤ **Why preview your textbook?**
Make it work to your advantage by learning how it is organized.

➤ **Why mark your textbook?**
Use it as a learning tool by marking the information that you need to know later.

➤ **How can other students help you learn?**
Talk to them about class assignments. Ask someone to be your study buddy. Review lecture notes with them and ask questions. Ask to read the papers of top-scoring students. Use technology to communicate with fellow students.

Form a five-member group and select one of the following activities. Brainstorm and then outline your major points on a transparency. Choose a member to present the group findings to the class.

➤ Make a list of the top ten ways college students waste time.

➤ Make a list of the top ten lifestyle (nutritional and fitness) errors made by college students.

➤ Make a list of the top ten ways to overcome procrastination.

➤ Write instructions for getting an e-mail address on your campus.

MyReadingLab (MRL) www.myreadinglab.com

➤ The MyReadingLab Web site contains many materials to help you advance your reading and study skills. MRL offers an excellent opportunity to improve your reading skills by building on your current strengths and working on weaknesses. In addition to the reading sections, you will find links to the Longman Vocabulary Web site, Longman Study Skills Web site and the Research Navigator.

Your professor will tell you if you will be using MRL as part of this course and, if so, provide instructions for creating an account.

If you will not be using MRL in the course, you can still purchase an access code and use the materials to practice your reading skills. Open your Web browser and go to www.myreadinglab.com. The instructions for purchasing an access code and setting up an account are available there.

When you have created an account and login, it is a good idea to take the diagnostic tests first. The program will create a personalized study plan based on the results. In the Skills section you will find practice exercises within modules that relate to each chapter in this book. In the Levels section, you will read interesting selections, answer questions about them, and see your reading level (Lexile) change. Your professor will tell you which parts you should use.

Take some time to explore the site and see what is available for you there.

The Reading *Workshop*

"Reading is to the mind what exercise is to the body."
—SIR RICHARD STEELE (1672–1729)

Common sense and reading experts tell us that reading is good for us. Not only does regular reading improve our ability to read well, it also expands our knowledge of many subjects, our schemata. In other words, the more we read, the better we read and the more we know. Add to that the lifelong pleasure that reading provides and you have a recipe for wisdom!

Your professor may incorporate into your course a novel, a biography, or another book that the entire class reads. Other professors may give students free choice of reading material beyond the textbook. Others still will ask only that you read the textbook. You don't have to wait for someone to assign a book to read. Just do it! You'll be glad you did.

If you are not already an avid reader, refer to the Everyday Reading Skill section on page 176 or the following list of books that other college students have liked to find something that will interest you.

Also, check out The Reading Workshop at the end of each chapter in this book for a tip to help you get the most out of your pleasure-reading experience. Pick a book, get started, and enjoy!

Albom, M. *Tuesdays with Morrie*

Beals, M. *Warriors Don't Cry*

Butler, O. E. *Kindred*

Cisneros, S. *The House on Mango Street*

Conley, D. *Honkey*

David, S., Jenkins, G., & Hunt, R. *The Pact*

Dawson, G. *Life Is So Good*

Ehreneich, B. *Nickel and Dimed*

Gaines, E. *A Lesson Before Dying*

Grealy, L. *Autobiography of a Face*

Grisham, J. *The Street Lawyer*

Harrison, J. *Revenge*

Hersey, J. *Hiroshima*

Hickam, H. *October Sky*

House, S. *Clay's Quilt*

Kingsolver, B. *Pigs in Heaven*

Kingsolver, B. *Small Wonder*

Kingsolver, B. *The Bean Trees*

Lord, W. *A Night to Remember*

Lott, B. *The Hunt Club*

McBride, J. *The Color of Water*

Mitchard, J. *Deep End of the Ocean*

Morrison, T. *The Bluest Eye*

O'Brien, T. *If I Die in a Combat Zone Box Me up and Ship Me Home*

Pelzer, D. *A Child Called "It": One Child's Courage to Survive*

Pelzer, D. *The Lost Boy: A Foster Child's Search for the Love of a Family*

Pelzer, D. *A Man Named Dave: A Story of Triumph and Forgiveness*

Redding, S. & Abagnale, F. *Catch Me If You Can: The True Story of a Real Fake*

Preston, R. *The Hot Zone*

Sinclair, U. *The Jungle*

Wiesel, E. *Night*

(This book list is a combination of suggestions from Betty Black at Texas A & M Kingsville, Jessica Bryant at Eastern Kentucky University, and the Kentucky Association for Developmental Education.)

Searching the Internet

The **Internet** is an electronic communication system that connects millions of computers worldwide. It was initially developed by the U.S. Defense Department in the 1960s. It is the backbone for an information network called the **World Wide Web (WWW)** or, simply, the Web.

The WWW is similar to an enormous library: the **Web sites** are like books, and the **Web pages** are like the pages in the books. These pages can contain written text, photographs, graphics, music, sound effects, movies, and animation. Although learning to use the Internet can be intimidating and frustrating at first, you will quickly become a proficient navigator.

For finding your way on the Web, you need specific directions, just as you need an address and zip code to mail a letter. A **uniform resource locator (URL)** provides those directions. A URL is similar to an e-mail address, except that it routes you to a source of information called a *Web page* or *Web site* rather than to the mailbox of an individual person. URLs are made up of several parts, as shown in the following address for the Web site for the Emory University Health Sciences Center Library:

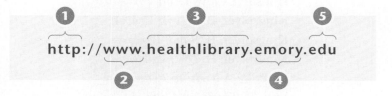

The following is a key to the numbered components of the sample URL.

1. **Protocol** This is standard for Web addresses and indicates *hypertext transfer protocol*, the type of language computers on the Internet use to communicate with each other. (Note it is not necessary to type "http://"; most browsers will automatically add the protocol "http://" before the address once you type it.)
2. **Server name** This indicates the computer network over which you will "travel" to reach the desired location. In most cases, this will be the World Wide Web.
3. **Directory path** This indicates a particular location within the Web site's host computer.
4. **Domain name** This is a name registered by the Web site owner.
5. **Domain type** This indicates the category to which the site owner belongs.

Such an address will take you to the site's **home page,** which you can think of as the main terminal through which you can reach other areas of the site. Like e-mail addresses, URLs must be typed with no mistakes.

Locate a Web Site

After you have entered the URL and reached the desired Web site, get an overview of what the site has to offer by scanning headlines, graphics, buttons, animation, category headings, site maps, and tables of contents. They will give you an idea of how the site is organized and where to go to find what you want. Look for the following elements to help you navigate:

Microsoft Internet Explorer reprinted with permission from Microsoft Corporation.

- **Headlines and Topic Headings** provide an overview of what the site has to offer. By clicking on them, you often move automatically to a subsequent section of the site, which might mean moving to another part of the same page or jumping to a new page or file within the same site.
- **Graphics** (including photos) enable you at a glance to understand how a site is organized. Clicking on them usually moves you to the section of the site they represent.
- **Buttons** are often shown next to headings or graphics; clicking them moves you to the desired location.
- **Hypertext Links,** or simply **links,** are phrases that appear as bold underlined text. Clicking on them not only moves you from one page to another within the site, but can also send you to other related Web sites. The words chosen and underlined as the link generally describe the information you are likely to find at that destination.

exercise 1

Research the following information about the National Aeronautics and Space Administration (NASA). First, go to the Web site (www.nasa.gov), click on the homepage, and examine the different headings. When you rest the cursor on the major headings, subtopics will appear. Use this navigational tool to answer the following questions.

1. What does NASA do? _____

_____

2. Name two ways that NASA's work impacts earth. _____

_____

_____

_____

_____

_____

3. What types of careers are available at NASA? _____

_____

_____

4. Check the latest NASA news items. List two. Write the categories under which you found them. _____

_____

_____

5. Use the "Search" feature to learn what significant event took place on July 20, 1969. _____

_____

Conduct a Search

The most intimidating part of navigating the Internet may be learning how to find the information you want. You do this by conducting a *search* for your topic. There are several steps that can help organize your search and make it more rewarding.

1. Make a Plan

Locating information on the Web requires using a **search engine,** which is a program that looks throughout the Internet for information. Several companies offer their own versions. They can be found at such Web sites as Google, Yahoo, AltaVista, Excite, Go.com, and Lycos. Thus, once you are connected to the Internet, you type in www.yahoo.com, or just yahoo.com, to get to the search engine.

Popular Search Engines and Their URLs

Google	www.google.com
Yahoo	www.yahoo.com
Excite	www.excite.com

Webcrawler	www.webcrawler.com
Lycos	www.lycos.com
Go.com	www.go.com
Ask.com	www.ask.com

No matter which search engine you choose, you will need to enter a keyword(s) or phrase in a search text box to describe the information you want. The search engine searches the Internet for sites that contain that word or phrase and displays a list of the first 10 to 25 sites (called *hits*). The more specific your description, the better. For example, entering "Star Spangled Banner" will result in a long list of sites about the song.

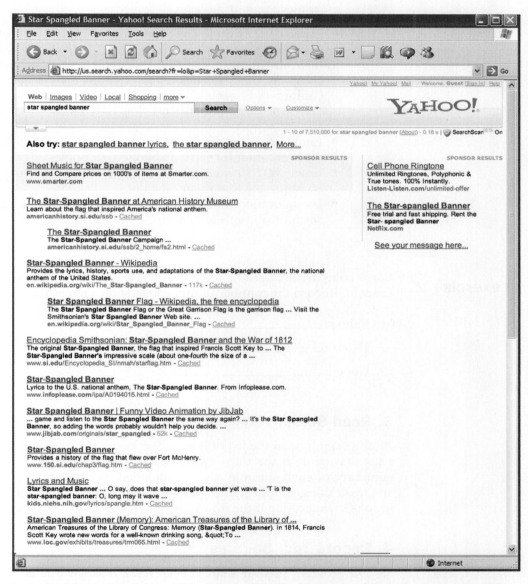

Reproduced with permission of Yahoo! Inc. ® 2008 by Yahoo! Inc. YAHOO! and the YAHOO! logo are trademarks of Yahoo! Inc. Microsoft Internet Explorer reprinted with permission from Microsoft Corporation.

2. Search and Search Again

Your initial search may be so specific that you get very few hits, or it may be so general that you get thousands, many of which are not appropriate to your research. Either way, you may have to try several searches before finding what you need. Making a list of any key terms that relate to your topic can be helpful. *Star Spangled Banner, Francis Scott Key,* and *the National Anthem,* for example, are all related topics that might help get you started. Scan a few of the hits your initial search produces to find other related terminology, names, and events that could be helpful.

Reader's *Tip* Limiting Your Search

- Enter *AND* or a plus (+) sign between each word of your search. For example, using the words *Apple Computer* for your search will turn up thousands of hits that include not only sites about the company, but also sites related to apple (the fruit) and sites about computers in general. Using *AND* in your key phrase (*Apple AND Computer*) will return sites that only contain both words in the phrase.
- Enter *OR* to broaden a search. *Apple OR Computer* will return sites that contain information about either apples or computers.
- Enter *NOT* to exclude items. *Apple AND Computer NOT fruit* will exclude sites that mention fruit.
- Use quotation marks when you want only hits that contain the exact phrase, such as "Apple Computer Financial Report for 2009."

exercise 2

For a comparison, use the following three search engines to look up Abraham Lincoln. Record the number of hits you find on each of them.

1. Yahoo _____
2. Excite _____
3. Google _____

3. Read Selectively

After a search, scan the list of hits to find keywords related to your research. The sites that contain the most appropriate information are usually listed first. A summary of each site may also be included. When you go to a particular Web site, read titles, subtitles, links, tables of contents, outlines, or introductory paragraphs to determine if the information is appropriate to your research.

4. Record Your Sources

As you progress in your search, keep track of keywords and phrases you have used as well as the results they produce. When you find a site to which you would like to return or one that you would like to use as a reference in your research, there are several options.

- *Write down* the URL next to the term used to find it so you can return to it later.
- *Print* the Web site material. You will have a hard (paper) copy to keep that usually lists the URL at the top of the printout.
- *Bookmark* or save the site. **Bookmarking** (or adding to *Favorites*, depending on your particular Web browser) lets you automatically return to the Web site with just one or two mouse clicks. If you will not have access to the same computer in the future, saving (or *exporting*, depending on your Web browser) a copy of the text of the Web page to disk will enable you to take it with you for reference on a different computer.

Reader's *Tip* Using Institutional Indexes

Indexes are *databases* that categorize articles according to topics for easy access. Check with your library for the following popular college databases that are paid for by your institution. Your college's Web site might have a direct link to the library's holdings.

Galileo
Periodical Abstracts
Newspaper Abstracts
Lexis-Nexis Academic Universe
MLA Bibliography
ABI Inform
Psyc FIRST
Social Science Abstracts
ERIC
MEDLINE

---

exercise 3

Using the search engine of your choice, locate three Web sites with information on well-known people such as Abraham Lincoln and Herman Cain. List each site and briefly describe the focus of the information.

1. syvum.com - achievements of leaders
2. annefrank.org - biography & home
3. stutteringhelp.org - overcoming disability

2 Stages of Reading

- What is reading?
- What is "knowing about knowing"?
- What is schema?
- What do good readers think about as they read?
- How can you remember what you read?

Everyday Reading Skills: Reading News and Feature Stories in the Newspaper

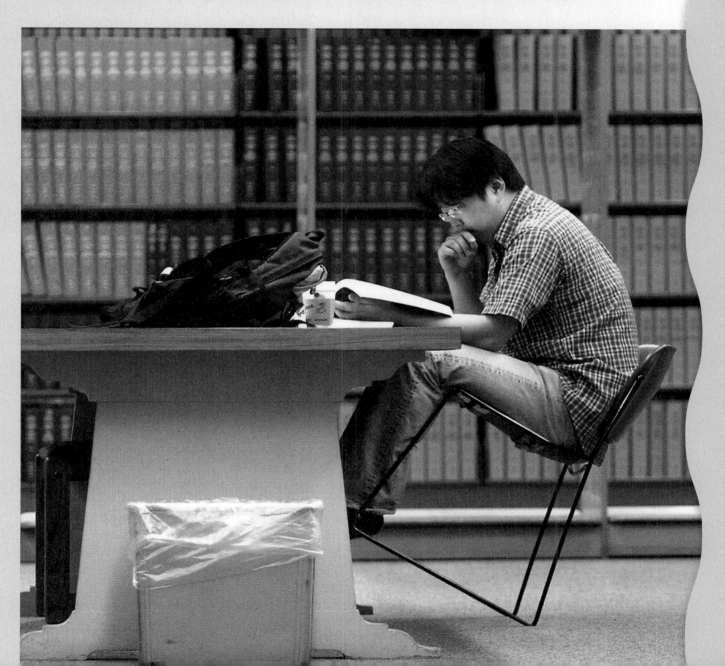

What Is the Reading Process?

In the past, experts thought of reading comprehension as a *product*. They assumed that if you could pronounce the words fluently, you would automatically be able to comprehend. Instruction focused on practicing and checking for the correct answers rather than on explaining comprehension skills. Newer approaches, by contrast, teach reading comprehension as a *process* in which you use your understanding of different skills and stages to achieve an understanding of the whole. Students are now taught how to predict upcoming ideas, activate existing knowledge, relate old information with new, form a main idea, and make inferences.

Stages of Reading

Good reading is divided into three thinking stages:

- **Before reading:** *Preview* to find out what the material is about, what you already know about the topic, and what you need to find out while reading.
- **During reading:** *Anticipate* upcoming information, visualize and integrate old and new knowledge, mark the text, and assess your own understanding in order to make adjustments.
- **After reading:** *Recall and react* to what you have learned.

Over the past fifty years, many experts have devised study skills strategies that break these three thinking stages into small steps. A historical example is SQ3R, which was devised by Francis P. Robinson at Ohio State University. The letters stand for Survey, Question, Read, Recite, and Review. Any such system can be successful, but all are designed to systematically engage the reader in thought *before, during,* and *after* reading.

Before
Preview
Set goals
Activate schema

After
Recall
React

During
Predict
Picture
Relate
Monitor
Correct
Annotate

Stage One: Previewing

Previewing is a method of assessing the material, your knowledge of the subject, and your goals for reading. Try to connect with the topic and get an overview of the assignment before starting on the first paragraph. At the beginning of each new course, preview the table of contents of your new textbook to get an overview of the scope of the material. Before reading a chapter, use the signposts such as subheadings, boldface or italic type, and summaries to anticipate what you will be learning.

Reader's Tip   Questions for Previewing

Use the following questions as guides to energize your reading and help you become an active learner.

1. What is the topic of the material?
2. What do I already know about the subject?
3. What is my purpose for reading?
4. How is the material organized?
5. What will be my plan of attack?

Signposts for Previewing. Consider the following typical features of college textbooks when previewing. These are the parts to read when previewing a textbook chapter:

Introductory Material. A textbook chapter usually begins with an introduction. This section prepares the reader for the major ideas that will be covered. Pay close attention to it!

Learning Questions. Many textbook chapters start with questions designed to heighten your interest and stimulate your thinking. Such questions directly relate to what the material covers and thus help you set goals.

Title. The title of a book, chapter, or article is the first clue to its meaning. Some titles are designed to be clever to attract attention, but most try to communicate the important thought in the text. Identify the *who, what,* or *why* of the title to anticipate the content of the material and its importance to you.

Headings and Subheadings. These are the titles of the sections and subsections within chapters that, like the major titles, describe the content. Usually headings and subheadings appear in bold or italic type and outline the author's message. Turn them into questions to anticipate what you will need to know from the reading. For example, the heading "Estimating Revenue Potential" in a marketing text could be changed to "How Do You Estimate Revenue Potential?."

Italics, Boldface, and Numbers. Italic and bold type highlight words that merit special emphasis. These words are usually terms that you will need to define and remember. Numbers are also used to list important details that you may need to learn.

Visual Aids or Marginal Notations. A biology professor at a major university tells his students to at least look at the illustrations and read the captions in the assigned material before coming to class, even if they don't read the assignment. He wants his students to have a visual overview. Authors use photos, charts, and graphs to enhance meaning, heighten interest, and help readers visualize information. Additional notations and definitions may be added in the page margins to further simplify the material for the reader.

Concluding Summary or Review. Most textbook chapters end with a summary of the most important points, which may be several paragraphs or a list of the important ideas. Regardless of its form, the summary helps you recall the material and reflect on its importance.

exercise 1

To get an overview of this chapter, look at the learning questions at the opening of the chapter on page 33. Read the Summary Points on pages 48–49 and scan to understand the headings, subheadings, and the boldfaced and italicized words. Spend a few moments reviewing the contents of the Reader's Tip Boxes. Preview the chapter to answer the following questions:

1. What is the purpose of previewing? _____

2. List the six thinking strategies good readers use during the reading process:

   _____

3. What is meant by recall? _____

   _____

   _____

   _____

4. How do good readers reflect? _____

   _____

   _____

5. Why would good readers keep records of their own learning progress?

   _____

The Power of Prior Knowledge. Experts say that prior knowledge is the most important factor in reading comprehension. Thus, if you know very little about a subject, the initial reading in that area will be difficult. The good news, however, is that the more you know, the easier it is for you to read and learn. Every new idea added to your framework of knowledge about a subject makes the next reading assignment on the topic a little bit easier.

Students who already know a lot about history may think that American history assignments are easy. But students who perhaps excel in science and know little history might disagree. Because of prior knowledge, most students would probably agree that senior-level college courses are much easier than freshman survey courses.

Previewing to Activate Schemata. Your prior knowledge on a subject is a schema. According to theory, a **schema** (plural, *schemata*) is the skeleton of knowledge in your mind on a particular subject. As you expand your knowledge, the skeleton grows. Here's another way to think about a schema: A schema is like a computer chip in your brain that holds everything you know on a particular subject. You pull it out when the need arises, add to it, and then return it to storage.

Your preview of the material will help you know which "computer chips" to activate. Call on what you already know and blend it with the new ideas. If you embellish the new thoughts with your past experience, your reading will become more meaningful.

Students tend to know more than they think they know. No matter how unfamiliar the topic may seem, you can probably provide some small link from your own experience. Pick up the signals from the written material and use them to retrieve prior knowledge and form a link of understanding with the next text.

Personal *Feedback* **1**   **Name** _____

1. What was your favorite subject in high school, and why? _____
   _____

2. What magazines do you like to read? _____
   _____

3. What sections do you like to read in the newspaper? _____
   _____

4. What magazines did your family subscribe to during your high school years?
   _____

5. What is the best book you have read? _____
   _____

6. What television programs do you watch regularly? _____
   _____

7. How does prior knowledge seem to relate to your areas of greatest interest?
   _____

Tear out and submit to your instructor.

EXAMPLE   Read the following sentence and activate your schema. Identify a knowledge link. Briefly describe an idea or image that comes to mind.

> Cuba became an obsession of American policy makers in 1959, when Fidel Castro and rebels of his 26th of July Movement ousted America's longtime ally Fulgencio Batista.
>
> —*A People and a Nation* by Mary Beth Norton et al.

EXPLANATION   You may know little Cuban history, but you probably know that Miami, Florida, has a large and flourishing Hispanic population, begun by people who left Cuba. Do you know why they left Cuba? Link this knowledge of Cubans in Florida to the new information.

Stage Two: Integrating Knowledge

If you watch two students reading silently, can you tell which student comprehends better? Probably not. The behaviors of good silent readers are thinking behaviors that cannot be observed or learned by watching others. These behaviors, however, need not be mysterious to college students.

Knowing About Knowing.   A myth in reading, probably inspired by the speed reading craze, is that good readers begin an assignment, race through it, and never stop until the last period. In fact, however, *good readers work hard* to assimilate the information they read. If they do not understand or if they get confused, they go back and reread to resolve the confusion. Good readers also understand the processes involved in reading and consciously control them. This awareness and control of the reading processes is called **metacognition,** which one expert defines as "knowing about knowing."[1]

Some students don't know when they don't know. They continue to read even though they are not comprehending. Poor readers tolerate such confusion because they either don't realize that it exists or don't know what to do about it. Poor readers focus on facts, whereas good readers try to assimilate details into a larger cognitive pattern. Good readers monitor their own comprehension. In other words, they supervise their own understanding of the material. They recognize inadequate comprehension and interrupt their reading to seek solutions.

Six Thinking Strategies of Good Readers. In order to find out what good readers do, Beth Davey studied the research on good and poor readers. She discovered that good readers, both consciously and subconsciously, use the five thinking strategies below.[2] In addition, a sixth strategy—annotating—will help you recall material you read.

1. Predict: Make Educated Guesses. Good readers make predictions about thoughts, events, outcomes, and conclusions. With the appearance of each new character in a James Patterson mystery novel, the reader makes a guess about who the culprit might be. Textbook predictions, although a little less dramatic, are equally important. While reading the facts in a science text, for example, you may be anticipating the concluding theory.

As you read, your predictions are confirmed or denied. If they prove invalid, you make new predictions. For example, in reading an economics text, you might predict that inflation hurts everyone. But after further reading, you discover that real estate investors make money by selling at the inflated prices. Thus your initial prediction proved invalid, and you readjusted your thinking on inflation. Your predictions involved you with the author's thinking and helped you learn.

EXAMPLE   What are your predictions for the rest of the section based on these beginning sentences?

> At least one bank recognized opportunity in this situation. Instead of classifying low-to-moderate-income Hispanics as credit risks to be avoided at all costs, Puerto Rico–based Banco Popular saw them as an untapped market for personal and business banking services. Having witnessed Banco Popular's success, mainstream banks such as Chase Manhattan and Citibank are . . .
>
> —*Business,* Sixth Edition, by Ricky Griffin
> and Ronald Ebert

EXPLANATION   The rest of this section explains how traditional banks are moving aggressively into the Hispanic market to offer banking services and win customers.

---

[1]Ann L. Brown, "The Development of Memory: Knowing, Knowing About Knowing, and Knowing How to Know," in *Advances in Child Development and Behavior* (vol. 2), ed. H. W. Reese (New York: Academic Press, 1975).

[2]Adapted from Beth Davey, "Think Aloud—Modeling the Cognitive Processes of Reading Comprehension," *Journal of Reading*, 27 (Oct. 1983): 44–47.

2. Picture: Form Images. For good readers, the words and the ideas on the page trigger mental images that relate directly or indirectly to the material. Because these mental images depend on the reader's experience, visualization is a highly individualistic process. One learner might read about Maine and picture the countryside and the rockbound coast, whereas another, with no experience in the area, might visualize the shape and location of the state on a map. Images are like movies in your head. You form a visualization to enhance the message in the text. Fiction quickly moves you into a new world of enjoyment or terror through visualization. Expository or textbook writing may require more imagination than fiction, but the images created also strengthen the message.

EXAMPLE   Describe your visualizations for the following passage.

> A dress so loud it hurts my eyes. There are yellows and oranges enough to throw back the light of the sun. I feel my whole face warming from the heat waves it throws out. Earrings gold, too, and hanging down to her shoulders. Bracelets dangling and making noises when she moves her arm . . .

> —*Everyday Use for Your Grandmama*
> by Alice Walker

EXPLANATION   Imagine a woman dressed in yellows and oranges that are perhaps too bright with long earrings and dangling bracelets. Depending on prior knowledge, you may visualize someone you know.

3. Relate: Draw Comparisons. When you relate your existing knowledge to the new information in the text, you are embellishing the material and making it part of your framework of ideas. A phrase or a situation may remind you of a personal experience that relates to the text. For example, a description of ocean currents may remind you of a strong undertow you once fought while swimming. Such related experiences help you digest the new experience as part of something you already know.

EXAMPLE   Describe any previous experience that the following excerpt brings to mind.

> How does aggressive driving lead to road rage? The process starts when another driver interferes with the feeling of freedom and well-being that comes from achieving control over one's environment. When a car suddenly moves in front of you, you are forced to change your behavior. This frustrates you and causes an emotional response.

> —Samuel E. Wood and Ellen R. Green, *The World of Psychology,* 4th ed. © 2002 (excerpt from page 490). Reproduced by permission of Pearson Education, Inc.

EXPLANATION   Have you ever felt angry at another driver? Has another driver ever expressed hostility toward you? Why do you think road rage is or is not a problem in your area?

4. Monitor: Check Understanding. Monitor your ongoing comprehension to test your understanding of the material. Keep an internal summary of the information as it is presented and how it relates to the overall message. Your summary will build with each new detail as long as the author's message is consistent. If, however, certain information seems confusing or erroneous, stop and seek a solution to the problem. Monitor and supervise your own comprehension.

Remember that poor readers continue to read even when confused, but good readers seek to resolve the difficulty. Good readers demand complete understanding and know whether it has been achieved.

EXAMPLE What is confusing about the following sentence?

"Another such victory like that on July 1," wrote Richard Harding Davis, "and our troops must retreat."

—*America and Its People*, Third Edition,
by James Martin et al.

EXPLANATION The words *retreat* and *victory* refer to opposite ideas. Usually the defeated army retreats. Davis must mean that the victory was too costly, and thus was hardly a victory at all. Davis must be speaking sarcastically, but a second reading might be necessary to figure this out.

5. Resolve Gaps in Understanding. Do not accept gaps in your reading comprehension. They may signal a failure to understand a word or a sentence. Stop and resolve the problem so you can continue to synthesize and build your internal summary. Seek solutions to confusion. Usually, this means rereading a sentence or looking back at a previous page for clarification. If an unknown word is causing confusion, the definition may emerge through further reading. Changing predictions is also a corrective strategy. For example, while reading a geography textbook you may be predicting that heavy rains saved a country from famine, but, as the conclusion emerges, it seems that fertilizers and irrigation were the saviors. If you cannot fill the gaps yourself, seek help from the instructor or another student.

EXAMPLE How could you seek to better understand the following paragraph?

Contemporaries cited more pressing needs. "We are a new country," a Boston doctor reminded his son, who wished to pursue a scientific career. "We have, as it were, just landed on these shores; there is a vast deal to be done; and he who will not be doing, must be set down as a drone."

—From Arms and Camp, *Biology: A Journey into Life*, 2nd ed.
© 1991 Brooks/Cole, a part of Cengage Learning, Inc.
Reproduced by permission. www.cengage.com/permissions

EXPLANATION Did the father want his son to study science or not? Do you know the meaning of *contemporaries* and *drone*? Do you understand the phrase *pressing needs*? Is the father's attitude different from attitudes today and thus unexpected? After using the correction strategies of defining and rereading, you should determine that the father said no to science.

6. Annotate the Text as You Read. By circling, underlining, and writing brief notes in the margin, you will be reacting to the material and highlighting the important information. This is a critical thinking process, that will help you understand and remember the material. Keeping your brain and your pen active while you read will help you stay focused and prevent your mind from wandering. An added bonus is that you will create a record of your thinking that you can return to when preparing for a test.

EXAMPLE   Notice how marking the text makes the major details stand out.

1990s rap

In the 1990s one of the elements of rap music shifted toward the DJs or (turntablists) who created sounds by manipulating the turntables on which LPs were played. The most commonly used technique involves moving the record rapidly back and forth while it is being played. DJs battle each other in displays of virtuosity. They work with two turntables simultaneously, cutting in and out of the sound made by (scratching), while the other LP is playing . . .

2 common techniques

(Sampling) involves the use of a short extract of a previous recording as a musical element in a new recording. The most commonly used samples are those of a recognizable riff or a catchy instrumental introduction from a song. Sung or spoken extracts can also be sampled . . .

—From *Understanding Music,* Fifth Edition,
by Jeremy Yudkin.

EXPLANATION As you read, did you notice that the passage describes a term, *turntablists,* and two characteristics of rap music? By circling the term and underlining its meaning, they are made visually clear. Similarly, circling the two characteristics and underlining the most important parts of their descriptions make the information stand out from the minor details. The marginal notes serve as labels for the marking. This process keeps the reader active and thinking. Plus, the annotations serve as a great aid to recall in the after reading stage. Whether you circle, underline, make marginal notes, or use some combination of these methods depends on the material itself and your purpose for reading.

Applying All Six Thinking Strategies. The following passage illustrates the use of the six thinking strategies. Some of the reader's thoughts appear as handwritten comments in the margins. Keep in mind that each person reacts differently. This example merely represents one reader's attempt to integrate knowledge.

EXAMPLE   Do the handwritten thoughts also represent your thoughts?

A BREATH FOR FASHION

In 1800s?

What is a diaphragm?

How did they breathe?

Is it healthy?

Are they victims of fashion?

Nineteenth-century doctors were taught that men and women breathed differently: men used their diaphragms to expand their chests, whereas women raised the ribs near the top of the chest. Finally, a woman doctor found that women breathed in this way because their clothes were so fashionably tight that the diaphragm could not move far enough to admit air into the lungs. Some women even had their lower ribs removed surgically so that they could lace their waists more tightly.

—From Arms and Camp, *Biology: A Journey into Life,* 2nd ed.
© 1991 Brooks/Cole, a part of Cengage Learning, Inc.
Reproduced by permission. www.cengage.com/permissions

EXPLANATION The handwritten comments model the reader's conscious and subconscious thoughts. Such an analysis may seem artificial and intrusive, but be aware that you do incorporate thinking strategies like these into your reading. The following exercises are designed to make you more aware of this interaction.

exercise 2   For the following passages, answer the questions and make a conscious effort to use the six strategies as you read:

1. Predict (develop hypotheses)
2. Picture (develop images)
3. Relate (link prior knowledge with new ideas)
4. Monitor (clarify ongoing comprehension)
5. Use corrective strategies (solve comprehension problems)
6. Annotate (mark the text)

Passage 1

ONCE UPON A SEPTEMBER DAY

Another meeting! One after another without coming up with a proposal that would fly.

This one took place in early September and (not surprisingly) only a few people showed up—12, to be precise. And so they talked for some days and finally came up with a plan for still another meeting, eight months hence. It was hoped this would offer sufficient time to generate interest in the matter.

They also moved the location. It was not that the September site had been unpleasant—on the contrary, the facilities were quite good—but variety in meeting places might induce more individuals to attend.

They were a relatively young group; the average age was 42. The youngest was 30 and the oldest 82 and prone to nod during long meetings. Although some were lackluster in ability, most were able and would later move to high executive positions.

They were together for 116 days, taking off only Sundays and 12 other days. And you might have guessed it: During a very hot summer they were without air conditioning. In addition to the formal sessions of the entire group, much of their work was done in committee and after hours.

There was still criticism of the final proposal. It was much too short, some argued—only 4,000 words. Four months of work and only 4,000 words! It was scarcely enough to fill a few sheets of paper. But 39 of them felt it was the best they could come up with. It was good enough to sign, which they did on the 17th day of September, 1787.

And they called their proposal the Constitution of the United States.

—Thomas V. DiBacco,
The Los Angeles Times, September 28, 1983

1. What did you predict to be the purpose of the meeting? _____

2. Who did you picture as the attendees of the meeting? _____

3. The passage mentions that the site of the meeting place had been changed with the hope that more individuals would attend. Have you experienced this same problem (a meeting at which not too many people showed up)? What sort of incentives are used to induce people to attend meetings?

_____

_____

_____

4. Why do you suppose the meeting was continued so many times?

_____

_____

_____

5. Underline any part of the passage you found confusing or needed to reread.

6. Did you annotate as you read? Now that you know the topic, go back and circle the clues.

Passage 2

THE "BUNNY" BREEDS RAPIDLY!

In Belarus, formerly part of the Soviet Union, the national currency is called the _zaichik_, or little hare. People in that country count their currency in "bunnies." The government there is fond of letting the bunnies breed rapidly, that is, printing more and more of them. Not long ago, the government announced that it would issue more bunnies to pay for the fall harvest. Not surprisingly, Belarus's domestic currency dropped in value. In one five-month period, it lost half of its purchasing power. In one week alone, it lost more than 10 percent. Foreign investors simply disappeared. The only country that Belarus has much trade with now is Russia, and most of that trade is through barter.

—_Economics Today_, 2001–2002 Edition, by Roger Leroy Miller

1. What is the connection between the title of this passage and the problem it describes? _____

_____

_____

_____

2. Why did Belarus print more currency? What other situations might cause a country to issue more currency? _____

_____

_____

3. Why would foreign investors leave? _____

_____

4. Why would Russia trade only in barter? _____

_____

_____

5. Underline any part of the passage that you found confusing.

6. Did you annotate to emphasize the important details?

Stage Three: Recall

Recall is your review of what you have read. Recall is self-testing and can be a silent, oral, or written recitation. When you recall, you take an additional few minutes to tell yourself what you have learned before you close the book. Poor readers tend to finish the last paragraph of an assignment, sigh with relief, and close the book without another thought. Study strategies developed by experts, however, stress the importance of a final recall or review stage. The experts emphasize that this final step improves both comprehension and memory.

As a part of monitoring your comprehension, maintain a running summary as you read. The end of an assignment is the time to give voice to this internal summary and review the material for gaps of knowledge. You can do the recall step in your head, aloud or on paper. To recall, talk to yourself and test your understanding. Pull the material together under one central idea or generalization, and then review the relevant details and commit them to memory.

Reader's *Tip* React and Reflect

After recalling what an author has said, evaluate its significance for you by answering the following questions:

- Did I enjoy the reading? Why or why not?
- Was the selection well-written? Explain specifics.
- Do I agree or disagree with the author? Why or why not?
- How many of the author's ideas do I accept?

Do not neglect this last stage. From a metacognitive point of view, you are adding related ideas to existing schemata and creating new knowledge networks or "computer chips" for storage. Recall makes a significant difference in what you retain from your reading.

How to Recall. The recall stage of reading can be silent or voiced, organized conversation with yourself or others, or a written reorganization. What method you choose depends on the difficulty of the material or your purpose for learning. Keep in mind that the goal is self-testing. Rather than wait for the professor's inquiry, answer your own question, "What did I get from this material?"

Think About It. What was the main point? What did you learn from each section? Do you have opinions or experiences related to this topic?

Talk About It. Say out loud, to yourself or to someone else, what you learned from the selection. Voice your opinions, questions, and experiences.

Write About It. If your purpose is to remember the information for the long term, for a test, perhaps, make notes on a separate sheet of paper. Use your text annotations as the basis for the notes. If your purpose is shorter term or general recall, so you can join a discussion with friends, for example, write a one- or two-sentence summary. You might also write any questions you want to discuss about the topic.

Feel free to accept or reject ideas according to your prior knowledge and the logic of the presentation. Your response is subjective, but as a critical thinker, you should base it on what you already know and what you have just found out.

EXAMPLE   Read the following passage and decide what it is about and whether you agree or disagree with the author.

> Access is a very important resource for an interest group. As we have noted, a person who makes a campaign contribution will often say something like this: "I don't want any special promise from you; all I want is the right to come and talk to you when I need to." This seemingly modest request may in fact be significant. Access is power.
>
> —*American Democracy*
> by Fred Harris

EXPLANATION   What is your position on the issue of access and power? You may agree with the author's position. The message is that if you can manage to talk to a powerful political figure, you have an excellent chance of influencing decisions. Because face-to-face contact can be convincing, access probably does give power.

exercise 3   Read the following passages and decide whether you agree or disagree with their messages. You are giving your *reactions* to the ideas, so there are no right or wrong answers. Think and react.

Passage 1

GENDER DIFFERENCES

> Men and women differ with respect to gossip, according to Deborah Tannen in *You Just Don't Understand: Women and Men in Conversation*. It isn't that one group gossips and the other does not. It is the subjects of their talks. "When most men talk to their friends or on the phone," Tannen says, "they may discuss what's happening in business, the stock market, the soccer match, or politics. For most women, getting together and talking about their feelings and what is happening in their lives is at the heart of friendship."
>
> Men and women differ when it comes to lecturing and listening. Experimental studies support Tannen in finding that "men are more comfortable than women in giving information and opinions and speaking in an authoritative way to a group, whereas women are more comfortable than men in supporting others."
>
> —*You Just Don't Understand: Women and Men in Conversation*
> by Deborah Tannen

1. What is the message? _____

   _____

2. Why do you agree or disagree with these assertions of gender differences on

   gossip, lecturing, and listening?

   (a) Gossip? _____

   (b) Lecturing? _____

   (c) Listening? _____

Passage 2

SEATBELT VIOLATION ARREST

By an unusual 5–4 split, with Justice David Souter writing the majority opinion, the Supreme Court said Fourth Amendment protection against unreasonable seizures does not cover Gail Atwater, who was ordered out of her pickup in 1997 for not using seatbelts for herself and her young children.

Atwater said she had let her daughter, 5, and son, 3, out of their belts as they were driving in Lago Vista so that they could better look for a toy that had dropped outside of the truck.

Bart Turek, the arresting officer, said Atwater told him she also did not have her license and insurance information, as required by Texas law, because her purse had been stolen the day before.

Turek cuffed Atwater, put her in a squad car and took her to jail, where she was forced to remove her shoes and empty her pockets and a "mug shot" was taken. Souter acknowledged that the officer engaged in "gratuitous humiliations." However, he said the law has long allowed police to arrest people if they believe a crime is being committed, no matter how small.

—From Joan Biskupic, "High Court Upholds Mom's Arrest in Seatbelt Violation: Cuffs, Jail Allowed in Minor Offenses," *USA Today,* April 25, 2001, p. A.01. Reprinted with permission.

1. What is the message? _____

   _____

   _____

2. Do you agree with the ruling? Why or why not? _____

3. Do you think that the manner in which the arresting officer treated the

   mother was appropriate? Explain your answer. _____

   _____

   _____

   _____

Assess Your Progress as a Learner

This textbook creates an artificial environment for you to learn about your own reading. Normally after reading, you do not answer ten comprehension questions and ten vocabulary questions. You read, reflect, and move on. In this book, however, the questions are provided to help you monitor your thinking. To improve your skills, reflect seriously on what you are getting right and what you are getting wrong. Making a good homework or classwork grade is part of the process, but it is not the real purpose. Understanding and improving are the goals, and they require your active participation as a learner. Assume responsibility for your own improvement.

Levels of Reading Comprehension

In order to give you more insight into your strengths and weaknesses, the comprehension questions at the end of each long reading selection in this text are labeled *main idea, detail,* and *inference.* These question types represent different levels of sophistication in reading that can be ranked and defined as follows.

1. Literal—What did the author say? These are detail questions about the facts, and the answers are clearly stated within the material. This is the beginning level of reading comprehension, the least sophisticated level. You might be able to answer detail questions and still not understand the overall meaning of the passage.

Example: Captain Thomas Hunt came to Plymouth Bay to capture Indians for the slave market. (True or False)

2. Interpretive—What did the author mean by what was said? These are main idea and inference questions. In order to answer, you must interpret

Personal *Feedback* 2

Name _____

1. Why do you think students are reluctant to recall (Stage 3) what they have read?

_____

2. What have you learned in this chapter that is positive about your reading habits?

_____

_____

3. What three immediate changes would you suggest for your own reading improvement?

(a) _____

(b) _____

(c) _____

4. What did you learn in this chapter about the reading process that surprised you?

_____

_____

5. What myths did you have about reading that no longer seem to be true?

_____

6. What is keeping you from becoming an excellent reader? _____

_____

7. What questions would you like to ask your instructor about the reading process?

_____

_____

Tear out and submit to your instructor.

the facts along with the author's attitude, using implied meaning to make assumptions and draw conclusions. At this level, you are considering both what is stated and what is unstated in order to figure out what the author is trying to say.

> *Example:* The author suggests that Squanto's Pawtuxet Indian tribe valued all of the following except (a) bravery, (b) endurance, (c) wealth, or (d) strength.

3. Applied—How does the author's message apply to other situations? These are questions that call for reaction, reflection, and critical thinking. This is the highest level of sophistication and involves analyzing, synthesizing, and evaluating. You are putting together what was said with what was meant and applying it to new situations and experiences. You are attempting to make wider use of what you have just learned.

> *Example:* Explain how the cultural values, goals, and ethics of the Native Americans as illustrated by Squanto in his youth differed from those of the European settlers and thus caused conflict.

Use the questions in this book as diagnostic information. What do your responses tell you about yourself? What kinds of questions do you always answer correctly? What do your errors tell you about your reading? Learn from your mistakes and begin to categorize your own reading strengths and weaknesses. Throughout the course, refer back to previous work as a reference for your own development. Keeping records and reflecting on your own learning are essential parts of your improvement plan.

Summary *Points*

➤ **What is reading comprehension?**
Reading comprehension is a process in which you use your understanding of the different skills and stages of reading to achieve an understanding of the author's words and suggestions.

➤ **What are the three stages of reading?**
Stage 1: Before reading, *preview* to find out what the material is about.
Stage 2: During reading, *anticipate* upcoming information and *integrate* knowledge.
Stage 3: After reading, *recall* and *react* to what you have learned.

➤ **What signposts are used for previewing?**
Readers use typical textbook features to preview, such as learning questions, the title, introductory materials, headings and subheadings, italics, boldface words, numbers, visual aids, marginal notations, concluding summaries, and reviews.

➤ **What do good readers anticipate?**
Good readers anticipate content, structure, and purpose.

➤ **Why is prior knowledge powerful?**
The more you know, the easier it is for you to read and learn.

➤ **What is schema?**
Schema is the skeleton of knowledge in your mind on a particular subject.

➤ **What are the six thinking strategies of good readers?**
Good readers predict, picture, relate, monitor, use corrective strategies, and annotate.

➤ **What is recall?**
After reading, good readers pull the material together as one central idea, review the relevant details, and summarize. They think about it, talk about it, and write about it.

➤ **How do good readers reflect?**
Good readers evaluate the significance of what they have read, and they accept or reject new ideas.

➤ **How do good readers assess reading progress?**
Good readers keep records of their own learning progress.

COLLABORATIVE   PROBLEM SOLVING

Form a five-member group and select one of the following activities. Brainstorm and then outline your major points on a transparency. Choose a member to present the group findings to the class.

➤ Make a list of five questions about your college at the literal level.

➤ Make a list of five questions about your college at the interpretive level.

➤ Make a list of five questions about your college at the applied level.

➤ Explain how recalling, connecting, and reacting help you remember what you have read.

PEARSON
myreadinglab

MyReadingLab (MRL) www.myreadinglab.com

➤ To practice the ideas and skills introduced in this chapter, go to the "Active Reading Strategies" module in the Skills section of MyReadingLab. To practice general reading comprehension, use the Levels section.

The Reading *Workshop*

"People say that life is the thing, but I prefer reading."
—LOGAN PEARSALL SMITH (1865–1946)

Have you selected a book and begun to read? Whatever you choose to read, it will be more fun if you allow enough time to get involved in the characters, the plot, and the setting. Find a comfortable, quiet place to curl up, and allow yourself at least 20 to 30 minutes at a time. If you are not immediately "hooked" on the book, give it at least two chapters to excite your interest. Some books are slow starters and draw the reader in gradually.

Just as thinking, talking, and writing about your textbook reading will help etch the material in memory, the same methods will heighten interest in your pleasure reading. Your professor may ask you to keep a Reading Workshop journal in which you write about your pleasure reading. Perhaps you will be given an opportunity to talk to a classmate or the whole class about it. Here are some suggestions.

Think about it, talk about it, write about it:

Is your book fiction or nonfiction? What is its topic? Why did you choose it? Did the author grab your interest in the first few lines or did it build slowly? What have you liked best about your book so far?

---

selection 1 🔬 Health

"You've got bad eating habits if you use a grocery cart in 7-Eleven . . ."

—Dennis Miller

College students need to eat on the run and on a budget, but can the food also be healthy? A McDonald's Double Quarter Pounder with Cheese at 730 calories with 40 grams of fat accompanied by an order of large fries at 570 calories with 30 grams of fat might not be the best nutritional choices. Is a chicken choice better? Not always. A Premium Crispy Chicken Club Sandwich weighs in at 680 calories with 29 grams of fat. How can you stretch your food dollars and still eat for good health?

THINKING BEFORE READING

Preview the selection for clues to content. What do you already know about good nutrition? Activate your prior knowledge. Anticipate the author's ideas and your purpose for reading. Think!

What fast-food choice do you make that is healthy?

What makes a food organic?

What do you eat on a weekly basis that is not a healthy choice?_____

I'll read this to find out _____

_____

VOCABULARY PREVIEW

Are you familiar with these words?

forages	constraints	maligned	discriminating	lard
opt	intolerance	triggers	hefty	pristine

Would you *opt* for a well-paying job that you didn't like or a low-paying job that you liked?

What types of *constraints* do people face when balancing work and family?

Your instructor may choose to give a true-false vocabulary review before or after reading.

THINKING DURING READING

As you read, use the six thinking strategies of a good reader: predict, picture, relate, monitor, correct, and annotate. Answer the questions in the margins that reflect your active thinking.

IMPROVED EATING FOR THE COLLEGE STUDENT

What are your nutritional challenges?

College students often face a challenge when trying to eat healthy foods. Some students live in dorms and do not have their own cooking or refrigeration facilities. Others live in crowded apartments where everyone forages in the refrigerator for everyone else's food.

Reader's *Tip* Reading and Studying Health

- Use learning aids provided within the text. Such items might include running glossaries on pages, checklists, discussion and application questions, and summaries.
- Answer any marginal questions placed within a chapter.
- Review and understand procedures by following the graphics provided.
- Design your own concept cards (see Chapter 3) to help learn new vocabulary.
- Draw simple figures or symbols to aid your understanding and recall of concepts.

Still others eat at university food services where food choices may be limited. Most stu-
5 dents have financial and time constraints that make buying, preparing, and eating healthy food a difficult task. What's a student to do?

FAST FOODS: EATING ON THE RUN

If your campus is like many others, you've probably noticed a distinct move toward fast-food restaurants in your student unions, so that they now resemble the food courts found in shopping malls. These new eating centers fit students' needs for a fast bite of food at a
10 reasonable price between classes and also bring in money to your school. But many fast foods are high in fat and sodium. Are they all unhealthy?

Not all fast foods are created equal, and not all are bad for you. Even at the often-maligned burger chains, menus are healthier than ever before and offer excellent choices for the discriminating eater. The key word here is *discriminating*. It really is possible to eat
15 healthy food if you follow these suggestions (see the Consumer Health box for even more ideas about how to eat healthily while eating out).

- Ask for nutritional analyses of items. Most fast-food chains now have them.

- Avoid mayonnaise, sauces, and other add-ons. Some places even have fat-free mayonnaise if you ask. Put a hold on extra ketchup.

20 - Hold the cheese. This extra contributes substantially to total fat but does not add a lot to taste.

- Order single, small burgers rather than large, high-calorie, bacon- or cheese-topped choices. Put on your own ketchup, and keep portions small.

What healthful choices could you 25 - Order salads, and be careful how much dressing you add. Many people think they are being health-smart by eating salad, only to load it with calorie- and fat-rich dressing.
make at a fast- Try the vinegar and oil or low-fat alternative dressings. Stay away from eggs and other
food restaurant? high-fat add-ons such as bacon bits.

- When ordering a chicken sandwich, order the skinless broiled version rather than the deep-fried version. Many people think that a deep-fried chicken sandwich is a healthier
30 choice when it really has more fat than a loaded double burger.

- If you must have fries, check to see what type of oil is used to cook them. Avoid lard-based or other saturated fat products.

- Order wheat bread, and ask them to hold the butter.

Consumer Health

What's Good on the Menu? While some restaurants offer hints for health-conscious diners, you're on your own most of the time. To help you order wisely, here are lighter options and high-fat pitfalls. Best choices contain fewer than 30 grams of fat, a generous meal's worth for an active, medium-size woman. "Worst" choices have up to 100 grams of fat.

Fast Food

BEST
Grilled chicken sandwich
Roast beef sandwich
Single hamburger
Salad with light vinaigrette

WORST
Bacon burger
Double cheeseburger
French fries
Onion rings

TIPS
Order sandwiches without mayo or "special sauce." Avoid deep-fried items like fish filets, chicken nuggets, and French fries.

Italian

BEST
Pasta with red or white clam sauce
Spaghetti with marinara or tomato-and-meat sauce

WORST
Eggplant parmigiana
Fettuccine alfredo
Fried calamari
Lasagna

TIPS
Stick with plain bread instead of garlic bread made with butter or oil. Ask for the waiter's help in avoiding cream- or egg-based sauces. Try vegetarian pizza, and don't ask for extra cheese.

Mexican

BEST
Bean burrito (no cheese)
Chicken fajitas

WORST
Beef chimichanga
Chili relleno
Quesadilla
Refried beans

TIPS
Choose soft tortillas (not fried) with fresh salsa, not guacamole. Special-order grilled shrimp, fish, or chicken. Ask for beans made without lard or fat and for cheeses and sour cream provided on the side or left out altogether.

Chinese

BEST
Hot-and-sour soup
Stir-fried vegetables
Shrimp with garlic sauce
Szechuan shrimp
Wonton soup

WORST
Crispy chicken
Kung pao chicken
Moo shu pork
Sweet-and-sour pork

TIPS
Share a stir-fry; help yourself to steamed rice. Ask for vegetables steamed or stir-fried with less oil. Order moo shu vegetables instead of pork. Avoid fried rice, breaded dishes, egg rolls and spring rolls, and items loaded with nuts. Avoid high-sodium sauces.

Japanese

BEST
Steamed rice and vegetables
Tofu as a substitute for meat
Broiled or steamed chicken and fish

WORST
Fried rice dishes
Miso (very high sodium)
Tempura

TIPS
Avoid soy sauces. Use caution in eating sashimi and sushi (raw fish) dishes to avoid possible bacteria or parasites.

Thai

BEST
Clear broth soups
Stir-fried chicken and vegetables
Grilled meats

WORST
Coconut milk
Peanut sauces
Deep-fried dishes

TIPS
Avoid coconut-based curries. Ask for steamed, not fried, rice.

Breakfast

BEST
Hot or cold cereal with 2% milk
Pancakes or French toast with syrup
Scrambled eggs with hash browns and plain toast

WORST
Belgian waffle with sausage
Sausage and eggs with biscuits and gravy
Ham-and-cheese omelette with hash browns and toast

TIPS
Ask for whole grain cereal or shredded wheat with 1% milk or whole wheat toast without butter or margarine. Order omelettes without cheese, fried eggs without bacon or sausage.

Sandwiches

BEST
Ham and Swiss cheese
Roast beef
Turkey

WORST
Tuna salad
Reuben
Submarine

TIPS
Ask for mustard; hold the mayo and cheese. See if turkey-ham is available.

Seafood

BEST
Broiled bass, halibut, or snapper
Grilled scallops
Steamed crab or lobster

WORST
Fried seafood platter
Blackened catfish

TIPS
Order fish broiled, baked, grilled, or steamed—not pan-fried or sauteed. Ask for lemon instead of tartar sauce. Avoid creamy and buttery sauces.

Sources: American Dietetic Association, 2002: www.eatright.org; *Health* 10 (November/December 1996): 79.

- Avoid fried foods in general, including hot apple pies and other crust-based fried
35 foods.

- Opt for places where foods are broiled rather than fried.

WHEN FUNDS ARE SHORT

Maintaining a nutritious diet within the confines of student life can be challenging. However, if you take the time to plan healthy meals, you will find that you are eating better, enjoying your food more, and actually saving money. Follow these steps to ensure a
40 healthy but affordable diet.

- Buy fruits and vegetables in season whenever possible for their lower cost, higher nutrient quality, and greater variety.

- Use coupons and specials to get price reductions.

What do you do to save money on food expenses?

- Shop at discount warehouse food chains; capitalize on volume discounts and no-frills
45 products.

- Plan ahead to get the most for your dollar and avoid extra trips to the store; extra trips usually mean extra purchases. Make a list and stick to it.

- Purchase meats and other products in volume; freeze portions for future needs. Or purchase small amounts of meats and other expensive proteins and combine them
50 with beans and plant proteins for lower cost, calories, and fat.

- Cook large meals, and freeze small portions for later use.

- Drain off extra fat after cooking. Save juices to use in soups and other dishes.

- If you find that you have no money for food, talk to staff at your county or city health department. They may know of ways for you to get assistance.

FOOD ALLERGY OR FOOD INTOLERANCE?

Do you have food allergies?

55 At some point in time, a *food allergy* or *food intolerance* will affect nearly everyone. You eat something, develop gas or have an unpleasant visit to the bathroom, and assume that it is a food allergy. One out of every three people today either say they have a food allergy or avoid something in their diet because they think they are allergic to it; in fact, only 3 percent of all children and 1 percent of all adults experience genuine allergic reactions to
60 what they eat. Surprised? Most people are when they hear this.

A **food allergy** or hypersensitivity is an abnormal response to a food that is triggered by the immune system. Reactions range from minor rashes to severe swelling in the mouth, tongue, and throat, to violent vomiting and diarrhea and occasionally death.

65　In adults, the most common foods to cause true allergic reactions are shellfish (such as shrimp, crayfish, lobster, and crab); peanuts, which can cause severe anaphylaxis (a sudden drop in blood pressure that can be fatal if not treated promptly); tree nuts such as walnuts; fish; and eggs. In children, food allergens that cause the most problems are eggs, milk, and peanuts.

How are food allergies and food intolerance different?

70　In contrast to allergies, in cases of **food intolerance** you may have symptoms of gastric upset but they are not the result of an immune system response. Probably the best example of a food intolerance is *lactose intolerance,* a problem that affects about one in every ten adults. Lactase is an enzyme in the lining of the gut that degrades lactose, which is in dairy products. If you don't have enough lactase, lactose cannot be digested and remains in the gut to be used by bacteria. Gas is formed, and you experience bloating,

75　abdominal pain, and sometimes diarrhea. Food intolerance also occurs in response to some food additives, such as the flavor enhancer MSG, certain dyes, sulfites, gluten, and other substances. In some cases, the food intolerance may have psychological triggers.

IS ORGANIC FOR YOU?

Due to mounting concerns about food safety, many people refuse to buy processed foods and mass-produced agricultural products. Instead, they purchase foods that are

80　**organically grown**—foods reported to be pesticide- and chemical-free. Less than a decade ago, buying organic foods meant going to a specialty store and paying premium prices for produce that was likely to be wilted, wormy, and smaller than its non-organic alternative. These products also came with no guarantee that they were really grown in organic environments. People who bought these foods did so out of a desire to eat

Are the benefits of eating organic foods worth the cost?

85　healthier produce and avoid the chemicals that they were increasingly being told caused cancer, immune system problems, and a host of other ailments.

Enter the organics of the twenty-first century—larger, more attractive, and fresher looking, but still carrying a hefty price tag. Is buying organic really better for you? Perhaps if we could put a group of people in a pristine environment and insure that they never ate,

90　drank, or were exposed to chemicals, we could test this hypothesis. In real life, however, it is almost impossible to assess the health impact of organic versus non-organic. Nevertheless, the market for organics has been increasing by 15 to 20 percent per year— 5 times faster than food sales in general. Nearly 40 percent of U.S. consumers now reach occasionally for something labeled organic, with sales topping $11 billion per year.

ANTIOXIDANTS AND YOUR HEALTH

How do antioxidants work?

95　**Antioxidants** are substances that are believed to protect active people from *oxidative stress* and resultant tissue damage at the cellular level. This damage is believed to occur in a complex process in which *free radicals* (molecules with unpaired electrons that are produced in excess when the body is overly stressed through exposure to toxic substances or events) either damage or kill healthy cells, cell proteins, or genetic material in the cells.

100　Antioxidants produce enzymes that destroy excess free radicals by scavenging them, slowing their formation, and/or actually repairing oxidative stress damage. Antioxidants are found in such food as blueberries, sweet potatoes, and chocolate.

There have been many claims about the benefits of antioxidants in reducing risks of cancer and heart disease, improving vision, and slowing or reversing the aging process.

105　Whether these claims produce scientifically validated evidence that a daily dose of antioxidants is truly beneficial remains to be seen. Initial results from numerous studies appear to support the benefits of at least some antioxidants.

(1,415 words)

—*Health: The Basics,* Sixth Edition,
by Rebecca J. Donatelle

THINKING AND WRITING AFTER READING

RECALL   Self-test your understanding.

Your instructor may choose to give you a true-false comprehension review.

REACT   What space do you have in your room to store food? How can a small refrigerator save dorm students money? _____

_____

_____

REFLECT   Why do fast-food chains have a bad reputation? What is your assessment of their food choices? _____

_____

THINK CRITICALLY   How have American eating habits changed over the last 20 years? What are the benefits and pitfalls? _____

_____

THINK AND WRITE   Prepare a meal plan for a week. List your choices for breakfast, lunch, dinner, and snacks. Be realistic about availability and taste.

Estimate the cost. _____

_____

_____

Interpret the Quote

Now that you have finished reading the selection, "Improved Eating for the College Student," go back to the beginning of the selection and read the opening quote again. What is the significance of using a grocery cart to shop in a convenience store such as 7-Eleven? Do convenience stores offer healthy food choices for college students? Write your responses on a separate sheet of paper.

Name _____

Date _____

COMPREHENSION QUESTIONS

Answer the following with *a, b, c,* or *d,* or fill in the blank. In order to help you analyze your strengths and weaknesses, the question types are indicated.

Main Idea _____ 1. The author's primary purpose in this passage is

    a. to explain the effects of poor nutrition on college students.
    b. to educate college students to make healthier food choices.
    c. to summarize the need for nutrition education at the college level.
    d. to discuss America's preoccupation with diet and nutrition.

Detail _____ 2. The author indicates that college students are challenged by all of the following *except*

    a. limited cooking facilities.
    b. lack of time for shopping and cooking.
    c. budgetary issues.
    d. too many food choices on campus.

Inference _____ 3. By saying "everyone forages in the refrigerator for everyone else's food," the author suggests that

    a. students buy nutritious food but it often spoils before they eat it.
    b. students who live together have little control over who eats the groceries they purchase.
    c. most students eagerly share food with roommates.
    d. students in apartments do not take the time to organize their food properly.

Detail _____ 4. The author notes that students can be healthier consumers at fast-food chains by doing all of the following *except*

    a. ordering broiled rather than fried foods.
    b. skipping the mayonnaise.
    c. requesting a burger with ketchup rather than with cheese and bacon.
    d. choosing a burger over a deep-fried chicken sandwich.

Detail _____ 5. A food intolerance can involve all of the following *except*

    a. gastric upset.
    b. the lack of an enzyme.
    c. an immune system response.
    d. diarrhea.

Detail _____ 6. According to the passage, the number of people who actually have food allergies is

    a. one out of every three.
    b. three out of every one hundred children.
    c. 3 percent of all adults.
    d. nearly everyone who develops gas or has an unpleasant bathroom visit.

Detail _____ 7. According to the passage, antioxidants

      a. have been proven to reduce cancer risks.

      b. destroy excess free radicals.

      c. significantly slow the aging process.

      d. are produced in excess when the body is under stress.

Answer the following with *T* (true) or *F* (false).

Inference _____ 8. If lactose-intolerant people drink milk, they will probably experience gas, discomfort, and bloating.

Inference _____ 9. The author implies that the rise in organic food sales is based more on psychological factors than scientific facts.

Inference _____ 10. The author concludes that students should not eat fast food.

VOCABULARY

Answer the following with *a, b, c,* or *d* for the word or phrase that best defines the boldface word used in the selection. The number in parentheses indicates the line of the passage in which the word appears.

_____ 1. "**forages** in the refrigerator" (3)

      a. glances

      b. eats

      c. searches

      d. shares

_____ 6. "**Opt** for places" (36)

      a. neglect

      b. choose

      c. destroy

      d. boycott

_____ 2. "time **constraints**" (5)

      a. restrictions

      b. goals

      c. periods

      d. persuasions

_____ 7. "food **intolerance**" (69)

      a. impatience

      b. disliking

      c. sensitivity

      d. freshness

_____ 3. "often-**maligned**" (13)

      a. eaten at

      b. insulted

      c. sued

      d. expanding

_____ 8. "psychological **triggers**" (77)

      a. bullets

      b. doctors

      c. tranquilizers

      d. stimuli

_____ 4. "**discriminating** eater" (14)

      a. overeating

      b. vegetarian

      c. healthy

      d. refined

_____ 9. "**hefty** price tag" (88)

      a. natural

      b. small

      c. polluting

      d. large

_____ 5. "Avoid **lard**-based" (32)

      a. unsaturated

      b. calorie

      c. animal fat

      d. fried

_____ 10. "**pristine** environment" (89)

      a. hospital

      b. clean

      c. regulated

      d. toxic

Your instructor may choose to give a true-false vocabulary review.

ASSESS YOUR LEARNING

Review questions that you did not understand, found confusing, or answered incorrectly. Seek clarification. Indicate beside each item the source of your confusion and notice the question type. Make notes beside confusing vocabulary items to help you remember them. Use your textbook as a learning tool.

selection 2 Science

". . . We have very little control over external forces such as tornadoes, earthquakes, floods, disasters, illness, and pain. What really matters is the internal force. How do I respond to those disasters?"

—Leo Buscaglia

In 2005 Hurricane Katrina hit the Gulf Coast and New Orleans with devastating results. Damage grew into the billions of dollars. People lost family, homes, businesses, jobs, possessions, and security. Survivors were scattered around the nation, and some bravely returned to rebuild. Was Katrina the worst disaster to hit the Gulf? The answer is no. In 1900 Galveston suffered the destruction of a similar storm. As in the case of Katrina, several factors came together to intensify the horror of the storm's rage.

THINKING BEFORE READING

Preview the selection for clues to content. Activate your schema, and anticipate what you will learn.

Have you experienced a hurricane, tornado, flood, or other natural disaster?

When is hurricane season?

How does television help save lives in a natural disaster_____?

I'll read this to find out _____.

VOCABULARY PREVIEW

Are you familiar with these words?

fatalities	barrier island	amiss	flocked	gawk
imminent	plummeted	flotsam	dredged	sediment

Is it polite to *gawk* at another person?

Is there a difference between *imminent* and *impending?*

Your instructor may choose to give a true-false vocabulary review before or after reading.

THINKING DURING READING

As you read, use the six thinking strategies of a good reader: predict, picture, relate, monitor, correct, and annotate. Answer the questions in the margins.

THE GALVESTON DISASTER

Why was this storm considered the United States' greatest natural disaster?

The greatest natural disaster to strike the United States was the tropical cyclone that hit Galveston, Texas, on the night of 8 September 1900. The combination of high wind, great waves, and storm surge killed about 8,000 people—more than the Johnstown Flood, the San Francisco Earthquake, the 1938 New England Hurricane, and the Great
5 Chicago Fire combined. Indeed this one event accounts for more than a third of all tropical storm- or hurricane-related fatalities ever recorded in the United States.

In 1900 Galveston, home to about 37,000 people, was one of the most important cotton markets in America. The island city was (and is) located at the eastern end of

Reader's *Tip* Reading and Studying Science

- Master a concept by explaining it in your own words.
- Draw your own scientific models and diagram the processes to reinforce learning them.
- Use illustrations as a reading and review tool before exams.
- Use chapter summaries as study checklists to be sure you have reviewed all the chapter material.
- Think like a scientist at the textbook Web site by participating in virtual research activities.
- Use mnemonics to memorize. For example—**M**any **P**eople **F**ind **P**arachuting **A**larming—to remember the five kingdoms, which are Monera, Protista, Fungi, Plantae, and Animalia.
- Know the theories you are applying in the lab and their significance.
- Blend lecture, lab, and textbook notes.

Describe the geography of Galveston Island.

Galveston Island, a low sand barrier island off the Texas coast about 48 kilometers (30
10 miles) long and 3.2 kilometers (2 miles) wide. When the hurricane struck, the highest point in Galveston was only 2.7 meters (8.7 feet) above sea level.

Why did Dr. Isaac Cline think something was wrong?

Unlike today, there were no geosynchronous satellites, ship-to-shore radios, or networks of weather forecasters to warn of the coming storm. Forecasting was done by experience and hunch, and few were better guessers than Dr. Isaac Cline, chief of the
15 U.S. Weather Bureau's Galveston station. On the evening of 7 September, as many of Galveston's residents were settling down to dinner, Cline became increasingly concerned about the 26-kilometer- (16-mile-) per-hour northerly wind that had blown steadily all day. Something was amiss—the wind was from the wrong direction, and high clouds at sunset were moving in nearly the opposite way, from the southeast. By midnight the wind
20 had shifted toward the northeast and had grown to about 60 kilometers (50 miles) per hour. At first light residents flocked to the shore to gawk at the monstrous waves crashing on the beaches. Then the water began to rise. Cline sensed a hurricane was imminent and believed he knew what was going to happen next, but as he spread emergency warnings to evacuate the island, a steamship was torn from its moorings and smashed through the
25 three bridges connecting the island to the mainland. There would be no escape.

The atmospheric pressure plummeted and the wind speed increased as the storm approached and intensified. The tropical cyclone's low pressure drew the ocean into a broad mound, and the winds drove this mound ashore—a phenomenon known as a storm surge. As misfortune would have it, the surge arrived at a time of high tide. Waters from the
30 Gulf of Mexico and Galveston Bay rose to meet each other. Residents scrambled to the second, third, or fourth stories of buildings to avoid the rising water. Winds that reached 200 kilometers (125 miles) per hour collapsed the structures, freeing masses of flotsam that hammered anyone outside. By the afternoon of 8 September, buildings crumbled and people were battered by debris and drowned. At 8:30 that evening, the water stood 3.4 meters
35 (11 feet) above Galveston Island's highest point. People died in the thousands, clinging to heaving rafts of wreckage and each other. Property damage was extraordinary.

Galveston was rebuilt. In 1902 residents began to construct a 5-meter- (16-foot-) thick, 5.2-meter- (17- foot-) high seawall covering 3 miles of oceanfront. (The seawall today extends for 16 kilometers, or 10 miles.) They also dredged enough sediment from
40 Galveston Bay to raise the island 2.5 meters (8 feet).

Between 80% and 90% of the residents of hurricane-prone areas have not experienced a major hurricane. The smaller storms they have seen often leave them with the false impression of a hurricane's true potential for damage. Galveston proves otherwise.

(591 words)

What is a storm surge?

How was Galveston changed to protect itself from future hurricanes?

—From Garrison, *Oceanography*, 5th ed. © 2005
Brooks/Cole, part of Cengage Learning, Inc. Reproduced
by permission. www.cengage.com/permissions

THINKING AND WRITING AFTER READING

RECALL Self-test your understanding.

Your instructor may choose to give you a true-false comprehension review.

REACT What factors combined to make the Galveston storm so deadly? _____

_____

REFLECT How can the experiences of Galveston be applied today in hurricane-

prone areas? _____

_____

THINKING CRITICALLY Compare the disaster of Galveston to the effects of Katrina

or another major hurricane. _____

_____

THINK AND WRITE How would you respond to a natural disaster where you live in

order to save your life and the lives of others? _____

_____

Interpret the Quote

Now that you have finished reading the selection "The Galveston Disaster," go back to the beginning of the selection and read the opening quote again. Do we have any control over disasters, such as earthquakes and floods? On a separate sheet of paper, list five reasons why you believe we do or do not have control during major disasters, and list five ways that we can appropriately respond to one.

Name _____

Date _____

COMPREHENSION QUESTIONS

Answer the following with *a, b, c,* or *d,* or fill in the blank. In order to help you analyze your strengths and weaknesses, the question types are indicated.

Main Idea _____ 1. The best statement of the main idea of this selection is:
   a. Galveston lacked an evacuation plan that could have saved thousands.
   b. A seawall could have saved the people of Galveston from the disaster of 1900.
   c. The residents of Galveston did not understand the potential force of a major hurricane.
   d. The Galveston storm was a huge disaster because of a combination of circumstances.

Detail _____ 2. The percentage of Galveston's population killed in the tropical cyclone disaster of 1900 was approximately
   a. 100%.
   b. 50%.
   c. 20%.
   d. 10%.

Inference _____ 3. The reader can conclude that some people survived the disaster by
   a. running to higher ground.
   b. staying on the first floor of their homes.
   c. floating.
   d. seeking government-provided shelter in small elementary schools.

Inference _____ 4. The author implies that Dr. Isaac Cline feared an unusual disaster because
   a. the waves were high on September 7.
   b. the winds were 16 miles per hour.
   c. the clouds were higher than usual at sunset.
   d. the water level, wind direction, and cloud direction changed from the usual.

Detail _____ 5. A storm surge is
   a. a violent wind.
   b. a wave of water.
   c. a mound of low pressure.
   d. the violent meeting of water from two sources.

Detail _____ 6. In the 1902 rebuilding of Galveston, residents
   a. built a protective seawall between Galveston Island and the mainland.
   b. deepened Galveston Bay to manage the tides.
   c. raised the land level of Galveston.
   d. raised the sea level of Galveston Island.

Inference _____ 7. The reader can conclude that most people in the Galveston disaster were killed by

    a. water.
    b. wind.
    c. floating wreckage.
    d. low pressure.

Answer the following with *T* (true) or *F* (false).

Inference _____ 8. The reader can conclude that low tide would have decreased the height of the storm surge.

Detail _____ 9. The island evacuation routes were destroyed by a steamship.

Inference _____ 10. The reader can conclude that the highest point in Galveston is now 20.7 feet above sea level.

VOCABULARY

Answer the following with *a, b, c,* or *d* for the word or phrase that best defines the boldface word used in the selection. The number in parentheses indicates the line of the passage in which the word appears.

_____ 1. "hurricane-related **fatalities**" (6)

    a. injuries
    b. deaths
    c. property destruction
    d. warnings

_____ 2. "**barrier island**" (9)

    a. underwater
    b. surface
    c. barricade
    d. rocky

_____ 3. "Something was **amiss**" (18)

    a. right
    b. windy
    c. crazy
    d. wrong

_____ 4. "residents **flocked**" (21)

    a. flew
    b. gathered
    c. left
    d. boycotted

_____ 5. "**gawk** at the monstrous waves" (21)

    a. surf
    b. escape
    c. stop
    d. stare

_____ 6. "a hurricane was **imminent**" (22)

    a. almost over
    b. miles away
    c. about to happen
    d. gone

_____ 7. "atmospheric pressure **plummeted**" (26)

    a. increased gradually
    b. increased quickly
    c. decreased gradually
    d. decreased quickly

_____ 8. "masses of **flotsam**" (32)

    a. houses
    b. wreckage
    c. boats
    d. people

_____ 9. "They also **dredged** . . . (39)

    a. drained
    b. filled
    c. dried
    d. detoured

_____ 10. enough **sediment**"(39)

    a. fishes
    b. bones
    c. deposits
    d. water

Your instructor may choose to give a true-false vocabulary review.

ASSESS YOUR LEARNING

Review confusing questions, seek clarification, and make notes in your text to help you remember new information and vocabulary.

selection 3 Criminal Justice

"The good of the people is the chief law."

—Cicero (106–43 BCE)

Psychological theories of criminal behavior focus on personality traits and behavior. Crime-control methods based on psychological views center on treating individuals with appropriate therapy to overcome their criminal tendencies. These methods rely on some measure of "dangerousness," or how likely the person is to do harm. Several important issues surround such psychological views. Should a mentally ill person be treated by the courts in the same way that a sane person is treated? What determines whether or not a person is insane? Can a mentally ill person who commits a crime be "cured" so that he or she can function safely in normal society?

THINKING BEFORE READING

Preview the selection for clues to content. Activate your schema, and anticipate what you will learn.

Have you heard news stories about people who have committed crimes and claimed that they were insane at the time?

What is the definition of *insanity*?

Why might society hesitate to punish mentally ill offenders in the same way that it punishes sane individuals?

This selection will probably tell me _____.

VOCABULARY PREVIEW

Are you familiar with these words and figures of speech?

abruptly	incarceration	took a dive	schizophrenia	severity
competent	acquittal	alluded	surmised	psychosis

Is there a difference between *surmised* and *inferred*?

Do you see a familiar word part in *psychosis* that might hint at the meaning?

Your instructor may choose to give a true-false vocabulary review before or after reading.

THINKING DURING READING

As you read, use the six thinking strategies of a good reader: predict, picture, relate, monitor, correct, and annotate. Answer the questions in the margins.

WAS ERIC CLARK INSANE OR JUST TROUBLED?

Have you had an experience so alarming that it seemed unreal?

The phone roused Terry Clark from sleep. She eyed the clock: 5 A.M. Who could be calling at this hour?

"Flagstaff Police Department," a voice announced abruptly. The next minutes and hours would pass like a slow-moving horror film where the evil emerges bit by bit.

3 selection

> ## Reader's *Tip* Reading and Studying Criminal Justice
>
> - Identify criminal acts in legal terms. Make lists to commit to memory.
> - Distinguish between the types of crimes and categories of criminals. Use charts to form groups.
> - Know the legal behaviors and responsibilities required for making an arrest and gathering evidence. Make timelines.
> - Understand the processes of the courts and the sequencing of legal actions. Create a flowchart for a visual display.
> - Relate possible legal decisions and police actions to the balance of police powers and democratic freedoms.

5　　At first, investigators told her only that a policeman had been shot. She heard a name, Officer Jeff Moritz. He was called to the neighborhood after residents reported a pickup circling round and round, blaring loud music.

　　Her son Gentry's pickup sat abandoned—driver's-side door flung open, keys in the ignition, a Dr. Dre CD in the player—next to the sidewalk where the police officer had

10　died.

　　Her son was the prime suspect. Not Gentry, though, who had been at home in bed, safe. Her other son, Eric. The one who had been a star football player and a good student with dreams.

　　The one who just two months earlier had called his mother and father aliens.

SLAYING SHOCKED TOWN

15　What happened in those early morning hours of June 21, 2000, left an entire town in shock. The victim was the only police officer ever killed in the line of duty in this mountain community north of Phoenix.

Whose side would the town probably take?

　　He was a caring cop who cut firewood for the handicapped and bought burgers for hungry transients he arrested. He was a husband and father with one young son and a

20　second on the way.

　　The accused was a 17-year-old high school senior who had a history of marijuana use and had been arrested two months earlier for drunken driving and drug possession. Police had found two dozen hits of LSD in his car.

　　A portrait quickly emerged of a drug-crazed teen with no regard for life. But as the

25　facts slowly surfaced so did a different picture of Eric Michael Clark—that of a decent boy from a stable family who had descended into schizophrenia.

　　With this revelation came a question: How do you measure justice when a killer is a mentally ill kid?

What was the verdict?

　　It took three years for Eric Clark to be found competent to stand trial. His lawyers

30　pushed for a verdict of "guilty except insane," meaning incarceration in a psychiatric facility. Instead, a judge found him guilty of first-degree, intentional murder and sentenced him to life in prison, where treatment isn't assured.

What were the legal issues in the U.S. Supreme Court case?

　　On Wednesday, the U.S. Supreme Court is scheduled to take up the case of *Clark* v. *Arizona* and the issue of just how difficult states can make it for criminal defendants to

35　prove insanity.

　　It's the first time the court has dealt with a direct constitutional challenge to the insanity defense since lawmakers around the country imposed new restrictions following John Hinckley's acquittal by reason of insanity in the 1981 shooting of President Reagan.

Eric Clark leaving the Coconino County Courthouse in Arizona prior to sentencing.

"When is it just to punish, or not?" says Richard Bonnie, director of the Institute of Law, Psychiatry and Public Policy at the University of Virginia. "There are some cases where a person was so mentally disturbed at the time of the offense that it would be inhumane and morally objectionable to convict and punish them."

SIGNPOSTS OF MENTAL ILLNESS

Looking back now, Terry Clark remembers things, little things, and wonders when it all started.

What were the signs of mental illness?

Eric was a gifted athlete who played soccer, baseball, basketball, football. As a running back at Flagstaff High, he was one of the young stars selected to play varsity and dreamed of becoming a professional athlete. Then he lost interest in sports.

He had been popular—a homecoming court nominee—but his friends quit calling. His grades, usually As and Bs, took a dive.

On June 21, 1999, Terry and her husband, Dave, had their son admitted to Aspen Hill, a local mental health facility. He'd abandoned his car on a road.

At Aspen Hill, Eric tested positive for marijuana, and Terry wondered whether drugs had triggered his behavior. But doctors alluded to something else—the possibility of schizophrenia. With no mental illness on either side of the family. Terry pushed that idea aside.

Eric seemed to improve and she had him discharged after only three days. "He's getting better," Terry convinced herself. He got worse.

That fall, Eric quit school. He became obsessed with Y2K, took his dad's debit card and charged $1,700 worth of survival gear. He wore layers upon layers of clothing and carried his possessions in a garbage bag.

When January 1, 2000, came and went, Eric's mood improved. He went back to high school. "He's getting better," Terry thought again—until Eric started mentioning "them."

That April, Eric suddenly referred to her as an alien. Eric called his father an alien, too. "If you'd go get some tools," he told them matter-of-factly, "I'd show you."

Terry now believed the doctors were right about schizophrenia. She was relieved when, that same month, Eric was arrested on drunken driving and drug charges; she thought that would lead to getting help. But authorities decided to postpone prosecution until Eric turned 18 later in the year.

She and Dave searched for counselors, but Eric refused to go. Terry left messages at treatment facilities that were never returned.

70   On June 19, 2000, Eric called his mother an alien again. "How would you like to be me," he said, "and never know who your real mother is?"

Terry contacted her lawyer and begged him to convince the county to pursue the drug charges. Prosecutors still wanted to wait until Eric was an adult, so he'd face longer prison time if convicted.

INTENT OR INSANITY?

75   Investigators surmise that sometime after 1:30 A.M. on June 21, 2000, Eric made his way home, sneaked into his brother Gentry's bedroom, took his keys and left in Gentry's truck.

What happened after that, and why, no one can know for certain; Eric never talked about the events of that morning.

At the 2003 trial, prosecutors and defense attorneys agreed that Eric suffered from
80   paranoid schizophrenia and was mentally ill. But legal insanity is another matter; Arizona law spells out its limited use as a defense.

"A person may be found guilty except insane if, at the time of the commission of the criminal act, the person was afflicted with a mental disease or defect of such severity that the person did not know the criminal act was wrong," the law states.

What are the arguments for the prosecution?

85   The Prosecutor, Assistant Attorney General David Powell, argued Eric did know. "Officer Moritz walked into . . . an ice-cold ambush," he said at trial.

Defense lawyers insisted Eric's psychosis was so severe he was incapable of hatching such a plan.

What are the arguments for the defense?

They noted that two months after the shooting, Eric called his parents from jail and
90   told them Flagstaff was a "platinum city" inhabited by 50,000 aliens. Before hanging up, he added: "The only thing that will stop aliens are bullets."

In his appeal to the U.S. Supreme Court, lawyer David Goldberg asserts that Arizona law is so restrictive that it violates a mentally ill defendant's right to a fair trial.

For one, he says, Arizona law prohibited the trial court from considering Eric's mental
95   illness in weighing whether he intentionally killed the police officer. Testimony about his mental illness was not permitted until the second phase of the two-part trial.

Goldberg also argues that Arizona's right-wrong test is too narrow in determining legal insanity. Eric might have known that killing was wrong in the abstract, Goldberg says, but if he believed Moritz was an alien, "he didn't understand the nature of what he was doing."

100   The Supreme Court's decision, expected later this year, could also mean a retrial for Eric Clark, something the Moritz family would see as unjust.

"An angry young man who sets out to kill a cop, or anybody else, ought to be locked up for the rest of his life," says the victim's father, Dan Moritz, a psychologist who questions whether Clark actually is a paranoid schizophrenic.

105   For the Clarks, a new trial would mean a chance for their son to receive psychiatric care.

"Lock him up for his crime," Terry Clark says, "but treat him for his mental illness, please. Eric didn't choose to be mentally ill. It chose him."

(1,361 words)

—Pauline Arrillaga, "Was Eric Clark Insane or Just Troubled?"
The Associated Press, April 15, 2006. Copyright © 2006 by The Associated Press. All rights reserved. Reprinted with permission.

THINKING AND WRITING AFTER READING

RECALL   Self-test your understanding.

Your instructor may choose to give you a true-false comprehension review.

Author's note: Eric Clark's conviction was upheld by the U.S. Supreme Court.

REACT Do you agree more strongly with Eric Clark's mother or with Officer Moritz's family? Why? _____

_____

_____

REFLECT Have you seen a movie or TV show about people who have a mental illness? Do you know anyone with a mental illness? What kind of therapy or treatment did they receive? Was it successful? _____

_____

_____

THINK CRITICALLY If you had been on the jury in Eric Clark's trial, how do you think you would have decided? _____

_____

_____

THINK AND WRITE Imagine that you are either the lawyer defending Eric Clark or the one prosecuting him. Write the main arguments you would present to support your case. _____

_____

_____

Interpret the Quote

Now that you have finished reading the selection, "Was Eric Clark Insane or Just Troubled?" go back to the beginning of the selection and read the opening quote again. How is the "good of the people" best served? By giving harsh sentences that do not allow for treatment of mentally ill criminals or by giving sentences that do allow for treatment? Explain your answer on a separate sheet of paper.

Name _____

Date _____

COMPREHENSION QUESTIONS

Answer the following with *a*, *b*, *c*, or *d*, or fill in the blank. In order to help you analyze your strengths and weaknesses, the question types are indicated.

Main Idea _____ 1. The best statement of the main idea of this selection is

a. Eric Clark's case involved Flagstaff's first death of a police officer in the line of duty.
b. Eric Clark's case highlights the difficulty of determining how the law should be applied to a mentally ill person who commits a crime.
c. Eric Clark stole a car and murdered a police officer.
d. People who commit murder should be punished in the same way whether or not they are insane.

Detail _____ 2. Which of the following statements describes Eric Clark before signs of mental illness appeared?

a. He had a difficult childhood and was often in trouble at school.
b. He was a quiet, sweet child who was shy in social situations.
c. He was a poor student who struggled in school.
d. He was a well-liked athlete.

Inference _____ 3. At about what age did Eric Clark begin to show signs of mental illness?

a. as an infant
b. age 5
c. age 16
d. age 18

Detail _____ 4. When Eric Clark was tried in Arizona, the court

a. found him not guilty by reason of insanity.
b. sentenced him to treatment in a mental health facility.
c. pronounced him guilty and sentenced him to death.
d. found him guilty and sentenced him to life in prison.

Inference _____ 5. The information in this selection suggests that

a. the laws in Eric Clark's state are more harsh toward mentally ill offenders than in other states.
b. the laws determining punishment for mentally ill offenders are the same throughout the United States.
c. the laws defining insanity are the same in all states.
d. the legal definition of insanity is very clear.

Detail _____ 6. The early signs of Eric Clark's mental illness included

a. a history of marijuana use.
b. seeing visions of people and things that were not there.
c. violent acts against his classmates.
d. loss of interest in athletics, friends, and school.

Inference _____ 7. The author suggests that the shooting of President Reagan by John Hinckley
   a. raised questions about whether insanity is an acceptable defense.
   b. had no bearing on Eric Clark's case.
   c. resulted in an incorrect punishment for Hinckley.
   d. made it clear that it is inhumane to convict and punish someone who is mentally ill.

Answer the following with *T* (true), *F* (false), or *CT* (can't tell).

Detail _____ 8. Eric and his brother Gentry were both involved in the murder.

Inference _____ 9. Eric had been arrested before the murder of Officer Moritz.

Detail _____ 10. The U.S. Supreme Court ruled in favor of Eric Clark.

VOCABULARY

Answer the following with *a, b, c,* or *d* for the word or phrase that best defines the boldface word used in the selection. The number in parentheses indicates the line of the passage in which the word appears.

_____ 1. "a voice announced **abruptly**" (3)
   a. quietly
   b. bluntly
   c. easily
   d. prettily

_____ 2. "to be found **competent**" (29)
   a. dead
   b. sick
   c. capable
   d. unable

_____ 3. "meaning **incarceration**" (30)
   a. freedom
   b. therapy
   c. imprisonment
   d. hospitalization

_____ 4. "John Hinckley's **acquittal**" (38)
   a. judgment of not guilty
   b. terrible act
   c. personality
   d. youth

_____ 5. "As and Bs **took a dive**" (49)
   a. improved
   b. went swimming
   c. were earned
   d. got worse

_____ 6. "But doctors **alluded** to" (53)
   a. referred
   b. demanded
   c. allowed
   d. tried

_____ 7. "the possibility of **schizophrenia**" (53–54)
   a. a kind of cancer
   b. a mental illness
   c. drug addiction
   d. heart disease

_____ 8. "Investigators **surmise**" (75)
   a. are sure
   b. state
   c. testify
   d. infer

_____ 9. "defect of such **severity**" (83)
   a. lightness
   b. evil
   c. seriousness
   d. unimportance

_____ 10. "Eric's **psychosis** was so severe" (87)
   a. serious mental illness
   b. jail time
   c. punishment
   d. reaction

Your instructor may choose to give a true-false vocabulary review.

selection

3

ASSESS YOUR LEARNING

Review confusing questions, seek clarification, and make notes in your text to help you remember new information and vocabulary.

ADDITIONAL VOCABULARY LESSONS

Use the vocabulary lessons in this textbook to expand your vocabulary. Each lesson follows a structural approach and links words through shared prefixes, roots, and suffixes. The words are organized into clusters or families to enhance memory, to organize your learning, and to emphasize that most new words are made up of familiar old parts. Strengthen your vocabulary by identifying your old friends in the new words. Then apply your knowledge of word parts to unlock and remember the meanings of the new words.

Your instructor may choose to introduce the words at the beginning of the week, assign review items for practice, and quiz your knowledge of the words at the end of the week. Learn over 200 words through this easy word-family approach.

Vocabulary *Lesson*

Not, Not, and Not

Study the following prefixes, words, and sentences.

Prefixes	*in, im*: not	*dis*: not	*un*: not

Words with in or im = not

Can invisible fences restrain pets? Will the inability to type help you with the computer?

- inadequate: not enough

  Having *inadequate* health care causes many flu victims to go untreated.

- inaccessible: not able to be reached

  Some mountain areas are *inaccessible* except by foot.

- inclement: not mild

  Keep an umbrella handy for *inclement* weather.

- intolerable: not bearable

  Children learn by suffering consequences for *intolerable* behaviors.

- inhospitable: not welcoming

  The *inhospitable* island was cold, windy, and barren.

- insatiable: cannot be satisfied

  Young readers have an *insatiable* desire for more Harry Potter.

- improbable: not likely to occur

  Because of overbooking, a doctor's appointment today is *improbable*.

- immoral: not conforming to accepted standards of right and wrong.

  The politician's *immoral* actions were scorned by the voters.

- impassable: blocked

  With the bridge washed out from the flood, the road was *impassable*.

- immortal: cannot die

  An *immortal* flame burns to honor the assassinated president.

- immobilized: rendered not able to move

  The zookeepers had to *immobilize* the lion before treating its infected foot.

Words with dis = not

Do the tabloids dishonor celebrities? Can you disclaim a relative?

- disarm: take weapons away

  The troops were *disarmed* after the surrender.

- disadvantage: handicap

  The major *disadvantage* of the sofa is that its light-colored fabric easily shows dirt.

- discredit: cause disbelief in

  To *discredit* his character, the opposition circulated a rumor of drugs.

- disgrace: shame

  With an indictment pending, the mayor resigned in *disgrace*.

- disloyal: unfaithful

  The *disloyal* employee revealed company secrets.

- distrust: doubt

  If you *distrust* the management, don't invest your money in the company.

- disconcerted: upset

  The workers were *disconcerted* and even angry about the computer virus.

- disregard: not pay attention to

  If you have already paid, please *disregard* this bill.

- dissolved: melted away

  The sugar *dissolved* into the hot espresso.

- disinherit: to deny an inheritance

  Few parents will *disinherit* a child.

Words with un = not

Is an unsaid rule clearly stated? Is an uneducated guess mostly luck?

- unable: not having the ability

  Because of a shortage, the company was *unable* to ship the software.

- unabridged: not shortened

  For the derivation of words, use an *unabridged* dictionary.

- unaffected: not touched

  Although we saw the funnel, our house was *unaffected* by the tornado.

- unaltered: not changed

  With no additional work, the original plans remain *unaltered*.

- untouchable: cannot be touched

  The children were told that the food was *untouchable* until the guests arrived.

Review

Part I

Answer the following with *T* (true) or *F* (false).

_____ 1. An abridged dictionary contains more than an unabridged dictionary.

_____ 2. Counties seek inaccessible voting locations for citizens.

_____ 3. A disinherited relative receives no gift from the deceased.

_____ 4. An invisible correction can be easily detected.

_____ 5. To discredit a source is to cast doubt on its worth.

_____ 6. Renters usually desire intolerant landlords.

_____ 7. An immobilized elephant is unlikely to charge.

_____ 8. An unaltered proposal remains in its original format.

_____ 9. Disloyal fans boost the morale of a team.

_____10. Powdered milk will dissolve in water.

Part II

Choose the best word from the list to complete each of the following sentences.

inadequate	disregard	unaffected	immoral	disgrace
impassable	disarm	inclement	untouchable	disconcerting

11. The three-foot snow left the roads _____.

12. Humor can _____ the anger of a complaining customer.

13. The _____ weather did not stop the snow skiers from skiing.

14. The _____ actions of the spouse were grounds for the divorce.

15. In a museum, signs indicate that the paintings are _____.

16. By not traveling, they were _____ by the hotel shortage.

17. The _____ protestors rudely interrupted the speaker.

18. Spenders who _____ money may soon be in debt.

19. To get good grades, do not take tests with _____ preparation.

20. When convicted of the crime, the defendant hung her head in

_____.

Reading News and Feature Stories in the Newspaper

What do you usually read first in your daily newspaper? You probably already have a pattern for reading your favorite parts. To help you locate different topics, newspapers are divided into *sections*: national and international news; local or regional news; sports; entertainment and the arts (including movies and television); classified ads; plus any other categories the editors believe are appropriate for the local community. The front page always carries the most important stories from all the categories. Those articles are often continued in a section in which other articles related to the lead story appear. Some newspapers include an index on the front page to help you locate high-interest articles or regular sections.

Understand the Evolution of Newspaper Style

To appreciate the organization of newspaper stories, you must first understand that the journalistic style of newspaper writing developed as a response to the telegraph machine, a new technology that could break down at any time.

As protection against a communication breakdown or a deadline cutoff, as well as to ensure that readers received the most important parts of the news story, reporters got into the habit of including only the most important points in the first paragraphs. The major and minor details of the story were then placed in the following paragraphs in *descending* order of importance. Thus the **inverted pyramid** format of news writing was invented. Although technology has improved dramatically, this format has continued.

News Stories

News stories are the front-page articles that objectively report facts in descending order of importance. The **lead** is the first paragraph, which catches the reader's attention, often summarizes the essential points of the story, and establishes a focus. Many leads contain the 5 *W*'s and one *H*: *Who, What, When, Where, Why*, and *How*? Think of the first paragraph as a condensed version of the event.

Reader's *Tip* Reading a News Story

- Get an overview from the headline and photographs.
- Answer the 5 *W*'s and the *H*.

Who is the story about?
What happened?
When did it happen?
Where did the event or events take place?
Why did this event occur?
How did this happen?

- Continue to read according to the amount of detail desired.

Subsequent paragraphs present details in a hierarchy of importance. A news story has no ending, but rather tapers down from major to minor details. As you read further, more complete information is given about the five basic questions. Your level of interest will determine how far you read for more details. The following is an example of the inverted pyramid format in a news story.

THE MONROE REPORTER

25¢　　　　　　　Monroe's Hometown Newspaper　　　　　Thursday, April 25, 2004

TWISTER HITS LYNCHBURG

Most important points

Lynchburg—A tornado slammed into this southern Virginia community early yesterday, leaving more than 400 people homeless and injuring more than 75. Two people were killed when their mobile home was hurled down an embankment.

Major details

The twister hit around 7:15 A.M. Wednesday, tearing the steeple off the Edgewood First Presbyterian Church, ripping glass out of storefronts, and overturning several cars at the Edgewood Forest Center next door. Arbor Park, a residential development directly across the street, was untouched.

Minor details

The storm system, which stretched from Georgia and the Carolinas to southern Maryland, dumped over 6 inches of rain on Lynchburg and the surrounding area in less than 3 hours. Flooding and tornado-related damage are expected to top $1 million. The governor's office immediately declared the region a disaster area and called in the National Guard for assistance.

exercise 1　Select a news story that you find interesting and clip it from the newspaper. Identify the who, what, when, where, why, and how on a separate sheet of paper. On the news clipping itself, draw an inverted pyramid over the most important points.

Feature Stories

Feature stories differ from news stories in their timeliness, style, and length. Whereas news stories cover breaking news, a feature story might discuss less time-sensitive issues, such as a profile of an actor or an important local businessperson, the reopening of a historical hotel, or a new lifestyle trend. In other words, articles such as these would have similar impact if you read them today or five days from now. Unlike the inverted pyramid style of news stories, the style of feature stories is characterized by a beginning, middle, and end, as well as a thesis. The feature may take up one or two complete pages of the newspaper. Other shorter articles related to the same primary topic often accompany feature stories.

Feature stories are usually found in the section appropriate to their subject. In the previous examples, an actor's profile would be found in *arts/entertainment*, the profile of a local businessperson would be in the *business section*, the refurbishing of a landmark hotel would be in *local news*, and new trends would be in the *lifestyle* or *living section*. They add a fresh angle to recent news by including overlooked or undisclosed information. *Exposés* are based on in-depth investigation to reveal or "expose" shocking or surprising information, such as abuses of power or the quality of public education in your area.

Reader's *Tip*   Reading a Feature Story

- How does the angle or focus of a feature story differ from that of a straight news story?
- How credible are the sources cited?
- Is it factual or sensationalized?
- Does the reporter show a bias?
- Does the reporter judge, or do you decide?

exercise 2

Locate a feature story that interests you and clip it from the newspaper. Discuss the factors that make this article a feature rather than a news story. In particular, think of timeliness (time-sensitivity), style, and length. What is the angle of the story, and why is it being printed now? Circle any credible sources that are cited, and underline sentences or phrases that show a positive or negative bias by the reporter.

3 Vocabulary

- What are context clues?
- What are roots, prefixes, and suffixes?
- How do you use the dictionary?
- Do words have "families"?
- What is a glossary?
- Why use a thesaurus?
- What comparisons form analogies?

Everyday Reading Skills: Getting News and Other Information from Web Sites and Forums

Learning New Words

Recognizing the meaning of words is essential to understanding what you read. If you have a weak vocabulary and stumble over unknown words when you read, you will lose your train of thought and end up concentrating on words rather than on meaning. A poor vocabulary severely limits your reading comprehension and speed.

Research tells us that you are already phenomenally successful at vocabulary acquisition. On the average, you have learned 3,000 to 5,000 words each year from kindergarten through twelfth grade. Experts estimate that only 300 new words are systematically taught each year by a teacher, so congratulate yourself that independently you have learned approximately 2,700 words every year! Were you afraid of new words? Apparently not, because during each of those years, you encountered 15,000 to 30,000 unknown words and you survived. That makes you a very efficient vocabulary builder. Continue to expand your vocabulary knowledge using those skills that have already made you an expert.

To the college reader, being able to recognize a large number of words is more important than being able to use each one of them. Studies show that we use only about 20 percent of the words we know. The average high school graduate recognizes about 50,000 words and uses only 10,000, whereas the average college graduate recognizes around 70,000 words and uses approximately 15,000. This means that during your years in college you probably will learn about 20,000 new words.

The English language contains about one million words. This number includes technical words in all disciplines, many of which the average person would never use. As a college student, however, you are becoming an expert in a particular field and a mini-expert in several areas. Each time you take a course in a new discipline, you face a vocabulary unique to that subject. It takes a little time and a lot of effort to master these new words. After overcoming the initial shock of vocabulary adjustment for each new course, you will find that reading becomes easier and comprehension improves.

Remembering New Words

As you read this section on remembering new words you might notice that memorizing words and definitions is not included. Memorizing is seldom effective for the long term. Instead, focus on understanding the meaning and recognizing the spelling and sound of the word. Think about how the word is used and repeat your exposure to it until it becomes part of your growing vocabulary.

Use Association

Certain new words, especially college-level words, are hard to remember because you don't hear them every day and can't easily work them into casual conversation. To latch on to a new word, form an association with it. Try to remember the word in the context in which it was used. Visualize the word or a situation pertaining to the word. Always try to think of a new word in a phrase, rather than in isolation. For example, do you know the word *surrogate*? Perhaps you encountered the word in psychology class when studying Harlow's experiments on the need for love in infants. The surrogates were wire models substituted for real monkey mothers to test the infant monkey's attraction. To remember the word *surrogate*, think of it in the phrase *surrogate mother* and visualize the infant monkey cuddling up to a wire artificial mother for love and affection. This association creates an indelible picture in your mind.

Use Concept Cards

You can also use concept cards to help you remember vocabulary. *Concept* means idea. On a concept card you expand the definition of a single word into a fully developed idea. You are creating an episode for the new word by providing a sentence, a picture, and a source reference.

Keep a concept card file of new words. Include more than the usual "mystery word" on the front of the card and the definition on the back. Use the technique of association, and on the front of the card write the word within a meaningful phrase or sentence, or both. Also on the front, note where you encountered the new word. On the back of the card, write the definition, and, to add a further

---

Personal *Feedback* **1**   Name _____

1. What is your present system for remembering new words?

   _____

   _____

2. For the ten vocabulary items following the selection in Chapter 2 on the Galveston disaster (p. 61), why do you think the line numbers are given for the words? _____

   _____

3. Why do instructors say that studying Latin is a useful way to increase your vocabulary? _____

   _____

4. What is the last new word you can remember learning? _____

   _____

5. What is a word that you frequently encounter but do not completely understand?

   _____

6. On a scale of 1 to 10, with 10 meaning *excellent at the college level*, how would you rate your vocabulary at present? _____

7. What do you feel are the benefits of having a large vocabulary?

   _____

   _____

8. List ten adjectives that describe you. Stretch your vocabulary and go beyond simple one- and two-syllable words. _____

   _____

   Tear out and submit to your instructor.

FRONT

surrogate mother

The baby monkey preferred
the terry cloth surrogate mother

Passage text on love

BACK

Def: substitute, as in the wire
mothers in experiments with
monkeys

memory link, draw a picture that illustrates the way you are using the word in your phrase or sentence. See the illustration above for an example.

When making concept cards, your limits depend only on your creativity and talent. For example, in *Vocabulary Cartoons,* a book by Sam, Max, and Bryan Burchers, the authors link the sounds within words to exaggerated visual images. The resulting cartoons, as shown below, depict the links and suggest the definitions by using sound associations and visual images, along with humor, to improve memory.

Practice Your New Words

Review your concept cards regularly. Look at the word on the front and quiz yourself on the definition. When you feel you have a clear understanding of the meaning, use your new word in writing or in conversation.

HOVEL
(HUV ul)
a small, miserable dwelling;
an open, low shed
Link: **SHOVEL**

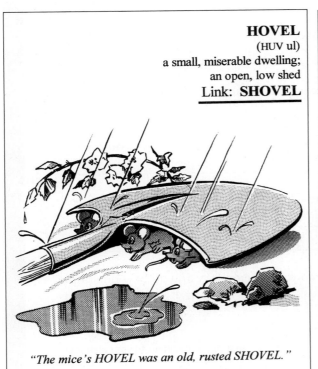

"The mice's HOVEL was an old, rusted SHOVEL."

EDIFICE
(ED uh fis)
a building, especially one of imposing
appearance or size
Link: **ATE A FACE**

"The Great Kong ATE the north FACE of the EDIFICE."

Notice the words around you. As you begin to pay attention to unfamiliar terms in print and in conversation, you will more than likely discover that you encounter many interesting new words.

Unlocking the Meaning of New Words

Use Context Clues

To figure out the meaning of a new word, do not immediately charge off to the dictionary and record a definition as if it were one more addition to a giant list of words. Contrary to what you may have heard, the dictionary is a *last* resort when you aren't sure what a word means. Instead, first try to figure out the meaning from the **context clues** in the sentence or paragraph in which the word is used. What do the surrounding words—the context—tell you about the new word?

Use Knowledge of Word Parts

Another way to discover the meaning of a word is to examine its parts. Do you recognize any prefixes, suffixes, or roots, such as *pseudo* (meaning *false*) or *nym* (meaning *name*) in the word *pseudonym*? If you know these word parts, you can easily figure out that *pseudonym* means a false name rather than a real one. Samuel Clemens's use of the name Mark Twain is an example of a pseudonym.

Use the Glossary and the Dictionary

If a word is specific to a subject area, such as the marketing term *promotional mix,* refer to the glossary in the back of the textbook for a definition that pertains specifically to that field. If all of these strategies fail to unlock the meaning of a new word and you can't understand what you are reading without a definition of the word, then go to the dictionary. But if the word is not essential to your general comprehension, skip it entirely or come back to it later. Your purpose for reading is to get meaning, not to collect vocabulary words. As you read more and encounter more new words, your vocabulary will naturally expand. Make a habit of noticing new words, and try to remember them by association.

Types of Context Clues

The first line of attack on a new word is to try to figure out the meaning from its *context*, or the way it is used in the sentence or paragraph. There are several types of context clues. The following examples show how each type can be used to figure out word meaning.

Definition

The unknown word is defined within the sentence or paragraph.

EXAMPLE   The explorers landed in an *alien* environment, a place both <u>foreign and strange</u> to their beloved homeland.

EXPLANATION   The definition is set off by a comma following the phrase in which the word appears. *Alien* means *strange* or *foreign.*

exercise 1   For each of the context clue exercises in this section, underline the context clue and mark *a, b, c,* or *d* for the meaning closest to that of the boldface word. Do not use a dictionary.

_____ 1. The CIA was engaged in **covert** activities in South America that were not made public.
   a. foreign
   b. dishonest
   c. dangerous
   d. hidden

FRONT

BACK

covert operations
in South America

CIA activities

hidden or secret

_____ 2. The meeting was brief, and the message was **concise** and to the point.
   a. laborious
   b. lengthy
   c. short
   d. important

_____ 3. If we have to have a pet around the house, get one that is **docile** and easy to manage.
   a. gentle
   b. short
   c. sick
   d. young

_____ 4. The professor gave an **ultimatum** about tardiness, saying today would be the last time anyone would be allowed to enter class late.
   a. final demand
   b. new proposal
   c. lecture
   d. choice

_____ 5. Checking the references in the bibliography for errors was **tedious** and uninteresting.

    a. educational
    b. necessary
    c. exhausting
    d. boring

Elaborating Details

Descriptive details suggest the meaning of the unknown word.

EXAMPLE

The natives were _hostile_ when the settlers approached their village. They lined up across the road and drew their weapons. The settlers were afraid to go farther.

EXPLANATION As described in the sentences after the word, _hostile_ must mean _unfriendly._

exercise 2

_____ 1. **Wearily**, the young woman climbed into bed after a long night shift for a well-deserved nap.

    a. relieved
    b. bored
    c. tired
    d. sadly

_____ 2. The gaping wound bled **profusely**, needing several bandages to absorb its flow.

    a. lightly
    b. unnoticeably
    c. slowly
    d. greatly

_____ 3. The boy received a **superficial** cut, the cat's claw having barely grazed his skin.

    a. shallow
    b. visible
    c. deep
    d. lengthy

_____ 4. The instructions left for the babysitter were **delineated** in several sentences with great detail.

    a. ignored
    b. described
    c. discovered
    d. questioned

_____ 5. The politician went on and on with his **harangue** while his fellow senators were forced to keep listening.

    a. noisy laughter
    b. simple explanation
    c. prolonged speech
    d. short conversation

Elaborating Examples

An anecdote or example before or after the word suggests the meaning.

EXAMPLE The bird's appetite is _voracious_. In one day he ate enough worms to equal three times his body weight.

    EXPLANATION Because the bird ate an extraordinary amount, _voracious_ means extremely _hungry_ or _greedy_.

exercise 3

_____ 1. The dancer's movements were not rehearsed but were a **spontaneous** response to the music.

    a. planned
    b. simple
    c. unpremeditated
    d. smooth

_____ 2. The embargo will **restrict** previously flourishing trade with the country and stop the goods from entering the seaport.

    a. promote
    b. enlist
    c. renew
    d. confine

_____ 3. The **affluent** members of the community live in big homes with swimming pools.

    a. powerful
    b. wealthy
    c. athletic
    d. political

FRONT

BACK

affluent people

wealthy: having lots of money

_____ 4. Because the employer had never heard of the three companies listed as references, she was **dubious** about the applicant's previous work history.

    a. relaxed
    b. unconcerned
    c. doubtful
    d. hopeful

_____ 5. The ophthalmologist gave a favorable **prognosis**, saying that in two weeks her vision would be clear, and she would no longer need the dark glasses.

    a. forecast
    b. prescription
    c. warning
    d. notification

Comparison

A similar situation suggests the meaning of the unknown word.

EXAMPLE

The smell of the flower was as *compelling* as a magnet's pull on a paper clip.

EXPLANATION Because a magnet will pull a paper clip to it, the comparison suggests that the smell of the flower had a strong attraction. *Compelling* means *forceful*.

exercise 4

_____ 1. I am as **skeptical** about its chances of success as I am about my chances of winning the lottery.

    a. doubtful
    b. confident
    c. remorseful
    d. hopeful

_____ 2. Confirming an appointment before leaving the office is as **prudent** as never letting your gas tank go lower than one-quarter full.

    a. annoying
    b. reckless
    c. rewarding
    d. wise

_____ 3. With a great deal of feeling, Ellen made an **impassioned** plea for her family to adopt the stray puppy.

    a. illogical
    b. soft-spoken
    c. emotional
    d. short-lived

_____ 4. Because there is always a first time for everything, each of us is a **novice** at some point in our lives.

    a. fool
    b. master
    c. manager
    d. beginner

_____ 5. If the climber is in fact a circus performer, it is **plausible** that he attempted such a dangerous feat on the tall building.

     a. doubtful
     b. impossible
     c. terrible
     d. believable

Contrast

An opposite situation suggests the meaning of the unknown word.

EXAMPLE   In America she is an *eminent* journalist, even though she is virtually unknown in England.

> **EXPLANATION**   The phrase *Even though* signals that an opposite is coming. Thus *eminent* means the opposite of *unknown*; it means *well-known* or *famous*.

exercise 5   _____ 1. Unlike **introverted** people, very talkative folks love crowds and conversation.

     a. quiet
     b. loud
     c. friendly
     d. hostile

_____ 2. His favorites were not the old stories of days gone by but the works of more **contemporary** authors.

     a. intelligent
     b. recent
     c. revolutionary
     d. meaningful

_____ 3. He did not mean to cause the problem. While looking for his hat, the young man **inadvertently** knocked over the lamp.

     a. purposely
     b. knowingly
     c. unintentionally
     d. suddenly

_____ 4. Now that she is an adult college student who is in control of her emotions, she no longer engages in the **infantile** outbursts that marked her behavior as a child.

     a. immature
     b. sudden
     c. angry
     d. short

_____ 5. Although she had had a crush on him all fall, Maria's interest in Michael began to **wane** when he asked two other girls to the holiday party.

a. grow
b. lessen
c. accelerate
d. intensify

WANE
(wain)
to decrease gradually
Link: **RAIN**

"Snowmen WANE in the RAIN."

exercise 6 Use context clues to determine the meanings of the boldface words, which appear frequently in health textbooks.

1. A condition such as arthritis can limit a person's **range of motion** in the shoulders, hips, wrists, and other joints. _____

2. Low **carbohydrate** diets are difficult to follow for lovers of sweets, baked goods, pasta, and potatoes. _____

3. Racehorses are sometimes given a **diuretic** to reduce body fluids before racing. _____

4. Exercise physiologists suggest that people who exercise at the appropriate level of **intensity** ought to be able to carry on a conversation at the same time. _____

5. Final exams would be excellent examples of **stressors** for most students.

_____

Multiple Meanings of a Word

Some words are confusing because they have several different meanings. For example, the dictionary lists more than thirty meanings for the word *run*. To determine the proper meaning, use the context of the sentence and paragraph in which the word occurs. Many of the multiple-meaning words are simple words that are used frequently. If you are puzzling over an unusual use of a common word, consider the context and be aware that the word may have another meaning.

exercise 7   The boldface words in the following sentences have multiple meanings. For each word, write a second sentence in which the word is used differently.

1. The puppy snuggled in the **covers**. _____

_____

2. The **pitch** was low and inside home plate. _____

_____

_____

3. Her neighbors objected to the dog **run** in her backyard. _____

_____

_____

4. I **suspect** it was your brother's mess. _____

_____

_____

5. Debbie had no **choice** in the matter, for it was already decided. _____

_____

6. The orchestra members took a **bow** at the end of the performance. _____

_____

7. Water spilled over the **stern** of the ship during the height of the storm.

_____

8. Nicholas prefers four slices of cinnamon **toast** for breakfast. _____

_____

9. The waves began to **break** along the beach. _____

_____

10. You cannot **hide** from the truth. _____

_____

Word Parts

Many words that at first may seem totally foreign to you are actually made up of words that you already know. One authority claims that learning approximately thirty key word parts will help you unlock the meaning of about 14,000 words. Although this claim may be exaggerated, it emphasizes the importance of roots, prefixes, and suffixes. Word parts are clues to the meaning of new words.

Look at the following family of words. Some may be familiar, and some may be new to you. You probably know the meaning of the first two words and thus can deduce that *ped* means *foot*. Try to figure out the meaning of the other *ped* words by applying your knowledge of closely related words.

Pedal: lever pressed by the foot

Pedestrian: person walking on foot

What do the following words mean? Use the clues to write the definitions.

quadruped: _____ (Hint: quadruplets?)

centipede: _____ (Hint: turn of the century?)

pedometer: _____ (Hint: speedometer?)

Roots

The **root** is the stem or basic part of the word. The roots that we use are derived primarily from Latin and Greek. For example, *port* is a root derived from Latin meaning *to carry,* as in the word *porter. Thermo* is a Greek word meaning *heat,* as in *thermometer.* In both cases, additional letters have been added to the word, but the meaning of the word has not changed. Knowing the definition of the root helps unlock the meaning of each word.

EXAMPLE

The root forms *duc, duct,* and *duce* mean *to lead.* This root branches out into a large word family. Use the root to supply appropriate words to complete the following three sentences.

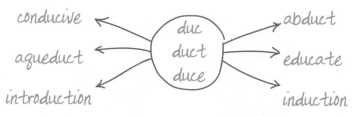

1. If the factory is ready, the new line of furniture will go into _____ in September.

2. The company is trying to cut down overhead in order to _____ expenses.

3. Legitimate business expenses can be _____ from your taxes if you keep the proper receipts.

EXPLANATION The correct answers are *production, reduce,* and *deducted.*

exercise 8 Complete the following sentences by using the given root to form an appropriate word.

grad, gred, gres: take steps, go, degree

1. The seniors will _____ from high school the first week in June.

2. The mountain trail began as a _____ climb and became steeper toward the top.

3. If we continue to work through lunch and all afternoon, we should make enough _____ on our project to finish by five o'clock.

port: carry

4. If we could _____ fewer goods into this country, our balance of payments would improve.

5. She wanted a _____ radio so she could listen to the game while riding in the boat on the lake.

6. Private contributions and volunteers _____ the efforts of the Salvation Army.

7. The organized _____ to and from the game will be by bus.

cred: believe

8. We could not believe what we saw; the feat was _____.

9. Some law schools in the country are not fully _____ by the state, and their courses do not transfer to other schools.

10. Derogatory remarks were made about his performance in an effort to _____ him.

Prefixes

A **prefix** is a group of letters with a special meaning that is added to the beginning of a word. For example, *ex* means *out of* and *im* means *into*. Adding these two prefixes to *port* gives two words that are opposite in meaning. *Export* means to send something out of the country, whereas *import* means to bring something in. Again, knowing the prefixes can help you identify the meaning.

EXAMPLE The prefix *trans* means *across*, *over*, and *beyond*. Write a word beginning with *trans* to complete each of the following three sentences.

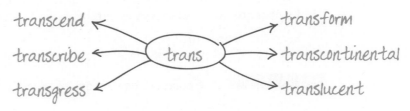

1. The radio station can now _____ programs to a wider audience.

2. Since she did not speak French, he acted as _____ while she conducted business in Paris.

3. When the business _____ was completed, the two executives shook hands.

EXPLANATION The correct answers are *transmit, translator,* and *transaction.*

exercise 9 Complete the following sentences by using the given prefix to form an appropriate word.

dis: take away, not, deprive of

1. When catching criminal suspects, the police carefully _____ them to remove any item that could be used as a weapon.

2. Because she missed the review in the last class before the final exam, the student was at a _____ in studying for the test.

3. Hospital employees are instructed to use special containers to _____ of used needles.

mis: wrong, bad

4. Because the child _____ in the restaurant, he was not allowed to go again.

5. The answer was not a lie, but it did _____ the truth.

6. Because of the lawyer's error, the judge declared a _____ and court was adjourned.

pre: before

7. Even a fortune-teller could not have _____ the fun we had scuba diving.

8. Police recommend alarm systems as a type of crime _____.

9. The student was so _____ with her mathematics assignment that she did not hear the doorbell ring.

10. If you order by phone, you will need a credit card to _____ for the concert tickets.

Suffixes

A **suffix** is a group of letters with a special meaning that is added to the end of a word. A suffix can alter the meaning of a word as well as the way the word is used in the sentence. For example, the *er* in *porter* means the *person who* and makes the word into the name of a person. But adding *able*, which means *capable of,* to *port* does not change the meaning as much as it changes the way the word can be used in the sentence. Some suffixes, therefore, have more meaning than others, but all alter the way the word can be used in a sentence.

EXAMPLE   The suffix *ist* means *one who* or *that which.* Write a word ending with *ist* to complete each of the following three sentences.

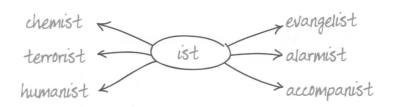

1. If you have a toothache, go to your _____ immediately.

2. The _____ struck the keys of the instrument with such force that the floorboards shook.

3. The picture was painted by a well-known American _____.

EXPLANATION   The correct answers are *dentist, pianist,* and *artist.*

exercise 10   Complete the following sentences by using the given suffix to form an appropriate word.

ion, sion, tion: act of, state of, result of

1. To honor his birthday, we invited his friends to a party and had a big

   _____.

2. If you don't clean out the wound and use a bandage, you are likely to get an

   _____.

3. The _____ bridge was held in the air by cables descending from two towers on either side of the river.

4. Use your _____ to visualize the festive atmosphere of music and outdoor dining.

ship: office, state, dignity, skill, quality, profession

5. After breaking her leg and missing two weeks of class, the student was advised to apply for a _____ withdrawal and make a fresh start the next semester.

6. The university also offered merit _____ that were not based on financial need.

7. The infantry soldier demonstrated excellent _____ by hitting the red mark with each shot.

less: without

8. Because the show was boring, I became _____ and could not sit still.

9. A baby lamb is _____ against fierce and determined predators.

10. Suffering from insomnia, she spent many _____ nights walking the halls.

The Dictionary

Use the dictionary as a last resort for finding the definition of a word while you are reading, unless the word is crucial to your understanding. Remember, stopping in the middle of a paragraph breaks your concentration and causes you to forget what you were reading. Mark unknown words with a dot in the margin, and then, when you have finished reading, look those words up in the dictionary.

Dictionaries contain more than just the definition of a word. They contain the pronunciation, the spelling, the derivation or history, the parts of speech, and the many different meanings a word may have. An entry may also include an illustration or give context examples of the use of the word in a phrase. Consider the following entry.

Source: By permission. From *Merriam-Webster's Collegiate® Dictionary, 11th Edition.*
© 2008 by Merriam-Webster Incorporated (www.Merriam-Webster.com).

ra·bil·i·ty \ˌad-m(ə-)rə-ˈbi-lə-tē\ n — ad·mi·ra·ble·ness \ˈad-m(ə-)rə-bəl-nəs\ n — ad·mi·ra·bly \-blē\ adv

ad·mi·ral \ˈad-m(ə-)rəl\ n [ME, fr. AF amiral commander & ML admiralis emir, admirallus admiral, fr. Ar amīr-al- commander of the (as in amīr-al-baḥr commander of the sea)] (15c) 1 archaic : the commander in chief of a navy 2 a : FLAG OFFICER b : a commissioned officer in the navy or coast guard who ranks above a vice admiral and whose insignia is four stars — compare GENERAL 3 archaic : FLAGSHIP 4 : any of several brightly colored nymphalid butterflies — compare RED ADMIRAL

admiral of the fleet (1660) : the highest-ranking officer of the British navy

ad·mi·ral·ty \ˈad-m(ə-)rəl-tē\ n (15c) 1 cap : the executive department or officers formerly having general authority over British naval affairs 2 : the court having jurisdiction over questions of maritime law; also : the system of law administered by admiralty courts

ad·mi·ra·tion \ˌad-mə-ˈrā-shən\ n (15c) 1 archaic : WONDER 2 : an object of esteem 3 : delighted or astonished approbation

ad·mire \əd-ˈmī(-ə)r\ vb ad·mired; ad·mir·ing [MF admirer, to marvel at, fr. L admirari, fr. ad- + mirari to wonder, fr. mirus astonishing] vt (1560) 1 : to regard with admiration 2 archaic : to marvel at ~ vi, dial : to like very much ⟨I would ~ to know why not —A. H. Lewis⟩ syn see REGARD — ad·mir·er n — ad·mir·ing·ly \-ˈmī-rin-lē\ adv

ad·mis·si·ble \əd-ˈmi-sə-bəl, ad-\ adj [F, fr. ML admissibilis, fr. L admissus, pp. of admittere] (1611) 1 : capable of being allowed or conceded : PERMISSIBLE ⟨evidence legally ~ in court⟩ 2 : capable or worthy of being admitted ⟨~ to the university⟩ — ad·mis·si·bil·i·ty \-ˌmi-sə-ˈbi-lə-tē\ n

ad·mis·sion \əd-ˈmi-shən, ad-\ n (15c) 1 a : the act or process of admitting b : the state or privilege of being admitted c : a fee paid at or for admission 2 a : the granting of an argument or position not fully proved b : acknowledgment that a fact or statement is true — ad·mis·sive \-ˈmi-siv\ adj

ad·mit \əd-ˈmit, ad-\ vb ad·mit·ted; ad·mit·ting [ME admitten, fr. L admittere, fr. ad- + mittere to send] vt (15c) 1 a : to allow scope for : PERMIT ⟨~s no possibility of misunderstanding⟩ b : to concede as true or valid ⟨admitted making a mistake⟩ 2 a : to allow entry (as to a place, fellowship, or privilege) ⟨an open window had admitted rain⟩ ⟨admitted to the club⟩ b : to accept into a hospital as an inpatient ⟨he was admitted last night for chest pains⟩ ~ vi 1 : to give entrance or access 2 a : ALLOW, PERMIT ⟨~s of two interpretations⟩ b : to make acknowledgment — used with to syn see ACKNOWLEDGE

ad·mit·tance \əd-ˈmi-tᵊn(t)s, ad-\ n (1536) 1 a : the act or process of admitting b : permission to enter 2 : the reciprocal of the impedance of a circuit

ad·mit·ted·ly \əd-ˈmi-təd-lē, ad-\ adv (1804) 1 : as has been or must be admitted ⟨an ~ inadequate treatment⟩ 2 : it must be admitted ⟨~, we took a chance⟩

ad·mix \ad-ˈmiks\ vt [back-formation fr. obs. admixt mingled (with), fr. ME, fr. L admixtus] (1533) : to mix in

ad·mix·ture \ad-ˈmiks-chər\ n [L admixtus, pp. of admiscēre to mix with, fr. ad- + miscēre to mix — more at MIX] (1605) 1 a : the action of mixing b : the fact of being mixed 2 a : something added by mixing b : a product of mixing : MIXTURE

ad·mon·ish \ad-ˈmä-nish\ vt [ME admonesten, fr. AF amonester, fr. VL *admonestare, alter. of L admonēre to warn, fr. ad- + monēre to warn — more at MIND] (14c) 1 a : to indicate duties or obligations to b : to express warning or disapproval to esp. in a gentle, earnest, or solicitous manner 2 : to give friendly earnest advice or encouragement to syn see REPROVE — ad·mon·ish·er n — ad·mon·ish·ing·ly \-ni-shin-lē\ adv — ad·mon·ish·ment \-mənt\ n

ad·mo·ni·tion \ˌad-mə-ˈni-shən\ n [ME amonicioun, fr. AF amonicion, fr. L admonition-, admonitio, fr. admonēre] (14c) 1 : gentle or friendly reproof 2 : counsel or warning against fault or oversight

ad·mon·i·to·ry \əd-ˈmä-nə-ˌtȯr-ē\ adj (1594) : expressing admonition : WARNING — ad·mon·i·to·ri·ly \-ˌmä-nə-ˈtȯr-ə-lē\ adv

ad·nate \ˈad-ˌnāt\ adj [L adnatus, agnatus, pp. of adgnasci to be born in addition, grow later — more at AGNATE] (1661) : grown to a usu. unlike part esp. along a margin ⟨a calyx ~ to the ovary⟩ — ad·na·tion \ad-ˈnā-shən\ n

ad nau·se·am \ad-ˈnȯ-zē-əm also -ˌam\ adv [L] (1647) : to a sickening or excessive degree

ad·nexa \ad-ˈnek-sə\ n pl [NL, fr. L annexa, neut. pl. of annexus, pp. of annectere to bind to — more at ANNEX] (1899) : conjoined, subordinate, or associated anatomical parts — ad·nex·al \-səl\ adj

ado \ə-ˈdü\ n [ME, fr. at do, fr. at + don, do to do] (14c) 1 : heightened fuss or concern : TO-DO 2 : time-wasting bother over trivial details ⟨wrote the paper without further ~⟩ 3 : TROUBLE, DIFFICULTY

ado·be \ə-ˈdō-bē\ n [Sp, fr. Ar al-ṭūb the brick, fr. Copt tōbe brick, fr. Egypt ḏbt] (1748) 1 : a brick or building material of sun-dried earth and straw 2 : a structure made of adobe bricks 3 : a heavy clay used in making adobe bricks; broadly : alluvial or playa clay in desert or arid regions — ado·be·like \-ˌlīk\ adj

ado·bo \ə-ˈdō-bō, ä-ˈthō-bō\ n, pl -bos [Sp] (ca. 1951) : a Philippine dish of fish or meat usu. marinated in a sauce containing vinegar and garlic, browned in fat, and simmered in the marinade

adobe 2

ad·o·les·cence \ˌa-də-ˈle-sᵊn(t)s\ n (15c) 1 : the state or process of growing up 2 : the period of life from puberty to maturity terminating legally at the age of majority 3 : a stage of development (as of a language or culture) prior to maturity

¹ad·o·les·cent \ˌa-də-ˈle-sᵊnt\ n [F, fr. L adolescent-, adolescens, prp. of adolescere to grow up — more at ADULT] (15c) : one that is in the state of adolescence

²adolescent adj (1785) 1 : of, relating to, or being in adolescence 2 : emotionally or intellectually immature — ad·o·les·cent·ly adv

Ado·nai \ˌä-də-ˈnȯi, -ˈnī\ n [Heb ʾădhōnāy] (bef. 12c) — used in place of YHWH as a name of the God of the Hebrews during prayer recitation

Ado·nis \ə-ˈdä-nəs, -ˈdō-\ n [L, fr. Gk Adōnis] (1565) 1 : a youth loved by Aphrodite who is killed at hunting by a wild boar and restored to Aphrodite from Hades for a part of each year 2 : a very handsome young man

adopt \ə-ˈdäpt\ vb [ME, fr. MF or L; MF adopter, fr. L adoptare, fr. ad- + optare to choose] vt (1500) 1 : to take by choice into a relationship; esp : to take voluntarily (a child of other parents) as one's own child 2 : to take up and practice or use ⟨~ed a moderate tone⟩ 3 : to accept formally and put into effect ⟨~ a constitutional amendment⟩ 4 : to choose (a textbook) for required study in a course ~ vi 1 : to adopt a child ⟨couples choosing to ~⟩ 2 : to sponsor the care and maintenance of ⟨~ a highway⟩ — adopt·abil·i·ty \-ˌdäp-tə-ˈbi-lə-tē\ n — adopt·able \-ˈdäp-tə-bəl\ adj — adopt·er n

syn ADOPT, EMBRACE, ESPOUSE mean to take an opinion, policy, or practice as one's own. ADOPT implies accepting something created by another or foreign to one's nature ⟨forced to adopt new policies⟩. EMBRACE implies a ready or happy acceptance ⟨embraced the customs of their new homeland⟩. ESPOUSE adds an implication of close attachment to a cause and a sharing of its fortunes ⟨espoused the cause of women's rights⟩.

adopt·ee \ə-ˌdäp-ˈtē\ n (1892) : one who is adopted

adop·tion \ə-ˈdäp-shən\ n (14c) : the act of adopting : the state of being adopted

adop·tian·ism \-shə-ˌni-zəm\ n, often cap (1874) : the doctrine that Jesus of Nazareth became the Son of God by adoption — adop·tion·ist \-sh(ə-)nist\ n, often cap

adop·tive \ə-ˈdäp-tiv\ adj (15c) 1 : made or acquired by adoption ⟨the ~ father⟩ 2 : of or relating to adoption — adop·tive·ly adv

ador·able \ə-ˈdȯr-ə-bəl\ adj (1611) 1 : worthy of being adored 2 : extremely charming ⟨an ~ child⟩ — ador·abil·i·ty \-ˌdȯr-ə-ˈbi-lə-tē\ n — ador·able·ness \-ˈdȯr-ə-bəl-nəs\ n — ador·ably \-blē\ adv

ad·o·ra·tion \ˌa-də-ˈrā-shən\ n (15c) : the act of adoring : the state of being adored

adore \ə-ˈdȯr\ vt adored; ador·ing [ME adouren, fr. AF aurer, adourer, fr. L adorare, fr. ad- + orare to speak, pray — more at ORATION] (14c) 1 : to worship or honor as a deity or as divine 2 : to regard with loving admiration and devotion ⟨adored his wife⟩ 3 : to be very fond of ⟨~s pecan pie⟩ syn see REVERE — ador·er n — ador·ing·ly adv

adorn \ə-ˈdȯrn\ vt [ME, fr. L adornare, fr. ad- + ornare to furnish — more at ORNATE] (14c) 1 : to enhance the appearance of esp. with beautiful objects 2 : to enliven or decorate as if with ornaments ⟨people of fashion who ~ed the Court⟩

syn ADORN, DECORATE, ORNAMENT, EMBELLISH, BEAUTIFY, DECK, GARNISH mean to enhance the appearance of something by adding something unessential. ADORN implies an enhancing by something beautiful in itself ⟨a diamond necklace adorned her neck⟩. DECORATE suggests relieving plainness or monotony by adding beauty of color or design ⟨decorate a birthday cake⟩. ORNAMENT and EMBELLISH imply the adding of something extraneous, ORNAMENT stressing the heightening or setting off of the original ⟨a white house ornamented with green shutters⟩, EMBELLISH often stressing the adding of superfluous or adventitious ornament ⟨embellish a page with floral borders⟩. BEAUTIFY adds to EMBELLISH a suggestion of counterbalancing plainness or ugliness ⟨will beautify the grounds with flower beds⟩. DECK implies the addition of something that contributes to gaiety, splendor, or showiness ⟨a house all decked out for Christmas⟩. GARNISH suggests decorating with a small final touch and is used esp. in referring to the serving of food ⟨an entrée garnished with parsley⟩.

adorn·ment \-mənt\ n (14c) 1 : the action of adorning : the state of being adorned 2 : something that adorns

ADP \ˌā-(ˌ)dē-ˈpē\ n [adenosine diphosphate] (1943) : a nucleotide $C_{10}H_{15}N_5O_{10}P_2$ composed of adenosine and two phosphate groups that is formed in living cells as an intermediate between ATP and AMP and that is reversibly converted to ATP for the storing of energy by the addition of a high-energy phosphate group — called also adenosine diphosphate

ad rem \(ˌ)ad-ˈrem\ adv or adj [L, to the thing] (1599) : to the point or purpose : RELEVANTLY

adren- or adreno- comb form [adrenal] 1 : adrenal glands ⟨adrenocortical⟩ 2 : adrenaline ⟨adrenergic⟩

¹ad·re·nal \ə-ˈdrē-nᵊl\ adj [ad- + renal] (1875) : of, relating to, or derived from the adrenal glands or their secretions ⟨~ steroids⟩

²adrenal n (1882) : ADRENAL GLAND

ad·re·nal·ec·to·my \ə-ˌdrē-nə-ˈlek-tə-mē\ n (ca. 1910) : surgical removal of an adrenal gland — ad·re·nal·ec·to·mized \-ˌmīzd\ adj

adrenal gland n (1875) : either of a pair of complex endocrine organs near the anterior medial border of the kidney consisting of a mesodermal cortex that produces glucocorticoid, mineralocorticoid, and androgenic hormones and an ectodermal medulla that produces epinephrine and norepinephrine — called also adrenal, suprarenal gland

Adren·a·lin \ə-ˈdre-nə-lən\ trademark — used for a preparation of levorotatory epinephrine

adren·a·line \ə-ˈdre-nə-lən\ n (1901) : EPINEPHRINE — often used in nontechnical contexts ⟨the fans were jubilant, raucous, their ~ running high —W. P. Kinsella⟩

adren·al·ized \ə-ˈdre-nə-ˌlīzd\ adj (1973) : filled with a sudden rush of energy : EXCITED

ad·ren·er·gic \ˌa-drə-ˈnər-jik\ adj [adren- + -ergic] (1934) 1 : liberating, activated by, or involving adrenaline or a substance like adrenaline ⟨an ~ nerve⟩ 2 : resembling adrenaline in physiological action ⟨~ drugs⟩ — ad·ren·er·gi·cal·ly \-ji-k(ə-)lē\ adv

ad·re·no·chrome \ə-ˈdrē-nə-ˌkrōm\ n (ca. 1913) : a red-colored mixture of quinones derived from epinephrine by oxidation

ad·re·no·cor·ti·cal \ə-ˌdrē-nō-ˈkȯr-ti-kəl\ adj (1936) : of, relating to, or derived from the cortex of the adrenal glands

---

\ə\ abut \ᵊ\ kitten, F table \ər\ further \a\ ash \ā\ ace \ä\ mop, mar \aů\ out \ch\ chin \e\ bet \ē\ easy \g\ go \i\ hit \ī\ ice \j\ job \ŋ\ sing \ō\ go \ȯ\ law \ȯi\ boy \th\ thin \t͟h\ the \ü\ loot \ů\ foot \y\ yet \zh\ vision, beige \k, ⁿ, œ, ᵫ, ᵁ\ see Guide to Pronunciation

Guide Words

The two words at the top of each dictionary page are called *guide words*. They represent the first and last word on the page. Because the words in the dictionary are in alphabetical order, you can use the guide words to determine quickly if the word you are looking for is on that particular page. The guide words for the sample entry are *skate* and *skid*.

Pronunciation

Each word is divided into sounds after the boldface main entry. Letters and symbols are used to indicate special sounds. A key to understanding the special sounds appears at the bottom of one of the two pages open to you.

Spelling

Spellings are given for the plural form of the word (if the spelling changes) and for any special endings. This is particularly helpful when letters are dropped or added to form the new word. In the sample entry, the plural of *ski* can be spelled correctly in two ways, either *skis* or *ski*. The first spelling is usually the preferred one.

Word Meaning

Frequently a word has many meanings. For example, *car* means automobile as well as the cargo part of an airship. In such a case, the dictionary uses a number to indicate each new meaning. In the sample entry, notice that a ski can be a narrow strip of wood or a piece of material that resembles a ski.

Parts of Speech

For each meaning of a word, the part of speech is given in abbreviated form. For example, *n* means *noun*, *adj* means *adjective*, *adv* means *adverb*, and *vi* or *vt* means *verb*. Other abbreviations are listed in the section in the front of your dictionary. In the example, *ski* is both a noun and a verb.

Word History

The language in which the word originally appeared is listed after the pronunciation or at the end of the entry. For example, *L* stands for Latin and *Gk* stands for Greek. Usually the original meaning is also listed. *Ski* is derived from the Norwegian (Norw) word *skith*, which means "stick of wood."

exercise 11   Consult the dictionary page on page 96 to label the statements as either *T* (true) or *F* (false).

———————   1. Garnish is a synonym for the word *adorn*.

———————   2. To *adulate* is also to flatter or admire.

———————   3. The word *Adonai* is taken from an ancient Greek myth.

———————   4. An *admonition* is a severe form of punishment.

_____ 5. The word *adobe* can be used to refer to both a structure and a type of clay.

_____ 6. If a topic is discussed *ad nauseam,* most listeners are likely to be tired of hearing about it.

_____ 7. The word *Adonis* is used to refer to a young man of great intelligence.

_____ 8. To *admire* someone is to dislike them.

_____ 9. *Adolescent* is a term used for young people in high school.

_____ 10. Someone who dislikes raw vegetables would be unlikely to *adore* fresh salads.

Word Origins

Words have ancestors. Some of the ancestors are words that were borrowed from other languages. *Shampoo,* for example, comes from a Hindi word meaning *to press,* and *moccasin* comes from the Algonquian Indian word for *shoe.* Other word ancestors include mythology, literature, people, places, and customs. The origin of the word *sadist,* which refers to a person who enjoys inflicting pain on others, is attributed to the Marquis de Sade, an eighteenth-century French author who wrote with pleasure about such cruelty.

Etymology

The study of word origins is called **etymology**. An etymologist traces the development of a word back to its earliest recorded appearance. In dictionaries, the etymology of a word is usually given in brackets. The extent to which the word origin is explained varies from one dictionary to another. Compare the information on the etymology of the word *mentor* given in three dictionaries.

This entry is from the small paperback edition of the *American Heritage Dictionary*:

> **men·tor** (mĕn′tôr′, -tər) *n.* A wise and trusted counselor or teacher. [< Gk. *Mentōr,* counselor of Odysseus. See **men-**.]

Source: Reprinted with permission from *American Heritage Dictionary of the English Language,* Third Paperback Edition.

This entry is from the textbook-size edition of *Merriam-Webster's Collegiate® Dictionary*:

> **¹men·tor** \\′men-ˌtȯr, -tər\\ *n* [L, fr. Gk *Mentōr*] (1616)   **1** *cap* : a friend of Odysseus entrusted with the education of Odysseus' son Telemachus   **2 a** : a trusted counselor or guide   **b** : TUTOR, COACH — **men·tor·ship** \\-ˌship\\ *n*
> **²mentor** *vt* (1976) : to serve as a mentor for : TUTOR

Source: By permission. From *Merriam-Webster's Collegiate® Dictionary,* 11th Edition. © 2008 by Merriam-Webster Incorporated (www.Merriam-Webster.com).

In both cases, the entries give information on the origin of the word, but the second explains the mythological background more clearly. Both dictionaries are abridged, which means that information has been condensed. An abridged dictionary is adequate for most college use. In special cases, however, you may desire more information on the origin or the past use of a word. If so, an unabridged, or unshortened, dictionary is necessary, but its large size dictates that you must go to it rather than carry it around with you. Consider the entry for *mentor* in the unabridged *Webster's Third New International® Dictionary:*

men·tor \\'men·ˌtȯ(ə)r, -ȯ(ə), -ntə(r)\\ *n* -s [after *Mentor*, tutor of Telemachus in the Odyssey of Homer, fr. L, fr. Gk *Mentōr*] **1 :** a close, trusted, and experienced counselor or guide ⟨every one of us needs a ~ who, because he is detached and disinterested, can hold up a mirror to us —P.W.Keve⟩ ⟨was much more than a ~; he supplied decisions —Hilaire Belloc⟩ ⟨has been my ~ since 1946 —Lalia P. Boone⟩ ⟨regarded by patrons ... as a personal friend as well as fashion ~ —*N. Y. State Legislative Committee on Problems of the Aging*⟩ **2 :** TEACHER, TUTOR, COACH ⟨a writer of monographs, and a ~ of seminars –*Atlantic*⟩ ⟨although he had never accepted a pupil ... she persuaded him to become her ~ —*Current Biog.*⟩ ⟨one of the game's most successful young ~s —*Official Basketball Guide*⟩

Source: By permission. From *Webster's Third New International® Dictionary, Unabridged.* © 1993 by Merriam-Webster Inc. (www.Merriam-Webster.com).

Your college library probably has several unabridged dictionaries in the reference room. Other excellent choices for etymological research include the *Random House Dictionary of the English Language* and the *American Heritage Dictionary of the English Language.*

Why Study Etymology? The more you know about a word, the easier it is to remember. The etymology gives you the history of a word, which can help you establish new relationships on your "computer chip," or schema, for that word. "Meeting the ancestors" can also help you create a rich visual image of the word by using the background information. For example, the word *trivial* means "of little worth or importance." It comes from the Latin words *tri* for *three* and *via* for *way*, which combine to mean "the crossing of three roads" in Latin. The Romans knew that people would stand and talk at such an intersection. Because many strangers would be listening to the conversations, it was advisable to talk only of small, or trivial, matters. This history of *trivial* can increase your enjoyment of the word while enhancing your ability to remember the definition.

exercise 12

Many English words have their roots in the names of characters in Greek mythology. The words represent a particular characteristic or predicament of the mythological person or creature. Read the entries here to discover their mythological origins, and answer the questions that follow.

at·las \\'at-ləs\\ *n* **1 a :** a book of maps often including descriptive text **b :** a book of tables, charts, or illustrations ⟨an *atlas* of anatomy⟩ **2 :** the first vertebra of the neck [*Atlas*, a Titan of Greek mythology]

△**origin** Atlas was one of the Titans or giants of Greek mythology whose rule of the world in an early age was overthrown by Zeus in a mighty battle. Atlas was believed to be responsible for holding up the sky, a task which he tried unsuccessfully to have Hercules assume. In his published collection of maps, the 16th century Flemish cartographer Gerhardus Mercator included on the title page a picture of Atlas supporting the heavens, and he gave the book the title *Atlas*. Other early collections of maps subsequently included similar pictures of Atlas, and such books came to be called *atlases*.

By permission. From *Webster's New Explorer College Dictionary* © 2003 by Federal Street Press, a division of Merriam-Webster Inc.

1. *Atlas* means _____

2. Explain the myth. _____

_____

> **od·ys·sey** \\'äd-e-sē\\ *n, pl* **-seys** : a long wandering usually marked by many changes of fortune [the *Odyssey*, epic poem attributed to Homer recounting the long wanderings of Odysseus]
>
> By permission. From *Webster's New Explorer College Dictionary* © 2003 by Federal Street Press, a division of Merriam-Webster Inc.

3. *Odyssey* means _____

_____

4. Explain the myth. _____

_____

Textbook Glossary

Some technical terms located within a textbook glossary may not be found in an ordinary dictionary. An example might be the term *coupled reactions*. One might locate each word separately within a dictionary, but the words combined (having a particular scientific meaning) might be found only within the glossary of a science textbook. The textbook **glossary** defines words and phrases as they apply to particular fields of study. Consult it before using the dictionary for words that seem to be part of the terminology of the discipline.

exercise 13   This exercise considers the types of words and the amount of information presented in a glossary. Notice that many of the words take on a special meaning within the particular field of study. Use the biology glossary on page 101 to answer the questions with *T* (true) or *F* (false).

_____ 1. *Continental drift* refers to a theory concerning how today's continents were formed.

_____ 2. *Cross bridges* were a means for ancient people to migrate to new places.

_____ 3. A major function of the *cranium* is to protect the brain.

_____ 4. *Cosmopolitan species* are found only in cities throughout the world.

conjugation (kon''jew-gay'shun)   (1) A sexual process in certain protists that involves exchange or fusion of a cell with another cell; (2) A mechanism for DNA exchange in bacteria that involves cell-to-cell contact.

connective tissue   Animal tissue consisting mostly of intercellular substance (fibers scattered through a matrix) in which the cells are embedded, e.g., bone.

consanguineous mating   A mating between close relatives.

conservation biology   A multidisciplinary science that focuses on the study of how humans impact organisms and on the development of ways to protect biological diversity.

constitutive gene   A gene that is constantly transcribed.

consumer   See *heterotroph*.

consumption overpopulation   A situation in which each individual in a human population consumes too large a share of resources; results in pollution, environmental degradation, and resource depletion. Compare with *people overpopulation*.

contest competition   See *interference competition*.

continental drift   The theory that continents were once joined together and later split and drifted apart.

contraception   Any method used to intentionally prevent pregnancy.

contractile root (kun-trak'til)   A specialized type of root that contracts and pulls a bulb or corm deeper into the soil.

contractile vacuole   A membrane-bounded organelle that is found in certain freshwater protists, such as *Paramecium,* and that appears to have an osmoregulatory function; it periodically fills with water, then contracts to expel the contents into the surroundings.

control group   In a scientific experiment, a group in which the experimental variable is kept constant. The control provides a standard of comparison used to verify the results of the experiment.

controlled mating   A mating in which the genotypes of the parents are known.

convergent circuit (kun-vur'jent)   A neural pathway in which a postsynaptic neuron is controlled by signals coming from two or more presynaptic neurons. Compare with *divergent circuit*.

convergent evolution (kun-vur'jent)   The independent evolution of structural or functional similarity in two or more distantly related species, usually as a result of adaptations to similar environments.

corepressor   Substance that binds to a repressor protein, converting it to its active form, which is capable of preventing transcription.

Coriolis effect (kor''e-o'lis)   The tendency of moving air or water to be deflected from its path to the right in the Northern Hemisphere and to the left in the Southern Hemisphere. Caused by the direction of Earth's rotation.

cork cambium (kam'bee-um)   A lateral meristem that produces cork cells and cork parenchyma; cork cambium and the tissues it produces make up the outer bark of a woody plant. Compare with *vascular cambium*.

cork cell   A cell in the bark that is produced outwardly by the cork cambium; cork cells are dead at maturity and function for protection and reduction of water loss.

cork parenchyma (par-en'kih-mah)   One or more layers of parenchyma cells produced inwardly by the cork cambium.

corm   A short, thickened underground stem specialized for food storage and asexual reproduction, e.g., crocus, gladiolus.

cornea (kor'nee-ah)   The transparent covering of an eye.

corolla (kor-ohl'ah)   A collective term for the petals of a flower.

corpus callosum (kah-loh'sum)   In mammals, a large bundle of nerve fibers interconnecting the two cerebral hemispheres.

corpus luteum (loo'tee''um)   The temporary endocrine tissue in the ovary that develops from the ruptured follicle after ovulation; secretes progesterone and estrogen.

cortex (kor'tex)   (1) The outer part of an organ, such as the cortex of the kidney; compare with *medulla*. (2) The tissue between the epidermis and vascular tissue in the stems and roots of many herbaceous plants.

cortical reaction   Process occurring after fertilization that prevents additional sperm from entering the egg; also known as the slow block to polyspermy.

cosmopolitan species   Species that have a nearly worldwide distribution and occur on more than one continent or throughout much of the ocean. Compare with *endemic species*.

cotransport   The active transport of a substance from a region of low concentration to a region of high concentration by coupling its transport to the transport of a substance down its concentration gradient.

cotyledon (kot''uh-lee'dun)   The seed leaf of a plant embryo, which may contain food stored for germination.

cotylosaurs   The first reptiles; also known as stem reptiles.

countercurrent exchange system   A biological mechanism that enables maximum exchange between two fluids. The two fluids must be flowing in opposite directions and have a concentration gradient between them.

coupled reactions   A set of reactions in which an exergonic reaction provides the free energy required to drive an endergonic reaction; energy coupling generally occurs through a common intermediate.

covalent bond   The chemical bond involving shared pairs of electrons; may be single, double, or triple (with one, two, or three shared pairs of electrons, respectively). Compare with *ionic bond* and *hydrogen bond*.

covalent compound   A compound in which atoms are held together by covalent bonds; covalent compounds consist of molecules. Compare with *ionic compound*.

cranial nerves   The ten to twelve pairs of nerves in vertebrates that emerge directly from the brain.

cranium   The bony framework that protects the brain in vertebrates.

crassulacean acid metabolism   See *CAM plant*.

creatine phosphate   An energy-storing compound found in muscle cells.

cretinism (kree'tin-izm)   A chronic condition due to lack of thyroid secretion during fetal development and early childhood; results in retarded physical and mental development if untreated.

cri-du-chat   A human genetic disease caused by loss of part of the short arm of chromosome 5 and characterized by mental retardation, a cry that sounds like a kitten mewing, and death in infancy or childhood.

cristae (kris'tee) (sing. *crista*)   Shelflike or finger-like inward projections of the inner membrane of a mitochondrion.

Cro-Magnons   Prehistoric humans *(Homo sapiens)* with modern features (tall, erect, lacking a heavy brow) who lived in Europe some 30,000 years ago.

cross bridges   The connections between myosin and actin filaments in muscle fibers; formed by the binding of myosin heads to active sites on actin filaments.

crossing-over   The breaking and rejoining of homologous (nonsister) chromatids during early meiotic prophase I that results in an exchange of genetic material.

—From Solomon, Berg, and Martin, *Biology* (with InfoTrac), 6th ed. © 2002 Brooks/Cole, a part of Cengage Learning Inc. Reproduced by permission. www.cengage.com/permissions

_____ 5. The brain is the only organ to have a *cortex*.

_____ 6. The *cornea* is a specialized section of a plant embryo.

_____ 7. *Connective tissue* is found in animals.

_____ 8. *Cotylosaurs* were one of the earliest forms of plant life.

_____ 9. *Creatine phosphate* helps plants store energy.

_____10. The *Coriolis effect* can probably impact weather patterns on Earth.

Thesaurus

Dr. Peter Mark Roget, an English physician, collected lists of related words as a hobby, and in 1852 the lists were published in a **thesaurus**, or treasury of words. In the book he related words because they were synonyms, such as *illegal* and *unlawful*, as well as antonyms, such as *peaceful* and *warlike*. This book, still called *Roget's Thesaurus* because of the man who first had the idea, has been revised frequently through the addition of new words and the deletion of obsolete ones.

Roget's Thesaurus is not a dictionary, and you would probably not use it while reading. Instead, it is a valuable source for writers who are stuck on using a particular word again and again and want a substitute. For example, if you are writing a history term paper and have already used the noun *cause* twice in one paragraph and hesitate to use it again, consult *Roget's Thesaurus* for other options. You will find noun alternatives such as *origin, basis, foundation, genesis,* and *root.* If you need a verb for *cause,* you will find synonyms that include *originate, give rise to, bring about, produce, create, evoke,* and many others. Probably over a hundred words are listed as relating to *cause,* but not all of them are synonymous. Select the one that fits your need in the sentence, adds variety to your writing, and maintains the shade of meaning that you desire.

The words in a thesaurus are ordinarily listed in alphabetical order, and familiar dictionary abbreviations are used for parts of speech. The following example shows an entry for the word *influence.*

---

influence, *n. & v.* —*n.* influentialness; IMPORTANCE, POWER, mastery, sway, dominance, AUTHORITY, control, ascendancy, persuasiveness, ability to affect; reputation, weight; magnetism, spell; conduciveness; pressure. *Slang,* drag, pull. —*v.t.* affect; move, induce, persuade; sway, control, lead, actuate; modify; arouse, incite; prevail upon, impel; set the pace, pull the strings; tell, weigh. *Ant.,* see IMPOTENCE.

Source: Morehead and Morehead,
The New American Roget's College Thesaurus.

When a word is printed in small capitals, such as IMPORTANCE, POWER, and AUTHORITY, it means that you can find additional synonyms by looking that particular word up in its alphabetical order. Explanations sometimes appear in brackets, and not every word in the dictionary is listed.

Reader's *Tip* Using an Electronic Thesaurus

Your word-processing program probably has a thesaurus. In many versions of Microsoft Word, for example, the thesaurus is found in the *Tools* pull-down menu, as one of the *Language* options. To use this, select the word for which you want alternatives by dragging the cursor over the word to highlight it and then clicking on the thesaurus. An array of words will appear, usually both in the *Meanings* box and in the *Replace with Synonyms* box, as indicated in the figure here displaying alternatives for the word *right*. Click and highlight a different word other than *just,* which is presently highlighted in the *Meanings* box, and you will get a different array of synonyms. For example, click on the word *sane* in the following illustration and your synonym options will be *normal, rational, sound, reasonable,* and *wise.*

This one word *right* has forty-nine synonym alternatives on this computer thesaurus in Microsoft Word. By moving the down arrow situated to the right of the word *claim,* you will uncover the word *Antonyms,* and the words *wrong, incorrect, erroneous,* and *lenient* will appear as options. Thus your computer thesaurus has many more words than appear at first glance. Search and choose an option that fits the context of your sentence. The procedure may vary depending on the version of Microsoft Word or other word-processing program you are using.

exercise 14   Use the thesaurus entry for *right* to select an alternative word that fits the meaning of *right* in the sentences that follow.

RIGHT, RIGHTNESS [922]

Nouns—**1,** rightness, right, what ought to be, what should be, fitness, propriety; JUSTICE, morality, PROBITY, honor, virtue, lawfulness.
2, privilege, prerogative, title, claim, grant, POWER, franchise, license.
3, rightness, correctness, accuracy, precision; exactness; TRUTH.
Verbs—**1,** be right, be just, stand to reason.
3, right, make right, correct, remedy, see justice done, play fair, do justice to, recompense, hold the scales even, give every one his due.
Adjectives—**1,** right, upright, good, just (see JUSTICE); reasonable, suitable, becoming.
2, right, correct, proper, precise, exact, accurate, true.
Adverbs—rightly, justly, fairly, correctly; in justice, in equity, in reason, without distinction of persons, on even terms.
Antonym, see WRONG.

Source: Morehead and Morehead,
The New American Roget's College Thesaurus.

1. The first amendment gives Americans the *right* of free speech. _____

2. It was not *right* for the government to force the Indians out of the Southeast in the Trail of Tears. _____

3. Can government payments help *right* some social wrongs of the past? _____

4. Do revolutionaries ignore the difference between *right* and wrong? _____

5. Employers want to make the *right* fit between employee skills and job demands. _____

Analogies

An **analogy** is a comparison that mimics a previously stated relationship. Perhaps the best explanation is an example.

EXAMPLE

Apple is to *fruit* as *potato* is to _____.

EXPLANATION The first step in solving an analogy is to pinpoint the initial relationship. What is the relationship between *apple* and *fruit?* Because an apple is

---

Reader's *Tip* **Categories of Relationships for Analogies**

Synonyms: Similar in meaning
  Start is to *begin* as *end* is to *finish.*

Antonyms: Opposite in meaning
  Retreat is to *advance* as *tall* is to *short.*

Function, use, or **purpose:** Identifies what something does. Watch for the object (noun) and then the action (verb).
  Car is to *drive* as *towel* is to *absorb.*

Classification: Identifies the larger group association
  Mosquito is to *insect* as *gasoline* is to *fuel.*

Characteristics and descriptions: Shows qualities or traits
  Sour is to *lemon* as *sweet* is to *sugar.*

Degree: Shows variations of intensity
  Walking is to *running* as *cool* is to *frozen.*

Part to whole: Shows the larger group
  Pupil is to *school* as *sailor* is to *navy.*

Cause and effect: Shows the reason (cause) and the result (effect)
  Work is to *success* as *virus* is to *illness.*

a member of the fruit group, you might say that it is one part of a larger whole. To complete the analogy, you must establish a similar relationship for *potato*. In what larger group does a potato belong? *Vegetable* is the answer.

Analogies are challenging and can be very difficult. They test logical thinking as well as vocabulary. Working through analogies is an experience in problem solving.

The preceding Reader's Tip explains the many different relationships that can be expressed in an analogy. Study both the list and the examples.

exercise 15

Study the following analogies to establish the relationship of the first two words. Record that relationship, using the categories just outlined. Then choose the word that duplicates that relationship to finish the analogy.

————— 1. *Leg* is to *table* as *wheel* is to —————————.

Relationship? —————————

a. chair
b. car
c. motor
d. steer

————— 2. *Soft* is to *firm* as *peaceful* is to —————————.

Relationship? —————————

a. pillow
b. kind
c. sleep
d. aggressive

————— 3. *Turnip* is to *vegetable* as *oak* is to —————————.

Relationship? —————————

a. wood
b. fuel
c. house
d. glass

————— 4. *Selling* is to *profit* as *germ* is to —————————.

Relationship? —————————

a. vaccination
b. carelessness
c. wealth
d. disease

————— 5. *Kind* is to *considerate* as *courage* is to —————————.

Relationship? —————————

a. soldier
b. bravery
c. fear
d. fighting

_____ 6. *Towel* is to *absorb* as *oven* is to _____.

Relationship? _____

a. safety
b. speed
c. cook
d. kitchen

_____ 7. *Tiny* is to *small* as *hot* is to _____.

Relationship? _____

a. summer
b. warm
c. cooking
d. temperature

_____ 8. *Soft* is to *pillow* as *humid* is to _____.

Relationship? _____

a. swamp
b. trip
c. camp
d. trees

_____ 9. *Work* is to *success* as *study* is to _____.

Relationship? _____

a. history
b. knowledge
c. professor
d. college

_____ 10. *Needle* is to *sew* as *bulb* is to _____.

Relationship? _____

a. lamp
b. illuminate
c. electricity
d. table

Easily Confused Words

Many pairs of words cause confusion because they sound exactly alike or almost alike but are spelled and used differently. *Principal* and *principle* are examples of this confusion. A common error is to write, "The new school principle is Mrs. Thompson." Remember, the *al* word is the person, or "pal," and the *le* word is the rule. To keep most of these words straight, memorize and associate. Study the following words that sound similar and learn their differences.

exercise 16   Circle the correct boldface word to fit the context of each sentence.

1. She exercised on a (**stationary, stationery**) bicycle.

2. Her brother devoured the (**hole, whole**) pizza by himself.

Reader's *Tip* Easily Confused Words

capital: city
capitol: building

hole: a depression in the ground
whole: entire

to: in the direction of
too: also

stationary: fixed position
stationery: paper

their: belonging to them
there: opposite of here
they're: they are

its: belonging to it
it's: it is

accept: receive
except: all but

your: belonging to you
you're: you are

cite: quote
sight: vision
site: place

threw: launched
through: in one side and out the
   other

3. The (**capital, capitol**) serves as a meeting place for both senators and representatives.

4. The line for the bookstore begins right (**their, they're, there**).

5. After such a late night, they were much (**to, too**) tired to wake up early.

6. In order to get (**threw, through**) college successfully, studying is necessary.

7. The overhead projector was placed directly in her (**cite, sight, site**) line for the speaker.

8. Sometimes it is difficult to (**accept, except**) the truth.

9. (**Your, you're**) first impression is often a lasting one.

10. (**Vain, vein**) students might spend extra time gazing at themselves in front of the mirror.

11. (**Its, It's**) not the best strategy to watch television while studying for a test.

Enriching Your Vocabulary

Most reading selections in this text are followed by practice for vocabulary development called Vocabulary Enrichment (see p. 153 for an example). In addition, Vocabulary Lessons using a structural approach appear at the end of most chapters, including this one. In these lessons, prefixes, roots, and suffixes are linked to new words. Plan to make vocabulary enrichment an exciting, lifelong activity.

Personal *Feedback* 2

Name _____

1. After reading this chapter, how will you change your system for remembering new words? _____

   _____

   _____

   _____

2. Why do you enjoy or dislike studying words? _____

   _____

   _____

   _____

3. Why is it not recommended that you look up unknown words as you read? _____

   _____

   _____

   _____

4. What is one word that your instructor uses frequently that you were not previously accustomed to hearing? _____

   _____

   _____

   _____

5. List ten adjectives to describe characteristics that you would like in a spouse. Again, stretch your vocabulary beyond easy words. _____

   _____

   _____

   _____

Tear out and submit to your instructor.

Summary *Points*

➤ **How many words does the average college graduate recognize?**
The average college graduate recognizes around 70,000 words and uses about 15,000.

➤ **How do context clues assist in unlocking word meaning?**
Use context clues from sentences in a passage to figure out the meaning of new words.

➤ **What should you include on a concept card?**
Put the word, the definition, a sentence, a picture, and the source on concept cards. Visualize associations to remember the new words.

➤ **How can you recognize new words by linking parts of old words?**
Identify old friends in new words by linking roots, prefixes, and suffixes.

➤ **How should you use a dictionary while reading?**
While reading mark words you don't know and then look them up after reading.

➤ **Why use a glossary?**
Locate words that are part of the terminology of the discipline in the textbook glossary in order to learn their meaning.

➤ **Why would you need a thesaurus?**
Use a thesaurus to find alternative words when writing.

➤ **What is the key to solving an analogy?**
First determine the category of the relationship.

COLLABORATIVE PROBLEM SOLVING

Form a five-member group and select one of the following activities. Brainstorm and then outline your major points on a transparency. Choose a member to present the group findings to the class.

➤ Make a list of ten words that have multiple meanings.

➤ Create a list of ten words that begin with the prefix *pre*.

➤ Create five analogies, one for each of the following relationships: synonyms, antonyms, function, part to whole, and cause and effect.

➤ Create a list of ten words that end with the suffix *ous*.

myreadinglab

MyReadingLab (MRL) www.myreadinglab.com

➤ To practice the ideas and skills introduced in this chapter, go to the "Vocabulary" module in the Skills sections of MRL.

➤ Extensive vocabulary exercises are also available through a direct link from MRL to the Longman Vocabulary Web site.

➤ To practice general reading comprehension, use the Levels section of MRL.

The Reading *Workshop*

Polonius: "What do you read my lord?"

Hamlet: "Words, words, words."

—SHAKESPEARE, *HAMLET*

One of the benefits of extensive reading is expanding your vocabulary. It stands to reason that the more words you see or hear, the more words you recognize. As you find interesting words in your Reading Workshop book, mark them for later additions to your concept cards. Don't stop the flow of your reading except to lightly mark the word with a pencil or sticky note and dog-ear the page.

Think about it, talk about it, write about it:

At the end of your reading session, make a list of the words you marked and make concept cards. Were you able to determine their meanings from the context or word structure clues? Try to use the words in conversation or in writing today. Don't be afraid of making a mistake. Your listener will be impressed by your broad vocabulary or at least appreciate your effort. Use the new words often and they will soon become familiar friends.

Your professor might ask you to submit a list of words for an individualized quiz or as an addition to a Reading Workshop journal.

Vocabulary Lesson

For or Against?

Study the prefixes, words, and sentences.

| **Prefixes** | *pro*: for, forward, forth | *anti, ant*: against | *contra*: against |

Words with *pro = for, forward, forth*

Do medical <u>procedures</u> require signed forms? Can you <u>proceed</u> inside with a ticket?

- Pro-choice: for abortion rights

  The *pro-choice* rally was held on the steps of the state capitol.

- Proponent: supporter

  Are you a *proponent* of building another oil pipeline in Alaska?

- Procure: to get or gain

  Campers need to *procure* supplies a week prior to departure.

- Profess: to openly admit

  I *profess* to enjoying double fudge chocolate brownie cake.

- Prolific: bringing forth young or fruit

  The *prolific* young couple had six small children.

- Proficient: showing skill

  To be *proficient* in Spanish requires a knowledge of grammar.

- Proliferate: to bring forth by rapid production

  Fast-food restaurants seem to *proliferate* near interstate highway exits.

Words with *anti* or *ant = against*

Do <u>antiabortionists</u> use signs? Will an <u>anticoagulant</u> stop bleeding?

- Antacid: a counteracting agent for acidity of the stomach

  Take an *antacid* tablet for a burning stomach.

- Antagonism: a strong feeling against a person or idea

  After they had shared several funny jokes, the *antagonism* between them evaporated.

- Antarctic: the opposite of the North Pole

  The *antarctic* region is south of the Arctic.

- Anticlimax: a letdown from a greater event

  After the previous night's celebration, New Year's day was an *anticlimax*.

- Antipathy: a strong feeling of dislike

  The business partner's *antipathy* toward the accused swindler was evident.

- Antithesis: a contrast of ideas

  The son's liberal ideas are the *antithesis* of his father's conservative policies.

- Antibody: a substance in the body opposing diseases

  The scientists worked to create an *antibody* for the new flu strain.

- Antidote: a remedy for poison

  Jungle travelers carry an *antidote* for snake bites.

- Antifreeze: a substance to slow the freezing process

  Check your car for *antifreeze* before the first frost.

Words with *contra = against*

Does sex education stress contraceptives? Are controversial issues frequently argued?

- Contraband: illegal

  Contraband items can be seized by the police.

- Contradict: to speak against

  To *contradict* a speaker, you must be sure of your facts.

- Contrarian: person who takes contrary views

  Reasoning with a *contrarian* is not always possible.

Review

Part I

Answer the following with *T* (true) or *F* (false).

_____ 1. An antidote is an amusing story.

_____ 2. A prolific plant bears many fruits.

_____ 3. Supplies can be procured by illegal means.

_____ 4. A contrarian would be comfortable in a role involving questioning.

_____ 5. Pro-choice advocates demonstrate against abortion clinics.

_____ 6. If you contradict the evidence, you disagree with the facts.

_____ 7. An athlete must be proficient to play on a professional team.

_____ 8. A sick person usually welcomes an antibody.

_____ 9. A controversial news story seldom generates further discussion.

_____10. For a peaceful relationship, mutual antagonism should be resolved.

Part II

Choose the best word from the list as a synonym for the following.

profess	antacid	antithesis	proponent	antifreeze
procedure	controversy	anticlimax	contraband	antipathy

11. Liquid solution for machines _____

12. Feeling of dislike _____

13. Smuggled drugs _____

14. Admit _____

15. Medication _____

16. Plan _____

17. Opposite _____

18. Disagreement _____

19. Supporter _____

20. Disappointment _____

Getting News and Other Information from Web sites and Forums

If you want up-to-the-minute news and other information, you can find it instantly on the Internet. A number of news sites headline current events and link in-depth stories with added details. For example, a CNN.com headline story on the Middle East struggle linked to an airplane interview with Secretary of State Condoleezza Rice, who had just changed into her warm-up outfit as she flew from Israel back to the United States. Some sites, such as CNN.com, further link to blogs, which are personal Web blogs, journals, or newsletters from people with an observation or opinion.

For information on specific groups of interest to you, you can visit online communities called forums, which will pinpoint your interests. For example, you could log on to a cooking forum, or to be more specific, a salmon cooking forum. If you log on to a salmon forum, you may be reading about environmental issues concerning saving the salmon, not grilling them.

News-Related Web sites

Searching for news stories is easy, using news-centered Web sites such as Google News <www.news.google.com> or CNN.com <www.CNN.com>. Both Google News and CNN offer home pages that list top news stories of the day and a search area where a topic or keywords can be typed in for related news stories. The sites also have separate sections for the United States and the world. You can get today's headline news in Rome, Mexico City, or Moscow. You can also search topics such as science/technology, sports, entertainment, and health.

You can also go to the Web sites of national newspapers, such as the *New York Times* <www.nytimes.com> and *USA Today* <www.usatoday.com>, to gather information. Your local newspaper probably has its own Web site. The newspaper sites require that you register with a password, but there is no charge for this service.

exercise 1 Go to either Google.com or CNN.com and explore news stories that interest you. Record the Web address of two news stories and, on a separate piece of paper, explain what information you found about each.

Forums

Forums, also known as online communities, provide free, up-to-date information about specific subjects. Forums may be maintained by a company or an individual and are interactive in that a subscriber can post questions and receive timely answers. There are forums for almost every subject. Here are just a few forums found on the Internet.

➤ Gardening forums feature the largest community of gardeners on the Internet.

Garden Web Forums   forums.gardenweb.com/forums

114

➤ Cooking forums offer experienced and inexperienced cooks information and tips on cooking.

DiscussCooking.com www.discusscooking.com

➤ Forums on bicycling offer a wealth of information for bicycle enthusiasts.

Cyclingforums.com www.cyclingforums.com

➤ iVillage Web site features a variety of forums related to women's issues, such as health and well-being, beauty and style, diet and fitness, and pregnancy and parenting.

ivillage.com www.ivillage.com

To find a forum, use a search engine such as Google. Type in a subject with the word *forum* next to it (for example, Fitness Forum). Then sample the choices offered to find the forum that suits you. When visiting or taking part in a forum,

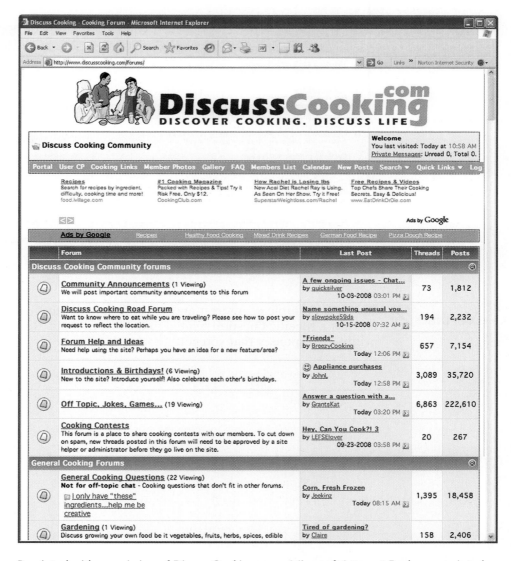

Reprinted with permission of DiscussCooking.com. Microsoft Internet Explorer reprinted with permission from Microsoft Corporation.

115

remember that these groups are open to all individuals, and some of the information may not have been verified. Keep an open mind as you participate in the forum, and do not accept every word as fact.

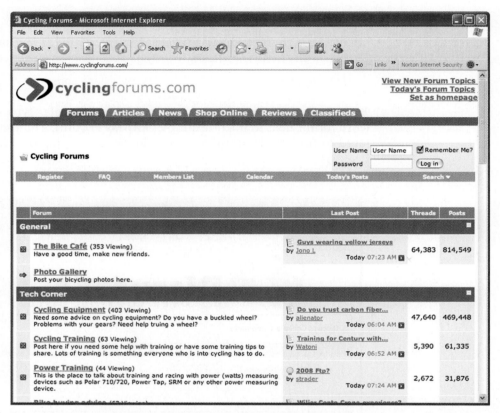

Copyright ©2001–2006 cyclingforums.com. Reprinted with permission. Microsoft Internet Explorer reprinted with permission from Microsoft Corporation.

exercise 2   Decide on a topic of interest and find a forum about this topic. Join the forum and ask a specific question related to the forum topic. Record your question and print any responses that you get.

4 Main Idea

- What is a main idea?
- What is a topic?
- How do you recognize the difference between general and specific ideas?
- What is a stated main idea?
- What is an unstated main idea?

Everyday Reading Skills: Selecting a Book

What Is a Main Idea?

The **main idea** of a passage is the core of the material, the particular point the author is trying to convey. The main idea of a passage can be stated in one sentence that condenses specific ideas or details in the passage into a general, all-inclusive statement of the author's message. In classroom discussions, all of the following words are sometimes used to help students understand the meaning of the main idea.

thesis

main point

central focus

gist

controlling idea

central thought

Whether you read a single paragraph, a chapter, or an entire book, many experts agree that your most important single task is to understand the main idea of what you read.

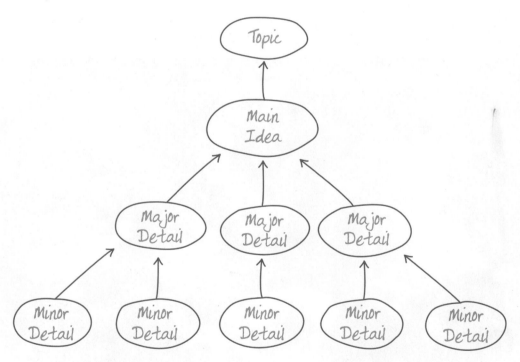

Recognize General and Specific Words

The first step in determining the main idea of a selection is to look at the specific ideas presented in the sentences and try to decide on a general **topic** or subject under which you can group these ideas. Before tackling sentences, begin with words. Pretend that the sentence ideas in a selection have been reduced to a short list of keywords. Pretend also that within the list is a general term that expresses an overall subject for the keywords. The general term encompasses or categorizes the key ideas and is considered the topic of the list.

EXAMPLE The following list contains three specific ideas with a related general topic. Circle the general term that could be considered the subject of the list.

satin

wool

fabric

silk

EXPLANATION Satin, wool, and silk are different types of fabric. Thus *fabric* is the general term or classification that could be considered the subject or topic.

exercise 1 Circle the general term or subject for each of the following related groups of ideas.

1. chimpanzees	2. cirrus	3. oats	4. Alps	5. shrimp
orangutans	clouds	wheat	Appalachians	crustacean
apes	cumulus	corn	mountains	crab
gorillas	stratus	grain	Rockies	lobster

Recognize General and Specific Phrases

Topics of passages are more often stated as phrases rather than single words. The following list contains a phrase that is a general topic and three specific ideas related to that topic. Circle the general topic that could be the subject.

EXAMPLE Turn on the ignition.

Press the accelerator.

Insert the key.

Start the car.

EXPLANATION The first three details are involved in starting a car. The last phrase is the general subject or topic.

exercise 2

Circle the phrase that could be the topic for each list.

1. totaling yearly income
   subtracting for dependents
   filing an income tax return
   mailing a 1040 form

2. paying fees
   buying books
   starting college
   going to class

3. picking up seashells
   vacationing at the beach
   walking in the surf
   riding the waves

4. pushing paper under sticks
   piling the logs
   building a fire
   striking a match

exercise 3

Read the lists of specific details and write a general phrase that could be the subject or topic for each group.

1. separate the white and dark clothes
   add one cup of detergent
   insert quarters into the machine
   General topic? _____

2. dribble the ball
   pass the ball down court
   shoot a basket
   General topic? _____

3. pull up alongside car
   back into space
   straighten out
   General topic? _____

4. switch on power
   select a program
   open a file
   General topic? _____

5. boil water in a large pot
   add salt and oil
   pour noodles into water
   General topic? _____

Recognize the General Topic for Sentences

Paragraphs are composed of sentences that develop a single general topic. The next practice exercises contain groups in which the sentences of a paragraph are listed numerically. After reading the sentences, circle the phrase that best expresses the topic or general subject of the sentences.

EXAMPLE

1. The law of demand is illustrated in an experiment conducted by the makers of M&M candy.
2. For a twelve-month period, the price of M&Ms remained the same in 150 stores, but the number of M&Ms in a package increased, which dropped the price per ounce.
3. In those stores, sales immediately rose by 20 to 30 percent.

Candy Maker's Experiment

M&Ms Drop in Price

M&Ms Prove the Law of Demand

EXPLANATION   The first phrase is too broad. The second relates a detail that is an important part of the experiment. The third links the candy with the purpose of the experiment and thus most accurately states the topic of the sentences.

exercise 4   Circle the phrase that best describes the topic or subject for each group of sentences.

Group 1

1. To provide a favorable climate for growing grapes, the winter temperature should not go below 15° F, and the summers should be long.
2. During the growing season, rainfall should be light.
3. A gentle movement of air is required to dry the vines after rains, dispel fog, and protect the vines from fungus disease.

Protecting Grapes from Disease

Appropriate Temperatures for Growing Grapes

Appropriate Climate for Growing Grapes

Group 2

1. For example, faced with fewer expansion opportunities within the United States, Wal-Mart opened new stores abroad and foreign sales reached $7.5 billion in three years.
2. As more and more companies engage in international business, the world is becoming a single, interdependent global economy.
3. In a plan to become a global giant, Chrysler, one of America's apple pie auto companies, merged with Germany's Daimler-Benz to become DaimlerChrysler.

International Auto Mergers

A Global Economy

Wal-Mart Expansion

Group 3

1. Oprah Winfrey's success has placed her in the top 0.5 percent of the population that owns more than a quarter of the nation's wealth.
2. Oprah's entertainment enterprises earn her over $250 million a year.
3. *Fortune* magazine has listed Oprah as one of the 400 richest Americans.

Rankings of Wealth

The Richest Americans

Oprah's Financial Success

Group 4

1. Salsa, the popular blend of Latin American music, is also the word for *sauce*.
2. According to stories, the expression was contributed to the music world by a Cuban orchestra conductor.
3. While practicing a mambo that needed more life, the orchestra leader told his musicians to "echale salsita" or "throw in the sauce."

Latin American Salsa Music

The Naming of Salsa Music

Contribution of Salsa

Group 5

1. Simply drinking water is the best way to prevent dehydration from sweating.
2. Taking salt tablets before drinking water can dehydrate the body even more by extracting water from body tissue.
3. Plain water is better than beverages containing sugar or electrolytes because it is absorbed faster.

Salt Tablets versus Water

Value in Plain Water

Preventing Dehydration

exercise 5 Read a group of three sentences, then write a phrase that best states the subject or general topic for the sentences.

Group 1

1. Psychologists conduct research with animals for several reasons.
2. Sometimes they simply want to know more about the behavior of a specific type of animal.
3. In other instances they want to see whether certain laws of behavior apply to both humans and animals.

General topic? _____

—*Psychology: Themes & Variations*, Sixth Edition,
by Wayne Weiten

Group 2

1. Scientists think that a more reasonably defined danger level would mean that only 50,000 homes have radon concentrations that pose a danger to occupants.
2. Scientists outside the EPA have concluded that the standards the EPA is using are too stringent.
3. The United States Environmental Protection Agency (EPA) regards 5 million American homes as having unacceptable radon levels in the air.

General topic? _____

_____

—*Physical Geology*, Fifth Edition,
by David McGeary et al.

Group 3

1. They resist accepting a warm pink body as a corpse from which organs can be "harvested."
2. The Japanese do not incorporate a mind–body split into their models of themselves; they locate personhood throughout the body rather than in the brain.
3. In Japan the concept of brain death is hotly contested, and organ transplants are rarely performed.

General topic? _____

—*Cultural Anthropology*, Eleventh Edition,
by William A. Haviland et al.

Recognize General and Supporting Sentences

Read the sentences in each of the following groups. The sentences are related to a single subject, with two of the sentences expressing specific support and one sentence expressing the general or main idea about the subject. Circle the number of the sentence that best expresses the general subject. Then read the three phrases and circle the one that best describes the subject of the sentences.

EXAMPLE

1. An accountant who prefers to work alone rather than as a team member may be an important part of the organization but will not become a leader.
2. A CEO who steers a company into increased profits but exhibits poor people skills by yelling at employees and refusing to listen will not keep her job.
3. Companies now demand of their top employees a high level of emotional intelligence (EI), which refers to skills in adaptability, self-control, conflict management, and teamwork.

IQ No Longer Matters

The Importance of Emotional Intelligence

Polite Changes in the Workplace

EXPLANATION The third sentence best expresses the general subject. The other two sentences offer specific supporting ideas. The second phrase, "The Importance of Emotional Intelligence," best describes the general subject of the material. The first phrase is not really suggested, and the last phrase is one of the details mentioned.

exercise 6   Circle the number of the sentence that best expresses the general subject, the main idea. Then read the three topic phrases and circle the phrase that best describes the subject of the sentences.

Group 1

1. African American and Hispanic teens are not as likely to use tobacco as Caucasian adolescents.
2. Each day approximately three thousand teens start smoking, and eventually one third of them will die from smoking.
3. Despite the proven danger, in the past decade tobacco usage among teens has increased.

Tobacco Usage Among Teens

Dangers Face Teens

Harms of Smoking

Group 2

1. Berry Gordy, an ex-boxer and Ford auto worker, borrowed $700 from his family and began to manufacture and sell his own records on the Hitsville USA (later called Motown, for "motor town") label.
2. The next year Smokey Robinson and the Miracles recorded "Shop Around," which was Gordy's first million-copy hit.
3. Gordy signed an 11-year-old boy to record for him under the name of Stevie Wonder.

Gordy's Success

Stevie Wonder at Motown

The Recording Artists at Motown

Group 3

1. The czar's wife believed that the devious and politically corrupt Rasputin, known as the "mad monk," was the only one who could save her son.
2. The son of Nicholas II was afflicted with hemophilia, a condition in which the blood does not clot properly.
3. In Russia during the reign of Nicholas II, hemophilia played an important historical role.

Rasputin's Charm

Hemophilia

Influence of Hemophilia on Russia

Group 4

1. By 2000 the world's population had moved past 6 billion people, and by 2050 it is expected to reach 9 billion.
2. The global statistics on population growth and the availability of food are alarming.
3. Biotechnologists estimate that the land available for raising crops will decrease by half in the next fifty years.

Biotechnology and Agriculture

Feeding the Poor

Population Growth and Food Production

Group 5

1. The success of Norman Rockwell's illustrations is based on his simple formula of drawing ordinary people doing ordinary things that make us laugh at ourselves.

2. Rockwell used humor to poke fun at situations but never at people.
3. Rockwell painted the people and children of the neighborhood, first from real life, then, in later years, from photographs.

Rockwell's Neighborhood

The Subjects of Rockwell's Paintings

Art from Photographs

exercise 7

For each group of sentences, write a phrase that states the topic; then circle the number of the sentence that best expresses the main idea.

Group 1

1. Four hundred Navajos were recruited as marine radio operators, and the codes based on the Navajo language were never broken by the enemy.
2. During World War II, over 25,000 Native Americans served in the armed forces and made amazing contributions toward the war effort.
3. The most famous Indian GI was a Pima Indian, the marine Ira Hayes, who helped plant the American flag on Iwo Jima.

General Topic? _____

Group 2

1. Germans view health as having several components.
2. Hard work, cleanliness, and staying warm aid in health maintenance.
3. Stress and germs as well as drafts, unhappiness, and a sedentary lifestyle are believed to cause illness.

General topic? _____

—Culture in Rehabilitation,
edited by Matin Royeen
and Jeffrey L. Crabtree

Group 3

1. Logically, the probability of having a "good Samaritan" on the scene would seem to increase as group size increases.
2. When it comes to helping behavior, many studies have uncovered a puzzling situation called the bystander effect: People are less likely to provide needed help when they are in groups than when they are alone.
3. Evidence that your probability of getting help *declines* as group size increases was first described by John Darley and Bibb Latane, who were conducting research on helping behavior.

General topic? _____

—Psychology: Themes & Variations, Sixth Edition,
by Wayne Weiten

exercise 8

Each of the following sentence groups contains three specific supporting sentences. Write a general sentence that states the overall *message* for each group. In addition, write a phrase that briefly states the general *topic* of that sentence.

Group 1

1. The battered woman does not want to believe the man she loves is violent.
2. She doesn't want to face the possibility that he may be violent for the rest of their lives together.
3. She wants to hold on to the hope that someday he will quit drinking and the relationship will change.

—Marriages and Families in a Diverse Society,
by Robin Wolf

General sentence stating the main idea? _____

_____

General topic? _____

Group 2

1. Decades before Jamestown was hailed as the first permanent settlement in America, Pedro Menendez de Aviles founded St. Augustine in Florida.
2. Menendez brought 800 soldiers and colonists to establish this first European settlement in America and to protect the land for Spain.
3. St. Augustine, so named because the landing occurred in the month of August, became a permanent and prosperous Spanish settlement.

General sentence stating the main idea? _____

_____

General topic? _____

Group 3

1. A big fear of banks and companies interested in introducing smart cards and digital cash has been the supposedly unsophisticated U.S. consumer.
2. Since the late 1990s, however, elementary school children in Westport, Connecticut, have been using smart cards to buy lunch at the school cafeteria.
3. Clearly, it doesn't take grown-up smarts to use smart cards.

—*Economics Today*, 2001–2002 Edition,
by Roger Leroy Miller

General sentence stating the main idea? _____

_____

General topic? _____

Differentiate Topic, Main Idea, and Supporting Details

We have said that a topic is a word or phrase that describes the subject or general category of a group of specific ideas. Frequently, the topic is stated as the title of a passage. The main idea, in contrast, is a complete sentence that states the topic and *adds the writer's position or focus on the topic*. The supporting details are the specifics that develop the topic and main idea.

Read the following example from a textbook paragraph and label the topic, the main idea, and a supporting detail.

EXAMPLE

_____ The Body Signaling Feeling

_____ Some signals of body language, like some facial expressions, seem to be "spoken" universally.

_____ When people are depressed, it shows in their walk, stance, and head position.

—*Psychology*, by Carole Wade and Carol Tavris

> **EXPLANATION** The first item is general enough to be the topic. The second item is a sentence that expresses the writer's point about the topic, and so it is the main idea. The third item is a specific example, so it is a detail.

exercise 9

Compare the items within each group and indicate which is the topic (T), the main idea (MI), and the specific supporting detail (D).

Group 1

_____ 1. Much in this American document comes from England's Magna Carta, which was signed in 1215.

_____ 2. British Roots in American Government

_____ 3. The American Constitution has its roots in the power of past documents.

Group 2

_____ 1. Children are highly valued in African American families.

_____ 2. Valuing Children

_____ 3. Like Latinos, African Americans view "children as wealth," believing that children are important in adding enjoyment and fulfillment to life.

—*Marriage and Families in a Diverse Society,*
by Robin Wolf

Group 3

_____ 1. The Fate of Mexican Americans

_____ 2. Some conquered Mexicans welcomed the Americans; many others, recognizing the futility of resistance, responded to the American conquest with ambivalence.

_____ 3. The 80,000 Mexicans who lived in the Southwest did not respond to the Mexican War with a single voice.

—*America and Its People*, Third Edition,
by James Martin et al.

Group 4

_____ 1. Her early research led to an understanding of how viruses infect the plant and destroy its tissues.

_____ 2. Esau's Early Career with Beets

_____ 3. Sugar beets played a major role in the career of Dr. Katherine Esau, one of this century's most productive plant scientists.

—*Biology: Concepts and Connections*, Fourth Edition,
by Neil Campbell, et al.

Group 5

_____ 1. Discrimination Against Women in Higher Education

_____ 2. Harvard, for example, was one of the last to give up sex discrimination and began admitting women to its graduate business program only in 1963.

_____ 3. In general, the more prestigious the educational institutions, the more strongly they discriminated against women.

—Sociology, Third Edition,
by Alex Thio

Differentiate Distractors in Main Idea Test Items

To gain insight into recognizing a correctly stated topic, categorizing incorrect responses to main idea questions can be helpful. When stating the topic or main idea of a passage, it is easy to make the mistake of creating a phrase or a sentence that is either too broad or too narrow. The same two types of errors occur when students answer main idea questions on standardized tests. A phrase that is too broad is too general and thus would suggest the inclusion of much more than is stated in the passage. A phrase that is too narrow is a detail within the passage. It may be an interesting and eye-catching detail, but it is not the subject of the passage.

EXAMPLE   After reading the following passage, decide which of the suggested titles is correct (C), too broad (TB), or a detail (D).

One interesting research finding shows that listeners can accurately judge the socioeconomic status (whether high, middle, or low) of speakers from 60-second voice samples. In fact, many listeners reported that they made their judgments in fewer than 15 seconds. Speakers judged to be of high status were also rated as being of higher credibility than speakers rated middle and low in status. Listeners can also judge with considerable accuracy the emotional states of speakers from vocal expressions.

—Human Communication, Sixth Edition,
by Joseph DeVito

_____ 1. Importance of Voice

_____ 2. Speaking

_____ 3. Making Judgments by Voice

_____ 4. Emotional States of Speakers

EXPLANATION   The third response most accurately describes the topic of the passage. The first two are too broad and would include much more than is in the paragraph. The last response is a detail that is part of one of the experiments with listeners.

exercise 10 Read the passage and label the suggested titles for the passage as correct (C), too broad (TB), or a detail (D).

Passage 1

In California, Mexican Americans were outnumbered and vulnerable to discrimination. During the early years of the Gold Rush, Mexican Americans were robbed, beaten, and lynched with impunity. The 1850 Foreign Miners' Tax imposed a $20 a month tax on Mexican American miners, even though the Treaty of Guadalupe Hidalgo had granted them citizenship. Many Mexicans were forced to sell land to pay onerous taxes that fell heaviest on the Spanish speakers.

—*America and Its People,* Third Edition,
by James Martin, et al.

_____ 1. Treaty of Guadalupe Hidalgo

_____ 2. Discrimination

_____ 3. Foreign Miners' Tax During the Gold Rush

_____ 4. Discrimination Against Mexican Americans in California

Passage 2

Humpback whales strain their food from seawater. Instead of teeth, these giants have an array of brushlike plates called baleen on each side of their upper jaw. The baleen is used to sift food from the ocean. To start feeding, a humpback whale opens its mouth, expands its throat, and takes a huge gulp of seawater. When its mouth closes, the water squeezes out through spaces in the baleen, and a mass of food is trapped in the mouth. The food is then swallowed whole, passing into the stomach, where digestion begins. The humpback's stomach can hold about half a ton of food at a time, and in a typical day, the animal's digestive system will process as much as 2 tons of krill and fish.

—*Biology: Concepts and Connections,* Fourth Edition,
by Neil Campbell, et al.

_____ 1. Humpback Whales

_____ 2. Baleen for Teeth

_____ 3. The Digestive System of the Humpback Whale

_____ 4. How Whales Filter Food

Passage 3

Tar and nicotine are not the only harmful chemicals in cigarettes. In fact, tars account for only 8 percent of tobacco smoke. The remaining 92 percent consists of various gases, the most dangerous of which is carbon monoxide. In tobacco smoke, the concentration of carbon monoxide is 800 times higher than the level considered safe by the U.S. Environmental Protection Agency (EPA). In the human body, carbon monoxide reduces the oxygen-carrying capacity of the red blood cells by binding with the receptor sites for oxygen. This causes oxygen deprivation in many body tissues.

—*Health: the Basics,* Fifth Edition,
by Rebecca J. Donatelle

_____ 1. Carbon Monoxide

_____ 2. Harmful Tars and Nicotine

_____ 3. Carbon Monoxide Dangers from Smoking

_____ 4. Tobacco and Smoking

Questioning for the Main Idea

To determine the main idea of a body of material, ask questions in the following three basic areas. (The order may vary according to how much you already know about the subject.) Usually, you decide on the general topic first, sometimes from the title and sometimes by considering the details. If you are familiar with the material, constructing a main idea may seem almost automatic. If the material is unfamiliar, however, you may need to connect the key thoughts to formulate a topic and then create your main idea statement.

1. Establish the Topic

Question: Who or what is this about? What general word or phrase identifies the subject? The topic should be broad enough to include all the ideas, but narrow enough to focus on the direction of the details. For example, identifying the topic of an article, such as "College Costs," "Change in College," or "Changing to Cut College Costs," might all be correct, but the last may be the most pointed and descriptive for the article.

2. Identify the Key Supporting Terms

Question: What are the important details? Look at the details that seem significant to see if they point in a particular direction. What aspect of the subject do they address? What seems to be the common message? In a passage on college costs, the details might describe benefits of larger classes, telecommunication networks, and video instruction. A common thread is that each idea relates to changes targeted at cutting the costs of college instruction.

3. Focus on the Message of the Topic

Question: What main idea is the author trying to convey about the topic? This statement should be:

- A complete sentence
- Broad enough to include the important details, and
- Focused enough to describe the author's slant

In the example about cutting college costs, the main idea might be "Several colleges experiment with ways to cut costs."

Stated Main Ideas

Research shows that readers comprehend better when the main idea is directly stated, particularly when it is stated at the beginning of a passage. Such an initial main idea statement, **thesis statement**, or **topic sentence** is a signpost for readers, briefing them on what to expect. This thesis or main idea statement provides an overview of the author's message and connects the supporting details. Read the following example and use the three-step method to determine the main idea.

EXAMPLE   Polygraph tests have been viewed as an invasion of privacy and criticized on ethical, legal, and scientific grounds. The physiological changes thought to reveal deception could result from anxiety about being interrogated, anger at being asked to take the test, or fear from pondering the consequences of "failing" the test. You might react in any of these ways if you were "hooked up" to a polygraph.

—*Psychology,* by Stephen F. Davis
and Joseph J. Palladino

1. Who or what is the topic of this passage? _____

2. Underline the key terms.

3. What point is the author trying to make? _____

_____

EXPLANATION   The topic of this passage is "Polygraph Tests." The details give specifics about how physiological changes caused by anxiety, anger, or fear can show up the same way on a polygraph test as a lie response. The author states the main idea in the first sentence.

Textbook authors do not always state the main idea in the first sentence. Stated main ideas may be the beginning, middle, or concluding sentence of a passage. Therefore, do not think of stating the main idea only as a search for a particular sentence. Instead, rely on your own skill in answering the three questions about topic, details, and focus. Connect the details to form your own concept of the main idea, and, if a specific sentence in the paragraph restates it, you will recognize it as the main idea.

exercise 11   Apply the three-question technique to identify the topic, key terms, and main idea of the following passages, all of which have stated main ideas.

Passage 1

To gain a better idea of what *social structure* is, think of college football. You probably know the various positions on the team: center, guards, tackles, ends, quarterback, running backs, and the like. Each is a *status*; that is, each is a social position. For each of these statuses, there is a *role*; that is, each of these positions has certain expectations attached to it. The center is expected to snap the ball, the quarterback to pass it, the guards to block, the tackles to tackle or block, the ends to receive passes, and so on. Those role expectations guide each player's actions; that is, the players try to do what their particular role requires.

—From James M. Henslin,
Sociology: A Down-to-Earth Approach, 7th ed.
© 2007 (excerpt from page 96). Reproduced by
permission of Pearson Education, Inc.

1. Who or what is the topic of this passage? _____
   _____

2. Underline the key terms.

3. What point is the author trying to make? _____
   _____

Passage 2

Many foods and beverages are produced with the help of microbial fermentation. Lactic acid bacteria are used in the production of acidophilus milk, yogurt, pickles, olives, and sauerkraut. Several types of bacteria are used to produce cheese. Bacteria are involved in making fermented meats such as salami and in the production of vinegar, soy sauce, chocolate, and certain B vitamins (B_{12} and riboflavin). Bacteria are also used in the production of citric acid, a compound added to candy and to most soft drinks.

—From Solomon, Berg, and Martin,
Biology (with InfoTrac), 6th ed,
© 2002 Brooks/Cole, a part of Cengage Learning, Inc.
Reproduced by permission. www.cengage.com/permissions

1. Who or what is the topic of this passage? _____

2. Underline the key terms.

3. What point is the author trying to make? _____
   _____

Passage 3

Today, many prosecutors, judges, and even mental health experts believe in the need for a verdict of "guilty but insane." Under this provision, if a person uses the insanity defense but a judge or jury finds the evidence insufficient for legal insanity, they can return a verdict of guilty but mentally ill. This indicates that the defendant is suffering from an emotional disorder severe enough to influence behavior but insufficient to render him or her insane. After such a finding, the court can impose any sentence it could have used on the crime charge. The convicted defendant is sent to prison, where the correctional authorities are required to provide therapeutic treatment. If the mental illness is cured, the offender is returned to the regular prison population to serve out the remainder of the sentence.

—*Introduction to Criminal Justice,* Ninth Edition, by Joseph J. Senna and Larry J. Siegel

1. Who or what is the topic of this passage? _____

2. Underline the key terms.

3. What point is the author trying to make? _____

_____

Passage 4

From the very beginning television ratings have been criticized for factors other than the small number of homes used in their computation. More important questions have to do with what ratings are measuring in the first place and how the results are used. Audimeter ratings did not measure whether anyone was actually *watching* at a given time. Its replacement technology, the peoplemeter, also has limitations. Punch-in protocols for nonfamily members are sufficiently complex that many users simply fail to acknowledge the presence of additional viewers, or they substitute a family member's code for the guest code. The diary is flawed as well; its value is dependent on the active involvement of viewers. Lack of interest, forgetfulness, and lying can and do occur. Equally important, diaries offer viewers no opportunity to comment on likes and dislikes.

—From Stanley J. Baran, *Introduction to Mass Communication,* Third Edition. Copyright © 2004 by The McGraw-Hill Companies. Reprinted by permission of The McGraw-Hill Companies.

1. Who or what is the topic of this passage? _____

_____

2. Underline the key terms.

3. What point is the author trying to make? _____

_____

Passage 5

Six Flags is a world-renowned theme park. The company owns and operates thirty-eight different parks spread out over North America, Latin America, and Europe. Locations include Mexico City, Belgium, France, Spain, Germany, and most major metropolitan areas in the United States. In fact, having a park in forty of the fifty major metropolitan areas in the United States has earned Six Flags the title of world's largest regional theme park company. Annually, more than 50 million visitors are reported to entertain themselves at Six Flags theme parks worldwide. The company prides itself in claiming that 98 percent of the U.S. population is within an 8-hour drive to any one of the numerous Six Flags theme parks.

—*Introduction to Hospitality,* Fourth Edition, by John R. Walker

1. Who or what is the topic of this passage? _____

2. Underline the key terms.

3. What point is the author trying to make? _____

_____

_____

Passage

Colleges and universities are denying access to third party credit card marketers in increasing numbers. There were 22 campuses that disallowed the practice in 1988. That number has increased dramatically and is expected to cross 400 in the next couple of years. Private sources that monitor college credit card marketing (*College Marketing Intelligence*) contend that the number is much higher, estimating that 750 to 1000 college campuses have already banned on-campus credit card marketing.

—*Taking Sides: Clashing Views on Controversial Issues in Marketing,* edited by Barton Macchiette and Abhijit Roy

1. Who or what is the topic of this passage? _____

   _____

2. Underline the key terms.

3. What point is the author trying to make? _____

   _____

   _____

Unstated Main Ideas

Research shows that only about half of the paragraphs in textbooks have directly stated main ideas. This should not be a problem if you understand the three-question technique for locating the main idea. The questions guide you in forming your own statement so that you are not dependent on finding a line in the text.

When the main idea is not directly stated, it is said to be *implied*, which means it is suggested in the thoughts that are revealed. In this case, the author has presented a complete idea, but for reasons of style and impact has chosen not to express it concisely in one sentence. As a reader, it is your job to systematically connect the details and focus the message.

In the following passage the main idea is not stated, but it may be determined by answering the three questions that follow.

EXAMPLE

In Australia and Belgium, nonvoters are subject to fines; not only the fine itself but the clear expectation that everyone is legally required to vote helps generate 90+ percent turnout rates. In Italy, nonvoters are not fined, but "Did Not Vote" is stamped on their identification papers, threatening nonvoters with the prospect of unsympathetic treatment at the hands of public officials should they get into trouble or need help with a problem.

—*The New American Democracy,* Election Update Edition,
by Morris Fiorina and Paul Peterson

1. Who or what is the topic of this passage? _____

   (This gives you the general topic or heading.)

2. What are the key terms or details? _____

   _____

3. What idea is the author trying to convey about nonvoting? _____

   _____

   (This is the main idea the author is trying to communicate.)

EXPLANATION The sentence stating the main idea might very well have been the first, middle, or last sentence of the paragraph. Having it stated, however, was not necessary for understanding the passage. In many cases, readers spend time searching for a single sentence that encapsulates the meaning rather than digesting the information and forming ideas. Instead, answer these three questions: "Who or what is this about?" "What are the key terms?" and "What point is the author trying to make?" This passage is about penalties for not voting. The key terms are "*giving fines in Australia and Belgium, and stamping 'Did Not Vote' on identification papers in Italy.*" The author's main idea is that in "*some countries nonvoters are penalized to encourage voting.*" Apply the three-question technique to determine the main idea.

exercise 12

Passage 1

Marilyn, a Southwest Airlines flight attendant, takes the mike as her plane backs away from the Houston terminal. "Could y'all lean in a little toward the center aisle please?" she chirps in an irresistible Southern drawl. "Just a bit, please. That's it. No, the other way, sir. Thanks."

Baffled passengers comply even though they have no idea why.

"You see," says Marilyn at last, "the pilot has to pull out of this space here, and he needs to be able to check the rearview mirrors."

Only when the laughter subsides does Marilyn launch into the standard aircraft safety speech that many passengers usually ignore.

—*Business Essentials,* Third Edition,
by Ronald Ebert and Ricky Griffin

1. Who or what is the topic of this passage? _____
2. Underline the key terms.
3. What point is the author trying to make? _____
   _____

Passage 2

Children have more taste buds than adults do, which may explain why they are often so picky about eating "grown-up" foods. Even among adults, individuals differ in their sensitivity to taste. Indeed, recent studies have shown that people can be divided into one of three groups: nontasters, medium tasters, and supertasters. Compared to most, supertasters use only half as much sugar or saccharin in their coffee or tea. They also suffer more oral burn from eating the active ingredient in chili peppers. Using videomicroscopy to count the number of taste buds on the tongue, researchers have found that nontasters have an average of 96 taste buds per square centimeter, medium tasters have 184, and supertasters have 425.

—*Psychology,* Second Edition, by Saul Kassin

1. Who or what is the topic of this passage? _____
2. Underline the key terms.

3. What point is the author trying to make? _____

_____

Passage 3

If the person is extremely important, you had better be there early just in case he or she is able to see you ahead of schedule. As the individual's status decreases, it is less important for you to be on time. Students, for example, must be on time for conferences with teachers, but it is more important to be on time for deans and still more important to be on time for the president of the college. Teachers, on the other hand, may be late for conferences with students but not for conferences with deans or the president. Deans, in turn, may be late for teachers but not for the president. Business organizations and other hierarchies have similar rules.

—*Human Communication,* Sixth Edition,
by Joseph DeVito

1. Who or what is the topic of this passage? _____

_____

2. Underline the key terms.

3. What point is the author trying to make? _____

_____

Passage 4

In his book *Bridges, Not Walls,* John Stewart dramatically illustrates the case of the famous "Wild Boy of Aveyron," who spent his early childhood without any apparent human contact. The boy was discovered in January 1800 while digging for vegetables in a French village garden. He showed no behaviors one would expect in a social human. The boy could not speak but uttered only unrecognizable cries. More significant than this absence of social skills was his lack of any identity as a human being. As author Roger Shattuck put it, "The boy had no human sense of being in the world. He had no sense of himself as a person related to other persons." Only after the influence of a loving "mother" did the boy begin to behave—and, we can imagine, think of himself as a human.

In 1970, authorities discovered a twelve-year-old girl (whom they called "Genie") who had spent virtually all her life in an otherwise empty, darkened bedroom with almost no human contact. The child could not speak and had no sense of herself as a person until she was removed from her family and "nourished" by a team of caregivers.

—*Understanding Human Communication,* Eighth Edition,
by Ronald B. Adler and George Rodman

1. Who or what is the topic of this passage? _____

   _____

2. Underline the key terms.
3. What point is the author trying to make? _____

   _____

Passage 5

A mother had a son who threw temper tantrums: lying on the floor, pounding his fists, kicking his legs, and whining for whatever he wanted. One day while in a supermarket he threw one of his temper tantrums. In a moment of desperation, the mother dropped to the floor, pounded her fists, kicked her feet, and whined, "I wish you'd stop throwing temper tantrums! I can't stand it when you throw temper tantrums!" By this time, the son had stood up. He said in a hushed tone, "Mom, there are people watching! You're embarrassing me!" The mother calmly stood up, brushed off the dust, and said in a clear, calm voice, "That's what you look like when you're throwing a temper tantrum." Sometimes, traditional approaches such as bribing, threatening, ignoring, or giving in seem so natural that we overlook the possibility that something different, such as embarrassment, might work too.

—*The Creative Problem Solver's Toolbox,*
by Richard Fobes

1. Who or what is the topic of this passage? _____

   _____

2. Underline the key terms.
3. What point is the author trying to make? _____

   _____

exercise 13 In some of the following passages the main ideas are stated. In others they are implied. Avoid simply searching for a sentence that states the main idea. Instead, apply the three-step method that you have learned and practiced throughout this chapter to determine the author's main point.

Passage 1

God's message to Muhammad in the form of the Qur'an (a "reciting") was clear: The Prophet is to warn his people against worship of false gods and all immorality, especially injustice to the poor, orphans, widows and women in general. At the end of time, on Judgment Day, every person will be bodily resurrected to face eternal punishment in hellfire or eternal joy in paradise, according to how he or she has lived. The way to paradise lies in gratitude to God for the bounties of creation, his prophetic and revelatory guidance, and his readiness to forgive the penitent. Social justice and obedient worship of the one Lord are required of every person. Each is to recognize his or her creatureliness and God's transcendence. The proper response is "submission" (*islam*) to God's will, becoming *muslim* ("submissive" or surrendering") in one's worship and morality.

—*The Heritage of World Civilizations Combined Edition,*
Sixth Edition, by Albert Craig, William Graham,
Donald Kagan, Steven Ozment, and Frank Turner

1. Who or what is the topic of this paragraph? _____

_____

2. Underline the key details.

_____ 3. Select the best statement of the main idea of the passage.

   a. The word "Qur'an" means a reciting, and "islam" means submission.
   b. God warned people against worship of false gods.
   c. Muhammad was a prophet who received a message from God that became known as the Qur'an.
   d. God's message to Muhammad was that he must tell people that the way to paradise is to live with concern for justice and submission to God.

Passage 2

The two most prominent centers of civilization—and the focus of this chapter—were Mesoamerica, in what is today Mexico and Central America, and the Andean region of South America. Both regions have a long, rich history of civilization that reaches back thousands of years. At the time of the European conquest of the Americas in the sixteenth century both regions were dominated by powerful expansionist empires—the Aztecs, or Mexica, in Mesoamerica, and the Inca in the Andes. In both regions Spanish conquerors obliterated the native empires and nearly succeeded in obliterating native culture. But in both, Native American traditions have endured overlaid and combined in complex ways with Hispanic culture, to provide clues to the pre-Hispanic past.

—*The Heritage of World Civilizations Combined Edition,* Sixth Edition,
by Albert Craig, William Graham, Donald Kagan,
Steven Ozment, and Frank Turner

1. Who or what is the topic of this paragraph? _____

_____

_____

2. Underline the key details.

_____ 3. Select the best statement of the main idea of the passage.
   a. The important, ancient cultures centered in Mesoamerica and the Andean region of south America produced recognizable traditions that are still visible today.
   b. The European conquest destroyed the Aztec and Inca civilizations.
   c. Mesoamerica was what is known as Mexico and Central America today.
   d. The Aztecs lived in Mesoamerica.

Passage 3

One hallmark of Chinese history is its striking continuity of culture, language, and geography. The Shang and Chou dynasties were centered in north China along the Yellow River or its tributary, the Wei. The capitals of China's first empire were in exactly the same areas, and north China would remain China's political center through history to the present. If Western civilization had experienced similar continuity, it would have progressed from Thebes in the valley of the Nile to Athens on the Nile; Rome on the Nile; and then, in time, to Paris, London, and Berlin on the Nile; and each of these centers of civilization would have spoken Egyptian and written in Egyptian hieroglyphics.

—*The Heritage of World Civilizations Combined Edition,* Sixth Edition, by Albert Craig, William Graham, Donald Kagan, Steven Ozment, and Frank Turner

1. Who or what is the topic of this paragraph? _____
_____

2. Underline the key details.

_____ 3. Select the best statement of the main idea of the passage.

   a. Western civilization began in Thebes in the valley of the Nile.
   b. China's first imperial capitals were in North China along the Yellow River and the Wei River.
   c. Chinese history has been amazingly consistent in its geography.
   d. Chinese and Western civilizations have developed in much the same way.

Passage 4

One of the most important things to realize about the restaurant industry is that you can't do it alone. Each person in your operation has to work together for you to be successful. The most important ingredient in managing people is to respect them. Many words can be used to describe a manager (coach, supervisor, boss, mentor), but whatever term is used, you have to be in the game to be effective. Managing a kitchen is like coaching a football team—everyone must work together to be effective. The difference between a football team and a kitchen is that chefs/managers cannot supervise from the sidelines; they have to be in the game. One of my favorite examples of excellent people management skills is that of the general manager of a hotel who had the ware-washing team report directly to him. When asked why, he indicated that they are the people who know what is being thrown in the garbage, they are the people who know what the customers are not eating, and they are the people most responsible for the sanitation and safety of an operation. There are many components to managing people—training, evaluating, nurturing, delegating, and so on—but the most important is respect.

—*Introduction to Hospitality,* Fifth Edition, by John Walker

1. Who or what is the topic of this paragraph? _____
   _____

2. Underline the key details.

_____ 3. Select the best statement of the main idea of the passage.

    a. Managing a kitchen is like coaching a football team.
    b. To be successful a restaurant manager must develop a team in which respect is the key ingredient.
    c. The people with the least-skilled jobs often know what the customers like and don't like.
    d. One hotel manager had the ware-washing team report directly to him.

Passage 5

Employability traits are those skills that focus on attitude, passion, initiative, dedication, sense of urgency, and dependability. These traits are not always traits that can be taught, but a good chef can demonstrate them by example. Most of the employers with job opportunities for students consider these skills to be more important than technical skills. The belief is that if you have strong employability traits, your technical skills will be strong.

—*Introduction to Hospitality*, Fifth Edition, by John Walker

1. Who or what is the topic of this paragraph? _____

2. Underline the key details.

_____ 3. Select the best statement of the main idea of the passage.

    a. Attitude is an important employability trait.
    b. Employability traits are often more important than technical skills.
    c. A good chef can teach by example.
    d. Employers like to employ students.

Getting the Main Idea of Longer Selections

Because of the great quantity of material included in a book, understanding the main idea of longer selections such as chapters and articles seems more difficult than understanding a single paragraph. Longer selections have several major ideas contributing to the main point and many paragraphs of supporting details. To pull the ideas together under one central theme, an additional step is necessary: Simplifying the material by organizing paragraphs or pages into manageable subsections and then deciding how each subsection contributes to the whole.

The following questions can help you determine the central theme for a longer selection.

1. What is the significance of the title? What does the title suggest about the topic?
2. How do the first paragraphs suggest the topic or thesis?
3. Under what subsections can the paragraphs and ideas be grouped?
4. How do these subsections support the whole?
5. What is the overall topic?
6. What point is the author trying to convey?

Personal *Feedback* **1**   Name _____

1. Describe the theme or main idea of a movie that you have seen recently, one that you liked, and give reasons for your positive evaluation.

   Movie Title: _____

   Theme or Main Idea: _____

   Reasons for Positive Evaluation: _____

2. Was there anything you did not understand about the main idea? _____

3. This chapter includes a longer reading selection on sleep. Approximately how many hours of sleep do you get each night? _____

4. What time do you usually go to bed? _____

5. What time do you get up? _____

6. Breakfast sends an early supply of glucose to the brain. When do you eat breakfast, and what do you eat for breakfast? _____

7. Typically what, when, and where do you eat the other meals of the day?

   Lunch: _____

   Dinner: _____

8. Exercise is recommended to reduce stress. What exercise do you get on a regular basis, and when do you do it? _____

   _____

9. Do you typically go out on weeknights? If so, typically when and where do you go?

   _____

10. Evaluate your energy level and concentration ability. _____

    _____

    _____

Tear out and submit to your instructor.

exercise 14   Search the Internet for articles on dreaming. Select an article that interests you, and on a separate sheet of paper, provide answers to the six questions pertaining to getting the main idea of longer reading selections on page 143.

Summary *Points*

➤ **What words are typically used to name the main idea?**
The main idea is also called the thesis, main point, central focus, gist, controlling idea, and central thought.

➤ **How do topics and details differ?**
The topic is the general subject, and the details are the specific supporting ideas.

➤ **What questions do you ask to find the topic of a passage?**
Ask "Who or what is the subject?"

➤ **What questions do you ask to find the main idea of a passage?**
Ask "What point is the author trying to make?"

➤ **How do stated and unstated main ideas differ?**
A stated main idea is a sentence within the passage. An unstated main idea is implied or suggested by thoughts revealed but not directly stated.

➤ **How do you get the main idea of longer selections?**
Break the material into subsections and determine how they support the whole.

COLLABORATIVE   PROBLEM SOLVING

Form a five-member group and select one of the following questions. Brainstorm and then outline your major points on a transparency. Choose a member to present the group findings to the class.

➤ Why is prior knowledge the best single predictor of reading comprehension?

➤ Why is comprehension better when the main idea is stated at the beginning of a test passage?

➤ Describe a passage that you might write that would have the main idea stated at the end.

➤ Why should the main idea of a passage be stated in a sentence rather than a phrase? Give examples.

myreadinglab

My ReadingLab (MRL) www.myreadinglab.com

➤ To practice the ideas and skills introduced in this chapter, go to the "Main Idea" module in the Skills section of MRL. To practice general reading comprehension, use the Levels section.

The Reading *Workshop*

"When I look back, I am so impressed again with the life-giving power of literature. If I were a young person today, trying to gain a sense of myself in the world, I would do that again by reading, just as I did when I was young."

—MAYA ANGELOU

Reading widely for pleasure can certainly enrich one's sense of self. Imagine the experiences available through books that may never be possible, or even desirable, for us to actually do. Traveling the world, seeing how other people think and behave, experiencing things we may never do otherwise—all of these help us see ourselves more clearly. (You may want to read something by Maya Angelou, well-known American author and poet. *I Know Why the Caged Bird Sings, A Song Flung Up to Heaven,* and *Even the Stars Look Lonesome* are three of her many books.)

Think about it, talk about it, write about it:

Whether you are reading fiction or nonfiction, consider what you have learned from your book:

➤ Why do you think a character acted like he or she did? Would you have done the same?

➤ What have you learned about a particular place or time period?

➤ Have you gained insights into a field of study or career?

➤ Have you learned new facts? How might you apply this new knowledge?

Your instructor might ask you to consider these questions or others in a Reading Workshop journal.

selection 1 Psychology

"Dreams say what they mean, but they don't say it in daytime language."

Gail Godwin

In studies conducted worldwide, modern dream scientists have found that dreams vary according to age, gender, and culture. Women tend to have more dreams of children, whereas men dream more of aggression, weapons, and tools. Americans are frequently embarrassed by nakedness in dreams, but such dreams rarely occur in cultures of people wearing fewer clothes. Mexican American college students dream of death more often than do Anglo American students, perhaps because death is more a part of life in Latin American cultures. The findings of such cross-cultural research supports the hypothesis that dreams reflect life events that are important to the dreamer.

THINKING BEFORE READING

Preview for content, activate your schema, and anticipate what you will learn.

Did you dream last night?

What dream or dreams have you had recently?

Can you explain the meaning of any of your dreams?

I think this reading will tell me _____.

VOCABULARY PREVIEW

Are you familiar with these words?

unconscious	paradox	convenient	symbolizes	bullied
idling	depriving	ascribed	critical	synchronized

Which word has the same root as *chronological*?

What is the definition of the prefix in *unconscious*?

Is the phrase "jumbo shrimp" a *paradox*?

Your instructor may choose to give a true-false vocabulary review before or after reading.

THINKING DURING READING

As you read, use the six thinking strategies of a good reader: predict, picture, relate, monitor, correct, and annotate.

> ## Reader's $\mathcal{T}ip$ Reading and Studying Psychology
>
> - Seek to understand abstract terms and confusing concepts through the concrete examples that illustrate them.
> - Relate psychological theories to yourself and visualize people you know as examples.
> - Memorize key terms with definitions and examples, especially for multiple-choice tests.
> - Test yourself by turning each boldface heading into a question, and recite your answer.
> - Because much of psychology is about theories, connect the names of researchers with their theories. Learn characteristics and examples for each theory.
> - Compare and contrast theories. For example, how do the social learning theorists differ from the behaviorists?
> - Reduce your notes to visual diagrams. For example, to study personality theories, draw charts to list the comparative elements.

SLEEPING AND DREAMING

The time when we are most obviously unconscious is when we are asleep. Yet we have dreams during that time. This implies that something is going on in our brain.

Is all sleep the same? Are there stages in sleep? When do humans dream? How can you tell if a person is dreaming? Why do people have dreams, anyway? These are the

5 questions to be answered in this section.

Researchers have learned more about sleep and dreaming in the past twenty-five years than in all of history up to that time. One major reason for this is the discovery that when people are asleep there are changes in the activity of their brain and eyes. These changes can be recorded.

10 Beth Smith lies down to sleep after a hard day. She drifts off. At first she is in a light kind of sleep. Her brain waves, if recorded on a brain-wave machine, show a pattern that is definitely different than when she is awake. After less than an hour, two things happen to Beth. Her brain waves change, so that they now look pretty much the way they do when she is awake. Yet she is still asleep. Also, although her eyelids are closed, her eyes

15 begin to move about rapidly under the lids. This lasts for twenty minutes. Then Beth returns to the sleep of easy brain waves and no eye movement.

Basically, there are two kinds of sleep. One is Rapid Eye Movement (REM) sleep. In this, the brain waves are similar to those of a waking person, and the eyes move about rapidly under the closed lids. The other kind of sleep is Non-Rapid Eye Movement sleep.

20 You can guess what that's like, right? Stop for a moment and describe REM and non-REM sleep to yourself.

REM sleep is also called *paradoxical sleep.* A paradox is something that seems contradictory within itself. What is the paradox about REM sleep? That the sleeper's brain waves would lead you to believe the person is awake, but in fact the person is asleep.

25 Now, the interesting thing is this. Suppose Beth is showing non-REM sleep. We wake her up and say: "Wake up, Beth! What are you dreaming?"

"Uh … nothing," Beth mumbles.

Disappointed, we let her go back to sleep. Later on, Beth begins to show REM sleep. Again, we wake her up. "What are you dreaming, Beth?"

30   "Uh . . . this man has ridden a camel into Mom's office. It's too big. The camel fills up the whole office. The man riding him is an Arab." She goes on with her dream.

Dreaming happens mainly in REM sleep. This is very convenient for researchers. They get volunteers to sleep in a bed in the laboratory. An electronic sensing device that registers eye movement is placed on the eyelids of the volunteers. Thus the researcher can tell

35   exactly when the volunteer is showing REM sleep.

"Wake up, volunteer! What are you dreaming?"

WHAT HAS BEEN LEARNED ABOUT DREAMING?

Everyone dreams about 20 percent of the time they are sleeping—that is, they show REM sleep about that much. Even people who say they never dream show about 20 percent REM sleep. If these "nondreamers" do their sleeping in a laboratory where the researcher

40   can wake them up, it turns out that they dream as much as others. They just don't remember the dreams in the morning, perhaps because memories for dreams fade fast and they are slow waking up.

People go back and forth between REM and non-REM sleep during the night. If something happens in their environment while they are sleeping, people may fit this into

45   the dream. Did you ever have the experience of someone calling you in the morning, but at first you thought it was part of a dream?

Events in daily life sometimes occur in symbolic form in dreams. For example, a boy was having a lot of difficulty on the school playground because a bigger boy kept bullying him. That night the smaller boy dreamed of being alone and unarmed in the African

50   grass country, facing a lion. The lion symbolizes the bully. At other times the dreaded event from daily life simply occurs in a dream in its real-life form—the boy dreams of being bullied by the bigger boy. How and when dream symbols are used is not yet understood.

WHY DO WE DREAM?

Do people actually need to dream? Or is it just the brain "idling its motor"? It's possible
55 that dreams are unimportant, just an accidental part of REM sleep.

One experimenter waked volunteers each time they started REM sleep. This meant
that he was also depriving them of their dreams. When they showed non-REM sleep, he
let them sleep on. Notice that by itself this experiment wouldn't prove much, even if
effects did occur. Why? Because the effects might result from just being waked up all the
60 time, rather than from just not being allowed to dream. The experimenters realized this,
so they used a second group of volunteers. These were waked exactly as much as the first
group, but no attention was paid to whether it was REM or non-REM sleep. Thus any differences could be ascribed to lack of REM sleep periods in the one group.

There were differences. People who were deprived of most of their REM sleep for
65 three nights in a row became irritable and somewhat disrupted in their actions. When on
the fourth night they were allowed to sleep on, so they could have REM sleep, they had it
about 30 percent of the time instead of the usual 20 percent. Apparently they were
"catching up" on their REM sleep. It looks as though people do, indeed, need REM sleep.
The critical question is: Is it the REM sleep that they need or the dreams? Do we have
70 REM sleep because it brings dreaming, or is dreaming just an accidental aspect of the
needed REM sleep? We don't know.

Why do people dream, then? We don't know that either. It does seem that REM sleep
is necessary. But are dreams? What do they accomplish? Some theorists have suggested
that we use dreaming to solve emotional problems, some have suggested that memories
75 are stored in the brain during sleep time and dream time. Some even suggest this is a
way of keeping our two eyes synchronized. Tomorrow we may know the answer. The discovery of rapid eye movements during dreaming has opened up the world of dreams for
research. Notice that the researchers here do something interesting. They go from an
observable behavior—the eye movements—to an internal condition—the dream. The
80 discovery of REM sleep helps bridge the gap between mental processes and the outside
world.

(1,124 words)

—*Psychology: What It Is/How to Use It,*
by David Watson

THINKING AND WRITING AFTER READING

RECALL Self-test your understanding.

Your instructor may choose to give you a true-false comprehension review.

REACT Why are sleep and dreaming important research topics for psychologists?

_____

_____

REFLECT Describe and try to interpret one of your recent or recurring dreams.

_____

_____

THINK CRITICALLY Would you predict any correlation between a good night's sleep
and a good quality of life? Why or why not? Write your answer on a separate
sheet of paper.

THINK AND WRITE   Researchers suggest that dreams differ according to age, gender, and culture. Do sleep patterns show similar differences? How would you predict that sleep patterns differ according to age, gender, and culture? _____

_____

_____

MAIN IDEA   Answer the following questions concerning the selection.

1. Who or what is the topic of the selection? _____

2. What point is the author trying to make? _____

_____

Interpret the Quote

Now that you have finished reading the selection, "Sleeping and Dreaming," go back to the beginning of the selection and read the opening quote again. What does Godwin mean when she says that dreams "say what they mean"? What is the difference between daytime language and the language of dreams? Answer both questions on a separate piece of paper.

Name ————————————————

Date ————————————————

COMPREHENSION QUESTIONS

Answer the following with *a, b, c,* or *d,* or fill in the blank. In order to help analyze your strengths and weaknesses, the question types are indicated.

Main Idea ———— 1. The best statement of the main idea of this selection is

    a. People become irritable when they do not have an adequate amount of dreaming.
    b. Through the discovery of REM, researchers have begun to learn about sleeping and dreaming, but many questions remain unanswered.
    c. Sleep is an observable behavior, whereas dreaming is an internal condition reflecting the mental processes.
    d. Dreams follow an irregular pattern, with people moving back and forth between REM and non-REM sleep all during the night.

Detail ———— 2. During REM sleep a person experiences

    a. different brain waves than when awake.
    b. the same brain waves as when awake.
    c. eye movement under closed lids.
    d. both *b* and *c*.

Inference 3. REM sleep is called paradoxical sleep because ——————————

————————————————————————

Detail ———— 4. Dreaming occurs

    a. during REM and non-REM sleep.
    b. during REM sleep.
    c. only during non-REM sleep.
    d. as people go back and forth between REM and non-REM sleep.

Detail ———— 5. Some people probably cannot remember dreams because

    a. they awaken in the middle of a dream.
    b. they are nondreamers.
    c. they experience only 20 percent REM sleep.
    d. they are slow waking up.

Inference ———— 6. The author implies that dreams do all of the following *except*

    a. symbolically reflect real-life problems.
    b. include experiences in the environment.
    c. relieve tension and irritability.
    d. normally occur in the last two hours of sleep.

Detail ———— 7. According to the passage, after several nights of interrupted REM sleep, people need to

    a. sleep longer.
    b. have a higher percent of REM sleep at the next sleeping time.
    c. have a higher percentage of non-REM sleep.
    d. sleep more frequently for brief periods of time.

Answer the following with *T* (true), *F* (false), or *CT* (can't tell).

Inference   _____ 8. Research shows that dreams are unimportant and just an accidental part of REM sleep.

Inference   _____ 9. The author feels that the discovery of rapid eye movement is the most significant finding thus far in dream research.

Inference   _____ 10. Dreams help people store memories.

VOCABULARY

Answer the following with *a, b, c,* or *d* for the word or phrase that best defines the boldface word as used in the selection. The number in parentheses indicates the line of the passage in which the word appears.

_____ 1. "most obviously **unconscious**" (1)

   a. alert
   b. daydreaming
   c. half-knowing
   d. not aware

_____ 2. "a **paradox** is" (22)

   a. mystery
   b. error
   c. contradictory truth
   d. reasoning

_____ 3. **convenient** for researchers" (32)

   a. logical
   b. easy to use
   c. necessary
   d. cooperative

_____ 4. "**symbolizes** the bully" (50)

   a. warns
   b. summarizes
   c. represents
   d. suspects

_____ 5. "**bullied** by the bigger boy" (52)

   a. intimidated
   b. befriended
   c. joined
   d. recognized

_____ 6. "**idling** its motor" (54)

   a. exhausting
   b. running without power
   c. withdrawing
   d. renewing

_____ 7. "**depriving** them of" (57)

   a. irritating
   b. educating
   c. encouraging
   d. preventing

_____ 8. "**ascribed** to lack of" (63)

   a. convened
   b. remembered
   c. credited
   d. returned

_____ 9. "the **critical** question is" (69)

   a. first
   b. general
   c. crucial
   d. most frequent

_____ 10. "keeping our two eyes" **synchronized**" (76)

   a. working simultaneously
   b. working vigorously
   c. focused
   d. slightly crossed

Your instructor may choose to give a true-false vocabulary review.

VOCABULARY ENRICHMENT

A. An acronym is an invented word formed by the initial letters of a compound term. REM, for example, is pronounced as a word that rhymes with *them*, rather than pronouncing the three letters separately to indicate rapid eye movement. Write an *A* beside the following letters that are pronounced as words and thus are acronyms.

_____ 1. HUD   _____ 3. FBI   _____ 5. NAFTA

_____ 2. UNICEF   _____ 4. CIA   _____ 6. radar

B. Study the following easily confused words, and circle the one that is correct in each sentence.

conscience: sense of right or wrong   **its:** ownership or possessive
conscious: awareness of self   **it's:** contraction of *it is*

to: toward
too: more than enough
two: the number 2

7. Let your **(conscience, conscious)** be your guide when faced with temptation to oversleep and cut class.

8. Over a lifetime, **(its, it's)** estimated we spend 25 years sleeping.

9. Sleeping for five hours is **(to, too, two)** little for most people.

C. Use the context clues in the following sentences to write the meaning of the boldface psychology terms.

10. Nightmares frequently reflect the frustration and **anxiety** felt in daily life.

_____

11. After years of practice, we **condition** ourselves to get up by the alarm clock.

_____

12. With the birth of the second child, the first child's desire for a bottle at bedtime was a sign of **regression.** _____

_____

13. Saying that you are too busy to sleep is only **rationalizing.**

_____

14. Dream therapy offers a **permissive** setting for revealing haunting and embarrassing nightmares. _____

15. Adequate sleep **reinforces** the immune system's ability to fight disease.

_____

ASSESS YOUR LEARNING

Review confusing questions, seek clarification, and make notes in your text to help you remember new information and vocabulary.

selection 2 Literature: Short Story

"The trouble with lying and deceiving is that their efficiency depends entirely upon a clear notion of the truth that the liar and deceiver wishes to hide."

Hannah Arendt

Jack Ritchie, born John George Reitci, was stationed in the Central Pacific during World War II. There, to pass the time, he read large numbers of crime stories and mystery fiction. Following the war, and with the help of a literary agent, he became a prolific short story writer whose work appeared in a wide variety of periodicals.

THINKING BEFORE READING

Preview the selection for clues to content. Activate your schema, and anticipate what you will learn.

What do you know about murder-for-hire?

How does a crime of passion differ from one that is premeditated?

I'll read this to find out _____.

VOCABULARY PREVIEW

Are you familiar with these words?

decanter	morbid	insight	davenport	authentic
commission	incorruptible	fortitude	pertinent	commiserate

Are *morbid* thoughts the same as irrational thoughts?

What is the difference between *insight* and oversight?

Your instructor may choose to give a true-false vocabulary review before or after reading.

THINKING DURING READING

As you read, use the six thinking strategies of a good reader: predict, picture, relate, monitor, correct, and annotate.

SHATTER PROOF

He was a soft-faced man wearing rimless glasses, but he handled the automatic with unmistakable competence.

I was rather surprised at my calmness when I learned the reason for his presence. "It's a pity to die in ignorance," I said, "Who hired you to kill me?"

5   His voice was mild. "I could be an enemy in my own right."

Reader's *Tip* Reading and Studying a Short Story

Ask yourself the following questions as you read a short story:

- How would you describe the main character? What other characters are well-developed? What is the purpose of the "flat" characters? What do the characters learn? How do the characters change?
- What is the main conflict in the story? What are the steps in the development of the plot? What is the climax? What is the resolution?
- What is the theme of the story? What universal truth did you learn from the story?
- When and where is the story set? How does the setting affect the theme?
- Who is telling the story? How does this point of view affect the message?
- What is the tone of the author? What mood is the author trying to create?
- What symbols provide vivid images that enrich the theme?
- What is your evaluation of the author's work?

I had been making a drink in my study when I had heard him and turned. Now I finished pouring from the decanter. "I know the enemies I've made and you are a stranger. Was it my wife?"

He smiled. "Quite correct. Her motive must be obvious."

10   "Yes," I said. "I have money and apparently she wants it. All of it."

He regarded me objectively. "Your age is?"

"Fifty-three."

"And your wife is?"

"Twenty-two."

15   He clicked his tongue. "You were foolish to expect anything permanent, Mr. Williams."

I sipped the whiskey. "I expected a divorce after a year or two and a painful settlement. But not death."

"Your wife is a beautiful woman, but greedy, Mr. Williams. I'm surprised that you

20 never noticed."

My eyes went to the gun. "I assume you have killed before?"

"Yes."

"And obviously you enjoy it."

He nodded. "A morbid pleasure, I admit. But I do."

25   I watched him and waited. Finally I said, "You have been here more than two minutes and I am still alive."

"There is no hurry, Mr. Williams," he said softly.

"Ah, then the actual killing is not your greatest joy. You must savor the preceding moments."

30   "You have insight, Mr. Williams."

"And as long as I keep you entertained, in one manner or another, I remain alive?"

"Within a time limit, of course."

"Naturally. A drink, Mr.... ?"

"Smith requires no strain on the memory. Yes, thank you. But please allow me to see
35 what you are doing when you prepare it."

"It's hardly likely that I would have poison conveniently at hand for just such an
occasion."

"Hardly likely, but still possible."

He watched me while I made his drink and then took an easy chair.

40 I sat on the davenport. "Where would my wife be at this moment?"

"At a party, Mr. Williams. There will be a dozen people to swear that she never left
their sight during the time of your murder."

"I will be shot by a burglar? An intruder?"

He put his drink on the cocktail table in front of him. "Yes. After I shoot you, I shall,
45 of course, wash this glass and return it to your liquor cabinet. And when I leave I shall
wipe all fingerprints from the doorknobs I've touched."

"You will take a few trifles with you? To make the burglar-intruder story more
authentic?"

"That will not be necessary, Mr. Williams. The police will assume that the burglar
50 panicked after he killed you and fled empty-handed."

"That picture on the east wall," I said. "It's worth thirty thousand."

His eyes went to it for a moment and then quickly returned to me. "It is tempting,
Mr. Williams, but I desire to possess nothing that will even remotely link me to you. I
appreciate art, and especially its monetary value, but not to the extent where I will risk
55 the electric chair." Then he smiled. "Or were you perhaps offering me the painting? In
exchange for your life?"

"It was a thought."

He shook his head. "I'm sorry, Mr. Williams. Once I accept a commission, I am not
dissuaded. It is a matter of professional pride."

60 I put my drink on the table. "Are you waiting for me to show fear, Mr. Smith?"

"You will show it."

"And then you will kill me?"

His eyes flickered. "It is a strain, isn't it, Mr. Williams? To be afraid and not to dare show it."

65 "Do you expect your victims to beg?" I asked.

"They do. In one manner or another."

"They appeal to your humanity? And that is hopeless?"

"It is hopeless."

"They offer you money?"

70 "Very often."

"Is that hopeless too?"

"So far it has been, Mr. Williams."

"Behind the picture I pointed out to you, Mr. Smith, there is a wall safe."

He gave the painting another brief glance. "Yes."

75 "It contains five thousand dollars."

"That is a lot of money, Mr. Williams."

I picked up my glass and went to the painting. I opened the safe, selected a brown envelope, and then finished my drink. I put the empty glass in the safe and twirled the knob.

80 Smith's eyes were drawn to the envelope. "Bring that here, please."

I put the envelope on the cocktail table in front of him.

He looked at it for a few moments and then up at me. "Did you actually think you could buy your life?"

I lit a cigarette. "No. You are, shall we say, incorruptible."

85 He frowned slightly. "But still you brought me the five thousand?"

I picked up the envelope and tapped its contents out on the table. "Old receipts. All completely valueless to you."

He showed the color of irritation. "What do you think this has possibly gained you?"

"The opportunity to go to the safe and put your glass inside it."

90 His eyes flicked to the glass in front of him. "That was yours. Not mine."

I smiled. "It was your glass, Mr. Smith. And I imagine that the police will wonder what an empty glass is doing in my safe. I rather think, especially since this will be a case of murder, that they will have the intelligence to take fingerprints."

His eyes narrowed. "I haven't taken my eyes off you for a moment. You couldn't have 95 switched our glasses."

"No? I seem to recall that at least twice you looked at the painting."

Automatically he looked in that direction again. "Only for a second or two."

"It was enough."

He was perspiring faintly. "I say it was impossible."

100 "Then I'm afraid you will be greatly surprised when the police come for you. And after a little time you will have the delightful opportunity of facing death in the electric chair. You will share your victims' anticipation of death with the addition of a great deal more time in which to let your imagination play with the topic. I'm sure you've read accounts of executions in the electric chair?"

105 His finger seemed to tighten on the trigger.

"I wonder how you'll go," I said. "You've probably pictured yourself meeting death with calmness and fortitude. But that is a common comforting delusion, Mr. Smith. You will more likely have to be dragged...."

His voice was level. "Open that safe or I'll kill you." I laughed. "Really now, Mr.
110 Smith, we both know that obviously you will kill me if I *do* open the safe."

A half a minute went by before he spoke. "What do you intend to do with the glass?"

"If you don't murder me—and I rather think you won't now—I will take it to a private detective agency and have your fingerprints reproduced. I will put them, along with

115   a note containing pertinent information, inside a sealed envelope. And I will leave instructions that in the event I die violently, even if the occurrence appears accidental, the envelope be forwarded to the police."

Smith stared at me and then he took a breath. "All that won't be necessary. I will leave now and you will never see me again."

120   I shook my head. "I prefer my plan. It provides protection for my future."

He was thoughtful. "Why don't you go direct to the police?"

"I have my reasons."

His eyes went down to his gun and then slowly he put it in his pocket. An idea came to him. "Your wife could very easily hire someone else to kill you."

125   "Yes. She could do that."

"I would be accused of your death. I could go to the electric chair."

"I imagine so. Unless . . . ."

Smith waited.

"Unless, of course, she were unable to hire anyone."

130   "But there are probably a half a dozen other. . . ." He stopped.

I smiled. "Did my wife tell you where she is now?"

"Just that she'd be at a place called the Petersons. She will leave at eleven."

"Eleven? A good time. It will be very dark tonight. Do you know the Petersons' address?"

135   He stared at me. "No."

"In Bridgehampton," I said, and I gave him the house number.

Our eyes held for half a minute.

"It's something you must do," I said softly. "For your own protection."

He buttoned his coat slowly. "And where will you be at eleven, Mr. Williams?"

140   "At my club, probably playing cards with five or six friends. They will no doubt commiserate with me when I receive word that my wife has been. . . shot?"

"It all depends on the circumstances and the opportunity." He smiled thinly. "Did you ever love her?"

I picked up a jade figurine and examined it. "I was extremely fond of this piece when

145   I first bought it. Now it bores me. I will replace it with another."

When he was gone there was just enough time to take the glass to a detective agency before I went on to the club.

Not the glass in the safe, of course. It held nothing but my own fingerprints.

I took the one that Mr. Smith left on the cocktail table when he departed.

150   The prints of Mr. Smith's fingers developed quite clearly.

(1,588 words)

—"Shatter Proof" by Jack Ritchie,
from *Manhunt Magazine*

THINKING AND WRITING AFTER READING

RECALL   Self-test your understanding.

Your instructor may choose to give you a true-false comprehension review.

REACT   Why do you think Mr. Williams will take the glass with the killer's finger prints to the detective agency before going to the club? _____

_____

REFLECT   How did Mr. Williams manage to trick and blackmail the killer? _____

_____

THINKING CRITICALLY Why did the author not end the story with the glass in the safe and the killer saying he would leave? Would it still have been a clever short story if it had ended at that point? _____

_____

THINK AND WRITE Irony is a twist that leads to the unexpected happening. In this story, what is the ironic twist for each of the three: Mr. Williams, the professional killer, and Mrs. Williams? _____

_____

Interpret the Quote

Now that you have finished reading the selection, "Shatter Proof," go back to the beginning of the selection and read the opening quote again. On a separate sheet of paper, explain the meaning of the quote. Do you think that Mr. Williams' deception was effective? Explain why.

Name ————————————————————

Date ————————————————————

COMPREHENSION QUESTIONS

Answer the following with *a*, *b*, *c*, or *d*. In order to help you analyze your strengths and weaknesses, the question types are indicated.

Main Idea ———— 1. The best statement of the main idea of the selection is
   a. Mr. Williams cleverly tricks a professional killer to change his own fate.
   b. Mr. Williams wanted to kill his wife and finally found a way to do it.
   c. Murder is a random game of chance.
   d. Dishonest people in polite society commit serious crimes and get away with it.

Inference ———— 2. The killer does not shoot Mr. Williams immediately because
   a. he wants more money.
   b. he takes pleasure in being entertained by the victim.
   c. he wants to give Mrs. Williams more time to establish her alibi.
   d. he does not enjoy killing but wants Mr. Williams to beg for his life.

Inference ———— 3. The main purpose for Mr. Williams' pointing to the painting and presenting the envelope was
   a. to switch the glasses.
   b. to divert the killer's eyes.
   c. to buy his life with the money.
   d. to get the $5,000 out of the safe.

Inference ———— 4. The killer did not shoot Mr. Williams because
   a. he had professional pride in accepting a commission.
   b. he believed Mr. Williams would give him the glass if he killed Mrs. Williams.
   c. he believed that Mrs. Williams also knew the combination to the safe.
   d. he believed he was trapped by the fingerprints in the safe.

Inference ———— 5. The killer will shoot Mrs. Williams because
   a. she might send someone else to kill Mr. Williams.
   b. he wants the glass returned by Mr. Williams.
   c. he plans to blame Mr. Williams for the murder.
   d. he realizes that he will not get any money from Mrs. Williams.

Inference ———— 6. Mr. Williams uses the jade figurine to describe
   a. his love for his wife.
   b. his present lack of interest in his wife.
   c. his long hatred for his wife.
   d. his wife's greed for money.

Inference _____ 7. The reader can most likely conclude that

   a. Mr. Williams will be convicted of his wife's murder.
   b. Mr. Williams will go to the police.
   c. The killer will not kill Mrs. Williams.
   d. Mr. Williams will keep the killer's fingerprints for his own protection.

Answer the following with *T* (true) or *F* (false).

Inference _____ 8. The reader can conclude that the professional killer's real name is Mr. Smith.

Detail _____ 9. Mr. Williams married a woman less than half his age.

Detail _____10. Mr. Williams discovered that the killer's weakness or vulnerable point was his fear of conviction and the electric chair.

VOCABULARY

Answer the following with *a*, *b*, *c*, or *d* for the word or phrase that best defines the boldface word as used in the selection. The number in parentheses indicates the line of the passage in which the word appears.

_____ 1. "from the **decanter**" (7)

   a. bowl
   b. glass
   c. vase
   d. ornamental bottle

_____ 2. "**morbid** pleasure"(24)

   a. healthy
   b. abnormal
   c. guilty
   d. happy

_____ 3. "you have **insight**" (30)

   a. time
   b. money
   c. education
   d. understanding

_____ 4. "sat on the **davenport**" (40)

   a. sofa
   b. table
   c. liquor cabinet
   d. bed

_____ 5. "story more **authentic**" (48)

   a. fake
   b. interesting
   c. slow
   d. genuine

_____ 6. "accept a **commission**" (58)

   a. client
   b. fee
   c. painting
   d. vote

_____ 7. "You are ... **incorruptible**" (84)

   a. not open to bribery
   b. dishonest
   c. clumsy
   d. innocent

_____ 8. "calmness and **fortitude**" (107)

   a. protest
   b. temper
   c. happiness
   d. courage

_____ 9. "containing **pertinent** information" (115)

   a. relevant
   b. insignificant
   c. misleading
   d. misspelled

_____10. "**commiserate** with me" (140–141)

   a. laugh
   b. sympathize
   c. wonder
   d. approve

Your instructor may choose to give a true-false vocabulary review.

VOCABULARY ENRICHMENT

A. Use the indicated prefix to write words from the word bank that complete each sentence in the groups.

in: not, in, into   **Word Bank:** incorruptible   insight   intruder

1. His wife had planned for Mr. Williams' murder to look like the act of a surprised _____ rather than a premeditated action.

2. Mr. Williams' _____ was that the hired gun did not particularly care for the act of killing.

3. Since the killer would not accept Mr. Williams' offer of a valuable painting in exchange for his life, Mr. Williams referred to him as _____.

pro: before, for   **Word Bank:** professional   protection   provided

4. Mr. Williams was able to convince the hit man to kill Mrs. Williams for his own _____.

5. Although unsettled by Mr. Williams' trick, the man stayed calm and collected because he was a _____ in his field.

6. Had Mr. Williams become a murder victim, his wife would probably have been _____ with a substantial estate.

re: back, again   **Word Bank:** remain   remotely return

7. Mr. Williams kept his would-be killer occupied as long as possible in order to _____ alive.

8. The murderer's initial plan was to shoot Mr. Williams, wash the glass he had used, and _____ it to the liquor cabinet.

9. Mr. Williams' offer of the painting was rejected partly because the criminal wanted no part of anything that would even _____ link him to the victim.

B. Use the context clues in the sentences to write the meaning of the boldface words.

10. **Narratives** never preach, but rather deliver a message to our emotions, senses, and imagination through a powerful shared experience.

_____

_____

11. The **theme** of a story about a college tennis champion might be that the journey to the top, including the hard work and discipline, was more meaningful than the final victory. _____

_____

12. Poisoned apples and talking mirrors may not seem realistic in a modern telephone conversation; however, in the context of Snow White, we easily find both **plausible.** _____

_____

13. E. M. Forster said that "The king died, and the queen died," is a narrative, but changing this to "The king died, and the queen died of grief," creates a **plot.** _____

_____

14. The **suspense** of a narrative is based on conflict, which perhaps starts out as mild and intensifies as each incident occurs. _____

_____

_____

15. Good writers select incidents and details that give **unity** to the story and advance the central theme. _____

_____

ASSESS YOUR LEARNING

Review confusing questions, seek clarification, and make notes in your text to help you remember new information and vocabulary.

selection 3 History

> "An individual who breaks a law that conscience tells him is unjust, and who willingly accepts the penalty of imprisonment in order to arouse the conscience of the community over its injustice, is in reality expressing the highest respect for the law."
>
> Martin Luther King, Jr.

A critical event in the struggle for equal rights occurred in Montgomery, Alabama, in 1955. Rosa Parks, a black seamstress who was returning from work and tired, sat down on a bus in a section reserved for whites. When asked to get up, she refused. Parks was arrested and ordered to stand trial. Black civil rights officials seized the issue and responded with a boycott of the bus system. Organizational meetings for the boycott were held in a Montgomery Baptist church where the young 27-year-old minister, Martin Luther King, Jr., took an active role in the protest. Soon the talented and articulate Dr. King emerged as the leading spokesman for the protest and for the civil and economic concerns of black Americans.

THINKING BEFORE READING

Preview for clues to the content. Activate your prior knowledge. Anticipate what is coming and think about your purpose for reading.

In what city is the Martin Luther King, Jr., homeplace and national memorial?

Where did Dr. King make his "I Have a Dream" speech?

What world leader inspired Dr. King's nonviolent tactics?

I want to learn _____.

VOCABULARY PREVIEW

Are you familiar with these words?

sweltering	centennial	oppressive	podium	resonant
galvanized	spurious	dire	recanted	compelled

What is a *centenarian*?

At what temperature do you *swelter*?

How do *compel*, *repel*, and *expel* differ?

Your instructor may chose to give a true-false vocabulary review before or after reading.

THINKING DURING READING

As you read, use the six thinking strategies of a good reader: predict, picture, relate, monitor, correct, and annotate.

> ## Reader's *Tip* Reading and Studying History
>
> - Know the *who, what, when, where,* and *why* for people, places, documents, and events.
> - Seek to understand the cause-and-effect relationship among events and their causes, results, and consequences.
> - Use time lines to familiarize yourself with chronologies to get an overall picture of parallel or overlapping events.
> - Learn significant dates to provide a framework for grouping and understanding events.
> - Look at maps of the region being studied.
> - Distinguish between fact and opinion, and compare your conclusions with the historian's interpretation.

THE DREAM OF NONVIOLENT REFORM

Perspiring in the sweltering heat of a Washington August afternoon, Martin Luther King, Jr., looked down from the steps of the Lincoln Memorial at the largest assembly ever congregated in the United States. Well over 200,000 people, 70 percent of them blacks, jammed the mile-long mall that swept away to the Washington Monument. Angry yet
5 hopeful, they had come to the nation's capital in 1963, the centennial of the Emancipation Proclamation, to personify black demands for equality in society. But the speakers and singers who preceded King had not been particularly effective, the heat and humidity were oppressive, and the great crowd was starting to thin around the edges. As he mounted the podium, King sensed this restlessness and the need for a focus. At first
10 his deep voice was husky, but it soon became resonant with a purpose that quieted and transfixed the multitude and the millions of television viewers. King's eloquence dramatized the anguish of black history. One hundred years after slavery, he pointed out, the black was still "an exile in his own land." It was the future, however, that mattered. "I have a dream," he cried repeatedly, as he sketched his vision of freedom, justice, and har-
15 mony. At the end of his speech King prophesied that one day all people would be able to join together in singing the words of an old Negro spiritual: "Free at last! Free at last! Thank God Almighty, we are free at last." There was an awed silence, then an ear-shattering roar: the crowd was applauding wildly. King had galvanized the massive assembly. At that moment he stood at the crest of a mounting wave of African American protest. Yet,
20 as King must have known, his dream would have an agonizing birth. Just five years after his Washington address, he lay dead on the balcony of a Memphis motel, the victim of the violence he had devoted his life to overcoming.

. . .

The Poor People's March was set for June 1968, but the whirlwind pace King had kept since the beginning of the decade allowed him only occasional participation in the
25 planning. One of the detours took him to Memphis, where a garbage strike threatened to evolve into a racial encounter of crisis proportions. Local black leaders wanted King to organize a peaceful demonstration, but once again he had difficulty working with Black Power militants. Uncontrollable black looters, arsonists, and street fighters were another source of difficulty. On March 28, they had transformed a nonviolent march into an orgy
30 of destruction that had provoked an even greater measure of police brutality. As a self-styled "riot preventer," King was sick at heart. If Memphis exploded, he feared, the

selection

3

approaching summer of 1968 would be chaos. Already, black leaders like Harlem congressman Adam Clayton Powell were arousing the urban masses and, as part of their campaign, making references to "Martin Loser King" and his Uncle Tom tactics.

35 Nonviolence, King felt, was on trial in Memphis.

On April 3, 1968, on the eve of the crucial Memphis march, King addressed a capacity crowd at the Masonic Temple located in that city. His mood was strangely somber and introspective. "Like anybody," he mused, "I would like to live a long life." But longevity, he added, was not his chief concern; he would rather do God's will. Some of his aides
40 were reminded of the great Washington rally of 1963, where King had expressed his belief that "if a man hasn't discovered something that he will die for, he isn't fit to live!" The following evening, on the way to yet another mass meeting, King walked onto the balcony of his hotel room and leaned over the railing to talk with a colleague. A moment later he crumpled to the ground. An assassin's bullet, fired from a hotel room across the
45 street, had pierced his skull. The killer, arrested two months later and identified as James Earl Ray, was a white drifter with a long criminal record.

Following Ray's confession, investigations of King's murder continued until 1977. Exhaustive reviews of the evidence seemed to prove conclusively that Ray had acted alone in the assassination, and there was no conspiracy. The research did reveal that the
50 Federal Bureau of Investigation, under orders of its director, J. Edgar Hoover, had complicated the last six years of King's life with a program of systematic harassment on the spurious grounds that he was under the influence of the Communist party. The conspiracy theory surrounding King's death reemerged in the 1990's when James Earl Ray, in prison and in dire health, recanted his confession. Talk of Ray being brought to trial—there had
55 been none due to his confession—ended abruptly when Ray died in early 1998.

The murder of Martin Luther King, Jr., moved the American people as had few events in recent years. The immediate response in all but the most prejudiced white minds was shame. Millions of whites felt compelled to apologize to black people as a whole and went to their churches for services honoring King. But even among the mourners, white
60 and black eyes did not meet easily. Everyone seemed to recognize that, with King's death, a powerful influence for interracial compassion and understanding had been eliminated—the basis of ordered change and reform.

(878 words)

—*From These Beginnings,* Sixth Edition, Volume Two,
by Roderick Nash and Gregory Graves

THINKING AND WRITING AFTER READING

RECALL   Self-test your understanding.

Your instructor may choose to give you a true-false comprehension review.

REACT   Aside from their stated reasons, why do you think the FBI would spend six years tracking Dr. King? _____

_____

REFLECT   What seemed to be the differences in philosophy among the civil rights leaders? _____

_____

THINK CRITICALLY   Why was Martin Luther King, Jr.'s birthday made a national holiday? _____

_____

THINK AND WRITE   Events often call for ordinary men and women to do extraordinary things. How were Rosa Parks and Martin Luther King, Jr., both ordinary and extraordinary? How did events converge to change their destinies and our history? _____

_____

MAIN IDEA

1. What is the topic of the first paragraph? _____

2. What is the topic of the last paragraph? _____

_____

Interpret the Quote

Now that you have finished reading the selection, "The Dream of Nonviolent Reform," go back to the beginning of the selection and read the opening quote again. Under what circumstances does Martin Luther King, Jr., believe it is acceptable to break the law? On a separate piece of paper, explain why you agree or disagree with Dr. King's views on breaking laws.

selection 3

Name ————————————————————

Date ————————————————————

COMPREHENSION QUESTIONS

Answer the following with *a, b, c,* or *d,* or fill in the blank. In order to help you analyze your strengths and weaknesses, the question types are indicated.

Main Idea   ———————   1. The best statement of the main idea of the selection is:

    a. Dr. King started the civil rights movement with his "I Have a Dream" speech in Washington.

    b. Though his life was taken violently, Dr. King was a moving speaker and a major force in the nonviolent movement for civil rights.

    c. Dr. King was killed violently by a drifter.

    d. Dr. King controlled the violence in Memphis but was killed for doing so.

Detail   ———————   2. The primary reason over 200,000 people had congregated in Washington in 1963 was

    a. to hear Dr. King speak.

    b. to urge legislators to pass the Emancipation Proclamation.

    c. to show strength in demanding equal treatment for African Americans in society.

    d. to honor Lincoln for freeing the slaves.

Detail   ———————   3. In his "I Have a Dream" speech, Dr. King's major thrust is to

    a. recall the hardships of the past.

    b. blame society for prejudice and hatred.

    c. ask God for forgiveness and strength.

    d. focus on the possibilities of the future.

Inference   ———————   4. The author implies that

    a. Black Power militants did not agree with Dr. King's tactics.

    b. Dr. King and Black Power militants shared the same philosophy and strategies.

    c. Adam Clayton Powell supported Dr. King's tactics.

    d. little friction existed among the different leaders supporting civil rights.

Inference   5. Dr. King felt that nonviolence was on trial in Memphis because

———————————————————————————————

———————————————————————————————

———————————————————————————————

Inference   ———————   6. The author suggests all of the following *except*

    a. Dr. King was willing to die for his cause.

    b. Dr. King had a premonition that he would not live a long life.

    c. Dr. King knew that fighting for his cause was dangerous.

    d. Dr. King was willing to back off from his nonviolent stand to get the support of other civil rights leaders.

Detail _____ 7. The author indicates that evidence suggests that
     a. Ray acted alone.
     b. Ray was part of a conspiracy.
     c. J. Edgar Hoover was involved in Dr. King's death.
     d. Ray was not the man who fired the shots from the hotel room.

Answer the following with *T* (true) or *F* (false).

Inference _____ 8. After Dr. King's death, the American people realized that he was indeed the "riot preventer."

Detail _____ 9. The garbage strike in Memphis was in June 1968.

Detail _____ 10. Ray was brought to trial after he took back his confession.

VOCABULARY

Answer the following with *a, b, c,* or *d* for the word or phrase that best defines the boldface word as used in the selection. The number in parentheses indicates the line of the passage in which the word appears.

_____ 1. "**sweltering** heat" (1)
    a. never-ending
    b. humid and sweaty
    c. permanent
    d. oncoming

_____ 2. "the **centennial** of the Emancipation Proclamation" (5)
    a. 10-year celebration
    b. 50-year celebration
    c. 100-year celebration

_____ 3. "heat and humidity were **oppressive**" (8)
    a. overpowering
    b. surprising
    c. brief
    d. energizing

_____ 4. "mounted the **podium**" (9)
    a. stairway
    b. top of the monument
    c. steps
    d. speaker's stand

_____ 5. "**resonant** with a purpose" (10)
    a. sensitive
    b. hoarse
    c. forceful and loud
    d. repetitious

_____ 6. "**galvanized** the massive assembly" (18)
    a. stopped
    b. excited
    c. frightened
    d. shamed

_____ 7. "on **spurious** grounds" (51–52)
    a. false
    b. evil
    c. criminal
    d. socialistic

_____ 8. "in **dire** health" (54)
    a. fair
    b. uncertain
    c. questionable
    d. terrible

_____ 9. "**recanted** his confession" (54)
    a. emphasized
    b. questioned
    c. regretted
    d. took back

_____ 10. "**compelled** to apologize" (58)
    a. nervous
    b. obliged
    c. angered
    d. manipulated

Your instructor may choose to give a true-false vocabulary review.

selection **3**

VOCABULARY ENRICHMENT

A. Use the indicated root to form words to complete each sentence.

voc, vok: voice, call

1. Dr. King's message of freedom and love for all mankind _____ a feeling of hope for racial unity in his audience.

2. Dr. King's brave manner of speaking out against injustice has inspired future generations to be more _____ about prejudice.

3. Dr. King's persuasive _____ included simple words like *dream* and *justice*.

gress, grad, gred: step, degree

4. Dr. King's inspiring words are often quoted to _____ in commencement speeches.

5. While Dr. King used peaceful methods of conflict resolution, Black Power militants tended to use more _____ tactics.

6. While many advocates for civil rights wanted instant change, Dr. King recognized that lasting change would be more _____.

spec, spect: see, watch

7. Over 200,000 _____ observed Dr. King's speech on the steps of the Lincoln Memorial.

8. An _____ of the assassination scene indicated that Dr. King had been shot from the window of a neighboring hotel.

9. The Memphis march was intended to be a _____ that would call national attention to the Civil Rights Movement.

B. Use context clues and mark *a, b, c,* or *d* for the meaning closest to that of the boldface word.

_____ 10. The fight for racial equality **signifies** a larger struggle for all human rights.
   a. indicates
   b. simplifies
   c. reduces
   d. warns of

_____ 11. Sit-ins by **diligent** believers in racial equality resulted in the desegregation of public facilities in a hundred southern cities.
   a. convincing
   b. hard-working
   c. older
   d. talkative

————— 12. The Civil Rights movement accomplished a **tangible** result when the Supreme Court ruled the Alabama segregated bus seating law unconstitutional.
    a. sizable
    b. tremendous
    c. actual
    d. movable

C. Study the following easily confused words, and circle the one that is correct in each sentence.

thorough: careful	**straight:** not curving	**loose:** not tight
threw: tossed	**strait:** narrow passage of water	**lose:** misplace
through: by means of		

13. Dr. King's "Letter from a Birmingham City Jail" did a (**thorough, threw, through**) job in explaining his vision to a group of Alabama clergymen.

14. Dr. King's doctrine of passive resistance required followers to stare and walk (**straight, strait**) ahead when confronted by violence.

15. Police often let attack dogs run (**loose, lose**) to menace Civil Rights protestors.

ASSESS YOUR LEARNING

Review confusing questions, seek clarification, and make notes in your text to help you remember new information and vocabulary.

selection

3

Personal *Feedback* **2**

Name _____

1. Review your responses to the three longer reading selections. Summarize and comment on your error patterns. _____
_____
_____

2. What selection, short or long, has held your attention the best? Why do you think it did so? _____
_____
_____

3. What are your major responsibilities other than going to college? _____
_____
_____

4. Did you receive any scholarships for college? If so, describe how you qualified for them. _____
_____
_____

5. Describe your mode of transportation and your average traveling time to class.
_____
_____

6. What unforeseen difficulties have you already encountered this term that have interfered with your ability to study? _____
_____
_____

Tear out and submit to your instructor.

Vocabulary Lesson

Before and After

Study the prefixes, words, and sentences.

| **Prefixes** | *ante*: before | *pre*: before | *post*: after |

Words with *ante* = *before*

Can <u>antenuptial</u> counseling strengthen marriages? Is an entry an <u>anteroom</u>?

- Antebellum: existing before the war

  The *antebellum* home with the white columns was built before the Civil War.

- Antecede: to go before

  Your good name can *antecede* your presence.

- Antecedent: word coming before the pronoun to which the pronoun refers

  The name *Valerie* is the *antecedent* of *her* in the sentence.

- Antediluvian: belonging to the time before the flood; very old

  She ignored the advice and regarded it as *antediluvian*.

- Antennae: feelers on the head of an insect used as organs of touch

  The insect's *antennae* inspected the food.

- Antescript: a note added before something such as a prefix to a letter

  The *antescript* indicated why the letter would be late arriving.

Words with *pre* = *before*

Can a <u>prefix predict</u> the meaning of a new word?

- Preamble: an introduction

  Schoolchildren learn the *Preamble* to the Constitution.

- Precede: to go before

  Queen Elizabeth should *precede* Prince Philip at state events.

- Predecessor: one who came before another in office

  Her *predecessor* helped orient the new chairperson to the job.

- Preeminent: supreme, before all others

  Our professor is the *preeminent* scholar in contemporary Russian literature.

- Prelude: a musical or dramatic introduction

  As the *prelude* began, the remaining ticket holders were seated in the audience.

- Premonition: a forewarning or omen

  When I heard the dog bark, I had a *premonition* that trouble was near.

- Prejudice: judgment before proof is given

  A lawyer tries to avoid choosing a potential juror who shows signs of *prejudice*.

- Precocious: having early development

  The *precocious* child could read at 2 years of age.

Words with *post = after*

Is the time ante meridian or post meridian?

- Posterity: descendants who come after

  Leave a gift for *posterity* and donate money to the college library.

- Posthumous: after death

  The *posthumous* award was given to the widow of the soldier.

- Postnatal: the time immediately after birth

  A *postnatal* examination monitors the health of the new mother.

- Postpone: delay or set the date back

  Let's *postpone* the meeting until tomorrow after lunch.

- Postscript: a note added to a letter after it has been signed

  Karen scribbled an afterthought in the *postscript* to her long letter.

Review

Part I

Choose an appropriate word from the list to complete each of the following sentences.

precocious	premonition	antebellum	prelude	postscript
predecessor	posthumous	preamble	postponed	preeminent

1. The ambassador is a _____ scholar in the history of Nigeria.

2. Shorten the _____ and begin the main point of your speech.

3. As a _____ athlete, the young Tiger Woods golfed on TV with adults.

4. The threat of a tornado _____ the game for three hours.

5. A _____ award honors a dead hero.

6. The couple restored the _____ home to its original 1850s appearance.

7. The musical _____ introduced the song to follow.

8. Bill Clinton was the immediate _____ of George W. Bush.

9. A superstitious person would see a black cat as a _____ of danger.

10. Sara's letter ended with her quickly remembered thoughts in a _____.

Part II

Answer the following with *T* (true) or *F* (false).

_____ 11. A prejudiced listener has trouble fairly evaluating both sides.

_____ 12. An antediluvian outfit is up to date.

_____ 13. A postnatal exam checks the growth of the fetus.

_____ 14. Antemeridian refers to the afternoon.

_____ 15. The antennae of an insect are usually attached to its tail.

_____ 16. The antescript is positioned in the main body of the letter.

_____ 17. An antecedent is a person, place, or thing.

_____ 18. Antenuptual arguments occur after the wedding day.

_____ 19. A presumed appointment needs to be double-checked for certainty.

_____ 20. Environmental regulations consider both the present and posterity.

EVERYDAY READING SKILLS

Selecting a Book

The next time you are in the market for a good read, enter a bookstore, feast your eyes on the colorful array of books, and remind yourself, "Don't judge a book by its cover." Like groceries and clothing, books are products—and the packaging matters. Book jackets are slick marketing tools designed by experts to entice you to make a purchase through pictures, testimonials, and exaggeration. Cut through the hype and decide if the book will be of interest to you. The introductory material on the cover can be helpful, but remember that exciting covers can be wrapped around boring books.

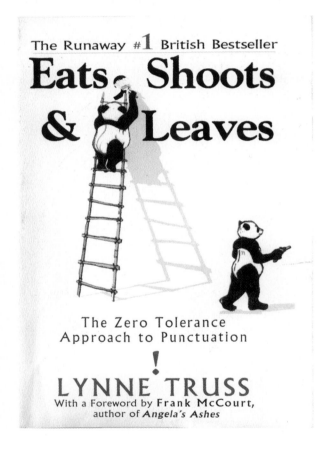

A panda walks into a café. He orders a sandwich, eats it, then draws a gun and fires two shots in the air.

"Why?" asks the confused waiter, as the panda makes towards the exit. The panda produces a badly punctuated wildlife manual and tosses it over his shoulder.

"I'm a panda," he says, at the door. "Look it up."

The waiter turns to the relevant entry and, sure enough, finds an explanation.

"**Panda.** Large black-and-white bear-like mammal, native to China. Eats, shoots and leaves."

So, punctuation really does matter, even if it is only occasionally a matter of life and death.

Sticklers unite!
What people are saying about *Eats, Shoots & Leaves*

"If Lynne Truss were Roman Catholic I'd nominate her for sainthood. As it is, thousands of English teachers from Maine to Maui will be calling down blessings on her merry, learned head."
–FRANK MCCOURT, author of *Angela's Ashes*

"There is a multitude of us riding this planet for whom apostrophe catastrophes, quotation bloatation, mad dashes, and other comma-tose errors squeak like chalk across the blackboard of our sensibilities. At last we who are punctilious about punctuation have a manifesto, and it is titled *Eats, Shoots & Leaves.*"
–RICHARD LEDERER, author of *A Man of My Words* and *Anguished English*

"At long last, a worthy tribute to punctuation's stepchildren: the neglected semicolon, the enigmatic ellipsis and the mad dash. Punc-rock on!"
–JAMES LIPTON, author of *An Exaltation of Larks* and writer and host of *Inside the Actors Studio*

ISBN 1-592-40087-6

51750

9 781592 400874

exercise 1 Refer to the preceding figure to answer the following questions.

1. Is this book on the British Best Sellers List? _____

_____

2. What is the book's topic? _____

3. Why is the comma misplaced in the panda anecdote? How does it alter the meaning of the sentence? _____

_____

_____

4. In this book an example of fiction or nonfiction? (See the definitions that follow if you are not sure.) Justify your response. _____

_____

_____

Reader's *Tip* Selecting a Book

After locating a book that looks interesting, investigate further using these strategies.

- Read the book jacket. Do the quotes from reviewers seem valid or clipped out of context? Do the blurbs introducing the book entice you? Has the author written other books that you have enjoyed? If the book is nonfiction, what are the author's credentials?
- Read the first page and at least one other page. Do you like the writing style? Is it comfortable for you to read? Does the first page grab your attention?
- If nonfiction, look at the illustrations and read the captions. Are you intrigued?
- If nonfiction, review the table of contents and scan the index. Is this material that you want to learn more about?

Consult Best-Seller Lists

If you want to know what books other people are buying, consult a best-seller list. Your bookstore or your city newspaper may publish one. If not, the *New York Times* Best Sellers List is nationally respected. Such lists are sometimes divided into best-selling fiction and nonfiction, and then further divided into hardbound books—which are published first and cost more—and paperbacks. Similar to a listing of top-grossing movies, a ranking on a best-seller list indicates quantity, but not necessarily quality. Bookstores often post their own lists of local best-selling suggestions.

Sample a Variety of Fiction and Nonfiction

Fiction is writing that has been invented by the imagination. The **novel,** the literary form for the imaginative and pleasurable stories of contemporary fiction, is longer than a short story but presents the same elements of plot, character, theme, setting, and tone.

Nonfiction is a piece of writing based on true events. The label of *nonfiction* includes biographies and books about travel, art, music, decorating, computers, cooking, and other special interests. Some are historical works in which dialogue may be invented based on known facts about the actual people and events of a given time period. Such books can be difficult to distinguish from fiction.

exercise 2   Visit a local bookstore or log on to an online bookstore and pretend you have $100 to spend on books. Review both fiction and nonfiction books and make your choices. Record the title and author of each book you select, as well as a one- or two-sentence summary of what you think the book will be about and why you may want to read it.

5 Supporting Details and Organizational Patterns

- What is a detail?
- How do you recognize levels of importance?
- What is a major detail?
- What is a minor detail?
- What organizational patterns are used in textbooks?
- How do transitional words signal organization?

Everyday Reading Skills: Selecting Magazines

What Is a Detail?

Details develop, explain, and prove the main idea. They are the facts, descriptions, and reasons that convince the reader and make the material interesting. Details answer questions and paint visual images so the reader has an experience with the author and sees what the author sees and understands. For example, in a passage on the validity of movie reviews, the supporting details might include information on the rating scale, the qualifications of the raters, and the influence of the production companies on the eventual reviews.

Details can be ranked by their level of importance in supporting a topic. Some details offer major support and elaboration, whereas others merely provide illustrations to relate the material to the reader's prior knowledge and make visualizing easier. All details play a part in our enjoyment of reading, but it is necessary to recognize their varying levels of importance.

Recognize Levels of Importance

To organize related words or ideas into levels of importance, the general topic is stated first, followed by subcategories of details, which may be further subdivided into specific examples. Outlines, diagrams, and **graphic organizers** can be used to help organize information into levels of importance.

EXAMPLE Notice that by using an outline and a diagram, the following list of words can be unscrambled to show relationships and levels of importance:

horses	grass	botany
zoology	cows	ants
bees	rabbits	entomology
branches of biology	flowers	mosquitoes
trees		

exercise 1 Major ideas and supporting details have been mixed together in the following lists of words. Think about how the ideas should be organized, and insert them in the outline or diagram form provided. The main idea or topic of each list appears either on the line above the outline or in the top box of the diagram.

List 1

elm, pine, conifers, maple, oak, deciduous, types of trees, spruce

Types of Trees

I. _____

    A. _____

    B. _____

II. _____

    A. _____

    B. _____

    C. _____

List 2

Maine, North Carolina, Southeastern, states in regions of the United States, New Mexico, Southwestern, Arizona, Rhode Island, Georgia, Connecticut, Florida, Northeastern

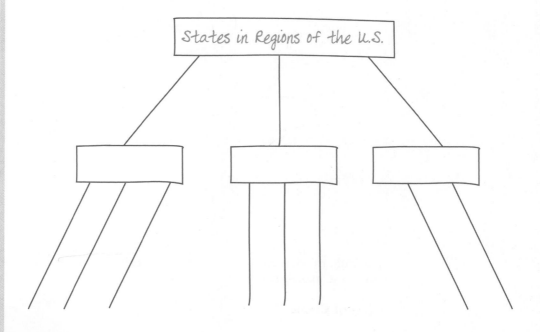

States in Regions of the U.S.

List 3

honest, personality, appearance, description of a person, shy, well-dressed, blond, straightforward, tall

Description of a Person

I. _____

    A. _____

    B. _____

    C. _____

II. _____

    A. _____

    B. _____

    C. _____

List 4

salsa, pasta, soy sauce, Mexican, ethnic foods, olive oil, fortune cookie, tacos, guacamole, Italian, egg rolls, Chinese

List 5

speeding, misdemeanor, felony, types of crime, murder, disorderly conduct, rape, gambling, armed robbery

Types of Crime

I. _____

    A. _____

    B. _____

    C. _____

II. _____
    A. _____
    B. _____
    C. _____

List 6

Angelina Jolie, Michael Phelps, Christina Aguilera, Movies, Celebrities, Tiger Woods, Russell Crowe, Carrie Underwood, Venus Williams, Sports, Chris Brown, Will Smith, Music

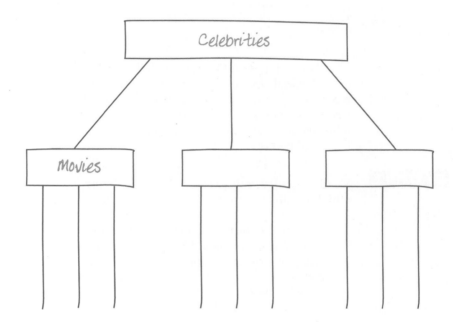

Distinguish Major and Minor Details

The outlines and diagrams on the preceding pages show that all details are not of equal importance. When reading textbooks, you may sometimes feel you are receiving an overload of details. Not only is it impossible to remember all of them, but doing so can be a waste of time. With practice, you will learn that some details are major and should be remembered, whereas others are of only minor significance in supporting the main idea. How do you determine the importance of a particular detail? It depends on what point the author is making, and it depends on *what information is essential to develop, explain, or prove that point*.

For example, in a passage about communication by sound, the reason a bird sings would be of major significance and gives primary support for the main idea, whereas the particular species of bird would be a minor detail the author included for secondary support. In a passage on the limitations of acupuncture, the date of origin of the technique would most likely be a minor detail, providing a secondary level of support. However, if the focus of the passage were on the history of acupuncture, the date of origin would be a major detail, giving primary support to the main idea.

Reader's *Tip* **Distinguishing Major and Minor Details**

To determine which details give major or minor support, first identify the author's main point and then ask yourself the following questions.

1. What details are needed to explain or prove the main idea? (These are major details that give primary support.)
2. What details are included just to make the passage more interesting? (These are minor details that provide a secondary level of support.)

Minor details add interest, help the reader understand by giving examples, create visual images, and generally fill out a passage. Perhaps the author could make the point without them, but minor details tend to enhance the quality of the work. Major details, however, directly support the main idea regardless of whether it is directly or indirectly stated, and they are vital to your understanding the passage.

EXAMPLE Read the following paragraph. First determine the main point and then decide which details are major and which are minor.

> John Quincy Adams was a chip off the old family glacier. Short (5 feet 7 inches; 1.7 meters), thickset, and billiard-bald, he was even more frigidly austere than his presidential father, John Adams. Shunning people, he often went for early morning swims, sometimes stark naked, in the then pure Potomac River. Essentially a closeted thinker rather than a politician, he was irritable, sarcastic, and tactless. Yet few men have ever come to the presidency with a more brilliant record in statecraft, especially in foreign affairs. He ranks as one of the most successful secretaries of state, yet one of the least successful presidents.
>
> —*The American Pageant,* by Thomas Bailey, and David Kennedy

1. What point is the author trying to make? _____

    _____

2. Are the following details major or minor in their support of the author's point?

    _____ a. He was 5 feet 7 inches tall.

    _____ b. He was thickset and bald.

    _____ c. He was a closeted thinker rather than a politician.

    _____ d. He swam naked in the Potomac River.

    _____ e. He came to the presidency with a brilliant record in statecraft.

EXPLANATION The author's main point is that John Quincy Adams had been a brilliant secretary of state but was a socially inept politician and thus one of the least successful presidents. Items *a* and *b* on appearance are minor details that add interest but lend only secondary support. Item *c* is a major detail because it shows Adam's isolation as a socially inept politician. Swimming naked (*d*) is an interesting minor detail, and the last item (*e*) is a major detail because it develops the main point.

Transitional Words to Signal Levels of Importance. Sometimes the following connecting words signal the importance of details:

Major (primary support):	first / second last / in addition
Minor (secondary support):	for example / to illustrate

exercise 2

For each of the following topics, three details are given. Determine which details offer major (primary) support to the topic and which offer minor (secondary) support. Write the appropriate word in the blanks.

1. Reducing the Fur Trade

   _____ a. Through advertising and publicity stunts, PETA, the world's largest animal rights group, has done much to convince the public that wearing fur is cruel.

   _____ b. Over the last fifteen years people have come to realize the suffering of animals, and the fur industry has declined dramatically.

   _____ c. For example, Tyra Banks and Cindy Crawford will not model fur.

2. Dorothea Dix's Humanitarian Reform

   _____ a. After visiting a jail to teach a Sunday school class to the female inmates and finding female patients in a mental hospital freezing in unheated, filthy cells, Dix started a lifelong campaign to improve conditions in such institutions.

   _____ b. From 1845 to 1885 she was directly responsible for establishing thirty-three mental hospitals at home and abroad.

   _____ c. Dix was born in Maine but moved to Boston at the age of 12 to live with her grandmother.

3. Diet of an Armadillo

   _____ a. The armadillo enjoys scorpions, tarantulas, and grasshoppers, but its favorite food is ants, including the eggs and larvae.

   _____ b. If pursued, the armadillo can outrun a human and quickly dig itself into the ground.

   _____ c. Sometimes it will eat fungus and wild berries or catch a lazy lizard, but the belief that the armadillo raids henhouses is unfounded.

4. Characteristics of the Millennium Generation (Born 1977–2002)

   _____ a. This group is also called Generation Y because it followed Generation X.

   _____ b. Members of this group have known digital technology all of their lives and are comfortable with it.

   _____ c. Millennials place a high value on making their jobs fit around their families and personal lives.

5. Larceny-theft

_____ a. Tires, wheels, hubcaps, radar detectors, stereos, CD players, cassette tapes, compact discs, and cellular phones account for many of the items reported stolen.

_____ b. Larceny-theft is the most frequently reported major crime.

_____ c. Larceny-theft may be the most underreported crime category, because small thefts rarely come to the attention of the police.

6. Preterm Neonates

_____ a. The immature development of preterm neonates makes them unusually sensitive to stimuli in their environment.

_____ b. Preterm neonates can easily be overwhelmed by the sights, sounds, and sensations they experience, and their breathing may be interrupted or their heart rates may slow.

_____ c. Such behavior is quite disconcerting to parents.

exercise 3

Distinguishing between major and minor details is important, whether you are studying a single paragraph, a chapter, or a whole book. After reading each of the following passages, first identify the author's main point. Then determine which of the details listed are major and which are minor in supporting that point. The skills you will use apply equally to these short readings and to the larger units of text you will be studying in college textbooks.

Passage 1

PRICE SETTING

The DeBeers Company of South Africa, a syndicate that controls most of the sales of raw diamonds, maximizes profits by determining what quantity of raw diamonds to offer on the world raw-diamond market. DeBeers markets diamonds through an unusual marketing procedure called a sight. About three weeks before each sight, DeBeers sends notices to the 300 largest diamond purchasers, who are asked to send in requests in carats for the amount of diamonds they wish to buy. Two days before the sight (held in London, Luzerne, and Kimberley, South Africa), the buyers are informed how many carats they have been allocated—an amount often below the quantity requested. At the sight each buyer is handed a container of raw diamonds. Buyers who refuse to purchase would run the risk of not being invited back. The market price of diamonds is regulated by the number of diamonds offered in each sight.

—_Essentials of Economics,_ by Paul Gregory

1. What point is the author trying to make? _____

_____

2. Which details are major and which are minor in supporting the author's point?

_____ a. The sight is held in London, Luzerne, and Kimberley.

_____ b. DeBeers invites the 300 largest diamond buyers to the sight.

_____ c. The buyers are offered fewer diamonds than the quantity they requested.

Passage 2

HEALTH FOOD?

When 35 million people in the United States gave their loved ones boxes of chocolates last Valentine's Day, they knew they were giving sweet comfort—but health food? Chocolate candy is certainly a significant source of fat and sugar calories, but recent research suggests that chocolate itself—the dark, bitter powder made from the seeds within cacao pods—may also be a significant source of protective molecules. Medical scientists have known for some time that many things that go wrong with our bodies can be traced to destructive molecules called *free radicals*. Many free radicals contain oxygen in a form that reacts strongly with, and damages, various biological molecules and their cellular structures. This process is called *oxidative stress*. So what's a person to do? Well, maybe eat more chocolate!

—*Biology: Life on Earth*, Sixth Edition, by Teresa Audesirk, Gerald Audesirk, and Bruce Byers

1. What point is the author trying to make? _____

_____

2. Which details are major and which are minor in supporting the author's point?

_____ a. Free radicals damage biological molecules and their cellular structure.

_____ b. About 35 million people in the United States gave chocolates on Valentine's Day.

_____ c. Chocolate is a source of fat and sugar calories.

Passage 3

GENDER AND COLLEGE PERFORMANCE

I registered for a calculus course my first year at DePauw. Even twenty years ago I was not timid, so on the very first day I raised my hand and asked a question. I still have a vivid memory of the professor rolling his eyes, hitting his head with his hand in frustration, and announcing to everyone, "Why do they expect me to teach calculus to girls?" I never asked another question. Several weeks later I went to a football game, but I had forgotten to bring my ID. My calculus professor was at the gate checking IDs, so I went up to him and said, "I forgot my ID but you know me, I'm in your class." He looked right at me and said, "I don't remember you in my class." I couldn't believe that someone who changed my life and whom I remember to this day didn't even recognize me.

—Patricia Ireland, quoted in *Failing at Fairness: How America's Schools Cheat Girls*, by Myra and David Sadker

1. What point is the author trying to make? _____

_____

2. Which details are major and which are minor in supporting the author's point?

_____ a. The author registered for a calculus course in her first year of college.

_____ b. When the author asked a question in class, her calculus professor responded in frustration, "Why do they expect me to teach calculus to girls?"

_____ c. The author attended a football game at which her calculus professor worked the gate checking IDs.

Passage 4

ASTEROIDS

Besides the eight major planets, thousands of smaller planetoids are also part of the solar system. These minor planets are called asteroids. There are more than 10,000 known asteroids, but many others are far too small to be seen even through the best telescopes. Most are found between the orbits of Jupiter and Mars, where the gravitational force of Jupiter prevented them from combining to form a single larger planet. The largest asteroid is only about 1000 km across.

—*Earth's Dynamic Systems*, Ninth Edition, by W. Kenneth Hamblin and Eric H. Christiansen

1. What point is the author trying to make? _____

_____

_____

2. Which details are major and which are minor in supporting the author's point?

_____ a. There are more than 10,000 known asteroids.

_____ b. There are eight major planets.

_____ c. The minor planets of the solar system are called asteroids.

Passage 5

INTEREST

When you deposit money in a bank—for example, in a savings account—you are permitting the bank to use your money. The bank may use the deposited money to lend customers the money to buy cars or make renovations on their homes. The bank pays you for the privilege of using your money. The amount paid to you is called interest. If you are the one borrowing money from the bank, the amount you pay for the privilege of using that money is also called interest.

—From Aufman/Barker/Lockwood, *Basic College Mathematics*, 8th Edition. © 2006 Brooks/Cole, a part of Cengage Learning, Inc. Reproduced by permission. www.cengage.com/permissions

1. What point is the author trying to make? _____

_____

2. Which details are major and which are minor in supporting the author's point?

_____ a. The bank lends money to customers who want to purchase cars or renovate their homes.

_____ b. The bank pays you for the privilege of using your money.

_____ c. When you deposit money in a bank you are permitting the bank to use your money.

Passage 6

STRESS RELIEF

Most of us have relieved stress by engaging in aggressive physical activity. Chopping wood when angry is one example. Exercise performed as an immediate response can help alleviate stress symptoms. However, a regular exercise program yields even more substantial benefits. Try to engage in at least 25 minutes of aerobic exercise three or four times a week. But simply walking up stairs, parking farther away from your destination, or standing rather than sitting helps to conserve and replenish your adaptation energy stores. Although it may not improve your aerobic capacity, a quiet walk can refresh your mind and calm your stress response. Plan walking breaks alone or with friends. Stretch after prolonged periods of study at your desk. A short period of physical exercise may provide the break you really need.

—_Health: The Basics_, Sixth Edition,
by Rebecca J. Donatelle

1. What point is the author trying to make? _____

   _____

2. Which details are major and which are minor in supporting the author's point?

   _____ a. Chopping wood when angry is an example of exercise used as stress relief.

   _____ b. Exercise performed as an immediate response to stress can help alleviate stress symptoms.

   _____ c. Walking with friends can be beneficial.

Follow Detailed Directions

Some of the normal rules of reading change dramatically when the task is to follow printed directions. Suddenly, all details are of equal importance, and you must switch gears to accomplish this new task. For example, every detail requires attention when you read the directions for a science experiment, a nursing procedure, or a computer program. You cannot read directions as you would a newspaper article.

Readers are not accustomed to attending to every single detail. For most reading, understanding the general idea and important details is adequate. However, this strategy does not work well when you are assembling a bicycle or following travel directions to a party. Confronted with a set of directions, you recognize that the task is different, even tedious, and then commit to reading step by step, sometimes even word by word and phrase by phrase. Consult any diagram that accompanies the directions, and read aloud if necessary. Remember that some people are better than others at visualizing graphic designs, so consider finding a partner if you think you need help.

Reader's *Tip* Following Directions

- Change your mindset from normal reading and commit to a different kind of task.
- Read to get an overview so you have a general idea of the task and can make a plan.
- Assemble the necessary equipment, estimate the time, and find a helper if needed.
- Read each step sequentially, and do as directed. Move from word to word and phrase to phrase for a clear understanding. Read aloud if necessary.
- Use numbers, letters, and guide words such as *first, next, before, after, then*, and *now* to maintain sequence. Insert your own numbers if steps are not sequenced.
- Visualize the process. Consult the diagram. Draw your own diagram if none exists.
- Think logically and keep your goal in mind.

EXAMPLE Select a friend and follow these directions together for calculating pulse rate.

1. Select a pulse point that is comfortable for you and the other person. You can take pulse rate on the inner surface of the wrist, in the fold of the arm opposite the elbow, on the side of the throat a few inches from the center, or in the bend of the leg behind the knee.
2. Press two or three fingers gently down over the selected pulse point. Do not use the thumb because it has a pulse of its own that could be mistaken for the client's pulse.
3. Once the pulsations are felt, use the second hand on your watch to count the pulsations for 30 seconds.
4. Multiply the number of pulsations by two to calculate the pulse rate per minute. Write down the rate.

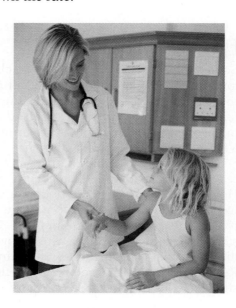

5. Wait a few minutes and repeat the procedure to obtain a second pulse rate. Write down the rate.
6. If the difference in the two pulse rates is more than two counts, repeat the procedure using a different pulse point. Write down this rate.

> **EXPLANATION** An overview of these directions indicates that you need a watch with a second hand, paper and a pen, and a willing friend. Find a comfortable pulsation point and calculate the pulse rate. Evaluate your results by considering that a normal resting pulse rate for an adult is 80 pulsations per minute with a range from 60 to 100.

exercise 4

Directions 1

Use the following directions to put numbers and signs on the line below.

_____

1. Put the number 8 in the middle of the line.
2. On the left end of the line, write a 5 and on the right end put a 7.
3. Equidistant between the 8 and the 7 write down the sum of the two numbers.
4. Equidistant between the number on the far left of the line and the number in the middle, write down the sum of all the numbers on the line.
5. On either side of the number in the middle of the line insert a minus.
6. To the right of the first number on the line and to the left of the last number, insert a plus.
7. Put an equals sign after the last number on the line and use the signs to calculate the total of the numbers listed. What is your total? _____

Directions 2

The American College of Sports Medicine (ACSM) recommends that you know how to determine your target heart rate in order to get the full benefit of exercise. Your **target heart rate** is the rate at which your heart should beat during any aerobic exercise such as running, cycling, fast walking, or participating in an aerobics class. According to the ACSM, you should reach your target rate and then maintain it for 20 minutes or more to achieve cardiovascular fitness. The intensity level varies for different individuals. A sedentary person might begin at the 60% level and gradually work up to 70%, whereas athletes and very fit individuals might work at the 85% level. The ACSM suggests that you calculate both 50% and 85% of your maximum heart rate. This will give you the low and high ends of the range within which your heart rate should stay.

To calculate your target heart rate:

	Example
Subtract your age from 220. This is your maximum heart rate.	$220 - 20 = 200$
Multiply your maximum heart rate by 50%. This is the low end of your range.	$200(0.50) = 100$
Divide the low end by 6. This is your low 10-second heart rate.	$100 \div 6 \approx 17$
Multiply your maximum heart rate by 85%. This is the high end of your range.	$200(0.85) = 170$
Divide the high end by 6. This is your high 10-second heart rate.	$170 \div 6 \approx 28$

1. Why are the low end and high end divided by 6 in order to determine the low and high 10-second heart rates? _____

   _____

   _____

2. Calculate your target heart rate, both the low and high end of your range.

   _____

Directions 3

> When in the Course of human Events, it becomes necessary for one People to dissolve the Political Bands which have connected them with another, and to assume, among the Powers of the Earth, the separate and equal Station to which the Laws of Nature and of Nature's God entitle them, a descent Respect to the Opinions of Mankind requires that they should declare the causes which impel them to the Separation.

Printed above is the first paragraph of the U.S. Declaration of Independence. As you can see, the rules for use of capital letters were different in 1776 than they are today.

Select any one of the first 20 words. Count the letters in it and call that number "n." Move ahead n words, beginning with the word after your selected word. When you reach that nth word, count its letters and move ahead as many words as the new letter count. Continue in this manner, counting letters and moving ahead words, until you stop on a word that is beyond the fourth line.

On what word did you stop? _____

—Martin Gardner, "Some Math Magic Tricks with Numbers," *Games Magazine*, May 1999

Directions 4

Use the compass directions and the grid shown below to complete the following exercise.

1. Begin in the southwest corner of cell X, and draw a line that extends north 4 cells.
2. Retrace this line south 2 cells, and then draw east 3 cells. Draw north 1 cell.
3. Draw a straight line northeast to the north center of this cell. Draw another straight line to the southeast corner of the cell.
4. Draw due east 1 cell and repeat step 3.
5. Draw south 3 cells. Draw west 6 cells.
6. Draw an oval in each of the full cells directly south of those in which you have drawn partial triangles.
7. Draw a line west to east across the center of the cell directly south of the cell between the ovals.

What have you drawn? _____

Write additional directions to complete the figure? _____

_____

Patterns of Organization

The logical presentation of details in textbooks tends to form several identifiable patterns. For example, introductory psychology texts tend to list many definitions and examples, whereas history texts present events in time order with numerous cause-and-effect conclusions. Recognizing these patterns helps you to read more efficiently and take notes for later study. They are blueprints for organizing your thinking.

Each organizational pattern can be predicted by key terms that signal the structure. Learn to use the patterns to mark your text and take notes for later study. Your markings and your notes are an organization of main ideas and major supporting details. The following are examples of the organizational patterns found most frequently in textbooks.

Simple Listing

To organize and condense material for the reader, introductory texts often enumerate key ideas. The listing technique may be used within one paragraph, or it may be used over three or four pages to pull material together. With a simple listing pattern, the items are of equal value, and thus the order in which they are presented is of no importance.

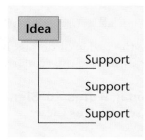

Reader's $\mathcal{T}ip$ Patterns of Organization and Signal Words

Addition (providing additional information): furthermore, again, also, further, moreover, besides, likewise

Cause and Effect (showing one element as producing or causing a result or effect): because, for this reason, consequently, hence, as a result, thus, due to, therefore

Classification (dividing items into groups or categories): groups, categories, elements, classes, parts

Comparison (listing similarities among items): in a similar way, similar, parallels, likewise, in a like manner

Contrast (listing differences among items): on the other hand, bigger than, but, however, conversely, on the contrary, although, nevertheless

Definition (initially defining a concept and expanding with examples and restatements): can be defined, means, for example, like

Description (listing characteristics or details): is, as, like, could be described

Generalization and Example (explaining with examples to illustrate): to restate, that is, for example, to illustrate, for instance

Location or Spatial Order (identifying the whereabouts of objects): next to, near, below, above, close by, within, without, adjacent to, beside, around, to the right or left side, opposite

Simple Listing (randomly listing items in a series): also, another, several, for example

Summary (condensing major points): in conclusion, briefly, to sum up, in short, in a nutshell

Time Order, Sequence, or Narration (listing events in order of occurrence): first, second, finally, after, before, next, later, now, at last, until, thereupon, while, during

Consider an addition problem:

Does the order of the numbers change the sum?

$$
\begin{array}{r} 4 \\ 7 \\ 2 \\ 5 \\ +\,9 \end{array}
\qquad\qquad
\begin{array}{r} 9 \\ 4 \\ 5 \\ 2 \\ +\,7 \end{array}
$$

Likewise, the order of details in a simple list pattern does not change the main point nor influence the reader's understanding of the passage.

Transitional Words to Signal Listing. Listed items usually begin with general phrases, such as these:

Many of the items included were . . .

A number of factors were . . .

Signal words used as transitional words to link ideas include:

in addition also several for example a number of

Also used are numbers such as *one, two, three* (or *first, second, third*) or positions such as *next, last,* or *finally*, where numerical order is not relevant.

Mark Your Text. After reading a listing, circle the topic of the list, that is, the words that best describe what the list contains. Next, insert numbers for each listed item and underline any key words that help explain the details listed. The following is an example of this technique.

EXAMPLE **INTERVIEWING FOR A JOB**

There are several tips one should remember (when interviewing for a job.) Be sure to ¹arrive on time and remember there is no excuse for being late. ²Attend to appearance and dress to look like a successful company employee. Also, ³do not smoke, chew gum, or accept candy, even if it is offered.

EXPLANATION Your Notes on "Interviewing for a Job" would be as follows:

Topic: Tips for job interviewing
1. Arrive on time.
2. Attend to appearance.
3. Don't smoke, chew gum, or eat.

exercise 5 For each of the following paragraphs, mark your text as if for later study. After reading, insert a topic onto the blank at the beginning of the passage. Take notes by first recording the topic and then listing the items. Respond with *T* (true) or *F* (false) to the comprehension items.

Passage 1

_____

College students may be especially vulnerable because they are in a period of transition in which they are often away from home for the first time, striking out on their own, and forging new relationships. From the moment they start packing for school, these transitions cause them to face key developmental tasks as their lives begin to make dramatic changes, such as achieving emotional independence from family, choosing and preparing for a career, preparing for a major relationship, commitment, and/or family life; facing economic independence; and developing their own values and ethical system. These tasks require the college student to develop new social roles and modify old ones. Such changes can result in role strain as they attempt to form a new identity and lead to chronic stress responses.

—*Health: The Basics*, Sixth Edition,
by Rebecca J. Donatelle

1. Mark your text; then take notes.

Topic: _____

(1) _____

(2) _____

(3) _____

(4) _____

(5) _____

_____ 2. Establishing financial independence is the largest source of stress for college students.

_____ 3. The many transitions involved in the lives of college students can make them more vulnerable to stress.

Passage 2

_____

During elections to Congress there are a number of advantages of incumbency (being currently in office). One big one is that incumbents can issue "official" statements or make "official" trips to their district. They can get a lot of free publicity that their opponents would have to pay for. For another advantage, members of the House have office and staff budgets of approximately $350,000 a year; senators are given at least that and often considerably more if their states are large. Both receive 32 government-paid round trips to their districts each year. Also, facilities for making television or radio tapes are available in Washington at a low cost. In addition, there is the *frank*, the privilege of free official mailing enjoyed by Congress. Two hundred million pieces of mail, much of it quite partisan, are sent free under the frank every year.

—*The Basics of American Politics,* by Gary Wasserman

1. Mark your text; then take notes.

Topic: _____

(1) _____

(2) _____

(3) _____

(4) _____

(5) _____

_____ 2. A *frank* privilege is a government-paid trip home.

_____ 3. Incumbents receive publicity paid for by taxpayers.

Classification

In order to simplify a complex topic, authors frequently begin introductory paragraphs by stating that the information which follows is divided into a certain number of groups or categories. The divisions are then named and the parts are explained.

Transitional Words to Signal Classification. Signal words often used for classification are the following:

two divisions   three groups   four elements   five classes

Mark Your Text. After reading, circle the group that will be classified and the number of categories you can expect. Underline any key words that help explain the major details listed. The following is an example of this technique.

EXAMPLE   **FIVE KINGDOMS**

Today most scientists believe that living things should be divided into five kingdoms. We begin by describing the largest groups, the kingdoms, and then discuss various representatives at lower levels in the taxonomic scheme. The five kingdoms generally accepted by biologists are monera, protista, fungi, plantae, and animalia.

—*Biology: The World of Life*, Seventh Edition, by Robert Wallace

exercise 6

For each of the following paragraphs, mark your text as if for later study. After reading, insert a topic onto the blank at the beginning of the passage. Take notes by first recording the topic and then listing relevant supporting items. Respond with *T* (true), *F* (false), or *CT* (can't tell) to the comprehension items.

Passage 1

_____

Fat cells consist of chains of carbon and hydrogen atoms. Those that are unable to hold any more hydrogen in their chemical structure are labeled **saturated fats.** They generally come from animal sources, such as meats and dairy products, and are solid at room temperature. **Unsaturated fats,** which come from plants and include most vegetable oils, are generally liquid at room temperature and have room for additional hydrogen atoms in their chemical structure. The terms *monounsaturated fat* (MUFA) and *polyunsaturated fat* (PUFA) refer to the relative number of hydrogen atoms that are missing. Peanut and olive oils are high in monounsaturated fats, whereas corn, sunflower, and safflower oils are high in polyunsaturated fats.

There is currently a great deal of controversy about which type of unsaturated fat is most beneficial. Although nutritional researchers in the 1980s favored PUFAs, today many believe that they may decrease beneficial HDL levels while reducing LDL levels. PUFAs come in two forms: omega-3 fatty acids and omega-6 fatty acids. MUFAs, such as olive oil, seem to lower LDL levels and increase HDL levels and thus are currently the preferred, or least harmful, fats. Nevertheless, a tablespoon of olive oil gives you a hefty 10 grams of MUFAs.

—Health: The Basics, by Rebecca J. Donatelle

1. Mark your text; then take notes.

   Topic: _____

   (1) _____
      (a) _____
      (b) _____
         i. _____
         ii. _____
            _____

_____ 2. Butter is an example of an unsaturated fat.

_____ 3. Fats are labeled according to the number of carbon atoms in their chemical structure.

Passage 2

_____

Three types of planets formed in our solar system. The inner planets are small and made mostly of silicates and iron metal. The outer planets are large and made largely of gaseous hydrogen and helium. The icy planets also lie in the outer solar system but are small and have surfaces dominated by water ice.

—Earth's Dynamic Systems, Ninth Edition, by W. Kenneth Hamblin and Eric H. Christiansen

1. Mark your text; then take notes.

Topic: _____

(1) _____

(2) _____

_____

(3) _____

_____

_____ 2. The icy planets are smaller than the outer planets.

_____ 3. The outer planets differ from the icy planets only in terms of size.

Definitions with Examples

In each introductory course, you enter a completely new field with its own unique concepts and ideas. These courses frequently seem to be the hardest because of the overload of information presented. In a single beginning course, you are expected to survey the field from one end to the other. Beyond simply learning vocabulary, you must learn the terminology for major ideas that create a framework for the entire course. You must create a new schema. For example, in an introductory psychology textbook, several paragraphs might be devoted to describing *schizophrenia, paranoia,* or a *manic-depressive cycle.* To remember these terms, you would mark your text and take notes defining the conditions. You would also include examples to help you visualize the terms.

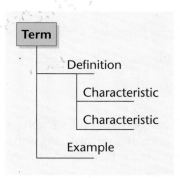

Transitional Words to Signal Definition and Examples. The new terms or concepts may appear as headings, or they may appear in quotation marks, boldface, or italics. Connecting words include the following:

for example	in this case	to illustrate
more specifically	in more precise terms	in one instance

Mark Your Text. After reading the definition of a new term, circle the term and then underline the *key defining words.* A word of caution here: Only underline *key* words. Refrain from underlining sentence after sentence, which leaves you with too much highlighted material for later reference. Mark *Ex* by the example that best helps you remember the term. The following paragraph illustrates this technique.

EXAMPLE   DISPLACEMENT

Father spanks son, who kicks the dog, who chases the cat. (Displacement) is the shifting of re-sponse from one object to another. The boss has yelled at the father, the father is angry at the boss but can't express it safely, so he ᴱˣdisplaces his anger to his son and spanks him. The son is angry at his father, but can't express it safely, so he ᴱˣdisplaces his anger to the dog and kicks it. The dog is "angry" at the son but can't express it safely, so he displaces his "ᴱˣanger" to the cat and chases it. In the mechanism of displacement, a feeling is dis-placed to a safer substitute.

—*Psychology: An Introduction to Human Behavior,*
Second Edition, by Morris Holland

Take Notes. For your study notes, jot down the term, define it in your own words, and list an example. Frequently, you will need to condense several sen-tences into a short phrase for your notes. If you think the text uses a clear and concise definition, it is permissible to use the same words, but don't let yourself fall into the "delayed learning" trap. If you simply copy textbook words that you do not understand, you won't be any better off weeks later when you study your notes for a midterm or final exam. The appropriate time to understand the term is when you first study and take notes on it.

Your notes on displacement might look like this:

Displacement: *Shifting the expression of a feeling from one object to another*

safe substitute

Example: *Son angry at father, so kicks dog*

exercise 7   Read the following paragraphs and write a topic for the beginning of each pas-sage. Circle the terms being defined, underline key phrases, and then write notes for later study. Respond to the comprehension items with *T* (true) or *F* (false).

Passage 1

_____

Large waves, known as seismic sea waves or by the Japanese term tsunami, originate from disturbances on the ocean floor. They are also commonly referred to as tidal waves, but they have no relationship with tides at all. **Tsunamis** can be caused by volcanic eruptions, submarine landslides, or even meteorite impact, but most result from earthquakes that displace the ocean floor. It is not surprising then that most tsunamis occur in the Pacific Ocean, which is circled by active volcanoes and intense seismicity, both of which result from a series of subduction zones surrounding the Pacific. For example, in 1999 a Magnitude 7.1 earthquake triggered in a subduction zone north of New Guinea created a tsunami that was 15 m high. When it struck the shore, it swept 2200 people to their deaths.

—*Earth's Dynamic Systems,* Ninth Edition,
by W. Kenneth Hamblin and Eric H. Christiansen

1. Mark your text; then take notes.

   Tsunamis: _____

   _____

   Example: _____

   _____

_____ 2. Most tsunamis occur in the Pacific Ocean because of its size, depth, and temperature.

_____ 3. Tsunamis are also referred to as tidal waves because they are dependent on the ebb and flow of tides.

Passage 2

_____

Most forget that there is also supposed to be a Type B, defined not by the personality traits its members possess but by the traits they lack. Type B people are the shadowy opposites of Type A people. They are those who are not so very Type A. They do *not* wear out their fingers punching that elevator button. They do *not* allow a slow car in the fast lane to drive their hearts to fatal distraction; in fact, they are at the wheel of that slow car.

—From *Faster, The Accelerarion of Just About Everything,*
by James Gleick

1. Mark your text; then take notes.

   Type B People: _____

   _____

   Example: _____

   _____

   _____

_____ 2. The author suggests that Type B behavior is defined more by what *isn't* than by what *is* (i.e., angry, impolite, rushed).

_____ 3. The author implies that Type A people are unlikely to demonstrate patience.

Description

Description is similar to listing; the characteristics that make up a description are no more than a definition or a simple list of details.

Transitional Words to Signal Description. Look for a list of defining details.

Mark Your Text. Circle the item being described and then underline the *key characteristic*. Only underline *key* words. The following paragraph illustrates this technique.

EXAMPLE **LIZARDS**

(Lizards) are the most successful living group of reptiles. There are [1]3,100 different species of lizards in comparison to the snakes, which have 2,000 species. Lizards range in [2]size from a gecko at 1.2 inches to monitor lizards at 15 feet. The [3]speed of a lizard varies with where it lives. The desert lizard is the fastest.

Take Notes. After marking your text, jot down the topic and underline the key characteristics. Your notes on the previous paragraph would be as follows:

Topic: Lizards

1. Most successful reptiles—3,100 different species
2. Size varies—gecko at 1.2 inches to monitor lizards at 15 feet
3. Speed varies—desert lizard fastest

exercise 8 Read the following paragraphs and write a topic for the beginning of each passage. Circle the item being described, underline key phrases, and then write notes for later study. Respond to the comprehension items with *T* (true) or *F* (false).

Passage 1

_____

Vertebrates of class Mammalia have hair, a characteristic as diagnostic as the feathers of birds. Hair insulates the body, helping the animal maintain a warm and constant body temperature. Mammals are endothermic, and their active metabolism is supported by an efficient respiratory system. Mammary glands that produce milk are as distinctively mammalian as hair. All mammalian mothers nourish their babies with milk. Most mammals are born rather than hatched, and mammals have larger brains than other vertebrates of equivalent size.

—*Biology,* Fourth Edition, by Neil Campbell

1. Mark your text; then take notes.

   Topic: _____

      (1) _____

      (2) _____

      (3) _____

      (4) _____

      (5) _____

_____ 2. Apes are mammals.

_____ 3. According to this information, chickens would be characterized as mammals.

Passage 2

_____

The shark is one of the most fabled, feared, and least understood large animals on earth. They have well-developed jaws and teeth and are reported to be totally humorless. The shark has a very short intestine and a large liver that helps with buoyancy. The body shape itself is quite streamlined, an important adaptation for coping with resistance.

—*Biology: World of Life,* Seventh Edition,
by Robert Wallace

1. Mark your text; then take notes.

   Topic: _____

      (1) _____

      (2) _____

      (3) _____

      (4) _____

_____ 2. The author exhibits a sense of humor in claiming that sharks have none.

_____ 3. The shark's liver helps it float.

Time Order, Sequence, or Narration

Items in time order, sequence, or narration are listed in the order in which they occurred or in a specifically planned order in which they must develop. Changing the order would change the results. For example, events in history are typically organized in time order or narration. Novels, biographies, and anecdotes are usually developed chronologically, and instructions and directions are usually developed in sequence.

A diagram or graphic organizer like the one below is a helpful tool for sorting details and especially for future study.

Topic:

When did it happen?	What happened?

Transitional Words to Signal Time Order or Sequence. Signal words often used for time order or sequence include:

first	second	afterward	after	before	when
until	at last	next	most important	finally	(dates)

Mark Your Text. After reading a time-ordered or sequenced section, first circle the topic and time indicators, such as dates or words like *later* or *the next year*. Insert numbers for each important stage and underline key words that explain each one. By its nature, history is full of time-ordered or chronological events. Be aware that every event is not of equal significance. History textbooks include many details that help you visualize but that you do not need to remember. Use the subheadings in the text to help you judge the importance of events.

EXAMPLE   **THE LOUISIANA PURCHASE**

The events surrounding the (Louisiana Purchase) occurred as follows: In (1795) [1]Spain granted western farmers the right to ship their produce down the Mississippi River to New Orleans, where their cargoes of corn, whiskey, and pork were loaded aboard ships bound for the East Coast and foreign ports. In (1800,) however, [2]Spain secretly ceded the Louisiana territory to France and closed the port of New Orleans to American farmers, who exploded with anger. The president sent James Monroe to France to purchase the land. Circumstances played into American hands when, also in (1800,) [3]slaves rebelled in Haiti, and France had to send troops to fight. After meeting with a determined resistance and mosquitoes carrying yellow fever, Napoleon exclaimed, "Damn sugar, damn coffee, damn colonies." He was then ready to sell. Finally, in (1803,) [4]the United States officially purchased all of the Louisiana Province, a territory extending from Canada to the Gulf of Mexico and westward as far as the Rocky Mountains. The American negotiators agreed on a price of $15 million, or about 4 cents an acre.

—*America and Its People*, Third Edition,
by James Martin et al.

Take Notes. After marking your text, jot down the topic and number the items that are relevant. Be brief. If these items need explanation, put key words underneath the item or in parentheses beside it. Your notes on the previous paragraph would be as follows:

Topic: Louisiana Purchase

When did it happen?	What happened?
1795	1. Spain allowed shipping
1800	2. Sold to France, which stopped shipping
	3. France failed to win in Haiti
1803	4. U.S. bought all land

 exercise 9 Read the following paragraphs and mark your text by writing a topic at the beginning of the passage, circling or numbering listed items, and underlining key phrases. Then write notes for later study. Respond to the comprehension items with *T* (true) or *F* (false).

Passage 1

She was the twentieth child in a black family of 22 in Clarksville, Tennessee. A weak and sickly infant, she was continually afflicted with childhood diseases, and at four she contracted polio. She was unable to walk without steel braces until she was nine and she continued to wear a supportive device in her shoes until age 11.

Both she and her mother were strong believers that fate was not something you had to resign yourself to, but that people could create their own vision and destiny. Together mother and daughter began a training program for those skinny, wobbly legs. Soon she was running. With renewed energy she began to formulate her own goals with a strategy plan. It did not take long until she was the fastest kid on the block . . . and then in the city, in the state, and even the nation.

At age 16 she qualified for the U.S. Olympic team and in 1956 she won a bronze medal in the 100-meter dash. In the 1960 Olympic Games she won three gold medals, for the 100- and 200-meter events and the 400-meter relay. In all three races she broke world records and established herself as the fastest woman on earth.

When asked how she did it, Wilma Rudolph answered, "No one has a life where everything that happened was good. I think the thing that made my life good for me is that I never looked back. I've always been positive no matter what happened."

—*Interpersonal Skills for Leadership,* Second Edition, by Susan Fritz et al.

1. Mark your text; then take notes.

Topic: _____

When did it happen?	What happened?
Childhood	
Age 16	
1956	
1960	

_____ 2. Wilma Rudolph began her vigorous training program in the hope of obtaining a college scholarship to Tennessee State University.

_____ 3. Rudolph views her success as a direct result of optimism in the face of hardship.

Passage 2

_____

Let us consider the deadly Ebola virus as an example of an emerging virus. Ebola outbreaks have occurred several times during the past few decades. The virus was first identified in 1976 in Zaire and Sudan (outbreaks that killed more than 400 people). During the 2000–2001 outbreak in Uganda several hundred people were infected, with a fatality rate of about 50%.

Early symptoms to Ebola infection resemble those of influenza or dysentery. Within about three days of infection, victims develop a fever and weakness, followed by a rash and vomiting. The victim hemorrhages internally, and bleeds from the mouth, eyes, ears, and other body openings. Internal organs shut down, and 50% to 90% of victims die within one to two weeks after infection. The disease is spread by contact with infected body fluids. Like many RNA viruses, Ebola makes frequent mistakes when it duplicates its RNA. The resulting high mutation rate leads to the rapid development of new strains, making it difficult for researchers to develop an effective vaccine.

—From Solomon, Berg, and Martin,
Biology (with InfoTrac), 6th ed. © 2002 Brooks/Cole,
a part of Cengage Learning, Inc. Reproduced by
permission. www.cengage.com/permissions

1. Mark your text; then take notes.

Topic:_____

When did it happen?	What happened?
_____	1. _____
_____	2. _____
	3. _____
	4. _____
	_____
	5. _____
_____	6. _____

_____ 2. According to the passage, there has been difficulty creating an effective vaccine to prevent the spread of Ebola because the majority of research funding is committed to finding a cure for HIV.

_____ 3. The passage suggests that, in its early stages, Ebola might be mistaken for the common flu.

Comparison and Contrast

Another pattern you will find in introductory texts is one that relates items according to existing comparisons and contrasts. To enrich your understanding of a topic, items are paired and then similarities or differences are listed.

Topic

Transitional Words to Signal Comparison and Contrast. Signal words often used for comparison or contrast include:

Comparison: similar   like   in the same way   likewise

Contrast: different   on the other hand   but   nevertheless   however
            although   instead   conversely

Mark Your Text. After reading the passage, record the topic and then write an abbreviation for similarities or differences in the margin. Circle the items being discussed, and underline key words. The following paragraph illustrates the technique.

EXAMPLE   CHICAGO AND CLEVELAND

Diff.

Sim.

Sim.

Chicago, at the southern tip of Lake Michigan, is a port city and an important commercial and industrial center of the Midwest. It is also an important educational, cultural, and recreational center, drawing thousands to its concert halls, art museums, and sports arenas. Cleveland, on the south shore of Lake Erie, is also a port city and a commercial and industrial center important to its area. Like Chicago, it has several important colleges and universities, a distinguished symphony orchestra, one of the fine art museums of the world, and many recreational centers. The location of the two cities undoubtedly contributed to their growth, but this similarity is not sufficient to explain their wide social diversity.

—*Short Essays*, edited by Gerald Levin

Take Notes. First, write in the topics being discussed. Then write the similarities and differences in the appropriate positions in the diagram. Some passages will be mostly comparisons and some will be mostly contrasts. The following illustration is an example.

Topic: Chicago and Cleveland

Chicago
Lake Michigan

Port city
Commercial &
   industrial center
Ed. center with colleges
Cultural center with
   symphony & art
Recreation-sports
   arenas

Lake Erie
   Cleveland

exercise 10 Read the paragraphs and write the topic at the beginning of the passage. Use an abbreviation to mark similarities or differences, underline key phrases, and then take notes for later study. Respond with *T* (true) or *F* (false) to the comprehension items.

Passage 1

_____

During World War II, Roosevelt was president of the United States and Churchill was prime minister of England. Both men had similar styles of leadership and were skilled in the uses of power. When in office, Roosevelt asked Congress for broad executive powers to deal with a national emergency even before war was declared. Similarly, Churchill immediately centralized the war in his own hands by becoming both the prime minister and the defense minister. Both leaders had magnetic personalities that drew people to them. Roosevelt was sensitive to people and their dreams, perhaps having learned from his own battle with polio. Churchill was fired with imagination and a love of language. Both were gifted speakers, Roosevelt with his homey illustrations and Churchill with his emotion and vivid imagery.

1. Mark your text and then take notes. Describe each of the political leaders.

Topic: _____

_____ 2. Churchill's sensitivity came from his battle with polio.
_____ 3. Roosevelt was both president and minister of defense.

Passage 2

_____

People talk about a new economy—one where the Internet is supposed to change everything. Now some even question whether a "new economy" exists, and if so, how it differs from the old economy.

The new economy is less concerned with physical goods. Almost 93 million workers (80 percent of the workforce) do not spend their days making things. Instead they work in jobs that require them to move things, process or generate information, or provide services to people. In the old economy, information flow was physical: cash, checks, invoices, reports, and face-to-face meetings. But in the new economy, information in all its forms becomes digital.

In the old economy, geography played a key role in determining who competed with whom. In the new economy, distance and time differences have vanished. Besides compressing distance, the Internet compresses time. In the new economy, the ability to innovate and get to market faster is a key competitive advantage. Consider this: In less than 18 months after its launch, Hotmail had signed up 12 million subscribers. A few days later its founders sold the company to Microsoft for $400 million in Microsoft stock. Today, with 50 million registered users, Hotmail is the largest Web-based e-mail service in the world.

In the old economy, setting up a nursery to sell plants might involve leasing a shed, buying various types of trees and plants, and more. But on the Internet, setting up a nursery can be as simple as registering a domain name, hiring an artist to design some Web pages, and making arrangements with a plant wholesaler. In short, barriers to entry for companies selling over the Internet are virtually nonexistent.

—*Business Today*, Tenth Edition,
by Michael Mescon et al.

1. Mark your text; then take notes.

Topic: _____

_____ 2. At the time of its purchase by Microsoft, Hotmail had 50 million subscribers.

_____ 3. The author suggests that online nurseries do not need to house their own plants.

Cause and Effect

In this pattern, one of several factors, or causes, is shown to lead to or result in certain events, or effects. Cause-and-effect patterns can be complex, because a single effect can have multiple causes and one cause can have many effects.

Topic:

Cause → Why did it happen?	Effect What happened?
→	
→	
→	

Transitional Words to Signal Cause and Effect. Signal words often used to indicate cause and effect include:

for this reason	consequently	on that account	thus
hence	because	made	therefore

Mark Your Text. Circle the topic, and remember there can be many causes and many effects. Therefore, give both labels and numbers to the causes and effects, as well as underlining key words to explain the items. The following paragraph illustrates the technique.

EXAMPLE   **EARLY JOBS**

The cause: (1) summer and (2) after-school jobs
Effects:
1. Money management
2. Skills
3. Belief in work
   a. Anxiety over free time
   b. Guilt over non-work activity

Aside from basic money management [*Eff*], what did I actually learn from all my summer and [*Cause*] after-school jobs? Each one may have given me some ²small skills [*Eff*] but the cumulative effect was to deepen my ³belief [*Eff*] that work was the essential aspect of grown-up life. Even now, I am sometimes filled with anxieties at the prospect of stretches of *free time*. When I do not immediately rush to fill that time with work, I have to fight off *guilt*, [*Eff*] struggling mentally against a picture of a Real Grown-up shaking a finger at me, someone with the droning voice of our high school career counselor, but with firm overtones of former employers, teachers, even my mother. "This," the voice beats relentlessly into my ear, "is your preparation for life."

—"Blooming: A Small-Town Girlhood,"
by Susan Allen Toth from *The Compact Reader*,
edited by Jane Aaron

Take Notes. Write the topic and then write headings to label causes and effects. List and number the causes and effects and add key words that are needed to explain. Note that an effect may also be the cause of something else. Arrows can indicate these relationships. Here is an example.

Topic: Effects of Early Jobs

Cause → Why did it happen?	Effect What happened?
Summer and after-school jobs → → →	1. Money mgt 2. Skills 3. Belief in work as essential to adult life ↓ 4. Anxiety over fun time; guilt over non-work

exercise 11 Read the following paragraphs. For each one, write the topic in the answer blank, label the causes and effects, underline key terms, and then take notes for later study. Respond with *T* (True) or *F* (False) to the comprehension items.

Passage 1

_____

Insects perform many roles vital to human life. Without bees and other insects, for instance, many flowering plants would never be pollinated—a prerequisite to producing crops such as apples, citrus fruits, berries, and cucumbers. Many beetles, ants, and flies are important decomposers, breaking down the dead bodies of plants and animals.

Nevertheless, people have devoted more time to killing insects than to praising them. It is perhaps unduly gloomy to conclude that we are losing the battle against insects, who will one day inherit the earth, but those who believe this have good reason for their opinion.

Insects destroy more than 10% of all crops in the United States, but the damage is even worse in the tropics, where hot weather throughout the year permits insects to grow and reproduce faster. In Kenya, officials estimate that insects destroy 75% of the nation's crops. A locust swarm in Africa may be 30 meters deep along a front 1500 meters long, and will consume every fragment of plant material in its path, leaving hundreds of square kilometers of country devastated.

Pesticides have not solved the insect problem. This is partly because pesticides act as selective pressures for the evolution of resistant strains of insects, which evolve too fast for expensive pesticide research to keep up.

—*A Journey into Life*, Second Edition, by Karen Arms and Pamela S. Camp

1. Mark your text; then take notes.

Topic:_____

Cause → Why did it happen?	Effect What happened?
_____ →	_____
_____	
_____ →	_____
_____ →	_____
	_____

_____ 2. Bees are considered decomposers.

_____ 3. Locusts can probably be eradicated in Africa with pesticides.

Passage 2

_____

Americans are also more conscious of what they are eating. The desire to reduce cholesterol intake has caused a shift away from red meat and dairy products. The trend was substantial enough to cause beef producers to band together and mount an educational campaign to convince consumers that beef is healthful. The trend to healthier foods has primarily affected product rather than promotional strategies. Producers of dairy foods are coming out with lines of low-cholesterol products, cereal companies with high-fiber products, and liquor manufacturers with lower alcohol lines to reflect the trend away from hard liquor.

The combined effects of better medical care and greater health awareness have resulted in increased longevity in the past twenty years. From 1970 to 1990, life expectancy of the average American went from 70 to 76 years reaching 80 by the turn of the century.

—*Consumer Behavior and Marketing Action,* Fourth
Edition, by Henry Assael

1. Mark your text; then take notes.

Topic: _____

Cause → Why did it happen?	Effect What happened?
_____	
_____ →	_____
→	_____
→	_____
→	_____

_____ 2. Americans are eating fewer dairy products.

_____ 3. Eating beef tends to lower cholesterol levels.

Clues to the Organizational Pattern

As shown in the previous explanations, readers have several clues to the organizational pattern of the material they are reading. Active readers use all of the clues rather than just one because they focus on the meaning.

1. *Signal words:* For example, repeated words, such as *because, as a result, therefore, for this reason*, suggest a cause-and-effect pattern. Be careful, though! Some signal words may be used in several different patterns.
2. *Diagrams or graphic organizers:* If the details fit into the diagram, the reader has more evidence that the predicted pattern is correct.
3. *Relationship among the details and the main idea:* This is the most reliable evidence a reader has to determine the organizational pattern, because it directly reflects the meaning of the material.

Mixed Patterns. In longer reading selections, authors often mix patterns. For example, a simple list pattern may be used in the introductory paragraph, a definition pattern in another paragraph, and a cause-and-effect pattern in yet another. Rather than be confused by this, readers should keep in mind the overall pattern—the pattern that best develops the author's main point.

exercise 12   Read the following beginning portions of paragraphs. Predict the dominant pattern(s) of organization to be used by the author. Select from the following list:

Simple listing	Definition	Description
Time order	Narration	Comparison-Contrast
Cause and effect		

1. Many psychologists believe that the basic structure of human personality is represented by five broad factors, known as the Big Five. They are neuroticism, extroversion, openness, agreeableness, and conscientiousness.

—Human Relations, Eighth Edition,
by Andrew J. DuBrin

Organizational pattern: _____

2. In some regions, such as Europe and South Asia, it is common for people to cluster in villages and towns; this contrasts with the dispersed settlement pattern of rural North America, where people tend to scatter across the countryside in individual farms and homesteads.

—Diversity and Globalization, Second Edition,
by Les Rowntree et al.

Organizational pattern: _____

3. To remain financially sound, Mega Music used the services of *headhunters*. They are paid recruiters who match hiring companies with employees or executives in order to find a new CEO. The headhunter found a young energetic Yankee named Bill Black. (A *Yankee* is a person from the northeastern region of the United States. The name originated during the Civil War because Yankees were soldiers from the north.)

—*Choices: A Basic Writing Guide with Readings,* Third Edition, by Kate Mangelsdorf and Evelyn Posey

Organizational pattern: _____

4. At last all the preparations for my wedding were almost completed and the day was fixed for August 21 of this year 1745. On the eve of the 21st we moved from the Summer to the Winter Palace.

—*Sources of the West,* Sixth Edition, edited by Mark A. Kishlansky

Organizational pattern: _____

5. If the people in your life treat you in an undesirable way, you're going to want to figure out what you are doing to reinforce, elicit, or allow that treatment. If you're involved in a relationship in which someone is consistently abusive, exploitive, or insensitive toward you, find out what you're doing to encourage that behavior, so that you can realign the relationship in a more healthy direction.

—*Celebrity Writing in America,* by William Vesterman

Organizational pattern: _____

6. *Comets* are small ice bodies that formed in the outer solar system. Some have elliptical orbits that take them near the Sun.

—*Earth's Dynamic Systems*, Ninth Edition, by W. Kenneth Hamblin and Eric H. Christiansen

Organizational pattern: _____

7. She holds a tall iced coffee in one hand, and her blond hair is piled high in a ponytail. Headphones hang above the stools, and computer screens are embedded in the countertop.

—Adapted from Alison Overholt, "Thinking Outside the Cup," *Fast Company* (July 2004)

Organizational pattern: _____

8. Within moments of sitting or lying down and pushing the "power" button, viewers report feeling more relaxed. Because the relaxation occurs quickly, people are conditioned to associate viewing with rest and lack of tension.

—Robert Kubey and Mihaly Csikszentmihalyi, "Television Addiction Is No Mere Metaphor," *Scientific American*, February 2002.

Organizational pattern: _____

9. A new cycle began in October when peasants prepared the ground for the planting of winter crops. In November came the slaughter of excess livestock because there was usually insufficient food to keep animals all winter. In February and March, the land was plowed for spring crops—oats, barley, peas, beans, and lentils.

—*Western Civilization I: To 1715*, Fifth Edition, by Jackson J. Spielvogel

Organizational pattern: _____

10. According to crime reports, individuals were the most common target of robbers. Banks, gas stations, convenience stores, and other businesses were the second most common target. Residential robberies accounted for only 13.5% of the total.

—*Criminal Justice Today*, Eighth Edition, by Frank Schmalleger

Organizational pattern: _____

Summary *Points*

➤ **What is a detail?**
A detail develops, explains, and proves the main idea. Details are facts, descriptions, and reasons that convince the reader and make the material interesting.

➤ **How do you distinguish between major and minor details?**
Major details are needed to explain or prove the main idea. Minor details are included to make the passage more interesting.

➤ **What is a simple listing pattern?**
Items of equal value are listed in a passage.

➤ **What is a classification pattern?**
In a classification pattern the divisions are named and the parts are explained.

➤ **What is a definition with examples pattern?**
A new term is defined and examples are added for clarification.

➤ **What is a chronological or sequence pattern?**
Events listed in the order in which they occur are in a chronological pattern or a sequence.

➤ **What is a comparison or contrast pattern?**
Items are compared or contrasted to show how they are alike or different.

➤ **What is a cause-and-effect pattern?**
Factors or causes are shown to lead to or result in certain consequences.

COLLABORATIVE   PROBLEM SOLVING

Form a five-member group and select one of the following activities. Brainstorm and then outline your major points on a transparency. Choose a member to present the group findings to the class.

➤ Write step-by-step directions for leaving your classroom and going to a place on campus to eat lunch.

➤ Create a diagram that shows several categories and subcategories for elected state government officials.

➤ Create a list or diagram of ideas that compares and contrasts your college with another college in the state.

➤ Provide two opening sentences stating the main idea for passages with a simple listing pattern of organization and two for a sequence pattern.

My ReadingLab (MRL) www.myreadinglab.com

➤ To practice the ideas and skills introduced in this chapter, go to the "Supporting Details" and "Patterns of Organization" modules in the Skills section of MRL. To practice general reading comprehension use the Levels section.

The Reading *Workshop*

"The more that you read, the more things you will know. The more you learn, the more places you'll go."

—Dr. Seuss, *I Can Read With My Eyes Shut!*

Is there somewhere you have always wanted to go? Something or someone you have wanted to know more about? Something you have always wanted to do? A trip to the library or bookstore might be just the thing to satisfy those desires. If you actually travel to that place, take a class, meet that person or find yourself in that situation, the experience will be richer for knowing more about it first. Spend a free afternoon or evening browsing in an actual or online bookstore or a public library and see what strikes your fancy.

Think about it, talk about it, write about it:

You should be well into your book by now. It's time to go beyond the literal details and think about the author's craft. If you are reading fiction, why is the story set where and when it is? Would a different setting significantly change the story line? If you are reading nonfiction, how would the book be different if it had been written ten years earlier or later?

Your instructor might ask you to consider these questions or others in a Reading Workshop journal.

Personal *Feedback* 1

Name _____

1. Describe a poster, painting, or photograph that you particularly like. What is the theme? How do the details support the theme? Why do you like it? _____

   _____

   _____

2. So far this term, have you collaborated on homework or projects with other class-mates? If so, describe your work. _____

   _____

   _____

3. In this class, who would you feel comfortable calling for assignment information?

   _____

   _____

4. What organizations have you joined? _____

   _____

   _____

5. What campus events or social functions have you attended? _____

   _____

   _____

6. When you have a break at school, where do you spend time? _____

   _____

   _____

7. What volunteer work have you recently done on or off campus? _____

   _____

   _____

8. What do you think "bonded to the college" means? _____

   _____

   _____

9. What would make you feel bonded to your college? _____

   _____

   _____

Tear out and submit to your instructor.

selection 1 🧠 Psychology

"Three grand essentials to happiness in this life are something to do, something to love, and something to hope for."

Joseph Addison

Many factors within our control contribute to good emotional health. One such factor is the social support or help provided in time of need by a spouse, friends, colleagues, and family. Research indicates that social support can have a positive influence on the body's immune system, reduce the impact of stress, and increase the probability of recovering from illnesses. How strong is your social network, and what other factors should you consider?

THINKING BEFORE READING

Preview for content and organizational clues. Activate your schema and anticipate what you will learn.

What is the happiest part of your day?

Why do you like hugs?

I think this will say _____

VOCABULARY PREVIEW

Are you familiar with these words?

pervasive	encounters	excessive	timidity	frailties
chronic	perspective	profoundly	competence	self-transcendence

What does the prefix *per* in *pervasive* and *perspective* mean?

How long does a *chronic* illness last?

Do you suffer from *timidity*?

Your instructor may choose to give a true-false vocabulary review before or after reading.

THINKING DURING READING

As you read, use the six thinking strategies of a good reader: predict, picture, relate, monitor, correct, and annotate.

BECOMING HEALTHY

How can you grow and eventually become fully functioning? How can you achieve that ideal stage of psychological health? You cannot be healthy simply by trying to be healthy; you cannot be happy simply by deciding to be happy.

Refer to the
Reader's *Tip*
for **Psychology** on
page 147.

5   Pleasure, happiness, and self-actualization cannot be effectively pursued; instead, they ensue, or automatically result, from your having satisfied a need, attained a goal, or grown toward health. Your deciding to be happy will not make you happy; happiness follows from what you *do*.

THREE THINGS TO AVOID

10   You have unpleasant feelings sometimes and this is quite natural. But if your unpleasant feelings are pervasive, unending, and tend to color your whole emotional life, then you want to stop feeling so bad. We are all sometimes blue, but if you are blue most of the time, then you want to change. As you grow toward health, you tend to experience fewer and fewer persistent unpleasant feelings. Three of these unpleasant feelings are doubt, dread, and depression.

15   ***Doubt.*** Self-doubt makes you feel worthless, stupid, and dull. Many persons have excessive doubts about their physical appearance; they consider themselves unattractive, ugly, and unlovable. They then retreat from dating and other interpersonal encounters and remain highly self-conscious about their appearance. Other persons have excessive doubts about their intelligence; they consider themselves uninteresting, ordinary, and dull. They act with great shyness and timidity when among other people, believing that

20   no one would want to listen to their ideas. Excessive self-doubt, in general, comes from a feeling that other people will not find you acceptable in some way; this feeling leads you not to accept yourself. Understanding yourself and others is one way to avoid self-doubt; you will discover that your frailties and fears are not unique. Being loved and prized by someone is another way to escape excessive self-doubt; to be wholly accepted by some-

25   one else makes it easier for you to accept yourself.

Dread. Dread is a feeling of anxiety or worry. You feel afraid, but you are not sure why. Dread makes you feel nervous, high-strung, restless, and irritable. The tension that you feel may show up physically in nail-biting, in crying spells, in chain-smoking, in frequent headaches or neck aches, or in chronic fatigue. The persistent feeling of dread is a

30   message, and the message is this: Relax, reduce the pressures in your life, and try to resolve some of your conflicts.

Relaxing is something you may have to practice and learn how to do. Here is something for you to try: Go to a quiet darkened room. Sit or lie in a comfortable position. Begin breathing deeply and slowly while you try to empty your mind of thoughts. Beginning with

35   your feet, tighten and then relax your muscles one by one, until all of the muscles of your body are relatively relaxed. Then close your eyes and imagine yourself floating in a tub of warm water. The pressures of your life can sometimes be reduced by getting away from them for a while—take a break and change your scene. For a change of pace take a walk every day or do some light reading. You can sometimes be helped in working out your prob-

40   lems and conflicts by talking to other people about them. As you listen to yourself, you may gain some insights. The feedback of other people may also give you a new perspective. Expressing your feelings to other people often in itself reduces the tension that you feel.

Depression. When you are depressed, you feel profoundly unhappy, blue, and sad. You are moody and pessimistic; you don't feel that things will get better in the near fu-

45   ture. You tend not to do things; your energy level is low. Things that once were significant now seem rather pointless. The persistent feeling of depression is a message, and the message is this: Become active, get to work, begin to be involved. Get a part-time job, start a project, volunteer as a helper in a clinic or community agency, join a club—do something. Depression is the opposite of involvement.

THREE THINGS TO DO

50   What you do and what happens to you are under your control. You are in charge. And what you do will determine whether you grow toward health or whether you stay as you are now. While you cannot attain psychological health by pursuing it directly, you can

grow in the direction of health through certain kinds of experiences, and these experiences are under your control. Some experiences move you toward health; some move
you away from health. To learn about yourself and others, to love and to be loved, and to
live actively and productively—all are growth-producing.

Learn. To learn about others you must be involved with them. You must have a relationship with them of mutual trust. For how can I learn about you unless you trust me
enough to disclose your "inner self" to me? And how can you trust me unless I am willing to reveal myself to you? You can help me understand myself, if I trust what you say
about me.

Self-understanding cannot easily be achieved in isolation; other people help us to define who we are. Our impression of ourselves depends upon how other people consistently react to us. My self-understanding and my knowledge of you thus depend upon
our relationship. If we do not have a trustful relationship, you may hide yourself from me.
You may "mystify" me by trying to create an impression that you are different from what
you really are. But if you allow me to know you, then you help me understand myself.
Knowing others and understanding yourself leads to self-acceptance. You discover that
the qualities in yourself that you have rejected are not unique to yourself; others are very
similar to you. And as you are accepted by others, you are led to accept yourself. Self-
understanding and self-acceptance are experiences of growth that make possible a state
of self-actualization.

Love. Experiences that confirm or validate who you are are health-producing experiences. Being loved by another is the most profound validation of yourself; for to be loved
means that someone knows you, that they accept the way you are, and that they value
and prize you. To be loved, and therefore validated, is health-producing because it leads
you to know, accept, and value yourself. And if you can do this, you are better able to
function in life and more likely to experience a continual feeling of well-being.

The capacity for love is a symptom of health. The ability to love depends upon the
extent to which you value yourself, have faith in your own powers, and are not afraid of
giving yourself.

Live. Living fully implies involvement with the world. When you actively do things, you
experience your self, your power, and your capacity. When you become intensely involved
in a job, hobby, cause, or other person, you tend to lose self-consciousness, develop feelings of competence, and invest yourself in something "outside your own skin." You have
feelings of purpose and meaningfulness and may taste the satisfaction of what has been
called "meaning fulfillment." When you become absorbed in something outside yourself,

you begin to experience a kind of self-transcendence, accompanied by a feeling of well-being. Thus the experience of active involvement is a growth experience.

(1,225 words)

—From Morris Holland, *Psychology: An Introduction to Human Behavior*, 2nd ed. © 1978 Wadsworth, a part of Cengage Learning, Inc. Reproduced by permission. www.cengage.com/permissions

THINKING AND WRITING AFTER READING

RECALL Self-test your understanding.

Your instructor may choose to give you a true-false comprehension review.

REACT How does someone you know well create unhappiness? _____

_____

REFLECT What makes you depressed? _____

_____

THINK CRITICALLY Discuss how learning can help you achieve good health. Write your answer on a separate sheet of paper.

THINK AND WRITE Describe your own social network and explain how its members contribute to your well-being. _____

_____

_____

DETAILS AND ORGANIZATIONAL PATTERNS Mark the following as major (*M*) or minor (*m*) details in support of the author's main point.

_____ 1. Self-doubt makes you feel worthless, stupid, and dull.

_____ 2. Tension may show up physically in nail-biting or headaches.

_____ 3. Learn about others.

_____ 4. Join a club to beat depression.

_____ 5. Live fully and be involved with the world.

6. What is the purpose of the first paragraph? _____

_____

7. What is the pattern of organization of the section entitled *Three Things to Avoid*? _____

8. What is the pattern of organization of the section entitled *Three Things to Do*? _____

Interpret the Quote

Now that you have finished reading the selection, "Becoming Healthy," go back to the beginning of the selection and read the opening quote again. Do you agree with Addison's three essentials to happiness? On a separate sheet of paper, list five essentials that bring you personal happiness.

Name _____

Date _____

COMPREHENSION QUESTIONS

Answer the following with *a, b, c,* or *d,* or fill in the blank. In order to help you analyze your strengths and weaknesses, the question types are indicated.

Main Idea _____ 1. The best statement of the main idea of this selection is:

    a. Negative and unpleasant feelings are natural but tend to ruin your emotional life.

    b. You can achieve health and happiness by avoiding negative feelings and focusing on certain positive experiences.

    c. In achieving good health, love and learning are more important than money.

    d. Pleasure, happiness, and self-actualization result as you grow toward health.

Inference _____ 2. The author's attitude toward becoming healthy is

    a. optimistic.

    b. pessimistic.

    c. sarcastic.

    d. sympathetic.

Inference _____ 3. The author believes that

    a. happiness can be pursued.

    b. happiness follows positive action.

    c. deciding to be happy can make you happy.

    d. setting realistic goals brings happiness.

Inference _____ 4. The author suggests that relaxation is a cure for

    a. self-doubt.

    b. anxiety.

    c. depression.

    d. timidity.

Inference 5. The author suggests that shyness is primarily a reflection of

_____

Detail _____ 6. The author views learning as

    a. getting a college degree.

    b. becoming involved in new hobbies.

    c. finding out about yourself and others.

    d. always actively pursuing knowledge.

Inference _____ 7. The author feels that being loved

    a. is more important than loving.

    b. is not as important as involvement with the world.

    c. is the single key to good health.

    d. gives a feeling of self-worth.

Answer the following with *T* (true), *F* (false), or *CT* (can't tell).

Inference _____ 8. The author is more concerned with the psychological than the physiological contributions to health.

Inference _____ 9. According to the author, involvement and activity help to prevent depression.

Detail _____10. Shy people can benefit from associating with self-confident, aggressive friends.

VOCABULARY

Answer the following with *a, b, c,* or *d* for the word or phrase that best defines the boldface word as used in the selection. The number in parentheses indicates the line of the passage in which the word appears.

_____ 1. "unpleasant feelings are **pervasive**" (9)

    a. upsetting
    b. uncharacteristic
    c. surprising
    d. widespread

_____ 2. "other interpersonal **encounters**" (16)

    a. meetings
    b. groups
    c. friendships
    d. circumstances

_____ 3. have **excessive** doubts" (17)

    a. endless
    b. needless
    c. more than usual
    d. inferior

_____ 4. "shyness and **timidity**" (19)

    a. nervousness
    b. meekness
    c. unreasonableness
    d. inconsistency

_____ 5. "your **frailties** and fears" (23)

    a. expectations
    b. unusual features
    c. hopes
    d. weaknesses

_____ 6. "**chronic** fatigue" (29)

    a. constant
    b. unwanted
    c. difficult
    d. nervous

_____ 7. "give you a new **perspective**" (41)

    a. interest
    b. view
    c. tension
    d. desire

_____ 8. "feel **profoundly** unhappy" (43)

    a. slightly
    b. briefly
    c. deeply
    d. frankly

_____ 9. "feelings of **competence**" (85)

    a. love
    b. ability
    c. belonging
    d. need

_____10. "a kind of **self-transcendence**" (88)

    a. excelling
    b. rejection
    c. inner analysis
    d. admiration

Your instructor may choose to give a true-false vocabulary review.

VOCABULARY ENRICHMENT

A. The purpose of many invented words is to form shorter expressions that carry the same meaning. Acronyms are words made from the initial letters of other words. Blends are words formed by combining parts of other words. *Abbreviations* are shortened forms of longer words. Write the definitions and elongated forms of the following words.

> **scu·ba** \'skü-bə\ *n, often attrib* [self-contained underwater breathing apparatus] (1952) : an apparatus utilizing a portable supply of compressed gas (as air) supplied at a regulated pressure and used for breathing while swimming underwater
>
> Source: By permission. From Merriam-Webster's *Collegiate*® *Dictionary, Eleventh Edition.* © 2008 by Merriam Webster Incorporated (www.Merriam-Webster.com).

(acronyms)

1. *Scuba* means _____

2. It comes from _____

> **Medi·care** \'me-di-ˌker\ *n* [blend of *medical* and *care*] (1955) : a government program of medical care esp. for the aged
>
> Source: By permission. From Merriam-Webster's *Collegiate*® *Dictionary, Eleventh Edition.* © 2008 by Merriam Webster Incorporated (www.Merriam-Webster.com).

(blends)

3. *Medicare* means _____

4. It comes from _____

> **¹ad** \'ad\ *n, often attrib* (1841) **1 :** ADVERTISEMENT 2 **2 :** ADVERTISING
> **²ad** *n* (1947) : ADVANTAGE 4
>
> Source: By permission. From Merriam-Webster's *Collegiate*® *Dictionary, Eleventh Edition.* © 2008 by Merriam Webster Incorporated (www.Merriam-Webster.com).

(abbreviations)

5. *Ad* means _____

6. It comes from _____

B. Use an unabridged dictionary in your college library to find the definitions and origins of the following words.

Achilles' heel

7. Definition: _____

8. Origin: _____

_____

maudlin

9. Definition: _____

10. Origin: _____

babel

11. Definition: _____

12. Origin: _____

_____

C. Circle the similar-sounding word that is correct in each sentence.

anecdote: story	**access:** entrance	**moral:** honorable
antidote: medicine	**excess:** more than needed	**morale:** spirit

13. The professor told an amusing (**anecdote, antidote**) about Queen Elizabeth.

14. The new key will give you easy (**access, excess**) to the computer room.

15. After the positive test grades were announced, the class (**moral, morale**) was high.

ASSESS YOUR LEARNING

Review confusing questions, seek clarification, and make notes in your text to help you remember new information and vocabulary.

selection 2 Criminal Justice

. . . If it sounds too good to be true, then you're dealing with an amateur con artist. . . .
                                                                    Dennis Marlock

The Internet has taken fraud to a larger audience. With a single click, you can lose money to a crook. Using a free gift as bait, scammers trap the unknowing into long-term Internet access contracts with big cancellation penalties simply by enticing the consumer to cash a check that arrived in the mail. For others, a free Web design or free adult entertainment is the bait, but the cost is then added to the consumer's telephone bill. How do such scammers operate without being apprehended?

THINKING BEFORE READING

Preview for content and organizational clues. Activate your schema and anticipate what you will learn.

Do con artists prey on certain sectors of the population?

Why are many swindles not reported to the police?

I think this will say that _____.

VOCABULARY PREVIEW

Are you familiar with these words?

annals	guile	frailties	monetary	swindle
sleight	fraudulent	phony	affluent	perishable

Is greed a human *frailty*?

Is a *fraudulent* check phony?

How does *sleight* of hand make a card trick possible?

Your instructor may choose to give a true-false vocabulary review before or after reading.

THINKING DURING READING

As you read, use the six thinking strategies of a good reader: predict, picture, relate, monitor, correct, and annotate.

CONFIDENCE GAMES MAY BE A SHELL GAME SCENE

Refer to the
Reader's *Tip*
for **Criminal Justice**
on page 66.

The confidence artist is a recurring figure in history and in fiction, police annals, and the literature of criminology. The confidence artist steals by guile in a person-to-person relationship. Most confidence artists have insight into human nature and its frailties, not least among which is the desire to get something for nothing or for a bargain.

5 Many people who read the details of some of the confidence games described below will find them hard to believe. How, they will ask, can anyone be so easily "conned"? But the police reports speak for themselves. The monetary loss and the number of confidence games very likely exceed the recorded figures because many victims are too embarrassed to make a police report.

THE PIGEON DROP

10 This swindle is operated by two people. A lone victim, usually elderly, is approached on the street by one of the swindlers, who strikes up a conversation. A wallet, envelope, or other item that could contain cash is planted nearby. The second swindler walks past, picking up the wallet or envelope within full view of the pair. The swindler approaches the partner and victim, saying that he or she has found a large sum of money and is will-
15 ing to divide it with them. But first the two must produce a large sum of money to show good faith. The victim is given no time to ponder and is urged to withdraw money from a savings account to show good faith. After withdrawing the money, the victim places it in an envelope provided by the first swindler. It is then shown to the second swindler who, by sleight of hand, switches envelopes, returning an identical envelope filled with
20 paper slips to the victim. Both swindlers then depart. The victim does not become aware of the con until he or she goes to deposit the newfound "money."

THE BANK EXAMINER SCHEME

The bank examiner scheme is one of the more sophisticated con games and requires knowing where targets bank. The con artist, usually a man, calls the victim—let us say an elderly woman—and introduces himself as a federal bank examiner, saying that there has
25 been a computer breakdown at the bank and that he wants to verify when she last deposited or withdrew money and her current balance. If she replies, for example, that there should be a deposit of $8,000 in the account, then the caller indicates that the bank records show a deposit of some lesser amount, perhaps $2,000. The caller then suggests that a dishonest teller may be tampering with the account and asks for help in ap-
30 prehending the teller. Once the victim agrees, the caller says that a cab will come and bring her to the bank. She is instructed that she should withdraw $7,000. One con man stays near the woman's house and observes her enter the cab. Another waits at the bank to verify the withdrawal and to be certain that bank officials or police are not alerted. After withdrawing the money, the woman gets back into the waiting cab and returns
35 home. One of the con men then telephones her to discuss the next phase of the bank's "investigation." While she is still on the phone, the second man knocks on the door. The man at the front door identifies himself as a bank employee, the woman lets him in, and lets him talk to the "bank examiner" on the telephone. After a short conversation, the con man hands the phone back to the woman. The caller instructs her to give her money
40 to the bank employee so that he can redeposit it with the suspected teller. Victim and money are soon parted—she may even be given a receipt.

INHERITANCE SCAM

In this scam, the victim's phone rings and, on the other end, a sweet-sounding person says, "You may be the recipient of a huge inheritance." But first some questions must be answered, such as birthday, birthplace, mother's maiden name, Social Security number—

45 all the information needed to withdraw money from the victim's bank account. When the victim answers the questions, the con artist says that he or she will deposit the inheritance in the victim's bank account. In the morning, a fraudulent check is deposited into the victim's account. In the afternoon, before the fraudulent check can be discovered, a withdrawal is made, and the victim has lost money.

50 One variation of the inheritance scam involves a victim who pays an inheritance tax before the inheritance is paid. Sometimes the caller tells the victim to mail the inheritance tax. Sometimes a well-dressed, official-looking gentleman collects the inheritance tax in cash before awarding the victim a phony cashier's check.

THREE-CARD MONTE

This scam is similar to the traditional shell game. The crook, using three "marked" play-
55 ing cards, shuffles the cards and coaxes the victim to pick the ace, queen of hearts, or whatever. In this case, the hands of the crook are usually quicker than the eyes of the victims. The cards are "marked"—sometimes by feel, such as folded edges—in some way that is recognizable to the shuffler. Initially permitted to win, thus receiving ego strokes, the victim is then cheated out of his or her money.

C.O.D. SCAM

60 The suspects usually pose as delivery employees. In an affluent neighborhood, the suspect spots an empty house and finds the resident's name. After writing a phony mailing

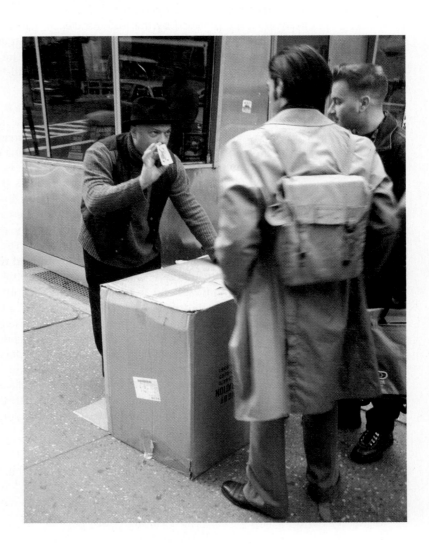

label, the suspect goes next door and asks the neighbor to accept a perishable package for the absent neighbor and to pay cash for C.O.D. charges.

65 A variant carried out on weekends involves demanding that a naïve teenage gas station attendant take cash register funds to pay for a package the owner supposedly ordered. Hoping to please the boss, who is off work for the weekend, the young employee pays the money. Of course, the boss ordered nothing, and the money is lost.

MONEY-MAKING-MACHINE SCAM

In this scam, a couple of con artists visit a local dice game to look for victims. They tell the victim that they have smuggled a secret formula out of Germany (or some other foreign
70 country) that will bleach the ink on $1 bills. Then the blank paper can be pressed against a $100 bill to form another $100 bill. In one case reported in Philadelphia, a victim brought 150 hundred-dollar bills from his bank to a motel room, where the money was washed and stuck in between pieces of tissue paper with "bleached" dollar bills. While the victim went drinking with some of the con artists, one went back to the motel room
75 and took the money. Another promised to look for the thieves and kept the victim from calling the police for a week. When the victim finally did call the police a week later, the suspects were long gone.

NIGERIAN OIL CON

In the Nigerian oil con, the suspects place an advertisement in a newspaper, claiming to have connections inside the Nigerian government. The price of oil that is quoted is usually
80 just a few cents per barrel below the current market price. The victim's confidence in the "good deal" is raised when the suspects dispatch to the victim "a succession of convincing telexes and documents," some even originating from the oil-carrying vessel itself.

The key to the con is the bill of lading. However, bills of lading are easy to fake. There are few ways to check the authenticity of such documents, and the demand to see
85 any additional papers will be of little concern to shipping con artists. If it is only one document that stands in the way of making a deal, then they will ask you what color you want it in.

Soon after the buyer begins negotiating for the cargo, typically worth millions of dollars, depending on the size of the oil tanker, the "supplier" will demand a cash ad-
90 vance of $250,000 to defray port costs and other expenses. After payment is made, that is usually the last time the buyer hears from the supplier. Both purchasers, the true purchaser and the conned purchaser, often meet at the dock, awaiting the arrival of the same oil tanker.

(1,359 words)

—From *Criminal Investigation*, 7th Edition, by Charles Swanson, Neil Chamelin, and Leonard Territo. Copyright © 2000 by The McGraw-Hill Companies, Inc. Reprinted by permission of The McGraw-Hill Companies.

THINKING AND WRITING AFTER READING

RECALL Self-test your understanding.

Your instructor may choose to give you a true-false comprehension review.

REACT Why do many people no longer put their names on their mailboxes?

_____

_____

REFLECT How do police locate, arrest, and obtain verdicts against con artists?

_____

_____

THINKING CRITICALLY The selection begins by asking how people can be so easily conned. After reading about the different scams, what factors do you think need to be present in order for a successful scam to be accomplished? Write your answer on a separate sheet of paper.

THINK AND WRITE How does the Internet provide a golden land of opportunity for scammers and fraud? _____

_____

DETAILS AND ORGANIZATIONAL PATTERNS

1. What is the purpose of the first paragraph? _____

   _____

2. After the first two paragraphs, what is the overall organizational pattern for

   the selection? _____

3. What is the organizational pattern of the section entitled Three-Card Monte?

   _____

4. The description of the pigeon drop is told in what order? _____

Mark the following as major (*M*) or minor (*m*) details in support of the author's main point.

_____ 5. In the pigeon drop the victim withdraws money from the bank to show good faith.

_____ 6. In the bank examiner scheme, a taxi waits while the victim withdraws money.

_____ 7. In the inheritance scam, the victim is assured of an inheritance.

_____ 8. In the Nigerian oil con, a bill of lading is produced to assure the victim.

Interpret the Quote

Now that you have finished reading the selection, "Confidence Games May Be a Shell Game Scene," go back to the beginning of the selection and read the opening quote again. What does this quote say about con artists? On a separate sheet of paper, list five characteristics of a good con artist and five red flags that should alarm honest people.

Name _____

Date _____

COMPREHENSION QUESTIONS

Answer the following with *a, b, c,* or *d,* or fill in the blank. In order to help you analyze your strengths and weaknesses, the question types are indicated.

Main Idea _____ 1. The best statement of the main idea of the selection is:

    a. confidence artists steal money from unsuspecting victims through a variety of scams.

    b. many victims are too embarrassed to report scams.

    c. in the literature of criminology, confidence scams are the most difficult to believe.

    d. most confidence scams rely on two people to complete the swindle.

Inference   2. The word *confidence* in the phrase *confidence artist* suggests that the "artist's" successful scam requires _____

_____

Detail _____ 3. In the pigeon drop swindle,

    a. two people must show good faith money for the promise of a three-way split.

    b. three people must produce good faith money for a two-way split.

    c. the wallet that is planted contains the victim's money for a three-way split.

    d. the victim withdraws money from a bank account for a three-way split.

Detail _____ 4. In the bank examiner's scheme,

    a. the con artists have bank records showing the victim's deposit amounts.

    b. the victim tries to deposit stolen money but is not successful.

    c. two con artists take the victim to the bank and deposit the victim's money in their account.

    d. the victim thinks that the money will be deposited but it is actually stolen.

Detail _____ 5. In one form of an inheritance scam described in the selection,

    a. the con artist wants to split the inheritance with the victim.

    b. the victim has a relative who has recently died, which prompts a call about an inheritance.

    c. the victim wants the inheritance, and the con artist wants the victim's personal identification information.

    d. the con artist gives the victim a portion of the inheritance prior to getting the identification information.

Detail _____ 6. In the money-making-machine scam example,

    a. the victim's $100 bills are bleached and duplicated.

    b. the victim's $100 bills are needed to press against bleached $1 bills.

    c. the victim delivers $100 bills and receives $1 bills.

    d. the victim delivers $1 bills and is promised $100 bills in return.

Detail _____ 7. In the Nigerian oil con example, all of the following are true *except*
a. shipment of oil actually is being delivered to a port.
b. the victim pays the con artist the total cost for the oil before delivery.
c. the victim responds to an advertisement that suggests profits.
d. the con artist supplies documents to validate the shipment.

Answer the following with *T* (true), *F* (false), or *CT* (can't tell).

Detail _____ 8. In three-card monte, the con artist first allows the victim to win money.

Inference _____ 9. In both the C.O.D. scam and the pigeon drop, the victim is motivated by good intentions rather than greed.

Detail _____ 10. In the pigeon drop, the swindler pretends to find money.

VOCABULARY

Answer the following with *a, b, c,* or *d* for the word or phrase that best defines the boldface word used in the selection. The number in parentheses indicates the line of the passage in which the word appears.

_____ 1. "police **annals**" (1)
a. rumors
b. records
c. conversations
d. anecdotes

_____ 2. "steals by **guile**" (2)
a. memory
b. contracts
c. cunning
d. brainwashing

_____ 3. "human nature and its **frailties**" (3)
a. weaknesses
b. secrets
c. wisdom
d. exceptions

_____ 4. "**monetary** loss" (7)
a. instant
b. financial
c. temporary
d. psychological

_____ 5. "**swindle** is operated" (10)
a. meeting
b. introduction
c. transaction
d. act of cheating

_____ 6. "**sleight of hand**" (19)
a. hidden movement
b. opening
c. repetition
d. return

_____ 7. "**fraudulent** check" (47)
a. large
b. fake
c. unsigned
d. hidden

_____ 8. "**phony** cashier's check" (53)
a. documented
b. fake
c. official
d. convenient

_____ 9. "**affluent** neighborhood" (60)
a. wealthy
b. elderly
c. suburban
d. nearby

_____ 10. "**perishable** package" (62)
a. stolen
b. unexpected
c. signature needed
d. likely to spoil

Your instructor may choose to give a true-false vocabulary review.

VOCABULARY ENRICHMENT

Transitional Words

Transitions are signal words that connect parts of sentences and lead readers to anticipate a continuation or a change in the writer's thoughts. They are the same signal words that suggest patterns of organization and are categorized as follows:

Signal *Addition*: in addition   furthermore   moreover

Signal *Examples*: for example   for instance   to illustrate   such as

Signal *Time*: first   secondly   finally   last   afterward

Signal *Comparison*: similarly   likewise   in the same manner

Signal *Contrast*: however   but   nevertheless   whereas   on the contrary   conversely   in contrast

Signal *Cause and Effect*: thus   consequently   therefore   as a result

Choose a signal word from the following words to complete the sentences:

however	consequently	for example	likewise	furthermore

1. Betty Shabazz, the widow of Malcolm X, recognized the value of a college education; _____, she returned to college to earn a doctorate and became a college teacher and administrator.

2. Anthropologists must be persistent. _____, Louis and Mary Leakey initially found primitive tools in Olduvai Gorge, but it was 28 years later that Mary discovered the first skull.

3. His real name was Samuel Langhorne Clemens; _____, millions know him as Mark Twain.

4. Plant hormones that regulate growth include auxins and gibberellins. _____, humans have important growth hormones.

5. People enjoy eating steaks rare. _____, some people use raw steak to cover an open wound, as did the ancient Egyptians.

nevertheless	therefore	in this case	similarly	moreover

6. Some vitamins act as antioxidants, which means they neutralize free radicals and _____ reduce the risk of cancer.

7. Despite the benefits of antioxidants, new research shows a danger because some minerals in multivitamins cause vitamin C to be released as a free radical.

8. More research on vitamins should be done. _____, doctors should be cautious in recommending vitamins that may not be needed.

9. At least five people were dead from botulism. _____, the poison could be traced to a swollen can of food that should have been discarded.

10. Hornwort is a bryophyta. _____, liverwort is also a bryophyta.

| on the other hand | for this reason | second |
| as an illustration | by the same token | |

11. A cut in the skin breaks the protective covering around the body and _____ can be dangerous.

12. To give CPR, first lift the neck and tilt the chin upward to open the airway. _____, check for breathing by holding your ear to the victim's mouth.

13. Dogs can be conditioned to respond to smell. _____, humans will sometimes salivate when smelling cookies baking.

14. Abnormal pituitary secretions can cause sudden increases in hormone production. Acromegaly, _____, is a condition known as dwarfism.

15. Plants store glucose in starch granules. Animals, _____, store glucose in glycogen molecules.

ASSESS YOUR LEARNING

Review confusing questions, seek clarification, and make notes in your text to help you remember new information and vocabulary.

selection 3 History

A Short History of Medicine
2000 BCE–"Here, eat this root."
1000 BCE–"That root is heathen, say this prayer."
1850 CE–"That prayer is superstition, drink this potion."
1940 CE–"That potion is snake oil, swallow this pill."
1985 CE–"That pill is ineffective, take this antibiotic."
2000 CE–"That antibiotic is artificial. Here, eat this root."

—Author Unknown

Unfortunately, it is likely that you know someone who has firsthand experience with cancer. You may have fought this difficult, yet all too common disease yourself or with someone close to you. According to the American Cancer Society and the Cancer Research Institute, cancer is the second leading cause of death in the United States. Some people mistakenly believe that cancer is a modern disease, but historic records show that it is a health issue that has afflicted people for more than 3,600 years. This article describes historical explanations of cancer. It provides useful information for the general reader and for readers interested in health science careers.

THINKING BEFORE READING

Preview for content and organizational clues. Activate your schema and anticipate what you will learn.

How have people explained the causes of cancer throughout history?

What progress has modern medicine made in understanding cancer?

I think this will say that _____.

VOCABULARY PREVIEW

Are you familiar with these words?

oncology	pathology	osteosarcoma	carcinoma	autopsy
lymph	chronic	trauma	mutations	carcinogens

Is *oncology* the study of cancer?

Is *pathology* the study of diseases?

Are *osteosarcoma* and *carcinoma* types of cancer?

How might an *autopsy* help oncologists and pathologists learn more about cancer?

Your instructor may choose to give a true-false vocabulary review before or after reading.

THINKING DURING READING

As you read, use the six thinking strategies of a good reader: predict, picture, relate, monitor, correct, and annotate.

THE HISTORY OF CANCER

Refer to the **Reader's** *Tip* for **History** on page 165.

Webster's *Encyclopedic Unabridged Dictionary of the English Language* defines cancer as "a malignant and invasive growth or tumor." It can affect nearly any organ or system of the body—bones, blood, skin, brain, breast, colon, etc. For thousands of years, people have struggled to explain this deadly disease. Physicians both ancient and modern have used
5   whatever tools and techniques available to understand its causes so that they could treat it more effectively. Along with advances in medical knowledge, the fields of oncology (study of tumors) and pathology (study of diseases) have grown.

OLDEST DESCRIPTIONS OF CANCER

Some of the earliest evidence of cancer is found among fossilized bone tumors, human mummies in ancient Egypt, and ancient manuscripts. Bone remains of mummies have re-
10   vealed growths suggestive of the bone cancer, osteosarcoma. In other cases, bony skull destruction as seen in cancer of the head and neck has been found.

     Our oldest description of cancer (although the team *cancer* was not used) was discovered in Egypt and dates back to approximately 1600 BCE. The Edwin Smith Papyrus, or writing, describes 8 cases of tumors or ulcers of the breast that were treated by cauteriza-
15   tion, with a tool called "the fire drill." The writing says about the disease, "There is no treatment."

ORIGIN OF THE WORD CANCER

The origin of the word *cancer* is credited to the Greek physician Hippocrates (460–370 BCE), considered the "Father of Medicine." Hippocrates used the terms *carcinos* and *carcinoma* to describe non-ulcer-forming and ulcer-forming tumors. In Greek these words
20   refer to a crab, most likely applied to the disease because the finger-like spreading projections from a cancer called to mind the shape of a crab. Carcinoma is the most common type of cancer.

CHANGING THEORIES OF CANCER CAUSES

From the earliest times, physicians have wondered about the cause of cancer. The Egyptians blamed cancers on the Gods.

25 **Humoral Theory:** Hippocrates believed that the body contained 4 *humors* (body fluids)—blood, phlegm, yellow bile, and black bile. A balance of these fluids resulted in a state of health. Any excesses or deficiencies caused disease. An excess of black bile collecting in various body sites was thought to cause cancer. This theory of cancer was passed on by the Romans and was embraced by the influential doctor Galen's medical
30 teaching, which remained the unchallenged standard through the Middle Ages for over 1300 years. During this period, the study of the body, including autopsies (examining a body after death) was prohibited for religious reasons, thus limiting knowledge.

Lymph Theory: Among theories that replaced the humoral theory of cancer was cancer's formation by another fluid, lymph. Life was believed to consist of continuous and
35 appropriate movement of the fluid parts through solids. Of all the fluids, the most important were blood and lymph. Stahl and Hofman theorized that cancer was composed of fermenting and degenerating lymph varying in density, acidity, and alkalinity. The lymph theory gained rapid support. John Hunter (1723–1792) agreed that tumors grow from lymph constantly thrown out by the blood.

40 **Blastema Theory:** In 1838, German pathologist Johannes Muller demonstrated that cancer is made up of cells and not lymph, but he was of the opinion that cancer cells did not arise from normal cells. Muller proposed that cancer cells arose from budding elements (blastema) between normal tissues. His student, Rudolph Virchow (1821–1902), the famous German pathologist, determined that all cells, including cancer cells, are de-
45 rived from other cells.

Chronic Irritation: Virchow proposed that chronic irritation was the cause of cancer, but he falsely believed that cancers "spread like a liquid." A German surgeon, Karl Thiersch, showed that cancers metastasize through the spread of malignant cells and not through some unidentified fluid.

50 **Trauma:** Despite advances in the understanding of cancer, from the late 1800s until the 1920s, cancer was thought by some to be caused by trauma. This belief was maintained despite the failure to cause cancer in experimental animals by injury.

Parasite Theory: A Nobel Prize was wrongly awarded in 1926 for scientific research documenting stomach cancer being caused by a certain worm. With the inability to con-
55 firm this research, scientists lost interest in the parasite theory.

MODERN DAY CARCINOGENS

More recently, other causes of cancer were discovered and documented. In 1911 Peyton Rous, at the Rockefeller Institute in New York, described a sarcoma in chickens caused by what later became known as the Rous sarcoma virus. He was awarded the Nobel Prize for that work in 1968. In 1915 cancer was induced in laboratory animals for the first time by
60 a chemical, coal tar, applied to rabbit skin at Tokyo University. One hundred and fifty years had passed since the most destructive source of chemical carcinogens known to man, tobacco, was first identified in London by the astute clinician John Hill. It was to be many years until tobacco was "rediscovered" as a carcinogen.

Today we recognize and avoid many specific substances that cause cancer: coal tars
65 and their derivatives such as benzene, some hydrocarbons, aniline (a substance used to make dyes), asbestos, and others. Radiation from a variety of sources, including the sun, is known to lead to cancer. To ensure the public's safety, the government has set occupational standards for many substances, such as benzene, asbestos, hydrocarbons in the air, arsenic in drinking water, radiation, and so on.

70   Several viruses are now linked to cancer:

- Long-standing liver infection with the hepatitis virus can lead to cancer of the liver.

- A variety of the herpes virus, the Epstein-Barr virus, causes infectious mononucleosis and has been implicated in non-Hodgkin's lymphomas and nasopharyngeal cancer.

- The human immunodeficiency virus (HIV) is associated with an increased risk of devel-
75   oping several cancers, especially Kaposi's Sarcoma and non-Hodgkin's lymphoma.

- Human papilloma viruses (HPVs) have been linked to cancers of the cervix, vulva, and penis.

Many of these associations were recognized long before scientists understood the mechanism by which the cancer was produced.

TWENTIETH-CENTURY UNDERSTANDING OF CANCER

80   By the middle of the 20th century, scientists had in their hands the instruments needed to begin solving the complex problems of chemistry and biology presented by cancer. James Watson and Francis Crick, who received the Nobel Prize for their work, had discovered the exact chemical structure of DNA, the basic material in genes.

DNA was found to be the basis of the genetic code that gives orders to all cells. After
85   learning how to translate this code, scientists were able to understand how genes worked and how they could be damaged by mutations (changes or mistakes in genes). These modern techniques of chemistry and biology answered many complex questions about cancer.

Scientists already knew that cancer could be caused by chemicals, radiation, and
90   viruses, and that sometimes cancer seemed to run in families. But, as our understanding of DNA and genes increased, we learned that it was the damage to DNA by chemicals and radiation or introduction of new DNA sequences by viruses that often led to the development of cancer. It became possible to pinpoint the exact site of the damage to a specific gene.

95   Further, scientists discovered that sometimes defective genes are inherited and that sometimes these inherited genes are defective at the same points that chemicals exerted their effect. In other words, most carcinogens caused genetic damage (mutations), mutations led to abnormal groups of cells (called clones), mutant clones evolved to even more malignant clones over time, and the cancer progressed by more and more genetic dam-
100 age and mutations. Normal cells with damaged DNA die; cancer cells with damaged DNA do not. The recent discovery of this critical difference answers many questions that have troubled scientists for many years.

Slowly, medical scientists are identifying genes that are damaged by chemicals or radiation and the genes that, when inherited, can lead to cancer. The recent discovery of
105 two genes that cause some breast cancers, BRCA1 and BRCA2, represents considerable promise because many people who have a higher probability of developing breast cancer can now be identified.

Other genes have been discovered that are associated with some cancers that run in families, such as cancers of the colon, rectum, kidney, ovary, esophagus, lymph nodes,
110 and pancreas and skin melanoma. Familial cancer is not nearly as common as spontaneous cancer, causing less than 15% of all cancers, but it is important to understand these cancers because with continued research in genetics we may be able to identify persons at very high risk.

SUMMARY

The growth in our knowledge of cancer biology and cancer treatment and prevention
115 has been staggering in recent years. Oncologists, pathologists and other scientists have learned more about cancer in the last decade of the 20th century than has been learned

in all the centuries preceding. This does not change the fact, however, that all scientific knowledge is based on the knowledge already acquired by the hard work and discovery of our predecessors.

(1,473 words)

—Adapted and reprinted by the permission of the American Cancer Society, Inc. from www.cancer.org. All rights reserved.

THINKING AND WRITING AFTER READING

RECALL   Self-test your understanding.

Your instructor may choose to give you a true-false comprehension review.

REACT   How does greater knowledge of cancer's history influence your understanding of the disease today? _____

REFLECT   How does current understanding of the causes of the disease affect treatment methods? _____

_____

THINKING CRITICALLY   The article mentions that in the Middle Ages medical science was restricted because of religious objections to autopsies. In what ways do religious beliefs affect medical research today? Write your answer on a separate sheet of paper.

THINK AND WRITE   Name two examples and explain how the invention of new equipment or technology affected advances in medical knowledge. _____

_____

_____

DETAILS AND ORGANIZATIONAL PATTERNS

1. What is the purpose of the first section? _____

_____

2. What two patterns of organization are used throughout this selection?

_____

3. Which pattern best reflects the main point of this selection? (Hint: Consider the title when you answer.) _____

4. What pattern is used in paragraph 1? _____

Mark the following as major (M) or minor (m) details in support of the author's main point.

_____ 5. The humoral theory, which lasted for more than 1300 years, explained cancer as stemming from an imbalance in bodily fluids.

_____ 6. The government has set occupational standards on certain cancer-causing substances to ensure public safety.

_____ 7. More recent discoveries connect some cancers to viruses.

_____ 8. Twentieth-century scientists have shown cancer to be linked to genetic mutations in DNA.

Interpret the Quote

Now that you have finished reading the selection, "The History of Cancer," go back to the beginning of the selection and read the opening quote again. What does the quote imply about advances in medical science? Do you agree with the author of the quote? Explain. It may be helpful to begin with a list of ways in which the quote is accurate and ways in which it is inaccurate. Write your responses on a separate sheet of paper.

Name _____

Date _____

COMPREHENSION QUESTIONS

Answer the following with *a, b, c,* or *d,* or fill in the blank. In order to help you analyze your strengths and weaknesses, the question types are indicated.

Main Idea ———— 1. The best statement of the main idea of this selection is:
   a. People once thought that cancer was caused by traumatic injuries.
   b. Scientists today know that cancer can be caused by viruses and by genetic mutations.
   c. Cancer can affect almost any part of the body.
   d. Understanding of cancer has changed with scientific advances throughout history.

Detail ———— 2. The theory that dominated for more than 1300 years was the
   a. Humoral Theory
   b. Lymph Theory
   c. Chronic Irritation Theory
   d. Parasite Theory

Detail ———— 3. According to the article, _____ is the most common type of cancer.
   a. breast cancer
   b. colon cancer
   c. carcinoma
   d. osteosarcoma

Inference ———— 4. The details in the article suggest that
   a. medical science has made significant progress in determining the causes of cancer.
   b. despite apparent advances we know little more today than we did centuries ago.
   c. the Lymph Theory is still accepted today.
   d. the Egyptians considered breast cancer untreatable.

Main Idea ———— 5. The main point of the section under the heading "Twentieth-Century Understanding of Cancer" is
   a. new instruments made further advances in medical science possible.
   b. the discovery of DNA led to the knowledge that genetic mutations are a critical cause of cancer.
   c. scientists discovered that viruses are the cause of some cancers.
   d. colon cancer has been linked with specific genes that run in families.

Detail ———— 6. _____ is considered the "Father or Medicine."
   a. Virchow
   b. Johannes Muller
   c. James Watson
   d. Hippocrates

selection 3

Inference _____ 7. We can infer from the selection that
 a. genetic research has little affect on curing cancer.
 b. further discovery of genes associated with cancer will enable doctors to better treat patients with a family history of certain cancers.
 c. before the discovery of DNA, scientists did not consider family history as a factor in cancer.
 d. radiation is less damaging to genes than chemicals.

Answer the following with *T* (true), *F* (false), or *CT* (can't tell).

Inference _____ 8. The ancient Egyptians had little scientific knowledge of cancer.

Detail _____ 9. According to the article, tobacco is the most destructive known source of chemical carcinogens.

Detail _____ 10. It is only in that last 50 years that tobacco has been linked to cancer.

VOCABULARY

Answer the following with *a, b, c,* or *d* for the word or phrase that best defines the boldface word used in the selection. The number in parentheses indicates the line of the passage in which the word appears. In addition to the context clues, use a dictionary to more precisely define the technical terms.

_____ 1. "the fields of **oncology**" (6)
 a. research in history
 b. scientific research
 c. study of tumors
 d. study of disease

_____ 2. "the field of **pathology**" (7)
 a. research in medicine
 b. scientific research
 c. cancer research
 d. study of diseases

_____ 3. "suggestive of **osteosarcoma**" (10)
 a. breast cancer
 b. brain cancer
 c. bone cancer
 d. blood cancer

_____ 4. "Hippocrates used **carcinoma** to" (19)
 a. a bone disease
 b. a disease spread by contact with crabs
 c. a condition common to ancient Egyptians
 d. non-ulcer and ulcer-forming tumors

_____ 5. "including **autopsies**" (31)
 a. laboratory tests
 b. examinations of a crime scene
 c. methods used often in the Middle Ages
 d. examinations of bodies after death

_____ 6. "**Lymph** Theory" (33)
 a. a body fluid that is discharged into the blood
 b. blood
 c. a type of tumor
 d. another word for "cancer"

_____ 7. "**chronic** irritation" (46)
 a. painful
 b. occurring often
 c. pleasant
 d. spreading

_____ 8. "caused by **trauma**" (51)
 a. poor eating habits
 b. injury to living tissue
 c. smoking
 d. lack of exercise

_____ 9. "of chemical **carcinogens**" (61)
   a. cures
   b. explanations
   c. cancer-causing agents
   d. reports

_____10. "damaged by **mutations**" (86)
   a. radiation
   b. injuries
   c. chemicals
   d. changes in genes

Your instructor may choose to give a true-false vocabulary review.

VOCABULARY ENRICHMENT

A. Study the similar-sounding words, then circle the one that is correct in each sentence.

alter: change	**coarse:** not smooth	**dual:** two
altar: platform in church	**course:** studies or path	**duel:** fight

   1. You must (**alter, altar**) your study habits to make better grades.

   2. To change a (**coarse, course**), you must go through a drop-add procedure.

   3. The two senators fought a (**dual, duel**) at dawn.

B. Use context clues to mark _a, b, c,_ or _d_ for for the meaning closest to that of the boldface word.

   _____ 4. From listening to her talk about the trip, I got **vicarious** pleasure and felt as if I had been there.
      a. selfish
      b. enormous
      c. secret
      d. secondhand

   _____ 5. The **cardiac** patient was waiting in surgery for a bypass operation.
      a. rested
      b. cancer
      c. emotion
      d. heart

   _____ 6. Because of his **phobia**, he did not want to climb to the top of the tower and look down.
      a. rash
      b. fear
      c. disease
      d. mood

C. Use the indicated root to write words to complete each sentence in the groups.
vis, vid: see

   7. When she plays tennis, she wears a _____ to keep the sun out of her eyes.

   8. From the description you have given me, I cannot _____ the actor's face.

9. The rip was so well-mended that the hole is now _____.

tin, ten, tent: hold, hold together

10. We cannot _____ the trip without stopping for gas.

11. The _____ crew cleans the floors at night when no one is in the building.

12. She has been _____ at her present job for a long time and is thus seeking other employment.

clud, clus: shut

13. She gradually became a _____ by staying in the house and not receiving visitors.

14. To _____ the interview, the manager stood up and shook her hand.

15. A correct address should _____ the zip code.

ASSESS YOUR LEARNING

Review confusing questions, seek clarification, and make notes in your text to help you remember new information and vocabulary.

Personal *Feedback* 2

Name _____

1. Approximately how much time do you spend each day studying for this class?

   _____

   _____

2. Where do you typically study? _____

   _____

3. How do you manage telephone calls during your scheduled study time?

   _____

4. Describe a time this week when you have procrastinated.

   _____

5. What were the consequences of your procrastination?

   _____

   Tear out and submit to your instructor.

selection **3**

Vocabulary Lesson

One Too Many

Study the prefixes, words, and sentences.

Prefixes	*mono, mon*: one	*bi, bin, bis*: two	*poly*: many

Words with *mono* or *mon* = *one*

Can a <u>monomaniac</u> be addicted to the Internet? Can a <u>monotone</u> put you to sleep?

- Monarchy: a government with only one ruler

  The power of the English *monarchy* has changed since the time of Elizabeth I.

- Monocle: an eyeglass for only one eye

  An 1800s *monocle* was more difficult to wear than the eyeglasses of today.

- Monogamy: marriage to one person only

  In the United States, *monogamy* is the legally accepted form of marriage.

- Monologue: a discourse by one person

  Jay Leno starts his late night show with a humorous *monologue*.

- Monochromatic: only one color

  A home decorated in beige has a *monochromatic* color scheme.

- Monotony: sameness

  Talking to customers breaks the *monotony* of working as a cashier.

Words with *bi, bin,* or *bis* = *two*

With cheap concert seats, carry <u>binoculars</u>. Are <u>biweekly</u> meetings every two weeks?

- Bimonthly: occurs every two months

  Regular *bimonthly* reports are required six times each year.

- Bifocal: having two lenses

  Initial use of *bifocal* lenses can be a difficult adjustment.

- Bigamy: marrying one person while already married to another

  Bigamy is illegal in the United States.

- Bilingual: using two languages

  In the United States most *bilingual* speakers know Spanish as well as English.

- Bipartisan: representing two parties

  A *bipartisan* committee would include both Democrats and Republicans.

- Biennial: something that occurs at two-year intervals or lasts two years

  Rather than every year, the class decided to have *biennial* reunions.

Words with *poly = many*

Can a <u>polytechnic</u> institute offer classes? Does the city have <u>polyethnic</u> districts?

- Polygon: closed figure with many angles

  A square is a *polygon* with four equal sides.

- Polyglot: a linguist who knows many languages

  Having lived abroad extensively, the student returned home a *polyglot*.

- Polygamy: custom of having more than one spouse at the same time.

  In cultures with *polygamy*, the additional wives function as servants.

- Polyandry: custom of having more than one husband at the same time.

  Polyandry is the exclusively female version of polygamy.

- Polychromatic: having many colors

  The *polychromatic* fabric emphasized reds and blues on a yellow background.

- Polydactyl: having more than the normal number of fingers or toes.

  The *polydactyl* abnormality was evident in three family members.

- Polymorphic: having many forms

  A *polymorphic* cartoon character can change from a cat to a tiger.

Review

Part I

Answer the following with (*T*) true or (*F*) false.

_____ 1. A polyglot is more than bilingual.

_____ 2. Two people talk to each other in a monologue.

_____ 3. A black piano has a monochromatic surface.

_____ 4. Bimonthly meetings occur twice each month.

_____ 5. Bipartisan politics suggests two parties willing to negotiate.

_____ 6. The biennial reports were due every January and July.

_____ 7. If white is a color, the U.S. flag is polychromatic.

_____ 8. An exclusively Italian area constitutes a polyethnic neighborhood.

_____ 9. Exciting people tend to enjoy monotony.

_____ 10. Bifocal lenses contain two separate eyeglass prescriptions.

Part II

Choose the best word from the list to fit the following descriptions.

monarch	monocle	monogamy	bilingual	polymorphic
bigamy	monotone	polyandry	polygon	polydactyl

11. More than ten toes _____

12. One tone of voice _____

13. Having two wives _____

14. Having two or more husbands _____

15. One eyeglass _____

16. Many forms _____

17. Speaking two languages _____

18. A queen _____

19. One spouse _____

20. A rectangle _____

Selecting Magazines

Visit the magazine section of a large local bookstore, and you will see specialty magazines on an amazing array of topics, from decorating to alternative medicine to scuba diving. Browse through the magazines to make your purchase choices. Publishers know that covers sell magazines, so check out the contents before spending your money.

News Magazines

News magazines are similar to newspapers in that they cover current events and areas of special interest, such as business, science and technology, and the arts. Because they are usually published weekly, they cannot cover breaking stories with the same immediacy as newspapers and television. What they can offer, however, is more detail and an analysis of events.

There are three main news magazines in the United States: *Time, Newsweek,* and *U.S. News & World Report*. They all contain the following elements:

News Stories. News magazine stories present the same 5 W's and H as newspapers do, but they include more details, use more colorful and dramatic language, and add amusing or touching anecdotes.

Feature Stories. The feature story for the week is usually displayed prominently on the cover to attract your attention. Most features include background information so you can understand how the current situation came to be. Colorful pictures, graphs, and survey results enrich the stories.

Editorials. The topics of these opinion essays in news magazines appeal to a broader national readership than those found in most newspapers. Rather than be isolated on a particular page, the editorials often appear beside the related stories.

Essays. News magazines also include essays that can either cover very serious matters or be whimsical and humorous. These pieces can be written by professional journalists, politicians, or readers—anyone who has an opinion or experience they want to share.

Critiques. News magazines include critiques or reviews of new movies, plays, music CDs, and books that summarize the work, state the critic's opinion, and predict the impact of the work.

exercise 1 Review current copies of *Time, Newsweek, People,* and *U.S. News & World Report* in your college library to answer the following questions.

1. Which magazine would you prefer to subscribe to and why?

2. What is the feature story in each, and why is each noteworthy?

3. Is *People* a news magazine? How would you categorize the stories in *People*?

Specialty Magazines

Specialty magazines cover almost every imaginable subject: fashion, business, technology, decorating, hobbies, health, and entertainment. Within these many categories, such publications can be very precise in their focus—not any type of guitar, but acoustic guitars. Although much of the content and terminology (jargon) may be difficult to follow for a new reader, there are usually columns and articles devoted to beginners.

Feature Articles. Feature articles are highlighted on the cover and in the table of contents. If you don't find the catchy summaries to be interesting, the articles probably won't be, either. Sometimes, rather than one feature story, a featured theme is addressed throughout an entire issue.

Letters to the Editor. If you are unfamiliar with a particular magazine, read the Letters to the Editor section. These letters, sent in by readers, will refer to past stories and can give you an idea of the audience to which the magazine appeals.

Brief News Updates. Most magazines begin with short summaries that are comparable to headline news updates on television and radio. No more than a paragraph or two in length, these updates cover news in the field on upcoming events, research findings, celebrity news, products, and trends.

Regular Columns. Columns appear regularly in magazines and are usually written by the same columnists each time, although guest writers can contribute as well. The columns are editorials about a current issue, event, or person in the magazine's field of interest, and reflect the writer's own biases.

Advertisements. Magazines make most of their revenue through selling advertising pages. Be aware that an advertisement for a particular product does not imply an endorsement of that product by the magazine. Conflicts of interest can arise between the editorial content of a magazine and its major advertisers. If a major advertiser's products and services always receive overwhelmingly positive reviews, take extra care to decide for yourself whether the findings are warranted based on the material presented. With some magazines, particularly fashion magazines, ask yourself if the publication is more interested in informing its readers or in maintaining advertising dollars.

Reader's *Tip* Choosing a Magazine

- Read the lead article headlines and the table of contents to find articles of interest to you.
- Flip through the magazine and read article titles and boxed article excerpts.
- Read several Letters to the Editor.
- Decide, purchase, and enjoy!

exercise 2 Select four specialty magazines that you would like to subscribe to if money were not an issue. For each magazine list the following:

1. Evaluate the quality of the feature articles.

2. Estimate the ratio or percentage of news and feature stories to advertisements.

3. Which regular articles particularly appeal to you?

Reading Casebook

What Is Beauty?

What is beauty? Are attractive people treated better than unattractive people? To what lengths will one go to achieve beauty? Who sets the standards for beauty? The answers to these questions depend on whom you ask and how that particular person views beauty.

It is safe to say that we all have different opinions about what makes someone beautiful. Many of these opinions are shaped by the images we see on TV, in fashion magazines, and on billboards. Our culture also defines how we perceive beauty. In the United States, for example, beauty and thinness often go hand in hand. Thinness isn't prized in all cultures, however. In some African cultures, for example, a person who carries extra weight is seen as beautiful and prosperous. Whatever your opinion of beauty is, use the three selections in this casebook to think critically about popular perceptions of beauty and to challenge your own perceptions of beauty. Begin by taking a personal inventory of your present perspectives.

Beauty Inventory 1

Answer the following questions on a separate sheet of paper:

1. What do you think makes someone or something beautiful?

2. What do you think makes someone unattractive?

3. Do you think you are attractive? Why or why not? If you think you are unattractive, what do you think would make you attractive?

4. How do images in the media shape your perceptions of beauty?

5. Do you think plastic surgery is a wise option to correct a physical flaw?

6. Do you think attractive people are treated better than unattractive people? Why or why not?

7. Whom do you think advertisers should employ to reflect beauty—supermodels or everyday people? Why?

8. Would you enter into a friendship or romantic relationship with someone solely because that person is attractive? Why or why not?

9. Do you treat attractive and unattractive people differently? Why or why not?

10. Do you think our society places too much emphasis on beauty?

Think Critically About Beauty: Which of the quotes below best reflects your views on physical beauty? On a separate sheet of paper, explain why you picked that quote to describe your views on beauty.

Beauty is not in the face; beauty is a light in the heart.

KAHLIL GIBRAN

Beauty is how you feel inside, and it reflects in your eyes. It is not something physical.

SOPHIA LOREN

Beauty comes in all sizes—not just size 5.

ROSEANNE

Always remember that true beauty comes from within—from within bottles, jars, compacts, and tubes.

PETER'S ALMANAC

It's beauty that captures your attention; personality which captures your heart.

ANONYMOUS

I'm in the public eye, so I don't care who knows what I get done. If I see something sagging, dragging, or bagging, I get it sucked, tucked, or plucked.

DOLLY PARTON

selection 1 Letters of Opinion

Are attractive people treated better than unattractive people? Research suggests that the answer to this question is yes. Studies show, for example, that attractive students get more attention and higher evaluations from their teachers, good-looking patients get more personalized care from their doctors, and handsome criminals receive lighter sentences than less attractive criminals. In business, research shows that plain people earn 5 to 10 percent less than people of average looks, who in turn earn 3 to 8 percent less than those deemed good-looking. What is most disturbing about these studies is that even parents treat attractive children better than unattractive children.

> ## Reader's *Tip* Reading and Studying Letters of Opinion
>
> Ask yourself the following questions as you read editorials or letters of opinion:
>
> - What event prompted the letter?
> - What is the thesis or opinion being promoted by the author?
> - Do the details prove the opinion?
> - What is left out?
> - Are the sources, facts, and other support credible?

ALL THAT GLITTERS* IS GOLD

I went out once with a guy who didn't care for his mother, partly because he felt she was not attractive enough. My brother Martin, on the other hand, tells our mom how proud he was when she picked him up from grade school because he thought she was the prettiest mother.

5   And we've seen those studies showing that aesthetics is hard-wired in the brain—that even babies have an innate sense of beauty, choosing to gaze longer at lovelier faces.

So it shouldn't be surprising to learn parents have the same bias. Still, the headline yesterday in *Science Times* was jolting: "Ugly Children May Get Parental Short Shrift." As Nicholas Bakalar wrote: "Canadian researchers have made a startling assertion: parents
10   take better care of pretty children than they do ugly ones."

Researchers at the University of Alberta observed that at the supermarket, less adorable tykes were more often allowed to engage in potentially dangerous activities—like standing up in the shopping cart or wandering off. Good-looking children, especially boys, got more attention from their parents and were kept closer at hand.

15   "When it came to buckling up, pretty and ugly children were treated in starkly different ways, with seat belt use increasing in direct proportion to attractiveness," the article said. "When a woman was in charge, 4 percent of the homeliest children were strapped in, compared with 13.3 percent of the most attractive children." With fathers, it was even worse, "with none of the least attractive children secured with seat belts, while
20   12.5 percent of the prettiest children were."

Haven't these parents heard of the ugly duckling? Do they read to pretty kids only about pretty ducklings?

Even if you're skeptical about supermarket science, the story conjures up poignant images of Pugsley-looking rugrats toddling off, or flying through the air and crashing into
25   the rotisserie chicken oven because they're not belted in.

*The word "glisters" in Ms. Dowd's original piece has been changed to "glitters."

Dr. Andrew Harrel, the research team's leader, put the findings in evolutionary terms: pretty children represent a premium genetic legacy, so they get top care. "Like lots of animals," he said, "we tend to parcel out our resources on the basis of value."

As Marilyn Monroe explained in "Gentlemen Prefer Blondes": "Don't you know that a man being rich is like a girl being pretty? You wouldn't marry a girl just because she's pretty, but my goodness, doesn't it help?"

A beauty bias against children seems so startling because you grow up thinking parents are the only ones who will give you unconditional love, not measure it out in coffee spoons based on your genetic luck—which, after all, they're responsible for.

But the world can be harsh. Surface matters more and more, and the world ignores Shakespeare's lesson from "The Merchant of Venice": "Gilded tombs do worms infold."

An analysis published last month by the Federal Reserve Bank of St. Louis suggests that the good-looking get more money and promotions than average-looking schmoes.

Quoting the economists Daniel Hamermesh and Jeff Biddle, the study notes that being tall, slender and attractive could be worth a "beauty premium"—an extra 5 percent an hour—while there is a "plainness penalty" of 9 percent in wages (after factoring out other issues).

Researchers report that taller men are more likely to win in business and—except for the hapless Al Gore and John Kerry—get elected president. Correlating 16-year-olds' height with their later salaries shows beanstalks grow up to earn about $789 more a year for each extra inch of height.

In his best seller "Blink," Malcolm Gladwell did a survey of half the Fortune 500 C.E.O.'s, and found that (Jack Welch notwithstanding—or notwithsitting) the average C.E.O., at 6 feet, is about 3 inches taller than the average American man.

As Randy Newman sang, "short people got no reason to live."

Research also shows that obese women get 17 percent lower wages than women of average weight and that dishy professors get better evaluations from their students.

There can be too much of a good thing. As Dan Ondrack, a professor at the University of Toronto, told *The Toronto Star*, there's a "Boopsey" effect—if women are too gorgeous, people assume they are airheads.

No one seems sure whether bosses discriminate against people because they're less attractive, or whether more attractive people develop more self-esteem and social finesse.

But one thing's for sure: it's hard to develop self-esteem when you're hurtling out of the supermarket cart toward the rotisserie oven.

—Maureen Dowd, "All That Glisters Is Gold," from *The New York Times*, May 4, 2005.

COMPREHENSION QUESTIONS

Answer the following questions with true (*T*) or false (*F*) or write a response.

_____ 1. Studies indicate that even babies have an inborn sense of beauty.

_____ 2. According to the article, pretty and ugly children were treated differently.

_____ 3. The selection reports that there seem to be more benefits to beauty and few negatives.

_____ 4. A correlation between height (at least for men) and income has been established by researchers.

_____ 5. The main purpose of this article is to explain the advantages experienced as a byproduct of being beautiful.

6. Are you familiar with the saying on which the author bases her title? (*All That Glitters Is Not Gold*) How would you interpret those words? _____

   _____

   _____

   _____

   _____

   _____

7. What evidence is presented that offers some proof that a lack of good looks may put children at a disadvantage? _____

   _____

   _____

   _____

   _____

8. How does the story of the ugly duckling relate to this passage? _____

   _____

   _____

   _____

   _____

   _____

9. What sort of an analogy is given in the Marilyn Monroe film quotation— *Don't you know that a man being rich is like a girl being pretty? You wouldn't marry a girl just because she's pretty, but my goodness, doesn't it help?* Is she equating beauty to wealth? Do you agree? _____

   _____

_____

_____

_____

10. How is the concept of beauty taken beyond the "pretty face" level in this pas-

sage? _____

THINKING AND WRITING AFTER READING

REACT What does the author mean by her final words: *It's hard to develop self-esteem when you're hurtling out of the supermarket cart toward the rotisserie oven?*

Do you agree? _____

_____

_____

REFLECT Is there a standard version of *beauty*? Do you think that most of us perceive the same sorts of things and people to be beautiful? _____

_____

THINK AND WRITE Can you think of some real-life examples of the ugly duckling/swan story? These examples might come from people you know or those you might have seen on television. Discuss how these people changed. Write your answer on a separate sheet of paper.

COMPARE This passage lists several ways in which beauty leads to good things for people with good looks. Can you think of any positives that might come

from a person being perceived as less than beautiful? _____

_____

_____

DEFINE Imagine that you are writing a dictionary entry for the word, *beauty*. What would you say? Would you include more than one definition? Write your

entry below. _____

_____

---

selection 2   Newspaper Feature Article

Being attractive to the opposite sex is important for the survival of most species. The colorful feathers and dramatic courtship dances of certain birds, for instance, are designed to attract the attention of a potential mate. Birds, however, don't usually endanger their health to entice a suitor. To what extremes do people go to make themselves attractive to the opposite sex? The answer depends largely on what their culture considers beautiful. In the United States, a slim, firm body is highly valued. In the western African country of Mauritania, however, the female ideal is quite different.

Reader's *Tip* Reading and Studying a News or Feature Article

- Preview the headline and photographs.
- Find the facts: *who, what, when, were, why* and *how.*
- Consider how the angle or focus of a feature story differs from a straight news story.
- Evaluate the credibility of the sources cited.
- When reading a feature story, observe the number of facts compared with the number of opinions.
- Look for the bias or judgment on the part of the reporter.

For more suggestions on reading news and feature articles in the newspaper, refer to the Everyday Reading skills on page 76.

IN MAURITANIA, SEEKING TO END AN OVERFED IDEAL

At the Olympics Sports Stadium here, a collection of dun-colored buildings rising mirage-like from the vast Sahara, about a dozen women clad in tennis shoes and sandals circled the grandstands one evening in late June, puffing with each step.

Between pants came brief explanations for their labors. "Because I am fat," said one,
5   a dark-eyed 34-year-old close to 200 pounds. Another, a 30-year-old in bright pink sneakers, said, "For myself, for my health and to be skinny." It is a typically Western after-work scene. But this is the Islamic Republic of Mauritania, the mirror opposite of the West on questions of women's weight. To men here, fat is sexy. And in this patriarchal region, many Mauritanian women do everything possible—and have everything possible done to
10   them—to put on pounds.

Now Mauritania's government is out to change that. In recent years, television commercials and official pronouncements have promoted a new message: being fat leads to diabetes, heart problems, high blood pressure and other woes. The joggers outside the Olympic stadium testify to their impact: Until lately, a Mauritanian woman in jogging
15   shoes was roughly as common as a camel in stiletto heels.

But in other respects, the message faces an uphill run. A 2001 government survey of 68,000 women found that one in five between ages 15 and 49 had been deliberately overfed. And nearly 70 percent—and even more among teenagers—said they did not regret it.
20   "That is a bad sign, especially among the younger generation," said Maye Mint Haidy, a government statistician who also runs a nongovernmental women's organization.

Other cultures prize corpulent women. But Mauritania may be unique in the lengths it has gone to achieve its vision of female beauty. For decades, the Mauritanian version of a Western teenager's crash diet was a crash feeding program, devised to cre-
25   ate girls obese enough to display family wealth and epitomize the Mauritanian ideal. Centuries-old poems glorified women immobilized by fat, moving so slowly they seemed to stand still, unable to hoist themselves onto camels without the aid of men's willing hands.

Girls as young as a 5 and as old as 19 had to drink up to five gallons of fat-rich
30   camel's or cow's milk daily, aiming for silvery stretch marks on their upper arms. If a girl refused or vomited, the village weight-gain specialist might squeeze her foot between sticks, pull her ear, pinch her inner thigh, bend her finger backward or force her to drink her own vomit. In extreme cases, girls died.

35 The practice was known as gavage, a French term for force-feeding geese to obtain foie gras. "There isn't a woman close to my age who hasn't gone through this, maybe not with the torture, but with the milk and other things," said Yenserha Mint Mohamed Mahmoud, 47, a top government women's affairs official.

Ms. Mahmoud insists that the use of torture has died out, though some say it lingers in remote areas. Still, Mauritania remains saddled with an alarming number of women 40 weighing 220 to 330 pounds, according to the Ministry for the Promotion of Women, Family and Children.

The same 2001 survey that documented overfeeding estimated that two in five women were overweight—not high by American standards, where government surveys show nearly three in five women are overweight—but remarkable for sub-Saharan Africa. 45 According to the International Obesity Task Force, a London-based research and advocacy group, Mauritania has the region's fourth highest percentage of overweight women. Government officials blame a concerted effort by all but the poorest families to pump girls full of milk, cream, butter, couscous and other calorie-rich foods.

In 2003, the women's ministry mounted a slim-down campaign, wielding messages 50 that were anything but subtle. One television and radio skit depicted a husband carting his fat wife around in a wheelbarrow. Another featured houseguests raiding the refrigerator because their host was too obese to get up to feed them. Doctors were recruited to explain health risks.

But messages spread slowly in the desert. Nearly three-fourths of Mauritanian 55 women do not watch television, and an even greater share do not listen to the radio, said Ms. Haidy, the statistician.

Nor is it easy, Ms. Mahmoud said, to change how the sexes view each other. "Men want women to be fat, and so they are fat," she said. "Women want men to be skinny, and so they are skinny." Indeed, according to Mauritanian stereotypes, porky men are 60 womanish and lazy.

Mohamed el-Moktar Ould Salem, a 52-year-old procurement officer, blames the brightly colored, head-to-toe mulafas that hide all but the most voluptuous female curves for shaping the men's preferences. A slender woman, he said, "just looks like a stick wrapped up."

65 Fatma Mint Mohamed, 35, a mother of five living in a village south of Nouakchott, the capital, agrees. She carries nearly 200 pounds on her five-foot frame. Her weight makes her husband "very happy, of course," she said, although her slimmer sister, 45 minutes away in the city, warns that it could kill her.

Mrs. Mohamed said she endured a comparatively mild form of gavage—"just 70 enough so our family did not get criticized or be thought of as poor"—and was proud to emerge with a praiseworthy, roly-poly figure. Her 9-year-old daughter, Selma, with curly dark hair, wide-set eyes and what her mother considers a distressingly slim figure, has so far escaped the treatment, in hopes that she will gain weight on her own.

Selma's sisters, now 20 and 14, were less fortunate. Mrs. Mohamed said she spared 75 them the "old-fashioned" techniques that made girls she grew up with scream in pain. "But to tell the truth, I did take them to the cows and made them overdrink," she acknowledged. "I did overfeed them, just a little bit, just so they could look like real Mauritanian girls. Forty days was enough to get them in the shape I wanted."

Other Mauritanian women have replaced gavage with thoroughly modern prescrip-80 tion drug abuse. At the capital's open-air market in late June last week, a male buyer easily secured a gold box of Indian-made dexamethasone tablets, a prescription steroid hormone that can cause sharp weight gain.

The black-turbaned seller, his wares displayed openly on a plastic sheet, warned that the drug was dangerous. But it would fatten up the man's wife fast, he promised.

85 Nouredine Françis, a pharmacist, refuses to sell that drug. But he said he could not keep a particular prescription antihistamine on his shelves because women had heard it made them drowsy, thus less active and more likely to add pounds.

He considers himself one of the few Mauritanian men who understand obesity's dangers. "Every day I see a woman come in here who has suffered from a stroke," he said. He
90 said he was trying to lose weight and did not push his wife to get fatter.

But his wife, an already-Rubenesque beauty-parlor worker, needs no pushing, he
said. "She says, 'Why don't you bring me any pills? You give them to other women but
you won't give them to me.'"

"Women are very sensitive about their weight," he said. "She just wants to keep up a
95 good image."

COMPREHENSION QUESTIONS

Answer the following questions with true (*T*) or false (*F*) or write a response.

_____ 1. The comments of the women at the Olympic Sports Stadium support the traditional ideal of female beauty.

_____ 2. Concern for women's health is the reason that the Mauritanian government is attempting to change the tradition of "gavage."

_____ 3. The author implies that Mauritania is alone in its belief that fat
women are more beautiful.

_____ 4. According to the statistics given in the article, a greater percentage
of Mauritanian women are overweight than American women.

_____ 5. Details in the article suggest that one reason fat women are preferred is to show that their families are wealthy enough to pay for
plenty of food.

6. What does the phrase "a Mauritanian woman in jogging shoes was roughly
as common as a camel in stiletto heels" mean? _____
_____

7. Why would teenage girls be less likely to object to overfeeding than older women? _____

_____

_____

8. Why is this a "bad sign," as the article comments? _____

_____

_____

9. What do Mauritanians consider the ideal for men? _____

_____

10. What modern methods of increasing weight have begun to replace the traditional methods? _____

_____

_____

THINKING AND WRITING AFTER READING

REACT Describe your first reaction to this article. _____

_____

_____

REFLECT List the statistics and comparisons of obesity in Mauritanian, sub-Saharan region, and American women. Which area has the greater percentage of obesity? _____

_____

_____

THINK AND WRITE Would you consider doing something so extreme to achieve a beautiful body? Make a list of the things Americans or people in your culture do to beautify themselves. What would you do to make yourself more attractive? Write your answers on a separate sheet of paper.

COMPARE In what ways are the traditional Mauritanian practices described in the article different or similar to what Americans do to achieve their idea of physical beauty? _____

_____

_____

DEFINE The article suggests that Mauritanian women gain weight to please men. Why might a culture evolve so that men define female beauty in this way? What purpose is served by valuing obesity in women? _____

_____

_____

---

selection 3 Business

For years, advertising firms have used impossibly thin supermodels in campaigns to sell everything from cars to cosmetics. Recently, however, some advertising firms are showcasing a more realistic version of beauty by using real women—with bodies that truly reflect what average women look like—to sell a variety of products. Whether or not this trend toward "real beauty" will continue remains to be seen.

Reader's *Tip* Reading and Studying Business

- Activate your schema with the introductory profiles and boxed material that describe an actual company with a current business dilemma. These illustrate the chapter concepts.
- Connect business theories with a real company's problems or solutions to make learning easier. Use the business illustrations to visualize the concepts.
- Cross-reference your reading with the illustrative photographs, tables, flow charts, figures, and copies of real advertisements. Sketch your own models of business and marketing processes and concepts. Use these visual learning tools to enhance your learning.
- Use the exercises to reinforce chapter topics, strengthen your research skills, and expand your knowledge. An instructional software disk may come with your text with practice quizzes and other instructional help.
- Use the tips that suggest how to market yourself by applying the chapter's concepts in your career search. For example, tips may offer advice on how to identify and access the major employment pipelines (*distribution channels*) for your product (you) in your career search.

EVERYDAY WOMEN

Madison Avenue is increasingly interested in using everyday women in advertising instead of just waifish supermodels.

The change comes after the Dove line of personal-care products sold by Unilever introduced what it called a "campaign for real beauty," which presents women in adver-
5   tisements as they are rather than as some believe they ought to be.

If the fad becomes a trend and shows legs, so to speak, it has the potential to fundamentally change decades of image-making on Madison Avenue. But that is a big if indeed. There have been many previous instances of ads that showed so-called real women in place of professional models, which receded as the allure of glamour again reared its
10 beautiful head.

This week, Nike is introducing a humorous print and online campaign for exercise gear, frankly glorifying body parts that until now were almost never seen in ads, much less celebrated. One ad, which begins boldly, "My butt is big," features an oversize photograph of the derrière in question.

15   Another Nike ad declares, "I have thunder thighs," while a third asserts: "My shoulders aren't dainty or proportional to my hips. Some say they are like a man's. I say, leave men out of it."

The Nike ads, by Wieden & Kennedy in Portland, Oregon, are arriving days after the Chicken of the Sea brand of tuna introduced a television commercial showing a gorgeous
20   young woman being ogled by the men in her office. She can escape their wolfish ways only in the elevator, which she enters alone, then breathes a sigh of relief—revealing that she really has a more-than-ample stomach, which she had been holding in.

The Nike campaign was in the works, executives say, well before the much-publicized arrival last month of Dove print and outdoor ads showing six women, none of them
25   models, sizes 4 to 12, smiling in their underwear. (The first of the Dove "real beauty" ads, showing older, wrinkled women, started appearing last fall.)

The Chicken of the Sea commercial is adapted from a spot that its parent, Thai Union Frozen Products, began running in Asia in 2001.

Even so, the arrival of all the ads at the same time suggests that change may be in
30   the air. "We've gotten tired of airbrushed pictures none of us can relate to or recognize," said Linda Kaplan Thaler, one of the most prominent women in advertising, whose agency, the Kaplan Thaler Group in New York, was not involved in creating any of the campaigns.

Advertisers are "loosening the reins," said Ms. Kaplan Thaler, who is chief executive
35   and chief creative officer at her agency, which is owned by the Publicis Groupe, in recognition of the reality that "women are the majority of consumers and are buying most of the products."

But those facts have been evident for years. Why the new style of ads now?

One reason, said Nathan Coyle, senior strategist at Brain Reserve in New York, a con-
40   sulting company, is the advent of reality television.

"Your neighbors, everyday people, are the new celebrities," Mr. Coyle said, which feeds the desire for marketers "to shift from depicting women who are unattainable to women who are attainable."

Kelly Simmons, president of a brand consulting company in Philadelphia named
45   Bubble, offered another reason: the aging of the baby-boom generation—the 76 million Americans born from 1946 to 1964—who have long set the pace for marketers and advertising agencies. The first baby boomers started turning 60 on Jan. 1, 2006.

"There's no question baby boomers feel better about their bodies," Ms. Simmons said, "and are determined to age beautifully," adding, "It feels there are real voices of
50   women coming through" in the Dove and Nike ads. "I applaud the trend."

Nancy Monsarrat, United States director for advertising at Nike in Beaverton, Oregon, said that in addition to the different attitudes about body image among boomer women, "younger women have a different perspective" from that of their counterparts a decade or two ago.

55   "They're more personally independent about who they can and should be," Ms. Monsarrat said, which is also reflected in the campaign's approach.

"One of the things we've noticed is if you go to an exercise class, if you go to a marathon, active women come in a lot of shapes and sizes," she added. "This can be a great celebration of that."

60   Fitness and health are also the focus of the Chicken of the Sea commercial, said John Signorino, the company's president and chief executive, in San Diego.

He imported the spot to the United States after consumers—including, he said, his wife—received overseas versions of it from friends by e-mail.

"It's an effort to show consumers, in an attention-getting way, that tuna, and
65   Chicken of the Sea, fit into a healthy lifestyle," Mr. Signorino said.

The commercial is being shown, or soon will be, on networks like ABC, CBS, HGTV and Oxygen, he added, and will be circulated through e-mail. The spot is adapted from the original version created by an agency in Bangkok named Chaiyo.

Ms. Monsarrat said the Nike campaign, which is also scheduled to appear on a Web
70   site (www.nikewomen.com), is in keeping with her company's efforts, dating back more

than a decade, to address issues about women's self-images in a positive way, without stereotypes.

She cited campaigns that carried themes like "This is not a goddess" and "If you let me play," all of which were intended, she said, to be "honest in how we communicate
75 with our target consumer."

Nike was not alone in the 1990's in running ads meant to question the conventional wisdom about images of women in advertising.

In 1997, the Body Shop gained international attention for a campaign carrying the theme "Love your body," which featured a Rubenesque plastic doll named Ruby.
80 The print ads and posters showed the voluptuous, even zaftig, Ruby reclining on a sofa under this headline: "There are 3 billion women who don't look like supermodels and only 8 who do."

And since 1997, the Advertising Women of New York club has presented awards to campaigns that its members deem to be breaking ground by portraying women in realis-
85 tic, nonstereotypical ways.

In addition to Nike, winners of such awards have included Adidas, Avon, Gatorade, John Hancock and Reebok.

The waxing and waning of so-called real women in advertising comes as marketers and agencies embrace the idea, then revert to traditional images when they believe it is
90 time for a new direction as consumers lose interest.

"Advertising sometimes starts trends, and sometimes it follows trends," Ms. Kaplan Thaler said.

Even if they do not turn up in ads, "real women have always been here, are here and continue to be here," she added. "I'm always happy to see advertising that does not dic-
95 tate a norm none of us can achieve."

Still, said Ms. Simmons of Bubble, who studies sex issues in marketing, more remains to be done before the stereotypes are banished.

"The emphasis is still on women's bodies" in the new ads, Ms. Simmons said. "It's not like we're looking at their irises."

—Stuart Elliott, "For Everyday Products, Ads Using the Everyday Woman."
From *The New York Times*, August 17, 2005. Copyright © 2005 The New York Times.

COMPREHENSION QUESTIONS

Answer the following questions with true (*T*) or false (*F*) or write a response.

_____ 1. The primary purpose of this selection is to describe one of the latest fads in the advertising world.

_____ 2. Madison Avenue is increasingly interested in using waifish women who are not supermodels.

_____ 3. The ad campaigns mentioned in the first half of the article (Dove, Nike, Chicken of the Sea) are targeting female consumers.

_____ 4. The everyday woman fad seems geared mostly toward Generation Xers.

_____ 5. According to the article, the everyday woman campaigns recognize the fact that women often do the bulk of the shopping for a family.

_____ 6. Dove was the first advertiser to focus on using real women (not professional models) in their campaigns.

7. Are these everyday woman ads designed to appeal to men as well as women?

_____

_____

_____

8. How does an advertiser earn an award from the Advertising Women of New York club? _____

_____

_____

9. Which sorts of companies have largely been using everyday women in their advertising campaigns? _____

_____

_____

_____

10. Why is at least one company (Dove/Unilever) not only marketing to the everyday woman, but to the older, wrinkled everyday woman? _____

_____

_____

_____

_____

THINKING AND WRITING AFTER READING

REACT Do you think that the advertising campaigns mentioned in the selection will result in greater sales of the products being marketed? Explain your reasoning.

_____

_____

REFLECT Do these ads appeal to you? Would you buy a product from a company using this approach? Explain why or why not._____

_____

THINK AND WRITE Would you agree that everyday women, such as those featured in the campaigns, have beauty? What exactly is _real_ beauty? Write your answer on a separate sheet of paper.

COMPARE Are there differences between _real_ beauty and _supermodel_ beauty? List the differences as you see them. _____

_____

DEFINE Has reading this selection changed the way in which you perceive beauty? If so, how and why? _____

_____

Beauty Inventory 2

Review your response to Beauty Inventory 1 in the introduction. How have your views changed? Answer the following questions to reflect your expanded knowledge and critical thinking about beauty.

1. What makes someone or something beautiful?

2. What makes someone unattractive?

3. What do you think is your most beautiful feature?

4. What specific images in the media shape your perceptions of beauty?

5. Would you undergo cosmetic surgery?

6. Do you think attractive people are treated differently than unattractive people?

7. Would you become romantically involved with someone solely because he or she is attractive?

8. Do you treat attractive people better than you treat unattractive people?

9. Would you treat a family member differently if you found that person unattractive?

10. Do you think society places too much emphasis on beauty?

Share your responses with class members. Notice any differences in your opinions of beauty.

6 Textbook Learning

- What is annotating?
- What is the Cornell method of notetaking?
- How do you write a summary?
- How can you use outlining?
- What is mapping?

Everyday Reading Skills: Reading Reference Materials

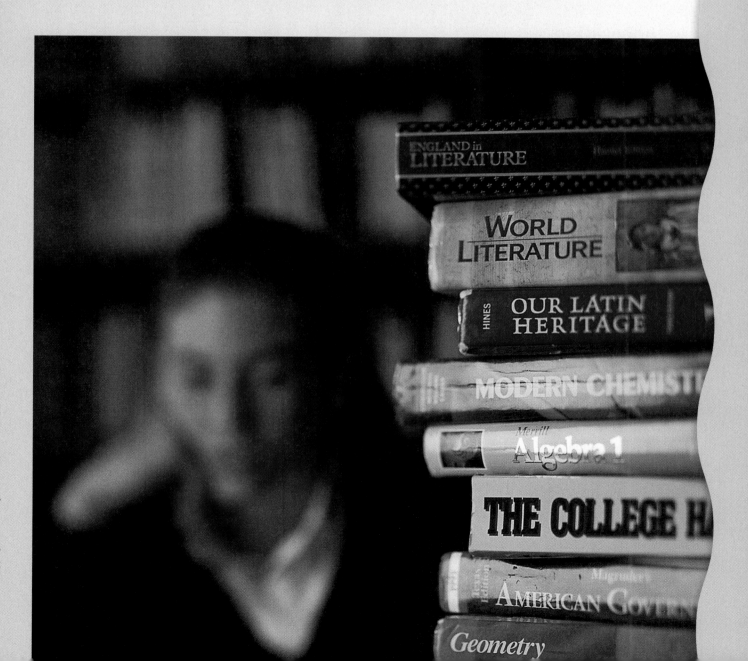

Expect Knowledge to Exist

Expect to know something after you have read a textbook assignment. Don't just watch the words go by. Use learning strategies to select key elements and to prepare for remembering. In the previous chapter, we discussed two such strategies—marking the text and taking notes. In this chapter, our discussion of those strategies continues with coverage of annotating, summarizing, outlining, and mapping.

The process of reading, marking, and organizing textbook information takes time. Many students ask, "How much do I need to do?" The answer to that question is, "Typically, the more you do, the more you learn." In other words, it is better to read the text than not to read the text. What's more, it is better to read and mark than only to read. Finally, it is better to read, mark, and take notes in some form (summary, Cornell notes, outline, or map) than just to read and mark. Your choices depend on the amount of time you can dedicate to learning. "Time on task" is a critical element in college success.

Annotating

Annotating is a system of marking that includes underlining and notations. It is the first and most basic step for all of the other organizing strategies.

When to Annotate

Annotate after a complete thought is presented. If you mark as you read, you tend to mark too much, and overmarking wastes valuable review time. Wait until a complete thought has been presented to separate the most important ideas from the least important ones. Such a thought unit may be as short as one paragraph or as long as an entire section under a subheading.

How to Annotate

The word *annotate* is used to suggest a notation system for selecting important ideas that goes beyond straight lines and includes numbers, circles, stars, and written comments, such as marginal notes, questions, and key words. With practice, students tend to form their own notation systems, which may include a variation of the following examples.

Symbol	Meaning	Symbol	Meaning
═══	Main idea (or write the topic in the margin beside the paragraph)	{ }	Section of material to reread for review
────	Supporting material	(1), (2), (3)	Numbering of important details under a major issue
☆	Major trend or possible essay exam question	?	Didn't understand and must seek advice
✓	Important smaller point to know for multiple-choice item	Topic, Def. or Ex.	Notes in the margin
⬭	Word that you must be able to define	How does it operate?	Questions in the margin
▭	A key issue to remember	↰	Indicating relationships

Unless you are reading a library book, annotate for study reading. For example, have you been annotating throughout this text as you have been reading? (The correct answer to this question should be yes!) If your instructor were to say at this moment, "Take fifteen minutes to review for a quiz on the last two chapters," could you quickly review your annotations? Remember, you can waste time reading for the purpose of learning if you do not annotate.

EXAMPLE The following passage represents information typically found in college psychology books. Notice a mixture of two organizational patterns: (1) definitions with examples, and (2) listing. Do you recognize signals that predict those patterns? Do the reader's markings help organize the material for later study?

PERSONALITY TYPES

According to Jung, Plato and Aristotle represent two fundamentally different tendencies
Introverts
2 types   in the human personality. Plato, concerned with the inner world, was an introvert, and
Extroverts
Aristotle, focusing his energies on the outer world, was an extrovert.

(Introverts) turn inward, seek isolation, and tend to withdraw from social engagements. They are reflective and introspective, absorbed with self-searching thoughts. They are self-critical and self-controlled, giving an outwardly cold appearance. They prefer to change the world rather than to adjust to it. (Extroverts) seek social contacts and are outgoing and accommodating. They appear friendly and outspoken and make friends easily. They are tolerant of others but relatively insensitive to the motivations and moods of their friends. They prefer to experience things rather than to read about them. Can you apply one of Jung's two personality types to yourself? How do you appear to others, as an introvert or an extrovert?

Mixture   Most people are a (mixture) of introvert and extrovert, being neither wholly one nor the other. This is one of the problems of classifying people into types. Unlike rocks, few people can be easily sorted into boxes according to type. We are just not that simple; each of us has the potential for behaving in different ways in different circumstances.

—From Morris Holland, *Psychology: An Introduction to Human Behavior*, 2nd ed.
©1978 Wadsworth, a part of Cengage Learning, Inc. Reproduced by permission.
www.cengage.com/permissions

The learner's task is not just to read but also to earmark relevant ideas for future study. To be an efficient learner, do not waste time.

exercise 1 Read the following passage and use the suggested annotations on page 268 to organize the material and mark key ideas for later study. Respond with *T* (true) or *F* (false) to the comprehension items.

SPATIAL DISTANCES

The way in which you treat space, a field of study called **proxemics**, communicates a wide variety of messages. Edward Hall distinguishes four distances that define the type of relationship between people and identifies the various messages that each distance communicates.

In *intimate distance,* ranging from actual touching to 18 inches, the presence of the other individual is unmistakable. Each person experiences the sound, smell, and feel of the other's breath. You use intimate distance for love-making and wrestling, for comforting and protecting. This distance is so short that most people do not consider it proper in public.

Personal distance refers to the protective "bubble" that defines your personal space, which measures from 18 inches to 4 feet. This imaginary bubble keeps you protected and untouched by others. You can still hold or grasp another person at this distance—but only by extending your arms—allowing you to take certain individuals such as loved ones into your protective bubble. At the outer limit of personal distance, you can touch another person only if both of you extend your arms.

At *social distance,* ranging from 4 to 12 feet, you lose the visual detail you have at personal distance. You conduct impersonal business and interact at a social gathering at this distance. The more distance you maintain in your interactions, the more formal they appear. Many people in executive and management positions place their desks so that they are assured of at least this distance from employees.

Public distance, measuring from 12 to more than 25 feet, protects you. At this distance, you can take defensive action if threatened. On a public bus or train, for example, you might keep at least this distance from a drunkard. Although you lose fine details of the face and eyes at this distance, you are close enough to see what is happening.

—*Essentials of Human Communication,* Fourth Edition,
by Joseph A. DeVito

Check your annotations with a study buddy. Could you study the essentials from the annotations without rereading the passage?

____F____ 1. Intimate distance is appropriate for social gatherings.

____T____ 2. The greater the social distance, the more formal the interaction appears.

Notetaking

Notetaking involves using your own words and a separate notebook to condense the key ideas you have marked in your text while annotating. Simply jotting these ideas down on paper is notetaking. In more elaborate systems, important ideas are written in sentences, then notes are inserted in the left margin for a quick topic reference.

When to Take Notes

Notetaking is useful for textbook study and class lectures. The marginal topic notes placed on the left are particularly helpful in organizing the study of a large body of material for a midterm or final exam.

How to Take Notes

The Cornell method, one of the most popular systems of notetaking, includes the following steps:

1. Draw a line down your paper 2.5 inches from the left edge to create a margin for noting key words and a wider area on the right for sentence summaries.
2. After reading a section, review your thoughts and write sentence summaries on the right side of your paper. Include the main ideas and key supporting details. Be brief and concise. Some students prefer to write phrases rather than sentences.
3. Review your summary sentences and underline key words. Write these key words in the column on the left side of your paper. These words can be used to stimulate your memory or quiz yourself.

Abbreviations. Use shortcuts. Develop your own system of abbreviations for notetaking, for both textbook and lecture notes. Some students mix shorthand symbols with their regular writing. Brainstorm with a study buddy and list abbreviations and symbols that can help you save time.

EXAMPLE   The following is an example of how the Cornell method might be used to organize notes for future study on the passage about Jung's theories.

2 Types	Jung believed in two types of personality
Introverts	<u>Introverts</u> turn inward, seek isolation, are reflective, and self-critical, and want to change the outside world.
Ex.	<u>Plato</u> is an example
Extroverts	<u>Extroverts</u> are outgoing, friendly, tolerant of others, and prefer to experience things rather than to read about them.
Ex.	<u>Aristotle</u> is an example
<u>Mixture</u>	Most people

exercise 2   Read the following passage about population growth in poorer nations. Annotate it, then use the Cornell method to take notes for future use. Write your notes in the box that follows the selection. Respond with _T_ (true) or _F_ (false) to the comprehension items.

POPULATION GROWTH

Why do people in the countries that can least afford it have so many children? We must take the role of the other so we can understand the world as _they_ see it. As our culture does for us, their culture provides a perspective on life that guides their choices. Let's consider three reasons why bearing many children plays a central role in the lives of millions upon millions of poor people around the world.

First is the status of parenthood. In the least industrialized nations, motherhood is the most prized status a woman can achieve. The more children a woman bears, the more she is thought to have achieved the purpose for which she was born. Similarly, a man proves his manhood by fathering children. The more children he fathers, especially sons, the better—for through them his name lives on.

Second, the community supports this view; many people share values and closely identify with one another. Children are viewed as a sign of God's blessing. Accordingly, a couple should have many children. By producing children, people reflect the values of their community and achieve status. The barren woman, not the woman with a dozen children, is to be pitied.

These factors certainly provide strong motivations for bearing many children. Yet, there is a third incentive. For poor people in the least industrialized nations, children are economic assets. These people have no Social Security or medical and unemployment insurance. This motivates them to bear *more* children, not fewer, for when parents become sick or too old to work—or when no work is to be found—they rely on their children to take care of them. The more children they have, the broader their base of support. Moreover, children begin contributing to the family income at a young age.

To those of us who live in the most industrialized nations, it seems irrational to have many children. And *for us it would be*. Understanding life from the framework of people who are living it, however—the essence of the symbolic interactionist perspective— reveals how it makes perfect sense to have many children. For example, consider the following incident, reported by a government worker in India:

> Thaman Singh (a very poor man, a water carrier) . . . welcomed me inside his home, gave me a cup of tea (with milk and "market" sugar, as he proudly pointed out later), and said: "You were trying to convince me that I shouldn't have any more sons. Now, you see, I have six sons and two daughters and I sit at home in leisure. They are grown up and they bring me money. One even works outside the village as a laborer. *You told me I was a poor man and couldn't support a large family. Now, you see, because of my large family I am a rich man.*"

Conflict theorists offer a different view of why women in the poor nations bear so many children. They would argue that these women have values that support male dominance. To father many children, especially sons, demonstrates virility, giving a man valued status in the community. From a conflict perspective, then, the reason poor people have so many children is that men control women's reproductive choices.

> —From James M. Henslin, *Sociology: A Down-to-Earth Approach*, 7th edition.
> ©2007 (excerpt from pages 583–585). Reproduced by
> permission of Pearson Education Inc.

____T____ 1. In poor countries throughout the world, poverty tends to increase rather than decrease the desire for a large number of children.

____F____ 2. A barren woman is a mother.

_____ T 3. In the least industrialized nations, an inability to bear children results in lower status for a woman.

_____ T 4. For poor people in the least industrialized countries, children are
viewed as their social security for old age.

Summarizing

A **summary** is a short, concise method of stating the main idea and significant
supporting details of the material. Think of it as the key words and phrases
linked by complete sentences and presented in paragraphs.

When to Summarize

Professors frequently ask students to take notes in the form of a summary on assigned readings. Such readings, which are usually in the library or on the
Internet, might include chapters from related texts, research articles from periodicals, or scholarly essays from books or periodicals. The preparation of a written
summary can demonstrate to the professor that you have a clear understanding
of the main points of the assignment. A summary can provide you with reference
notes for later study; and it can be useful when you are compiling information
from several sources for a long research paper.

How to Summarize

When you write a summary, put the ideas into your own words. If you need to
quote an author directly, place quotation marks around the *exact* wording to
avoid plagiarism. Keep in mind the purpose of your summary. The way you will
use the information will influence the number of details you include. Generally,
be brief but make your point. A summary is usually just one paragraph. A summary should never be as long as the piece it is summarizing!

Reader's *Tip* How to Write a Summary

- Remember your purpose; be brief.
- Underline the key ideas in the text you want to include.
- Begin your summary with a general statement, the main idea, that unites the key ideas.
- Include the key ideas that support the general statement. Link these ideas in sentences, and show their significance.
- Delete irrelevant or trivial information.
- Delete redundant information.
- Use your own words to show your understanding of the material. Don't try to camouflage a lack of comprehension by copying from the original.
- Do not include your opinions or anything that is not in the original.

EXAMPLE The following is a summary of the passage on Jung's personality types (p. 269). Notice that the first sentence states the main ideas and the others concisely state the major supporting details.

> Jung believed in two types of personality and that most people are a mixture of each. Introverts turn inward, seek isolation, are reflective and self-critical, and want to change the outside world. Plato is an example. Extroverts, on the other hand, are friendly, tolerant of others, and prefer to experience things rather than to read about them. Aristotle is an example. Most people are a combination of the two types.

exercise 3 Annotate the following passage and then write a summary of it. Include only the most important details in your summary and exclude the irrelevant ones. For example, this passage is dramatized by an anecdote, but does the information belong in the summary? Respond with *T* (true) or *F* (false) to the comprehension items.

RATTLESNAKE SURPRISE

David Chiszar, a professor in the psychology department at the University of Colorado, got a big surprise when he walked into his laboratory in 1995. His laboratory shelves are lined with dozens of glass cases; behind the glass, the subjects of Dr. Chiszar's research coil a safe distance from the professor and any visitors brave enough to enter. Although most are eerily silent, an occasional research subject emits a dry, rattling sound when the professor passes by. Dr. Chiszar is a herpetologist—in particular, he studies snakes. The day of the surprise, he went to the glass case that held a 14-year-old female timber rattlesnake. Timber rattlesnakes are poisonous but relatively unaggressive snakes that are found only in the eastern half of the United States. Severe declines in timber rattlesnake populations have led several states, including New York and Massachusetts, to list it as a threatened or endangered species, making it illegal to harass, kill, or collect timber rattlesnakes.

Dr. Chiszar had raised this timber rattlesnake since she was a two-day-old baby, not much bigger than an earthworm. Now, as he peered into her cage, he was astonished to see a tiny rattlesnake baby next to the $2^1/_2$-foot-long female snake. Even though she had never been in contact with a male snake, she had given birth to a male timber rattlesnake. Like other pit vipers, timber rattlesnakes don't lay eggs, but bear their young alive. Genetic studies showed that the baby snake really was the offspring of the 14-year-old rattler and that he didn't have a "father" in the usual sense of the word.

Although it may surprise you, such events are not all that rare in the world of reptiles, some birds, and insects. In fact, some species of whiptail lizards and geckos lack males entirely. The females of these species routinely produce offspring without the requirement for fertilization.

—*Biology: Life on Earth* by Teresa Audesirk,
Gerald Audesirk, and Bruce Byers

Written Summary

Timber rattlesnakes _____

_____

_____

_____

_____ 1. The female timber rattlesnake produced a male offspring without any contact with a male.

_____ 2. The 14-year-old mother rattlesnake had been isolated in captivity since it was two days old.

exercise 4 Annotate the following passage and write a summary of it. Respond with *T* (true) or *F* (false) to the comprehension items.

YOUTH IN CRISIS

Problems in the home, the school, and the neighborhood have placed a significant portion of American youth at risk. Youths considered at risk are those who engage in dangerous conduct such as drug abuse, alcohol use, and precocious sexuality. Although it is impossible to determine precisely the number of at-risk youths in the United States, one estimate is that 25 percent of the population under age 17, or about 17 million youths, are in this category. The most pressing problems facing American youth revolve around four issues.

Poverty. Though the number of American children living in poverty is dropping, the U.S. Census Bureau finds that there are still more than 12 million indigent children (the Census Bureau defines poverty as an income below $13,290 a year, or the equivalent of $1,108 a month for a family of three). While the percentage of children living in poverty in America is at its lowest level since 1979, the percentage of poor children in working families continues to climb, with 77 percent of poor children living in families where someone is working; this indicates that many working families are still struggling to stay afloat.

Family Problems. Divorce strikes about half of all new marriages, and many families sacrifice time with each other to afford more affluent lifestyles. Research shows that children are being polarized into two distinct economic groups: those in affluent, two-earner, married-couple households and those in poor, single-parent households.

Urban Decay. Adolescents living in deteriorated urban areas are prevented from having productive and happy lives. Many die from random bullets and drive-by shootings. Some are homeless and living on the street, where they are at risk of drug addiction and sexually transmitted diseases (STDs) including AIDS. One study of street kids in New York City found that 37 percent earned money through prostitution and almost one-third had contracted an STD.

Inadequate Education. The U.S. educational system seems to be failing many young people. We are lagging behind other developed nations in critical areas such as science and mathematics. The rate of *retention* (being forced to repeat a grade) is far higher than it should be. Retention rates are associated with another major problem: dropping out. It is estimated that about 14 percent of all eligible youths do not finish high school. In addition, poor and minority-group children attend the most underfunded schools, receive inadequate educational opportunities, and have the fewest opportunities to achieve conventional success.

—From Larry J. Siegel, *Juvenile Delinquency,* 1st ed.© 2002 Wadsworth, a part of Cengage Learning, Inc. www.cengage.com/permissions.

Written Summary

Begin with a general statement about youth in crisis. Link the key ideas and do not include irrelevant information.

_____

_____

_____

_____

_____

_____

_____ 1. The author suggests that children who experience any of the four at-risk factors have a higher probability of becoming drug or alcohol abusers than those without such experiences.

_____ 2. The author suggests that having a job is not a guarantee of avoiding poverty.

exercise 5 Annotate the following passage and write a summary of it. Respond with *T* (true) or *F* (false) to the comprehension items.

BUSINESS ETIQUETTE

A major component of managing your impression is practicing good etiquette. **Business etiquette** is a special code of behavior required in work situations. *Manners* has an equivalent meaning. Both manners and etiquette generally refer to behaving in a refined and acceptable manner. Business etiquette is much more than knowing how to use the correct utensil or how to dress in a given situation. Businesspeople today must know how to be at ease with strangers and with groups, be able to offer congratulations smoothly, know how to make introductions, and know how to conduct themselves at company social functions. Studying etiquette is important because knowing and using proper business etiquette contributes to individual and business success. People who are considerate of the feelings of others, and companies who are courteous toward customers, are more likely to succeed than their rude counterparts.

Business etiquette includes many aspects of interpersonal relations in organizations. What is considered proper etiquette and manners in the workplace changes over time and may vary with the situation. At one time, addressing one's superior by his or her first name was considered brash. Today it is commonplace behavior. A sampling of etiquette guidelines is nevertheless helpful. A general principle of being considerate of the feelings of work associates is more important than any one act of etiquette or courtesy.

ETIQUETTE FOR WORK BEHAVIOR AND CLOTHING

General work etiquette includes all aspects of performing in the work environment, such as completing work on time, punctuality, being a good team player, listening to others, and following through. For instance, having the courtesy to complete a project when it is due demonstrates good manners and respect for the work of others.

Clothing might be considered part of general work behavior. The casual standards in the information technology field, along with dress-down days, have created confusion about proper office attire. A general rule is that *casual* should not be interpreted as sloppy, such as torn jeans or a stained sweatshirt. Many companies have moved back toward emphasizing traditional business attire, such as suits for men and women. In many work situations, dressing more formally may constitute proper etiquette.

INTRODUCING PEOPLE

The basic rule for introductions is to present the lower-ranking person to the higher-ranking person regardless of age or sex. "Ms. Barker (the CEO), I would like you to meet my new coworker, Reggie Taylor." If the two people being introduced are of equal rank, mention the older one first. Providing a little information about the person being introduced is considered good manners. When introducing one person to the group, present the group to the individual. "Sid Foster, this is our information systems team." When being introduced to a person, concentrate on the name and repeat it soon, thus enhancing learning. A fundamental display of good manners is to remember people's names and to pronounce them correctly. When dealing with people senior to you or of higher rank, call them by their last name and title until told otherwise. (Maybe Ms. Barker, above, will tell you, "Please call me Kathy.")

It is good manners and good etiquette to remember the names of work associates to whom you are introduced, even if you see them only occasionally. If you forget the name of a person, it is better to admit this than to guess and come up with the wrong name. Just say, "I apologize, but I have forgotten your name. Tell me once more, and I will not forget your name again."

A major change in introducing people is that men and women are now both expected to extend their right hand when being introduced. Give a firm, but not overpowering, handshake, and establish eye contact with the person you are greeting.

—*Human Relations: Interpersonal, Job-Oriented Skills*, Eighth Edition, by Andrew J. DuBrin

Written Summary

Begin with a general statement about business etiquette. Link the key ideas and do not include irrelevant information.

_____

_____

_____

_____

_____

_____

_____

_____

_____ 1. The passage indicates that *etiquette* and *manners* have about the same meaning.

_____ 2. In introductions, present the higher ranking person to the lower ranking one.

Outlining

Outlining is a form of notetaking that gives a quick display of key issues and essential supporting details. Outlining uses indentations, numbers, and letters to show levels of importance. The outline forces you to sort out significant details and decide on levels of importance. Being able to outline shows that you understand main ideas and can distinguish between major and minor supporting details.

Reader's *Tip* Creating an Outline

The following is the format for a model outline. Notice how the numbers, letters, and indentations show the importance of an idea.

Main Point or Topic

I. Primary supporting idea
   A. Secondary supporting detail
   B. Secondary supporting detail
   C. Secondary supporting detail

II. Primary supporting idea #2
   A. Secondary supporting detail
   B. Secondary supporting detail
      1. Minor supporting detail or example
      2. Minor supporting detail or example

III. Primary supporting idea #3
   A. Secondary supporting detail
   B. Secondary supporting detail

When to Outline

Outlining can be used to take notes on a textbook chapter or a class lecture or for brainstorming the answer for a possible essay question.

How to Outline

Letters, numbers, and indentations are used in an outline to show levels of importance. In a standard outline, Roman numerals mark items of greatest importance and letters indicate supporting details. The greater distance from the left margin an item is listed, the less significance it is afforded. Your outline need not be picture perfect, but it should use indentation and some form of enumeration. Always remember that you are outlining to save time for later study and review. Don't cram all your facts on half a sheet of paper when you need several sheets. Give yourself plenty of room to write. You want to be able to look back quickly to get a clear picture of what is important and what supports it.

When taking notes in outline form, be brief and to the point. Use phrases rather than sentences. Record the main points, including key explanatory words, but leave out the insignificant details or "fillers."

Remember, making a picture-perfect outline is not critical; the important thing is to distinguish between the primary supporting ideas and the secondary supporting details. In an informal study outline, you can show the same levels of importance with indentations and bullets.

EXAMPLE The following example shows how the passage on Jung's theories (see p. 269) might be outlined for future study.

Jung's Personality Types

    I. Introverts

        A. turn inward, seek isolation

        B. reflective and introspective (self-searching)

        C. self-critical and self-controlled

        D. wish to change world rather than adjust

        E. ex. Plato

    II. Extroverts

        A. seek social contacts, outgoing

        B. friendly and outspoken

        C. tolerant of others

        D. prefer to experience than read about

        E. ex. Aristotle

   III. Most people are a mixture

EXPLANATION Notice that even though Plato and Aristotle are mentioned in the first paragraph, they fit logically as examples of each personality type. The "filler" is left out of the outline, but enough information is included so that rereading the passage won't be necessary.

exercise 6

Make a study outline for the following material. Annotate first, and then organize your notes into an informal outline with numbers or bullets.

THE SIX TYPES OF LOVE

EROS: BEAUTY AND SENSUALITY

Erotic love focuses on beauty and physical attractiveness, sometimes to the exclusion of qualities you might consider more important and more lasting. The erotic lover has an idealized image of beauty that is unattainable in reality. Consequently, the erotic lover often feels unfulfilled. In defense of eros, however, it should be noted that both male and female eros lovers have the highest levels of reward and satisfaction when compared with all other types of lovers (Morrow, Clark, & Brock 1995).

LUDUS: ENTERTAINMENT AND EXCITEMENT

Ludus love is seen as fun, a game to be played. To the ludic lover, love is not to be taken too seriously; emotions are to be held in check lest they get out of hand and make trouble. Passions never rise to the point at which they get out of control. A ludic lover is self-controlled and consciously aware of the need to manage love rather than to allow it to control him or her. The ludic lover is manipulative, and the extent of one's ludic tendencies has been found to correlate with the use of verbal sexual coercion (Sarwer, Kalichman, Johnson, Early, et al. 1993). Ludic-oriented sexually coercive men also experience less happiness, friendship, and trust in their relationships than do noncoercive men (Kalichman, Sarwer, Johnson, & Ali 1993). Ludic lover tendencies in women are likewise related to a dissatisfaction with life (Yancey & Berglass 1991).

STORGE LOVE: PEACEFUL AND SLOW

Like ludus love, **storge love** lacks passion and intensity. Storgic lovers do not set out to find lovers but to establish a companion-like relationship with someone they know and with whom they can share interests and activities. Storgic love develops over a period of time rather than in one mad burst of passion. Sex in storgic relationships comes late, and when it comes it assumes no great importance. Storgic love is sometimes difficult to separate from friendship; it is often characterized by the same qualities that characterize friendship: mutual caring, compassion, respect, and concern for the other person.

PRAGMA: PRACTICAL AND TRADITIONAL

The **pragma lover** is practical and wants compatibility and a relationship in which important needs and desires will be satisfied. In its extreme, pragma may be seen in the person who writes down the qualities wanted in a mate and actively goes about seeking someone who matches up. The pragma lover is concerned with the social qualifications of a potential mate even more than personal qualities; family and background are extremely important to the pragma lover, who relies not so much on feelings as on logic. The pragma lover views love as a necessity—or as a useful relationship—that makes the rest of life easier. The pragma lover therefore asks such questions about a potential mate as, "Will this person earn a good living?" "Can this person cook?" and "Will this person help me advance in my career?"

MANIC LOVE: ELATION AND DEPRESSION

The quality of mania that separates it from other types of love is the extremes of its highs and lows, its ups and downs. The **manic lover** loves intensely and at the same time worries intensely about and fears the loss of the love. With little provocation, for example, the manic lover may experience extreme jealousy. Manic love is obsessive; the manic lover has to possess the beloved completely—in all ways, at all times. In return, the manic lover wishes to be possessed, to be loved intensely. It seems almost as if the manic lover is driven to these extremes by some outside force or perhaps by some inner obsession that cannot be controlled.

AGAPE: COMPASSIONATE AND SELFLESS

Agape is a compassionate, egoless, self-giving love. Agape is nonrational and nondiscriminative. Agape creates value and virtue through love rather than bestowing love only on that which is valuable and virtuous. The agapic lover loves even people with whom he or she has no close ties. This lover loves the stranger on the road, and the fact that they will probably never meet again has nothing to do with it. Jesus, Buddha, and Gandhi practiced and preached this unqualified love. Agape is a spiritual love, offered without concern for personal reward or gain. The agapic lover loves without expecting that the love will be returned or reciprocated. For women, agape is the only love style positively related to their own life satisfaction (Yancy & Berglass 1991).

—Human Communication, Sixth Edition,
by Joseph A. DeVito

Six Types of Love

I. Eros: Beauty and Sensuality

   A. Focus: _____

   B. _____

   C. _____

   D. _____

II. Ludus: Entertainment and Excitement

   A. Focus: _____

   B. _____

   C. _____

   D. _____

III. Storge: Peaceful and Slow

   A. Focus: _____

   B. _____

   C. _____

   D. _____

IV. Pragma: Practical and Traditional

   A. Focus: _____

   B. _____

   C. _____

   D. _____

V. Manic: Elation and Depression

   A. Focus: _____

   B. _____

C. _____

D. _____

VI. Agape: Compassionate and Selfless

A. Focus: _____

B. _____

C. _____

D. _____

exercise 7

Make a study outline for the following material. Annotate first, and then organize your notes into an informal outline with numbers or bullets.

DRUG TESTS

Employers bear a crushing economic burden—estimates run as high as $100 billion—owing to drug and alcohol abuse by employees. These costs arise from high turnover, poor work performance, absenteeism, increased medical claims, low morale, theft, and other factors.

The drug-abusing employee is late three times as often as his coworkers, asks for time off twice as often, has two and one-half times as many absences of eight or more days, is five times more likely to file a workers' compensation claim, and is involved in accidents more than three times as often.

Typical on-the-job symptoms of drug abuse are inability to pay attention, difficulty with simple arithmetic, prolonged trips to the restroom, frequent absenteeism, poor personal hygiene, lapses in memory, and inattention to detail.

Given the social gravity and bottom-line expense of the drug problem, it is understandable that most American companies now screen for drug abuse during the pre-employment process. In most cases, this testing takes place as an ordinary and relatively inexpensive part of the pre-employment physical.

—Interviewing for Success,
by Arthur H. Bell and Dayle M. Smith

Drug Abuse by Employees

I. Costs to Employers

A. _____

B. _____

C. _____

D. _____

E. _____

F. _____

G. _____

II. Symptoms of Drug-Abusing Employees

A. _____

B. _____

C. _____

D. _____

E. _____

F. _____

G. _____

exercise 8   Make a study outline for the following material. Annotate first, and then organize your notes into an informal outline with numbers or bullets.

BUILDING SKILLS TO REDUCE STRESS

Dealing with stress involves assessing all aspects of a stressor, examining your response and how you can change it, and learning to cope. Often we cannot change the requirements at our college, assignments in class, or unexpected stressors. Inevitably, we will be stuck in classes that bore us and for which we find no application in real life. We feel powerless when a loved one dies. Although the facts cannot be changed, we can change our reactions to them.

ASSESSING YOUR STRESSORS

After recognizing a stressor evaluate it. Can you alter the circumstances to reduce the amount of distress you are experiencing or must you change your behavior and reactions to reduce stress levels? For example, you may have five term papers due for five different courses during the semester, but your professors are unlikely to drop such requirements. However, you can change your behavior by beginning the papers early and spacing them over time to avoid last-minute panic.

CHANGING YOUR RESPONSES

Changing your responses requires practice and emotional control. If your roommate is habitually messy and this causes you stress, you can choose from among several responses. You can express your anger by yelling; you can pick up the mess and leave a nasty note; or you can defuse the situation with humor. The first reaction that comes to mind is not always the best. Stop before reacting to gain the time you need to find an appropriate response. Ask yourself, "What is to be gained from my response?"

LEARNING TO COPE

Everyone copes with stress in different ways. Some people drink or take drugs; others seek help from counselors; and still others try to forget about it or engage in positive activities, such as exercise. **Stress inoculation,** one of the newer techniques, helps people prepare for stressful events ahead of time. For example, suppose you are petrified about speaking in front of a class. Practicing in front of friends or in front of a video camera may inoculate you and prevent your freezing up on the day of the presentation. Some health experts compare stress inoculation to a vaccine given to protect against a disease. Regardless of how you cope with a situation, your conscious effort to deal with it is an important step in stress management.

DOWNSHIFTING

Today's lifestyles are hectic and pressure-packed, and stress often comes from trying to keep up. Many people are questioning whether "having it all" is worth it, and they are taking a step back and simplifying their lives. This trend is known as **downshifting.** Moving from a large urban area to a smaller town, exchanging the expensive SUV for a modest four-door sedan, and a host of other changes in lifestyle typify downshifting. Some dedicated downshifters have given up television, phones, and even computers.

Downshifting involves a fundamental alteration in values and honest introspection about what is important in life. When you consider any form of downshift or perhaps even start your career this way, it's important to move slowly and consider the following.

a. *Determine your ultimate goal.* What is most important to you, and what will you need to reach that goal? What can you do without? Where do you want to live?

b. *Make a short-term and a long-term plan for simplifying your life.* Set up your plan in doable steps, and work slowly toward each step. Begin saying no to requests for your time, and determine those people with whom it is important for you to spend time.

c. *Complete a financial inventory.* How much money will you need to do the things you want to do? Will you live alone or share costs with roommates? Do you need a car, or can you rely on public transportation? Pay off credit cards and eliminate existing debt, or consider debt consolidation. Get used to paying with cash.

—*Health: The Basics,* Sixth Edition,
by Rebecca J. Donatelle

Building Skills to Reduce Stress

I. Assessing Your Stressors

    A. _____

    B. _____

    C. _____

II. Changing Your Responses

    A. _____

    B. _____

III. Learning to Cope

    A. _____

    B. _____

    C. _____

IV. Downshifting

    A. _____

    B. _____

Mapping

Mapping visually condenses material to show relationships. A map is a diagram that places important topics in a central location and connects major points and supporting details in a visual display that shows degrees of importance. The previous study methods are linear in nature, whereas mapping uses space in a free and graphic manner.

When to Map

A map provides a quick reference for overviewing a chapter to stimulate prior knowledge, emphasize relationships, and aid recall. College students use maps or charts to reduce information for memorizing from lecture notes and the text.

How to Map

To prepare a map, do the following:

1. Draw a circle or a box in the middle of a page, and in it write the subject or topic of the material.
2. Determine the main ideas that support the subject, and write them on lines radiating from the central circle or box.
3. Determine the significant details, and write them on lines attached to each main idea. The number of details you include will depend on the material and your purpose.

Maps are not restricted to any one pattern but can be formed in a variety of creative shapes, as the following diagrams illustrate.

The following is an example of how the passage on Jung's theories might be mapped for future study.

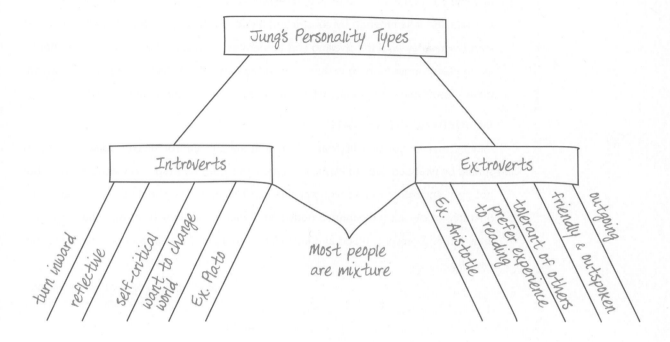

exercise 9   Read the following passage and map the key ideas. The structure of the map is provided. Insert the main idea first, then arrange the supporting ideas to radiate appropriately.

RELIEF FOR INJURIES

For the past several hundred years many injuries were treated with heat—steaming baths where leisurely soaking was encouraged, hot water bottles, or electric heating pads or wraps. It was assumed that since heat speeded up metabolism, it would also speed the healing process. Today's researchers have proved that just the opposite is true. . . . Heat does speed up body processes but it also stimulates injured tissue and dilates blood vessels. In turn, this causes swelling to increase and enlarges the pools of blood and fluid, actually slowing healing. Even if there is no injury, heat after exercising can cause aches and pains. A quick, cool shower is recommended after your jog rather than a hot tub.

Four basic first aid procedures are used in treating the majority of runners' injuries.

STOP ACTIVITY

The first and most critical is to stop jogging as soon as the symptom appears. About the only pain you can run through is a side stitch. Joggers who insist on running with pain or walking off an injury usually incur further harm. Even though the pain does not become more intense, continuing the activity may aggravate the injury and prolong healing.

APPLY COLD

Cold packs are now universally accepted as the best first aid for virtually any jogging injury and constitute the second step in treatment. Chilling numbs the pain and minimizes swelling and inflammation by constricting blood and lymph vessels. Apply cold packs at least twice a day until the swelling and tenderness disappear. The ice pack should not be left in place longer than 30 minutes at one time. Muscle cramps are one of the few conditions associated with jogging where heat instead of cold should be applied.

IMMOBILIZE AND ELEVATE

Injuries that would benefit from being immobilized and/or given additional support should be wrapped with an elastic Ace-type bandage. This wrapping should be snug, but not tight enough to inhibit blood circulation. This third step should be taken before the final step of elevating the injured body part. Elevation not only helps drain fluid from the area, but also prevents blood and fluid from rushing to the area, thereby causing further swelling.

— *Jogging Everyone,* by Charles Williams
and Clancy Moore

exercise 10 Read the following passage and map the key ideas. The structure of the map is provided. Insert the topic first, then arrange the supporting ideas to radiate appropriately.

TYPES OF CRIME

In the United States, the Federal Bureau of Investigation gathers information on criminal offenses and regularly reports the results in a publication called *Crime in the United States.* Two major types of crime make up the FBI "crime index."

Crimes against the person are *crimes that direct violence or the threat of violence against others.* Such violent crimes include murder and manslaughter (legally defined as "the willful killing of one human being by another"), aggravated assault ("an unlawful attack by one person upon another for the purpose of inflicting severe or aggravated bodily injury"), forcible rape ("the carnal knowledge of a female forcibly and against her will"), and robbery ("taking or attempting to take anything of value from the care, custody, or control of a person or persons by force or threat of force or violence and/or putting the victim in fear").

Crimes against property encompass *crimes that involve theft of property belonging to others.* Property crimes include burglary ("the unlawful entry of a structure to commit a [serious crime] or a theft"), larceny-theft ("the unlawful taking, carrying, leading, or riding away of property from the possession of another"), auto theft ("the theft or attempted theft of a motor vehicle"), and arson ("any willful or malicious burning or attempt to burn the personal property of another").

A third category of offenses, not included in major crime indexes, is **victimless crimes,** *violations of law in which there are no readily apparent victims.* Also called "crimes without complaint," they include illegal drug use, prostitution, and gambling. The term "victimless crime" is misleading, however. How victimless is a crime when young people have to steal to support a drug habit? What about a young pregnant woman who smokes crack and permanently harms her baby? Perhaps it is more correct to say that people who commit such crimes are both offenders and victims.

—*Sociology*, Tenth Edition,
by John J. Macionis

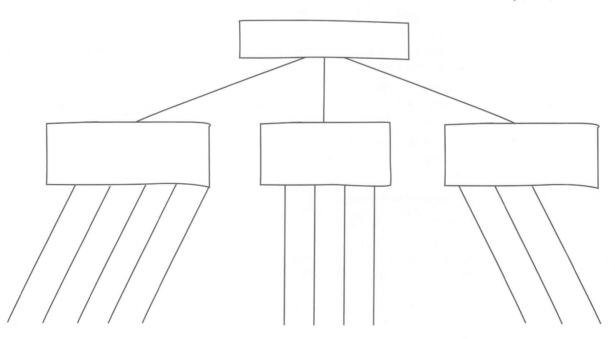

exercise 11   On a separate sheet of paper, make a study map or chart to diagram the essential information in the passage titled *The Six Types of Love* (see Exercise 6).

Take Organized Lecture Notes

Develop an efficient system for organizing class lectures. Professors speak rapidly yet expect students to remember important information. The Cornell method uses marginal notes to emphasize main points, whereas the outline format shows importance through indentation. Whichever system you use, allow yourself plenty of room to write. Considering your investment in college, paper is inexpensive. Use a pen, not a pencil, to avoid smudges. Try writing on only one side of the paper so you can backtrack later to add information when the professor summarizes. Compare your lecture notes with those of other students. Why would some professors say, "I can tell how much a student understood by looking at his or her lecture notes"?

exercise 12   Choose a study buddy and divide the work in order to compare the two notetaking systems, the Cornell method and the modified outline format. Ask permission and, if possible, both of you visit a regular history, psychology, sociology, or political science class. One of you should take notes using the Cornell method and the other using an informal version of the outline format. After class, compare notes and decide which method works better for you.

Summary *Points*

➤ **What is annotating?**
Annotating is a system of marking that includes underlining and notations for future study.

➤ **What is the Cornell method of notetaking?**
The Cornell method includes writing summaries with marginal notes.

➤ **What is a summary?**
A summary is a short, concise passage that states the main idea and significant supporting details.

➤ **What is outlining?**
Outlining gives a quick graphic display of key issues and can be used to brainstorm answers to essay exam questions.

➤ **What is mapping?**
Mapping visually depicts material to show relationships.

COLLABORATIVE   PROBLEM SOLVING

Form a five-member group and select one of the following activities. Brainstorm and then outline your major points on a transparency. Choose a member to present the group findings to the class.

➤ List ten tips for taking good lecture notes.
➤ List ten items you can purchase that will help you get organized for successful study.
➤ List ten shorthand terms or abbreviations that will help you take lecture notes rapidly.
➤ List ten reasons not to cut a class.

MyReadingLab (MRL) www.myreadinglab.com

➤ To practice the ideas and skills introduced in this chapter, go to the "Reading Textbooks," "Outlining and Summarizing," and "Note Taking and Textbook Highlighting" modules in the Skills section of MRL. To practice general reading comprehension, use the Levels section.

The Reading *Workshop*

"There are many little ways to enlarge your child's world. Love of books is the best of all."

—JACQUELINE KENNEDY

"Reading aloud with children is known to be the single most important activity for building the knowledge and skills they will eventually require for learning to read."
—MARILYN JAGER ADAMS, READING EXPERT

Did someone read to you when you were a child? This is one of the best ways for a child to learn the rhythm and sounds of written language. Even the youngest child learns that reading is fun through the experience of sharing it with someone. Read to a child today or tomorrow! It will give you both great pleasure.

Think about it, talk about it, write about it:

Did you have a favorite book as a child? What was it? Did you visit the library or a bookstore? Write about your reading experiences, or lack of them, in your childhood.

Write about the experience of reading to a child. What did you read? Did she or he enjoy it? What did you gain from the experience?

Your professor might ask you to discuss these topics or others in a Reading Workshop journal.

Personal *Feedback* **1**

Name _____

1. What format do you prefer for notetaking? Why? _____
    _____
    _____

2. What has been your experience with highlighting? How would you evaluate your
    own highlighting as compared with other methods of annotating? _____
    _____
    _____

3. Why should you take lecture notes on one side of a notebook page only? _____
    _____
    _____

4. How do you reward yourself during study breaks? _____
    _____
    _____

5. What is the most useful thing you have learned from this chapter? _____
    _____
    _____

6. What is the most interesting thing you have learned so far from your instructor?
    _____
    _____
    _____

7. What do you feel are the five major differences in academic expectations between
    high school and college? _____
    _____
    _____

Tear out and submit to your instructor.

selection 1   Health

"People's behavior makes sense if you think about it in terms of their goals, needs, and motives."
—Thomas Mann

Dr. Bernard Suran reports in the Florida Bar News that when asked, "Would you like to become a better person?" most people surprisingly respond with a resounding "maybe" rather than an enthusiastic "of course." Why bother to change if life is not holding your feet to the fire in a reaction to circumstances? Genuine change is difficult, requiring a firm commitment and an organized plan. Dr. Suran says, "What motivates best is the realm of possibility, if we allow ourselves to consider the prospect of becoming even more awesome than we already are."

THINKING BEFORE READING

Preview for content and organizational clues. Activate your schema and anticipate what you will learn.

What circumstances can give people the impetus to change unwanted behaviors?

What is a positive reinforcement?

How do Olympic athletes use imagery and psychology to excel?

I think this will say that _____.

VOCABULARY PREVIEW

Are you familiar with these words?

coaxed	acknowledgment	languish	vigilance	commitment
scenario	inducement	premise	irrational	resort

How can someone be *coaxed* into a *commitment* they do not want to make?

What *scenario* might cause someone to *resort* to an extreme lifestyle change?

Your instructor may choose to give a true-false vocabulary review before or after reading.

THINKING DURING READING

As you read, use the six thinking strategies of a good reader: predict, picture, relate, monitor, correct, and annotate.

ANNOTATING

Annotate the selection in order to make an outline of significant elements in behavior change.

BEHAVIOR CHANGE

Refer to the
Reader's *Tip*
for **Health** on page
51.

Mark Twain said that "habit is habit, and not to be flung out the window by anyone, but coaxed downstairs a step at a time." The chances of successfully changing negative behavior improve when you make gradual changes that give you time to unlearn negative patterns and to substitute positive ones.

STAGING FOR CHANGE

5 On any given day, countless numbers of us get out of bed and resolve to begin to change a given behavior "today." Whether it be losing weight, drinking less, exercising more, being nicer to others, managing time better, or some other change in a negative behavior, we start out with high expectations. In a short time, however, a vast majority of people fail and are soon doing whatever it was they thought they shouldn't be doing.

10 After considerable research, Dr. James Prochaska and Dr. Carlos DiClimente believe that behavior changes usually do not succeed if they start with the change itself. Instead, they believe that we must go through a series of "stages" to adequately prepare, or ready, ourselves for that eventual change.

Precontemplation. People in the precontemplation stage have no current intention
15 of changing. They may have tried to change a behavior before and may have all but given up, or they may just be in denial and unaware of any problem.

Contemplation. In the contemplation stage, the person recognizes that he or she has a problem and begins to think about the need to change. Despite this acknowledgment, people can languish in this stage for years, knowing that they have a problem but
20 never finding the time or energy to make the change.

Preparation. Most people in this stage are close to taking action. They've thought about several things they might do and may even have come up with a plan.

Action. In the action stage, the individual begins to follow the action plan he or she has put together. Unfortunately, too many people start behavior change here rather than
25 going through the first three stages. Without a plan, without enlisting the help of others, or without a realistic goal, failure is likely.

Maintenance. Maintenance requires vigilance, attention to detail, and long-term commitment. Many people reach their goals, only to relax and slip back into the undesired behavior.

30 **Termination.** In this stage, the behavior is so ingrained that the current level of vigilance may be unnecessary. The new behavior has become an essential part of daily living.

CHOOSING A BEHAVIOR-CHANGE STRATEGY

Once you have analyzed all the factors that influence what you do, you must decide which behavior-change technique will work best for you. These techniques include
35   shaping, visualization, modeling, controlling the situation, reinforcement, and changing self-talk.

Shaping.

Regardless of how motivated you are, some behaviors are almost impossible to change immediately. To reach your goal, you may need to take a number of individual steps, each designed to change one small piece of the larger behavior. This process is known as shaping.
40   For example, suppose that you have not exercised for a while. You decide that you want to get into shape, and your goal is to jog three to four miles every other day. So you start slowly and build up to your desired fitness level gradually.

Visualization.

Mental practice and rehearsal can help change unhealthy behaviors into healthy ones. Athletes and others use a technique known as **imagined rehearsal** to reach their goals.
45   By visualizing their planned action ahead of time, they are better prepared when they put themselves to the test.

For example, suppose you want to ask someone out on a date. Imagine the setting (walking together to class) for the action. Then practice exactly what you're going to say ("Minh, there's a great concert this Sunday and I was wondering if") in your mind and
50   out loud. Mentally anticipate different responses ("Oh, I'd love to, but I'm busy that evening") and what you will say in reaction ("How about if I call you sometime this week?"). Careful mental and verbal rehearsal—you could even try out your scenario on a friend—will greatly improve the likelihood of success.

Modeling.

Modeling, or learning behaviors through careful observation of other people, is one of
55   the most effective strategies for changing behavior. For example, suppose that you have trouble talking to people you don't know very well. One of the easiest ways to improve your communication skills is to select friends whose "gift of gab" you envy. Observe their social skills. Do they talk more or listen more? How do people respond to them? Why are they such good communicators?

Controlling the Situation.

60   Sometimes, the right setting or right group of people will positively influence your behaviors. Many situations and occasions trigger certain actions. The term **situational inducement** refers to an attempt to influence a behavior by using situations and occasions to control it.

The man in this photo lost nearly half his body weight as a result of participating in the Weight Watchers program. He rewarded himself for his weight loss by purchasing a new wardrobe.

For example, you may be more apt to stop smoking if you work in a smoke-free office, a positive situational inducement. By carefully considering which settings will help

65 and which will hurt your effort to change, you will improve your chances for change.

Reinforcement.

A **positive reinforcement** is a reward that is given to increase the likelihood that a behavior change will occur. Each of us is motivated by different reinforcers. Although a special T-shirt may be a positive reinforcer for young adults entering a race, it would not be for a 40-year-old runner who dislikes message-bearing T-shirts.

Changing Self-Talk

70 **Self-talk,** or the way you think and talk to yourself, can also play a role in modifying health-related behaviors. Here are some cognitive procedures for changing self-talk.

Rational-Emotive Therapy—This form of cognitive therapy or self-directed behavior change is based on the premise that there is a close connection between what people say to themselves and how they feel. According to psychologist Albert Ellis, most emotional

75 problems and related behaviors stem from irrational statements that people make to themselves when events in their lives are different from what they would like them to be.

For example, suppose that after doing poorly on an exam, you say to yourself, "I can't believe I flunked that easy exam. I'm so stupid." By changing this irrational,"cata-strophic" self-talk into rational, positive statements about what is really going on, you can

80   increase the likelihood that positive behaviors will occur. Positive self-talk might be phrased as follows: "I really didn't study enough for that exam, and I'm not surprised I didn't do very well. I'm certainly not stupid. I just need to prepare better for the next test." Such self-talk will help you to recover quickly from disappointment and take posi-tive steps to correct the situation.

85   **Meichenbaum's Self-Instructional Methods**—Behavioral psychologist Donald Meichenbaum is perhaps best known for a process known as stress inoculation, which subjects clients to extreme stressors in a laboratory environment. Before a stressful event (e.g., going to the doctor), clients practice individual coping skills (e.g., deep breathing exercises) and self-instruction (e.g., "I'll feel better once I know what's causing my pain").

90   Meichenbaum demonstrated that clients who practiced coping techniques and self-instruction were less likely to resort to negative behaviors in difficult situations. In Meichenbaum's behavioral therapies, clients are encouraged to give themselves "self-instructions" ("Slow down, don't rush") and "positive affirmations" ("My speech is going fine—I'm almost done!") instead of self-defeating thoughts ("I'm talking too fast—my

95   speech is terrible") whenever a situation seems to be getting out of control.

      Blocking/Thought Stopping—By purposefully blocking or stopping negative thoughts, a person can concentrate on taking positive steps toward behavior change. For example, suppose you are preoccupied with your ex-partner, who has recently deserted you for someone else. You consciously stop dwelling on the situation and force yourself to

100 think about something more pleasant (e.g., dinner tomorrow with your best friend). By refusing to dwell on negative images and forcing yourself to focus elsewhere, you can save wasted energy, time, and emotional resources and move on to positive change.

                                                                    (1,321 words)

                                                      —*Health: the Basics*, Fifth Edition,
                                                              by Rebecca J. Donatelle

STUDY OUTLINE

Use your annotations to make an outline of significant elements in behavior change.

THINKING AND WRITING AFTER READING

RECALL   Self-test your understanding.

Your instructor may choose to give you a true-false comprehension review.

REACT   Why are positive role models important for success? How has your behavior been affected by negative role models? Who has been a positive role model for you? _____

_____

REFLECT   Why are people reluctant to initiate behavior change? How do past experiences temper enthusiasm? _____

_____

THINK CRITICALLY   What behavior would you most like to change? Outline your plan for success.

THINK AND WRITE   Why do we engage in negative self-talk? How can negative self-talk be self-defeating and positive talk be uplifting? What does self-talk say about the power of language? How would you like to change your own self-talk?

_____

_____

_____

Interpret the Quote

Now that you have finished reading the selection, "Behavior Change," go back to the beginning of the selection and read the opening quote again. Do you agree that people's behavior is shaped by their goals, needs, and motives? On a separate sheet of paper, list five personal goals and, for each goal, explain how your behavior is related to each goal.

Name _____

Date _____

COMPREHENSION QUESTIONS

Answer the following with *a, b, c,* or *d,* or fill in the blank. In order to help you analyze your strengths and weaknesses, the question types are indicated.

Main Idea _____ 1. The best statement of the main idea of the selection is:
   a. Behavior change is the science of learning new, positive patterns to replace previous negative actions.
   b. Successful behavior change begins with precontemplation, and then other stages follow.
   c. Shaping, visualization, and modeling are the significant strategies for behavior change.
   d. Successful behavior change begins with adequate preparation and continues with a variety of strategies and techniques to gradually alter thoughts and actions.

Inference 2. What did Mark Twain mean by saying, "habit is habit, and not to be flung out the window by anyone, but coaxed downstairs a step at a time"? _____

_____

_____

Inference _____ 3. Establishing realistic goals, identifying rewards for milestones, and seeking support from friends is the stage of change labeled
   a. precontemplation.
   b. contemplation.
   c. preparation.
   d. termination.

Detail _____ 4. The strategy of learning behaviors through watching other people is called
   a. shaping.
   b. visualization.
   c. modeling.
   d. reinforcement.

Inference _____ 5. To achieve a weight loss goal, not making your usual weekly purchase of M & M's is an example of the behavior-changing strategy called
   a. shaping.
   b. modeling.
   c. controlling the situation.
   d. reinforcement.

Detail _____ 6. Rational-emotive therapy is based on the premise that
   a. feelings are manipulated by what we tell ourselves.
   b. coping techniques such as deep breathing can reduce stress.
   c. forcing yourself to focus elsewhere removes the negative thought.
   d. language is more powerful than thought.

Inference _____ 7. For a weight loss goal, replacing thoughts of chocolate candy with thoughts of the Friday night basketball game is an example of

    a. rational-emotive therapy.

    b. self-instruction.

    c. Meichenbaum's coping strategy.

    d. blocking.

Answer the following with *T* (true), *F* (false), or *CT* (can't tell).

Detail _____ 8. Prochaska and DiClimente believe that failure occurs when people start with the change itself.

Detail _____ 9. In Meichenbaum's self-instructional method, clients pretend to experience the dreaded event in order to practice coping skills.

Detail _____ 10. Visualization is the observation and imitation of positive behaviors of others.

VOCABULARY

Answer the following with *a, b, c,* or *d* for the word or phrase that best defines the boldface word used in the selection. The number in parentheses indicates the line of the passage in which the word appears.

_____ 1. "**coaxed** downstairs" (2)

    a. forced

    b. persuaded

    c. thrown

    d. scattered

_____ 2. "Despite this **acknowledgment**" (18–19)

    a. denial

    b. fulfillment

    c. opportunity

    d. admission

_____ 3. "people can **languish**" (19)

    a. pine away

    b. progress

    c. contemplate

    d. evolve

_____ 4. "requires **vigilance**" (27)

    a. courage

    b. watchfulness

    c. intelligence

    d. energy

_____ 5. "long-term **commitment**" (28)

    a. confidence

    b. frustration

    c. management

    d. obligation

_____ 6. "try out your **scenario**" (52)

    a. enactment

    b. dream

    c. argument

    d. sentences

_____ 7. "situational **inducement**" (61)

    a. stop

    b. error

    c. enticement

    d. replacement

_____ 8. "based on the **premise**" (73)

    a. hope

    b. feeling

    c. idea

    d. emotion

_____ 9. "**irrational** statements" (75)

    a. illogical

    b. angry

    c. hateful

    d. threatening

_____ 10. "**resort to** negative behaviors" (91)

    a. escape through

    b. go back to

    c. hide under

    d. yearn for

Your instructor may choose to give a true-false vocabulary review.

VOCABULARY ENRICHMENT

A. **Context Clues:** Select the word from the list that best completes the sentences.

coaxed	acknowledgment	languish	vigilance	commitment
scenario	inducement	premise	irrational	resort

1. Without becoming a "warrior against pleasure," you do not want to silently watch a friend _____ to undesired behaviors.

2. Money can be a strong and effective _____ to motivate behavior changes.

3. Denial can cause people to _____ in a state of indecision and fail to embrace change.

4. Entering the termination stage is an _____ that maintenance has been successful.

5. During the contemplation stage of change, a gentle nudge from a friend may have _____ the contemplator to get started.

6. Emotive therapy or self-talk can calm the nerves and help prevent _____ behavior.

7. Without proper _____, a dieter can slip back into old habits of snacking and not exercising.

8. Significant others can assist a loved one in making a _____ to lasting change.

9. If you accept the _____ that positive reinforcements promote change, seek to individualize incentives for maximum motivation.

10. Write a _____ in which you are tempted to revert to your old bad habits, but instead you skillfully conquer the demons.

B. **Thesaurus:** Use a thesaurus, either the computer or book version, to find four alternative words for each of the following:

1. indication _____

2. habit _____

3. beginning _____

4. agreement _____

5. respect _____

ASSESS YOUR LEARNING

Review confusing questions, seek clarification, and make notes in your text to help you remember new information and vocabulary.

> **"If you do the right job then money will come to you. Because people who need you will request, will ask for you, will attract you, and will be willing to pay you for your services."**
>
> —Jose Silva

The odds for the failure of small businesses are initially quite high. Despite the slight margin for success, some companies have taken off and soared. One such company is Goya Foods. Established in 1936 by a Spanish immigrant, Prudencio Unanue, Goya continues to prosper. In addition to its financial success, Goya is known as a company that believes in giving back to the community. Goya executives have made commitments to humanitarian efforts ranging from donating food for soup kitchens to creating scholarships for college students. Perhaps part of the company's key to success lies in Goya's partnerships with the communities it serves.

THINKING BEFORE READING

Preview for content and organizational clues. Activate your schema and anticipate what you will learn.

What ethnic foods do you enjoy?

Where in your grocery store would you find either salsa or soy sauce?

Where do you find "health foods" in your grocery store? How do you think special shelving increases health food sales?

After reading this I will probably know _____.

VOCABULARY PREVIEW

Are you familiar with these words?

consumer	forefront	trend	dominated	positioned
strives	gauging	demographic	garner	core

As a college student, what are your *core* goals?

Is there a difference between a *consumer* and a customer?

Are you good at *gauging* the amount of money you spend each day?

Your instructor may choose to give a true-false vocabulary review before or after reading.

THINKING DURING READING

As you read, use the six thinking strategies of a good reader: predict, picture, relate, monitor, correct, and annotate.

ANNOTATING AND OUTLINING

Annotate as you read, and then make an informal study outline to answer this essay exam question: Discuss the reasons for Goya Foods' success.

GOYA FOODS

Refer to the
Reader's *Tip*
for **Business** on
page 262.

At the ShopRite supermarket in Jersey City most of the goods are organized as they are at any big U.S. grocery store—by aisle, according to product type. One section differs slightly from that pattern. It carries a variety of goods—desserts, beans, and sauces among them. Unusually, one company is in control: the Hispanic-food powerhouse Goya.

5   "Our research has shown that that's the way our consumer likes to buy," says Andy Unanue, chief operating officer of the closely held Goya Foods Inc., and a grandson of the company founder, Prudencio Unanue. "They know that everything they need to cook is in that section."

    Goya is at the forefront of a trend seen in neighborhoods across the land that are
10 dominated by a specific ethnic group. At the ShopRite, almost 50 percent of the population within a half a mile is Latino. So Goya has positioned itself as a kind of shop within a shop that offers everything a Hispanic consumer might want. Its products, which include basic ingredients like Spanish olive oil, seasonings like Mexican chiles, and Caribbean fruit juices, are imported from all over Latin America and sold under the Goya brand.

15   Key to its approach are some 500 independent brokers—out of about 2,300 employees it has in the United States. They work directly with store managers to help them decide where and how to sell Goya products. The company strives to grab as much

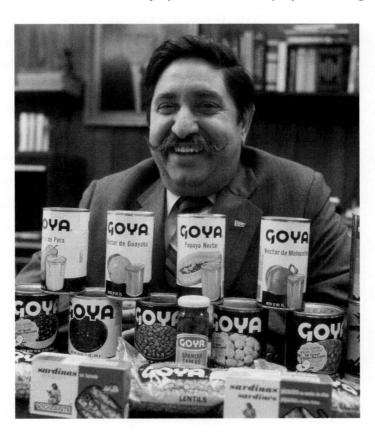

retail space as it can get without occupying so much that the retailer loses money, says Mr. Unanue.

20　　　Typically, retailers charge a "slotting fee" related to the space a product occupies within the store. Industry observers say the fee helps retailers make a profit on products that might not be consistent sellers. "Retailers don't want to use shelf space for a product that isn't proven," says Cesar Melgoza, president of Geoscape International Inc., a marketing company that specializes in Hispanic retailing strategy.

25　　　But given the skill of its sales team in gauging market demand, and the swelling Hispanic demographic, Goya "has never paid a slotting fee," Mr. Unanue says. Big retailers in particular aren't experts at serving the Hispanic market, while Goya Foods has had plenty of practice.

　　　"The knowledge of who are your key consumers, where they live and where they 30　buy, is the intellectual capital that can work as a substitute to slotting fees as well as an insurance against the risks of introducing new products in the market," Mr. Melgoza says.

　　　Yet there's a downside to the all-in-one-aisle strategy that Goya pursues most of the time. Its products don't garner as many crossover sales as they could when people compare the quality and prices of similar products from different makers, Mr. Unanue ac-35　knowledges. Although Goya has in the past made a big push toward serving the broader U.S. market, 75 percent of its clients remain Latinos, most of them recent immigrants or traditional families that eat Hispanic food at home. "What we may lose in the crossover market, we gain more in making our core clients happy," argues Mr. Unanue.

　　　Other big Hispanic food makers are trying to follow a similar tack. The Unilever unit 40　Iberia Foods, which has about $40 million in annual sales, is one of them, as is the closely held La Cena Fine Foods Ltd. of Saddle Brook, New Jersey, which sells about 400 different products under its brand name.

　　　These ethnic-brand merchandisers are increasingly pushing on an open door at the nation's most important retailers, who have taken notice of recent studies that highlight 45　the attractiveness and loyalty of Latino shoppers. One study, carried out by the Cultural Access Group Inc. for the Washington-based Food Marketing Institute, indicates that 85 percent of Latinos do most of their shopping in supermarkets and that 80 percent of them say brands are very important in deciding where they shop.

　　　What's more, Latinos, with an estimated buying power approaching half a trillion 50　dollars yearly, visit grocery stores an average of 4.7 times a week, compared with 2.2 times for the average American. They also outspend other Americans, $117 to $87 per week in grocery shopping, according to the study.

　　　Prudencio Unanue recognized the opportunity early. In 1936 he and his wife Carolina moved to the United States from Spain. They missed the foods of Spain and

55 started a small business in lower Manhattan to sell olives, olive oil, and sardines to the Hispanic people who were living in the area. From this small storefront, the business grew to selling globally and has evolved into the largest family-owned company in the United States.

Goya has shown leadership and civic responsibility in local and national organiza-
60 tions that help Hispanic communities. For example, in a drive to improve safety in the bodegas in New York City, Goya became the lead sponsor for "Operation Safe Store." In a recent exhibit on Portraits of Latino Achievement, the Smithsonian Museum named Prudencio Unanue as one of the twenty-four outstanding Hispanics in America.

(827 words)

—From Alejandro Bianchi and Gabriel Sama, "Goya Foods Leads an Ethnic Sales Trend." Reprinted with permission of *The Wall Street Journal*, Copyright © 2002 Dow Jones & Company, Inc. All Rights Reserved Worldwide.

THINKING AND WRITING AFTER READING

RECALL Self-test your understanding.

Your instructor may choose to give you a true-false comprehension review.

REACT What factors point to the continuing growth of Goya Foods? _____

_____

REFLECT How does the marketing of Goya Foods compare with the marketing strategies for other items you might purchase at the grocery store? _____

_____

THINK CRITICALLY What other products employ the "shop within a shop" market-ing technique successfully? Would this strategy work best within food stores alone, or can other markets be tapped equally well? _____

_____

THINK AND WRITE How has the charitable policy of giving back to the commu-nity worked to help Goya Foods remain a leader in the Hispanic food market?

_____

_____

Interpret the Quote

Now that you have finished reading the selection, "Goya Foods," go back to the beginning of the selection and read the opening quote again. On a separate sheet of paper, describe how Goya Foods did the "right job" in attracting consumers to its products.

Name _____

Date _____

COMPREHENSION QUESTIONS

Answer the following with *a*, *b*, *c*, or *d*, or fill in the blank. In order to help you analyze your strengths and weaknesses, the question types are indicated.

Main Idea _____ 1. The best statement of the main idea of the selection is:

    a. Goya Foods dominates the Hispanic food market through its shelving and marketing strategies.

    b. Goya Foods has successfully avoided paying slotting fees to its retailers.

    c. Consumers favor Goya Foods for its commitment to customer service.

    d. Goya Foods is aggressively seeking to increase sales in the crossover market.

Detail _____ 2. According to the selection, the reason Goya Foods employed the one-aisle marketing approach was

    a. the intuition of Goya CEO Andy Unanue.

    b. observation of the strategy's success when used by other Latino food companies.

    c. research findings indicating its consumers preferred a designated section for all cooking goods.

    d. retailers prefer that ethnic foods be grouped together.

Inference _____ 3. The reader can conclude that the major reason for Goya's not paying a slotting fee is that

    a. retailers do not want shelf space used for unproven products.

    b. the Goya products consistently make money for retailers.

    c. the independent brokers control the retail space.

    d. Goya pioneered the shelving strategies before fees were being charged.

Inference _____ 4. The author implies that Goya's drive for the crossover business

    a. is tempting the company to abandon the special shelving strategy.

    b. is driven by competition from Unilever.

    c. is lukewarm because of satisfaction among Latino clients.

    d. is expected to change as Latino immigrants become Americanized.

Detail _____ 5. In comparison with the average American grocery shopper, Latinos

    a. shop for groceries more than twice as often.

    b. spend twice as much money on groceries.

    c. spend almost a half trillion dollars on groceries in a year.

    d. do more of their shopping in supermarkets than in small stores.

Inference _____ 6. By saying that ethnic-based merchandisers are "pushing on an open door" at retailers, the author implies that ethnic-based merchandisers

    a. meet initial resistance.

    b. must provide a powerful sales record.

    c. are welcomed by retailers.

    d. must push to compete with Goya Foods.

Inference _____ 7. The best example of Goya's community involvement is

  a. the fact that the business remains family-owned.
  b. the company's exhibit at the Smithsonian Institute.
  c. the company's role in Operation Safe Store.
  d. the company's reputation as a multinational firm.

Answer the following with *T* (true), *F* (false), or *CT* (can't tell).

Detail _____ 8. The founder of Goya Foods immigrated to New York City from South America and thus knew the Latino market.

Detail _____ 9. The ethnic food competitors of Goya Foods are not using the same shelving strategy as Goya to meet the Latino market.

Inference _____ 10. The author implies that the slotting fee is intended to offset losses rather than primarily to increase profits.

VOCABULARY

Answer the following with *a, b, c,* or *d* for the word or phrase that best defines the boldface word used in the selection. The number in parentheses indicates the line of the passage in which the word is located.

_____ 1. "**consumer** likes to buy" (5)

  a. shopper
  b. relative
  c. citizen
  d. store

_____ 2. "at the **forefront**" (9)

  a. end
  b. beginning
  c. position
  d. outside

_____ 3. "of a **trend**" (9)

  a. aversion
  b. habit
  c. moving
  d. direction

_____ 4. "land that are **dominated** by" (10)

  a. populated
  b. traveled
  c. loved
  d. built

_____ 5. "**positioned** itself" (11)

  a. bought
  b. constructed
  c. placed
  d. decorated

_____ 6. "company **strives**" (17)

  a. hates
  b. tries
  c. reaches
  d. fails

_____ 7. "**gauging** market demand" (25)

  a. speculating
  b. decreasing
  c. measuring
  d. gouging

_____ 8. "Hispanic **demographic**" (26)

  a. family
  b. history
  c. children
  d. population

_____ 9. "don't **garner**" (33)

  a. sell
  b. like
  c. find
  d. collect

_____ 10. "**core** clients" (38)

  a. expensive
  b. basic
  c. negative
  d. personal

Your instructor may choose to give a true-false vocabulary review.

VOCABULARY ENRICHMENT

A. Study the following definitions and then circle the similar-sounding word that is correct in each sentence.

conscience: sense of right and wrong	**fair:** just or right
conscious: aware	**fare:** fee for transportation

1. Goya's involvement in community affairs indicates that the company has a social (**conscience, conscious**).

2. Some in the foods business may feel that exempting Goya from paying slotting fees gives the company an advantage which is not (**fair, fare**) to their competitors.

B. **Analogies:** Supply a word that completes each analogy, then state the relationship that has been established.

3. *Knife* is to *cut* as *gun* is to _____

    Relationship? _____

4. *Old* is to *ancient* as *new* is to _____

    Relationship? _____

5. *Eye* is to *see* as *ear* is to _____

    Relationship? _____

6. *Go* is to *come* as *sell* is to _____

    Relationship? _____

7. *State* is to *governor* as *city* is to _____

    Relationship? _____

8. *Skin* is to *person* as *fur* is to _____

    Relationship? _____

9. *Smart* is to *intelligent* as *chilly* is to _____

    Relationship? _____

10. *Razor* is to *sharp* as *cement* is to _____

    Relationship? _____

11. *Winter* is to *summer* as *wet* is to _____

    Relationship? _____

C. **Words from Literature:** The names of certain characters in literature have dropped their capital letters and taken on special meaning in the English language. The following are from Spanish and English literature, respectively. Read the entries to determine their definitions and origins.

quix·ot·ic \kwik-'sä-tik\ *adj* [Don *Quixote*] (1718)   **1** : foolishly impractical esp. in the pursuit of ideals; *esp* : marked by rash lofty romantic ideas or extravagantly chivalrous action   **2** : CAPRICIOUS, UNPREDICTABLE   *syn* see IMAGINARY — **quix·ot·i·cal** \-ti-kəl\ *adj* — **quix·ot·i·cal·ly** \-ti-k(ə-)lē\ *adv*

Source: By permission. From *Merriam-Webster's Collegiate® Dictionary, 11th Edition.* © 2008 by Merriam-Webster Incorporated (www.Merriam-Webster.com).

12. *Quixotic* means _____.

13. The origin of the word is _____.

Lil·li·put \'li-li-(ˌ)pət\ *n* (1726) : an island in Swift's *Gulliver's Travels* where the inhabitants are six inches tall
Lil·li·pu·tian \ˌli-lə-'pyü-shən\ *adj* (1726)   **1** : of, relating to, or characteristic of the Lilliputians or the island of Lilliput   **2** *often not cap* **a** : SMALL, MINIATURE ⟨a ∼ camera⟩ **b** : PETTY
Lilliputian *n* (1726)   **1** : an inhabitant of Lilliput   **2** *often not cap* : one resembling a Lilliputian; *esp* : an undersized individual

Source: By permission. From *Merriam-Webster's Collegiate® Dictionary, 11th Edition.* © 2008 by Merriam-Webster Incorporated (www.Merriam-Webster.com).

14. *Lilliputian* means _____.

15. The origin of the word is _____.

ASSESS YOUR LEARNING

Review confusing questions, seek clarification, and make notes in your text to help you remember new information and vocabulary.

selection 3 Communication

"An eye can threaten like a loaded and leveled gun, or it can insult like hissing or kicking; or, in its altered mood, by beams of kindness, it can make the heart dance for joy."
—Ralph Waldo Emerson

We draw conclusions about people through what their eyes communicate. A lifted eyebrow suggests surprise, and a narrowed gaze hints at skepticism. We say "Look me straight in the eye" to search for truth. On the other hand, a furtive glance arouses suspicion. To both lubricate and protect the eyes, we normally blink an average of fifteen times a minute, but excessive blinking can cause us to question sincerity. The eyes have been called the "mirrors of the soul." How accurate are we in reading the eyes?

THINKING BEFORE READING

Preview for content and organizational clues. Activate your schema and anticipate what you will learn.

Why does the expression "The couple locked eyes" suggest romance?

When speaking to a group, do you make eye contact with each member of the audience?

When do your pupils become dilated?

After reading this I will probably know _____.

VOCABULARY PREVIEW

Are you familiar with these words?

duration	gaze	perceive	compensate	avert
auditory	intuitive	dilated	constricted	profound

Why do you want to be *compensated* for your hard work?

How is *intuitive* related to *intuition*?

Is a *profound* statement worthy of remembering?

Your instructor may choose to give a true-false vocabulary review before or after reading.

THINKING DURING READING

As you read, use the six thinking strategies of a good reader: predict, picture, relate, monitor, correct, and annotate.

OUTLINING

Annotate the selection and then make an informal study outline to prepare for an essay exam.

Reader's *Tip* Reading and Studying Communication

Ask yourself the following questions as you read a communications text.

- How can I improve as a communicator and a conversationalist?
- How do I react to other people? Am I open to new ideas?
- How can I become a more valuable group member or a more productive group leader?
- Am I afraid to speak in public? How can I lessen that fear?
- What actions and expressions should be avoided in opening and closing a speech?

EYE COMMUNICATION

The messages communicated by the eyes vary depending on the duration, direction, and quality of the eye behavior. For example, in every culture there are rather strict, though unstated, rules for the proper duration for eye contact. In much of England and the United States, for example, the average length of gaze is 2.95 seconds. The average

5   length of mutual gaze (two persons gazing at each other) is 1.18 seconds. When eye contact falls short of this amount, you may think the person is uninterested, shy, or preoccupied. When the appropriate amount of time is exceeded, you may perceive this as showing high interest.

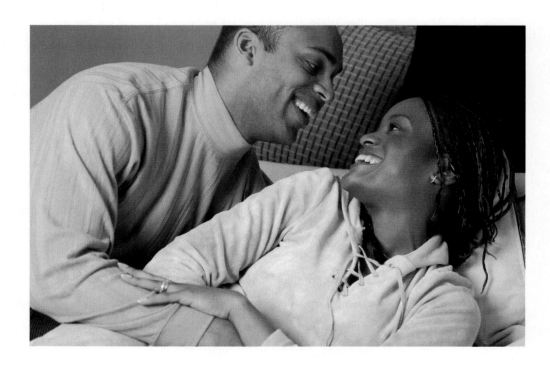

In much of the United States direct eye contact is considered an expression of
10 honesty and forthrightness. But the Japanese often view this as a lack of respect. The
Japanese will glance at the other person's face rarely and then only for very short periods.
In many Hispanic cultures, direct eye contact signifies a certain equality and so should be
avoided by, say, children when speaking to a person in authority. Try visualizing the potential misunderstandings that eye communication alone could create when people from
15 Tokyo, San Francisco, and San Juan try to communicate.

The direction of the eye also communicates. Generally, in communicating with another person, you would glance alternatively at the other person's face, then away, then
again at the face, and so on. When these directional rules are broken, different meanings
are communicated—abnormally high or low interest, self-consciousness, nervousness
20 over the interaction, and so on. The quality—how wide or how narrow your eyes get
during interaction—also communicates meaning, especially interest level and such emotions as surprise, fear, and disgust.

EYE CONTACT

You use eye contact to serve several important functions. You can use eye contact to
monitor feedback. For example, when you talk with someone, you look at the person
25 intently, as if to say, "Well, what do you think?" or "React to what I've just said." You also
look at speakers to let them know that you're listening. Studies show that listeners gaze at
speakers more than speakers gaze at listeners. The percentage of interaction time spent
gazing while listening, for example, ranges from 62 percent to 75 percent; the percentage of time spent gazing while talking, however, ranges from 38 percent to 41 percent.
30 When these percentages are reversed—when a speaker gazes at the listener for longer
than "normal" periods or when a listener gazes at the speaker for shorter than "normal"
periods—the conversational interaction becomes awkward. You may wish to try this with
a friend. Even with mutual awareness, you'll notice the discomfort caused by this seemingly minor communication change.

35 When you speak with two or three other people, you maintain eye contact to *secure
the attention and interest* of your listeners. When someone fails to pay attention you will
increase attention. When making an especially important point, you would look intently
at your listeners—assuming what nonverbal researchers call "visual dominance behavior"—
almost as a way of preventing them from devoting any attention to anything but what
40 you're saying.

Eye communication can also *regulate or control the conversation.* For example, with
eye movements you can inform the other person that the channel of communication is
open and that she or he should now speak. A clear example of this occurs in the college
classroom, where the instructor asks a question and then locks eyes with a student.

45 Without any verbal message, it's assumed that the student should answer the question. Similarly, when you're nearing the end of what you want to say, you'll probably focus eye contact on the person you think wants to speak next and then turn over the conversation to that person.

Eye communication also helps *signal the nature of the relationship* between two
50 people—for example, one of positive or negative regard. In the United States when you like someone, you increase your eye contact. When eye contact exceeds 60 percent in an interaction, the people are probably more interested in each other than in the verbal messages being exchanged.

Eye contact in the higher primates is often used to signal status and aggression.
55 Among many younger people, prolonged eye contact from a stranger is taken to signify aggressiveness and has frequently prompted physical violence, just because one person looked perhaps a little longer than is considered normal in that specific culture. A less extreme way to assert one's position is with visual dominance behavior. The average person maintains a higher level of eye contact while listening and a lower level while speaking.
60 When people want to signal dominance, they may reverse this pattern and maintain a high level of eye contact while talking but a much lower level while listening. Another way people try to signal dominance is to lower their eyebrows. Research does support this general interpretation of behavior. For example, faces with lowered eyebrows, in both cartoons and photographs, were judged to communicate greater dominance than
65 raised eyebrows. Eye movements may also signal whether the relationship between two people is amorous, hostile, or indifferent.

Eye movements are often used to *compensate for increased physical distance*. By making eye contact, we overcome psychologically the physical distance between us. When we catch someone's eye at a party, for example, we become psychologically close even
70 though we may be separated by considerable physical distance. Eye contact and other expressions of psychological closeness, such as self-disclosure and intimacy, have been found to vary in proportion to each other.

EYE AVOIDANCE

The eyes, sociologist Erving Goffman observed in *Interaction Ritual* (1967), are "great intruders." When you avoid eye contact or avert your glance, you allow others to maintain
75 their privacy. You probably do this when you see a couple arguing in the street or on a bus. You turn your eyes away as if to say, "I don't mean to intrude; I respect your privacy." Goffman refers to this behavior as **civil inattention**.

Eye avoidance can also signal lack of interest—in a person, a conversation, or some visual stimulus. At times, like the ostrich, we hide our eyes to try to cut off unpleasant
80 stimuli. Notice, for example, how quickly people close their eyes in the face of some

extreme unpleasantness. Interestingly enough, even if the unpleasantness is auditory, we tend to shut it out by closing our eyes. At other times, we close our eyes to block out visual stimuli and thus heighten our other senses; for example we often listen to music with our eyes closed. Lovers often close their eyes while kissing, and many people prefer to
85 make love in a dark or dimly lit room.

PUPIL DILATION

In the fifteenth and sixteenth centuries, Italian women used to put drops of belladonna (which literally means "beautiful woman") into their eyes to enlarge the pupils so that they would look more attractive. Contemporary research supports the intuitive logic of these women; dilated pupils are in fact judged more attractive than constricted ones.

90   In one study, photographs of women were retouched. In one set of photographs, the pupils were enlarged, and in the other they were made smaller. Men were then asked to judge the women's personalities from the photographs. The photos of women with small pupils drew responses such as cold, hard, and selfish; those with dilated pupils drew responses such as feminine and soft. However, the male observers could not verbalize the
95 reasons for the different perceptions. **Pupil dilation** and reactions to changes in the pupil size of others both seem to function below the level of conscious awareness.

        Pupil size also reveals your interest and level of emotional arousal. Your pupils enlarge when you're interested in something or when you're emotionally aroused. When homosexuals and heterosexuals were shown pictures of nude bodies, the homosexuals' pupils
100 dilated more when viewing same-sex bodies. These papillary responses are unconscious and are even observed in persons with profound mental retardation. Perhaps we judge dilated pupils more attractive because we judge them as indicative of a person's interest in us. That may be why models, Beanie Babies, and Teletubbies have exceptionally large pupils.

105   Although belladonna is no longer used, the cosmetics industry has made millions selling eye enhancers—eye shadow, eyeliner, false eyelashes, and tinted contact lenses that change eye color. These items function (ideally, at least) to draw attention to these most powerful communicators.

(1,394 words)

—From Joseph A. DeVito, *The Interpersonal Communication Book,* 12th edition.
Published by Allyn and Bacon/Merrill Education, Boston, MA. Copyright © 2009 by
Pearson Education. Adapted by permission of the publisher.

STUDY OUTLINE

Use your annotations to make an outline of significant elements in behavior change.

THINKING AND WRITING AFTER READING

RECALL Self-test your understanding.

Your instructor may choose to give you a true-false comprehension review.

REACT Why do you feel uncomfortable when locked in a mutual gaze for over 1.18 seconds? _____

_____

REFLECT Try the suggested experiment of adjusting the percentage of interaction time for gazing. With another student, first let the speaker gaze for 62 to 75 percent of the time, and then have the speaker gaze for only 38 to 41 percent of the time. Next, try the same percentages for the listener. Describe the difficulties and your reactions. _____

_____

THINK CRITICALLY How do college instructors use eye contact to enhance instruction? Give examples of a variety of effective strategies that you have observed. _____

_____

THINK AND WRITE Why do you agree or disagree that the eyes are the "mirrors to the soul"? Give examples of when you feel you have been both correct and incorrect in "reading the eyes." _____

_____

_____

Interpret the Quote

Now that you have finished reading the selection, "Eye Communication," go back to the beginning of the selection and read the opening quote again. On a separate sheet of paper, describe what Emerson means when he says that an eye can "threaten like a loaded and leveled gun." Also, describe two situations in which you used your eyes to communicate joy or anger.

Name _____

Date _____

COMPREHENSION QUESTIONS

Answer the following with *a, b, c,* or *d,* or fill in the blank. In order to help you analyze your strengths and weaknesses, the question types are indicated.

Main Idea   _____   1. The best statement of the main idea of the selection is:

    a. Eye contact in different cultures varies according to duration, direction, and quality.

    b. Eye contact communicates several different messages that vary according to duration, direction, and quality.

    c. When the rules are broken for eye contact, the messages can range from self-consciousness to fear and disgust.

    d. The appropriateness of eye contact can be measured in the length of seconds of duration and the percentage of time gazing while listening.

Detail   _____   2. Direct eye contact is considered a sign of equality in

    a. Japan.

    b. England.

    c. the United States.

    d. Latin America.

Detail   _____   3. For a speaker to be considered within the "normal" range, an appropriate percentage of time spent gazing while talking is

    a. 39 percent.

    b. 45 percent.

    c. 62 percent.

    d. 75 percent.

Inference   _____   4. The author suggests that in the United States a short duration of eye contact will most likely be interpreted as

    a. aggression.

    b. status for the speaker.

    c. love interest.

    d. inattention.

Inference   5. In what cases might civil inattention be inappropriate? _____

    _____

    _____

Detail   _____   6. Belladonna was all of the following *except*

    a. eye drops used by Italian women.

    b. a fifteenth- and sixteenth-century beauty enhancer.

    c. eye medication with beautifying side effects.

    d. an Italian word meaning "beautiful woman."

selection **3**

Detail _____ 7. According to research findings discussed in the passage, the general viewer's pupil dilation reactions when viewing pictures of nude bodies were all of the following *except*

    a. varying in emotional arousal for different groups.
    b. emotionally arousing for homosexuals viewing same-sex pictures.
    c. emotionally arousing for heterosexuals viewing same-sex pictures.
    d. made without conscious awareness.

Answer the following with *T* (true), *F* (false), or *CT* (can't tell).

Detail _____ 8. In referring to the quality of eye communication, the author is describing how wide or narrow the eyes are during interaction.

Detail _____ 9. The eyes can silently be used by a speaker to indicate the next to speak.

Detail _____10. A high level of eye contact by the listener shows a lack of status for the speaker.

VOCABULARY

Answer the following with *a, b, c,* or *d* for the word or phrase that best defines the boldface word as used in the selection. The number in parentheses indicates the line of the passage in which the word appears.

_____ 1. "depending on the **duration**" (1)

    a. strength
    b. length
    c. ability
    d. meaning

_____ 2. "length of **gaze**" (4)

    a. look
    b. clarity
    c. direction
    d. quality

_____ 3. "may **perceive** this" (7)

    a. deny
    b. dismiss
    c. object to
    d. recognize

_____ 4. "used to **compensate** for" (67)

    a. calculate
    b. make up
    c. detract
    d. vary

_____ 5. "**avert** your glance" (74)

    a. turn toward
    b. intensify
    c. extend
    d. turn away

_____ 6. "unpleasantness is **auditory**" (81)

    a. seen
    b. imagined
    c. heard
    d. real

_____ 7. "**intuitive** logic" (88)

    a. instinctive
    b. ancient
    c. stylish
    d. historic

_____ 8. "**dilated** pupils" (89)

    a. colored
    b. narrowed
    c. enlarged
    d. painted

_____ 9. "**constricted** ones" (89)

    a. narrowed
    b. enlarged
    c. closed
    d. unadorned

_____10. "**profound** mental retardation" (101)

    a. slight
    b. deep
    c. recent
    d. confusing

Your instructor may choose to give a true-false vocabulary review.

selection 3

VOCABULARY ENRICHMENT

A. Use context clues and word parts to determine the meaning of the boldface words from a popular communications textbook.

1. When speaking, avoid **adaptors,** such as scratching your face while speaking, that interfere with effective communication. _____
   _____

2. Be specific and use examples to clarify points so that your audience is not confused by **ambiguity**. _____

3. Express **empathy** as a listener by actively involving your face to reflect the feelings that you think the speaker is experiencing. _____
   _____

4. Use a **euphemism** when appropriate. Rather than saying "I am sorry your father died," say "I am sorry he passed away." _____
   _____

5. In using a **feedforward** to alert your listener, be brief and always follow through on what you promised. _____
   _____

6. In an interpersonal conflict, stick to the specific topic and avoid **gunnysacking** previous grievances. _____
   _____

7. In analyzing the supplied information, the speaker solved the problem by **deduction**. _____

8. In a conversation, be sensitive to the **leave-taking cues** of others and politely end the exchange. _____
   _____

9. **Emphatic communication**—"Hello," "How are you?" and "I'm fine"—is traditional in American culture. _____
   _____

10. Those who study **proxemics** in foreign countries find variations in the accepted distances for personal interaction and even the organization of space in homes and offices. _____
    _____

B. **Analogies:** Supply a word that completes each analogy, then state the relationship that has been established.

11. *Music* is to *piano* as *explosion* is to _____

    Relationship? _____

12. *Whale* is to *mammal* as *ant* is to _____

    Relationship? _____

13. *Bones* are to *leg* as *freckles* are to _____

    Relationship? _____

14. *Attract* is to *repel* as *pretty* is to _____

    Relationship? _____

15. *Tiger* is to *meat* as *cow* is to _____

    Relationship? _____

ASSESS YOUR LEARNING

Review confusing questions, seek clarification, and make notes in your text to help you remember new information and vocabulary.

selection 3

Personal *Feedback* **2**

Name _____

1. Would you describe yourself as a spontaneous person or a person who plans?

   _____

   _____

   _____

2. What type of noise bothers you when you study? _____

   _____

   _____

3. Have you been generally happy or unhappy this week? Explain why.

   _____

   _____

   _____

4. What has happened this week to make you laugh at yourself? _____

   _____

   _____

5. List three questions that you have asked in any of your classes during the past two weeks. _____

   _____

   _____

6. What routine do you usually follow at night to get ready for the next day at school?

   _____

   _____

   _____

7. What has pleasantly surprised you about your college experience? _____

   _____

   _____

   _____

8. How did you waste time this past week? _____

   _____

   _____

Tear out and submit to your instructor.

Vocabulary Lesson

See, Hear, and Voice Your Concerns

Study the roots, words, and sentences.

Roots	*Vis, vid*: see	*aud, aus*: hear or listen	*voc, vok*: voice or call

Words with *vis* or *vid* = *see*

What did Julius Caesar mean by, "Veni, <u>vidi</u>, vici,"? Can <u>invisible</u> ink be seen?

- Visible: can be seen

  On clear nights, stars are more *visible* in the countryside than in cities.

- Visionary: one who sees visions or dreams of the future

  Be both a *visionary* and a good businessperson to create a successful company.

- Visor: a brim to protect the eyes so you can see better

  Wear a *visor* for tennis so the sun doesn't interfere with your performance.

- Evident: can easily be seen

  The solution was *evident* to those who had previously encountered the problem.

- Visa: a passport endorsement giving the bearer the right to enter a country

  Prior to visiting certain countries, tourists must apply for a *visa*.

- Vista: a view from a distance

  The *vista* from a mountaintop on an autumn day can be breathtaking.

- Envision: to see in one's mind

  Try to *envision* the furniture in the empty room.

Words with *aud* or *aus* = *hear* or *listen*

Does an <u>audience</u> sit in an <u>auditorium</u>? Can <u>inaudible</u> words be heard?

- Audible: can be heard

  Because she speaks so softly, her voice is barely *audible*.

- Audition: a hearing to try out for a role

  The actor nervously began the *audition* for a part in the Broadway musical.

- Audio: sound made by electronic or mechanical reproduction

  The *audio* on my television is not clear.

- Auditory: relating to hearing

  The *auditory* nerves are damaged and thus hearing is impaired.

- Audit: a formal examination of accounts made by an accountant

  Citizens fear an *audit* by the Internal Revenue Service.

Words with *voc* or *vok* = *voice* or *call*

How can you voice your ideas on vocabulary? Are vocal people heard?

- Evoke: call out from the past

  The ceremony was designed to *evoke* the memory of past heroes.

- Vocation: a call to serve in a particular profession

  Although my plans may change, I am preparing for a *vocation* in nursing.

- Vociferous: making a noisy outcry

  The opponent's remarks drew *vociferous* objections.

- Avocation: a hobby or second calling

  My money comes from banking, but music is my *avocation*.

- Convocation: an assembly or calling together

  The *convocation* celebrated the 75th anniversary of the college.

- Invocation: solemn prayer or divine blessing

  The religious service began with an *invocation*.

- Invoke: to call forth

  The witness *invoked* the Fifth Amendment to avoid answering questions.

Review

Part I

Choose the best word from the list to complete each of the following sentences.

invocation	audience	vocation	vista	visor
vocal	convocation	audit	avocation	visa

1. If customers are _____, they can make their complaints heard.

2. From the cruise ship, the travelers could see a mountain _____.

3. Our chorus sang at the _____ honoring our new college president.

4. A company _____ indicated funds were incorrectly allocated.

5. The _____ clapped after the performance.

6. The priest gave a brief _____ at the beginning of the assembly.

7. A _____ is required to enter Israel.

8. Recreational golfing can become a serious and challenging _____.

9. After thirty years, the electrical engineer retired from his lifelong

   _____.

10. Wear a _____ to protect your eyes from the sun.

Part II

Answer the following with *T* (true) or *F* (false).

_____ 11. Parents invoke their authority to get their children to go to bed.

_____ 12. A vociferous group is quiet and orderly.

_____ 13. A visionary might seek to make a dream become a reality.

_____ 14. The taillights on a motor vehicle should be visible at night.

_____ 15. To promote a cause, activists usually want a vocal spokesperson.

_____ 16. For most people, gardening is an avocation rather than a vocation.

_____ 17. Landing a part in a play usually requires an audition.

_____ 18. Financial records are reviewed in a company audit.

_____ 19. The person who provokes an argument is called a troublemaker.

_____ 20. Teens usually prefer background music to be inaudible.

Reading Reference Materials

Whether you are researching a topic for a term paper or an automobile purchase decision, you want to find relevant and reliable data to support your final conclusions and recommendations. The material you use for support will depend on your project, your goals, and the research tools available to you.

Begin with Encyclopedias

Encyclopedias will provide you with background information about your topic, define key words used in the field, and, in certain cases, mention important researchers in the area under consideration. Many different encyclopedias are available for specific topics, such as the *Encyclopedia of African American Religions*, *Encyclopedia of Earth Sciences*, and *The Cambridge Encyclopedia of Astronomy*. For college research, general encyclopedias such as *Americana*, *Colliers*, and *Britannica* may be helpful in your preliminary efforts at defining your research topic, but they will probably not include enough in-depth information to support your premise.

Your college or university library probably has a subscription to several encyclopedias on the Web. Some popular ones are the following:

Encarta	encarta.msn.com
Encyclopedia Britannica	britannica.com
Grolier	go.grolier.com

Keep in mind that free general encyclopedias online are not as comprehensive as subscription-based online encyclopedias or encyclopedias in print. Try www.freeality.com/encyclop.htm or www.encyclopedia.com for hot links to other online sources.

exercise 1   Visit your college library and locate two specialty encyclopedias, excluding general encyclopedias such as the **Encyclopedia Britannica**. It may be possible to do this remotely from the library link at your college's Web site. Take notes on an interesting entry from each and share the notes with your classmates.

Use Indexes to Scholarly and Popular Publications

Most research topics can be approached from the viewpoints of several academic disciplines. For example, sexual assault can be addressed from a legal, medical, sociological, psychological, or educational vantage point. Decide on the academic discipline for your research paper, and ask a reference librarian to help you select an appropriate index. Then use the index to locate appropriate articles in the *periodical literature*. **Periodical** is a term used to describe all publications that come out on a regular schedule. They include popular sources and scholarly journals.

Articles in **popular sources** (usually newspapers and magazines) are aimed at the general public and written by professional journalists who are usually not specialists in the field. On the other hand, articles in **scholarly journals** contain research results of experts and always include a **bibliography**, a list of the

Reader's *Tip* Defining Your Topic

To define your research topic, consider:

- **Geography:** Pick a specific area.
- **Time Frame:** Limit the time period under examination.
- **Interest Groups:** Narrow your research by appropriate descriptors such as age, gender, or occupation.
- **Academic Discipline:** What college or department would study this subject?

sources consulted by the author of the article. For most college research, you will need to use primarily scholarly journals.

Many articles that you find in indexes will not be relevant to your specific needs. Use the information that appears in the index entries to save time and make decisions. Each entry will display a **citation** to the article that includes the title, author(s), name of the periodical, volume and page numbers, issue date, and descriptive notes or key search terms. Usually the entry will also include an abstract.

If the article title and the date look appropriate to your search, read the abstract. The **abstract** is a short paragraph that summarizes the article, stating the premise the authors set out to prove, the subjects or location of the project, and the conclusions. If the abstract sounds as if the article will be relevant to your research, print the entry page or record the information so you can locate a copy of the article. In some cases the database provides a link to the complete text of the article. However, remember that the best articles for your topic may not be available electronically, but they may be easily accessible in the library collection.

Use the Internet

For researching, the Internet has both advantages and limitations. The advantages are the up-to-date coverage and the ease with which you can search, access, and download information. The Internet is often more informative and current than the library on topics relating popular trends, computer science, and government reports. You can use a **search engine**, an index of World Wide Web locations, to find a list of up-to-date Web sites that include your search term(s). The Web sites listed will vary with the search engine you use. See Chapter 1 for Internet search directions.

Each search engine works slightly differently: Some group links from the same site, some rank the links based on relevancy, and some allow you to limit your search by date, language, or domain type. Examples of search engines include Yahoo! Search, Google, Dogpile, Altavista, Hotbot, Go.com, and Lycos. There are dozens of search engines available, and a good list is available through *Yahoo*! (www.yahoo.com). *Infomine* (infomine.ucr.edu) provides links to sources especially useful for academic research.

Because the Internet is open to everyone, always question the accuracy, reliability, and bias of online information. With the Internet, there are no gatekeepers. By contrast, the scholarly journals previously mentioned have editors, usually a group of experts in the field, who decide what gets published or rejected.

New York Times Graphics. Reprinted with permission. Microsoft Internet Explorer reprinted with permission from Microsoft Corporation.

exercise 2 Answer the following questions based on the Internet article "Monkeys Control a Robot Arm With Their Thoughts."

1. Would the Internet article be relevant if you were making a class presentation on medical technology? _____

2. Has this article been written for a scholarly journal? _____
   _____

3. Is the information in this article current enough to be useful? _____

4. What key words could you use to find similar articles about breakthroughs in medical technology? _____
   _____
   _____

7 Test-Taking Strategies

- Can your physical condition affect your test score?
- Are test questions predictable?
- How can you keep your mind on what you are reading?
- How are standardized test items made especially tricky?
- How do you organize an essay response?

Everyday Reading Skills: Using Mnemonics

Achieve Your Highest Potential

Are you now at the midpoint of your courses and preparing to take tests? Can insight improve your performance? High test scores should reflect your knowledge and ability, not your use of tricks or gimmicks. Awareness of test-taking strategies, however, can help you achieve your highest potential.

In college you face basically two types of tests: content exams and standardized tests. A content exam measures your knowledge on a subject that you have been studying. For example, the final exam in Psychology 101 measures your understanding and retention of what was taught throughout the course. The score becomes a major part of your final grade in the course. A standardized test, in contrast, measures your mastery of a skill that has developed over a long period of time, such as reading or mathematics. The scores on standardized tests usually help you qualify for entering or exiting specific college programs.

This chapter will help you improve your test scores by becoming aware of what is expected in the test-taking situation. Many of the following suggestions are obvious, but it is surprising how frequently students overlook them. Some relate to your physical and mental readiness for peak performance, whereas others explore means for coping with the challenging demands of the testing situation. Technical aspects of test construction are presented with opportunities for application and practice. Awareness and practice can indeed improve test scores and give you that winning edge!

Be Prepared

exercise 1

Read the passage, then write *agree* or *disagree* for the statements that follow.

Ed was earning money for college by working at a local convenience store in the late afternoon and early evening. On Wednesday night his boss asked him to work long past midnight for an employee who had called in sick. Because Ed needed money for his car payments, he agreed. He did not tell his boss that he had an important test early the next morning.

Thursday morning Ed slept through the alarm but fortunately was awakened by the telephone a half-hour later. He arrived at the exam as the test booklets were being distributed, having missed the professor's introductory remarks and responses to students' questions. Ed spent the first part of the test settling down mentally and physically. He was surprised by some of the material on the test. As he began to read and answer questions, he worried that he would not do well.

_____ 1. Ed was mentally alert after a good night's sleep.

Ed made a poor decision in not telling his boss that he needed adequate sleep on the night before his big test. Being alert rather than drowsy can make the difference in correctly answering one item or more. That correct item, for example, could make the difference in a failing score of 68 or a passing score of 70. Don't take chances when the stakes are high. Being alert can make a difference. *Set yourself up for success, and get plenty of sleep the night before a test.*

_____ 2. Because Ed arrived while the test was being distributed, his lateness did not work against him.

Ed could not immediately begin to work on the test because he had to calm himself first. If you arrive late and flustered, you lose valuable time and begin at a disadvantage.

Do your nerves a favor and avoid close calls. *Arrive five or ten minutes early for a test, and get settled.* Find a seat, greet your friends, and take out a pen or pencil.

_____ 3. Ed knew what to expect on the test.

Ed expressed surprise over some of the material on the test. Always check to be sure you know exactly what the test will cover. Know the format of the test. Will it be essay or multiple choice? Study with the format in mind. *Know what to expect on the test.*

_____ 4. Ed had probably asked how the test would be scored.

Because Ed arrived late and missed the professor's introductory remarks, he probably did not know about the scoring. Sometimes, but not very often, guessing is penalized in the scoring. When scores are based on answering all questions, you are better off guessing than leaving items blank. To be safe, ask if omitted items count against you. Also, sometimes some items are worth more points than others; this information is usually stated on the test itself. *Be aware of how the test will be scored.*

_____ 5. Ed approached the test with a positive mental attitude.

Ed had unnecessarily hurt himself and thus lost confidence. Preparation breeds self-confidence, and the lack of it breeds anxiety. Be prepared and plan for success. Give yourself good reasons to be optimistic. *Have confidence in your abilities.*

Stay Alert

exercise 2

Read the passage, then write *agree* or *disagree* for the statements that follow.

After reading the first passage on the comprehension test, Julie realized that she had no idea what she had read. She had seen all the words, but her mind was not on the message. She was excited and wanted to do well, but she was having trouble focusing on the material. She moved to the questions, hoping—erroneously—that they would provide clues to the meaning. They did not, and so she began rereading the passage with greater determination.

Julie finally gained control over the test and was doing fine until her classmates began to leave. She panicked. She was not finished, but others were turning in their tests. She was stuck on an item that she had reread three times. She looked at her watch and saw she had ten minutes left. That would be plenty of time to finish the last passage, if she could only regain her composure.

_____ 1. Julie was unable to concentrate when she began the test.

Julie could not initially focus her attention and comprehend the material. She was anxious and excited. *Concentration is essential for comprehension.* If you are distracted, take a few deep breaths to relax and get your mind on track. Tune out internal and external distractions, and focus on the meaning. Visualize the message and relate it to what you already know. *Follow directions,* and proceed with confidence. Use your pen as a pacer to concentrate on the passage. (For more on this technique of rhythmically following the words, see Chapter 8.) If anxiety is a consistent problem, seek help from the campus counseling center.

_____ 2. Julie was smart to wear a watch to the test.

Time is usually a major consideration on a test, so always wear *and use* a watch. *Size up the task and schedule your time.* Look over all parts of the test when you receive it. Determine the number of sections to be covered and allocate your time accordingly. Check periodically to see if you are meeting your time goals.

On a midterm or final exam, the number of points for each item sometimes varies greatly. Spend the most time on the items that yield the most points.

_____ 3. Julie should be sure of her answer to each item before moving to another.

Do not waste time that you may need later by pondering an especially difficult question. Mark the item with a dot and move on to the rest of the test. If you have a few minutes at the end, return to the marked items. *On a test every minute counts, so work rapidly.* Be aggressive and alert in moving through the test.

_____ 4. Changing an answer usually makes it wrong.

If you have time at the end of the test, *go back to the items you were unsure about.* If careful rethinking indicates another response, change your answer. Research shows that scores can be improved by making such changes.[1]

_____ 5. Students who finish a test early make the best grades.

The evidence indicates no correlation between high scores and the time taken to complete a test.[2] Speed does not always equal accuracy. *Don't be intimidated by students who finish early.* Schedule your time and meet your goals.

Seek Feedback

After a test, investigate your errors, if possible. On many standardized tests, only the score is reported, so you are unable to review the test itself. But when feedback is available, take advantage of the opportunity. Analyze your mistakes so you can learn from them and avoid repeating the same errors. Wrong answers give you valuable diagnostic information. If you do not understand the error in your thinking, seek advice from another student or the professor. Never merely look at your grade and forget the test if feedback is available.

Standardized Reading Tests

Students take standardized reading comprehension tests for a variety of reasons. Tests such as the SAT or the ACT are required for admission to many colleges. Computerized tests such as the Compass are used by many colleges for placement. Some states require additional testing for entering students, such as the CLAST in Florida. In Georgia, students must take a test with a reading component, the Regents Exam, before they are allowed to graduate. Thus, for college students, performing well on standardized tests can be critical to success.

[1]Marshal A. Geiger, "Changing Multiple-Choice Answers: Do Students Accurately Perceive Their Performance?" *Journal of Experimental Educating* 59 (1991): 250–257.

[2]Robert K. Bridges, "Order of Finish, Time to Completion, and Performance on Course-Based Objective Examinations: A Systematic Analysis of Their Relationship on Both Individual Exam Scores and Total Score Across Three Exams," Annual Meeting of the Eastern Psychological Association, Baltimore, MD, April 1982.

Personal *Feedback* **1**

Name _____

1. Depending on which test you were required to take, what were your scores on the SAT, the ACT, or a college placement test? _____

   _____

2. How do you feel you could improve your scores if you took the test again? _____

   _____

3. What state- or college-mandated tests will you need to take before college graduation?

   _____

   _____

4. What skills are included in those mandated tests? _____

   _____

5. What class activities do you feel you need to help you improve your standardized test scores? _____

   _____

6. What individual assistance could your instructor offer to help you improve?

   _____

   _____

7. Review the comprehension questions you missed in previous chapters. What question types do you tend to miss most often? Why? _____

   _____

8. What do you feel is the biggest misconception about standardized tests? _____

   _____

   _____

Tear out and submit to your instructor.

The following strategies will help you perform better on standardized reading tests.

Read to Comprehend

Read for the main idea of the passage. Don't fixate on details. Read to understand the author's message. Students ask, "Should I read the questions first and then the passage?" Experts differ in their opinions, but most advise reading the passage first and then answering the questions. If you read the questions first, you have five or six purposes for reading. Reading thus becomes fragmented and lacks focus. Read with one purpose: to understand the main idea rather than initially focusing on details.

Interact

Use the thinking strategies of good readers to interact with the passage. Predict the topic and activate your schema. Visualize the message and relate it to what you already know. Monitor and self-correct. Apply what you already know about the reading process to each test passage.

Anticipate

Anticipate what is coming. Test passages are frequently untitled and thus offer no clue to content. To activate your schema before reading, glance at the passage for a repeated word, name, or date that might signal its subject.

Read the first sentence carefully. Reread if necessary. The first sentence usually sets the stage for what is to come. It sometimes states the central theme or simply stimulates your curiosity. In any case, the first sentence starts you thinking about what you will be reading. Continue to anticipate throughout the passage. Some of your guesses will be right and some will be wrong. Double-check information and self-monitor.

Relax

Don't allow yourself to feel rushed. Work with control and confidence. That anxious, pressured feeling tends to occur at the beginning, middle, and end of a test. In the beginning, you are worried about not being able to concentrate immediately and thus having to reread. In the middle, you may be upset because you are only half finished, which is where you should be. When the first student finishes the test, you may again feel rushed and lose your concentration. To combat this feeling, use your pen as a pointer to focus your attention both mentally and physically on the printed page. Plan your time, relax, and concentrate.

Read to Learn

Test passages are not always dull. They may never compete with steamy novels, but some are quite interesting and informative. Rather than reading with the artificial purpose of only answering questions, read to learn and enjoy. You may surprise yourself!

Recall

Pull the passage together before pulling it apart. Remind yourself of the author's main point, rather than wait for questions to prod you. This final monitoring step in the reading process takes only a few seconds.

exercise 3 Using the suggestions just outlined, read the following passage as if it were part of a reading comprehension test. The handwritten side notes will help make you aware of a few aspects of your thinking.

A what?
How could she get out of there?

One of the most remarkable women in world history, famed for her vices as well as for her strong and able rule, governed China from about 660 to 705. The Empress Wu began her career as a concubine in the harem of the third T'ang emperor. When the emperor died, Wu and all the other concubines, according to custom, had their heads shaved and entered a Buddhist convent. Here they were expected to pass the remainder of their lives. Wu, however, was too intelligent and beautiful—as well as too unscrupulous—to accept such a fate. Within a year she had won the new emperor's heart and had become his concubine. According to a hostile tradition, she first met the new emperor in a lavatory when he was paying a ceremonial visit to the convent.

Where?

Wu accused empress and took power

Evil?

Puppets?

Full power

Evil monks wanting power manipulated scripture.

Does the author think it's O.K.?

Surprise!

Expanded empire Weaknesses?

Lover?

One too many Downfall

Wu rose steadily in the new emperor's favor until, after accusing the empress of engaging in sorcery, murdering her baby daughter, and plotting to poison her husband, she was herself installed as empress. According to the official history of the age, "The whole sovereign power passed into her hands. Life and death, reward and punishment, were determined by her word. The Son of Heaven merely sat upon his throne with hands folded."

After the death of the emperor twenty years later, Wu installed two of her sons as successive puppets. She ruthlessly employed secret police and informers to suppress conspiracies against her. Finally, in 690 at the age of sixty-two, she usurped the imperial title and became the only woman ever to rule China in name as well as in fact.

To legitimize her usurpation, the empress was aided by a group of unscrupulous Buddhist monks, one of whom is reputed to have been her lover. They discovered in Buddhist scriptures a prophecy that a pious woman was destined to be reborn as the ruler of an empire that would inaugurate a better age and to which all countries would be subject. Not only did the monks identify Wu as the woman in the prophecy, but they acclaimed her as a divine incarnation of the Buddha. The T'ang capital was renamed the Divine Capital, and Wu assumed a special title—"Holy Mother Divine Imperial One."

Despite her ruthlessness—understandable in the totally unprecedented situation of a woman seeking successfully to rule a great empire—the Empress Wu was an able ruler who consolidated the T'ang Dynasty. She not only avenged earlier Sui and T'ang defeats at the hands of the northern Koreans who had been subject to the Han, but she made all of Korea a loyal vassal state of China. Yet because she was a woman and a usurper, she found little favor with Chinese Confucian historians. They played up her vices, particularly her many favorites and lovers whom she rewarded with unprecedented honors.

Among those who gained great influence over the aging empress was a peddler of cosmetics, famous for his virility, who was first made abbot of a Buddhist monastery, then palace architect, and finally commander-in-chief of the armies on the northern frontier. At the age of seventy-two, her favorites—and reputed lovers—were two young brothers of a type known as "white faces" (men who were physically attractive but otherwise of no account), whose powdered and rouged faces were a common sight around the palace. When the empress appointed a younger brother of her two favorites to an important governorship, her leading ministers successfully conspired to put her son back on the throne. The two brothers were decapitated in the palace and the Empress Wu, the founder and only member of the Wu Dynasty, was forced to abdicate.

—*Civilization Past and Present,* by Walter Wallbank et al.

Understand Major Question Types

Test questions follow certain predictable patterns. For example, almost all passages are followed by one question on the main idea. Learn to recognize the types of questions and understand how they are constructed. What techniques does the test writer use when creating correct answers and incorrect distractors? Well-written distractors are tempting incorrect responses that draw attention, cause confusion, and thus force the test taker to use knowledge and logic. This section discusses each major question type, offers insight into their construction, and gives you an opportunity to play the role of test writer.

Main Idea Questions

Main idea questions ask you to identify the author's main point. These questions are often stated in one of the following forms:

The best statement of the main idea is . . .

The best title for this passage is . . .

The author is primarily concerned with . . .

The central theme of the passage is . . .

Incorrect responses to main idea items fall into two categories: (1) Some are too broad or general. They suggest that the passage includes much more than it actually does. For example, for a passage describing the hibernation of goldfish in a pond during the winter, the title "Fish" would be much too general to describe the specific topic. (2) Other incorrect answers are too narrow. They focus on details within the passage that support the main idea. The details may be attention-getting and interesting, but they do not describe the central focus. They are tempting, however, because they are direct statements from the passage.

If you have difficulty understanding the main idea of a passage, reread the first and last sentences. Sometimes, but not always, one of these sentences will give you an overview or focus.

EXAMPLE Answer the following main idea items on the passage about Empress Wu. Then read the handwritten remarks describing the student's thinking involved in judging whether a response is correct.

_____ 1. The best statement of the main idea of this passage is:

a. Buddhist monks bring Wu to power.

(Important detail, but the focus is on her.)

b. Women in China were not equal to men.

(Too broad and general, or not really covered.)

c. Empress Wu's ambition for her young lovers leads to her downfall.

(Very interesting, but a detail.)

d. Empress Wu ruthlessly usurped power but became an able ruler of a great empire.

(Yes, includes all major points and sounds great!)

_____ 2. Which is the best title for this passage?

a. Confucians Defeat Wu

(Detail.)

b. Empress Wu and Her Lovers

(Very interesting, but a detail.)

c. Empress Wu, Ruler of China

(Sounds best.)

d. Rulers of China

(Too broad; this passage is about only one woman.)

exercise 4 For further practice on main idea items, read the following passage and answer the two questions. After each possible answer, write why you did or did not choose that response. For main idea distractors, the reasons might be that the incorrect response is *too broad, too narrow, a detail,* or *not in the passage.*

In the United States, every state has laws prohibiting some type of relatives from marrying each other. Today there is universal agreement when it comes to prohibiting mother–son marriage and preventing full siblings from marrying, but the laws vary when it comes to more distant relatives. Thirty states prohibit first cousins from marrying, while twenty do not. Furthermore, the prohibitions are not limited to people related by birth. A dozen states forbid some types of in-laws from intermarrying.

—*Cultural Anthropology: The Human Challenge,*
Eleventh Edition, by William A. Haviland et al.

_____ 1. The best title for this passage is:

a. Marriage Laws _____

b. Marriage Prohibitions Among Relatives in the United States

_____

c. Mother-son Marriage Prohibitions _____

_____

d. Cultural Taboos Forbidding Intermarrying _____

_____

_____ 2. The best statement of the main idea of this passage is:

a. There is no disagreement with preventing marriage between

brothers and sisters. _____

_____

b. Twenty states allow first cousins to marry. _____

c. There are laws forbidding citizens from marrying relatives in

every state in the U.S. _____

d. Intermarriage results in increased health problems for the

children of such marriages. _____

Detail Questions

Detail questions check your ability to understand material that is directly stated in the passage. To find or double-check an answer, note a key word in the question and then quickly glance at the passage for that word or synonym. When you locate the term, reread the sentence for clarification. Detail questions fall in the following patterns:

The author states that . . .

According to the author . . .

According to the passage . . .

All of the following are true except . . .

A person, term, or place is . . .

Incorrect answers to detail questions tend to be false statements. Test writers like to use pompous or catchy phrases stated directly from the passage as distractors. Such phrases may sound authoritative but mean nothing.

EXAMPLE

Answer the following detail question on the passage about Empress Wu (see pages 332–333). Then note the handwritten remarks reflecting the thinking involved in judging whether a response is correct.

_____ 1. Empress Wu did all the following *except*

(Note the use of "except"; look for the only false item to be the correct answer.)

   a. consolidate the T'ang Dynasty.

   (True, this is stated in the fifth paragraph.)

   b. accuse the empress of sorcery.

   (True, this is stated in the second paragraph.)

   c. appoint the brother of a young favorite to an important governorship.

   (True, this is stated in the last paragraph.)

   d. poison her husband.

   (She did not do this, so this is the correct answer.)

exercise 5

For further practice on details, read the following passage and answer the detail question. Indicate beside each response why you did or did not choose the item.

> Be quite sure that there isn't a woman who cannot be won, and make up your mind that you will win her. Only you must prepare the ground. Sooner would the birds cease their song in the springtime, or the grasshopper be silent in the summer, . . . than a woman resist the tender wooing of a youthful lover. . . .
>
> In the first place, it's best to send her a letter, just to pave the way. In it you should tell her how you dote on her; pay her pretty compliments and say all the nice things lovers always say. . . . And promise, promise, promise. Promises will cost you nothing. Everyone's a millionaire where promises are concerned. . . .
>
> If she refuses your letter and sends it back unread, don't give up; hope for the best and try again.
>
> —From *The Love Books of Ovid,* translated by J. Lewis May

_____ 1. The author recommends the following to capture the heart of a young woman:

   a. Playing hard to get. _____

   b. Flattery. _____

   c. Total honesty. _____

   d. Gifts. _____

Inference Questions

An inference is something that is suggested but not directly stated. Clues in the passage lead you to make assumptions and draw conclusions. Items testing implied meaning deal with the attitudes and feelings of the writer that emerge as if from behind or between words. Favorable and unfavorable descriptions suggest positive and negative opinions toward a subject. Sarcastic remarks indicate the motivation of characters. Look for clues that help you develop logical assumptions. Inference questions may be stated in one of the following forms:

The author believes (or feels or implies) . . .

It can be inferred (deduced from clues) from the passage . . .

The passage (or author) suggests . . .

It can be concluded from the passage that . . .

Base your conclusion on both what is known and what is suggested. Incorrect responses to implied meaning items tend to be false statements that lack logical support.

EXAMPLE Answer the following inference questions on the passage about Empress Wu. Then note the handwritten remarks reflecting the thinking involved in judging whether a response is correct.

_____ 1. The author implies that Empress Wu

   a. was a devout Buddhist.

   (She was aided by Buddhists, but her religious preference is not suggested.)

   b. killed the first empress's baby daughter.

   (No; she accused the former empress of doing this.)

   c. let her vices lead to her downfall.

   (True, rewarding her young lovers probably hurt the empire.)

   d. conquered Korea to satisfy the Confucian historians.

   (She did conquer Korea, but it is not suggested that she tried to satisfy the Confucian historians.)

exercise 6 For further practice on inference, read the following passage and answer the inference question. In the blank, indicate the reason for your answer choice.

[We were invited to a banquet with Attila.] When the hour arrived we went to Attila's palace, along with the embassy from the western Romans, and stood on the threshold of the hall in the presence of Attila. The cup-bearers gave us a cup, according to the national custom, that we might pray before we sat down. Having tasted the cup, we proceeded to take our seats, all the chairs being ranged along the walls of the room on either side. Attila sat in the middle on a couch; a second couch was set behind him, and from it steps led up to his bed, which was covered with linen sheets and coverlets. . . .

[First the king and his guests pledged one another with the wine.] When this ceremony was over the cup-bearers retired and tables, large enough for three or four, or even more, to sit at, were placed next the table of Attila, so that each could take of the food on the dishes without leaving his seat. The attendant of Attila first entered with a dish full of meat, and behind him came the other attendants with bread and other dishes, which they laid on the tables. A luxurious meal, served on a silver plate, had been made ready for us and the other guests, but Attila ate nothing but meat on a wooden platter. In everything else, too, he showed himself temperate; his cup was of wood, while to the guests were given goblets of gold and silver. His dress, too, was quite simple, affecting only to be clean.

—Priscus, quoted in *Western Civilization,* Fifth Edition,
by Jackson J. Spielvogel

_____ 1. The author implies that

    a. although luxuries are available to him, Attila chooses a simpler lifestyle.

    b. Attila ordered a victory feast for his leaders before a day of battle.

    c. the Roman peasants were starving while the food and drink flowed at Attila's palace.

    d. while he enjoys the banquet, the author is also fearful of Attila.

    Reason for choice: _____

_____

_____

_____

Purpose Questions

The purpose of a passage is not usually stated. Instead, it is implied and is related to the main idea. In responding to a purpose item, you are answering the question, "What was the author's purpose in writing this material?" You might restate this question as, "What did the author do to or for me, the reader?"

EXAMPLE

Reading comprehension tests tend to include three basic types of passages, each of which suggests a separate set of purposes. Study the outline of the three types shown in the Reader's Tip box, and answer the question on the Empress Wu passage. Then note the handwritten remarks reflecting the thinking involved in judging whether an answer is correct.

_____ 1. The purpose of the passage on Empress Wu is

    a. to argue.

      (No side is taken.)

    b. to explain.

      (Yes, because the material is factual, like a textbook.)

    c. to condemn.

      (The reading is not judgmental.)

    d. to persuade.

      (No point of view is argued.)

Reader's *Tip*   Types of Test Passages

Factual Passages

What?	Science, sociology, psychology, or history articles
How to Read?	Read for the main idea, and do not get bogged down in details. Remember, you can look back.
Author's Purpose?	• To inform • To explain • To describe

Example: Textbooks

Opinion Passages

What?	Articles with a particular point of view on a topic
How to Read?	Read to determine the author's opinion on the subject. Then judge the value of the support included and decide whether you agree or disagree.
Author's Purpose?	• To argue • To persuade • To condemn • To ridicule

Example: Newspaper editorials

Fiction Passages

What?	Articles that tell a story
How to Read?	Read to understand what the characters are thinking and why they act as they do.
Author's Purpose?	• To entertain • To narrate • To describe • To shock

Examples: Novels and short stories

exercise 7

For further practice, read the following passage and answer the purpose question. In the blank, indicate the reason for your answer choice.

During the Victorian age women were often considered frail and delicate creatures, at least partly because they seemed prone to fainting spells. Did they faint because of their "inner natures" or for some other reason? Consider the fact that many of these women wore extremely tight corsets to give them tiny waists. In fact, the corsets were so tight that women could only take shallow breaths—if they took a deep breath, they ran the risk of being stabbed by the whalebone "stays" in the corset. These stays were thin and very sharp, and not only could they cause a bloody wound, but they could also puncture a lung! One consequence of continued shallow breathing is dizziness—hence the fainting spells common among stylish Victorian women.

—*Psychology,* Second Edition, by Stephen M. Kosslyn
and Robin S. Rosenberg

_____ 1. The author's primary purpose in this passage is

     a. to argue.

     b. to condemn.

     c. to entertain.

     d. to explain.

     Reason for response: _____

     _____

     _____

Vocabulary Questions

Vocabulary items test your general word knowledge as well as your ability to figure out meaning by using context clues. Vocabulary items are usually stated as follows.

As used in the passage, the best definition of _____ is . . .

Both word knowledge and context are necessary for a correct response. Go back and reread the sentence before the word, the sentence with the word, and the sentence after the word to be sure that you understand the context and are not misled by unusual meanings. Be suspicious of common words such as *industry,* which seems simple on the surface but can have multiple meanings.

EXAMPLE Answer the following vocabulary question on the passage about Empress Wu. Then note the handwritten remarks reflecting the thinking involved in judging whether an answer is correct.

_____ 1. As used in the third paragraph of the passage, the best definition of *usurped* is

     (Reread the sentence. Look also at the use of "usurpation" in the fourth paragraph.)

     a. earned.

     (This is too positive to describe her ruthless behavior.)

     b. won.

     (Again, this is too positive for her negative actions.)

     c. bought.

     (No payoff is suggested.)

     d. seized.

     (Yes, she took control and then tried to make it legal.)

exercise 8 For further practice, read the following passage and answer the vocabulary question. In the blank, indicate the reason for your answer choice.

> Pennsylvania plans to begin paying the relatives of organ donors $300 toward funeral expenses. It would be the first jurisdiction in the country to reward organ donation. Indeed, it might even be violating a 1984 federal law that declares organs a national resource not subject to compensation. Already there are voices opposing the very idea of pricing a kidney.
>
> —"Yes, Let's Pay for Organs,"
> by Charles Krauthammer

_____ 1. As used in the passage, the best definition of *compensation* is

a. discussion.

b. regulation.

c. authority.

d. payment.

Reason for choice: _____

_____

_____

_____

_____

_____

Hints for Taking Multiple-Choice and True-False Tests

Study the following hints and answer the items on the passage about Empress Wu with *a, b, c,* or *d,* or *T* (true) or *F* (false) before reading the explanation in italics.

Read All Options

Even if the first answer seems undisputedly correct, read all the options. Be careful, and consider each answer. Multiple-choice tests usually ask for the *best* answer, not for any one that is reasonable.

_____ 1. The author suggests that

a. the empress wanted the emperor dead.
b. the sons of the empress were disobedient.
c. Wu's sons plotted against the emperor.
d. the emperor gave the empress immense power.
(Although the first option may be tempting, the last answer is implied by the quote describing her power and thus is correct.)

Predict the Correct Answer

As you read the stem (or beginning) of a multiple-choice item, anticipate what you would write for a correct response. Develop an answer in your mind before you read the options, and then look for a choice that corresponds to your thinking.

_____ 2. At the end of her reign, the Empress Wu was

    a. decapitated.
    b. married.
    c. pushed from power.
    d. imprisoned.
    (It says in the last sentence that she "was forced to abdicate." The third option most closely matches this answer.)

Avoid Answers with "100 Percent" Words

All and *never* mean 100 percent, without exception. In a true-false question, a response containing either word is seldom correct. Rarely can a statement be so definitely inclusive or exclusive. Other "100 percent" words to avoid are *no, none, only, every, always,* and *must.*

_____ 3. Empress Wu was hated by all the Chinese Confucian historians.
    (All means 100 percent, and thus is too inclusive. Surely one or two Confucians might not have felt so strongly against Wu.)

Consider Answers with Qualifying Words

Words such as *sometimes* and *seldom* suggest frequency but do not go so far as to say *all* or *none.* Such qualifying words can mean more than none and less than all. By being so indefinite, they are difficult to dispute. Therefore, qualifiers are more likely to be included in a correct response to a true-false question. Other qualifiers are *few, much, often, may, many, some, perhaps,* and *generally.*

_____ 4. Empress Wu was hated by many of the Chinese Confucian historians.
    (The phrases "she found little favor" with Confucians and "They played up her vices" suggest dislike. The statement is true.)

Do Not Overanalyze

Try to follow the thinking of the test writer rather than overanalyze minute points. Don't make the question harder than it is. Use your common sense, and answer what you think was intended.

_____ 5. Empress Wu fought Korea and won.
    (Of course Empress Wu was not standing on the front line of battle with a sword, but as the leader of China she was ultimately responsible for the victory. Thus the answer is true.*)*

True Statements Must Be True Without Exception

A statement is either totally true or it is incorrect. Adding an incorrect *and, but,* or *because* phrase to a true statement makes it false and thus an unacceptable answer. If a statement is half true and half false, mark it false.

_____ 6. The Chinese Confucian historians plotted against Empress Wu because they were concerned about the welfare of the poor people of China.
(It is true that the Confucians plotted against Wu, but their reasons for doing so are not stated. The statement is half true and half false, so it is false.)

If Two Options Are Synonymous, Eliminate Both

If two items say basically the same thing but only one answer is possible, then neither can be correct. Eliminate the two and spend your time on the others.

_____ 7. The purpose of this passage is

   a. to argue.
   b. to persuade.
   c. to inform.
   d. to entertain.
   (Because "argue" and "persuade" are basically synonyms, you can eliminate both and move on to other options.)

Figure Out the Difference Between Similar Options

If two similar options appear, frequently one of them will be correct. Study the choices to see the subtle difference intended by the test maker.

_____ 8. Empress Wu was

   a. supported by many Buddhists.
   b. supported by all the Buddhists.
   c. beloved by the poor.
   d. the greatest ruler of the T'ang Dynasty.
   (The last two answers are not suggested. Close inspection shows that the word all *is the only difference between the first and second answers and is the reason that the second is untrue. Thus the first answer, with the qualifying word, is correct.)*

Use Logical Reasoning When Two Answers Are Correct

Some tests include the option *all of the above* and *none of the above*. If you see that two of the answers are correct and are unsure about a third, *all of the above* would be a logical response.

_____ 9. Empress Wu was a

   a. concubine.
   b. mother.
   c. wife.
   d. all of the above.
   (If you recall that Wu was a concubine and a mother but are not sure that she was a wife, "all of the above" would be your logical option because you know that two of the choices are correct.)

Look Suspiciously at Directly Quoted Pompous Phrases

In searching for distractors, test makers sometimes quote a pompous phrase from the passage that doesn't make much sense. Such a phrase may include lofty, ornate, and seemingly important language from the passage, yet still be incorrect. However, you may read the phrase and think, "Oh yes, I saw that in the passage. It sounds good, so it must be right." Be sure authoritative phrases make sense before choosing them.

_____10. Wu was installed as empress because

  a. the Son of Heaven folded his hands.
  b. the imperial title was suppressed in conspiracy.
  c. the prophecy in Buddhist scriptures identified her by name.
  d. the brilliant conniving of an ambitious woman was successful.
  (The first two are pompous and do not make sense. The third is false because of the phrase "by name." The last is the correct answer.)

Simplify Double Negatives by Canceling Out Both

Double negatives are confusing and time-consuming to unravel. Simplify a double-negative statement by first canceling out both negatives. Then reread the statement without the confusion of the two negatives, and decide on the accuracy of the statement.

_____11. Empress Wu was not unscrupulous.
  (Cancel out the two negatives, not and un. Reread the sentence without the negatives: "Empress Wu was scrupulous." This is a false statement.)

Certain Responses Are Neither True nor False

For some items, you are not given the clues necessary for judging their accuracy. There is not sufficient evidence to indicate whether they are true or false.

_____12. Empress Wu was loved by the Chinese people.
  (The passage does not provide clues to indicate that she was loved or not loved by the Chinese people.)

Validate True Responses

If you are told that all the answers are correct except one, verify each response and, by the process of elimination, find the one that does not fit.

_____13. Empress Wu was all of the following *except*

  a. a scheming concubine.
  b. a ruthless woman.
  c. the first woman to rule China.
  d. the founder of the T'ang Dynasty.
  (Always note the "except" and look for the response that is false. The first three answers are true and the last is untrue, so it is the correct answer.)

Recognize Flaws in Test Making

Professionally developed reading tests are usually well-constructed and do not contain obvious clues to the correct answers. However, some teacher-made tests are hastily written and thus may have errors in test making that can help you find the correct answer. Do not, however, rely on these flaws to make a big difference in your score, for such errors should not occur on a well-constructed test.

Grammar. Eliminate responses that do not have subject-verb agreement. The tense of the verb as well as modifiers such as *a* or *an* can also give clues to the correct response.

_____ 14. Wu's ambition was to become an

  a. concubine.
  b. empress.
  c. lover.
  d. Buddhist.
  (The an *suggests an answer that starts with a vowel. Thus "empress" is the obvious answer.)*

Clues from Other Parts of the Test. Information in one part of the test may help you with an uncertain answer in another section.

_____ 15. During Wu's reign, China defeated

  a. Vietnam.
  b. India.
  c. Russia.
  d. Korea.
  (A previous question mentions the conquest of Korea.)

Length. On poorly constructed tests, longer answers are more frequently correct.

_____ 16. The author suggests that Wu promoted the cosmetics peddler to commander-in-chief because he

  a. was a good soldier.
  b. knew how to sell.
  c. had been a Buddhist monk.
  d. was her lover and she wanted to give him favors.
  (In an effort to be totally correct without question, the test maker has written the last—and longest—answer.)

Absurd Ideas and Emotional Words. Avoid distractors that contain absurd ideas or emotional words. The test maker probably got tired of trying to think of distractors and in a moment of weakness included a nonsense answer.

_____ 17. As used in the passage, the best definition of *concubine* is

  a. wife.
  b. child.
  c. mistress.
  d. dog.
  (The last answer is totally absurd. The test maker should take a break.)

Hints for Taking Essay Exams

In many ways, essay tests are more demanding than multiple-choice tests. Rather than simply recognizing correct answers, you must recall, create, and organize. You face a blank sheet of paper instead of a list of options, and, to write an appropriate response, you must remember ideas and present them in a logical and well-organized manner. The following suggestions can help you respond effectively.

Reword the Statement or Question

Sometimes the statement or question you are asked to discuss is written in a confusing or pompous manner. Be sure you understand the meaning, then rephrase it in your own words. If it is a statement, put it in the form of a question. If it is a question, simplify it and, if possible, divide it into parts.

Decide on the approach you will use in making your response. Will you define, describe, explain, or compare? For example, suppose you were asked to support the following statement:

> Wu rose to power through unscrupulous deception, and she fell through her own vice and weaknesses.

First rephrase the statement as a question, using words such as *why, what,* or *how*:

> *How did Wu rise to power through unscrupulous deception and fall through her own vice and weaknesses?*

The question really contains two parts, which you can list separately:

1. *How did Wu rise to power through unscrupulous deception?*
2. *How did Wu fall from power through her own vice and weaknesses?*

How will you answer the question? Use two approaches:

1. List her unscrupulous acts of deception that put her in power.
2. Explain the reasons for her fall.

Answer the Question

Answer the question that is asked—not some other question. This may seem obvious, but students frequently get off track. Do not write a summary of the material, include irrelevant information, or repeat the same idea over and over again. Focus on the question and write with purpose.

The following is an example of an incorrect response to the question about Wu's rise and fall. It is a summary of the material rather than a direct answer:

> Empress Wu became the only woman to rule China in name as well as fact. Her rule lasted for 45 years. She began her rise to power as a concubine of the third T'ang emperor.

Organize Your Answer

Think before you write. This is perhaps the most important step in test taking, but it is the one you may least want to take the time to do. Plan what you are going to say before you say it.

Brainstorm Ideas. Reread the question and jot down words or phrases to indicate the ideas you want to include in the answer. Number your ideas in the order in which you want to discuss them. On reconsidering, you may find that some of your brainstorming ideas overlap and others are examples of larger ideas. This is a chance for you to look at your possibilities and come up with a plan. When you use a plan, the writing is a lot easier and more logical.

Establish your purpose in the first sentence, and direct your writing specifically to answer the question. List specific details that support, explain, prove, and develop your point. In a concluding sentence, reemphasize your arguments and restate your purpose. Divide your writing with numbers or subheadings whenever possible, because they simplify the answer for the reader and show the organization. If time runs short, use an outline or a diagram to express your remaining ideas.

The following example shows the plan for answering the question on Empress Wu. The brainstormed ideas have already been organized into a concise, working outline. Remember to think before you write; that is the most important step.

Rise
1. Left convent
2. Plots against wife (sorcery, daughter, poison)
3. Made empress
4. After his death—2 sons
5. Took power
6. Monks made her divine ruler

Fall
1. Made ministers mad
2. Rewarding lovers & favorites
   - Cosmetics peddler
   - Young brothers (governorship)

Use a Formal Writing Style

A college professor, not your best friend, will be reading and grading your answer. Be respectful, direct, and formal. Do not use slang expressions. Do not use phrases such as *as you know* or *well*. They may be appropriate in conversation but not in formal writing.

Avoid empty words and thought. Adjectives such as *good, interesting,* and *nice* say little. Be direct and descriptive in your writing.

State your thesis or main point, supply proof, and use transitional phrases to tie your ideas together. Words such as *first, second,* and *finally* add transition and help to organize your answer. Other terms, such as *however* and *in contrast,* show a shift in thought. Remember, you are pulling ideas together, so use phrases and words to help the reader see relationships.

The following example illustrates a poor response to the question on Empress Wu. Note the total lack of organization, the weak language, the slang phrase, and the failure to use transition words in this paragraph.

Empress Wu was very sneaky. She did many dishonest things. She told lies about the empress that were so bad that the emperor dumped the empress. Well, then Wu rose like a bird to fill the new shoes.

Be Aware of Appearance

Research has shown that, on the average, essays written in a clear, legible hand receive a grade-level higher score than essays written somewhat illegibly.[3]

---

[3]Charles A. Sloan and Iris McGinnis, "The Effects of Handwriting on Teachers' Grading of High School Essays," Eric No. ED 220 836, 1978.

Be particular about appearance and be considerate of the reader. Proofread for correct grammar, punctuation, and spelling.

Predict and Practice

Predict possible essay items by using the table of contents and subheadings of your text to form questions. Practice brainstorming to answer these questions. Review old exams for insight into both the questions and the kinds of answers that received good marks. Outline answers to possible exam questions. Do as much thinking as possible to prepare yourself to take the test before you sit down to begin writing.

Notice Key Words

Following is a list of key words of instruction that appear in essay questions, with hints for responding to each word.

Compare: List the similarities.

Contrast: Note the differences.

Criticize: State your opinion and stress weaknesses.

Define: State the meaning and use examples so the term is understood.

Describe: State the characteristics so the image is vivid.

Diagram: Make a drawing that demonstrates relationships.

Discuss: Define the issue and elaborate on the advantages and disadvantages.

Evaluate: State positive and negative views and make a judgment.

Explain: Show cause and effect and give reasons.

Illustrate: Provide examples.

Interpret: Explain your own understanding of and opinions on a topic.

Justify: Give proof or reasons to support an opinion.

List: Record a series of numbered items.

Outline: Sketch the main points with their significant supporting details.

Prove: Use facts to support an opinion.

Relate: Connect items and show how one influences another.

Review: Give an overview with a summary.

Summarize: Retell the main points.

Trace: Move sequentially from one event to another.

Write to Earn Points

Essay exam grades seem much more subjective and mysterious than multiple-choice test grades. Some students feel they deserve to pass for filling the page with writing. They wonder what they did wrong when their paper is returned with a low score.

Professors use objective measures to grade essay tests. They look for you to cover a certain number of points for a passing score. If you do not make the minimum number of points, the paper fails. Answer an essay question to earn points; do not waste your time including personal experiences or irrelevant facts. Stick to the question, and demonstrate to the professor that you know the material.

The professor will use the following checklist to score the essay on Empress Wu. A checklist such as this is often called a **rubric**.

Rise (60 points)

1. Left convent
2. Plots against wife
3. Installed as empress
4. Sons on throne
5. Took power
6. Monks made her divine

Fall (40 points)

1. Ministers angry
2. Rewarding lovers
3. Examples—peddler and brothers

Grades

All passing exams must have items on both her rise and her fall.

C = Minimum of 5 items

B = Minimum of 6 items

A = Minimum of 7 items

Read an "A" Paper for Feedback

When your professor returns a multiple-choice exam, reread the items. Use what you know about test construction to analyze your errors to figure out what you did wrong. An essay exam, however, is not so easy to review. Sometimes essay exams have only a grade on the front and no other comment. The professor may discuss in class what was needed for an "A" answer, but without your seeing it pulled together, a perfect paper is difficult to visualize.

Ask to see an "A" paper. Maybe it will be yours. If so, share it with others. If not, ask your classmates or professor. The "A" paper becomes a model from which you can learn. Compare this paper with your own, and draw conclusions about the professor's expectations. Study and learn from the model so you will not repeat your mistakes.

Read and assign a grade of A, B, C, D, or F to each of the following essay responses to the Empress Wu question. Explain your reasons for each grade and include any suggestions you would offer to the student who wrote the paper.

Paper 1

Empress Wu did many bad things in order to get the power. The things she did were against the people in power. She did not want to stay with the Buddhists because she wanted to be with the new emperor. He died and her sons became puppets. She worked against the people who did not like her.

She was finally forced out of power because she had lovers. One of the lovers became a governor. The two brothers that she liked were decapitated. She fell from power and thus was no longer the empress.

Paper 2

Empress Wu rose to power through tricks and deception. She was intelligent enough to devise a way to meet the new emperor, get him attracted to her, and thus escape her lifetime sentence in the convent. She rose in the new emperor's favor and plotted dishonestly against his wife. Wu falsely accused the emperor's wife of sorcery, murdering her own daughter, and plotting to poison her husband. Wu was soon made empress and given great power. When the emperor died, she ruled through her two sons. Finally, she took the throne herself. Buddhist monks helped her devise a scheme using the scriptures to validate her power. They said she was a divine incarnation of the Buddha.

Wu fell from power because of her weakness for men as lovers. She rewarded her lovers with power and thus angered her ministers. She made a cosmetics peddler an abbot, architect, and then commander-in-chief. Her final appointment of a younger brother of two of her favorites to an important governorship was too much for the ministers. They forced her from power.

Remember: Brainstorm before you write. Jot down the ideas you will use to answer the question and number them. Stick to the question, organize your response, and use logic.

Personal *Feedback* **2**

Name _____

1. Do you prefer multiple-choice or essay exams? Why? _____
   _____

2. What are the weaknesses of your essay responses? _____
   _____

3. How did your last English course prepare you for essay exam responses? _____
   _____

4. Describe an activity that could be done in this course to help you on essay
   responses. _____
   _____

5. Name a student who writes excellent essay responses. _____
   _____

6. Have you ever outlined a possible essay question before a test? If so, for what class?
   _____
   _____

7. Describe the best paper you have ever written. _____
   _____

8. Grading essay responses is more subjective than grading multiple-choice items.
   What system do you think professors use to arrive at accurate grades? _____
   _____

Tear out and submit to your instructor.

Summary *Points*

➤ **How can you prepare to be mentally alert on a test?**
Get plenty of sleep the night before a test. Arrive early for a test and know what to expect. Concentrate and schedule your time.

➤ **What should you know about the organization of an exam prior to taking it?**
Find out the distribution of question types, whether short answer, multiple-choice, or essay. Know how many points each question counts in grading.

➤ **How should you read standardized reading test passages?**
Concentrate and read the first sentence carefully. Use the six thinking strategies of good readers.

➤ **What are the major question types on standardized reading tests?**
They are main idea, detail, inference, purpose, and vocabulary.

➤ **How should you organize essay exam responses?**
Brainstorm first to organize ideas into a concise outline. Answer each question directly.

➤ **Why should you seek feedback after an exam?**
On multiple-choice and short-answer item tests, seek feedback so you will not repeat your mistakes. Read an "A" essay response so that you know what the professor expects.

Form a five-member group and select one of the following activities. Brainstorm and then outline your major points on a transparency. Choose a member to present the group findings to the class.

➤ List ten feelings you have when you begin to take an important test.

➤ List ten tips for successfully writing essay exam responses in a history course.

➤ List ten reasons why you would not want to take a course that only had one test, the final exam.

➤ List standardized tests that you or your classmates may have to take in the future. Include tests for admission to professional schools, for graduate schools, and for jobs.

MyReadingLab (MRL) www.myreadinglab.com

➤ To practice the ideas and skills introduced in this chapter, go to the "Reading Textbooks," "Memorization and Concentration," and "Test Taking" modules in the Skills section of MRL. To practice general reading comprehension, use the Levels section.

The Reading *Workshop*

"The things I want to know are in books. My best friend is the man who'll get me a book I [haven't] read."

—ABRAHAM LINCOLN

When we read for pleasure, we learn many things almost accidentally. Reading for the purpose of learning, though, requires working with the material in a deeper and more active way. When we know that we will be tested, we read more carefully. Put yourself in the teacher's position, and, as you read, predict and answer the questions that might be included on a test. You may find that you pay closer attention!

Think about it, talk about it, write about it:

Create a brief test that might be given to someone who has read the book you are reading. Write one question for each type of question discussed in this chapter—main idea, detail, author's purpose, inference, and vocabulary—and include an essay question and an answer key.

Your professor might ask you to include your test in a Reading Workshop journal.

Vocabulary Lesson

Call Out and Remember to Send

Study the roots, words, and sentences.

> **Roots**   *claim, clam*: declare, call out   *mem*: remember   *mitt, miss*: send

Words with *claim* or *clam* = *declare* or *call out*

Can an <u>exclamation</u> point end a sentence? What is <u>unclaimed</u> freight?

- Clamor: a racket

  The suitcases made a *clamor* as they fell off the rack.

- Reclaim: regain or demand the return of

  After recovering from an injury, the tennis star *reclaimed* the championship.

- Disclaim: cut off, deny

  If you insult the host, I will *disclaim* ever knowing you.

- Exclaim: cry out

  At the celebration, the patriots *exclaimed* in their joy of victory.

- Irreclaimable: cannot be restored

  The moving company declared that the broken furniture was *irreclaimable*.

- Proclamation: a notice to the public

  A *proclamation* concerning taxation was published in the newspaper.

- Claimant: one who makes a claim

  The *claimant* told the insurance company a tree hit the car in a hurricane.

Words with *mem* = *remember*

Are most *memos* short? Do holidays jog <u>unremembered</u> feelings?

- Memento: something to make one remember

  The small statue is a *memento* of my trip to Italy.

- Memoir: a record to remember

  The soldier's *memoirs* gave a personal perspective to the war.

- Memorandum: a note or reminder

  Because a *memorandum* is a business correspondence, make it short.

- Memorable: worth remembering

  With the family together, Thanksgiving dinner was a *memorable* event.

- Memorabilia: things valued for the memories associated with them.

  Elvis *memorabilia* are sold at Graceland.

- Commemorate: to observe and remember

  Display a flag to *commemorate* Independence Day.

- Memorial: a reminder of a distinguished person or a great event

  The fountain was a *memorial* to the founder of the city.

Words with *mit* or *miss* = send

Do you <u>admit</u> errors? Will you <u>permit</u> me to use you as a reference?

- Missile: something sent through the air

  The *missile* was directed toward enemy territory.

- Emissary: a messenger sent on a mission

  She sent an *emissary* to the French government.

- Remiss: careless

  I would be *remiss* if I did not remind you that the gates close at midnight.

- Remit: pay

  The phone company asked me to *remit* another thirty dollars.

- Submit: surrender

  He had to *submit* to a body search at the airport.

- Emit: to send out

  The car seems to be *emitting* pollution.

Review

Part I

Answer the following with *T* (true) or *F* (false).

_____ 1. An exhaust emissions check measures auto pollution.

_____ 2. Veterans Day commemorates those who served our country.

_____ 3. To receive an insurance payment, the claimant must suffer a loss.

_____ 4. Irreclaimable goods are fixed rather than replaced.

_____ 5. A "We are not responsible for" statement is a company disclaimer.

_____ 6. To reclaim checked goods, you usually need a ticket.

_____ 7. To be remiss is to neglect a duty.

_____ 8. A memoir is nonfiction.

_____ 9. Olympic memorabilia include collectors' pins for the events.

_____10. If you remit money, you refuse to pay.

Part II

Choose the best word from the list as a synonym for the following.

| memorandum | emissary | proclamation | exclamation | memoir |
| clamor | memorial | remittance | missile | memento |

11. book   _____

12. Washington Monument   _____

13. person   _____

14. keepsake   _____

15. correspondence   _____

16. noise   _____

17. explosive   _____

18. official announcement   _____

19. cry   _____

20. payment   _____

Using Mnemonics

Mnemonics is a technique that helps you organize and recall. It works by stimulating your senses through pictures, sounds, rhythms, and other mental "tricks" to create extrasensory "handles" or hooks that make it easier for your brain to arrange and retrieve information. Given a list of twelve nouns to remember, students who link them in a story remember more than students who just try to memorize them as unrelated items. Weaving such a story is called *narrative chaining*, because the technique links, organizes, and gives meaning to unrelated items. The following are suggested mnemonic techniques for college learning.

Reading Out Loud

Although you may not think of this as a mnemonic, you use additional senses when you read out loud. Memory experts explain that your eyes *see* the material on the page, and your ears *hear* the information. Your mouth, tongue, lips, and throat *feel* the sensation of speaking the words. This is particularly effective for studying lecture notes after class or before an exam.

Writing It Down

Writing works in a similar way to reading aloud, because you feel your hand transcribing the information. Thus summarizing, annotating, notetaking, outlining, and mapping add sensory steps to learning. Always take class lecture notes to reinforce the spoken information.

Creating Acronyms

Create words using the first letter of each word you want to remember. A well-known example of this technique is using HOMES to remember the great lakes: *H*uron, *O*ntario, *M*ichigan, *E*rie, *S*uperior.

Creating Acrostics

Form a sentence in which the first letter of each word corresponds to the first letter of each word in a list you want to remember. For example, *members must jump unless neighbors enlist very soon* is an acrostic for remembering the eight planets in our solar system: *M*ercury, *M*ars, *J*upiter, *U*ranus, *N*eptune, *E*arth, *V*enus, *S*aturn. If you need to remember the planets in the order they orbit the sun, create a different sentence. Silly and unusual acrostics can be easy to remember.

Using Rhythms, Rhymes, and Jingles

Use rhythms, rhymes, and jingles to create additional handles for your brain to use to process and retrieve. Most students never forget the year Christopher

Columbus came to America because they learned the rhythmic rhyme, "In four-teen-hundred-and-ninety-two/Columbus sailed the ocean blue."

Making Associations

Make a connection between seemingly unrelated ideas by using pictures, nonsense ideas, or connected bits of logic. For example, two easily confused words are *stationary*, which means standing still, and *stationery*, meaning letter-writing paper. To remember the difference, note that *stationary* is spelled with an "a," which relates to the "a" in *standing still*; *stationery* is spelled with an "e," which relates to *letters*.

Conjuring Mental Images

Create a picture, perhaps a funny picture, just as you would on a vocabulary concept card. Picture a *voracious* reader as a shark greedily eating a book.

Using Key Word Images

To learn foreign language vocabulary, use the sound of the new word to relate to an image of a known word. For example, the Spanish word for horse is *caballo*, which is pronounced *cab-eye-yo*. Associate *eye* as the key word and picture a horse with only one large eye looking into a taxi cab.

exercise 1

1. Create an association to remember that *cereal* is a breakfast food and *serial* is a numerical order. _____

   _____

2. Create an acrostic to remember the elements that make up the vast majority of molecules in living things: carbon, hydrogen, nitrogen, oxygen, phosphorus, and sulfur. _____

   _____

3. Create a rhyme or jingle to remember that World War II ended in 1945.

   _____

   _____

Reader's *Tip* Remembering Information

- Hook it to mental signs that are easy to remember.
- Link it to other information you already know.
- Sense it by touching, writing, or speaking.
- Rehearse it by writing and speaking to yourself.

8 Efficient Reading

- What is your reading rate?
- How fast should you read?
- How can you increase your reading speed?

Everyday Reading Skills: Managing Workplace Reading

What Is Your Reading Rate?

If you are not zipping through a book at 1,000 words per minute, does it mean you are a slow reader? No, of course not. You do not need to be reading as fast as you can turn the pages. Yet many college students are concerned about their reading rate. This chapter explains factors that contribute to a fast or slow reading rate and suggests techniques that can help you improve your reading efficiency.

exercise 1

Read the following selection at your normal reading speed. Time your reading so you can calculate your words-per-minute rate. Use a stopwatch or a watch with a second hand. Record your starting time in minutes and seconds. When you have completed the selection, record your finishing time in minutes and seconds. Answer the questions that follow, and use the chart to determine your rate.

Starting time: _____ minutes _____ seconds

COLLEGE YEARBOOK PHOTOS AS INDICATORS

What does your yearbook photo say about you?

More than you might think. In fact, how people appear in their college yearbooks may predict whether they will be married 5 years later and even whether they will be happy in their marriages 30 years later.

There's nothing particularly special or magical about people's yearbook photos for forecasting their futures. They're just photographs—but photographs can be useful indicators of people's positive emotional expression. That is, people who tend to be more happy and joyful also tend to produce more intense and sincere smiles, which can be distinguished by careful analysis of facial features in photographs. Positive emotions, in turn, may be able to influence how people's lives unfold.

Researchers interested in the long-term functions of positive emotions wanted to make use of data collected over a 30-year period. The data included personality measures and reports of marriage, family, and career outcomes taken when the women were 21, 27, 43, and 52 years old. In order to explore how the women's positive emotional expressions in young adulthood related to their later personality development and life outcomes, the researchers studied the women's college yearbook photos.

The women who showed more positive emotional expression in their yearbook photos tended to express higher degrees of belonging and ability, personality traits that indicate good relationship and thinking skills. These women also tended to express increased ability over time and to become more organized, focused, and achievement oriented. They furthermore tended to report less negative emotionality and to experience decreased negative emotionality over time.

In addition, the women who expressed more positive emotion in their yearbook photos were more likely to be married at age 27 and more likely to report feeling satisfied with their marriages at age 52. They also tended to report fewer psychological and physical problems, better relations with others, and better life satisfaction throughout young and middle adulthood.

Why might positive emotions in young adulthood predict such favorable outcomes in later years? People with more positive emotions tend to be more outgoing and active. They are more likely to think broadly, to explore their environment, and to interact with others. Furthermore positive emotions smooth interactions with others. People who smile more also seem more approachable and are perceived by others more favorably. These advantages of positive emotions may contribute to better relationships and to a sense of well being.

What seems particularly surprising about this research is that such a restricted and seemingly unimportant measure of positive emotion in young adulthood could predict the course of personality development and life events over such a long period. Of course, nearly all the women smiled for their yearbook photographs. The key difference was how they smiled—whether the rest of their face, especially the area around their eyes, indicated that the smile was a genuine expression of positive emotion or merely a response to being photographed.

(482 words)

—Development Across the Life Span, Fourth Edition, by Robert S. Feldman

Finishing time: _____ *minutes* _____ *seconds*

Reading time in seconds = _____

Words per minute = _____ *(see Time Chart)*

TIME CHART

Time in Seconds and Minutes	Words per Minute
60 (1 min.)	482
80	362
90	321
100	290
110	263
120 (2 min.)	241
130	222
140	207
150	193
160	181
170	170
180 (3 min.)	160
190	152

Answer the following with *T* (true) or *F* (false).

_____ 1. Research findings indicated that subjects judged to have sincere yearbook smiles tended to be more achievement oriented.

_____ 2. This study includes both men and women.

_____ 3. Researchers felt they distinguished genuine from insincere yearbook smiles through a careful analysis of facial features.

_____ 4. Researchers collected data on the subjects at four different ages.

_____ 5. The author concludes that the early sincere smile brings a more favorable reaction from others that results in positive relationships.

What Is an Average Reading Rate?

Rate calculations vary according to the difficulty of the material. Research indicates, however, that on relatively easy material, the average adult reading speed is approximately 250 words per minute at 70 percent comprehension. For college students, the rate is sometimes estimated at closer to 300 words per minute.

Because this selection was not particularly difficult, the average adult reading speed of 250 words per minute at 70 percent comprehension would apply.

If you are reading below this rate, you may have trouble finishing standardized tests and finishing assignments. The suggestions in this chapter can help you become a more efficient reader.

How Can You Increase Your Reading Speed?

Be Aggressive—Attack!

Grab that book, sit up straight, and try to get some work done. Don't be a passive reader who watches the words go by but lacks understanding and involvement. Be active. Look for meaning with a strong intellectual curiosity, and try to get something out of what you read. Drive for the main idea.

Faster reading does not mean poorer comprehension. Moderate gains in speed usually result in improved comprehension because you are concentrating and thinking more.

The following exercises will help increase your awareness of speed and give you a sense of haste. Time yourself on each exercise and then compare your time with those of other members of the class. If possible, do these exercises as a class or group, with one person calling out the time at five-second intervals.

Personal *Feedback* 1

Name _____

1. When you read the timed reading, how many times did you have to reread? _____

_____

2. If your mind wandered during the timed reading, what were you thinking about?

_____

_____

3. Describe why reading speed is or is not a problem for you. _____

_____

4. What kind of easy reading would you choose for practicing and improving your reading rate? _____

_____

5. Describe any previous instruction that you have had on improving your reading rate. _____

_____

6. What do you think is the greatest misconception about reading speed? _____

_____

Tear out and submit to your instructor.

exercise 2

In the following lists, the key word is in boldface in the column at the left. It is then repeated in the group of words to the right. As rapidly as possible, locate the identical word, check it, and then move to the next line. Try to do most of this visually rather than saying each word to yourself. When you have finished each list, record your time and compare your performance with that of fellow classmates.

List 1

1. **lip**	lid	long	left	lip	lap
2. **stand**	start	stand	strong	torn	stop
3. **wander**	willow	wanton	waiting	wander	worry
4. **vain**	vale	vain	vane	vague	value
5. **most**	mort	most	might	host	mast
6. **divide**	divine	devoted	divide	have	doing
7. **someone**	somewhere	someone	sooner	somehow	somebody
8. **week**	weak	meek	week	leak	seek
9. **hazy**	hazy	hazard	hamper	lazy	dizzy
10. **mold**	mole	mound	mold	mind	hold
11. **sight**	height	right	might	sight	light
12. **aide**	aid	aide	add	also	hide
13. **reform**	remake	reclaim	malformed	reform	form
14. **bubble**	raffle	baffle	bubble	rubber	blubber
15. **scarce**	source	sacred	scarce	scorn	serious
16. **fabulous**	famous	fabulous	fashion	false	fasten
17. **reservation**	preservation	occupation	realization	reservation	reserve
18. **reality**	really	reaction	finality	reality	rational
19. **tranquilizer**	transfer	relaxation	tranquilizer	transcribe	transit
20. **phenomena**	pneumonia	phenomena	paralysis	feminine	phrases

Time in seconds = _____

List 2

1. **wing**	wig	wring	wing	with	ring
2. **cram**	crash	carry	ram	ham	cram
3. **like**	mike	like	land	load	hike
4. **sandal**	saddle	sandal	ramble	soften	sweet
5. **prime**	proud	prim	prime	prissy	rime
6. **manage**	mingle	manager	mangle	manner	manage
7. **rash**	rash	rush	race	lush	rich
8. **trace**	trance	trace	trade	train	trail
9. **saline**	saloon	salmon	saline	short	slowly
10. **revenge**	regain	ravenous	rancid	revamp	revenge
11. **tired**	tried	trend	tread	tired	torn
12. **withdrawn**	without	withdraw	within	withdrawn	witness
13. **powerful**	power	potential	powerful	potent	palate
14. **indignant**	indigenous	indigent	distinguish	indignant	indulge
15. **remember**	dismember	remain	reminisce	remission	remember
16. **condescending**	condemning	condense	concise	coherent	condescending
17. **magnanimous**	magnificent	magnanimous	magnetic	malformed	magnify
18. **humorous**	human	hormone	hammock	hammer	humorous
19. **civilization**	civilized	citizenry	civic	civilization	centered
20. **ingenious**	ingenuous	injurious	ingenious	ignoble	engine

Time in seconds = _____

Concentrate

Our eyes cannot actually read. We read with our minds. Thus getting information from the printed page ultimately comes down to concentration. The faster you read, the harder you must concentrate. It is like driving a car at 75 miles per hour as opposed to 35 miles per hour. You are covering more ground at 75, and it requires total concentration if you are to keep the car on the road. Faster reading is direct, purposeful, and attentive. There is no time to think about anything except what you are reading.

As Professor Clayton Pinette at the University of Maine says, "Concentration requires lots of energy. Health, rest, and physical and mental well-being are necessary for good concentration. Rest breaks are important and so are personal rewards."[1]

Both external and internal distractions interfere with concentration. External distractions are the physical things around you. Are you in a quiet place? Is the television going? Can you hear people talking on the telephone? Are you being interrupted by someone asking you questions? You can control most external distractions by prior planning. Be careful in selecting your time and place to study. Choose a quiet place and start at a reasonable hour. Set yourself up for success.

Internal distractions, however, are much more difficult to control. They are the thoughts in your mind that keep you from concentrating. Again, prior planning will help. Keep a "To Do" list as described in Chapter 1. Making a list and knowing that you will check back over it will help you stop worrying about your duties and responsibilities. Make an effort to spend more time *doing* something than *worrying* about something.

Visualizing can also help concentration. If you are reading about ostriches, visualize ostriches. As much as possible, try to see what you read as a movie. Use your imagination and all five of your senses to improve your comprehension.

exercise 3

In the lists here, the key word is in boldface. Among the words to the right, locate and mark the one most similar in meaning to the key word. In this exercise, you are not just looking at the shapes of words, but you are looking quickly for meaning. This will help you think fast and effectively. When you have finished each list, record your time, check your answers, and compare your performance with those of others in the class.

List 1

1. **recall**	read	guide	remember	fail	forgive
2. **sanitary**	new	fine	equal	clean	straight
3. **physician**	health	doctor	coward	elder	teacher
4. **motor**	car	horse	wagon	shine	engine
5. **first**	primary	last	finally	only	hard
6. **look**	stick	serve	glance	open	wait
7. **usual**	common	neat	best	cruel	kindness
8. **quick**	noisy	near	fast	finish	give
9. **annoy**	logic	make	win	disturb	set
10. **shout**	cry	action	most	fear	force
11. **friend**	family	mother	soldier	farmer	comrade
12. **carry**	plan	instruct	take	deal	rank

[1]Clayton Pinette, personal communication, February 1994.

13. sincere	style	genuine	safe	future	simple
14. valuable	dear	unstable	truthful	ancient	broken
15. diminish	season	promote	forward	reduce	marry
16. anxious	appear	sight	nervous	mean	helpful
17. liquid	clear	running	pipes	kitchen	fluid
18. prestige	program	status	mission	natural	report
19. core	side	nation	heart	event	process
20. harness	control	appear	build	mark	attend

Time in seconds = _____

List 2

1. ill	sin	die	skill	sick	mind
2. calm	envy	breeze	peaceful	early	far
3. nice	pleasant	needed	new	smooth	plastic
4. emotion	drain	feeling	heat	silent	search
5. close	cost	tall	mild	flow	near
6. gun	knife	rifle	handle	metal	hold
7. expert	rule	sort	believer	follower	specialist
8. obtain	get	feature	delay	injure	adapt
9. discuss	sense	divide	order	talk	find
10. moisture	dampness	sample	screen	dark	dirty
11. village	mountain	town	river	country	moving
12. bravery	origin	voluntary	courage	means	social
13. loyal	client	faithful	definite	legal	scale
14. convert	swim	chief	movement	policy	change
15. celebrate	attain	learn	century	rejoice	statement
16. argument	fund	quarrel	meeting	democracy	voice
17. preserve	opportunity	solar	system	save	signal
18. hilarious	funny	horrible	drama	sensible	even
19. imitate	difficult	confer	strike	language	copy
20. danger	general	fair	position	risk	army

Time in seconds = _____

Stop Regressions

A **regression** is the act of going back and rereading what you have just finished. Does this ever happen to you? Certainly some textbook material is so complex that it requires a second reading, but most of us regress even when the material is not that complicated. The problem is simply "sleeping on the job." Your mind takes a nap or starts thinking about something else while your eyes keep moving across the page. Hence halfway down the page, you wonder, "What am I reading?" and you plod back to reread and find out. Then, after an alert rereading, the meaning is clear, but you have lost valuable time.

Regression can be a habit. You know you can always go back and reread. Break yourself of the habit. The next time you catch yourself going back to reread because your mind has been wandering say, "Halt, I'm going to keep on reading." This will put more pressure on you to pay attention the first time.

Sleeping through only one or two paragraphs in an entire chapter probably won't hurt your comprehension that much. Sleeping through much more than that, however, could be a problem. Remember, reading the assignment twice takes double the time. Try to reread only when it is necessary because of the complexity of the material.

Avoid Vocalization

Vocalization means moving your lips as you read. It takes additional time and is generally a sign of an immature reader. A trick suggested by specialists to stop lip movement is to put a slip of paper in your mouth. If the paper moves, your lips are moving, and you are thus alerted to stop the habit.

Subvocalization refers to the little voice in your head that reads out loud for you. Even though you are not moving your lips or making any sounds, you hear the words in your mind as you read. Some experts say that subvocalization is necessary for difficult material, and others say that fast readers are totally visual and do not need to subvocalize. The truth is probably in between the two. You may find that in easy reading you can eliminate some of your subvocalization and only hear the key words, whereas on more difficult textbook material, the subvocalization reinforces the words and gives you better reading comprehension. Because your work will be primarily with textbook reading, do not concern yourself with subvocalization at this time. In fact, sometimes you may need to read particularly difficult textbook passages aloud in order to understand them fully.

Expand Fixations

Your eyes must stop for you to read. These stops, which last for a fraction of a second, are called **fixations.** If you are reading a page that has twelve words to a line and you need to stop at each word, you have made twelve fixations, each of which takes a fraction of a second. If, however, you can read two words with each fixation, you will make only half the stops and thus increase your total reading speed.

You might say, "How can I do this?" and the answer has to do with peripheral vision. To illustrate, hold up your finger and try to look only at that finger. As you can see, such limited vision is impossible. Because of peripheral vision, you can see many other things in the room besides your finger. Research has shown that the average reader can see approximately 2.5 words per fixation.

Read the following phrase:

in the barn

Did you make three fixations, one on each word, or did you fixate once? Now read the following word:

entertainment

How many fixations did you make? Probably one, but as a beginning reader in elementary school, you most likely read the word with four fixations, one for each syllable. Your use of one fixation for *entertainment* dramatizes the progress you have already made as a reader and indicates the ability of the eyes to take in a number of letters at one time. The phrase *in the barn* has nine letters, whereas *entertainment* has thirteen. Does it make any sense to stop three times to read nine letters and once to read thirteen? Again, the reason we do so is habit. If you never expected or tried to read more than one word per fixation, that is all you are able to do.

The key to expanding your fixations is to read phrases or thought units. Some words seem to go together automatically and some don't. Words need to be grouped according to thought units. Your fixation point, as shown in the following example, will be under and between the words forming the thought unit, so your peripheral vision can pick up what is on either side of the point.

Read the following paragraph by fixating at each indicated point. Notice how the words have been divided into phrase units.

FASTER READING

A faster   reading speed   is developed   through practice

and concentration.   Your reading rate   also depends

on how much   you know   about a subject.

exercise 4

In the following lists, the key phrase is in boldface. Among the words on the line below, locate and mark the phrase that is most similar in meaning to the key phrase. Record your time, check your answers, and compare your performance with those of others in the class. This exercise will help you increase your eye span and grasp meaning quickly from phrases.

List 1

1. **to have your own**
   wish for more   share with others   keep for yourself   be harmed by fire
2. **finish a task**
   lessen the impact   clean the attic   turn on the lights   complete a job
3. **sing a song**
   hum a tune   work for pleasure   leave for vacation   wish on a star
4. **manage a business**
   lose your job   lock the door   seek employment   run a company
5. **sit for a while**
   make ends meet   rest in a chair   learn new ways   fall into bed
6. **clear and concise**
   engaging in conversation   ordering a change   easy to understand   complex and difficult
7. **reach a goal**
   achieve an objective   call a meeting   change your mind   open a hearing
8. **free your mind**
   leave a spot   clear the head   turn the motor   remember a date
9. **walk down the road**
   meet in the car   support rapid transit   call the taxi   stroll in the street
10. **hold some money back**
    rush to the bank   drop a dime   accumulate savings   remain at work

Time in seconds = _____

List 2

1. **sense a disaster**
   sleep with ease   feel danger near   yearn for adventure   seek your fortune
2. **hurry to leave**
   walk in the rain   spill the coffee   lower the rent   rush out the door
3. **seek legal advice**
   engage an attorney   earn a living   move your address   give to charity
4. **forget to call**
   scream and yell   open an account   send by mail   neglect to phone
5. **offer your services**
   get in the way   ask to help   quit your job   waste your time
6. **listen to music**
   play in a band   buy a piano   hear a tune   turn off the radio

7. **notice a change**
   see a difference   buy a new shirt   work on a project   meet new people
8. **lose money gambling**
   pay for a product   not win a bet   cut expenses   make an offer
9. **clean up a spill**
   go in the kitchen   add more water   wipe away a stain   tear a rag
10. **leap with delight**
    sing a high note   turn the page   ask for help   jump for joy

Time in seconds = _____

Use a Pen as a Pacer

Using a pen to follow the words in a smooth, flowing line can help you set a rhythmical pace for your reading. In elementary school you were probably taught never to point at words, so this advice may be contrary to what you have learned. However, it can be an effective speed-reading technique.

The technique of using a pen as a pacer is demonstrated in the following paragraph. Use a pen to trace the lines shown, so it goes from one side of the column to the other and returns in a *Z* pattern. Because you are trying to read several words at a fixation, it is not necessary for your pen to go to the extreme end of either side of the column. After you have finished, answer the comprehension questions with *T* (true) or *F* (false) and compare your speed with that of others.

EXAMPLE **BREAKING FOR MEMORY**

Researchers have found that taking a series
of short breaks during a long
study period can enhance memory
and thus improve your recall
of the information. The breaks should be
a complete rest from the task
and should be no longer than
ten minutes. You may choose
to break every forty or fifty minutes.
During your break, you will experience
what experts call memory consolidation
as the new information is linked
and organized into knowledge networks.
According to some experts, deep breathing
and relaxation exercises can also help
by improving the flow of oxygen to the brain.

(100 words)

Time in seconds = _____

_____ 1. Fifty-minute breaks are recommended during long study periods.

_____ 2. Memory consolidation means improving the flow of oxygen to the brain.

EXPLANATION The answers are (1) *false* and (2) *false*. Although it may seem awkward at first, practice using a pen to read in a Z pattern on light material such as newspaper or magazine articles to get accustomed to the technique. It will not only force you to move your eyes faster, it will also improve your concentration and keep you alert and awake.

Try using your pen as a pacer for the first five or ten minutes of your reading to become familiar with the feeling of a faster, rhythmical pace. When you tire, stop the technique, but try to keep reading at the same pace. If, later in the reading, you feel yourself slowing down, resume the technique until you have regained the pace. This is a simple technique that does not involve expensive machines or complicated instruction, and *it works*! Pacing with the Z pattern *will* increase your reading speed.

exercise 5 Read the following passages (using your pen as a pacer in the Z pattern in Passages 1, 2, and 3). Answer the comprehension questions with *T* (true) or *F* (false), then record your reading time and compare your performance with that of other students.

Passage 1

NATURAL GAS SAFETY

Natural gas   is odorless   so,   in the early days
of using   natural gas   to heat buildings   and cook,
someone would occasionally   light a match   without realizing that
a gas leak   had filled   the air   with gas.   Poof!
Inventors quickly   began designing devices   that would detect
the presence   of natural gas   in the air   and sound
an alarm.   However,   the best solution   was not
a detection device.   Instead,   a gas   that could be
easily smelled   was added   to the odorless   natural gas
so that   a leak   could be detected   easily   by a human's
built-in   gas detector,   the nose!

(98 words)

—*A Creative Problem Solver's Toolbox,* by Richard Fobes

Time in seconds = _____

_____ 1. Another gas was mixed with natural gas to create a smell.

_____ 2. Originally natural gas was odorless.

Passage 2

NETIQUETTE

The rules   and guidelines   for acceptable behavior   on the Net

are called netiquette.   Be careful   to say   what you mean

and to say it   with care.   You cannot   double-click   and take

it back.   Keep your   messages short   and to the point.   People who

receive hundreds   of e-mails   each day are more likely   to respond

to short ones.   Although you   are hidden   from view,   appearances

are important.   Proofread   your messages.   Other people   will judge

your intelligence   and education   by the spelling,   grammar,   punctuation,

and clarity   of your messages.   If you   want your messages   to be taken

seriously,   present your   best face.

(100 words)

—*Computer Confluence,* Third Edition, by George Beekman

Time in seconds = _____

_____ 1. According to the author, once a message is sent you can double-click and retract it.

_____ 2. The author suggests that grammar and punctuation are not important in e-mail messages to close friends.

Passage 3

TYPING KEYBOARD

The earliest typewriters   usually jammed   when a key

was pressed   too soon   after the previous key

was released.   Most people   weren't willing

to tolerate   this flaw,   so early typewriters

were used   mostly by blind people   and others

who couldn't write   easily by hand.   Christopher Sholes

created a clever   supporting enhancement   that overcame

this jamming tendency.   He arranged   the letters

on the keys   awkwardly!   He put   the frequently

typed letters   E, T, O, N, R, and I   on keys

that required   finger movement   to reach them,

and assigned   frequently typed   pairs of letters,

such as E and D,   to the same finger.   His innovation worked!

It successfully   slowed down   a person's typing speed,

thereby reducing   the tendency for   his typewriters to jam.

Unfortunately,   because Sholes' typewriters   became so popular,

this awkward   keyboard arrangement   is the one

we still   use today!

(139 words)

—*The Creative Problem Solver's Toolbox,* by Richard Fobes

Time in seconds = _____

_____ 1. Our present typing keyboard was adopted to enhance speed.

_____ 2. Early typewriters were used by blind people.

Passage 4

I HAVE A SENSE OF HUMOR

According to the journalist Norman Cousins, laughing is internal jogging, and when you laugh, you are exercising all your internal organs. Not only does laughter feel good, it is essential to good health and a sense of well-being. Cousins has good reason to believe this. Some years ago he was diagnosed with a terminal illness and given just two months to live. Instead of spending his precious time remaining in the hospital, he checked into a hotel and watched, read, or listened to every humorous movie, book, and audiotape he could get his hands on. He virtually laughed himself well. Many years later, still in excellent health, Cousins was convinced, as were his doctors, that laughter accounted for his recovery! In fact, the medical school at UCLA invited him to join its faculty to teach interns how to lighten up.

Cousins' amazing story holds a lesson for all of us. We can all stand to lighten up a little—to find the genuine humor in an embarrassing moment, in a mistake, in a situation that is so serious that we need to laugh to keep from crying. Humor at its best means being able to laugh at yourself. Look for opportunities to see the lighter side of life and to share the experience of being human with others who can laugh with you, not at you. Cultivate the habit of walking on the "light" side of life.

(237 words)

—*The Career Fitness Program,* Seventh Edition,
by Diane Sukiennik et al.

Time in seconds = _____

_____ 1. Norman Cousins had humorous movies, books, and tapes brought to his hospital room to speed his recovery.

_____ 2. Cousins was invited to teach student interns about humor.

Passage 5

WHERE ARE THE WOMEN?

Charles A. O'Reilly III, professor of organizational behavior at the Stanford Graduate School of Business, has been interested in women's career attainment and the problem of why, despite gains in education and experience, women are still not in the top ranks of American corporations. In 1986, he began following a group of University of California, Berkeley MBAs to see if he could see those qualities that led to a corner office. His conclusion is simple: Success in a corporation is less a function of gender discrimination than of how hard a person chooses to compete. And the folks who tend to compete the hardest are generally the stereotypical manly men.

Think of careers as a tournament, he says. In the final rounds, players are usually matched pretty equally for ability. At that point, what differentiates winners from losers is effort—how many backhands a tennis player hits in practice, how many calls a sales rep is willing to make. He says, "Those most likely to be promoted are those who both have the skills and are willing to put in the effort. Individuals who are more loyal, work longer hours, and are willing to sacrifice for the organization are the ones who will be rewarded."

Today's women, he says, are equal to their male counterparts in education, experience, and skill. But when it's a painful choice between the client crisis and the birthday party, the long road trip and the middle schooler who needs attention, the employee most likely to put company over family is the traditional, work-oriented male. Interestingly, the women in O'Reilly's study reported levels of career satisfaction equal to those of their more-driven male peers, even if they were not as outwardly successful. In other words, women may be happier not gunning for power positions if it means they can work less and have a life.

(309 words)

—From Linda Tischler, "Where Are the Women?" *Fast Company*, Issue 79 (February 2004), p. 52. Copyright 2004 by Mansueto Ventures LLC. Reproduced with permission of Mansueto Ventures LLC in the format Textbook via Copyright Clearance Center.

Time in seconds = _____

_____ 1. According to O'Reilly's research, upper-level male and female employees are equally skilled.

_____ 2. O'Reilly found that females and males are equally likely to place a family event, such as a child's birthday, above business commitments.

Preview Before Reading

Do not start reading without looking over the material and thinking about what you need to accomplish. Think about the title and glance over the material for key words and phrases. Read the boldface and italic type. Decide what you think the selection is going to be about and what you want to know when you finish it. A few minutes spent on such an initial survey will help you read more purposefully and thus more quickly.

Activate your schema. What is your prior knowledge on the subject? Pull out your computer chip and prepare to add new information or change existing ideas.

Set a Time Goal for an Assignment

For each of your textbooks, estimate the approximate number of words per page. Write this estimate in the front of your book so you can refer to it during the course. Knowing your reading rate, you can approximate how many minutes it will take you to read a page. Remember, your speed will vary with different textbooks according to the difficulty of the material. Toward the middle of the book, as you become more familiar with the subject, you will read faster than you did in the beginning.

Each time you sit down to do an assignment, count the number of pages you need to complete. Calculate the amount of time it will probably take you, and then look at the clock and write down your projected finishing time. Make your goal realistic and pace yourself so you can make it. Having an expectation will help you speed up your reading and improve your concentration. Do not become an all-night victim of Parkinson's law, which states that the job expands to fit the time available. Don't allow yourself all night or all weekend to read twenty-five pages. Set a goal and then try to meet it. Rather than leisurely sauntering through an assignment, develop a sense of urgency.

Be Flexible

Inefficient readers are overconscientious, too often giving equal time to all words and all types of reading. As mentioned, you should be able to read a newspaper article in much less time than it would take you to read a science or economics passage, especially if you have already heard the news highlights on television or radio. Textbooks are more difficult and less familiar than news stories. Don't read everything at the same rate. Be willing to switch gears and select the appropriate speed for the job.

Sometimes you may need to look over material for a detail or a specific point. In this case, don't read all the words. Skim until your eyes locate the information you need and then move on to the next task. This is a case of adjusting your speed to your purpose. For example, if you are told to read a history chapter for an exam, read it carefully and spend some time studying it. But if you have been told to write a half-page summary of five articles in the library, you can probably just skim the material for the main ideas and a few supporting details. Again, adjust your speed to your purpose.

Practice

You cannot improve your running speed unless you get out and run. The same is true with reading. To learn to read faster, practice faster reading techniques every day. As the following paragraph explains, *wishing* and *willing* are not the same:

The *wish* to learn is diffuse and general. The *will* to learn is concentrated and specific. The wish to learn means that we repeat a thing again and again hoping for something to happen. The will to learn means that we dig down and analyze, that we try to find out exactly what is wrong and exactly how to put it right.

—*Streamline Your Mind,* by James Mursell

Summary Points

➤ **What is the average adult reading speed?**
The average speed is approximately 250 words per minute at 70 percent comprehension.

➤ **How can you improve your concentration for faster reading?**
Be an aggressive reader. Learn to control internal and external distractions so you can concentrate.

➤ **What is regressing?**
Regressing is rereading what you have just finished, usually because you haven't been concentrating. Regressing can be a crutch or a habit; don't do it.

➤ **What is subvocalization?**
Subvocalization is the little voice in your head that reads out loud for you.

➤ **What are fixations?**
Fixations are the stops your eyes must make to read. You group several words into thought units to be read in each fixation.

➤ **How do you use your pen as a pacer?**
Use a pen to follow the words in a smooth, flowing line, setting a rhythmical pace for your reading and improving concentration.

➤ **How can you set pace goals?**
Preview an assignment and estimate the number of words per page. Knowing your reading rate, you can approximate how long it will take you to read each page and complete the assignment.

➤ **How does speed adjust to purpose?**
Be flexible. Vary your speed according to the difficulty of the material and what you need to know when you have finished it.

COLLABORATIVE **PROBLEM SOLVING**

Form a five-member group and select one of the following activities. Brainstorm and then outline your major points on a transparency. Choose a member to present the group findings to the class.

➤ Create a "Top Ten" list of suggestions for improving your reading speed.

➤ Create a "Top Ten" list of reasons why students have trouble concentrating on what they are reading.

➤ List reasons why prior knowledge influences reading rate.

➤ List reasons why you should not expect to read a textbook at the same reading rate as a novel.

PEARSON
myreadinglab

MyReadingLab (MRL) www.myreadinglab.com

➤ To practice the ideas and skills introduced in this chapter, go to the "Reading Rate" module in the Skills section of MRL. To practice general reading comprehension, use the Levels section.

The Reading *Workshop*

"I am not a speed reader. I am a speed understander."
—ISAAC ASIMOV, SCIENCE FICTION AUTHOR

Reading efficiently is all about selecting the method and speed to accomplish your purpose. When reading for pleasure most people naturally settle into a comfortable, medium rhythm. When reading for long-term recall and study, as in most textbook reading, the pace slows considerably. When scanning for one small piece of information, we can read with lightning speed. Think about your purpose and set your "readometer" accordingly.

Think about it, talk about it, write about it:

Set up a little experiment. First, check your reading speed on Exercise 1 in this chapter. Second, count out an equal number of words (482) in something you are reading for pleasure with no need for long-term recall, and check your words-per-minute rate. Third, do the same check with a difficult textbook chapter. Create a small chart in which you record your rates in the three different situations. Write a brief paragraph to compare and explain the results.

The next time you read something, set a realistic time goal that is based on your purpose for reading.

Your professor might ask you to include this discussion in a Reading Workshop journal.

timed reading 1 Business

Preparing for an interview can be challenging. Interviewees often practice answering questions and think about how to present themselves in the best possible light for the jobs they are seeking. Occasionally, a question might be asked that not only borders on the personal but might actually be against the law.

Use your pen as a pacer and time your reading of the following selection.

Starting time: _____ minutes _____ seconds

WHEN INTERVIEW QUESTIONS TURN ILLEGAL

Refer to the
Reader's *Tip*
for **Business** on
page 262.

You're probably aware that interviewers are not supposed to ask you certain questions. There are five areas of special sensitivity in selection interviewing. Our goal here is twofold: to point out these illegal areas of questions, and to suggest strategic ways to handle them if they occur in your interview.

5   Our aim here is not to turn you into a "legal eagle" on constant alert for any cause to accuse or sue an interviewing company. In truth, many instances of illegal interview questions (such as, "Are you married?") occur in the course of ordinary getting-to-know-you small talk during an interview and aren't intended by the interviewer as an intrusion into your privacy. But innocent or not, illegal interview questions can land a company in court

10   when a job seeker claims discrimination in the interview process.

Learning to avoid illegal questions as an interviewer and handling them well as an interviewee is the focus of what follows.

WHO MAKES THE RULES FOR INTERVIEW QUESTIONS?

No single federal, state, or local agency or court defines for all cases which interview questions are legal or illegal. Instead, a plethora of court rulings, legislative decisions,

15   agency regulations, and constitutional laws combine to produce the often confusing and frequently changing list of what you can and can't ask a job applicant.

HOW TO ANSWER DIFFICULT QUESTIONS

Following are our suggestions for some of the more difficult areas in which the employer must exercise caution when asking questions—and you must be equally careful in how or if you answer.

MARITAL CIRCUMSTANCES

20   Courts have ruled that it's none of the company's business how many children an applicant has; whether he or she is married, single, divorced, or engaged; whether the applicant plans to become pregnant at any time in the future; how the applicant's spouse or partner feels about overnight travel; or what plans the applicant has made for child care during the workday.

25   Managers stumble into trouble in this area when making small talk, especially of a disclosing or "sharing" nature with the candidate. Manager: "My wife and I have lived here for about 10 years. We love it—especially the school system. Do you have kids?" Innocent? Or course. But if relations turn litigious, the manager will have to admit in court that he inquired about children as part of the selection interview.

WHAT TO DO

30   If you are asked an illegal question in this area, you can give a general response, said graciously: "I would prefer to stick to job-related questions." Or you can be more pointed:

"Are children a requirement for this position?" And, of course, you can always decide simply to play along, but as minimally as possible: "Yes, we have one child. Shall we talk about your requirements for this position?"

AGE

35 To prevent age discrimination in hiring, courts have disallowed these sorts of questions: "How old are you?" "In what year were you born?" "When did you graduate from high school?" and so forth. You do have the right to ask whether the applicant meets the legal age requirements for work in your city or state.

    Managers stray into trouble here when they talk about the average age of their work-
40 force in relation to the candidate: "Our typical employee is probably 8 to 10 years older than you. Do you anticipate problems managing people older than yourself?" You can imagine the later court scene. *Manager:* "But, Your Honor, I never asked her age!" *Candidate/plaintiff:* "My age seemed to be one of his key concerns about my ability to manage." Verdict goes to the plaintiff, with back pay, damages, and court costs.

WHAT TO DO

45 If asked an illegal question having to do with your age, you can respond, with a smile: "Age has never been a consideration for me in my work life." Or you can turn the knife a bit: "Is my age being considered as part of my application?" And, of course, you can simply answer, if you wish: "I'm 27, but my age hasn't been a consideration in past jobs."

DISABILITIES

50 Companies are forbidden by law from asking an applicant if he or she has mental or physical disabilities. Nor can they inquire about the nature or severity of disabilities, no matter how apparent they seem in the hiring process. Any physical or mental require-ments a company establishes as a prerequisite for hiring must be based on "business ne-cessity" and the safe performance of the job.

55   Managers are misled here by their best intentions: "We have many people with dis-abilities working for us and we support their needs in every way possible. For example, we could overcome the problem you have with your hands by giving you an automated speech recognition word processor." If the candidate with disabilities does not get the job, the manager's assumptions about the candidate's typing abilities could come back to
60 haunt in an expensive way.

WHAT TO DO

If you are asked an illegal question having to do with disabilities, you can refer the inter-viewer to Americans with Disabilities Act (ADA) guidelines: "I believe that under current ADA law you can't make this issue a part of the hiring process." Or you can take the edge off a bit with a general answer: "I know of nothing that will prevent me from fulfilling the
65 job requirements of this position."

SEX AND PHYSICAL APPEARANCE

An employer cannot ask questions about the person's gender unless the job specifications strictly require either a male or a female. The burden of proof is on the employer to demon-strate that only a man or a woman can do the job. Employers should beware: Courts and the Equal Employment Opportunity Commission have interpreted very narrowly the notion
70 that only one gender can perform a particular job. In addition, employers should avoid questions about the person's physical appearance, including height, weight, grooming, and dress, unless these bear clearly upon job requirements.

    Again, a manager's small talk in the job interview is the unhappy hunting ground for mistakes in this area of questioning. *Manager to a woman applicant:* "We have a fitness
75 facility here at the plant. But you seem to be pretty fit already." Oops.

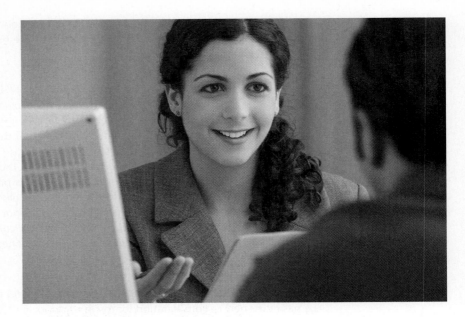

WHAT TO DO

If quizzed about matters of gender or physical appearance, you can respond in a general way: "I'm fully prepared to take on these job responsibilities, and I don't think gender or appearance plays a role." Or you can return the question with a question: "Are gender and appearance being considered as part of this hiring process?" These responses need
80 not be said in a snarlish way (though the interviewer may well deserve your anger). You can preserve your chances for the job by handling the questions professionally.

CITIZENSHIP AND NATIONAL ORIGIN

A company cannot legally inquire into the applicant's place of birth, ancestry, native language, spouse's or parents' birthplace, or residence. Nor can an employer ask directly, "Are you a U.S. citizen?" or "Do you have naturalization papers?" Prior to the decision to
85 hire, these questions may tend to reveal racial or ethnic factors that may bias the employer. Companies should request names or *persons* to notify in case of an emergency rather than specifying *relatives*. Employers should not require that the applicant's photograph be submitted prior to the hiring decision.

Managers often misstep into this pitfall when inquiring about a candidate's second
90 language capability. *Manager:* "You say on your resume that you speak Spanish fluently. Did you grow up in Mexico?" A person's land of birth cannot be grounds for a hiring decision. Clearly, this question strays into legally hazardous areas.

WHAT TO DO

If asked about your national origin, you can answer "My family history and heritage are getting us off the topic, don't you think? I would rather talk about job requirements." Or
95 you can be more direct: "I assume that where my parents came from isn't one of the requirements for this job."

(1,318 words)

—*Interviewing for Success,* by Arthur H. Bell and
Dayle M. Smith

Finishing time: _____ *minutes* _____ *seconds*

Total time: _____ *minutes* _____ *seconds*

Rate = words per minute _____ *(see time chart)*

TIME CHART

Time in Seconds and Minutes	Words per Minute	Time in Seconds and Minutes	Words per Minute
180 (3 min.)	439	340	233
220	359	350	226
230	344	360 (6 min.)	220
240 (4 min.)	329	370	214
250	316	380	208
260	304	390	203
270	293	400	197
280	282	410	193
300 (5 min.)	263	420 (7 min.)	188
310	255	430	184
320	247	440	180
330	239	450	176

Answer the following with *T* (true) or *F* (false).

_____ 1. According to the passage, the list of legal and illegal interview questions frequently changes with new regulations.

_____ 2. Illegal interview questions often request personal information.

_____ 3. Interviewers cannot legally ask questions regarding whether or not an applicant is a parent.

_____ 4. Companies may ask questions about an applicant's physical disabilities if they relate to job safety.

_____ 5. If the company offers a child care program for employees, the interviewer may ask about the number of children who might participate.

_____ 6. It is not permissible for an interviewer to ask whether or not an applicant is a U.S. citizen,

_____ 7. School administrators are permitted to ask questions regarding planned pregnancies of teacher applicants, since a maternity leave would directly affect schoolchildren.

_____ 8. While interviewers cannot directly ask an applicant's age, they can ask when the applicant graduated from high school.

_____ 9. Employers have the right to ask whether or not job applicants meet the legal age requirements for work in their city or state.

_____ 10. The reader can conclude that many of the questions which have been determined to be illegal were found to be so on the basis that the answers to such questions could be used to discriminate against job applicants.

THINK AND WRITE

Why might it not be in the best interests of job applicants to tell their interviewers they are asking illegal questions? _____

_____

_____

_____

_____

timed reading 2   History

Have you ever wondered why a red carpet is rolled out for celebrities and royalty? Why not green, yellow or blue? As with most traditions, there is a reason for this one, and it is rooted in ancient history.

Use your pen as a pacer and time your reading of the following selection.

Starting time: _____ minutes _____ seconds

THE RED CARPET

Refer to the **Reader's** *Tip* for **History** on page 165.

GREAT FEETS

Hollywood actors are often considered American royalty and as it turns out, they have the carpeting to match. The first mention of the red carpet we could find dates back to the story of *Agamemnon,* written by the Greek playwright Aeschylus in 485 B.C.E. In the play, Mycenaean King Agamemnon's wife tricks him into walking across a red carpet fit only
5   for the "feet of the gods."

Red-tinted colors, especially deep purplish reds, were especially admired in the early Greek and Roman societies because they were both expensive and scarce. In fact, throughout recorded history, royals and others of high rank have used the colors red and purple to symbolize how important and wealthy they were. The use of the red carpet ap-
10 peared again in the 1600s, however, when Jahangir, a Mughal emperor, visited his brother-in-law on New Year's Day. His brother-in-law carpeted the road from the palace to his house with gold brocades and rich velvets (color unknown) to prevent royal feet from ever touching the ground.

AMERICANS SEE RED

Over time, rolling out the red carpet for special or honored people trickled down from
15 royalty. In 1821, U.S. president James Monroe became the first to receive the treatment with a red carpet rolled out to the river to guide his path. New York Central's luxury train, the 20th Century Limited, debuted in 1902 establishing the "red carpet treatment" not only for royals and dignitaries but for anyone receiving special treatment. The train traveled the smooth water-level route from New York to Chicago and the railroad rolled out a
20 red carpet to welcome passengers onto the train.

As for Hollywood, the red carpet first emerged in 1922 when the famous exhibitor Sid Grauman opened up the Egyptian Theatre (seven years before the first Academy Awards ceremony). And while the Academy Awards have become the best known use of the red carpet in history, with virtually every famous star walking its length at one
25 time or another, the question remains: So, how does Oscar's red carpet arrive each year?

The answer is; not very glamorously but plenty safe, in dozens of rolls wrapped in plastic on flatbed trucks. Strangely enough, the actual shade of red is a secret, designed by the academy to be a slightly purplish red that appears more reddish on TV.

ROLLING IT OUT

30 Though the process of rolling out a carpet sounds like it would be simple enough, the process takes hours of meticulous labor. The crew unrolls the rugs on their hands and knees, then cut the edges with a huge putty knife to make sure they match perfectly. Another worker follows the process to scoop up the remnants to make sure they can't be stolen for color copying or eBay sales. In all, it takes more than 20 men a full two days to
35 install the carpet (including ironing every seam after everything is in place). Just like celebrities keep stylists on hand in case of emergency, so does the carpet itself. One expert always appears at the show in tuxedo to ensure that the carpet looks its best and never forms a rumple that might trip someone famous. In all, the modern-day film stars probably receive a more detailed and luxurious red carpet welcome than any monarch or
40 dignitary in history.

(560 words)

—"The Red Carpet," p. 159, entire page, from *Mental Floss presents In the Beginning* by Mary Carmichael, Will Pearson, and Mangesh Hattikudur. Copyright ©2007 by Mental Floss, LLC. Reprinted by permission of HarperCollins Publishers.

Finishing time: _____ *minutes* _____ *seconds*

Total time: _____ *minutes* _____ *seconds*

Rate = words per minute _____ *(see time chart)*

TIME CHART

Time in Seconds and Minutes	Words per Minute	Time in Seconds and Minutes	Words per Minute
60 (1 min.)	560	190	177
70	483	200	168
80	421	210	160
90	373	220	152
100	335	230	146
110	306	240 (4 min.)	140
120 (2 min.)	280	250	135
130	259	260	129
140	240	270	124
150	224	280	120
160	210	290	116
170	198	300 (5 min.)	112
180 (3 min.)	187		

Answer the following with *T* (true) or *F* (false).

_____ 1. According to the article, the earliest reference to the red carpet is in an ancient Greek play.

_____ 2. We can infer from the article that red and purple dyes were plentiful in ancient times.

_____ 3. In the Hollywood movie industry, the tradition of the red carpet began with the first Academy Awards ceremony.

_____ 4. The formula for the red of the Academy Awards carpet is a closely guarded secret.

_____ 5. Installing the red carpet for the Academy Awards is accomplished quickly and efficiently.

Comprehension = (% correct) _____

THINK AND WRITE

Why do people often treat celebrities like royalty?_____

_____

_____

Eleanor Roosevelt redefined the role of First Lady. During World War II she visited soldiers in Europe and Asia to boost morale and report conditions first-hand to her husband. During peacetime she worked tirelessly to improve working conditions, made speeches for social justice, and championed the hiring of qualified women and African Americans in government. She was always courageous, but her critics claimed she had too much power.

Use your pen as a pacer and time your reading of the following selection.

Starting time: _____ minutes _____ seconds

ELEANOR ROOSEVELT

Refer to the
Reader's *Tip*
for **History** on
page 165.

Eleanor Roosevelt's emergence as a public figure was spurred on by family tragedy. In August 1921, Franklin Roosevelt was stricken with infantile paralysis, or poliomyelitis. While on vacation at their Campobello retreat in New Brunswick, Canada, the family often went sailing. One day in August, they spotted a forest fire and put ashore to fight it. After the ex-
5 hausting battle was over, Franklin went swimming in a landlocked lake near the family home. Later that day he complained of chills and went to bed. The following day he developed a mild fever that worsened. Soon his arms and legs were paralyzed. When specialists arrived, they diagnosed him as having what was commonly called polio. If Franklin did survive, the family was told, he would probably be an invalid for the rest of his days. After the
10 initial shock, Eleanor gathered her composure and saw to her husband's needs. With strong family support and extraordinary determination, Franklin Roosevelt began to recover, first regaining the use of his upper torso and arms. And though he never walked unaided again, within two years of his illness he was back in politics. Franklin and Eleanor now had a new relationship, probably unique in political history. Although they would never again share the
15 love of their earliest years together, they still needed one another. Franklin would work his way back into the political limelight, and Eleanor would be "his eyes and ears." [The following example illustrates her strength and commitment.]

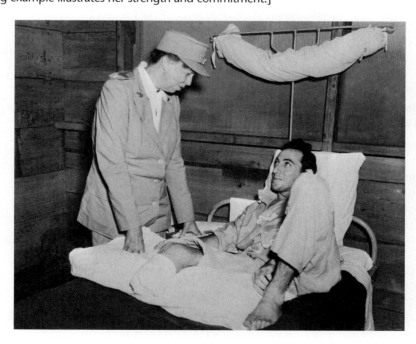

The door to the hospital tent was so low that the tall woman, dressed in a standard Red Cross uniform, had to duck considerably to enter. It was good to be sheltered from the blaz-
20 ing tropical sun of Christmas Island, in the South Pacific, on that fall day of 1943. But her senses were quickly overcome by the combined odors of antiseptic, bandages, and wounded men. There was little time on this stopover, yet it was important that she spend a few moments with a marine whose torso had been horribly mangled by a mortar shell blast. Extremely worried about the young man's survival, the doctors had asked First Lady Eleanor
25 Roosevelt to sit with him for a while and hopefully brighten his spirits and strengthen his will to live.

Recovering her poise after the initial shock of the hospital scene, she smiled, adjusted her cap, walked to the bedside of the boy shrouded in bandages, and introduced herself as "Mrs. Roosevelt." Heavily drugged and barely conscious, the boy took the hand of the
30 kindly woman, who leaned forward to kiss him on the forehead. In the same unhurried, sincere, and caring manner with which she had spoken to hundreds of Allied soldiers fighting in World War II, Eleanor Roosevelt gently reassured the boy that he would fully recover and come home to the United States. The time was short, and the troop trans- port plane, on which she had traveled throughout the Pacific, was ready to depart for
35 Honolulu. But she stayed until the very last moment, holding the boy's hand and speak- ing softly to him. She even promised to visit his mother when she returned to the States. Only when he fell asleep did the first lady leave his bedside.

Some months later, the same young soldier called on Eleanor Roosevelt at the White House to express his deep gratitude for her visit. Her remarkable impact on his recovery—
40 and on the morale of tens of thousands of Allied soldiers fighting in World War II— symbolizes the person who has been called the most important public woman of the twentieth century. The wife of President Franklin Roosevelt poured the same kind of boundless energy and tireless concern for the betterment of the world into all of her hu- manitarian interests. Eleanor Roosevelt was a pacesetter for the expansion of rights for
45 minorities, the disabled, and especially women. Still, she remained an embodiment of the characteristics that defined the traditional Victorian American woman.

(658 words)

—*From These Beginnings,* Sixth Edition, Volume Two,
by Roderick Nash and Gregory Graves

Finishing time: _____ *minutes* _____ *seconds*

Total time: _____ *minutes* _____ *seconds*

Rate = words per minute _____ *(see time chart)*

TIME CHART

Time in Seconds and Minutes	Words per Minute	Time in Seconds and Minutes	Words per Minute
60 (1 min.)	658	180 (3 min.)	219
70	564	190	208
80	494	200	197
90	439	210	188
100	395	220	179
110	359	230	172
120 (2 min.)	329	240 (4 min.)	165
130	304	250	158
140	282	260	152
150	263	270	146
160	247	280	141
170	232	300 (5 min.)	132

Answer the following with *T* (true) or *F* (false).

_____ 1. The author suggests that Eleanor Roosevelt performed the presidential tasks of mingling with the people while the president stayed close to home.

_____ 2. On the day Franklin Roosevelt became ill, he had helped fight a forest fire and swam in a cold lake.

_____ 3. After contracting polio, Franklin Roosevelt was never able to leave his wheelchair or travel away from home.

_____ 4. The wounded young man whom Eleanor Roosevelt visited died after she left.

_____ 5. Franklin Roosevelt was president of the United States during World War II.

Comprehension = (% correct) _____

THINK AND WRITE

Why would critics claim Eleanor Roosevelt had too much power? _____

_____

_____

_____

Managing Workplace Reading

Everyone works at some point. Perhaps you had a full-time job before you entered college, or perhaps you work part time when you are not studying. In any event, all occupations demand some amount of reading. In fact, companies frequently hire expensive consultants to advise employees on efficient methods for meeting workplace reading demands. Typically, these consultants first urge employees to put their reading demands in perspective and set priorities. Memos, for example, may need to be read immediately, but annual reports can probably wait until later. As a next step, the experts strongly suggest handling a piece of paper only once. Their advice is "Do not open a letter and then set it aside to be handled later. If you open a letter, read it and take action." The three action options are: respond to it, throw it in the trash, or file it to be used later with other material on the same subject.

Reader's *Tip* Managing Workplace Reading

- Set priorities before reading.
- Strive to handle a piece of paper only once.
- Respond to it, discard it, or file it.

Types of Workplace Reading

Work-related documents usually make points quickly, have a serious tone, and are written to inform rather than to entertain. The importance of a document is determined by the way in which the information it contains can affect your job performance, so only you can set priorities.

E-mail

In many workplaces, communication is done mainly by e-mail. This can be an efficient and convenient way to transmit information, discuss ideas, and issue work orders. Sometimes the number of e-mails that employees must process takes an excessive amount of time. Experienced employees use several time-saving methods to manage their e-mail.

First, they disable the tone that signals an incoming message and read their e-mail only two or three times a day. Second, they read messages once and immediately respond, delete, or file as needed; they try to have no messages in their inboxes at the end of the day. Third, they store important messages in folders with logical names.

For responding to e-mail, experts advise employees to keep their messages brief, polite, and not to "reply to all" unless it is necessary; to re-read outgoing messages before sending them; and to avoid rushing with an e-mail response to an important message by sending a courteous, one-sentence e-mail saying they will reply at a later time.

Specific types of workplace reading such as those described below are often sent to employees via e-mail.

Memos

A memo is a brief message used to update co-workers, announce meetings, ask questions, request assistance, or announce decisions. Memos are written in a concise, direct style and can be formal or informal, depending on the sender's level of seniority and the sender's relationship with the recipient. Used correctly, memos are intended for internal messages among company employees and are not generally used for communicating with those outside the organization. They are frequently sent by e-mail.

Memos are usually only a few sentences long but can sometimes continue for several pages. The most important information is given at the beginning (see the illustration below). Notice dates, times, places, and requests for a response or action. Special formatting such as numbered or bulleted lists may be applied to other important items to make them stand out.

1. What is the reason for the memo? _____

_____

2. What is the necessary action? _____

TO: Market Designs Personnel
FROM: Sergio Rodriguez, Director of Personnel Services
DATE: March 1, 2009
CC: Veronica Menser, General Manager
RE: Direct Deposit of Paychecks

Please note that beginning with the second pay period in April, all nonsalaried employees will have the option of direct deposit of their paychecks. In order to take advantage of this option, you must fill out a Direct Deposit Request Form (sample is attached) and return it to the Accounting Department by no later than March 15. Implementation of the direct deposit option will be delayed one month for those employees who submit their requests after that date. If you have any questions, please contact me at extension 225.

Letters

A letter is somewhat more formal than a memo and therefore more appropriate for communication outside a company. Use a letter to give or request information, to congratulate or express appreciation, to register complaints, or to emphasize an action. Like memos, business letters are relatively short and written in a concise, direct manner.

Newsletters

Newsletters are documents published by businesses, organizations, clubs, or schools that combine news, editorial columns, letters, stories, and graphics on subjects of interest to group members. They look like mini-newspapers or multi-page stapled letters. The purpose of a newsletter is to build group spirit, bind members together, recognize member achievement, and chronicle group events. Each member of the particular group usually receives the newsletter.

Newsletters are basically *propaganda* (persuasive public relations information) for the organization. They tend to report on the past and rarely have any critical information that demands action. If there is a table of contents, use it to guide your reading. If not, read the headings and beginning paragraphs to determine what you care to read.

Reader's *Tip* Reading Newsletters

- Read selectively. You may want to read all of the newsletter or none of it.
- Read critically. You cannot consider the information in a newsletter to be objective, because it contains information beneficial only to the company or organization. Unflattering information is not included, so the coverage is not balanced.
- Note items that are highlighted; set off by numbers, bullets, or capital letters; or that appear in boldface or italic type.

9 Analytical Reasoning

- What is good thinking?
- What are the characteristics of unsuccessful students?
- What are the characteristics of successful students?
- What is involved in good problem solving?
- How do graphic illustrations condense complex information?

Everyday Reading Skills: Reading Direct Mail Advertisements

Identify Analytical Thinking

According to researchers, good thinkers have developed a logical and sequential pattern of working through complex material, whereas poor thinkers lack this habit of analysis. Good thinkers work persistently, believing they will find answers. They draw on their old knowledge to solve new problems and thus relate, interpret, and integrate what they already know with what they want to learn. Poor thinkers, in contrast, merely collect facts and are unaware of relationships. They cannot put old and new information together to draw conclusions. They seem to have no logical method for problem solving.

Mastering each new college subject offers you both immediate and future benefits. For example, after you struggle through and finally understand an introductory biology text, those same new habits of thinking transfer to the next biology course, which then will be easier to understand. You can also apply these thinking skills to new and different tasks. For instance, the very act of thinking through the complexities of biology will make it easier for you to tackle chemistry and physics. Thinking, like everything else, requires practice, and the more you do, the better you become. You gradually develop the ability to educate yourself.

Two researchers, Bloom and Broder, studied both academically successful and academically unsuccessful college students at the University of Chicago.[1] They described the thinking processes of each (see the lists that follow).

Before reading further, think of a student you know personally who is not successful in school. Check to see if the following characteristics describe that student.

An Unsuccessful Student

1. Has no method of attacking new material.
2. Misunderstands or skips directions.
3. Fails to keep the purpose in mind.
4. Is unable to apply present knowledge to new situations.
5. Is passive in thinking and answers questions on the basis of few clues.
6. Uses "impression" or "feeling" to arrive at answers.
7. Is careless in considering details and jumps around from one to another.
8. After making a superficial attempt to reason, gives up and guesses.

Who do you know who is a very successful student? How many of the following characteristics describe that student?

A Successful Student

1. Is careful and systematic in attacking the problem.
2. Can read directions and immediately choose a point at which to begin reasoning.
3. Keeps sight of goals while thinking through the problem.
4. Pulls out key terms and tries to simplify the material.
5. Breaks larger problems into smaller subproblems.
6. Is active and aggressive in seeking meaning.
7. Applies relevant old knowledge to the problem.
8. Is persistent and careful in seeking solutions.

What kind of student are you? Go back to both lists and circle the characteristics that apply to you.

---

[1]B. S. Bloom and L. Broder, *Problem-Solving Process of College Students* (Chicago: University of Chicago Press, 1950).

Successful students aggressively and systematically attack their studying, and they persist to a logical conclusion. As you can see, Bloom and Broder's list of characteristics might just as easily apply to successful problem solving in everyday life as to success in the academic world. These characteristics thus contribute not only to college success but to the long-lasting personal success that is the ultimate reason for going to college. Start developing them!

Personal *Feedback* 1

Name _____

1. If you won the lottery, what would you do with the money? _____
   _____
   _____

2. Why were you glad to leave high school? _____
   _____
   _____

3. What do you miss most about high school? _____
   _____
   _____

4. What does *delayed gratification* mean and how does it apply to college? _____
   _____
   _____

5. What causes you the most stress? _____
   _____
   _____

6. How can a professor make you feel you are an important part of the class? _____
   _____
   _____

7. Describe a problem at home, work, or school that you enjoyed attacking and solving systematically. _____
   _____
   _____

8. What do you feel is your greatest problem-solving strength? _____
   _____
   _____

Tear out and submit to your instructor.

Engage in Problem Solving

Another researcher, Arthur Whimbey, studied good and poor readers. He noted two prominent features of poor college readers.

> First, there is one-shot thinking rather than extended, sequential construction of understanding; and second, there is a willingness to allow gaps of knowledge to exist, in effect, an attitude of indifference toward achieving an accurate and complete comprehension of situations and relations.[2]

Whimbey and other researchers believe that all students can learn the characteristic behaviors of good readers by increasing their analytical reasoning skills through problem solving. Through analytical reasoning they break problems into small parts and use logic to arrive at a solution. Breaking a complex word problem into sequential steps for solution requires thinking skills similar to those used in breaking a paragraph down to get a main idea, draw a conclusion, or trace the details of a process.

EXAMPLE Read the following word problem and think about how you would figure out the answer.

> Mary is shorter than Carol but taller than Kathy. Sue is taller than Mary but shorter than Carol. Which girl is tallest?

Although the problem may seem rather confusing at first reading, when it is broken down in sequential steps, the answer is simple. The best way to solve this problem is to draw a diagram so you can visualize the relative height of each girl. Reread the problem and place each girl in a position on a vertical line.

Mary is shorter than Carol,
    Carol
    Mary

but taller than Kathy.
    Carol
    Mary
    Kathy

Sue is taller than Mary,
but shorter than Carol.
    Carol
    Sue
    Mary
    Kathy

EXPLANATION The diagram indicates that the tallest girl is Carol.

Whimbey found that analytical reasoning skills can be taught through practice. He devised a variety of word problems similar to those that follow to help students learn. The thinking strategies used to solve these problems apply in every academic task, not just in reading textbooks. Break each problem in the exercise into parts and work sequentially toward a solution. You may want to do the first exercise with someone else so you can discuss the steps leading to a solution, then try the rest on your own.

---

[2]Arthur Whimbey, *Intelligence Can Be Taught* (New York: E. P. Dutton, 1975), 55.

exercise 1 Collaborate with a study buddy to answer the following questions. Share your steps in thinking with each other.

_____ 1. Which set of letters is different from the other three?

   a. GHIF   b. MNOK   c. RSTQ   d. CDEB

_____ 2. Face the south and turn to your right. Make another right turn and then an about-face. In which direction are you now facing?

_____ 3. According to the pattern, which letters should come next in the series?

   KL NO QR T __ __ __

_____ 4. A train arrived at its destination at 7:45, which was 3 hours and 50 minutes after its departure. What time was its departure?

_____ 5. According to the pattern, which numbers should come next in the series?

   1 2 4 5 7 8 10 11 __ __ __

_____ 6. Write the word _manage_. If deleting the first three letters or the last three letters leaves an actual word, circle the second _a_ in the original word. If not, circle the first _a_.

_____ 7. According to the pattern, what numbers should come next in the series?

   1 6 11 16 21 __ __ __

8. Sylvia needed dental work in a small town with only two dentists. She met them both. Dr. Drill had beautiful teeth, but Dr. Fill's teeth needed work. Using logic, which dentist should Sylvia choose?

   _____

   _____

9. Ellen, Carolyn, and Betsy each finished the road race at a different time. Their last names, not in order, are King, Wilson, and Harris. Wilson finished before Harris but after King. Betsy came in before Carolyn, and Ellen was last. What are the last names of Betsy and Ellen?

   _____

10. Fran, Sally, and Marsha collect old books from different countries. Together they have a total of eighteen books. Six of the books are from Spain, with one more than that being the total from India and one less being the total from Holland. Sally has two books from Spain, and Fran has an equal number from India. Marsha has twice as many books from India as Fran has. Both Marsha and Fran have only one book each from Holland, and Fran has only one from Spain. How many books does Sally have? How many does Marsha have?

   _____

	Holland	Spain	India	**Total**
Fran	1	1	2	4
Sally	3	2	1	6
Marsha	1	3	4	8
Total	5	6	7	18

Do you prefer working alone or do you benefit more from working with a study buddy? _____

Analytical Reasoning in Textbooks

Apply analytical reasoning to every page of every textbook you read. Reading is problem solving, and reading is thinking. Get in the habit of working through complex ideas carefully and systematically. Simplify the material, and break it into smaller, more manageable ideas. Draw on what you already know, and actively and aggressively seek to understand.

To help you visualize complex ideas, textbooks frequently include maps, charts, diagrams, and graphs. These illustrations condense a lot of information into one picture. Refer to such graphic illustrations while you read; the material will then be easier to understand.

This chapter presents exercises on graphic illustrations and problems that require logical and sequential thinking. Before doing the exercises, read the hints in the Reader's Tip.

Reader's Tip   Thinking About Maps, Charts, Graphs, and Diagrams

1. Read the title to determine the subject.
2. Read any information in italics or boldface.
3. Read the footnotes to determine the source of the information.
4. Read the labels to determine what each mark, arrow, figure, or design means.
5. Figure out the legend, the key on a map that shows what the markings represent.
6. Notice numbers indicating units of measurement, such as percentages, dollars, thousands, millions, or billions.
7. Notice trends and extremes. What is the average, and what are the highs and lows?
8. Refer back and forth to the text to follow a process or label parts.
9. Draw conclusions based on the information.
10. Do not read more into the illustration than is supported by fact. In other words, don't draw conclusions that cannot be proved.

exercise 2 Make notes or diagrams to help you solve the following problems.

1. Which set of letters differs from the other three? _____

   _____

         a. ABCD   b. EFGH   c. IJKL   d. MNOP

2. What number would be next in this sequence?

   _____

         3   4   6   9   13

   —*The Great Book of Math Teasers,* by Robert Muller

3. **The nine-dot problem:** Without lifting your pencil from the paper, draw no more than four straight lines that will cross through all nine dots.

   —*Conceptual Blockbusting: A Guide to Better Ideas,* Fourth edition, by James L. Adams

4. **The matchstick problem:** Move two matches to form four squares of equal size.

   —*Basic Psychology,* by Howard H. Kendler

5. **Analogy:** What word completes the analogy?

      Merchant: Sell : : Customer: _____

      Lawyer: Client : : Doctor: _____

6. **String problem:** You are in the situation depicted below and given the task of tying the two strings together. If you hold one string, the other is out of reach. Can you do it?

_____

_____

_____

—From Richard J. Gerrig and Philip G. Zimbardo, *Psychology & Life,* 17th ed., figure 8.13D (page 266) and figure 18.14D (page 268). ©2005 Pearson Education, Inc. Reproduced by permission of Pearson Education, Inc.

7. **Anagram:** Rearrange the letters to make an English word.

      RWAET _____

      KEROJ _____

8. **Series completion:** What number or letter would be next in each series?

      1 2 8 3 4 6 5 6 _____

      A B M C D M _____

—Items 5, 7, 8 from Wayne Weiten, 6th ed.
©2005 Wadsworth, a part of Cengage Learning, Inc.
Reproduced by permission. www.cengage.com/permissions

exercise 3   Collaborate with a study buddy to answer the following questions.

Percentage Population Change in the States Between 1990 and 2000
The United States Bureau of the Census reports that the population of the states changed substantially in the 1990s. Census data are collected every ten years.

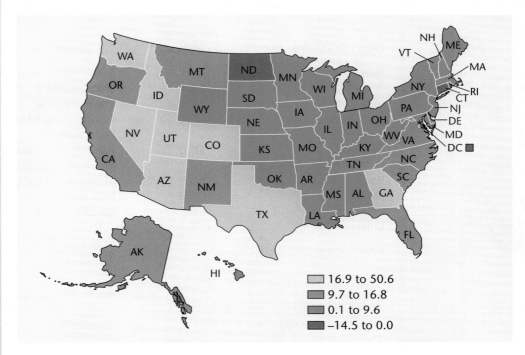

16.9 to 50.6
9.7 to 16.8
0.1 to 9.6
–14.5 to 0.0

Source: U.S. Bureau of the Census.

—*The Struggle for Democracy*, 6th ed.
by Edward Greenberg and Benjamin Page

The purpose of the map is to show _____

_____

Use the map to answer the following with *T* (true), *F* (false), or *CT* (can't tell).

_____ 1. North Dakota was the only state that experienced no population growth during the ten-year period.

_____ 2. Eight states experienced population growth between 16.9% and 50.6%.

_____ 3. Texas was the only state to have a population growth of 50.6% during the ten-year period.

_____ 4. Florida, California, Alaska, and Alabama experienced a population growth within the same 9.7% to 16.8% range.

_____ 5. Over half of the states in the United States experienced a population growth of 9.7% or above in the ten-year period.

6. Although the map does not show reasons, why do you think states indicated in yellow saw such dramatic population increases? _____

_____

exercise 4 Collaborate with a study buddy to review the table and answer the questions that follow.

THE WORLD'S TEN LARGEST URBAN AREAS, 1980 AND 2015

1980		2015 (Projected)	
Urban Area	Population (in Millions)	Urban Area	Population (in Millions)
New York, U.S.A.	16.5	Tokyo–Yokohama, Japan	26.4
Tokyo–Yokohama, Japan	14.4	Mumbai, India	26.1
Mexico City, Mexico	14.0	Lagos, Nigeria	23.2
Los Angeles–Long Beach, U.S.A.	10.6	Dhaka, Bangladesh	21.1
		São Paulo, Brazil	20.4
Shanghai, China	10.0	Karachi, Pakistan	19.2
Buenos Aires, Argentina	9.7	Mexico City, Mexico	19.2
Paris, France	8.5	Shanghai, China	18.0
Moscow, U.S.S.R.	8.0	New York, U.S.A.	17.4
Beijing, China	8.0	Calcutta, India	17.3
Chicago, U.S.A.	7.7		

Source: United Nations (2001).

—*Social Problems,* Second edition, by John J. Macionis

The purpose of this table is _____

_____

Use the table to answer the following with *T* (true), *F* (false), or *CT* (can't tell).

_____ 1. The number of U.S. metropolitan areas ranking in the world's ten largest urban areas of population drops from three to one in the thirty-five-year period projected by the table.

_____ 2. The New York City metropolitan area would increase in population but fall from first place to last in the ranking of the world's ten largest urban areas of population over the thirty-five-year period shown.

_____ 3. Only four metropolitan areas listed in the top ten for 1980 are also listed in the world's ten largest urban areas of population in 2015.

_____ 4. In the year 2006, the Tokyo metropolitan area had over 20 million people.

_____ 5. The reader can assume that the population of Mumbai will have to have more than doubled from 1980 to meet its projection for 2015.

6. The table does not show the reasons for population growth. Why do you think the six areas listed after Tokyo in 2015 are expected to have such a dramatic increase in population and no European area is listed on the 2015 chart?

_____

_____

exercise 5   **Graphs That Spin**

Graphs, which often show an upward or downward trend over time, are a good way to present data. But using graphs also gives people the opportunity to "spin" data in various ways. The trend depends in part on the time frame used. During the past ten years, for instance, the U.S. crime rate has fallen. But if we were to look at the past fifty years, we would see an opposite trend: The crime rate pushed sharply upward.

The scale used to draw a graph is also important because it lets a researcher "inflate" or "deflate" a trend. Both graphs shown here present identical data for College Board SAT critical reading scores between 1967 and 2006.

—*Sociology*, 10th Edition, by John J. Macionis

People use graphs to spin the truth. Especially in newspapers and other popular media, we find statistics in the form of charts and graphs.

The purpose of these graphs is to _____

_____

_____

Use the graphs to answer the following with *T* (true), *F* (false), or *CT* (can't tell).

_____ 1. Both graphs show that the 1985 SAT critical reading scores were slightly higher than 500.

_____ 2. The lines on the two graphs appear different because the years listed on each are different.

_____ 3. From 1995 to 2000 the average critical reading SAT scores remained approximately the same.

_____ 4. From 1970 to 1990 critical reading SAT scores decreased by approximately 35 points.

_____ 5. The SAT math scores were lower than the verbal scores in 1985.

exercise 6 Collaborate to study the pie graphs and to answer the questions.

Country of Origin of U.S. Latinos

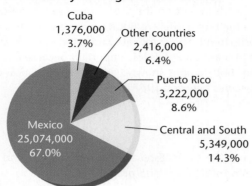

Source: By the author. Based on *Statistical Abstract* 2005:Table 40.

Where U.S. Latinos Live

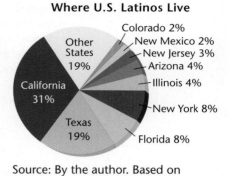

Source: By the author. Based on *Statistical Abstract* 2005:Table 21.

Today, Latinos are the largest minority group in the United States. There are millions more Latinos in the United States than there are Canadians in Canada (33 million). As shown, two-thirds of Latinos live in just four states: California, Texas, Florida, and New York.

—From James M. Henslin, *Essentials of Sociology: A Down-to-Earth Approach*, 6th ed. ©2006 (excerpts from pages 226 and 227 and figures 9.6 and 9.7). Reproduced by permission of Pearson Education, Inc.

The purpose of these pie graphs is to show _____

_____

_____

Use the graph to answer the following with *T* (true), *F* (false), or *CT* (can't tell).

_____ 1. Over half of the Latino immigrants in the United States live in California and Texas.

_____ 2. The majority of the 3 million plus Puerto Rican immigrants live in Florida.

_____ 3. The number of Latino immigrants living in New York is greater than the Latino immigrant populations of Colorado, New Mexico, and New Jersey combined.

_____ 4. By the 2010 census, the number of immigrants from Mexico will pass the 30,000,000 mark.

_____ 5. Over twice as many immigrants come from Central and South America as come from Cuba.

6. Although these graphs do not show the reasons for immigration,

why do you suppose the majority of Latino immigrants to the United

States come from the country of Mexico? _____

_____

_____

exercise 7 Collaborate to study the bar graph and to answer the questions.

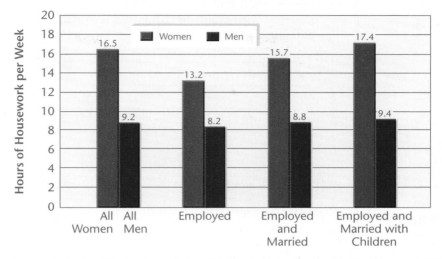

Source: Based on Stapinsky, *American Demographics*, vol. 20, no. 11 (November 1998).

GENDER AND HOUSEWORK

Just as patriarchy gives men control of the workplace, it also assigns women most of the housework. In Japan, probably the most patriarchal of all high-income nations, women do almost all the shopping, cooking, cleaning, and child care. In the United States, where having two incomes is the norm among married couples, women still do most of the housework (or they pay other women to do it). The bar graph shows that the amount of housework people do depends on whether they are single or married, working for pay or staying at home.

—*Social Problems*, Third Edition, by John J. Macionis

The purpose of this graph is _____

_____

_____

Use the graph to answer the following with *T* (true), *F* (false), or *CT* (can't tell).

_____ 1. The graph indicates that employed, married women and men do more housework if they have children.

_____ 2. The amount of housework done by employed men varies greatly depending on whether they are married or married with children.

_____ 3. Employed, married women with children spend close to twice as much time doing housework than employed, married men with children.

_____ 4. Unemployed, married women with children do more housework than employed married women with children.

_____ 5. The pair of bars closest to the left side represents the averages of the data for men and women in the three categories to the right.

6. Based on the data in the graph, how might you explain the greater increase in the amount of housework done by employed women who are married or married with children compared to the amount done by men in the same categories?

_____

_____

_____

_____

exercise 8   Read the passage and use the drawing to help visualize your thoughts.

THE KINDEST CUT

After thanking the donor for a bouquet of flowers and sniffing them appreciatively, the next step is to find a vase and put them in water. The florist usually sends a message to cut off an inch or two of stem first; purists even instruct that this should be done while the stem is immersed in water.

Three stems were cut from the same plant at the same time. Stem 1 was placed in water immediately. Stem 2 was left for half an hour, and then a two-inch length was cut off the bottom end. It was then placed in water. Stem 3 was also left for half an hour and then placed in water without further treatment.

Stem 3 is distinctly wilted, whereas the other two look normal.

The figure shows why Stems 1 and 2 have fared so much better: in both, the column of water in the xylem is continuous with the water in the container. As the leaves transpire, the water lost from the plant is replaced by pulling more water into the xylem from the container. While Stems 2 and 3 were left out of water, transpiration from the leaves pulled the water column in the xylem up into the stem, leaving room for air to enter the base of the xylem. Cutting Stem 2 the second time removed this air-filled xylem, permitting the water still in the xylem to link up with the water in the container. However, Stem 3 was left with an air bubble at the base of its xylem, which blocks the entry of water from the container. As the leaves transpire, they lose water faster than the dwindling xylem contents can replace it. Water is pulled out of other cells in the leaves until they no longer fill their walls. Without this internal support the walls buckle and the plant wilts.

—From Arms and Camp, *Biology: A Journey into Life,* 2nd ed. © 1991
Brooks/Cole, a part of Cengage Learning, Inc.
Reproduced by permission. www.cengage.com/permissions

Use the passage and the diagram to answer the following questions with *T* (true) or *F* (false).

_____ 1. Stem 2 would not be receiving water unless it had been cut a second time.

_____ 2. The flow of water in Stem 1 is not blocked by an air bubble.

_____ 3. The xylem is in the stem of the plant.

_____ 4. The xylem of Stem 2 was blocked before the second cut.

_____ 5. If cut immediately above the air bubble and placed in water, Stem 3 might recover freshness.

exercise 9 Answer the following questions from an Interpersonal Communications textbook, and then analyze your responses in order to learn about your listening skills. Compare your results with those of your classmates.

ASSESSING YOUR LISTENING SKILLS

The purpose of this questionnaire is to assess your listening skills. Respond to each statement with a number as follows: 1 for always false, 2 for usually false, 3 for sometimes false, 4 for usually true, and 5 for always true.

_____ 1. I have a difficult time separating important and unimportant ideas when I listen to others.

_____ 2. I check new information against what I already know when I listen to others.

_____ 3. I have an idea what others will say when I listen to them.

_____ 4. I am sensitive to others' feelings when I listen to them.

_____ 5. I think about what I am going to say next when I listen to others.

_____ 6. I focus on the process of communication that is occurring between me and others when I listen to them.

_____ 7. I cannot wait for others to finish talking so I can take my turn.

_____ 8. I try to understand the meanings that are being created when I communicate with others.

_____ 9. I focus on determining whether others understand what I said when they are talking.

_____ 10. I ask others to elaborate when I am not sure what they mean.

SCORING

To find your score, first reverse your responses for the odd-numbered items. (If you wrote 1, make it 5; if you wrote 2, make it 4; if you wrote 3, leave it as 3; if you wrote 4, make it 2; if you wrote 5, make it 1.) Next, add the numbers next to each statement. Scores range from 10 to 50. The higher your score, the better your listening skill.

—*Interpersonal Communication*, Third Edition, by
Steven Beebe, Susan Beebe, and Mark Redmond

Write a brief description of the strengths and weaknesses of your listening skills.

I am _____

_____

_____

exercise 10

Experience the specialization of the cerebral hemispheres by performing the following activity. Then respond to the True-False items.

RIGHT AND LEFT HEMISPHERE FUNCTIONS

Get a meter stick or yardstick. Try balancing it vertically on the end of your left index finger, as shown in the drawing. Then try balancing it on your right index finger. Most people are better with their dominant hand—the right for right-handers, for example. Is this true for you?

Now try this: Begin reciting the ABCs out loud as fast as you can while balancing the stick with your left hand. Do you have less trouble this time? Why should that be? The right hemisphere controls the act of balancing with the left hand. However, your left hemisphere, though poor at controlling the left hand, still tries to coordinate your balancing efforts. When you distract the left hemisphere with a steady stream of talk, the right hemisphere can orchestrate more efficient balancing with your left hand without interference.

—From Samuel E. Wood and Ellen R. Green Wood, *The World of Psychology*,
4th ed. ©2002 (excerpt and drawing from page 62).
Reproduced by permission of Pearson Education, Inc.

———— 1. To successfully balance the yardstick, right-handers want the right hemisphere to be in control.

———— 2. To successfully balance the yardstick, right-handers use talk to distract the left hemisphere so that the right hemisphere can take control for balance.

Summary oints

➤ **What do good thinkers do?**
Good thinkers work persistently in a logical and sequential pattern, drawing on old knowledge to solve new problems while they relate, interpret, and integrate what they know with what they are learning.

➤ **What are the characteristics of successful students?**
Successful students systematically identify goals and break larger problems into smaller problems. They pull out key terms and simplify problems. They are persistent, active, and aggressive. They apply relevant old knowledge to create new solutions.

➤ **What are the characteristics of unsuccessful students?**
Unsuccessful students engage in one-shot thinking and allow gaps of knowledge to exist. They fail to work with purpose and have no method of attacking new material. They are passive, careless in considering details, superficial in reasoning, and allow impressions to reign rather than logic.

➤ **How do graphic illustrations condense complex information?**
Graphs and charts condense complicated information into a single picture to dramatize differences and allow for quick comparisons.

Form a five-member group and select one of the following activities. Brainstorm and then outline your major points on a transparency. Choose a member to present the group findings to the class.

➤ Record the month in which each class member was born. Create a bar graph showing the number of class birthdays in each month. Put the months on the horizontal line and indicate the number of birthdays in each month on the vertical line.

➤ Record the month in which each class member was born. Create a bar graph showing the number of class birthdays in each month. Indicate the number of birthdays on the horizontal line and put the months on the vertical line.

➤ Record the date of the month on which each class member was born. Create a bar graph showing the number of class birthdays on each date. Put the dates on the horizontal line and indicate the number of birthdays on each date on the vertical line.

➤ Record the date of the month on which each class member was born. Create a bar graph showing the number of class birthdays on each date. Indicate the number of birthdays on the horizontal line and put the dates on the vertical line.

PEARSON myreadinglab

MyReadingLab (MRL) www.myreadinglab.com

➤ To practice the ideas and skills introduced in this chapter, go to the "Graphs and Visual Aids" module in the Skills section of MRL. To practice general reading comprehension, use the Levels section.

The Reading *Workshop*

"There is more treasure in books than in all the pirate's loot on Treasure Island."

—WALT DISNEY

It may be difficult to convince a nonreader of this, but once a person is "hooked on books," he or she knows it is a true statement. Reading opens treasure troves of knowledge and entertainment.

Think about it, talk about it, write about it:

Analyze the author's style in a book you are reading for pleasure. How does the author gain, or fail to gain, the reader's interest? If you are reading fiction, think about how the author has set the pace of the plot. In other words, how quickly do major events occur? Does the author drop hints to allow the reader to predict what might happen? Is some information withheld? Does the interest lie primarily in the characters, the plot, or the setting?

If you are reading nonfiction, think about how the author organized the information. Are there logical sections and headings to break up the text and to guide the reader? Have appropriate illustrations and graphics helped to illustrate the information? Has the author provided all the information you want? Too much? Too little?

Your professor may ask you to record your responses to these questions in a Reading Workshop journal.

selection 1 Science

"Like the linkage of the oppositions of continent and ocean in the thermal exchanges of the atmosphere, our linked system of oppositions can generate good harvests and tornadoes, tourist paradises and hurricanes, as well as a global warming and a new Ice Age."
—William I. Thompson

Hurricane specialists can accurately forecast the path of a hurricane with just an 85-mile margin of error when a hurricane is 24 hours away. Forecasting the strength of the storm, however, is more difficult. A Category 5 monster could wallop a community that was expecting a weaker Category 1 tropical storm. Computers cannot accurately show the details of the storm's eye, which changes in shape and intensity as it moves over water and thunderstorms build. The need for accurate forecasting is vital to build the public trust necessary for defensive preparations and forced evacuations.

THINKING BEFORE READING

Preview for content and organizational clues. Activate your schema and anticipate what you will learn.

What type of natural disaster most threatens your area?

What was the name of last year's most destructive hurricane?

How are hurricanes named?

This selection will probably tell me _____.

VOCABULARY PREVIEW

Are you familiar with these words?

tranquil	rotary	precipitation	deceptive	liberated
aloft	barrage	debris	torrential	advent

What does the prefix in *advent* mean?

Why is the pronunciation of *debris* unexpected?

What is the opposite of *torrential*?

Your instructor may choose to give a true-false vocabulary review before or after reading.

THINKING DURING READING

As you read, use the six thinking strategies of a good reader: predict, picture, relate, monitor, correct, and annotate.

PROFILE OF A HURRICANE

Refer to the **Reader's** *Tip* for **Science** on page 60.

Most of us view the weather in the tropics with favor. Places like Hawaii and the islands of the Caribbean are known for their lack of significant day-to-day variations. Warm breezes, steady temperatures, and rains that come as heavy but brief tropical showers are expected. It is ironic that these relatively tranquil regions sometimes produce the most
5   violent storms on Earth.

These intense tropical storms are known in various parts of the world by different names. In the western Pacific, they are called *typhoons,* and in the Indian Ocean, including the Bay of Bengal and Arabian Sea, they are simply called *cyclones.* In the following discussion, these storms will be referred to as hurricanes. The term *hurricane* is derived
10   from Huracan, a Carib god of evil.

Although many tropical disturbances develop each year, only a few reach hurricane status. By international agreement a hurricane has wind speeds of at least 119 kilometers[1] per hour and a rotary circulation. Mature hurricanes average about 600 kilometers across, although they can range in diameter from 100 kilometers up to about 1500 kilometers.
15   From the outer edge of the hurricane to the center, the barometric pressure has sometimes dropped 60 millibars, from 1010 to 950 millibars. The lowest pressures ever recorded in the western hemisphere are associated with these storms.

At the very center of the storm is the eye of the hurricane. This well-known feature is a zone where precipitation ceases and winds subside. The eye offers a brief but deceptive
20   break from the extreme weather in the enormous curving wall clouds that surround it. The air within the eye gradually descends and heats by compression, making it the warmest part of the storm. Although many people believe that the eye is characterized by clear blue skies, this is usually not the case because the subsidence in the eye is seldom strong enough to produce cloudless conditions. Although the sky appears much brighter
25   in this region, scattered clouds at various levels are common.

A hurricane is a heat engine that is fueled by the latent heat liberated when huge quantities of water vapor condense. The amount of energy produced by a typical hurricane in just a single day is truly immense—roughly equivalent to the entire electrical energy production of the United States in a year.

THE 20 DEADLIEST U.S. HURRICANES, 1900–2005

Ranking	Hurricane	Year	Category	Deaths
1.	Texas (Galveston)	1900	4	8000*
2.	Florida (Lake Okeechobee)	1928	4	1836
3.	Katrina	2005	4	1300**
4.	Florida (Keys)/S. Texas	1919	4	600†
5.	New England	1938	3	600
6.	Florida (Keys)	1935	5	408
7. (tie)	Audrey (SW Louisiana/Texas)	1957	4	390
7. (tie)	NE United States	1944	3	390†
9.	Louisiana (Grand Isle)	1909	4	350
10. (tie)	Louisiana (New Orleans)	1915	4	275
10. (tie)	Texas (Galveston)	1915	4	275
12.	Camille (Mississippi/Louisiana)	1969	5	256

*May actually have been as high as 10,000 to 12,000.

**Estimated figure.

†Over 500 of these lost on ships at sea; 600 to 900 estimated deaths.

†Some 344 of these lost on ships at sea.

---

[1] 1 kilometer is equal to approximately 0.62 mile.

30   Hurricanes develop most often in the late summer when ocean waters have reached temperatures of 27°C or higher and are thus able to provide the necessary heat and moisture to the air. This ocean-water temperature requirement is thought to account for the fact that hurricanes do not form over the relatively cool waters of the South Atlantic and the eastern South Pacific.

35   Hurricanes diminish in intensity whenever they (1) move over ocean waters that cannot supply warm, moist tropical air, (2) move onto land, or (3) reach a location where the large-scale flow aloft is unfavorable. In addition, because the land is usually cooler than the ocean, the low-level air is chilled rather than warmed. Moreover, the increased surface roughness over land results in a rapid reduction in surface wind speeds.

STORM SURGE

40   Without question, the most devastating damage in the coastal zone is caused by the storm surge. It not only accounts for a large share of coastal property losses, but it is also responsible for 90 percent of all hurricane-caused deaths. A storm surge is a dome of water 65 to 80 kilometers wide that sweeps across the coast near the point where the eye makes landfall. If all wave activity were smoothed out, the storm surge is the height of the
45   water above normal tide level. In addition, tremendous wave activity is superimposed on the surge. We can easily imagine the damage that this surge of water could inflict on low-lying coastal areas.

WIND DAMAGE

Destruction caused by wind is perhaps the most obvious of the classes of hurricane damage. For some structures, the force of the wind is sufficient to cause total ruin. Mobile
50   homes are particularly vulnerable. In addition, the strong winds can create a dangerous barrage of flying debris.

INLAND FLOODING

The torrential rains that accompany most hurricanes represent a third significant threat—flooding. Whereas the effects of storm surge and strong winds are concentrated in coastal areas, heavy rains may affect places hundreds of kilometers from the coast for sev-
55   eral days after the storm has lost its hurricane-force winds.

DETECTING HURRICANES

The advent of weather satellites has largely solved the problem of detecting tropical storms and has significantly improved monitoring. However, satellites are remote sensors, and it is not unusual for wind-speed estimates to be off by tens of kilometers per hour.

(773 words)

—*The Atmosphere,* 7th Edition,
by Frederick Lutgens and Edward Tarbuck

Note: On September 13, 2008, Hurricane Ike made U.S. landfall at Galveston, Texas, within a few miles of Houston. Ike devastated Galveston Island and Bolivar Peninsula and spread its fury north all the way into Ohio and beyond. Although Ike was a Category 2 storm at landfall, its large size and estimated 15-ft. storm surge accounted for its place as the third costliest tropical cyclone in U.S. and Atlantic basin history, behind Andrew in 1992 and Katrina in 2005. Ike is blamed for 164 deaths in Haiti and the U.S.; as of December 2008, 202 people were still missing.

THINKING AND WRITING AFTER READING

RECALL Self-test your understanding.

Your instructor may choose to give you a true-false comprehension review.

REACT Why are mobile homes particularly vulnerable to hurricane damage?

_____

_____

REFLECT Under what conditions might an area benefit from a hurricane?

_____

_____

_____

THINKING CRITICALLY Considering the factors involved in the development of a hurricane, why are Florida and the east coast so vulnerable to hurricanes? Write your answer on a separate sheet of paper.

THINK AND WRITE Why is accurate forecasting to build the public trust necessary for defensive preparations and forced evacuations? Describe the possible short-term and long-term results of inaccurate forecasting. _____

_____

_____

ANALYTICAL REASONING

Use the table on page 408 to answer the following items with *T* (true) or *F* (false).

_____ 1. Most of the deadliest U.S. hurricanes occurred before 1970.

_____ 2. According to the table, Katrina was the deadliest hurricane of 2005.

_____ 3. More than three times as many people were killed in the Galveston hurricane of 1900 than were estimated to be killed by Katrina.

_____ 4. According to the chart, category 5 hurricanes cause more deaths than category 4 storms.

_____ 5. From the list of the deadliest hurricanes, two have been in the northeastern United States.

Interpret the Quote

Now that you have finished reading the selection, "Profile of a Hurricane," go back to the beginning of the selection and read the opening quote again. What does the quote say about opposites? On a separate sheet of paper, list three situations in which something positive happens as a result of something negative, or something negative happens as a result of something positive.

Name _____

Date _____

COMPREHENSION QUESTIONS

Answer the following with *a, b, c,* or *d,* or fill in the blank. In order to help you analyze your strengths and weaknesses, the question types are indicated.

Main Idea _____ 1. The best statement of the main idea of the selection is:

    a. Calm places can produce intense tropical storms.

    b. Hurricanes cause intense damage and leave many people homeless each year.

    c. A hurricane is an intense tropical storm that develops over warm tropical waters and can cause extreme damage from winds and water on land.

    d. A hurricane is a heat engine that produces electricity.

Detail _____ 2. By international agreement, a hurricane is defined by all of the following *except*

    a. wind speed of 119 kilometers per hour.

    b. rotary circulation.

    c. a drop in barometric pressure.

    d. an eye with a clear blue sky.

Detail _____ 3. The eye of a hurricane

    a. has the most damaging winds.

    b. produces torrential rains.

    c. is the warmest part of the storm.

    d. signals the end of the storm.

Inference _____ 4. According to the passage, hurricanes probably begin developing in late summer because

    a. the season will soon be changing to autumn.

    b. the ocean water temperature is highest.

    c. cool winds from the South Atlantic reach the Caribbean.

    d. typhoons and cyclones occur during the winter.

Detail _____ 5. All of the following will diminish the intensity of a hurricane *except*

    a. cold ocean water.

    b. land.

    c. warm ocean air.

    d. cold land air.

Detail 6. What is the purpose of the table on page 408? _____

_____

_____

Detail _____ 7. The storm surge is characterized by all of the following *except*

    a. it pushes ocean water across coastal property.

    b. it occurs near where the eye of the hurricane hits land.

    c. it always occurs at low tide.

    d. it surges and floods.

Answer the following with *T* (true), *F* (false), or *CT* (can't tell).

Inference   _____ 8. The author implies that typhoons, cyclones, and hurricanes are all about the same.

Detail   _____ 9. High winds from a hurricane usually kill more people than the storm surges.

Detail   _____ 10. The storm surge can be as much as 80 kilometers high.

VOCABULARY

Answer the following with *a*, *b*, *c*, or *d* for the word or phrase that best defines the boldface word as used in the selection. The number in parentheses indicates the line of the passage in which the word appears.

_____ 1. "**tranquil** regions" (4)

   a. warm
   b. calm
   c. breezy
   d. tropical

_____ 2. "**rotary** circulation" (13)

   a. intense
   b. random
   c. rapid
   d. circular

_____ 3. "**precipitation** ceases" (19)

   a. rain
   b. heat
   c. temperature
   d. winds

_____ 4. "**deceptive** break" (19)

   a. fearful
   b. uneventful
   c. turbulent
   d. deceiving

_____ 5. "heat **liberated**" (26)

   a. added
   b. freed
   c. mixed
   d. multiplied

_____ 6. "large-scale flow **aloft**" (37)

   a. below
   b. around
   c. overhead
   d. downhill

_____ 7. "dangerous **barrage**" (51)

   a. circle
   b. wall
   c. blast
   d. barrier

_____ 8. "flying **debris**" (51)

   a. dirt
   b. insects
   c. water
   d. trash

_____ 9. "**torrential** rains" (52)

   a. sudden
   b. frequent
   c. annoying
   d. fierce

_____ 10. "**advent** of weather satellites" (56)

   a. advertisement
   b. appearance
   c. location
   d. idea

Your instructor may choose to give a true-false vocabulary review.

VOCABULARY ENRICHMENT

Context Clues

Select the word from the list that best completes each sentence.

tranquil	rotary	precipitation	deceptive	liberated
aloft	barrage	debris	torrential	advent

1. After the storm, the shore was littered with _____.

2. When the summer tourists come to Maine, the small coastal towns are no longer _____.

3. _____ women do not mind speaking out on issues, even when their opinions are unpopular.

4. Five days of _____ rain created flooding in the fields and threatened the livestock.

5. The forecast for the evening is for _____ in the form of snow or sleet.

6. With the _____ of more accurate hurricane forecasting, people are hoping for fewer evacuations.

7. The pickpocket had a _____ way of smiling and asking unsuspecting tourists for directions.

8. The scientists sent a weather balloon _____ to record data for the experiment.

9. The speaker was hit by a _____ of questions about where evacuees would be housed.

10. The _____ fan above the bed moves the air enough to keep the room cool on moderate spring nights.

ASSESS YOUR LEARNING

Review confusing questions, seek clarification, and make notes in your text to help you remember new information and vocabulary.

"Almost all the ideas we have about being a man or being a woman are so burdened with pain, anxiety, fear and self-doubt. For many of us, the confusion around this question is excruciating."

—Andrew Cohen

The ever changing issues of gender, and their accompanying status concerns, affect social institutions by solving some problems and usually creating others. For example, in the 1960s women were underrepresented in the colleges. Advocates for women voiced concerns. In 2005 approximately 213,000 more women than men graduated with bachelor's degrees from colleges in the United States. In 2011 the estimated graduation numbers will further widen to 273,000 more women than men. Are these numbers a victory for advocacy, or do they define another problem? In another social institution, marriage, the ages are shifting upward. In 1960 the median age for a first marriage was 20 for women and 22 for men. In 2005 the median age was 25 for women and 27 for men. How does this significant shift in age affect the institution, the status of the members, and the culture?

THINKING BEFORE READING

Preview for content and organizational clues. Activate your schema and anticipate what you will learn.

How do parents encourage different behaviors for sons and daughters?

How do teachers treat females and males differently?

What jobs tend to be typically male or typically female?

I think this selection will say that _____.

VOCABULARY PREVIEW

Are you familiar with these words?

humdrum	conventional	stereotypes	bias	banning
spectators	subtle	competence	pout	rural

Do you live in a *rural* area?

Is there a political *bias* in elections?

Does it take *competence* to fly an airplane?

Your instructor may choose to give a true-false vocabulary review before or after reading.

THINKING DURING READING

As you read, use the six thinking strategies of a good reader: predict, picture, relate, monitor, correct, and annotate.

Reader's *Tip* Reading and Studying Sociology

- Think broadly about society and social organizations. Search for the historical reasons for human behavior and organizational structures. Make cause-and-effect connections among history, culture, and social organizations.
- Compare and contrast customs and social behaviors across cultures.
- Remain open-minded and be tolerant of cultural differences. Avoid biased value judgments.
- Think objectively and scientifically to evaluate the problems of society.

GENDER AND SOCIAL INSTITUTIONS

At countless bridal showers, women celebrate a friend's upcoming marriage by showering her with useful gifts. But the scene is very different at bachelor parties, where men give their friend one last fling before he must settle down to the humdrum routines of married life. We find the same pattern among singles: Contrast the positive image of a
5 carefree bachelor with the negative one of the lonely spinster.

On the face of it, it seems that marriage is a *solution* for women and a *problem* for men. But is this really the case? Research indicates that in general, marriage is good for people, not only raising levels of personal happiness but improving health and boosting income, too. But researcher Jessie Bernard points out that the benefits of traditional mar-
10 riage are greater for men than for women. Bernard claims that there is no better prescription for a man's long life, good health, and overall happiness than having a wife devoted to caring for him and keeping an orderly home. That is why divorced men are less happy than divorced women and are more eager to remarry.

But for many women, Bernard continues, marriage reduces happiness and increases
15 the risk of depression or other personality disorders. Why? Bernard explains that the problem is not marriage in general but the fact that conventional marriage places men in charge and saddles women with most of the housework.

In the past, marriages based on conventional ideas about gender were more common than they are today. So why have women always seemed so eager to marry?
20 Bernard explains that at a time when women were all but shut out of the labor force, "landing a man" was the only way a woman could gain economic security.

Today, however, women with more economic opportunity also have more choices about marriage. This is one reason that more couples are sharing responsibilities more equally. As Bernard sees it, breaking away from conventional ideas about gender is mak-
25 ing both women and men happier and healthier.

GENDER AND EDUCATION

By the time they begin school, children have learned a great deal about gender from books. Children's books used to be full of gender stereotypes, showing girls and women mostly in the home while boys and men did almost everything else outside the home. Newer children's books present the two sexes in a more balanced way, although some
30 antifemale bias remains.

And what of school itself? Today's primary and secondary schools do a pretty good job of providing equal education to both boys and girls. In addition, 57 percent of all college students are now women, and some professional schools (such as law) now graduate

as many women as men. Even so, gender stereotyping still steers women toward college
35 majors in English, dance, drama, or sociology while pushing men toward physics, economics, biology, mathematics, and computer science.

Gender is at work on the playing fields as much as in the classroom. In the past,
extracurricular athletics was a male world in which females were expected to watch
instead of play. In 1972, Congress passed Title IX, the Educational Amendment to the
40 Civil Rights Act, banning sex discrimination in any educational program receiving federal
funding. In recent years, colleges and universities have also tried to provide an equal
number of sports to both women and men. Even so, men benefit from higher-paid
coaches and enjoy larger crowds of spectators. In short, despite the federal policy outlaw-
ing gender bias, in few athletic programs is gender equality a reality.

GENDER AND THE MASS MEDIA

45 With some 250 million television sets in the United States and people watching an average of four-and-one-half hours of TV each day (U.S. Bureau of the Census, 2006), who
can doubt the importance of the mass media in shaping how we think and act? What
messages about gender do we find on TV?

When television became popular in the 1950s, almost all the starring roles belonged
50 to men. Only in recent decades have television shows featured women as central characters. But we still find fewer women than men cast as talented athletes, successful executives, brilliant detectives, and skilled surgeons. More often than not, women have
supporting roles as wives, assistants, and secretaries. Music videos also come in for criticism: Performing groups are mostly all men, and when women do appear on stage, they
55 are there for little more than their sex appeal. And today's song lyrics reinforce men's
power over women.

What about advertising? In the early years of television, advertisers targeted women
during the day because so many women were at-home wives (the fact that most of
the commercials advertised laundry and household products is the reason daytime TV
60 dramas are still called "soap operas"). On television and in newspaper and magazine advertising, most ads continue to use male models to pitch products such as automobiles, banking services, travel, and alcoholic beverages to men and female models to sell products
such as clothing, cosmetics, cleaning products, and food to women. Ads have always been
more likely to show men in offices or in rugged outdoor scenes and women in the home.
65 Gender biases in advertising can be subtle. Research shows that ads almost always
present men as taller than women, and women (but never men) often lie on sofas and
beds or sit on the floor like children.

In addition, men's facial expressions suggest competence and authority, whereas
women laugh, pout, or strike childlike poses. Finally, the men featured in advertising
70 focus on the products they are promoting; women, as often as not, pay attention to men.

GENDER AND THE MILITARY

Women have been part of the military since the Revolutionary War. During World War II,
when the government officially opened the military to both sexes, women made up just
2 percent of the armed forces. By the Gulf War in 1991, that share rose to almost 7 percent, and 5 of the 148 soldiers killed were women. Women have been 15 percent of the
75 U.S. military fighting in Iraq, and 62 women are included among the 3,000 fatalities (as
of January 6, 2007).

Today, almost all military assignments are open to women. But there is still resistance
to expanding the role of women in the military. The traditional explanation for limiting
women's opportunities is the claim that women are not as strong as men, although this
80 argument makes much less sense in a high-technology military that depends less and less
on muscle power. The real reason people oppose women in the military has to do with
gender itself. Many people have difficulty with the idea of women—whom our culture
defines as nurturers—being put in a position to kill and be killed.

Women and Men in the U.S. Labor Force

Over the last fifty years, the share of men in the labor force has gone down (with men retiring earlier and living longer), while the share of women working for income has gone up rapidly.

Source: U.S. Department of Labor (2006).

GENDER AND WORK

85 Many people still think of different kinds of jobs as either "men's work" or "women's work." A century ago in the United States, in fact, most people did not think women should work at all, at least not for pay. Back then, as the saying used to be, "a woman's place is in the home," and in 1900, just one woman in five worked for income. By 2005, as the graph above shows, this share jumped to three in five (59 percent), even as the share of adult men in the labor force declined. About three-fourths of women in today's 90 labor force work full time (U.S. Department of Labor, 2006).

What accounts for this dramatic rise in the share of working women? Many factors are involved. At the beginning of the twentieth century, a majority of the U.S. population lived in rural areas largely without electric power, where women typically spent long hours cooking, doing housework, and raising large families. Today's typical home has a 95 host of appliances, including washers, vacuums, and microwaves, that have dramatically reduced the time needed for housework.

In addition, today's average woman has just two children, half the number that was typical a century ago. Having young children does not prevent most women from working: Fifty-nine percent of married women with children under age six work, as do 76 percent of married 100 women with children six to seventeen years old. From another angle, more than half of today's married couples have both partners working for income (U.S. Census Bureau, 2005).

Even though more women now work for pay, the range of jobs open to them is still limited, and our society still labels most jobs as either feminine or masculine. Work that our society has defined as "masculine" involves physical danger (such as firefighting and 105 police work), strength and endurance (construction work and truck driving), and leadership roles (clergy, judges, and business executives). Work defined as "feminine" includes support positions (secretarial work or medical assisting) or occupations requiring nurturing skills (child care and teaching young children).

Gender discrimination was outlawed by the federal Equal Pay Act of 1963 and Title 110 VII of the Civil Rights Act of 1964. This means that employers cannot discriminate between men and women in hiring or pay. But gender inequality is deeply rooted in U.S. society; officials investigate thousands of discrimination complaints every year, and few doubt that the real number of cases of discrimination is far higher.

(1525 words)

—*Social Problems*, Third Edition, by John J. Macionis

THINKING AND WRITING AFTER READING

RECALL Self-test your understanding.

Your instructor may choose to give you a true-false comprehension review.

REACT The author is harsh in criticizing gender stereotyping. How have you been persuaded to think about a "masculine job" or a "feminine job"? Did any of the stereotyping stick?_____

_____

REFLECT Why do economic opportunities drive something as basic as the relationship between a husband and wife?_____

_____

THINKING CRITICALLY In recent years, young brides have been going to Las Vegas or Miami for exciting bachelorette parties with their close girlfriends. How does this mark a change in culture? What does it imply about a breaking away of conventional ideas? Why do you think this change is occurring? _____

_____

THINK AND WRITE Statistically the people who live in the greatest poverty in the United States are single mothers with children. What can be done to empower them? How did they get into their impoverished situation? Are they victims of gender discrimination? How can such situations be prevented? How can they gain financial independence? _____

_____

Interpret the Quote

Now that you have finished reading the selection, "Gender and Social Institutions," go back to the beginning of the selection and read the opening quote again. Do you agree that how we think of ourselves in terms of our gender is "burdened with pain, anxiety, fear, and self-doubt"? On a separate sheet of paper, write a paragraph on what you think it means to be a man or woman.

Name _____

Date _____

selection 2

COMPREHENSION QUESTIONS

Answer the following with *a*, *b*, *c*, or *d*, or fill in the blank. In order to help you analyze your strengths and weaknesses, the question types are indicated.

Main Idea _____ 1. The best statement of the main idea of the selection is:

a. Current research indicates that women have nearly achieved social equality with males.
b. Bias against women continues to be promoted by societal institutions.
c. The majority of Americans believe that women and men deserve equal pay.
d. Mothers and fathers in the United States remain unbiased in their parenting duties.

Inference _____ 2. The author's primary objection to bachelor parties in comparison with bridal showers is that

a. women give gifts to the couple to be used in the marriage.
b. women are eager to solve problems through marriage.
c. men "celebrate" a loss rather than a positive gain.
d. men raise their levels of personal happiness through marriage.

Inference _____ 3. The author would consider a conventional idea about marriage to be all of the following *except*

a. women doing the laundry.
b. men washing the dishes.
c. women cooking breakfast.
d. men working to provide income.

Detail _____ 4. Despite the passage of Title IX in 1972, the author feels that colleges still discriminate against women by

a. giving women little chance to play.
b. banning sex discrimination in any educational program receiving federal funding.
c. the number of spectators who show up to watch the games.
d. paying coaches for male sports more than coaches for female sports.

Detail _____ 5. Daytime television dramas are called "soap operas" because

a. they appeal to at-home wives.
b. the content is soapy with gossip and sex.
c. women were targeted during the day.
d. most began by advertising cleaning products.

Inference _____ 6. The author suggests that women still face limited opportunities in the military primarily because of

a. the physical demands of military assignments.
b. the high technology now used by the military.
c. the public perception of the role of women.
d. the inability of women to perform many military maneuvers.

Inference _____ 7. The reader can conclude that sociologists consider all of the following social institutions *except*

    a. the family.
    b. the schools.
    c. recreation.
    d. work.

Answer the following with *T* (true) or *F* (false).

Detail _____ 8. According to the passage, 80 percent of women with children under the age of six work outside the home.

Inference _____ 9. The author suggests that economic opportunity for women is the primary and underlying reason for the weakening of conventional ideas about gender and marriage.

Inference _____10. The author implies that a help wanted advertisement cannot legally specify the desire for a male or female applicant.

Answer the following with *T* (true) or *F* (false), referring to the graph on page 417.

_____ 1. In 1955 the percentage of men in the labor force was more than twice the percentage of women.

_____ 2. In this graph, if you were 16 years old in 2000 and without a job, you were considered a nonworker.

_____ 3. From 1950 to 2005, the increase in the number of women in the workforce was more than twice as much as the decline in the number of men working.

_____ 4. From 1950 to 1965, the decrease in men working was 5 percentage points.

_____ 5. For every year indicated on the graph, women showed an increase in their percentage of the workforce.

VOCABULARY

Answer the following with *a*, *b*, *c*, or *d* for the word or phrase that best defines the boldface word used in the selection. The number in parentheses indicates the line of the passage in which the word appears.

_____ 1. "**humdrum** routines" (3)

    a. inspiring
    b. dull
    c. connected
    d. wonderful

_____ 3. "gender **stereotypes**" (27)

    a. typical representations
    b. caricatures
    c. editorial cartoons
    d. tendencies

_____ 2. "**conventional** ideas" (18)

    a. novel
    b. institutional
    c. strange
    d. traditional

_____ 4. "antifemale **bias**" (30)

    a. basis
    b. prejudice
    c. inference
    d. happenings

2 selection

_____ 5. "**banning** sex discrimination"
(40)
   a. highlighting
   b. prohibiting
   c. exposing
   d. hiding

_____ 6. "crowds of **spectators**" (43)
   a. players
   b. owners
   c. scouts
   d. onlookers

_____ 7. "can be **subtle**" (65)
   a. easy to identify
   b. costly
   c. obvious
   d. hard to understand

_____ 8. "suggest **competence**"
(68)
   a. completeness
   b. ownership
   c. skill
   d. total helplessness

_____ 9. "women laugh, **pout**" (69)
   a. talk
   b. tease
   c. smile
   d. show displeasure

_____ 10. "**rural** areas" (93)
   a. foreign
   b. elegant
   c. city
   d. country

Your instructor may choose to give a true-false vocabulary review.

VOCABULARY ENRICHMENT

Context Clues

Select the word from the list that best completes each sentence.

humdrum	conventional	stereotypes	bias	banning
spectators	subtle	competence	pout	rural

1. People in _____ India value sons because they can work in the fields.

2. Does a cultural _____ exist regarding women in combat?

3. Advertisers often place males in roles that suggest _____ and authority.

4. It could be said that people following the same routines day after day may be leading a _____ sort of existence.

5. _____ career choices for women were once largely limited to professions such as teaching and nursing.

6. The superior positioning of male actors and models in advertisements may be a more _____ example of gender bias.

7. _____ reinforce the myths that all women are good cooks and love housework.

8. Although laws have been passed _____ sex discrimination in the workplace, women continue to be underrepresented in boardrooms across America.

9. In many cases, the number of _____ at men's college sports events greatly exceeds those in attendance at women's games.

10. Television is full of examples of females who _____ to get what they want instead of simply stating their wishes.

Thesaurus

Use a thesaurus, either a computer or a book version, to find three alternative words or phrases for each of the following. Answers may vary according to the thesaurus used.

11. primary _____

12. devoted _____

13. restrict _____

14. nurturing _____

15. dramatic _____

ASSESS YOUR LEARNING

Review confusing questions. Seek clarification and make notes in your text to help you remember new information and vocabulary. Use visuals such as symbols, diagrams, and pictures to reinforce your learning.

selection 3   Business

"Shoot for the moon. Even if you miss, you'll land among the stars."

—Brian Littrell

What makes workers tick? Surprisingly, money is not the only motivator. Different workers are motivated by different factors. Motivation to work hard can be inspired by the recognition that comes with a simple thank you, an award, or a public acknowledgment for a job well done. For employees who enjoy learning and find repetition dull, new projects and new challenges stimulate enthusiasm for work. Self-starting employees thrive in a flexible environment; they do not like to be micromanaged. To become a successful manager, the trick is to find the appropriate motivator for each employee.

THINKING BEFORE READING

Preview for content and organizational clues. Activate your schema and anticipate what you will learn.

Why are you motivated to make good grades in college?

If you were a millionaire, would you get a college degree?

This selection will probably tell me _____.

VOCABULARY PREVIEW

Are you familiar with these words?

stifled	inspire	proponent	premise	pinnacle
crux	deemphasis	hygienic	grievances	verbalizing

How do the prefixes *pre* and *pro* differ?

Are people who get to the *pinnacle* usually inspired?

What committees in your college are set up to hear student *grievances*?

Your instructor may give a true-false vocabulary review before or after reading.

THINKING DURING READING

As you read, use the six thinking strategies of a good reader: predict, picture, relate, monitor, correct, and annotate.

MOTIVATING YOURSELF

Refer to the **Reader's** *Tip* for **Business** on page 262.

"It is asking too much to suggest that people motivate themselves in the work environment. Motivation should come from the supervisor, special rewards, or the job itself."

    Many people would disagree with the preceding quotation. They would claim that self-motivation is an absolute necessity in many work environments. They would also

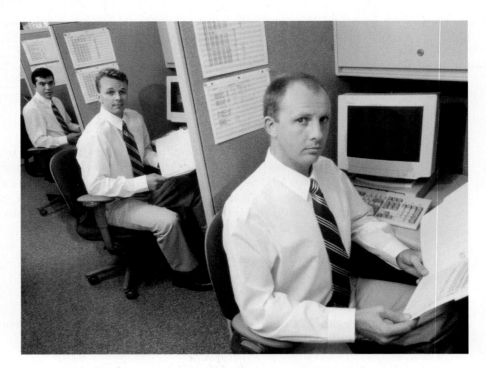

5 claim that the more you can learn about motivation, the more you understand yourself and, as a result, the more you will be in a position to inspire your own efforts.

Let's assume that you find yourself in a job where things are not going well. You feel stifled and "boxed in." You may, for example, be much more capable than the job demands. Perhaps too, the pay and benefits are only average, your immediate supervisor
10 is difficult to deal with, and some other factors are not ideal. Even so, you consider the organization a good one and you recognize that by earning promotions your long-term future can be excellent.

How can you inspire yourself to do a better-than-average job despite the temporary handicaps? How can you motivate yourself to live close to your potential despite a nega-
15 tive environment? How can you keep your attitude from showing? How can you keep from injuring important human relationships?

There are many theories or schools of thought on why people are motivated to achieve high productivity on the job. Most of these are studied by managers so that they will be in a better position to motivate the employees who work for them. In this chapter
20 we are going to reverse the procedure. We are going to show you how to motivate yourself. *If your supervisor can be trained to motivate you, why can't you learn to motivate yourself?*

THEORY 1: SELF-IMAGE PSYCHOLOGY

This is frequently called the PsychoCybernetics School. The proponent of this theory is Dr. Maxwell Maltz, a plastic surgeon. The basic idea is that, in order to be properly motivated
25 to achieve certain goals, an individual must recognize the *need* for a good self-image. Dr. Maltz discovered in his work as a plastic surgeon that some patients became much more self-confident and far more motivated after having their faces greatly improved. Why? Maltz came to the conclusion that the image the individual had of himself (or herself) *inside* was more motivating than the changes he had made *outside.* In short, the way an
30 individual *thinks* he or she looks can be more important than the way he or she actually looks to others.

How Can You Use This Theory to Motivate Yourself? Learn to picture yourself in a more complimentary way. First, research has shown that most people who have poor self-images actually *do* look better to others than they do to themselves. If this is true of

35 you, you might try concentrating on your strong features instead of the weak ones, thus developing a more positive outlook and a better self-image.

Second, you might consider improving yourself on the outside as well as on the inside. You may not want to go as far as plastic surgery, but you could change your hair-style, dress differently, lose or gain weight, exercise, and many other things. According to
40 the theory, however, unless you recognize and accept the improvement, nothing may happen. PsychoCybernetics is, of course, a do-it-yourself project. You do all the work—and you get all the credit, too!

THEORY 2: MASLOW'S HIERARCHY OF NEEDS

This is a very old theory developed by Abraham Maslow in his book *Motivation and Personality*. The premise here is that you have certain needs that must be fulfilled if you are
45 to be properly motivated. These needs are built one on top of the other as in a pyramid.

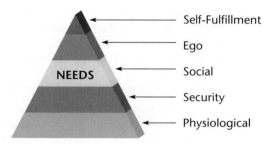

The bottom need is physiological—food, good health. The next is safety and security. The third from the bottom is social needs: one needs to be accepted and enjoy the company of others. Next are ego needs—recognition from others. Finally, at the pinnacle, is one's need for self-fulfillment or self-realization.
50 The crux of this theory is that the bottom needs must be fulfilled before the others come into play. In other words, you must satisfy your need for food and security *before* social needs become motivating. You must satisfy social and ego needs before self-fulfillment is possible.

How Can You Use This Idea to Motivate Yourself to Reach Goals? If you believe
55 Maslow is right, it would be self-defeating to reverse the pyramid or "skip over" unsatisfied needs to reach others. Chances are good, however, that your first two needs are being adequately satisfied so you could make a greater effort to meet new people and make new friends. This could, in turn, help to satisfy your ego needs. With both your social and ego needs better satisfied you might be inspired to attempt greater creative
60 efforts which could eventually lead you to greater self-realization.

THEORY 3: PSYCHOLOGICAL ADVANTAGE

This school was founded by Saul W. Gellerman. It contends that people constantly seek to serve their own self-interests, which change as they grow older. People can make their jobs work for them to give them a psychological advantage over other people at the same level. The way to create a psychological advantage in a starting job that is beneath
65 your capacity is to learn all there is about that job. That way, you can use the job as a springboard to something better, a position that will give you more freedom and responsibility.

How Could You Use This to Inspire Yourself? The best way, perhaps, is to be a little selfish about your job. Work for the organization and yourself at the same time. Instead of
70 letting your job control you, perhaps pulling you and your attitude down, use it as a

launching pad. Use it to build human relations that will be important later on. Study the structure of your organization so you will understand the lines of progression better than the other employees. Study the leadership style of your supervisor and others so that you will have a better one when your turn comes.

THEORY 4: MOTIVATION-HYGIENIC SCHOOL

75 This theory was developed by Professor Frederick Herzberg. Basically it claims that undesirable environmental factors (physical working conditions) can be dissatisfiers. Factors of achievement, recognition, and freedom, on the other hand, are satisfiers. All working environments have both negative and positive factors.

How Can You Take Advantage of This Theory? People who maintain positive atti-
80 tudes under difficult circumstances do so through attitude control. They concentrate *only* on the positive factors in their environment. You can, for instance, refuse to recognize the demotivating factors in your job and concentrate only on those things that will satisfy your needs better.

This could mean a deemphasis on physical factors and more emphasis on psycholog-
85 ical factors such as social, ego, and self-fulfillment needs. One individual puts it this way: "I work in a very old building with poor facilities. Even so I have learned that I can be happy there because of the work I do and the great people I work with. One quickly gets used to fancy buildings and facilities and begins to take them for granted anyway."

THEORY 5: THE MAINTENANCE-MOTIVATION THEORY

This school is much like Herzberg's hygienic approach and was developed by M. Scott
90 Myers of Texas Instruments, Inc. His research found that employees usually fall into one of two groups: motivation-seekers and maintenance-seekers. In short, some people look for those factors that are motivating to them and are constantly pushing themselves toward fulfillment. Others are concerned with just staying where they are. Maintenance-seekers spend much time talking about working conditions, wages, recreational programs,
95 grievances, and similar matters and do little or nothing to motivate themselves. Motivation-seekers, on the other hand, look beyond such matters.

How Might You Use This to Improve Your Own Motivation? The obvious answer is, of course, to keep yourself out of the maintenance-seeker classification. To do this you should try not to overassociate with those in the maintenance classification. Without your
100 knowing it, they could pull you into their camp. Try also to talk about positive things instead of being a complainer. Verbalizing negative factors often intensifies the dissatisfaction one feels. Turn your attention to things you can achieve on the job—not to the negative factors.

(1,338 words)

—Your Attitude Is Showing, Ninth Edition,
by Elwood N. Chapman and Sharon Lund O'Neil

THINKING AND WRITING AFTER READING

RECALL Self-test your understanding.

Your instructor may choose to give you a true-false comprehension review.

REACT If you could have plastic surgery, what would you have done and what do you think it would do for you? _____

_____

REFLECT   For each of Maslow's five levels of needs, name and describe a person that you know who fits the level. _____

_____

THINKING CRITICALLY   Why would a plastic surgeon be the author of a book on self-image and motivation? Write your answer on a separate sheet of paper.

THINK AND WRITE   Assuming that your salary is appealing and that you are willing to work, describe what you would consider the perfect work environment for you. What factors would be strong motivators, and what factors would be disincentives? _____

_____

ANALYTICAL REASONING

Use your analytical reasoning skills on the following business problem.

After having worked for the same corporation for over three years, Norman decided that he had made a major mistake. He had been accepted into a formal management training program directly out of college. He had received his first supervisory role before his first year was up, but after that nothing else happened. He had been on a plateau for over two years. In recent months he had been feeling extremely frustrated, stifled, and somewhat hostile. He admitted that his attitude was showing. He admitted that his personal productivity had stagnated.

Norman knew the primary reason for his lack of upward progress. His company had been going through a consolidation process and had put a freeze on hiring new employees. Very few middle- and upper-management positions were opening. Nevertheless, Norman finally came to the uncomfortable conclusion that he had to do something about his situation. He had to force some kind of action, even if it was difficult.

He then sat down and listed the advantages and disadvantages of his role with the company:

Advantages	Disadvantages
Good geographical location	Corporation not expanding
Good benefits	Salary only fair
Job security	Limited learning opportunities
Good personnel policies	Overconservative management
Good physical working conditions	Poor supervisor
Little commuting time	Already made some human relations mistakes
Good home neighborhood	Limited opportunities for upward communication with management
Enjoyable type of work	Boring fellow supervisors

After carefully going over the pros and cons of his job—and considering his three-year investment—Norman decided he had the following options:

1. Go to the personnel department and discuss his frustration about being on a plateau.
2. Submit a written request for a transfer involving a promotion.

3. Start a serious search for a new job in a new company.
4. Resign with two weeks' notice and start looking for a new job.
5. Talk to his supervisor and ask for more responsibility.
6. Motivate himself so that management will recognize a change in attitude and consider him for the next promotion.
7. Relax, continue present efforts, and wait it out.
8. Motivate himself for three months. Then if nothing happens, resign.
9. After telling his boss his intentions, go to the president of the company with the problem.
10. Go to the president of the company to discuss his personal progress.

Assume you are Norman. First, on a separate sheet of paper, list which of the listed options you would consider. Second, put them in the order in which you would undertake them. Third, add any steps you would take that are not on the list. Fourth, justify your decisions.

Interpret the Quote

Now that you have finished reading the selection, "Motivating Yourself," go back to the beginning of the selection and read the opening quote again. How does the quote relate to motivation? On a separate sheet of paper, list three situations in your life when motivation helped you achieve a goal. Also, list three situations in which you could use motivation to reach a goal.

Name _____

Date _____

COMPREHENSION QUESTIONS

Answer the following with *a, b, c,* or *d* or fill in the blank. In order to help you analyze your strengths and weaknesses, the question types are indicated.

Main Idea _____ 1. The best statement of the main idea is:

    a. Motivation comes from within and cannot be taught.
    b. People can use different theories of motivation to motivate themselves.
    c. People who are not motivated lose their jobs.
    d. Motivation in an organization is the responsibility of management.

Inference _____ 2. The purpose of this selection is to

    a. improve management.
    b. criticize supervisors.
    c. encourage self-motivation.
    d. analyze mistakes.

Detail _____ 3. According to Maltz's theory, many people make mistakes by

    a. thinking they look worse than others think they do.
    b. trying to look as good as others.
    c. thinking they look better than they do.
    d. trying to hide their weaknesses from others.

Inference _____ 4. In Maslow's hierarchy of needs, winning sales trophies satisfies the

    a. security need.
    b. social need.
    c. ego need.
    d. self-fulfillment need.

Inference _____ 5. Gellerman's theory of psychological advantage is based primarily on

    a. competition.
    b. self-interest.
    c. group cooperation.
    d. the needs of management.

Inference _____ 6. According to the motivation-hygienic theory, a person should

    a. work only in a positive environment.
    b. motivate supervisors to clean up the environment.
    c. ignore the negative factors in the environment and focus on the positive factors.
    d. seek a job with only positive factors.

Inference _____ 7. According to the maintenance-motivation theory, someone who wants to stay in a position for a few more years until retirement is a

_____

Answer the following with *T* (true) or *F* (false).

Inference   _____ 8. The author seems to agree with the quotation on lines 1 and 2 at the beginning of the selection.

Inference   _____ 9. In Maslow's hierarchy, the need to feel that you are using all of your talents to the best of your ability is the self-fulfillment need.

Inference   _____ 10. Maltz's theory is exactly the opposite of Herzberg's theory.

VOCABULARY

Answer the following with *a*, *b*, *c*, or *d* for the word or phrase that best defines the boldface word used in the selection. The number in parentheses indicates the line of the passage in which the word appears.

_____ 1. "feel **stifled**" (8)

    a. useless
    b. smothered
    c. angry
    d. sick

_____ 6. "The **crux** of this theory" (50)

    a. crucial point
    b. beginning
    c. solution
    d. reward

_____ 2. "**inspire** yourself" (13)

    a. motivate
    b. force
    c. command
    d. instruct

_____ 7. "**deemphasis** on physical factors" (84)

    a. renewed response
    b. less stress
    c. complete drop
    d. minor stress

_____ 3. "**proponent** of this theory" (23)

    a. scholar
    b. attacker
    c. advocate
    d. manager

_____ 8. "**hygienic** approach" (89)

    a. scientific
    b. analytical
    c. healthful
    d. resourceful

_____ 4. "The **premise** here" (44)

    a. signal
    b. mistake
    c. meaning
    d. supposition

_____ 9. "**grievances**, and similar matters" (95)

    a. successes
    b. contests
    c. enrichments
    d. complaints

_____ 5. "at the **pinnacle**" (48–49)

    a. bottom
    b. crucial time
    c. peak
    d. most noticeable point

_____ 10. "**Verbalizing** negative factors" (101)

    a. hiding
    b. talking about
    c. overlooking
    d. remembering

Your instructor may choose to give a true-false vocabulary review.

VOCABULARY ENRICHMENT

A. Study these easily confused words and circle the correct one for each sentence.

wares: goods sold	**decent:** morally good	**allusion:** reference in
wears: puts on clothes	**descent:** move downward	literature
where: a place	**dissent:** disagreement	**illusion:** false idea

1. The (**wares, wears**) of the company were posted on the Web site before customers received catalogs.

2. The (**decent, descent, dissent**) between the two employees grew into a major confrontation that hurt company morale.

3. He is operating under the (**allusion, illusion**) that I am going to write the corporate report and then let him take credit for it.

B. Refer to Appendix 2 and use the doubling rule to form the following words.

4. regret + ing = _____

5. swim + ing = _____

6. excel + ent = _____

7. ship + ed = _____

C. Suffixes: Use the boldface suffix to supply an appropriate word for each group of sentences.

ment: act of, state of, result of action

8. Like another _____ to the constitution, theories of motivating can change as researchers document new results with innovative techniques.

9. Just as the mind needs stimulation, an energetic worker needs to eat the right foods so the body gets the proper _____.

10. My _____ with the manager was postponed until tomorrow at two o'clock.

ence: action, state, quality

11. The therapist showed great _____ in working with the man for hours to achieve a tiny degree of success.

12. While previous authoritarian managers may have valued _____ in following orders, now managers want workers who can problem-solve and share in decision making.

13. A capable and nurturing manager can have a great _____ on your success in a company.

able, ible: can do

14. Highly motivated employees seek extra responsibility and make themselves highly _____ to corporate decision makers.

15. Being a _____ employee means meeting deadlines and getting to meetings on time with the necessary information.

ASSESS YOUR LEARNING

Review confusing questions, seek clarification, and make notes in your text to help you remember new information and vocabulary.

Vocabulary *Lesson*

Turn and Throw

Study the roots, words, and sentences.

| **Roots** | *vers, vert:* turn | *jac, jec, ject:* throw, lie |

Words with *vers* or *vert* = *turn*

Is sex in advertisements controversial? Is the coat reversible?

- Convert: win over; persuade

  With mind-controlling strategies, the student was *converted* to a cult.

- Revert: turn back to

  Reformed smokers are frequently tempted to *revert* to old habits.

- Divert: turn away from

  The driver's attention was *diverted* by the accident on the roadside.

- Invert: turn upside down

  If you want to divide a fraction, you need to *invert* and multiply.

- Averse: turned against

  They were divorced, but she was not *averse* to seeing him at parties.

- Introvert: shy and quiet; introspective

  Being an *introvert*, the writer rejected offers to read his poems in public.

- Extrovert: outgoing; gregarious

  An *extrovert* like Oprah Winfrey enjoys the energy of a large studio audience.

- Ambivert: having both introverted and extroverted tendencies

  Most *ambiverts* enjoy both being with people and having some quiet time.

- Pervert: turned to an improper use

  Because of a shoe fetish, the thief was regarded as *perverted*.

- Obverse: facing the opponent; front surface

  The head of the president was depicted on the *obverse* side of the coin.

- Conversant: knowledgeable about a subject

  After another semester of economics, I hope to be more *conversant* on the euro.

- Versatile: having many skills; can turn from one thing to another

  A *versatile* jacket can be worn with several different pants and shirts.

- Subversive: undermining

  The terrorists were engaged in *subversive* activities.

- Vertigo: a dizzy spell when things seem to be turning

  Avoid roller-coasters if you have a tendency toward *vertigo*.

- Version: an adaptation or translation of the original form

  The children's *version* of the Bible had pictures and large print.

- Versus: against

  The next trial was *State of Texas versus John Doe*.

- Vortex: both a whirling and a suction motion, as in a whirlpool

  Watching the whirling water from the cliff, he threw a log into the *vortex*.

Words with *jac, jec, ject = throw* or *lie*

Do you have an objection to leaving early? Does rejection hurt?

- Inject: insert

  Students appreciate professors who *inject* humor into lectures.

- Eject: to throw out

  If the plane is on fire, the fighter pilot can push the *eject* button.

- Dejected: low in spirits

  After failing two tests, the *dejected* student finally sought help in the lab.

- Adjacent: next to

  Consumers save time when a dry cleaner is *adjacent* to a grocery store.

- Conjecture: to form an opinion; guess

  The statement that the new president will step down is merely *conjecture*.

- Interject: throw a word in between others

  Because renters were talking, I could not *interject* a word about a deposit.

- Projection: thrown forward

  At the year's end, the company had not met its profit *projections*.

- Abject: degraded

  In the Rio Barrio the children live in *abject* poverty.

Review

Part I

Answer the following with (*T*) true or (*F*) false.

_____ 1. A conjecture is a fact rather than an opinion.

_____ 2. If a proposal is rejected, it is no longer under consideration.

_____ 3. Subversive activity is clearly evident.

_____ 4. Water in the vortex sprays up like a fountain.

_____ 5. If it is stated as *Wiley versus Rogers*, the two sides are in opposition.

_____ 6. If you are conversant in Spanish history, you know the subject well.

_____ 7. A versatile athlete can play several sports well.

_____ 8. If you invert a cup of coffee, the liquid is likely to spill.

_____ 9. A dejected worker is not a happy employee.

_____10. A controversial topic draws little disagreement.

Part II

Select the word from the list that best completes each sentence.

diverted	averse	projections	pervert	extroverted
converted	vertigo	version	adjacent	introverted

1. Inner ear problems can cause loss of balance and _____.

2. The _____ sculptor enjoyed his meditative time alone outdoors.

3. The developer _____ the stream to build on the property.

4. The _____ professor gave lively lectures and enjoyed students.

5. The sex offender's unacceptable behavior labeled him as a _____.

6. By remodeling with glass windows, the porch was _____ to a usable room.

7. Unfortunately I can hear the TV in the room _____ to mine.

8. The population _____ for 2025 will influence mass-transit decisions.

9. The sign indicates the home owners are _____ to smoking on the premises.

10. Did you hear the rock singer or the movie star _____ of the story?

Reading Direct Mail Advertisements

How much "junk" mail do you receive each week? If you have no interest in a piece of advertising, put it in a recycle bin or throw it away. If you are interested, always remember the old saying, "If it sounds too good to be true, it probably is."

Do not succumb to the glitz. Recognize that if you do not really need the product or service, saving 40 percent will not be beneficial. If you are intrigued, however, read to clarify your total commitment and exactly what you will receive in return. Read the fine print.

Credit Cards

Credit card promotions (see figure on facing page) have become such a problem at colleges that some institutions are banning the advertisers from their campuses. You have probably already received many promotions saying that you are preapproved for a certain credit limit. Some students, enticed by the easy credit and low monthly payments, charge themselves into serious debt with crippling finance charges that take years to repay. Thus the misuse of credit cards can be deadly.

Proper use of a credit card, however, can be extremely convenient. Before committing to one, know first that you have the means and the discipline to pay your bill before the due date. If always paid promptly, your only cost for this financial convenience will be the annual fee, which is typically $50 or less (and for many cards there is no annual fee).

Reader's *Tip* Evaluating a Credit Card Offer

- How much is the annual fee for the card?
- What is the finance charge rate? Annual rates typically run from 18% to 22%, so finance charges can add up quickly.
- Does the rate start low and change after an initial introductory period? The balance may be subject to a higher interest rate after the initial period as the low rate expires.
- Why do you need it? If you already have one card, why do you need another one?

1. How long will the introductory rate be available on the Hamilton Premier MasterCard advertised on page 437? _____

2. After the introductory period, what is the best annual percentage rate (APR) you could get if your account balance is less than $2,500? _____

3. If your application is transferred to Hamilton Southwest, what is the highest fixed annual percentage rate (APR) you might have to pay? _____

3.99%
Introductory APR

THE CARD YOU'VE BEEN WAITING FOR
THE BENEFITS YOU NEED
THE RATE YOU WANT

Dear Stephanie Albert,

This card is not for everyone. It's for people like you who are just starting out and have already demonstrated responsibility with their credit. Because you've shown that kind of special care, Hamilton Bank can make this special offer to you—a Hamilton Premier MasterCard.

The rate shown above is one of the lowest of any major credit card issuer. There's no gimmick here—the fixed rate of 3.99% is yours for nine months and will not increase if the Prime Rate changes.* After nine months, you'll still save with a variable Annual Percentage Rate as low as Prime +5.49%—right now that's only 13.24%.*

This rate saves you money on new purchases and on outstanding balances, too. Move those high rate balances to your Hamilton Premier MasterCard—who knows how much you'll save?

With a Hamilton Premier MasterCard, you'll also enjoy these benefits:
- Credit line up to $100,000
- No annual fee
- Optional Travel Accident Insurance, Lost Luggage Insurance, Auto Rental Insurance, Credit Card Registration and Merchandise Protection

*By filling out the following application, you agree that we reserve the right, based upon your evaluation, to open a Hamilton Standard MasterCard account if you do not qualify for a Hamilton Premier MasterCard account or, if you do not qualify, not to open any account. If we do not open an account, we may submit your application to our subsidiary, Hamilton Southwest, which will consider you for an Excel or Regular MasterCard account with the pricing terms shown below.

HAMILTON BANK SUMMARY OF TERMS

Annual Percentage Rate for Purchases	Variable Rate Information
Preferred Pricing: 3.99% Introductory APR for 9 months. Thereafter, for Hamilton MasterCard: 13.24% if your balances are greater than or equal to $2,500/15.24% if your balances are less than $2,500. For Hamilton MasterCard: 17.24%. *Non-Preferred Pricing:* 22.74%	Annual Percentage Rate is fixed at 3.99% for the first 9 months your account is open. Thereafter, your Annual Percentage Rate may vary. For Hamilton Premier MasterCard, the rate is determined monthly by adding 5.49% if your balances are greater than or equal to $2,500 or 7.49% if balances are less than $2,500 (for Hamilton Standard MasterCard: 9.49% for all balances), to the Prime Rate as published in *The Wall Street Journal.* *Non-Preferred Pricing:* Your Annual Percentage Rate may vary. The rate is determined monthly by adding 14.99% to the Prime Rate. This rate will not be lower than 19.8%.

HAMILTON SOUTHWEST SUMMARY OF TERMS

Annual Percentage Rate for Purchases	Variable Rate Information
Preferred Pricing: For Excel MasterCard: 23.15%. For Regular MasterCard: 27.15%. These rates will not be lower than 21.9% or higher than 29.9% *Non-Preferred Pricing:* Fixed 29.9% APR.	*Preferred Pricing:* Your Annual Percentage Rate may vary. For Excel MasterCard accounts, the rate is determined quarterly by adding 15.4% to the Prime Rate as published in *The Wall Street Journal.* For Regular MasterCard accounts, the rate is determined quarterly by adding 19.4% to the Prime Rate.

437

10 Inference

- What is implied meaning?
- Why would meaning be implied rather than stated directly?
- What is slanted language or connotation of words?
- What kinds of clues imply meaning?
- How do good readers draw conclusions?

Everyday Reading Skills: Reading Newspaper Editorials

What Is an Inference?

An *inference* is a meaning that is suggested rather than directly stated. Inferences are implied through clues that lead the reader to make assumptions and draw conclusions. For example, instead of making a direct statement, "These people are rich and influential," an author could imply that idea by describing a palatial residence, expensive heirlooms, and prominent friends. Understanding an inference is what we mean by "reading between the lines," because the suggestion, rather than the actual words, carries the meaning.

Inference from Cartoons

Cartoons and jokes require you to read between the lines and make a connection. They are funny because of the unstated rather than the stated. When listeners catch on to a joke, it simply means they have made the connection and recognized the unstated inference. For example, what inference makes the following joke funny?

> *Sam:*   Do you know how to save a politician from drowning?
> *Joe:*   No.
> *Sam:*   Good.

Taxpayers like to dislike politicians, and this joke falls into that category. As a rule, when you have to explain the inference in a joke, the fun is lost. You want your audience to make the connection and laugh uproariously.

EXAMPLE   Look at the following cartoon. What do you know about a jury? What is being implied about this one?

"*Eleven hamburgers, one frank. Eleven coffees, one tea. Eleven apple pies, one chocolate cake. . . .*"

—*Elements of Public Speaking,* by Joseph DeVito

EXPLANATION A jury is composed of twelve people who are trying to reach consensus on a verdict of guilty or not guilty. The implication in this cartoon is that eleven of the jurors are in agreement on everything, including what to eat, and one juror is totally opposed. Ordering food implies that the discussion may drag on for a long and difficult time. Frequently, a point that takes some figuring out and taps our imagination has a greater impact on us than one that is obviously stated.

exercise 1   The following cartoon contains many details that imply meaning. Use the details to figure out the meaning of the cartoon and answer the questions.

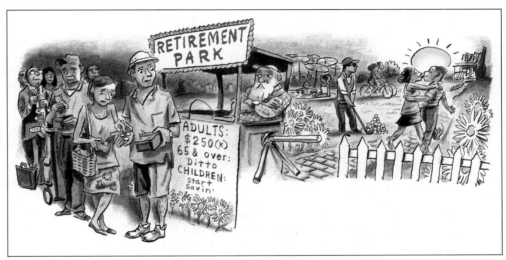

© Rob Shepperson

1. What are the people in line hoping to do in "Retirement Park?" _____

   _____

   _____

2. What is the significance of the setting sun in the background? _____

   _____

   _____

3. Why do the people waiting in line look so distressed? _____

   _____

4. What message does this cartoon have for young people? _____

   _____

5. What are many older people doing now to supplement their retirement

   income? _____

   _____

   _____

6. What is the main point of the cartoon? _____

   _____

Recognizing Suggested Meaning

In reading, as in everyday life, information may or may not be stated outright. For example, someone's death would seem to be a fact beyond question. An author could simply state, "He is dead," but often it is more complicated than that. In literature and in poetry, such a fact might be divulged in a more dramatic manner, and the reader is left to put the clues together and figure out what happened. Read the following excerpt from a story about a shipwrecked crew's struggle to shore. What clues tell you that the oiler is dead?

> In the shallows, face downward, lay the oiler. His forehead touched sand that was periodically, between each wave, clear of the sea.
>
> —*The Open Boat,* by Stephen Crane

The oiler's head is face down in the shallow water. When the waves rush in to shore, his face is in the water, and when they wash out, his face or forehead touches the sand. He is bobbing at the water's edge like a dead fish and cannot possibly be alive with his face constantly underwater or buried in the sand. The man must be dead, but the author doesn't directly state that.

Two paragraphs later in the story the author writes:

> The welcome of the land to the men from the sea was warm and generous; but a still and dripping shape was carried slowly up the beach, and the land's welcome for it could only be the different and sinister hospitality of the grave.
>
> —*The Open Boat,* by Stephen Crane

The "still and dripping shape" and the "sinister hospitality of the grave" support your interpretation of the clues, even though the author still has not directly stated, "The oiler is dead." Implying the idea is perhaps more forceful than making a direct statement.

Connecting with Prior Knowledge

Authors, like cartoonists, use inferences that require linking old knowledge to what is being read at the time. Clues that imply meaning may draw on an assumed knowledge of history, current issues, or social concerns. Just as in making the connection to understand the punch line of a joke, the reader must make a connection in order to understand the inference.

EXAMPLE   **A TURNING POINT**

> More than 3,000 people were killed, thousands more were wounded, and the loss of property was unprecedented in the worst terrorist attack in history. The events horrified people around the world who understood that two symbols of American global financial and military dominance had been singled out in a carefully planned and executed mission of destruction. The event was immediately compared to the Japanese attack on Pearl Harbor in 1941.
>
> —*Civilization in the West,* Fifth Edition, by Mark Kishlansky, Patrick Geary, and Patricia O'Brien

1. What was the symbol of financial dominance that is not named here? Where was the attack?
2. What is the symbol of military dominance? Where was the destruction?

3. When did these terrorist attacks occur?
4. Why was the attack compared to the Japanese attack on Pearl Harbor in 1941?

Personal *Feedback* **1**

Name _____

1. Who supplied your references for college admission or for your last job? _____

   _____

   _____

   _____

2. What professor would you ask to write you a letter of reference for an award or

   scholarship? Why would you choose that particular professor? _____

   _____

   _____

3. Describe how textbooks differ from literature books. _____

   _____

   _____

4. Katharine Hepburn told Barbara Walters that she would describe herself as an oak

   tree. What plant would you choose to describe yourself? _____

   _____

   _____

5. Describe the personal dynamics of your reading class. _____

   _____

   _____

6. What have you added to the class? _____

   _____

   _____

7. What preparation have you done for next term? What courses do you plan to take

   and why? _____

   _____

   _____

Tear out and submit to your instructor.

EXPLANATION The symbol of financial dominance was the twin towers of the World Trade Center in New York City. The symbol of military dominance was the Pentagon in Washington, D.C. The attacks occurred on September 11, 2001, when terrorists hijacked passenger planes and used them to bomb buildings. The attacks precipitated a war, just as the Japanese attack on Pearl Harbor brought the United States into World War II. The following exercise illustrates how authors expect readers to connect with prior knowledge.

exercise 2

Link prior knowledge to answer the questions that follow each passage.

Passage 1

THE BEGINNING OF THE SHOOTING

After seeing the light in the North Church, Paul Revere and William Dawes rode through the countryside alerting the colonists that British troops were moving across the back bay. In Concord and Lexington, trained militiamen were waiting to respond.

Where and approximately when was this? _____

_____

_____

Passage 2

FOOT BINDING

Foot binding was a form of violence against women. The woman's tiny feet, which made it difficult for her to walk, were a "marker" of status, indicating that her husband was wealthy and did not need her labor. It also made her dependent on him.

—*Essentials of Sociology*, Fourth Edition,
by James Henslin

Although not directly stated, foot binding was practiced in what country?

_____

Passage 3

TELLING THE STORY

The account of that morning some weeks later belongs to history. Three planes take off during the night of 6 August from Tinian in the Mariana Islands. Paul Tibbets is the group's commander. Eatherly opens the formation. There are no bombs in his plane; as for the others, no one suspects what a terrible device is hidden inside the *Enola Gay*. A bigger contrivance, they think, nothing more. Eatherly's job is to pinpoint the target with maximum accuracy. He must establish whether weather conditions allow for the center to be Hiroshima, Kokura or Nagasaki, or whether they should continue towards secondary targets. He tells the story of that morning's events in a voice devoid of emotion which suggests that the recitation is the thousandth one.

—"Telling the Story: The Man from Hiroshima," by Maurizio Chierici,
first published in *Granta* 22, Autumn 1987

1. What is the "bigger contrivance"? _____

_____

2. What was the mission assignment of Tibbets and Eatherly? _____

_____

Recognizing Slanted Language

Writers choose words to manipulate the reader and thus to control the reader's attitude toward a subject. Such words are referred to as having a particular **connotation** or **slant.** The dictionary definition of a word is its *denotation,* but the feeling or emotion surrounding a word is its *connotation.* For example, a real estate agent showing a rundown house to a prospective buyer might refer to the house as "neglected" rather than "deteriorated." Both words mean rundown. *Neglected* sounds as if a few things have been forgotten, whereas *deteriorated* sounds as if the place is rotting away and falling apart.

Some words in our society seem to have an automatic positive or negative slant. Words such as *socialist, cult member,* and *welfare state* have a negative emotional effect; words such as *the American worker, democracy,* and *everyday people* have a positive effect. The overall result of using slanted language is to shift the reader's attitude toward the point of view, positive or negative, advocated by the author.

exercise 3

Label the following phrases as either *P* (slanted positively) or *N* (slanted negatively).

_____ 1. warm and winning ways

_____ 2. an engaging smile

_____ 3. appearing remote and self-involved

_____ 4. a savvy salesperson

_____ 5. candid and open

_____ 6. the picture of efficiency

_____ 7. weak and sickly

_____ 8. words like daggers

_____ 9. a loose cannon

_____10. spoken without thinking

_____11. not the sharpest knife in the drawer

_____12. a creased brow

_____13. an exasperated look

_____14. wise beyond her years

_____15. a nurturing mother

_____16. an easy mark

_____17. a hostile takeover

_____18. a dream fulfilled

_____19. the promise of tomorrow

_____20. the brotherhood of man

exercise 4   Indicate whether the boldface words in the following passages are *P* (positive) or *N* (negative), and explain your answer.

_____ 1. Opponents forecast that the increased labor cost from a large minimum-wage hike would jeopardize hundreds of thousands of **unskilled jobs.** _____

_____

—Microeconomics for Today, Fourth Edition, by Irvin B. Tucker

_____ 2. One of the best *Candid Camera* illustrations of the subtle power of social situations to control behavior is the "elevator caper." A person riding a rigged elevator first obeys the usual silent rule to face the front, but when a group of other passengers all face the rear, the **hapless victim** follows the group and faces the rear as well.

_____

—Life-Span Development, Ninth Edition, by John W. Santrock

_____ 3. In the United States and other **highly developed** countries, infectious disease accounts for about 4% to 8% of deaths, compared with death rates of 30% to 50% in developing regions. _____

_____

_____

—Biology, Sixth Edition, by Eldra P. Solomon et al.

_____ 4. Early on in your approach to cooking—or in running a restaurant— you have to determine whether or not you are willing to commit fully and completely to the idea of **the pursuit of excellence. I** have always looked at it this way: if you strive for perfection—an all out assault on total perfection—at the very least you will hit a high level of excellence, and then you might be able to sleep at night. _____

_____

—Introduction to Hospitality, Fourth Edition, by John R. Walker

_____ 5. Finding Mozart a job was not easy. Most of his prospective employers thought that he was too young and too talented ("**overqualified**" is the word we would use today) for a normal position. Indeed, any music director would have been threatened by this brash and brilliant youngster. _____

_____

—Understanding Music, Fourth Edition,
by Jeremy Yudkin

exercise 5

Write a word or phrase with a positive connotation that could be substituted for each of the following negative words. For example, positive substitutes for the word *criticism* might be *feedback* and *advice*. Answers may vary.

1. strange _____

2. wild _____

3. shy _____

4. bossy _____

5. skinny _____

6. nosy _____

7. hyperactive _____

8. slow _____

9. old _____

10. tree-hugger _____

Drawing Conclusions

Readers use both stated and unstated ideas to draw logical conclusions. They use the facts, the hints, and their prior knowledge to piece together meaning. The facts and clues lead to assumptions, which then lead to conclusions. Read the following passage and explain how the conclusion is suggested.

EXAMPLE   **MY HOUSE**

My master still went to school every day and, coming home, he'd still bottle himself up in his study. When he had visitors he'd continue to complain about his job.

I still had nothing to eat so I did not become very fat but I was healthy enough. I didn't become sick like Kuro and, always, I took things as they came. I still didn't try to catch rats, and I still hated Osan, the maid. I still didn't have a name but you can't always have what you want. I resigned myself to continue living here at the home of this school-teacher.

—Excerpt from I Am a Cat, by Natsume Soseki

Conclusion: The narrator of the book is a cat.

What clues suggest this conclusion? _____

EXPLANATION The term *my master* may lead to an initial suspicion of a pet, and "try to catch rats" clearly suggests a cat. The option of continuing to live in the home supports the idea of a cat. The book, as you might guess, is titled *I Am a Cat*.

exercise 6

In passages 1 through 3, identify the clues that lead to the stated conclusions. In passages 4 and 5, state the conclusion and identify the clues.

Passage 1

CULTS: THE PEOPLE'S TEMPLE

A **cult** is usually united by total rejection of society and extreme devotion to the cult's leader. The People's Temple is a dramatic example. In the 1970s their leader, Jim Jones, preached racial harmony, helped the poor, established drug-rehabilitation programs, staged protest demonstrations against social injustices, and helped elect sympathetic politicians. He moved his cult from San Francisco to Jonestown, Guyana, because, he said, evil people in the United States would try to destroy the Temple. He told his flock that to build a just society required a living God—namely, himself. To prove his deity, he "healed parishioners by appearing to draw forth cancers" (which actually were bloody chicken gizzards). He claimed that he had extraordinary sexual gifts, required Temple members to turn over all their possessions to him, and insisted that they call him "Dad" or "Father." Then the People's Temple shocked the world. In November 1978 more than 900 members committed mass suicide at the order of their leader.

—*Sociology*, Third Edition, by Alex Thio

Conclusion: Jim Jones brainwashed cult members into total submission.

What clues suggest this conclusion? _____

_____

_____

_____

Passage 2

THE TOBACCO CRAZE

The first European smoker, Rodrigo de Jerez, was with Columbus. Jerez was jailed by the Spanish Inquisition for seven years because of his bad habit, but he was the wave of the future. Slowly, inexorably, the practice of "drinking" tobacco smoke spread throughout Europe. James I, who found smoking "loathsome" and forbade it in his presence, could not stop it. Nor could the Sultan of Turkey, who threatened to execute puffers.

The lure of the exotic—the trendy—has always been potent among the leisured classes, and some European physicians seized on tobacco as a miracle drug—"the holy, healing herb," "a sovereign remedy to all diseases"—prescribing it liberally to their patients. Throughout the 1500s, the Spanish were pleased to meet Europe's demand from their West Indian plantations.

—*The American Past,* Fifth Edition, by Joseph Conlin

Conclusion: Although initially rejected by political leaders, tobacco became an accepted and sought after commodity.

What clues suggest this conclusion? _____

_____

_____

Passage 3

NICHOLAS II (1894–1917)

Last of the Romanov tsars, Nicholas II was in almost every respect an unfortunate man. Besides having been influenced by a reactionary father and a strong-willed mother, he was dull, weak, stubborn, insensitive, and totally devoid of the qualities required for successfully administering a great empire. The day following his coronation, in conformity with tradition, he scheduled a banquet celebration for the people of the capital. A huge throng, possibly half a million souls, turned out for the great event. At one point the crowd surged forward and more than a thousand people were trampled to death. But Nicholas and the tsarina attended a ball at the French embassy that night and apparently spent a most enjoyable evening.

—A History of the Western World, by Solomon Modell

Conclusion: Nicholas and the tsarina had a total lack of concern for the welfare of the people.

What clues suggest this conclusion? _____

_____

_____

Passage 4

THE FUTURE OF M-COMMERCE

M-commerce has everything to do with speed and location, with short requests for information and prompt, relevant replies. Consider a scenario from the near future. Customers entering a butcher shop are offered a discount for waving their cell phone through an infrared sensor that records the telephone's number. Business at the store is brisk throughout the day. But near closing time, the butcher is anxious to get rid of some prime cuts of Argentine beef.

— Business Today, Tenth Edition,
by Michael Mescon et al.

What conclusion does the author imply? _____

_____

_____

_____

What clues suggest this conclusion? _____

_____

_____

Passage 5

LANDMINES

Cheap and easy to deploy, many fighting forces routinely use mines to defend a frontier, deny opponents the use of a road, and many other purposes. Often these landmines remain active long after the fighting has ceased, posing a significant threat to the safety of the civilian population. The magnitude and horror of this problem sparked a grassroots effort to ban landmines.

The campaign received a major boost in 1996 when Diana, Princess of Wales, joined in the effort, going to places most affected by land mines, comforting victims, and bringing the issue to the attention of millions. When Princess Diana died in a car crash in August 1997, sorrow often turned into commitments to support her charitable interests, including the effort to ban mines. Only a few nations remain opposed to the landmine convention.

—*American Government,* 1999 Edition,
by Karen O'Connor and Larry Sabato

What conclusion does the author imply? _____

_____

_____

What clues suggest this conclusion? _____

_____

_____

---

exercise 7 Use a combination of inference skills to read the following passages and answer the questions.

Passage 1

TEXAS TOUGH

Lyndon Baines Johnson was a complex man—shrewd, arrogant, intelligent, sensitive, vulgar, vain, and occasionally cruel. He loved power, and he knew where it was, how to get it, and how to use it. "I'm a powerful sonofabitch," he told two Texas congressmen in 1958 when he was the most powerful legislator on Capitol Hill. Everything about Johnson seemed to emphasize or enhance his power. He was physically large, and seemed even bigger than he was, and he used his size to persuade people. The "Johnson Method" involved "pressing the flesh"—a back-slapping, hugging sort of camaraderie. He also used symbols of power adroitly, especially the telephone which had replaced the sword and pen as the symbol of power. "No gunman," remarked one historian, "ever held a Colt. 44 so easily" as Johnson handled a telephone.

A legislative genius, Johnson had little experience in foreign affairs. Reared in the poverty of the Texas hill country, educated at a small teachers' college, and concerned politically with domestic issues, before becoming president LBJ had expressed little interest in foreign affairs. "Foreigners are not like the folks I am used to," he often said, and whether it was a joke or not he meant it. He was particularly uncomfortable around foreign dignitaries and ambassadors, often receiving them in groups and scarcely paying attention to them. "Why do I have to see them?" he once asked. "They're [Secretary of State] Dean Rusk's clients, not mine."

—*America and Its People*, Third Edition,
by James Martin et al.

Answer with *T* (true) or *F* (false).

———— 1. LBJ had an enormous ego.

———— 2. LBJ used the telephone to influence votes.

———— 3. LBJ quickly learned to perform in international situations.

———— 4. LBJ's background is reflected in both his genius and his flaws.

———— 5. LBJ was the right person to be president during the Vietnam War.

———— 6. The phrase *replaced the sword* suggests a negative connotation.

Passage 2
THE REIGN OF LOUIS XVI (1774–1793)

A plain, fat, rather stupid young man, who loved to hunt and tinker with locks, Louis XVI succeeded his grandfather (whose one legitimate son, Louis XVI's father, died in 1765) at the age of twenty. His modesty and inherent kindness did not serve him well. He was far too simple, possessed an almost total lack of self-confidence, and could be made to change his mind with relative ease. His wife, Marie Antoinette, an Austrian princess, was pretty, not well educated, shallow, and selfish. Totally unconcerned with the people's welfare, she devoted herself to jewels and costly clothes, gambling and flirtation, masques and balls. Not completely satisfied with court life, she insisted on interfering in governmental affairs and sabotaged, to the extent that she could, whatever chance existed for the reformation of French life. Her liberal emperor-brother, Joseph II of Austria, reprimanded her, but his words went unheeded.

—*A History of the Western World,* by Solomon Modell

Answer with *T* (true) or *F* (false).

———— 1. Louis XVI and his wife were probably loved and respected by his people.

———— 2. Despite his wife's influence, Louis XVI had many of the qualities of a great leader.

———— 3. Louis XVI was firm in his decisions.

———— 4. Marie Antoinette's extravagance was probably resented by the people.

———— 5. Joseph II understood the possible repercussions of Marie Antoinette's actions.

———— 6. The reformation of French life would probably have been a benefit to the people.

———— 7. The phrase *tinker with locks* suggests hard work.

Passage 3
"LIZZIE BORDEN TOOK AN AX"

Andrew [Borden] was rich, but he didn't live like a wealthy man. Instead of living alongside the other prosperous Fall River citizens in the elite neighborhood known as The Hill, Andrew resided in an area near the business district called the flats. He liked to save time as well as money, and from the flats he could conveniently walk to work. For his daughters Lizzie and Emma, whose eyes and dreams focused on The Hill, life in the flats was an intolerable embarrassment. Their house was a grim, boxlike structure that lacked comfort and privacy. Since Andrew believed that running water on each floor was a wasteful luxury, the only washing facilities were a cold-water faucet in the kitchen and a laundry room water tap in the cellar. Also in the cellar was the toilet in the house. To make matters worse, the house was not connected to the Fall River gas main. Andrew preferred to use kerosene to light his house. Although it did not provide as good light or burn as cleanly as gas, it was less expensive. To save even more money, he and his family frequently sat in the dark.

The Borden home was far from happy. Lizzie and Emma, ages thirty-two and forty-two in 1892, strongly disliked their stepmother Abby and resented Andrew's penny-pinching ways. Lizzie especially felt alienated from the world around her. Although Fall River was the largest cotton-manufacturing town in America, it offered few opportunities for the unmarried daughter of a prosperous man. Society expected a woman of Lizzie's social position to marry, and while she waited for a proper suitor, her only respectable social outlets were church and community service. So Lizzie taught a Sunday School class and was active in the Woman's Christian Temperance Union, the Ladies' Fruit and Flower Mission, and other organizations. She kept herself busy, but she wasn't happy.

In August 1892, strange things started to happen in the Borden home. They began after Lizzie and Emma learned that Andrew had secretly changed his will. Abby became violently ill. Abby told a neighborhood doctor that she had been poisoned, but Andrew refused to listen to her wild ideas. Shortly thereafter, Lizzie went shopping for prussic acid, a deadly poison she said she needed to clean her sealskin cape. When a Fall River druggist refused her request, she left the store in an agitated state. Later in the day, she told a friend that she feared an unknown enemy of her father's was after him. "I'm afraid somebody will do something," she said.

On August 4, 1892, the maid Bridget awoke early and ill, but she still managed to prepare a large breakfast of johnnycakes, fresh-baked bread, ginger and oatmeal cookies with raisins, and some three-day-old mutton and hot mutton soup. After eating a hearty meal, Andrew left for work. Bridget also left to do some work outside. This left Abby and Lizzie in the house alone. Then somebody did something very specific and very grisly. As Abby was bent over making the bed in the guest room, someone moved into the room unobserved and killed her with an ax.

Andrew came home for lunch earlier than usual. He asked Lizzie where Abby was, and she said she didn't know. Unconcerned, Andrew, who was not feeling well, lay down on the parlor sofa for a nap. He never awoke. Like Abby, he was slaughtered by someone with an ax. Lizzie "discovered" his body, still lying on the sofa. She called Bridget, who had taken the back stairs to her attic room: "Come down quick; father's dead; somebody came in and killed him."

Experts have examined and reexamined the crime, and most have reached the same conclusion: Lizzie killed her father and stepmother. In fact, Lizzie was tried for the gruesome murders. However, despite a preponderance of evidence, an all male jury found her not guilty. Their verdict was unanimous and was arrived at without debate or disagreement. A woman of Lizzie's social position, they affirmed, simply could not have committed such a terrible crime.

Even before the trial started, newspaper and magazine writers had judged Lizzie innocent for much the same reasons. As one expert on the case noted, "Americans were certain that well-brought-up daughters could not commit murder with a hatchet on sunny summer mornings."

Jurors and editorialists alike judged Lizzie according to their preconceived notions of Victorian womanhood. They believed that such a woman was gentle, docile, and physically frail, short on analytical ability but long on nurturing instincts.

Too uncoordinated and weak to accurately swing an ax and too gentle and unintelligent to coldly plan a double murder, women of Lizzie's background simply had to be innocent because of their basic innocence.

—*America and Its People*, Third Edition,
by James Martin et al.

Answer with *T* (true) or *F* (false).

———— 1. Andrew Borden's family suffered from his efforts to save money.

———— 2. Abby was probably correct in telling the doctor that her illness was due to poison.

———— 3. Andrew was killed when he discovered his wife dead.

———— 4. The jury did not carefully consider the evidence against Lizzie.

———— 5. The Victorian stereotyping of women worked in Lizzie's favor.

———— 6. The author believes that Lizzie was not guilty.

———— 7. The quotation marks around the word *discovered* change the connotation of the word.

Personal *Feedback* **2**

Name ————————————

1. What characteristics do you have that are important for leadership? ——————

———————————————————————————

2. During this term, what have your leadership roles been? ————————————

———————————————————————————

3. As the term has progressed, how has your thinking about college changed? ————

———————————————————————————

4. How are your friends and loved ones affecting your academic success? ————————

———————————————————————————

5. What is most irritating about your roommates or people you live with? ——————

———————————————————————————

6. What will you remember most from this class? ————————————————

———————————————————————————

Tear out and submit to your instructor.

Summary *Points*

➤ **What is an inference?**
An inference is an implied meaning that is not directly stated but can be deduced from clues. Inferences require linking old knowledge to what is being read at the time.

➤ **Why are jokes funny?**
Jokes and cartoons are funny because of the implied meaning understood by the teller and the audience.

➤ **What is the effect of slanted language?**
Slanted language manipulates the reader's attitude in a positive or negative manner toward a subject.

➤ **What are conclusions?**
Conclusions are generalized meaning based on clues that incorporate what you already know with what you have just discovered.

COLLABORATIVE PROBLEM SOLVING

Form a five-member group and select one of the following activities. Brainstorm and then outline your major points on a transparency. Choose a member to present the group findings to the class.

➤ Use details, dialogue, and characters to create a cartoon about poorly performing public high schools that blames *teachers* for the problems.

➤ Use details, dialogue, and characters to create a cartoon about poorly performing public high schools that blames *students* for the problems.

➤ Use details, dialogue, and characters to create a cartoon about poorly performing public high schools that blames *parents* for the problems.

➤ Use details, dialogue, and characters to create a cartoon about poorly performing public high schools that blames a *lack of money* for the problems.

PEARSON myreadinglab

MyReadingLab (MRL) www.myreadinglab.com

➤ To practice the ideas and skills introduced in this chapter, go to the "Inferences" module in the Skills section of MRL. To practice general reading comprehension, use the Levels section.

The Reading *Workshop*

"The only books that influence us are those for which we are ready, and which have gone a little farther down our particular path than we have yet got ourselves."
—E.M. FORSTER

Have you been "stretched" by the books you are reading for pleasure? If not, consider selecting something just a bit more challenging next time. This might mean venturing into a subject, genre, or length that you have hesitated to try but that intrigues you. Beware: Growth may occur!

Think about it, talk about it, write about it:

What inferences did the author of your book expect you to make to understand the action or point? For example, in a suspense novel there are usually clues that allow the reader to speculate about the outcome. Sometimes the author plants false clues or "red herrings" to lead the reader to incorrect conclusions. Also consider the significance of the book's title. Does it directly label the content of the book, or does it reflect a significant theme or meaning within the book?

Your professor may ask you to discuss these questions in a Reading Workshop journal.

"Deception is a cruel act . . . It often has many players on different stages that corrode the soul."

—Donna A. Favors

The training to be a physician is long, rigorous, and expensive. Most young doctors finally emerge in their 30s, ready for a job and burdened with debt. However, their financial opportunities appear rosy. Based on almost 3,000 replies to Physicians Search, doctors with three years of experience in practice are making money. On the high end of the salary range, the survey indicates the following yearly base salaries without benefits or bonuses for these specialties: psychiatrist at $189,000; family practice physician at $197,000; pediatrician at $201,000; emergency medicine at $250,000; dermatologist at $407,000; plastic surgeon at $411,000; radiologist at $429,000; cardiologist at $450,000; oncologist at $473,000; neurosurgeon at $713,000. Thus, for someone who is oriented toward science and gifted in medicine, the choices of a specialty are compelling. How does a young doctor decide, even with the special training needed, which is the best career path to pursue?

THINKING BEFORE READING

Preview the selection for content and organizational clues. Activate your schema and anticipate the story.

How much medical attention do prisoners receive?

What types of crime do FBI agents investigate?

After reading this, I will probably know _____ .

VOCABULARY PREVIEW

Are you familiar with these words?

| deceptively | acknowledged | extradition | financier | limp |
| manipulations | distracting | stashed | extracted | trance |

Have you ever had a tooth *extracted*?

Do you think driving while talking on a cell phone is *distracting*?

Do you sometimes feel as though you are in a *trance*?

Your instructor may choose to give a true-false vocabulary review before or after reading.

THINKING DURING READING

As you read, use the six thinking strategies of a good reader: predict, picture, relate, monitor, correct, and annotate.

THE BEST PLACE

Refer to the
Reader's *Tip*
for **a Short Story** on
page 155.

Dr. Jason Whitney saw the two federal agents enter the crowded restaurant. Their rumpled suits and stubble-covered cheeks betrayed the fact that they had been too busy to think of appearances for some time. They moved wearily toward him along the line of booths against the wall, looking for an empty one. When they reached the booth where
5 the young doctor was sitting alone, he spoke to the agent he recognized, a deceptively soft-looking man in his forties.

"Hello, Tom. Have a seat." He indicated the place opposite him with a sweep of his hand. "There probably aren't any empty booths at this hour. A lot of people stop here for breakfast on their way to work."

10 Tom Campbell slid heavily into the booth and was followed by his look-alike companion. "I'd like you to meet my partner, Joe Moffet, Dr. . . . Dr. . . ." Campbell snapped his fingers, trying to dislodge the name from his memory.

"Whitney. Jason Whitney," the doctor offered with a smile, not the least offended at not being remembered.

15 "Yeah, that's right," Campbell acknowledged with a nod as Joe Moffet and the young doctor clasped hands briefly.

"You men look like you've had a hard night," the doctor said.

"You can say that again," Campbell answered. "We haven't been out of our clothes in two days. Just brought a man back from Spain."

20 "Extradition?"

Campbell gave a wry smile. "You could call it that. Our man was staying in Andorra, that little postage-stamp country on the border between Spain and France. They'd have let him stay there until his money ran out, which would've taken a couple of thousand years or so. We have no treaty with them."

25 "So what happened?"

"The usual. We pretended we'd lost interest in him and waited for him to get careless. When he made the mistake of taking a walk too close to the Spanish border, we were ready. Next thing he knew, Joe and I each had one of his arms and were marching him past the Spanish customhouse. We tossed him into a car and rushed him to a plane we had waiting
30 at one of our bases. The Spanish authorities pretended they didn't see a thing."

"Seems like a lot of trouble and expense over just one man," Dr. Whitney said.

"It was Henry Hammond." Campbell had a touch of pride in his tone.

A waitress came to take their breakfast orders. As soon as she was gone, the doctor repeated the name. "Henry Hammond . . . It *does* sound a bit familiar. Should I know the
35 name?"

"He's the big-shot financier who jumped bail and skipped the country a couple of years ago. He'd built himself an empire, using phony balance sheets and illegal manipulations. He got away with just about every nickel from his companies' treasuries."

"Oh, yes, now I remember. It made quite a splash in the papers at the time. What
40 did you do with him?"

"Dropped him off at your place ten minutes ago," Campbell said.

The second agent, Joe Moffet, had been sitting quietly, but now he twisted his face into a puzzled expression and said, "Huh?"

Campbell turned to him. "The doctor is in charge of the infirmary at the Federal
45 House of Detention on West Street," he explained. "He'll probably be giving our friend a physical examination today."

"I check all new prisoners," Dr. Whitney agreed.

The waitress returned with their orders. They didn't say much until they had settled back to enjoy their coffee. Then the conversation returned to Henry Hammond.
50 "Do you think he'll return the money he stole?" the doctor asked.

"That's something you'll have to ask Hammond. We couldn't get a word out of him all the way across the Atlantic. He probably has it safely stashed away in a couple of dozen Swiss banks. One thing's sure—no one will ever see it again unless he wants them to."

"I wonder what makes a man decide to be a criminal?" the doctor mused.

55 Campbell shrugged. "Who knows? People don't always do the things you'd expect, or fit into patterns the way you think they should. Take yourself, for instance. What's a bright young guy like you doing in the Public Health Service? There's no military draft anymore, so you didn't choose it as an alternative service the way doctors and dentists have in the past. I'll bet you could have had your pick of the private hospitals."

60 "Yes, I probably could have, but I'm happy where I am. I think it's the best place for me. If I didn't, I'd go somewhere else or do something else. That's the way you feel about your job, isn't it, Tom? That active police work is the best occupation for you?"

"You certainly have Tom figured out," Joe Moffet said. "And you put it into words better than he does, too. He's turned down two promotions in the last year. He could 65 have a comfortable desk job in D.C., but he prefers to transport fugitives. Everyone thinks he's crazy, but he says he's happy where he is."

They exchanged small talk for a few more minutes, then left the restaurant together. They paused to say good-bye on the sidewalk outside, and Tom Campbell's face clouded with confusion and embarrassment. "I'm terribly sorry, Doctor, but I—uh—I've forgotten 70 your name again."

Jason Whitney smiled. "That's all right. You'd be surprised how many people have trouble remembering me. The next time you're at the House of Detention stop by my office to say hello. I always have a pot of coffee on the hot plate." He turned to the other agent. "That goes for you, too, Mr. Moffet. Stop in any time. It's been nice meeting 75 you."

Jason Whitney waited until ten that morning before having Henry Hammond called to the infirmary. He chose that time because the morning sick call had been taken care of by then, and his assistants were enjoying a coffee break.

"Good morning, Mr. Hammond. I'm Dr. Whitney, the Chief Medical Officer here. I'm 80 in charge of the health and physical well-being of you and the other prisoners. It's my job to examine each new arrival and determine whether or not he'll require treatment of any kind."

Hammond nodded his understanding. He had dark circles under his eyes and stood nervously in the doorway of the infirmary. He clenched and unclenched his right fist in an 85 uneven rhythm, and his eyes swept back and forth, taking in all the cabinets and equipment. It was obvious his sudden arrest and transportation to the United States had been a severe shock.

"Step this way, please," Whitney said, leading the way to a side room.

Here there were bare white walls and the only furniture was an examination table for 90 the patient. There was nothing that might prove distracting.

"Lie down, please. I'm going to take your blood pressure. I'm sure you've had it done before."

The doctor wrapped the instrument around Hammond's arm, and squeezed the bulb to pump air into it.

95 "Be as quiet as you can. I want the lowest reading possible. Relax as much as you can and try not to think of anything in particular."

Whitney busied himself with the instrument.

"Your reading is a bit high, Mr. Hammond. I think you're a little too tense. If you don't mind, I'll show you how to relax. Just close your eyes. That's right, close your eyes 100 and relax the eyelids. I think you can get the feeling of complete relaxation if you'll follow my suggestions. Relax your eyelids completely. Now turn your attention to your arms. Let them become completely limp. Think of them as a pair of limp rags and when I lift them let them fall back to the table just as a couple of limp rags would. That's very good. Now we'll do the same with your legs. See, you're much more relaxed and at 105 ease now.

"I'll just take your blood pressure again and see how well you've done. Oh, that's very good. That's very, very good. You're far more relaxed than before. Let's try it again, Mr. Hammond, and this time keep your eyes closed all the while. That will aid the relaxation process.

110   "Okay, now, relax your eyes. Now your arms. Let them become as limp as rags. Now your legs. Relax them. Just relax your whole body. Let your whole body go limp. Let your whole body become heavy. Get completely comfortable. Now, if you are truly relaxed, you will find that your eyelids won't open. Relax your eyelids and body completely. When you feel you're completely relaxed you may try to open your eyes. If you are completely

115   relaxed, they won't open. If you cannot open your eyes, you will be completely relaxed. That's fine. Now try to open your eyes. See—you cannot open them. You are completely, deeply relaxed and you cannot open your eyes. Your arms and legs are heavy and limp and you cannot lift or move them."

       As quickly and easily as that, without once using the words sleep or hypnosis, Dr.
120   Jason Whitney placed Henry Hammond into a deep trance.

       In the next half hour he deepened the trance still further, then extracted from Hammond the code numbers and balances of ten secret bank accounts. Immediately before allowing the man to wake up, he directed Hammond to forget forever that the secret accounts had ever existed. "And you will never be able to remember my name," he told him.

125   That reminded Whitney of Agent Tom Campbell. When he had hypnotized Campbell a year before and instructed the man to keep him informed about criminals with hidden money; he had neglected to order him always to come to the restaurant alone. He would have to rectify that oversight at the first opportunity.

       As Hammond left the infirmary to return to his cell, Dr. Whitney watched him walk
130   away and felt a wave of satisfaction. This *was* the best place for him. He didn't have to work the long hours a hospital might have demanded, and he was collecting far, far more money in a single year than his professional hypnotist parents had earned in their lifetimes.

(1,714 words)

—by A. F. Oreshnik

THINKING AND WRITING AFTER READING

RECALL   Self-test your understanding.

Your instructor may choose to give you a true-false comprehension review.

REACT   At what point in the story did you guess what was going to happen?

_____

_____

REFLECT   Why is the blood pressure deception an excellent choice for Dr. Whitney?

_____

THINKING CRITICALLY   What factors must combine to make Dr. Whitney's scheme a perfect and profitable crime? _____

_____

THINK AND WRITE   Define *irony*, and describe how it applies to three of the characters. _____

_____

INFERENCE QUESTIONS

1. What does the author mean by the phrase "a deceptively soft-looking man"?

   _____

   _____

   _____

   _____

2. What is the irony in Jason Whitney's statement to the agents, "I wonder what makes a man decide to be a criminal?" _____

   _____

3. Why does Dr. Whitney never mention the words *sleep* and *hypnosis*? _____

   _____

4. What can be inferred from Dr. Whitney's remark to Tom Campbell, "You'd be surprised how many people have trouble remembering me"? _____

   _____

   _____

   _____

5. Why did Dr. Whitney wait until his assistants were on their coffee break before meeting with Henry Hammond? _____

   _____

   _____

Interpret the Quote

Now that you have finished reading the selection, "The Best Place," go back to the beginning of the selection and read the opening quote again. On a separate sheet of paper, explain the acts of deception that are most apparent in the story. Who were the players in this deception?

Name _____

Date _____

COMPREHENSION QUESTIONS

Answer the following with *a, b, c,* or *d,* or fill in the blank. In order to help you analyze your strengths and weaknesses, the question types are indicated.

Main Idea _____ 1. The cliché that best reflects the main idea of this selection is:

    a. Crime does not pay.
    b. Honesty is the best policy.
    c. You can't judge a book by its cover.
    d. A penny saved is a penny earned.

Detail _____ 2. Dr. Whitney is not offended when Agent Campbell fails to recall his name because

    a. Dr. Whitney is a modest man.
    b. Dr. Whitney does not want to embarrass the agent.
    c. Dr. Whitney has hypnotized Agent Campbell and told him to forget the name.
    d. Dr. Whitney knows Agent Campbell usually has trouble remembering names.

Inference _____ 3. Dr. Whitney needs to maintain a relationship with Agent Campbell because

    a. Campbell is his source for criminals with money.
    b. he considers Campbell a friend.
    c. Dr. Whitney and Agent Campbell are partners in crime.
    d. both men are employed by the same federal agency.

Inference _____ 4. The irony of the story is that

    a. Hammond is guilty.
    b. Hammond was captured by the FBI.
    c. Dr. Whitney is a criminal.
    d. Joe Moffet believes his partner.

Inference _____ 5. The reader can most likely conclude that Tom Campbell turned down two promotions because

    a. he was hypnotized to do so.
    b. he enjoys the travel in transporting fugitives.
    c. he did not want to move to D.C.
    d. he makes more money in his present job of transporting fugitives.

Inference _____ 6. The reader can conclude that Henry Hammond was most likely arrested

    a. inside Spain.
    b. by Spanish customs officials.
    c. during the night when officials were not watching.
    d. while still in Andorra.

Inference _____ 7. The author uses the story's title, *The Best Place,* to apply ironically to the situations in the lives of:

a. Dr. Whitney and Tom Campbell.
b. Tom Campbell and Joe Moffet.
c. Dr. Whitney, Tom Campbell, and Joe Moffet.
d. Dr. Whitney, Tom Campbell, Joe Moffet, and Henry Hammond.

Answer the following with *T* (true) or *F* (false).

Inference   _____ 8. The reader can conclude that Dr. Whitney most likely got his job in the Federal House of Detention by accident.

Inference   _____ 9. The reader can conclude that the FBI agents question Dr. Whitney about his job choice because they are suspicious of him.

Inference   _____10. The reader can conclude that Henry Hammond's blood pressure was high.

VOCABULARY

Answer the following with *a, b, c,* or *d* for the word or phrase that best defines the boldface word used in the selection. The number in parentheses indicates the line of the passage in which the word appears.

_____ 1. "**deceptively** soft-looking" (5)

  a. honestly
  b. misleadingly
  c. plainly
  d. happily

_____ 2. "**acknowledged** with" (15)

  a. smiled
  b. remembered
  c. recognized
  d. choked

_____ 3. "**Extradition**?" (20)

  a. exile
  b. forced removal
  c. relation
  d. stay

_____ 4. "big-shot **financier**" (36)

  a. drug lord
  b. criminal
  c. waiter
  d. money manager

_____ 5. "illegal **manipulations**" (37–38)

  a. schemes
  b. money
  c. adjustments
  d. companies

_____ 6. "safely **stashed**" (52)

  a. sent
  b. found
  c. buried
  d. hidden

_____ 7. "prove **distracting**" (90)

  a. examining
  b. comforting
  c. drawing attention elsewhere
  d. truthful

_____ 8. "completely **limp**" (102)

  a. lifeless
  b. rigid
  c. clean
  d. tense

_____ 9. "a deep **trance**" (120)

  a. sleeplike state
  b. alertness
  c. awareness
  d. panic

_____10. "**extracted** from" (121)

  a. followed
  b. removed
  c. made up
  d. helped

Your instructor may choose to give a true-false vocabulary review.

VOCABULARY ENRICHMENT

Idiom

An *idiom* is a phrase used mainly in conversation that has meaning other than the literal meaning of the words themselves. For example, the phrase "My eyes were bigger than my stomach" is an idiom. The exact, literal meaning of the words is anatomically impossible. In our culture, however, the phrase is a creative way of saying, "I took more food on my plate than I can possibly eat." Other languages may not have this exact same expression, but they may have different idioms to express the same idea. Students who learn English as a second language find our idioms confusing when they look for an exact translation.

Idioms are slang phrases, clichés, and regional expressions. Their popularity changes with the times. Grandparents may use idioms that would make a college student shudder. Professional writers try to avoid idioms because they are considered informal.

Write the meaning of the boldface idioms in the following sentences.

1. Thomas's first-born son is **a chip off the old block**. _____
   _____

2. It was getting late, and the mother decided to **hit the road** with her children.
   _____

3. With that inappropriate comment to his students, the professor really
   crossed the line. _____
   _____

4. Many inventors and entrepreneurs are experts at **thinking outside the box**.
   _____
   _____

5. Her father can be demanding and outspoken, but Suzanne knows that **his
   bark is worse than his bite**. _____
   _____

6. Cynthia's dog has taken obedience class three times yet remains untrained;
   he is definitely **not the sharpest knife in the drawer**. _____
   _____

7. When she learned that her son had made online purchases using her debit
   card, the mother **raked him over the coals**. _____
   _____

8. After seeing the negative effects of his dishonesty, the student vowed to **turn
   over a new leaf** and turn in only his own work. _____
   _____

9. The new coach is in favor of discipline and hard work; he makes his players **toe the line**. _____

10. Students who have jobs and attend college full-time often find themselves **burning the candle at both ends**. _____

_____

ASSESS YOUR LEARNING

Review confusing questions, seek clarification, and make notes in your text to help you remember the new information and vocabulary.

Literature: Short Story

"... I have been married for forty-seven years and not once have we had an argument serious enough to consider divorce; murder, yes, but divorce, never."

—Jack Benny

The term alchemist *conjures up visions of medieval wizards who mixed chemistry with the supernatural. The occult art or pseudoscience of alchemy was veiled in magic and superstition. The exceedingly optimistic goals of alchemists were to transmute or turn base metals into gold, to create a potion to cure all ills, and to discover an elixir to extend life. Alchemists were both sought after and persecuted for their secrets. Today these first practitioners of chemistry might be seen as New Age spiritualists exploring homeopathy, aromatherapy, or astrology.*

THINKING BEFORE READING

Preview the selection for content and organizational clues. Activate your schema and anticipate the story.

What is an alchemist?

Were alchemists viewed positively or negatively? Why?

After reading this, I will probably know _____ .

VOCABULARY PREVIEW

Are you familiar with these words?

| alchemist | baser metals | autopsy | insomnia | hot grog |

Can chemists turn *baser metals* into gold?

What ingredients are in *hot grog*?

Your instructor may choose to give a true-false vocabulary review before or after reading.

THINKING DURING READING

As you read, use the six thinking strategies of a good reader: predict, picture, relate, monitor, correct, and annotate.

THE ALCHEMIST'S SECRET

Sitting quietly in his little herb shop on a crooked street in the shadow of Notre Dame, Doctor Maximus did not look like a very remarkable man. But he was. Five hundred years before, he might have busied himself changing the baser metals into gold. But in Paris of the nineties, it is said, he worked at a more subtle alchemy. He changed dreams into realities—provided, of course, you could pay.

5

Refer to the
Reader's *Tip*
for **a Short Story**
on page 155.

The man who came into the gaslit shop this early October evening in 1891 was prepared to pay. He stood just inside the door, blotting his forehead with a silk handkerchief
although actually the weather was rather cool. He was holding a heart-shaped package
tightly under one arm. "You are Monsieur le Doctor Maximus?"

10   The Doctor bowed respectfully.

"I have a problem," said the visitor nervously. "I am told you might help me with it."

"Indeed?" said the Doctor mildly. "Who told you that?"

The newcomer glanced around uneasily at the dim shelves, the leathery tortoise dangling from a string, the small stuffed crocodile with its dust-filmed eyes. "Last night we

15   had a dinner guest. A foreign diplomat. First secretary of the—"

"Ah, yes, Pechkoff. It is true I did him a small service."

"He was not very specific, you understand. But after a few glasses of cognac he
talked rather freely. I got the impression . . ."

"Yes?"

20   "That if it weren't for your—er—assistance he would still be married, most unhap-
pily, to his first wife."

Doctor Maximus took off his glasses and polished the spotless lenses. "She died, I
believe, poor woman. Quite suddenly."

"Yes," said the visitor, "she did. So suddenly that there was an autopsy. But they dis-

25   covered nothing wrong."

"Of course not," said Doctor Maximus, smiling gently.

"My wife," said the visitor with a certain agitation, "is a very beautiful woman.
Naturally, she has many admirers. She has always ignored them until recently, but now
there is one—I don't know which one—a younger man, no doubt. She admits it! She

30   demands that I make some settlement. I will not—"

Doctor Maximus raised his hand. "The details," he murmured, "do not concern me."

The visitor's face was tight and dangerous. "I am not a man to be made a fool of!"

"No," said the Doctor, "I can see that."

"Madame," said the visitor abruptly, "is very fond of candy." He unwrapped the

35   heart-shaped package and placed it on the counter. It was a box of chocolates. "I thought
perhaps you might—ah—improve the candies at your convenience and then post them to

her. She would be very pleased. I have even prepared a card to enclose." He took out a small rectangle of cardboard. On it was printed in neat capitals: FROM AN ADMIRER.

Doctor Maximus took the card and sighed. "My fees are not inconsiderable."

40   "I did not expect them to be," the visitor said stiffly. He did not flinch when the price was named. He paid it, in gold coins. He blotted his forehead once more with the silk handkerchief. "Will you be able to send the candy tonight?"

"Perhaps," said the Doctor noncommittally. "We shall see. And where should it be sent?"

45   "Ah, yes," said the visitor. "Of course." And he gave Madame's name and address.

Doctor Maximus wrote the information on a slip of paper. Then he scribbled three digits on another slip and handed it over. "You sir, are customer 322. If there are any difficulties, kindly refer to that number. Not," he added, "that there will be any."

With one hand on the doorknob, the visitor hesitated. "It won't be—" he wet his
50   lips—"it won't be painful, will it?"

"Not at all," said Dr. Maximus. He peered over his spectacles in a benign and sympathetic fashion. "You seem rather upset. Do you want me to give you something to make you sleep?"

"No, thank you," said his visitor nervously. "I have my own prescription for insomnia:
55   a hot grog before going to bed."

"Ah, yes," said Dr. Maximus. "An excellent habit."

"Good night," said the visitor, opening the door into the narrow, ill-lit street.

"Good-bye," murmured Dr. Maximus.

Taking the box of chocolates in one hand and the slip of paper in the other, he went
60   into the little room at the rear of the shop. From the shelf above his test tubes and retorts he took a big black book, opened it, and looked at the record of the previous transaction. There it was, entered only that afternoon in his spidery handwriting: *Customer 321. Complaint: the usual. Remedy: six drops of the elixir, to be administered in husband's hot grog at bedtime . . .*

65   Dr. Maximus sighed. Then, being a man who honored his commitments, he opened the box of chocolates and went to work. There was no great rush. He would post the parcel in the morning.

In the herb shop, as in life, you got just about what you paid for. But his motto was, First come, first served.

(867 words)

—by Arthur Gordon

THINKING AND WRITING AFTER READING

Inference Questions

1. Where did the couple learn of Dr. Maximus? _____

    _____

2. How was Dr. Maximus connected to Pechkoff's wife? _____

    _____

3. Why was the husband who drank grog unhappy with his wife? _____

    _____

4. How did Dr. Maximus realize that the husband was his next victim? _____

    _____

    _____

5. What can be concluded about Customer 321? _____

6. Why is the motto "First come, first served" ironic in this story? _____

_____

_____

7. Why is the phrase "being a man who honored his commitments" sarcastic?

_____

_____

8. What is the theme of this story? _____

_____

THINK AND WRITE

Considering the three goals of alchemists, why do you think they were both sought after and persecuted for their secrets? _____

_____

_____

Interpret the Quote

Now that you have finished reading the selection, "The Alchemist's Secret," go back to the beginning of the selection and read the opening quote again. What can you infer from Jack Benny's quote about his marriage? On a separate sheet of paper, explain how this quote relates to the relationship between the husband and wife depicted in the story.

VOCABULARY ENRICHMENT

Literary Devices

A. **Personification.** In personification, an inanimate object is given human characteristics. Personification can embellish an image and create a mood. In the sentence "The wind sang through the trees," the word *sang* gives the wind a human characteristic that adds a soft, gentle mood to the message.

Write the meaning, mood, or feeling the boldface personification adds to the message in the following sentences.

1. As the alchemist scraped the bar of gold, her skin **crawled**. _____

_____

2. The glowing fireplace was the **heart** of the tiny shop selling health remedies.

_____

3. The sun **kissed** the window and brightened the dark laboratory. _____

_____

4. The shelves **stretched** to make room for more new youth potions. _____

_____

5. As he reached for the poison potion, the stars **flirted** with the drifting sand.

_____

B. **Irony.** Irony is saying one thing but meaning another. It may be used to show humor or to be sarcastic and ridicule others. The trick in irony is to be able to recognize that the speaker does not really mean what he or she says. The context in which the statement is made gives clues to the speaker's true attitude. Gullible people have trouble picking up irony and are subsequently sometimes fooled and embarrassed. For example, after a basketball game, someone may say to a player who scored only once in seventeen tries, "You're a great shot." Here irony is used to ridicule the poor shooting.

Complete the story in each of the following sentences by choosing the response that best shows irony.

_____ 6. Each time the professor called on Larry to answer a question, he gave the wrong response. After class Frances said to Larry,

   a. "We need to study hard."
   b. "Here's the guy with the brains."
   c. "I hope you weren't embarrassed."

_____ 7. Sue missed only one item on a chemistry exam that almost everyone else failed. When congratulated, Sue retorted,

   a. "Maybe next time I'll study."
   b. "I'm glad I studied."
   c. "My major is chemistry."

_____ 8. As newlyweds, Betsy and Fred moved to a tiny New York apartment. When their parents came to visit, a sign on the door said,

   a. "Welcome to our new place."
   b. "Welcome to the Caribbean Hilton."
   c. "Welcome to our friends and family."

_____ 9. Because George's apartment was so dirty, his friends called him

   a. the Slob.
   b. George the Unclean.
   c. Mother's Helper.

_____ 10. Chris was known to be cheap, so friends started calling him

   a. Mr. Rockefeller.
   b. Mr. Scrooge.
   c. Mr. Chips.

ASSESS YOUR LEARNING

Review confusing questions, seek clarification, and make notes in your text to help you remember the new information and vocabulary.

selection 3 Literature: Short Story

"Diamonds are nothing more than chunks of coal that stuck to their jobs."
—Malcolm Forbes

Diamonds have value because they sparkle and are cherished in the marketplace. That value, or price, is determined by the four Cs of diamonds: cut, clarity, color, and carat weight. If you are searching for specific prices, the range varies. For example, one company lists its one-carat round cut diamonds from $5,000 to $17,000 according to clarity and color. Another company offers one-carat stones with the same round cut for $3,000 to $16,000. For three-carat diamonds with round cuts, the range is $14,000 to $112,000 or $7,000 to $41,000. High prices make diamonds particularly attractive to thieves. Stones are also difficult to trace and easy to sell on the black market. Robbing a jewelry store may be easier than robbing a bank, and some people may think that both produce sure money.

THINKING BEFORE READING

Preview for content and organizational clues. Activate your schema and anticipate the author's opinion.

What factors contribute to the appeal and the price of diamonds?

Why are stolen diamonds easy to resell without being traced?

After reading this, I will probably want to _____ .

VOCABULARY PREVIEW

Are you familiar with these words?

strolled	fashion-plate	reluctantly	commotion	cooler
previous	mingled	dapper	confirmed	wading

Is Beyoncé a *fashion-plate*?

Do you *reluctantly* go to the doctor?

When was the last time you *mingled* with people you didn't know?

Your instructor may choose to give a true-false vocabulary review before or after reading.

THINKING DURING READING

As you read, use the six thinking strategies of a good reader: predict, picture,
relate, monitor, correct, and annotate.

A DEAL IN DIAMONDS

Refer to the
Reader's *Tip*
for **a Short Story**
on page 155.

It was seeing a girl toss a penny into the plaza fountain that gave Pete Hopkins the idea. He was always on the lookout for money-making ideas, and they were getting tougher to find all the time. But as he looked up from the fountain to the open window of the Downtown Diamond Exchange, he thought he had found a good one at last.

5   He strolled over to the phone booth at the other side of the plaza and called Johnny Stoop. Johnny was the classiest dude Pete knew—a real fashion-plate who could walk into a store and have the clerks falling over themselves to wait on him. Better yet, he had no record here in the east. And it was doubtful if the cops could link him to the long list of felonies he had committed ten years ago in California.

10   "Johnny? This is Pete. Glad I caught you in."

"I'm always in during the daytime, Pete boy. In fact, I was just getting up."

"I got a job for us, Johnny, if you're interested."

"What sort?"

"Meet me at the Birchbark Bar and we'll talk about it."

15   "How soon?"

"An hour?"

Johnny Stoop groaned. "Make it two. I gotta shower and eat breakfast."

"Okay, two. See you."

The Birchbark Bar was a quiet place in the afternoons—perfect for the sort of meet-
20   ing Pete wanted. He took a booth near the back and ordered a beer. Johnny was only ten minutes late and he walked into the place as if he were casing it for a robbery or a girl he might pick up. Finally he settled, almost reluctantly, for Pete's booth.

"So what's the story?"

The bartender was on the phone yelling at somebody about a delivery, and the rest
25   of the place was empty. Pete started talking. "The Downtown Diamond Exchange. I think we can rip it off for a quick handful of stones. Might be good for fifty grand."

Johnny Stoop grunted, obviously interested. "How do we do it?"

"*You* do it. I wait outside."

"Great! And I'm the one the cops grab!"

30   "The cops don't grab anyone. You stroll in, just like Dapper Dan, and ask to see a tray of diamonds. You know where the place is, on the fourth floor. Go at noon, when there's always a few customers around. I'll create a commotion in the hall, and you snatch up a handful of stones."

"What do I do—swallow them like the gypsy kids used to do?"

35   "Nothing so crude. The cops are wise to that, anyway. You throw them out the window."

"Like hell I do!"

"I'm serious, Johnny."

"They don't even keep their windows open. They got air conditioning, haven't they?"

40   "I saw the window open today. You know all this energy-conservation stuff—turn off the air conditioner and open the windows. Well, they're doing it. They probably figure four flights up nobody's goin' to get in that way. But something can get *out*—the diamonds."

"It sounds crazy, Pete."

"Listen, you toss the diamonds through the window from the counter. That's maybe
45   ten feet away." He was making a quick pencil sketch of the office as he talked. "See, the window's behind the counter, and you're in front of it. They never suspect that you threw 'em out the window because you're never near the window. They search you, they question you, but then they gotta let you go. There are other people in the store, other suspects. And nobody saw you take them."

50   "So the diamonds go out the window. But you're not outside to catch them. You're in the hall creating a diversion. So what happens to the stones?"

"This is the clever part. Directly beneath the window, four stories down, is the fountain in the plaza. It's big enough so the diamonds can't miss it. They fall into the fountain

and they're as safe as in a bank vault till we decide to get them. Nobody noticed them hit
55   the water because the fountain is splashing. And nobody sees them *in* the water because
they're clear. They're like glass."

"Yeah," Johnny agreed. "Unless the sun—"

"The sun don't reach the bottom of the pool. You could look right at 'em and not
notice 'em—unless you knew they were there. We'll know, and we'll come back for them
60   tomorrow night, or the next."

Johnny was nodding. "I'm in. When do we pull it off?"

Pete smiled and raised his glass of beer. "Tomorrow."

On the following day, Johnny Stoop entered the fourth floor offices of the Downtown
Diamond Exchange at exactly 12:15. The uniformed guard who was always at the door
65   gave him no more than a passing glance. Pete watched it all from the busy hallway outside, getting a clear view through the thick glass doors that ran from floor to ceiling.

As soon as he saw the clerk produce a tray of diamonds for Johnny, he glanced across
the office at the window. It was open about halfway, as it had been the previous day. Pete
started walking toward the door, touched the thick glass handle, and fell over in an
70   apparent faint. The guard inside the door heard him fall and came out to offer assistance.

"What's the matter, mister? You okay?"

"I—I can't—breathe . . ."

He raised his head and asked for a glass of water. Already one of the clerks had come
around the counter to see what the trouble was.

75   Pete sat up and drank the water, putting on a good act. "I just fainted, I guess."

"Let me get you a chair," one clerk said.

"No, I think I'd better just go home." He brushed off his suit and thanked them. "I'll
be back when I'm feeling better." He hadn't dared to look at Johnny, and he hoped the
diamonds had gone out the window as planned.

80   He took the elevator downstairs and strolled across the plaza to the fountain. There
was always a crowd around it at noon—secretaries eating their lunches out of brown-paper
bags, young men casually chatting with them. He mingled unnoticed and worked his way
to the edge of the pool. But it was a big area, and through the rippling water he couldn't
be certain he saw anything except the scattering of pennies and nickels at the bottom.
85   Well, he hadn't expected to see the diamonds anyway, so he wasn't disappointed.

He waited an hour, then decided the police must still be questioning Johnny. The
best thing to do was to head for his apartment and wait for a call.

It came two hours later.

"That was a close one," Johnny said. "They finally let me go, but they still might be
90   following me."

"Did you do it?"

"Sure I did it! What do you think they held me for? They were goin' crazy in there. But I can't talk now. Let's meet at the Birchbark in an hour. I'll make sure I'm not followed."

Pete took the same booth at the rear of the Birchbark and ordered his usual beer.

95 When Johnny arrived the dapper man was smiling. "I think we pulled it off, Pete. Damn if we didn't pull it off!"

"What'd you tell them?"

"That I didn't see a thing. Sure, I'd asked for the tray of stones, but then when there was the commotion in the hall I went to see what it was along with everyone else. There

100 were four customers in the place and they couldn't really pin it on any one of us. But they searched us all, and even took us downtown to be X-rayed, to be certain we hadn't swallowed the stones."

"I was wondering what took you so long."

"I was lucky to be out as soon as I was. A couple of the others acted more suspicious

105 than me, and that was a break. One of them even had an arrest record for a stolen car." He said it in a superior manner. "The dumb cops figure anyone who stole a car would steal diamonds."

"I hope they didn't get too good a look at me. I'm the one who caused the commotion, and they just gotta figure I'm involved."

110 "Don't worry. We'll pick up the diamonds tonight and get out of town for a while."

"How many stones were there?" Pete asked expectantly.

"Five. And all beauties."

The evening papers confirmed it. They placed the value of the five missing diamonds at $65,000. And the police had no clue.

115 They went back to the plaza around midnight, but Pete didn't like the feel of it. "They might be wise," he told Johnny. "Let's wait a night, in case the cops are still snoopin' around up there. Hell, the stones are safe where they are."

The following night, when the story had already disappeared from the papers, replaced by a bank robbery, they returned to the plaza once more. This time they waited till

120 three A.M., when even the late crowd from the bars had scattered for home. Johnny carried a flashlight and Pete wore wading boots. He'd already considered the possibility that one or two of the diamonds might not be found, but even so they'd be far ahead of the game.

The fountain was turned off at night, and the calmness of the water made the search easier. Wading in the shallow water, Pete found two of the gems almost at once. It took

125 another ten minutes to find the third one, and he was ready to quit then. "Let's take what we got, Johnny."

The flashlight bobbed. "No, no. Keep looking. Find us at least one more."

Suddenly they were pinned in the glare of a spotlight, and a voice shouted, "Hold it right there! We're police officers!"

130 "Damn!" Johnny dropped the flashlight and started to run, but already the two cops were out of their squad car. One of them pulled his gun and Johnny stopped in his tracks. Pete climbed from the pool and stood with his hands up.

"You got us, officer," he said.

"Damn right we got you," the cop with the gun growled.

135 "The coins in that fountain go to charity every month. Anybody that would steal them has to be pretty low. I hope the judge gives you both ninety days in the cooler. Now up against the car while we search you!"

(1,000 words)

—by Edward D. Hoch, from *Ellery Queen's Mystery Magazine*

THINKING AND WRITING AFTER READING

RECALL   Self-test your understanding.

Your instructor may choose to give you a true-false comprehension review.

REACT Greed prompted the robbery, but how did excessive greed figure into the arrest? _____

_____

REFLECT What could Pete and Johnny have done when the police caught them to escape charges for the diamond robbery?_____

_____

THINKING CRITICALLY This story was first published in 1975. What modern changes in building construction and security might make such a heist far less probable today? Write your answer on a separate sheet of paper.

THINK AND WRITE What better or "safer" plan might have been devised for getting diamonds out of the fountain? Explain your ideas. _____

_____

INFERENCE QUESTIONS

1. Why does Pete want Johnny rather than himself to steal the diamonds?

   _____

   _____

2. Why does Pete's plan call for retrieving the diamonds a night or two after they are stolen? _____

   _____

   _____

3. What is the meaning of the phrase "Dapper Dan"? _____

   _____

4. Why was Johnny not arrested as a suspect in the crime? _____

   _____

   _____

5. What is suggested by the phrase "Pete didn't like the feel of it"? _____

   _____

   _____

Interpret the Quote

Now that you have finished reading the selection, "A Deal in Diamonds," go back to the beginning of the selection and read the opening quote again. In the story, Pete and Johnny go to great lengths to steal the diamonds, yet what does Malcolm Forbes' quote say about the value of diamonds? On a separate sheet of paper, list three things (other than diamonds) that become valuable over time, and explain why.

Name _____

Date _____

COMPREHENSION QUESTIONS

Answer the following *T* (true) or *F* (false).

Inference _____ 1. The diamond heist could have taken place in New York but not in Las Vegas.

Inference _____ 2. Johnny Stoop would have been detained longer by the police if the robbery had been in California.

Inference _____ 3. Pete gambled correctly that office workers having lunch around the fountain would not see the falling diamonds.

Inference _____ 4. The irony of the story is that the police arrested the right men for the wrong reasons.

Inference _____ 5. The reader can conclude that Johnny and Pete will be charged with the diamond robbery.

Inference _____ 6. The security guard was suspicious of Pete's fainting spell.

Inference _____ 7. The reader can conclude that one of the suspected Diamond Exchange customers confessed to a previous arrest.

Inference _____ 8. The two men were worried that the police might find the diamonds in the fountain if they waited longer than a night or two to collect them.

Detail _____ 9. Pete and Johnny found four of the diamonds before they were arrested.

Inference _____ 10. The police officers suspected that they had apprehended the men responsible for the diamond theft.

VOCABULARY

Answer the following with *a, b, c,* or *d* for the word or phrase that best defines the boldface word used in the selection. The number in parentheses indicates the line of the passage in which the word appears.

_____ 1. "**strolled** over" (5)
    a. walked slowly
    b. called
    c. walked quickly
    d. looked

_____ 2. "a real **fashion-plate**" (6)
    a. set of dinner dishes
    b. well-dressed person
    c. jerk
    d. criminal

_____ 3. "almost **reluctantly**" (22)
    a. happily
    b. willingly
    c. quietly
    d. unenthusiastically

_____ 4. "create a **commotion**" (32)
    a. play
    b. job
    c. interest
    d. disturbance

5. "**previous** day" (68)
a. subsequent
b. prior
c. following
d. later

8. "**confirmed** it" (113)
a. reported
b. proved
c. valued
d. ignored

6. "He **mingled**" (82)
a. blended
b. walked
c. talked
d. shopped

9. "**Wading** in" (124)
a. walking
b. looking
c. finding
d. hiding

7. "**dapper** man" (95)
a. grubby
b. smelly
c. elegant
d. happy

10. "in the **cooler**" (136)
a. refrigerator
b. freezer
c. drink
d. jail

Your instructor may choose to give a true-false vocabulary review.

VOCABULARY ENRICHMENT

Figurative Language

Writers and speakers use figurative language to spark the imagination and make the message more sensual and visual. The words create images in the mind and activate associations stored in memory. Figurative language is challenging, because figuring out the meaning demands logical and creative thinking.

A. **Simile.** A simile uses the words *like* or *as* to compare two unlike things. The purpose of a simile is to strengthen the message by adding a visual image. Similes usually dramatize the characteristics of nouns. As a reader, you must figure out the unique characteristic the simile is describing. In the sentence, "The new teacher stood like a statue in front of the class," what does the simile add to the meaning? "Like a statue" describes the teacher as "stiff and unmoving." The simile adds humor and visual interest to the sentence.

Write the meaning of the boldface similes in the following sentences.

1. The boys were **like two peas in a pod** working on their handheld electronic devices. _____

2. My grandmother claims to be **as old as the hills**. _____
   _____

3. Her face was **as fresh as the morning dew**. _____
   _____

4. When he walked into the arcade, the little boy smiled **like a fox in a henhouse**. _____

5. Looking for the missing check was **like trying to find a needle in a haystack**. _____

B. **Metaphor.** Whereas a simile uses the words *like* or *as* to compare two unlike things, a metaphor does not use those words but instead states the comparison directly. For example, "The soccer player was a tiger" is a metaphor that dramatizes the player's aggressive spirit. If the statement had been, "The girl plays soccer like a tiger," the figure of speech would be a simile, but the meaning would remain the same.

Write the meaning of the boldface metaphors in the following sentences.

6. Superman is **made of steel**. _____

7. Her words were **daggers** directed toward his heart. _____

_____

8. She was a **willow** in the winds of time. _____

_____

9. The woman had **built a wall** between herself and others. _____

_____

10. He was her **world**. _____

ASSESS YOUR LEARNING

Review confusing questions, seek clarification, and make notes in your textbook to help you remember the new information and vocabulary.

Vocabulary Lesson

Come Together, Hold Together, and Shut

Study the roots, words, and sentences.

Roots	*greg*: come together, group	*clud, clus*: shut
	ten, tent, tain, tinu: hold together, hold	

Words with *greg* = *come together, group*

Does a congregation sing hymns? Have men's clubs desegregated?

- Congregate: to flock together

  Students usually *congregate* in the gym prior to the first class period.

- Gregarious: outgoing; enjoying groups

  Gregarious people enjoy parties.

- Aggregation: a collection or union

  The steering committee was an *aggregation* of members of six sororities.

- Egregious: conspicuous; the worst of the group

  The *egregious* error was easy to detect but costly to fix.

- Segregate: to separate from the group

  Before eating M&Ms, do you *segregate* the red ones?

Words with *ten, tent, tain, tinu* = *hold together, hold*

Will a lock secure the contents? Is daily maintenance needed?

- Tenant: one who holds a lease on a house or apartment

  The present *tenant* pays his rent early.

- Tenacity: quality of holding together for a purpose

  Do you have the drive and *tenacity* to run for public office?

- Contented: easy in mind or satisfied

  A *contented* dog is usually one that is well fed.

- Contentment: satisfaction with one's lot

  Money is not essential for *contentment*, but it does help.

- Intent: purpose, concentration, holding one's mind on a single matter

  What is the *intent* of this lengthy proposal?

- Retain: to hold secure

  With a majority in the Senate, the Republicans can *retain* power.

- Continuously: without stopping

  In summer, the Niagara River flows *continuously* over Horseshoe Falls.

- Tenable: able to be held or defended

  Paying for the damage is a *tenable* resolution to the accident.

- Untenable: cannot be held

  Continuing a relationship after being abused is *untenable*.

- Discontented: not content

  I am *discontented* with my grades, because I know I can do better.

Words with *clud* or *clus* = *shut*

Should <u>conclusive</u> evidence result in a conviction? Is your <u>conclusion</u> final?

- Recluse: one who shuts himself or herself away from others, a hermit

  The *recluse* left the island only to get provisions.

- Exclude: to shut out

  Do not *exclude* your friends from your joys or sorrows.

- Inclusive: counting everything

  The quoted price is *inclusive* of tax and shipping.

- Seclude: to remove, shut off

  In order to recuperate, he wanted to *seclude* himself from visitors.

- Preclude: to close beforehand or hinder

  Having a mobile phone does not *preclude* the need for an answering machine on your home telephone.

Review

Part I

Answer the following with true (*T*) or false (*F*).

_____ 1. Gregarious students are usually shy.

_____ 2. If you segregate your socks by color, you mix them in one group.

_____ 3. When students congregate in the doorway, entrance can be difficult.

_____ 4. An egregious boor is usually a desirable companion.

_____ 5. Desegregated schools bring together students of different backgrounds.

_____ 6. Contented babies cry excessively.

_____ 7. If you retain your job, you keep your position.

_____ 8. A winning lawyer has a tenable case.

_____ 9. To seclude yourself is to join the group for the celebration.

_____10. An inclusive organization welcomes entry to many.

Part II

Choose the best word from the list as a synonym for the following.

| intent | tenacity | contents | recluse | conclusion |
| maintenance | aggregation | tenant | congregation | contentment |

11. hermit   _____

12. renter   _____

13. happiness   _____

14. collection   _____

15. purpose   _____

16. final statement   _____

17. flock   _____

18. determination   _____

19. upkeep   _____

20. belongings   _____

Reading Newspaper Editorials

Editorials. Unlike news stories, **editorials** are one of the few types of articles in newspapers that are subjective—that is, they express the opinion of a person or organization. A newspaper's editorial pages feature the views of its management and editors. Issues discussed in these pieces are usually related to particular local, national, or international news stories.

Although the style of editorials varies as widely as people's opinions, the basic format is usually the same: Two or three brief paragraphs describe a scene or provide historical background leading up to the main theme the writer intends to discuss. After stating a position, the writer follows up with examples, data, and analysis to support the position. Once the case has been made, alternative ideas and solutions may be provided and may also include the writer's prediction of what will happen if the current situation is not changed. The final paragraphs summarize and restate the main idea of the editorial.

Remember that editorials *always express opinions*, and regardless of how persuasive the writer's argument might be, you are free to reject it. Newspapers encourage readers to express their own opinions—either for or against editorials—in Letters to the Editor. Selected letters are published in the newspaper, usually in the same section with the editorials, and they often feature the views of readers who disagree with recent editorials or with the way in which a news story has been reported.

Reader's Tip   Reading Editorials

While reading editorials, ask yourself the following questions:

- What event prompted the editorial?
- What is the thesis or opinion being promoted by the author?
- Do the details prove the thesis?
- Is the author liberal or conservative?
- What is left out?
- Are the sources, facts, and other support credible?

exercise 1

Read the following editorial to answer the questions.

1. What event does the writer describe to introduce the main idea? _____

_____

_____

2. What is the writer's main idea? _____

_____

Tuesday, April 25, 2008

EDITORIAL PAGE

Political Poverty

In a recent speech to the Linville Chamber of Commerce, Mayor Anderson praised the city council for its "new direction" and its efforts to eliminate city programs that "throw money" at social problems. The audience found this statement to their liking and responded enthusiastically.

However, one phrase in the mayor's speech was quite revealing. He believes it is wrong to expect "governments . . . to take over the upbringing of all who choose the low road to poverty."

What sort of misguided thinking is this—not only to blame those who are "grossly neglected" (as the Mayor characterized them) and who have "special needs for their predicaments," but to further stigmatize them by calling theirs "the low road"?

People do not choose poverty. People do not choose the obstacles they must overcome any more than they choose the family into which they are born. The physically challenged, the culturally deprived, and those lacking sufficient education can certainly take the responsibility for changing their circumstances, but cannot be blamed for those circumstances—no matter how convenient it may be for addressing the city's fiscal difficulties.

A moral society bears responsibility for providing aid and education to the less fortunate. We all contribute to this effort by paying our taxes. However, all too often our culture also rushes to blame victims for their own predicaments. This is because we have an unrealistic sense of our own immunity and invulnerability, believing we can avoid or surmount any challenge—in other words, always thinking "that could never happen to me." Perhaps we would feel more humble if we were the ones trying to overcome catastrophic illness without adequate medical care, trying to find a job without the skills provided by a sound public education system, or trying to feed a family on a minimum-wage salary. In such circumstances, the luxury of being as smug and self-assured as the mayor, the city council, and the Chamber members are would certainly be lost.

Proponents of this so-called new direction absolve themselves too easily of moral responsibility when the low road that they have chosen is one of convenience and callous indifference toward those already burdened and less fortunate than themselves.

3. What one example does the writer give that would help the mayor better understand this position? _____

_____

4. Is the author liberal or conservative? _____

5. Is the main idea supported primarily by facts or opinions? _____

exercise 2 Locate an editorial that interests you in a local, city, or national newspaper. Cut out the editorial and answer the following questions:

1. What event prompted the editorial? _____

2. What is the author's opinion on the issue? _____

3. Do the details prove the thesis? Are they credible? _____

4. What has been left out? _____

11 Critical Reading

- What is an author's purpose or intent?
- What is point of view?
- What is bias?
- What is tone?
- How do you distinguish between fact and opinion?
- What are fallacies?

Everyday Reading Skills: Evaluating Internet Information

What Do Critical Readers Do?

Critical readers do not accept the idea that "If it's in print, it must be true." They do not immediately accept the thinking of others. Rather, they use direct statements, inferences, prior knowledge, and language clues to assess and evaluate. They think for themselves, analyze written material in their search for truth, and then decide how accurate and relevant the printed words are.

Recognize the Author's Purpose or Intent

Authors write with a particular **purpose** or **intent** in mind. For example, you might be instructed to write a scientific paper on environmental pollution with the ultimate purpose of inspiring classmates to recycle. In writing the paper, you must both educate and persuade, but your overriding goal is persuasion. Therefore, you will choose and use only the facts that support your argument. Your critical reading audience will then carefully evaluate your scientific support, recognizing that your purpose was to persuade and not really to educate, and thus decide whether to recycle all or some combination of paper, glass, aluminum, and plastic. The author's reason for writing can alert the reader to be accepting or suspicious. These are three common purposes for writing:

- **To inform.** Authors use facts to inform, to explain, to educate, and to enlighten. The purpose of textbooks is usually to inform or explain, but sometimes an author might venture into persuasion, particularly on topics such as smoking or recycling.
- **To persuade.** Authors use a combination of facts and opinions to persuade, to argue, to condemn, and to ridicule. Editorials in newspapers are written to argue a point and persuade the reader.
- **To entertain.** Authors use fiction and nonfiction to entertain, to narrate, to describe, and to shock. Novels, short stories, and essays are written to entertain. Sometimes an author may adopt a guise of humor in order to entertain and achieve a special result.

EXAMPLE For each of the following topic sentences, decide whether the author's main purpose is to inform (*I*), to persuade (*P*), or to entertain (*E*).

_____ 1. Telling secrets in the form of public confessions on television talk shows is detrimental to building healthy, satisfying relationships. Such talk shows reveal the worst in human behavior and should be taken off the air.

_____ 2. Self-disclosure in communication means revealing information about yourself, usually in exchange for information about the other person.

_____ 3. Daytime viewers don't seem too surprised to find that Sam has been married to two other women while he has been dating Lucinda, who is carrying his third child and is having an affair with Sam's best friend.

EXPLANATION The purpose of the first sentence is to persuade the reader to condemn such programs for the harm they can cause the participants. The purpose of the second sentence is simply to inform or educate by giving a definition. The last sentence exaggerates in order to entertain.

exercise 1   Identify the main purpose of each of the following as to inform (*I*), to persuade (*P*), or to entertain (*E*).

_____ 1. Lucy and Rachel were both 11 years old when they met in the textile mill for work. When they were not changing the bobbins on the spinning machines, they could laugh with each other and dream of trips back home.

_____ 2. Samuel Slater opened a new textile mill in Rhode Island in 1790 and employed seven boys and two girls between the ages of 7 and 12. The children were whipped with a leather strap and sprayed with water to keep them awake and alert. Consolidating such a workforce under one roof, the children could produce three times as much as whole families working at home.

_____ 3. The textile mills of the late eighteenth century in America were not unlike the sweatshops of Central America today. Children were employed for pennies under the supervision of an adult who was concerned about profit. Today, however, enlightened Americans are buying the product of the labor of foreign children. Perhaps Americans should think before buying.

_____ 4. To be successful in the future, retail companies must embrace e-commerce and establish creative Web sites that are easy for customers to use. Learn to use the Internet for advertising, marketing, and retailing.

_____ 5. In response to a drop in profits, Gap Inc. opened Old Navy stores targeted at discount shoppers. This created a three-tiered organization. The company's Banana Republic is designed to appeal to high-end shoppers, The Gap to a middle market searching for quality casual clothing, and Old Navy for the bargain hunters.

_____ 6. She quickened her pace as the footsteps behind her became louder. Was he following her, or did he just happen to be turning down Grove Street, too?

exercise 2   Read the passages and identify the author's purpose for each by responding with *a, b, c,* or *d.*

Passage 1

KEEP YOUR EYES ON FINLAND

Despite its small size and relative isolation in the Arctic Circle, Finland leads the pack in mobile phone technology and its applications. The country is a laboratory of eager users and will soon pioneer the use of so-called third-generation mobile phones that boast lightning-quick access to the Internet. Part of the reason for Finland's advancement is its geography. When telecommunications developed in the 1970s, Finns were more inclined to pursue wireless options because the costs of running cable to isolated pockets of a vast and frozen nation were daunting. Thus wireless technology became a priority for the government and the private sector.

—*Business Today,* Tenth Edition,
by Michael Mescon et al.

_____ 1. The primary purpose of this passage is to

    a. support fast mobile phone access to the Internet.
    b. explain why Finland is the leader in mobile phone technology.
    c. argue against Finland's leadership in mobile phone technology.
    d. compare cable phones with wireless options.

_____ 2. The author describes Finland as a "vast and frozen nation" in order to

    a. compliment the Finns on their struggle with nature.
    b. show that employment is difficult and the industry provides jobs.
    c. explain the cause-and-effect relationship that has motivated excellence in the industry.
    d. show how Finns have reduced spending to increase profits.

Passage 2

JANE ADDAMS

Without knowing why, Jane Addams opened her eyes. It was pitch-black in her bedroom, and at first, she heard nothing more than the muted night noises of the Chicago streets surrounding Hull House. Then she saw what had disturbed her sleep. A burglar had pried open the second-story window and was rifling her bureau drawers. Jane spoke quietly, "Don't make a noise." The man whirled around, then prepared to leap out the window. "You'll be hurt if you go that way," Jane calmly observed. A conversation ensued in the darkness. Addams learned that the intruder was not a professional thief, but simply a desperate man who could find no employment that winter of 1890 and had turned to crime to survive. Hull House had been founded the previous fall as a social "settlement" to serve just such people. It testified to Jane Addams's belief that only unfavorable circumstances stood between the innate dignity and worth of every individual and their realization. Moreover, Addams believed that as a well-to-do, cultivated lady she had a special responsibility for alleviating the social ills accompanying the nation's growth. So she was in earnest when she promised her unexpected visitor that if he would come back the next morning, she would try to help. The burglar agreed, walked down the main stairs, and left by the front door. At 9 A.M. he returned to learn that Jane Addams had found him a job.

—From These Beginnings, Sixth Edition,
by Roderick Nash and Edward Graves

_____ 1. The primary purpose of this passage is to

    a. explain how Hull House operated on a daily basis.
    b. illustrate Jane Addams's courage and commitment to her cause.
    c. argue the need for social settlements to assist the needy.
    d. educate the public on the reasons for crime.

_____ 2. The author implies that Hull House was designed primarily to serve

    a. drug users.
    b. the mentally ill.
    c. criminals after release from jail.
    d. people down on their luck.

Passage 3

POPULARITY OF PART-TIMERS

Some experts claim that full-time, core employees are paid for eight hours of work but actually work closer to six or seven. This discrepancy is because it may take ten minutes or more for them to get ready to work, two fifteen-minute breaks are required, and often employees start getting ready to leave before the end of their work day. In contrast, part-timers employed for four hours may actually work at top performance for almost the entire period.

Part-time workers can be divided into three classifications: (1) full-time students who seek "peak period" jobs for approximately twenty hours per week to help with educational expenses, (2) housewives who seek part-time work so they can devote more time to children, and (3) retired people who wish to supplement their retirement incomes.

Many supervisors claim that part-timers are a welcome challenge when it comes to weaving them into the general mix of employees. They like the enthusiasm, energy, and flexibility they bring with them. Others claim that the high turnover rate of part-timers negates their advantages. All agree that it takes additional time and energy from the supervisor to convert part-timers into productive members of a work team.

—*Supervisor's Survival Kit,* Ninth Edition,
by Elwood N. Chapman and Cliff Goodwin

_____ 1. The primary purpose of this passage is to

    a. condemn society's reliance on part-time workers.
    b. explain the downside of relying on part-timers in the workforce.
    c. discuss methods employees can use to increase the productivity of part-time workers.
    d. discuss the pros and cons of part-time work for both employers and employees.

_____ 2. The author implies that

    a. employers are split in their opinions of the advantages of part-time workers.
    b. full-time workers put in fewer hours because part-timers are more committed to getting the job done.
    c. part-time work can be considered to range from twenty to forty hours per week.
    d. the majority of part-time employees are students.

Recognize the Author's Point of View or Bias

If you were reading an article analyzing George W. Bush's achievements as president, you might ask, "Is this written by a Republican or a Democrat?" The answer would help you understand the point of view or bias from which the author is writing and thus help you evaluate the accuracy and relevance of the message.

Point of view refers to the opinions and beliefs of the author or of the reader, and a critical reader must recognize how those beliefs influence the message. Students sometimes find the term *point of view* confusing because, when discussing literature, point of view refers to the narrative voice the author is using: first, second, or third person. In this chapter, however, point of view refers to an opinion or position on a subject. For example, if you were reading an article on UFOs you would ask, "Does the author write from the point of view of a believer or a nonbeliever in aliens?"

Bias is a word closely related to point of view. However, the term *bias* tends to be associated with prejudice, and thus it has a negative connotation. A bias, like a point of view, is an opinion or a judgment. Either may be based on solid facts or on incorrect information, but a bias suggests that an author leans to one side, unequally presenting evidence and arguments. All authors write from a certain point of view, but not all authors have the same degree of bias.

Because both writers and readers are people with opinions, their biases interact on the printed page. Thus critical readers need to recognize an author's bias or point of view as well as their own. For example, a reader might fail to understand an author's position on legalizing prostitution because the reader is totally opposed to the idea. In such a case, the reader's bias or point of view on the subject can interfere with comprehension.

EXAMPLE

Respond to the following statement by describing the author's point of view or bias, as well as your own.

African animals are endangered and should not be killed for their fur to make coats. Minks, however, are a different story and should be considered separately. Minks are farmed animals that are produced only for their fur.

Explain the author's point of view/bias. _____

Explain your own position on the topic. _____

EXPLANATION The author implies that minks are not endangered and should be used in making fur coats. Your position may be the same, or you may think that being on the endangered list is not the only issue. You may feel that animals should not be used for clothing.

exercise 3

The following statements adamantly express only one side of an issue. Read each statement and mark whether you agree (*A*) or disagree (*D*). Then describe the point of view/bias of the author and your own position.

_____ 1. Citizens deserve to be protected from pornography on the Internet. Although pictures of child pornography are now prohibited on the Internet, lessons on how to seduce grade school children are perfectly legal in chat rooms and news groups. First Amendment rights should not outweigh our need to protect the population from deviant behaviors.

Explain the author's point of view/bias. _____

_____

Explain your own point of view/bias. _____

_____

_____ 2. Reproductive technology has outpaced the law and is in need of record keeping. In a fertility laboratory, the sperm of one anonymous donor is united with the egg of another anonymous donor. Then the fertilized product is implanted into a hopeful parent who never knows the identity of either donor. Considering that such donors usually make multiple contributions, how can children be sure in future years that they are not marrying brothers or sisters?

Explain the author's point of view/bias. _____

_____

Explain your own point of view/bias. _____
_____

_____ 3. An overwhelming amount of this nation's land is owned by the government in the form of national parks and forests. This is especially true in the West. Much of this land is not needed for public recreation and could be sold to private enterprise, with the proceeds going to pay off part of the national debt.

Explain the author's point of view/bias. _____
_____

Explain your own point of view/bias. _____
_____

_____ 4. Is a parent responsible for a child's actions? Because some parents neglect their parental duties when signs of danger are obvious, public interest in parental duty laws is increasing. Under such laws, parents can no longer look the other way while society suffers the consequences.

Explain the author's point of view/bias. _____
_____

Explain your own point of view/bias. _____
_____

_____ 5. Cities that have teen curfews violate the rights of responsible teens. Those teens who obey are forced to curtail wholesome activities while violators continue as if there were no curfew.

Explain the author's point of view/bias. _____
_____

Explain your own point of view/bias. _____
_____

exercise 4

Read the following description of Napoleon Bonaparte from a freshman history textbook. Keep in mind that Napoleon is generally considered one of the great heroes of France and one of the greatest conquerors of the world. Does this passage say exactly what you would expect? Analyze the author's point of view, and answer the questions that follow with *T* (true) or *F* (false).

Passage 1

Napoleon was a short, swarthy, handsome man with remarkable, magnetic eyes. Slender as a youth, he exhibited a tendency toward obesity as he grew older. He was high-strung, and his manners were coarse. Militarily, he has been both denigrated and extolled. On the one hand, his success has been attributed to luck and the great skill of his professional lieutenants; on the other, he has been compared with the greatest conquerors of the past. Politically, he combined the shrewdness of a Machiavellian despot with the majesty of a "sun king." It is generally conceded that he was one of the giants of history. He had an exalted belief in his own destiny, but as an utter cynic and misanthrope felt only contempt for the human race. He once exclaimed, "What do a million men matter to such as I?" The world was Napoleon's oyster. He considered himself emancipated from moral scruples. Yet this man, who despised humanity, was worshiped by the millions he held in such contempt. To his soldiers he was the invincible hero, a supreme ruler over men, literally a *demi-god.* He came from nowhere, but was endowed with an extraordinary mind and the charisma required for masterful leadership. He used democracy to destroy democracy. He employed the slogans of revolution to fasten his hold on nations. His great empire collapsed, but his name will never be forgotten.

—*A History of the Western World,*
by Solomon Modell

_____ 1. The author wants to present Napoleon as a demigod.

_____ 2. The author shows Napoleon as the greatest military leader in history.

_____ 3. The author feels that Napoleon effectively used propaganda for his own benefit.

_____ 4. The author wants to show the differences between the public and the private views of Napoleon.

_____ 5. The author feels that Napoleon adhered to a strict moral code.

_____ 6. The author feels that Napoleon matured into a handsome, well-mannered gentleman.

_____ 7. The author believes that Napoleon's success was due primarily to good luck.

_____ 8. The author feels that Napoleon had little regard for the average person.

_____ 9. The author feels that Napoleon is undeserving of a prominent place in history.

_____ 10. The author feels that Napoleon used ruthless tactics to get what he wanted.

The author gives a cynical description of Napoleon. For example, he relates a quote attributed to Napoleon that shows him in an unfavorable light. The critical reader needs to be aware that other accounts show Napoleon as a great leader who was concerned for his soldiers and wanted the best for France.

Read Passage 2 for a somewhat different view of Napoleon. Then answer the questions that follow.

Passage 2

Few men in Western history have compelled the attention of the world as Napoleon Bonaparte did during the fifteen years of his absolutist rule in France. Schooled in France and at the military academy in Paris, he possessed a mind congenial to the ideas of the Enlightenment—creative, imaginative, and ready to perceive things anew. His primary interests were history, law, and mathematics. His particular strengths as a leader lay in his ability to conceive of financial, legal, or military plans and then to master their every detail; his capacity for inspiring others, even those initially opposed to him; and his belief in himself as the destined savior of the French. That last conviction eventually became the obsession that led to Napoleon's undoing. But supreme self-confidence was just what the French government lacked since the first days of the revolution. Napoleon believed both in himself and in France. That latter belief was the tonic France now needed, and Napoleon proceeded to administer it in liberally revivifying doses.

—*Western Civilizations,*
by Edward McNall Berns et al.

_____ 1. This author has a more positive opinion of Napoleon than did the previous author.

_____ 2. This author believes that Napoleon's initial self-confidence was unwelcome in France.

_____ 3. This author suggests that Napoleon developed a mental obsession about being a destined savior that led to his decline.

_____ 4. This author does not imply that Napoleon hated humanity.

_____ 5. This author believes that Napoleon failed to attend to details and thus lost power.

Recognize the Author's Tone

The author's **tone** describes the writer's attitude toward the subject. An easy trick to distinguish tone is to think of tone of voice. When someone is speaking, voice sounds usually indicate whether the person is angry, romantic, or joyful. In reading, however, you cannot hear the voice, but you can pick up clues from the choice of words and details.

As a critical reader, tune in to the author's tone, and thus let attitude become a part of evaluating the message. For example, an optimistic tone on water pollution might make you suspicious that the author has overlooked information, whereas an extremely pessimistic article on the same subject might overwhelm you, causing you to discount valuable information.

EXAMPLE Identify the tone of the following passage.

Tiger Woods doesn't just play golf well, he plays better than anyone in the world. His father, Earl, taught the 1-year-old Tiger to putt, and the next year Tiger beat Bob Hope at putting on a national television show. By age 3, the amazing Tiger shot a 48 for 9 holes, and at age 8 he won an international junior tournament.

_____ 1. The author's tone is

a. nostalgic.
b. ironic.
c. admiring.

EXPLANATION The details chronicle Tiger's amazing early success with wonder and admiration. The tone is admiring of his exceptional talent.

Reader's *Tip* Recognizing the Author's Tone

The following list of words with explanations can describe an author's tone or attitude:

- **absurd, farcical, ridiculous**: laughable or a joke
- **ambivalent, apathetic, detached**: not caring
- **angry, bitter, hateful**: feeling bad and upset about the topic
- **arrogant, condescending**: acting conceited or above others
- **awestruck, admiring, wondering**: filled with wonder
- **cheerful, joyous, happy**: feeling good about the topic
- **compassionate, sympathetic**: feeling sorrow at the distress of others
- **complex**: intricate, complicated, and entangled with confusing parts
- **congratulatory, celebratory**: honoring an achievement or festive occasion
- **cruel, malicious**: meanspirited
- **cynical**: expecting the worst from people
- **depressed, melancholy**: sad, dejected, or having low spirits
- **disapproving**: judging unfavorably
- **distressed**: suffering strain, misery, or agony
- **evasive, abstruse**: avoiding or confusing the issue
- **formal**: using an official style
- **frustrated**: blocked from a goal
- **gentle**: kind or of a high social class
- **ghoulish, grim**: robbing graves or feeding on corpses; stern and forbidding
- **hard**: unfeeling, strict, and unrelenting
- **humorous, jovial, comic, playful, amused**: being funny
- **incredulous**: unbelieving
- **indignant:** outraged
- **intense, impassioned**: extremely involved, zealous, or agitated
- **ironic**: the opposite of what is expected; a twist at the end
- **irreverent**: lack of respect for authority
- **mocking, scornful, caustic, condemning**: ridiculing the topic
- **objective, factual, straightforward, critical**: using facts without emotions
- **obsequious**: fawning for attention
- **optimistic**: looking on the bright side
- **outspoken**: speaking one's mind on issues
- **pathetic**: moving one to compassion or pity
- **pessimistic**: looking on the negative side
- **prayerful**: religiously thankful
- **reticent**: shy and not speaking out
- **reverent:** showing respect
- **righteous**: morally correct
- **romantic, intimate, loving**: expressing love or affection
- **sarcastic**: saying one thing and meaning another
- **satiric**: using irony, wit, and sarcasm to discredit or ridicule
- **sensational**: overdramatized or overhyped
- **sentimental, nostalgic**: remembering the good old days
- **serious, sincere, earnest, solemn**: being honest and concerned
- **straightforward**: forthright
- **subjective, opinionated**: expressing opinions and feelings
- **tragic**: regrettable or deplorable mistake
- **uneasy**: restless or uncertain
- **vindictive**: seeking revenge

exercise 5   Mark the letter that identifies the tone for each of the following sentences.

_____ 1. Baseball was invented as an urban game in order for owners to make money, players to become arrogant, and spectators to drink overpriced beer.

    a. objective
    b. nostalgic
    c. cynical

_____ 2. The Puritans came to the new land for religious freedom, yet they allowed their followers little freedom. Anne Hutchinson was banished from the colony for preaching that salvation can come through good works.

    a. optimistic
    b. ironic
    c. sentimental

_____ 3. When I study now, I'm in a lab with fifty noisy computers. What happened to the quiet chair in a corner with a table for your books, papers, and pencils?

    a. objective
    b. cheerful
    c. nostalgic

_____ 4. According to a recent study in a book called _Living Well_, sexually active partners who do not use contraceptives stand an 85 percent chance of conceiving within a year.

    a. subjective
    b. objective
    c. sarcastic

_____ 5. If given the funding, scientists could trace most aggressive behavior, crime, and violence to either too much testosterone or low blood sugar.

    a. sentimental
    b. subjective
    c. objective

_____ 6. On hot summer days, the health risks increase as auto exhaust from rush hour traffic pollutes the air, threatens our lungs, and damages the ozone layer.

    a. disapproving
    b. reverent
    c. incredulous

_____ 7. Aging can be isolating and lonely. As mobility becomes more limited, the elderly patiently wait for the excitement of a friend's call or a child's next visit.

    a. evasive
    b. righteous
    c. sympathetic

_____ 8. Is the top of the world as crowded as Times Square? According to official records, the greatest number of people to reach the summit of Mount Everest on a single day is 89. The number of corpses still remaining on Everest is 120.

    a. sarcastic
    b. optimistic
    c. indignant

exercise 6

Read the passages and answer the questions that follow by writing in the blanks or answering with *a, b, c,* or *d.*

Passage 1

TECHNO-BORES

Techno-bores are like chemically altered bores in that their condition (infatuation with technology—often computers) blinds them to the possibility that *your* reality simply isn't theirs. Details about the latest software or synthesizer are lost on you.

    The curious thing about computer-obsessed bores is that their behavior appears to have been directly influenced by the machines they love—you can see little floppy disks spinning in their eyes when they speak; their sentences come out in a robotic cadence. Don't even consider launching a personal question in the direction of a techno-bore—you may cause a short circuit.

—"The Ten Most Memorable Bores,"
by Margot Mifflin

1. What is the tone of the passage? _____

2. What clues reveal the author's tone? _____

_____

Passage 2

STONE CRABS

One of the more regrettable circumstances attendant upon the tourist invasion of Dade County, Florida, of recent winters, was the discovery by visitors of the stone crab.

    The home folks in Dade County, Florida, have long esteemed the stone crab, the greatest of native delicacies, and can remember when they were so numerous that a man could dip a foot anywhere in Biscayne Bay and come up with a stone crab hanging on each toe. Or lacking the energy to dunk a pedal he could buy more stone crabs for a few bits than a horse could lug.

    Since the winter visitors got on to the stone crab, however, the crustaceans have become scarce and costly. They now sell by the karat. They are so expensive that the home folks are inclined to leave them off their menus. The visitors eat more of the stone crab nowadays and this is all the more deplorable when you reflect that stone crabs are really too good for visitors. A certificate of at least four years residence in Dade County should be required of every person desiring stone crabs.

—"The Brighter Side," by Damon Runyon

_____ 1. The author's tone is

    a. bitter.
    b. serious.
    c. humorous.
    d. sympathetic.

_____ 2. The author's primary purpose is to

    a. educate.
    b. entertain.
    c. narrate.
    d. shock.

Passage 3

TAKING THE TEST

For the next two weeks I ate bacon cheeseburgers almost daily, a series of last meals. Every time the phone rang, at home or at the office, I felt an electric anxiety. My doctor had promised he would not call, but I kept hoping he'd break our agreement and phone to say I was negative. That way I could sleep at night. He didn't call. I grew more obsessed daily. Even though for hours at a time I'd forget to anticipate my test results, my fear would ambush me like a bowel-loosening punch in the gut. I told myself that I wouldn't die the very day the doctor told me the bad news. My HIV-positive friends, and those who had been diagnosed with AIDS, were still alive—mostly. They'd coped. I'd cope too. Cold comfort.

—"Taking the Test," by David Groff

_____ 1. The author's tone is

    a. bitter.
    b. fearful.
    c. sarcastic.
    d. intellectual.

_____ 2. The author's primary purpose is

    a. to argue.
    b. to criticize.
    c. to describe.
    d. to entertain.

Passage 4

ZOO DOO

Sometimes, companies don't realize how valuable their by-products are. For example, most zoos don't realize that one of their by-products—their occupants' manure—can be an excellent source of additional revenue. Sales of the fragrant by-product can be substantial. So far, novelty sales have been the largest, with tiny containers of Zoo Doo (and even "Love, Love Me Doo" valentines) available in 160 zoo stores and 700 additional retail outlets. For the long-term market, Zoo-Doo looks to organic gardeners who buy 15 to 70 pounds of manure at a time. Zoo-Doo is already planning a "Dung of the Month" club to reach this lucrative by-products market.

—_Principles of Marketing,_ Ninth Edition,
by Philip Kotler and Gary Armstrong

_____ 1. The authors' tone is

    a. cynical.
    b. disapproving.
    c. incredulous.
    d. playful.

_____   2. The authors' primary purpose is

      a. to argue.
      b. to criticize.
      c. to educate.
      d. to narrate.

Passage 5

COSTCO

But this isn't a story about Wal-Mart. It's about Costco, the red-hot warehouse retailer that competes head-on with Wal-Mart's Sam's Club. Sam's Club is huge. With more than 550 stores and $40 billion in revenues, if Sam's Club were a separate company, it would be the seventh-largest U.S. retailer. But when it comes to warehouse retailing, it's Costco that's the bully, not the other way around.

With about the same number of members but 50 fewer stores, Costco outsells Sam's Club by 50 percent. Its $60 billion in sales makes Costco the nation's third-largest retailer, behind only Wal-Mart and Home Depot and one step ahead of Target. And unlike Wal-Mart and Sam's Club, Costco is growing at a torrid pace. In just the past four years, Costco's sales have surged 55 percent; profits are up 57 percent. Costco's same-store sales are growing at more than twice the rate of Wal-Mart's. How is Costco beating Sam's Club at its own low-price game? The two retailers are very similar in many ways. But inside the store, Costco adds a certain merchandising magic that Sam's Club just can't match.

—*Marketing, An Introduction,* Ninth Edition,
by Gary Armstrong and Philip Kotler

_____   1. The author's tone is

      a. admiring.
      b. nostalgic.
      c. serious.
      d. amused.

_____   2. The author's primary purpose is

      a. to entertain.
      b. to criticize.
      c. to narrate.
      d. to convince.

Passage 6

DECIMAL NOTATION

The set of arithmetic numbers, or nonnegative rational numbers, consists of the whole numbers 0, 1, 2, 3, 4, 5, 6, 7, 8, 9, 10, and so on, and fractions like 1/2, 2/3, 7/8, 17/10, and so on. Note that we can write the whole numbers using fraction notation. For example, 3 can be written as 3/1 We studied the use of fraction notation for arithmetic numbers in Chapter 2.

In Chapter 3, we will study the use of *decimal notation*. The word *decimal* comes from the Latin word *decima,* meaning a tenth part. Although we are using different notation, we are still considering the nonnegative rational numbers. Using decimal notation, we can write 0.875 for 7/8; for example, or 48.97 for 48 97/100.

—Developmental Mathematics: College Mathematics
and Introductory Algebra, Seventh Edition,
by Marvin L. Bittinger and Judith A. Beecher

———— 1. The author's tone is

       a. satiric.
       b. objective.
       c. irreverent.
       d. cheerful.

———— 2. The author's primary purpose is

       a. to narrate.
       b. to argue.
       c. to instruct.
       d. to describe.

Passage 7

THE GIFT

To pull the metal splinter from my palm
my father recited a story in a low voice.
I watched his lovely face and not the blade.
Before the story ended, he'd removed
the iron sliver I thought I'd die from.

I can't remember the tale,
but hear his voice still, a well
of dark water, a prayer.
And I recall his hands,
two measures of tenderness
he laid against my face,
the flames of discipline
he raised above my head.

Had you entered that afternoon
you would have thought you saw a man
planting something in a boy's palm,
a silver tear, a tiny flame.
Had you followed that boy
you would have arrived here,
where I bend over my wife's right hand.

Look how I shave her thumbnail down
so carefully she feels no pain.
Watch as I lift the splinter out.
I was seven when my father
took my hand like this,
and I did not hold that shard
between my fingers and think,

> *Metal that will bury me,*
> christen it Little Assassin,
> Ore Going Deep for My Heart.
> And I did not lift up my wound and cry,
> *Death visited here!*
> I did what a child does
> when he's given something to keep.
> I kissed my father.

—*The Gift,* by Li-Young Lee

_____ 1. The author's tone is

     a. loving.
     b. humorous.
     c. irreverent.
     d. cheerful.

_____ 2. The author's primary purpose is

     a. to narrate.
     b. to criticize.
     c. to instruct.
     d. to entertain.

Distinguish Fact from Opinion

The reader who cannot distinguish between fact and opinion will always remain gullible. By contrast, the critical reader realizes that most writing contains a combination of facts and opinions and is able to tell one from the other. A **fact** is a statement that can be proven true or false, whereas an **opinion** is a statement of feeling or belief that cannot be proven right or wrong.

EXAMPLE Mark the following stand-alone statements as *F* (fact) or *O* (opinion).

_____ 1. George Washington was the first president of the United States.

_____ 2. George Washington was the best president of the United States.

_____ 3. The author states that George Washington was the best president of the United States.

_____ 4. It is a fact that George Washington was the best president of the United States.

The first and third are statements of fact that can be proven, but the second and fourth are opinions, even though the fourth tries to present itself as a fact. In psychology, for example, it is a fact that Freud believed the personality is divided into three parts; however, it is only an opinion that there are three parts of the human personality. Others may believe the personality should be divided into two parts or ten parts.

Dr. Beatrice Mendez-Egle, a professor at the University of Texas–Pan American, further clarifies the distinction between fact and opinion with the following definitions and table.

A **fact** is an observation that can be supported with incontrovertible evidence. An **opinion,** on the other hand, is a commentary, position, or observation based on fact but that represents a personal judgment or interpretation of these facts.

Fact	Opinion
3/4 of the students in this class are making A's.	This class is really smart.
The temperature in the class is 78°.	This classroom is always hot and stuffy!
George W. Bush won the presidency with fewer popular votes than Al Gore in 2000.	George W. Bush doesn't deserve to be president because fewer than half the voters who voted in the 2000 presidential election voted for him.

The first two opinions are clearly judgments that would probably be obvious to most readers. The third opinion, however, is mixed with fact; and thus the judgment portion of "doesn't deserve to be president" needs the sharp eye of a critical reader to recognize it as an opinion. In order to achieve a certain purpose, a writer can support a particular bias or point of view and attempt to confuse the reader by blending facts and opinions so that both sound like facts.

exercise 7

Mark the following statements from textbooks as *F* (fact) or *O* (opinion).

_____ 1. I maintain it is much safer to be feared than loved, if you have to do without one of the two.

> —Machiavelli, quoted in *Western Civilization,* Fifth Edition, by Jackson J. Spielvogel

_____ 2. Everyone complains about federal, state, and local taxes.

> —*We the People: An Introduction to American Politics,* Fourth Edition, by Benjamin Ginsberg et al.

_____ 3. The technical name for our gigantic social insurance program is Old Age, Survivors, and Disability Health Insurance, or OASDHI.

> —*Micro Economics for Today,* Fourth Edition, by Irvin B. Tucker

_____ 4. At first, young children were barred from the factories, and older ones were allowed to work only a partial adult shift.

> —*A Brief History of Western Civilization*, Fourth Edition, by Mark Kishlansky et al.

_____ 5. Taxi drivers have been found to have unusually large hippocampi (a brain structure that plays a special role in spatial memory)—and the longer a driver has worked, the larger they are.

> —*Psychology,* Second Edition, by Steven M. Kosslyn and Rogin S. Rosenberg

_____ 6. Leopold Mozart, father of the illustrious Wolfgang Amadeus Mozart, sacrificed his own considerable career to further that of his son.

> —*Understanding Music,* Fourth Edition,
> by Jeremy Yudkin

_____ 7. English, the language of globalization, is both savior and villain in Europe.

> —*Diversity and Globalization,* Second Edition,
> by Les Rowntree et al.

_____ 8. In the 1920s, Cleveland, Ohio, and Chicago, Illinois, were among the first major cities to perform crime surveys.

> —*Criminal Justice,* by James A. Fagin

_____ 9. Longshoremen, who are on their feet all day and lift, push, and carry heavy cargo, have about half the risk of fatal heart attack as coworkers like crane drivers and clerks.

> —*Life-Span Development,* Ninth Edition,
> by John W. Santrock

_____ 10. Self-confidence, perhaps more than any other factor, is the secret to success and happiness.

> —*The Career Fitness Program,* Seventh Edition,
> by Diane Sukiennik et al.

exercise 8 The following passage from a history textbook describes Thomas Jefferson. Notice the mixture of facts and opinions the author uses to develop a view of Thomas Jefferson. Mark the items that follow as (*F*) fact or (*O*) opinion.

> Jefferson hardly seemed cut out for politics. Although in some ways a typical, pleasure-loving southern planter, he had in him something of the Spartan. He grew tobacco, but did not smoke, and he partook only sparingly of meat and alcohol. Unlike most planters he never hunted or gambled, though he was a fine horseman and enjoyed dancing, music, and other social diversions. His practical interests ranged enormously—from architecture and geology to natural history and scientific farming—yet he displayed little interest in managing men. Controversy dismayed him, and he tended to avoid it by assigning to some thicker-skinned associate the task of attacking his enemies. Nevertheless, he wanted to have a say in shaping the future of the country, and once engaged, he fought stubbornly and at times deviously to get and hold power.
>
> —*The American Nation,* Tenth Edition,
> by John Garraty and Mark Carnes

_____ 1. Jefferson hardly seemed cut out for politics.

_____ 2. Jefferson was a typical, pleasure-loving southern planter.

_____ 3. Jefferson grew tobacco, but did not smoke.

_____ 4. Controversy dismayed Jefferson.

_____ 5. Jefferson fought deviously to get and hold power.

Recognize Valid and Invalid Support for Arguments

When evaluating persuasive writing, critical readers realize that support for an argument or a position can be in the form of both facts and opinions. For example, valid reasons for a career change or a vacation destination can be a combination of both facts and feelings. The trick is to recognize which reasons validly support the point and which merely confuse the issue with an illusion of support.

A **fallacy** is an error in reasoning that can give an illusion of support. On the surface, a fallacy can appear to add support, but closer inspection shows it to be unrelated and illogical. For example, valid reasons for buying running shoes might be comfort and price, whereas invalid reasons might be that "everybody has them" and a sports figure said to buy them.

Fallacies are particularly prevalent in **propaganda,** a form of writing designed to convince the reader by whatever means possible. Propaganda can be used to support a political cause, advertise a product, or engender enthusiasm for a college event.

Experts have identified and labeled over 200 fallacies or tricks of persuasion. The following list describes some of the most common ones.

Testimonials: Celebrities who are not experts state support.

Example: Tiger Woods appears in television advertisements endorsing a particular credit card.

Bandwagon: You will be left out if you do not join the crowd.

Example: All the voters in the district support Henson for senator.

Transfer: A famous person is associated with an argument.

Example: George Washington indicated in a quote that he would have agreed with us on this issue.

Straw Person: A simplistic exaggeration is set up to represent the argument.

Example: The professor replied, "If I delay the exam, you'll expect me to change the due dates of all papers and assignments."

Misleading Analogy: Two things are compared as similar that are actually distinctly different.

Example: Studying is like taking a shower; most of the material goes down the drain.

Circular Reasoning: The conclusion is supported by restating it.

Example: Papers must be turned in on time because papers cannot be turned in late.

exercise 9 | Identify the fallacy in each of the following statements: (a) testimonial, (b) bandwagon, (c) transfer, (d) straw person, (e) misleading analogy, (f) circular reasoning.

_____ 1. Purchase her new novel, *Growing Up Latino,* which is written in the tradition of outstanding novelist Richard Rodriguez, who wrote *Hunger of Memory: The Education of Richard Rodriguez.*

_____ 2. The first semester of college is like the premiere of a Batman movie because both require the use of imagination.

_____ 3. Customs booklets warn that Cuban cigars are not legally allowed in the United States because the government will not let you bring them into the country.

_____ 4. Pele, the famous soccer player who led Brazil to three World Cup championships, recommends multivitamins by Zip to add energy to your life and strength to your body.

_____ 5. Purchase tickets immediately because everyone in school has signed up for the event and it will soon be sold out.

_____ 6. A student who is late for class would probably be late for a job interview and thus be a failure.

_____ 7. Use the cosmetics advertised by Jennifer Lopez because she says they work for her.

_____ 8. Writing a term paper is like brewing coffee when your crushed beans turn into a flow of ideas.

_____ 9. Join a club to meet new friends because you will meet people that you do not know.

_____ 10. George W. Bush points out that the first president of the United States was another George W.

exercise 10 | To practice your critical thinking skills, read the passages and answer the questions that follow.

Passage 1

BEETHOVEN'S WORK HABITS

As Beethoven grew older and withdrew more and more from society, he became wholly absorbed in his art. He would habitually miss meals, forget or ignore invitations, and work long into the night. He himself described his "ceaseless occupations." Beethoven felt the strongest urge to produce the music within him, and yet he suffered the same creative anxiety as lesser mortals. "For some time past I have been carrying about with me the idea of three great works. . . . These I must get rid of: two symphonies, each different from the other, and also different from all my other symphonies, and an oratorio. . . . I dread beginning works of such magnitude. Once I have begun, then all goes well."

We are fortunate in possessing many of the sketchbooks in which Beethoven worked out his musical ideas. They present a vivid picture of the composer at work.

—*Understanding Music,* Fourth Edition,
by Jeremy Yudkin

Answer the following with *T* (true) or *F* (false) or with *a*, *b*, *c*, or *d*.

_____ 1. The author wishes to show Beethoven as both a preoccupied genius and a person who dreaded a big project.

_____ 2. The author suggests that the sketchbooks reveal some of the thought processes of Beethoven.

_____ 3. The author's tone is condemning.

_____ 4. The author conveys an appreciation for Beethoven as a creative artist.

_____ 5. The author implies that Beethoven did not write down his symphonies until they were completed in his head.

_____ 6. Each of the following words has a negative connotation *except*

    a. vivid
    b. withdrew
    c. anxiety
    d. dread

Mark the following statements as *F* (fact) or *O* (opinion).

_____ 7. "He became wholly absorbed in his art."

_____ 8. "He would habitually miss meals . . . and work long into the night."

_____ 9. "Beethoven felt the strongest urge to produce the music within him, and yet he suffered the same creative anxiety as lesser mortals."

Passage 2

ALEXANDER THE LEADER

The army was crossing a desert of sand. The sun was already blazing down upon them, but they were struggling on under the necessity of reaching water, which was still far away. Alexander, like everyone else, was tormented by thirst, but he was nonetheless marching on foot at the head of his men. It was all he could do to keep going, but he did so, and the result (as always) was that the men were better able to endure their misery when they saw that it was equally shared. As they toiled on, a party of light infantry which had gone off looking for water found some—just a wretched little trickle collected in a shallow gully. They scooped up with difficulty what they could and hurried back, with their priceless treasure, to Alexander. Then, just before they reached him, they tipped the water into a helmet and gave it to him. Alexander, with a word of thanks for the gift, took the helmet and, giving it full view of his troops, poured the water on the ground. So extraordinary was the effect of this action that the water wasted by Alexander was as good as a drink for every man in the army. I cannot praise this act too highly. It was a proof, if anything was, not only of his power of endurance, but also of his genius for leadership.

—From *The Campaigns of Alexander* by Arrian,
translated by Aubrey de Sélincourt.

Answer the following with *T* (true) or *F* (false).

_____ 1. The author's purpose is to compliment Alexander's troops for giving him the treasured water.

_____ 2. The author implies that part of Alexander's success as a leader was his understanding and endurance of the same hardships as his soldiers.

_____ 3. The author implies that Alexander was willing to die of thirst with his soldiers.

_____ 4. The author's tone is respectful of Alexander.

_____ 5. The reader can conclude that this account could contribute to the positive propaganda about Alexander.

_____ 6. In using the words *extraordinary* and *genius,* the author intends a positive slant.

Mark the following statements as *F* (fact) or *O* (opinion).

_____ 7. "The army was crossing a desert of sand."

_____ 8. "Alexander, with a word of thanks for the gift, took the helmet and, giving it full view of his troops, poured the water on the ground."

_____ 9. "It was a proof, if anything was, not only of his power of endurance, but also of his genius for leadership."

Passage 3

`OPTIMISM`

One measure of how helpless or effective you feel is where you stand on optimism-pessimism. How do you characteristically explain negative and positive events? Perhaps you have known students whose *attributional style* is negative—who attribute poor performance to their lack of ability ("I can't do this") or to situations enduringly beyond their control ("There is nothing I can do about it"). Such students are more likely to persist in getting low grades than are students who adopt the more hopeful attitude that effort, good study habits, and self-discipline can make a difference. Although mere fantasies tend not to fuel motivation and success, genuine positive expectations do.

In their study of professional achievement, psychologists Martin Seligman and Peter Schulman compared sales made by new life insurance representatives who were more or less optimistic in their outlooks. Those who put an optimistic spin on their setbacks—seeing them as flukes or as a means to learning a new approach, rather than viewing them as signs of incompetence—sold more policies during their first year and were half as likely to quit. Seligman's finding came to life for him when Bob Dell, one of the optimistic recruits who began selling for Metropolitan Life after taking Seligman's optimism test, later dialed him up and sold him a policy.

Health, too, benefits from a basic optimism. A depressed hopelessness dampens the body's disease-fighting immune system. In repeated studies, optimists have outlived pessimists or lived with fewer illnesses.

—David G. Myers, *Psychology,* 7th Edition. Copyright 2004 by Worth Publishers Inc. Reproduced with permission of Worth Publishers Inc. in the format Textbook via Copyright Clearance Center.

Answer the following with *T* (true) or *F* (false).

_____ 1. The author's purpose is to discuss a positive relationship between optimism and achievement.

_____ 2. The author's tone in telling the Bob Dell story is humorous.

_____ 3. The author indicates that pessimists are likely to receive lower grades than optimists.

_____ 4. According to the passage, optimistic students can achieve better grades even without good study habits and self-discipline.

_____ 5. The author suggests that pessimism affects motivation but does not physically affect the body.

_____ 6. The author implies that an optimist would believe that "It happens when it happens."

Mark the following statements as *F* (fact) or *O* (opinion).

_____ 7. "In their study of professional achievement, Seligman and Peter Schulman compared sales made by new life insurance representatives . . . ".

_____ 8. "Those who put an optimistic spin on their setbacks . . . sold more policies during their first year and were half as likely to quit."

_____ 9. "In repeated studies, optimists have outlived pessimists or lived with fewer illnesses."

Passage 4

SIMPLICITY

Clutter is the disease of American writing. We are a society strangling in unnecessary words, circular constructions, pompous frills and meaningless jargon.

Who can understand the clotted language of everyday American commerce: the memo, the corporation report, the business letter, the notice from the bank explaining its latest "simplified" statement? What member of an insurance or medical plan can decipher the brochure explaining his costs and benefits? What father or mother can put together a child's toy from the instructions on the box? Our national tendency is to inflate and thereby sound important. The airline pilot who announces that he is presently anticipating experiencing considerable precipitation wouldn't think of saying it may rain. The sentence is too simple—there must be something wrong with it.

But the secret of good writing is to strip every sentence to its cleanest components. Every word that serves no function, every long word that could be a short word, every adverb that carries the same meaning that's already in the verb, every passive construction that leaves the reader unsure of who is doing what—these are the thousand and one adulterants that weaken the strength of a sentence. And they usually occur in proportion to education and rank.

During the 1960s the president of my university wrote a letter to mollify the alumni after a spell of campus unrest. "You are probably aware," he began, "that we have been experiencing very considerable potentially explosive expressions of dissatisfaction on issues only partially related." He meant that the students had been hassling them about different things. I was far more upset by the president's English than by the students' potentially explosive expressions of dissatisfaction. I would have preferred the presidential approach taken by Franklin D. Roosevelt when he tried to convert into English his own government's memos, such as this blackout order of 1942:

Such preparations shall be made as will completely obscure all Federal buildings and non-Federal buildings occupied by the Federal government during an air raid for any period of time from visibility by reason of internal or external illumination.

"Tell them," Roosevelt said, "that in buildings where they have to keep the work going to put something across the windows."

—From "Simplicity" from *On Writing Well,* Seventh Edition, by William Zinsser. Published by Collins, an imprint of HarperCollins Publishers. Copyright © 1976, 1980, 1988, 1990, 1994, 1998, 2001, and 2006 by William K. Zinsser. Reprinted by permission of the author.

Answer the following with *T* (true) or *F* (false) or with *a, b, c,* or *d.*

_____ 1. The author's main purpose is to criticize wordy writing.

_____ 2. The author quotes Franklin D. Roosevelt to show how simply the blackout order could have been stated.

_____ 3. The author quotes the president of his university to show that educated people usually communicate clearly.

_____ 4. The author feels that the airline pilot avoids using the word *storm* because it may frighten the passengers.

_____ 5. The overall tone of the passage is serious.

_____ 6. All of the following words are negatively slanted *except*

      a. clutter.
      b. jargon.
      c. decipher.
      d. brochure.

Mark the following statements as *F* (fact) or *O* (opinion).

_____ 7. "Clutter is the disease of American writing."

_____ 8. "We are a society strangling in unnecessary words . . . ".

_____ 9. ". . . the secret of good writing is to strip every sentence to its cleanest components."

Passage 5

THEODORE ROOSEVELT AND THE ROUGH RIDERS

Brimming with enthusiasm, perhaps a bit innocent in their naiveté, the Rough Riders viewed Cuba as a land of stars, a place to win great honors or die in the pursuit. Like many of his men, TR believed "that the nearing future held . . . many chances of death, of honor and renown." And he was ready. Dressed in a Brooks Brothers uniform made especially for him and with several extra pairs of spectacles sewn in the lining of his Rough Rider hat, Roosevelt prepared to "meet his destiny."

In a land of beauty, death often came swiftly. As the Rough Riders and other soldiers moved inland toward Santiago, snipers fired upon them. The high-speed Mauser bullets seemed to come out of nowhere, making a *z-z-z-z-z-eu* as they moved through the air or a loud *chug* as they hit flesh. Since the Spanish snipers used smokeless gunpowder, no puffs of smoke betrayed their positions.

During the first day in Cuba, the Rough Riders experienced the "blood, sweat and tears" of warfare. Dr. Church looked "like a kid who had gotten his hands and arms into a bucket of thick red paint." Some men died, and others lay where they had been shot, dying. The reality of war strikes different men differently. It horrifies some, terrifies others, and enrages still others. Sheer exhilaration was the best way to describe Roosevelt's response to death and danger. Even sniper fire could not keep TR from jumping up and down with excitement.

On July 1, 1898, the Rough Riders faced their sternest task. Moving from the coast toward Santiago along the Camino Real, the main arm of the United States forces encountered an entrenched enemy. Spread out along the San Juan Heights, Spanish forces commanded a splendid position. As American troops emerged from a stretch of jungle, they found themselves in a dangerous position. Once again the sky seemed to be raining Mauser bullets and shrapnel. Clearly the Heights had to be taken. Each hour of delay meant more American casualties.

The Rough Riders were deployed to the right to prepare to assault Kettle Hill. Once in position, they faced an agonizing wait for orders to charge. Most soldiers hunched behind cover. Bucky O'Neill, however, casually strolled up and down in front of his troops, chain-smoked cigarettes, and shouted encouragement. A sergeant implored him to take cover. "Sergeant," Bucky remarked, "the Spanish bullet isn't made that will kill me." Hardly had he finished the statement when a Mauser bullet ripped into his mouth and burst out of the back of his head. Even before he fell, Roosevelt wrote, Bucky's "wild and gallant soul has gone out into the darkness."

—*America and Its People,* Third Edition,
by James Martin et al.

Answer the following with *T* (true) or *F* (false) or with *a, b, c,* or *d.*

_____ 1. The author's main purpose is to persuade.

_____ 2. The author feels that the Rough Riders had a glorified view of war.

_____ 3. The author shows sarcasm in mentioning the "Brooks Brothers uniform."

_____ 4. In view of his subsequent death, Bucky O'Neill's remark about a Spanish bullet was ironic.

_____ 5. The overall tone of the passage is humorous.

_____ 6. Which of the following phrases is negatively slanted?

    a. sheer exhilaration
    b. jumping up and down
    c. sternest task
    d. casually strolled

Mark the following statements as *F* (fact) or *O* (opinion).

_____ 7. ". . . the Spanish snipers used smokeless gunpowder . . .".

_____ 8. "Dr. Church looked 'like a kid who had gotten his hands and arms into a bucket of thick red paint.'"

_____ 9. "Some men died, and others lay where they had been shot, dying."

Passage 6

SHYNESS AS A NEW DISEASE

A fast-growing number of people are doing something they would not have thought of doing before: going to their doctors for a prescription drug to cure their shyness.

In the past, many people knew that they were shy, but it never crossed their minds that shyness was a pathology, a disease that requires medical treatment. Recently, though, a number of social forces have converged to turn shyness into a mental disorder. First, in 1980, the psychiatric profession labeled extreme shyness as a *social phobia* or *social anxiety disorder*. At that time, the condition was regarded as a *rare* disorder, as it involved experiencing not only a distracting nervousness at parties or before giving a speech but also a powerful desire to avoid these social situations altogether. Next, some movie stars, big-name athletes, and other celebrities appeared on talk shows, in magazines, and on other media to disclose their struggles with shyness. Finally, the pharmaceutical company Smith Kline Beecham entered the picture by advertising and selling its antidepressant Paxil as a medicine for shyness. And thus, Americans were left with the impression that shyness is far more serious and widespread than they had ever realized.

As a result, many people today regard shyness as a disease, a medical problem serious enough to require treatment with a drug. But shyness is a serious problem only for a very few—those who are extremely bashful or truly incapacitated by fears of others' disapproval and need relief through the use of psychoactive drugs. For the majority, however, shyness is only a mild problem. According to a recent survey, nearly half of all Americans consider themselves shy and still manage to carry on a normal social life. Also consider the fact that many of these Americans may actually not be shy at all. In American culture today, it is difficult *not* to feel shy given the ubiquitous media full of immodest and even brazen talkers, just as it is difficult not to feel fat with the media presentation of extremely thin beauties.

In short, what was once considered a personality trait is now labeled as a disease and treated with drugs.

—From *Sociology: A Brief Introduction*, Sixth Edition, by Alex Thio.

Answer the following with *T* (true) or *F* (false) or with *a*, *b*, *c*, or *d*.

_____ 1. The author's primary purpose is to discuss solutions for shyness.

_____ 2. The author's overall tone is skeptical.

_____ 3. The author writes from the point of view of a shy person who has sought treatment.

_____ 4. The author suggests that Smith Kline Beecham had a role in perception of shyness as a treatable disease.

_____ 5. The words *pathology* and *disorder* convey negative connotations regarding shyness.

_____ 6. All of the following words are positively slanted *except*

a. movie stars.
b. big-name athletes.
c. celebrities.
d. ubiquitous media.

Mark the following statements as *F* (fact) or *O* (opinion).

_____ 7. "In 1980s, the psychiatric profession labeled extreme shyness as a *social phobia* or *social anxiety disorder.*"

_____ 8. "Americans were left with the impression that shyness is far more serious and widespread than they had ever realized."

_____ 9. "In American culture today, it is difficult *not* to feel shy . . .".

Passage 7

EXCERPTS FROM "HOW TO TAME A WILD TONGUE"

. . . I remember being caught speaking Spanish at recess—that was good for three licks on the knuckles with a sharp ruler. I remember being sent to the corner of the classroom for "talking back" to the Anglo teacher when all I was trying to do was tell her how to pronounce my name. "If you want to be American, speak 'American.' If you don't like it, go back to Mexico where you belong."

"I want you to speak English. *Pa'hallar buen trabajo tienes que saber hablar el inglés bien. Qué vale toda tu educación si todavía hablas inglés con un* 'accent,'" my mother would say, mortified that I spoke English like a Mexican. At Pan American University, I, and all Chicano students were required to take two speech classes. Their purpose: to get rid of our accents.

Attacks on one's form of expression with the intent to censor are a violation of the First Amendment. *El Anglo con cara de inocente nos arrancó la lengua.* Wild tongues can't be tamed, they can only be cut out.

Overcoming the Tradition of Silence

Ahogadas, escupimos el oscuro.
Peleando con nuestra propia sombra
el silencio nos sepulta.

En boca cerrada no entran moscas. "Flies don't enter a closed mouth" is a saying I kept hearing when I was a child. *Ser habladora* was to be a gossip and a liar, to talk too much. *Muchachitas bien criadas,* well-bred girls don't answer back. *Es una falta de respeto* to talk back to one's mother or father. I remember one of the sins I'd recite to the priest in the confession box the few times I went to confession: talking back to my mother, *hablar pa' 'trás, repelar. Hocicona, repelona, chismosa,* having a big mouth, questioning, carrying tales are all signs of being *mal criada.* In my culture they are all words that are derogatory if applied to women—I've never heard them applied to men. . . .

—Excerpted from Gloria Anzaldúa, *Borderlands/La Frontera: The New Mestiza.* Copyright © 1987, 1999.

Answer the following with *T* (true) or *F* (false) or with *a, b, c,* or *d.*

_____ 1. The author's purpose is to persuade the reader that it is wrong to try to control how a person speaks.

_____ 2. The overall tone is contented.

_____ 3. The author implies that Hispanic culture expects men and women to keep silent.

_____ 4. The author's words imply that *only* Chicano students were required to take two speech classes.

_____ 5. The author writes from the perspective of an Anglo-American woman.

_____ 6. All of the following expressions have a negative slant *except:*

    a. "talking back."
    b. mortified.
    c. "spoke English like a Mexican."
    d. well-bred girls.

Mark the following statements as *F* (fact) or *O* (opinion).

_____ 7. "All Chicano students were required to take two speech classes."

_____ 8. "If you want to be an American, speak 'American.'"

_____ 9. "Well-bred girls don't answer back."

Summary Points

➤ **What do critical readers do?**
Critical readers think for themselves, analyze, and evaluate the accuracy and relevance of the printed word before accepting it.

➤ **What is an author's *purpose* or *intent*?**
Authors write with a particular goal in mind, which may be to inform, persuade, or entertain.

➤ **What is the author's *point of view*?**
Point of view refers to the writer's opinions and beliefs about the subject.

➤ **What is *bias*?**
Bias is an opinion or judgment and is thus similar to point of view. Bias is associated with prejudice and thus has a negative connotation. Both writers and readers bring bias to the printed page.

➤ **What is *tone*?**
Tone refers to the author's attitude toward the subject.

➤ **What is a *fact*?**
A fact is a statement that can be proven true or false.

➤ **What is an *opinion*?**
An opinion is a statement of feeling or belief that cannot be proven right or wrong.

➤ **What is a *fallacy*?**
A fallacy is an error in reasoning designed to give the illusion of support.

➤ **What is *propaganda*?**
Propaganda is a form of writing that uses fallacies to convince readers.

COLLABORATIVE PROBLEM SOLVING

Form a five-member group and select one of the following activities. Brainstorm and then outline your major points on a transparency. Choose a member to present the group findings to the class.

➤ List five facts and five opinions that could be used to support the argument that people should not smoke.

➤ Write five different statements regarding rap music, each with one of the following tones: humorous, angry, ironic, sarcastic, and nostalgic.

➤ Create a fallacy for each of the six types listed in this chapter: testimonial, bandwagon, transfer, straw person, misleading analogy, and circular reasoning.

➤ List five points that you would make in an argument for capital punishment and five points that you would make in an argument against capital punishment.

MyReadingLab (MRL) www.myreadinglab.com

➤ To practice the ideas and skills introduced in this chapter, go to the "Critical Thinking" module in the Skills section of MRL. To practice general reading comprehension, use the Levels section.

The Reading *Workshop*

"I have often reflected upon the new vistas that reading opened to me. I knew right there in prison that reading had changed forever the course of my life. As I see it today, the ability to read awoke in me some long dormant craving to be mentally alive."

—MALCOLM X

That is a powerful statement! What is it about reading that so inspired this civil rights activist? Perhaps you can think of ways in which you have benefitted from something you have read. There is something yet to be read that could change the course of your life—look for it!

Think about it, talk about it, write about it:

Whether they are reading fiction or nonfiction, critical readers are alert to the often subtle evidence of the author's biases and point of view. What words best describe the overall tone of the book you are reading? Is the author's purpose solely to entertain, to persuade or to inform, or do you detect a mixture of purposes? Does the author reveal any biases? Defend your responses with evidence from the book.

Your professor may ask you to discuss these questions in a Reading Workshop journal.

selection 1 Literature: Short Story

The emotional, sexual, and psychological stereotyping of females begins when the doctor says, "It's a girl."

—Shirley Chisholm

Irony is a literary technique used to entertain or educate a reader. Irony occurs when there is a contrast between what is said or expected and what actually happens. There are three basic types of irony: verbal, dramatic, and situational. In verbal irony, you say one thing when you mean another. Sarcasm is a type of verbal irony when you mean the precise opposite of what you say. The second type of irony, dramatic irony, occurs when the reader has information that the characters do not. For example, in Romeo and Juliet *the reader knows that Juliet is not dead but Romeo thinks she is dead. The third type of irony is situational irony, in which both the characters and the audience are unaware of certain important information. This type of irony results in surprise endings to stories as the characters and the reader both become aware of the missing information.*

THINKING BEFORE READING

Preview for content and organizational clues. Activate your schema and anticipate what you will learn.

Why were British colonists in India in the early 1900s?

Why do people scream at the unexpected?

What makes you scream?

I think this story will be about _____.

VOCABULARY PREVIEW

Are you familiar with these words?

| colonial | attachés | naturalist | veranda | spacious |
| contracting | summons | impulse | commotion | forfeit |

What is an *attaché* case?

What type of science does a *naturalist* study?

What happens to your money if you *forfeit* a deposit?

Your instructor may give a true-false vocabulary review before or after reading.

THINKING DURING READING

As you read, use the six thinking strategies of a good reader: predict, picture, relate, monitor, correct, and annotate.

THE DINNER PARTY

Refer to the **Reader's** *Tip* for a **Short Story** on page 155.

The country is India. A colonial official and his wife are giving a large dinner party. They are seated with their guests—army officers and government attachés and their wives, and a visiting American naturalist—in their spacious dining room, which has a bare marble floor, open rafters, and wide glass doors opening onto a veranda. A spirited discussion
5 springs up between a young girl who insists that women have outgrown the jumping-on-a-chair-at-the-sight-of-a-mouse era and a colonel who says they have not.

"A woman's unfailing reaction in any crisis," the colonel says, "is to scream. And while a man may feel like it, he has that ounce more of nerve control than a woman has. And that last ounce is what counts."

10 The American does not join in the argument but watches the other guests. As he looks, he sees a strange expression come over the face of the hostess. She is staring straight ahead, her muscles contracting slightly. With a slight gesture she summons the servant standing behind her chair and whispers to him. The servant's eyes widen, and he quickly leaves the room.

15 Of the guests, none except the American notices this or sees the servant place a bowl of milk on the veranda just outside the open doors.

The American comes to with a start. In India, milk in a bowl means only one thing—bait for a snake. He realizes there must be a cobra in the room. He looks up at the rafters—the likeliest place—but they are bare. Three corners of the room are empty, and
20 in the fourth the servants are waiting to serve the next course. There is only one place left—under the table.

His first impulse is to jump back and warn the others, but he knows the commotion would frighten the cobra into striking. He speaks quickly, the tone of his voice so arresting that it sobers everyone.

25 "I want to know just what control everyone at this table has. I will count three hundred—that's five minutes—and not one of you is to move a muscle. Those who move will forfeit fifty rupees. Ready!"

The twenty people sit like stone images while he counts. He is saying ". . . two hundred and eighty . . ." when, out of the corner of his eye, he sees the cobra emerge and
30 make for the bowl of milk. Screams ring out as he jumps to slam the veranda doors safely shut.

"You were right, Colonel!" the host exclaims. "A man has just shown us an example of perfect control."

"Just a minute," the American says, turning to the hostess. "Mrs. Wynnes, how did
35 you know that cobra was in the room?"

A faint smile lights up the woman's face as she replies: "Because it was crawling across my foot."

(466 words)

—"The Dinner Party," by Mona Gardner,
Saturday Review of Literature

THINKING AND WRITING AFTER READING

RECALL Self-test your understanding.

Your instructor may choose to give you a true-false comprehension review.

REACT How would this incident have affected you? _____

_____

REFLECT How did Mrs. Wynnes and the American act as a team? What might

have happened if each had acted in a different manner? _____

_____

THINKING CRITICALLY What do you think the young girl will say to the colonel
after the incident? How do you think the colonel and the guests replied? How
does the author feel about the gender argument? Write your answer on a separate sheet of paper.

THINK AND WRITE How does the situational irony in this story entertain and edu-

cate? How is irony used to attack a bias? _____

_____

CRITICAL READING

Write your response to the following questions.

1. What is the difference of opinion at the beginning of the story between the

   young girl and the colonel? _____

   _____

   _____

2. What is the bias of the host of the party? _____

   _____

3. As the dinner party unfolds, what action or fact emerges to support the

   opinion of the young girl? _____

   _____

Mark the following statements as *F* (fact) or *O* (opinion).

_____ 4. "A woman's unfailing reaction in any crisis is to scream."

_____ 5. The American does not join in the argument but watches the other guests.

_____ 6. "A man has just shown us an example of perfect control."

Interpret the Quote

Now that you have finished reading the selection, "The Dinner Party," go back to the beginning of the selection and read the opening quote again. What stereotypes about women does the colonel promote in this story? On a separate sheet of paper, list four common stereotypes for men and four stereotypes for women. Next to each stereotype, write whether you believe the stereotype is true or false and explain why.

1 selection

Name _____

Date _____

COMPREHENSION QUESTIONS

Answer the following with *a, b, c,* or *d,* or fill in the blank. In order to help you analyze your strengths and weaknesses, the question types are indicated.

Main Idea _____ 1. The best statement of the main idea of the selection is:

   a. Women appreciate courage in men more than men appreciate courage in women.
   b. In a crisis the real character of a person is displayed.
   c. Arguments of gender differences can be proven true or false.
   d. In a crisis, a woman can have as much nerve as a man.

Inference _____ 2. During the argument, when the American noted Mrs. Wynnes's strange expression, the hostess was reacting to

   a. the colonel's negative words about women.
   b. the cobra crossing her foot.
   c. the young girl's opinion in support of women.
   d. the bowl of milk brought by the servant.

Inference _____ 3. The American was perhaps more attuned than the average person to the habits of a snake because

   a. his profession involved the study of nature.
   b. he had been born in India.
   c. the cobra is indigenous or native to America.
   d. army officers were trained to react appropriately to such dangers.

Inference _____ 4. From Mrs. Wynnes's reaction to the crawling snake and the American's challenge to the dinner guests, the reader can assume that a cobra

   a. attacks when it cannot find milk.
   b. can be agitated into an attack by movement.
   c. attacks at the sound of a human voice.
   d. is more attracted to the warmth of the human body than to a favorite food.

Inference 5. What does the description "A faint smile lights up the woman's face as she replies . . ." suggest about the feelings of Mrs. Wynnes?

   _____

   _____

   _____

   _____

Inference _____ 6. The guests at the dinner party participated in the five-minute challenge by the American because they

   a. knew there was a snake under the table.
   b. saw that Mrs. Wynnes was also greatly disturbed.
   c. wanted to win fifty rupees.
   d. were inspired by the American's voice and sensed the importance of the challenge.

selection

1

Inference _____ 7. The author implies that Mr. Wynnes

    a. chose to disregard his wife's contribution to the dilemma.

    b. did not fully understand that two people were involved in the successful solution.

    c. remained firm in his opinions even after recognizing the facts of the incident.

    d. knew that the American had not acted alone.

Answer the following with *T* (true) or *F* (false).

Detail _____ 8. The setting of the story suggests that the people at the dinner party were members of the upper crust.

Inference _____ 9. The author suggests that the American is initially biased toward the gender opinion of the colonel.

Inference _____ 10. The milk was most likely placed on the veranda because the doors could be closed when the snake crawled out.

VOCABULARY

Answer the following with *a, b, c,* or *d* for the word or phrase that best defines the boldface word as used in the selection. The number in parentheses indicates the line of the passage in which the word appears.

_____ 1. "**colonial** official" (1)

    a. wealthy

    b. native of India

    c. residing in a colony

    d. authoritarian

_____ 2. "government **attachés**" (2)

    a. diplomatic staffers

    b. friends

    c. generals

    d. contractors

_____ 3. "American **naturalist**" (3)

    a. liberal

    b. scientist of nature

    c. conservative

    d. inspector

_____ 4. "**spacious** dining room" (3)

    a. clean

    b. large

    c. decorated

    d. crowded

_____ 5. "muscles **contracting**" (12)

    a. relaxing

    b. not reacting

    c. increasing in size

    d. tightening

_____ 6. "**summons** the servant"(12)

    a. seizes

    b. holds

    c. calls for

    d. nods to

_____ 7. "**veranda** just outside" (16)

    a. porch

    b. room

    c. entry

    d. stairs

_____ 8. "first **impulse**" (22)

    a. attempt

    b. information

    c. association

    d. urge

_____ 9. "**commotion** would frighten" (22)

    a. jump

    b. argument

    c. turmoil

    d. bait of milk

_____ 10. "**forfeit** fifty rupees" (26)

    a. give up

    b. earn

    c. gamble

    d. borrow

Your instructor may choose to give a true-false review.

VOCABULARY ENRICHMENT

A. Study the similar-sounding words and circle one for each sentence.

accent: speech pattern	**elicit:** draw out	**eminent:** well-known
ascent: climb upward	**illicit:** improper	**imminent:** about to happen

1. British colonists in India spoke with a slight (**accent, ascent**).

2. The young girl will surely (**elicit, illicit**) an apology from the colonel.

3. The hostess felt that with a sudden movement a snake bite would be (**eminent, imminent**).

B. Use context clues, word parts, and, if necessary, the dictionary, to write the meaning for each of the boldface words from a sociology textbook.

4. As foreigners, the ruling British colonists were not quickly **assimilated** into the society of India. _____

5. In order to live together in harmony, society demands **conformity** from its members. _____

6. In the story, the American sees a **correlation** between the milk and a snake.

   _____

7. The American naturalist was held in high **esteem** for his quick thinking.

   _____

8. Except for the young girl, the other guests at the dinner party seem to be members of the same age or **peer** group. _____

9. Because India is densely populated, most people live in **urban** areas.

   _____

10. Because of their governing positions, British colonists enjoyed many perks of their high **status.** _____

C. Identify the boldface phrase as simile, metaphor, or personification and explain the meaning.

11. George Washington was the **father of his country** but he had no children of his own. _____

12. Glaciers are melting **like warm ice cream** because pollution is trapping heat to the earth. _____

13. Some birds migrate over two continents, perhaps **singing their songs** in both English and Spanish. _____

   _____

14. Because of 200 mph winds that strike **like tornadoes,** climbers can ascend Mount Everest only during two months of the year. _____

_____

15. Poetry **speaks to** both the heart and the brain. _____

_____

ASSESS YOUR LEARNING

Review confusing questions, seek clarification, and make notes in your text to help you remember new information and vocabulary.

selection 2 Essay

Fortunately, the time has long passed when people liked to regard the United States as some kind of melting pot, taking men and women from every part of the world and converting them into standardized, homogenized Americans. We are, I think, much more mature and wise today. Just as we welcome a world of diversity, so we glory in an America of diversity—an America all the richer for the many different and distinctive strands of which it is woven.

—Hubert H. Humphrey, vice president of the United States, 1967

From the birth of the United States in the late 1700s until the late 1900s, one purpose of public education was to "Americanize" its students, many if not most of whom were from other parts of the world. The goal was to create a unified nation proud of its common history and heritage. In addition to singing patriotic songs, honoring the flag and learning stories about historical heros, this also meant that schools often forbade students from speaking any language other than English, and they observed only Christian and uniquely American holidays. Textbooks presented a view of U.S. history that centered largely on the contributions of white, Anglo-Saxon Protestants. In the 1960s and '70s, however, a trend emerged called multi-culturalism. Since then, the focus in public schools has gradually broadened to acknowledge and celebrate the multitude of cultural, racial, ethnic and religious groups that have shaped and continue to shape the American nation. Korean immigrant, Yuh Ji-Yeon, a professor of history at Northwestern University in Illinois, describes her views on multiculturalism in this essay. It first appeared in the Philadelphia Inquirer *in 1991.*

THINKING BEFORE READING

Preview the selection for clues to content. Activate your schema, and anticipate what you will learn.

What is the ethnic origin of your family?

Did your history textbooks accurately depict all aspects of past events?

Do you believe there is one "American" culture?

I think this essay will make the following point: _____.

VOCABULARY PREVIEW

Are you familiar with these words?

industrialists	scalpers	adapted	abolitionists	migration
indigenous	inconsistencies	dissenting	ethnicity	bolster

In this essay, does the word *scalpers* have something to do with a person's scalp or with selling tickets to an event?

What did *abolitionists* want to abolish?

What are *inconsistencies*?

Your instructor may choose to give a true-false vocabulary review before or after reading.

THINKING DURING READING

As you read, use the six thinking strategies of a good reader: predict, picture, relate, monitor, correct, and annotate.

Reader's *Tip* **Reading and Studying an Essay**

Ask yourself the following questions:

- What is the theme, thesis, or main idea?
- How do the details and examples develop the theme?
- How does the title aid in understanding the essay?
- What is the author's attitude toward the subject?
- What images contribute to the theme of the essay?
- What is the conclusion? How is it significant?

LET'S TELL THE STORY OF ALL AMERICA'S CULTURES

I grew up hearing, seeing and almost believing that America was white—albeit with a little black tinge here and there—and that white was best.

The white people were everywhere in my 1970s Chicago childhood: Founding Fathers, Lewis and Clark, Lincoln, Daniel Boone, Carnegie, presidents, explorers and
5 industrialists galore. The only black people were slaves. The only Indians were scalpers.

I never heard one word about how Benjamin Franklin was so impressed by the Iroquois federation of nations that he adapted that model into our system of state and federal government. Or that the Indian tribes were systematically betrayed and massacred by a greedy young nation that stole their land and called it the United States.
10 I never heard one word about how Asian immigrants were among the first to turn California's desert into fields of plenty. Or about Chinese immigrant Ah Bing, who bred the cherry now on sale in groceries across the nation. Or that plantation owners in Hawaii imported labor from China, Japan, Korea and the Philippines to work the sugar cane fields. I never learned that Asian immigrants were the only immigrants denied U.S. citizenship,
15 even though they served honorably in World War I. All the immigrants in my textbook were white.

I never learned about Frederick Douglass, the runaway slave who became a leading abolitionist and statesman, or about black scholar W.E.B. Du Bois. I never learned that black people rose up in arms against slavery. Nat Turner wasn't one of the heroes in my
20 childhood history class.

I never learned that the American Southwest and California were already settled by Mexicans when they were annexed after the Mexican-American War. I never learned that Mexico once had a problem keeping land-hungry white men on the U.S. side of the border.

So when other children called me a slant-eyed chink and told me to go back where
25 I came from, I was ready to believe that I wasn't really an American because I wasn't white.

America's bittersweet legacy of struggling and failing and getting another step closer to democratic ideals of liberty and equality and justice for all wasn't for the likes of me, an immigrant child from Korea. The history books said so.
30 Well, the history books were wrong.

Educators around the country are finally realizing what I realized as a teenager in the library, looking up the history I wasn't getting in school. America is a multicultural nation, composed of many people with varying histories and varying traditions who have little in common except their humanity, a belief in democracy and a desire for freedom.

35   America changed them, but they changed America too.

A committee of scholars and teachers gathered by the New York State Department of Education recognizes this in their recent report, "One Nation, Many Peoples: A Declaration of Cultural Interdependence."

They recommend that public schools provide a "multicultural education, anchored
40   to the shared principles of a liberal democracy."

What that means, according to the report, is recognizing that America was shaped and continues to be shaped by people of diverse backgrounds. It calls for students to be taught that history is an ongoing process of discovery and interpretation of the past, and that there is more than one way of viewing the world.

45   Thus, the westward migration of white Americans is not just a heroic settling of an untamed wild, but also the conquest of indigenous peoples. Immigrants were not just white, but Asian as well. Blacks were not merely passive slaves freed by northern whites, but active fighters for their own liberation.

In particular, according to the report, the curriculum should help children "to assess
50   critically the reasons for the inconsistencies between the ideals of the U.S. and social realities. It should provide information and intellectual tools that can permit them to contribute to bringing reality closer to the ideals."

In other words, show children the good with the bad, and give them the skills to help improve their country. What could be more patriotic?

55   Several dissenting members of the New York committee publicly worry that America will splinter into ethnic fragments if this multicultural curriculum is adopted. They argue that the committee's report puts the focus on ethnicity at the expense of national unity.

But downplaying ethnicity will not bolster national unity. The history of America is the story of how and why people from all over the world came to the United States, and
60 how in struggling to make a better life for themselves, they changed each other, they changed the country, and they all came to call themselves Americans.

E pluribus unum. Out of many, one.

This is why I, with my Korean background, and my childhood tormentors, with their lost-in-the-mist-of-time European backgrounds, are all Americans.
65   It is the unique beauty of this country. It is high time we let all our children gaze upon it.

(809 words)

—Ji-Yeon Yuh, *The Philadelphia Inquirer*

THINKING AND WRITING AFTER READING

RECALL Self-test your understanding.

Your instructor may choose to give you a true-false comprehension review.

REACT Do you agree with the author that history textbooks do not accurately depict all sides of historical events? Why or why not? _____

_____

_____

REFLECT Did you learn something new about some cultural groups in the U.S.? List at least one detail from the essay that you did not learn from your K–12 history classes.

_____

_____

_____

THINK CRITICALLY Do you think that presenting both positive and negative facts about historical events discourages or encourages students to develop respect and love of their country? On a separate sheet of paper, explain and support your position.

THINK AND WRITE Is it a good idea to emphasize multiculturalism in schools? Yuh Ji-Yeon presents support in favor of it and also the reasons to oppose it. List the pros and cons given in the essay, and then state your opinion on the issue.

In favor of multiculturalism   *Opposed to multiculturalism*

_____   _____

_____   _____

_____   _____

_____   _____

My opinion: _____

CRITICAL READING

1. Describe the author's purpose in writing this essay. Be more specific than simply saying it is to persuade, inform, or entertain. _____

   _____

   _____

   _____

2. The author's tone changes near the end of the essay. Select two or three words to describe the tone in the first part and two or three more words to describe the tone near the end. _____

   _____

   _____

3. Does the author's background as an immigrant to the United States influence the credibility of her argument? Explain. _____

   _____

   _____

   _____

   _____

4. Why does the author use so many personal experiences and memories in her essay? What effect do they have as support for her point? _____

   _____

   _____

5. List five examples from the essay of negatively slanted language and five examples of positively slanted language. _____

   _____

   _____

   Negatively slanted language: _____

   _____

   Positively slanted language: _____

   _____

Mark the following statements as *F* (fact) or *O* (opinion).

_____ 6. "Asian immigrants were among the first to turn California's desert into fields of plenty."

_____ 7. "The American Southwest and California were already settled by Mexicans when they were annexed after the Mexican-American War."

_____ 8. "Downplaying ethnicity will not bolster national unity."

Interpret the Quote

Now that you have finished reading the selection, "Let's Tell the Story of All America's Cultures," go back to the beginning of the selection and read the opening quote again. Do you believe that in the United States we "glory in an America of diversity"? On a separate sheet of paper, list as many cultural, racial, and ethnic groups as you can that make up the community in which you live.

Name _____

Date _____

COMPREHENSION QUESTIONS

Answer the following with *a, b, c,* or *d,* or fill in the blank. In order to help you analyze your strengths and weaknesses, the question types are indicated.

Main Idea   _____   1. The best statement of the main idea of this selection is:

   a. Textbooks present a one-sided account of U.S. history.
   b. Some immigrant children grow up believing that America was shaped only by whites.
   c. A committee of educators published a report called "One Nation, Many Peoples: A Declaration of Cultural Interdependence."
   d. All of America's cultures should be included in U.S. history instruction.

Detail   _____   2. Where did the author learn about the aspects of U.S. history that were not taught in school?

   a. at the library
   b. from her parents
   c. in college
   d. from information of the Internet

Inference   _____   3. The reader can infer that the author came to the United States from Korea _____ .

   a. as a college student
   b. when she was a young child
   c. to educate her own children
   d. to marry

Detail   _____   4. The report from the committee assembled by the New York State Department of Education said that a multicultural curriculum would do all of the following *except:*

   a. split the nation into separate ethnic divisions.
   b. help students see that there is more than one way to view the world.
   c. develop students' ability to think critically.
   d. give children skills to improve their country.

Inference   _____   5. At the end of the essay, when the author refers to the children who bullied her as having "lost-in-the-mist-of-time European backgrounds," she means that

   a. they were not born in the United States but in Europe.
   b. their European cultures did not make as strong a contribution as her culture.
   c. their European ancestors came to the U.S. so long ago that their traditions are not clearly remembered.
   d. she is more American than they are.

Detail   _____   6. According to the author, opponents of a multicultural school curriculum

   a. say that it creates students who are unpatriotic.
   b. believe that only whites had an important role in shaping U.S. history.
   c. agree that it will encourage students to think critically.
   d. fear that it will create greater divisions among ethnic groups.

Inference _____ 7. What does the author believe is the "unique beauty of this country"?

    a. the diverse cultures that together have created this nation

    b. the contributions made by people of Korean and European backgrounds

    c. a belief in democracy and a desire for freedom

    d. the inconsistencies between American ideals and reality

Answer the following with *T* (true), *F* (false), or *CT* (can't tell).

Inference _____ 8 The author agrees with the recommendation of the committee appointed by the New York State Department of Education.

Detail _____ 9. A Mexican immigrant bred the Bing cherry.

Inference _____ 10. The author probably felt left out of mainstream America as a child.

VOCABULARY

Answer the following with *a, b, c,* or *d* for the word or phrase that best defines the boldface word used in the selection. The number in parentheses indicates the line of the passage in which the word appears.

_____ 1. "**industrialists** galore" (5)

    a. factories

    b. managers of big businesses

    c. bankers

    d. busy, active people

_____ 2. "the only Indians were **scalpers**" (5)

    a. people who resell tickets

    b. people who wear feathered headdresses

    c. people who cut the skin and hair from victims' heads

    d. people who trade with settlers

_____ 3. "**adapted** that model" (7)

    a. tested

    b. invented

    c. rejected

    d. fit

_____ 4. "leading **abolitionist**" (18)

    a. slave owner

    b. legislator

    c. person who opposed slavery

    d. government official

_____ 5. "the westward **migration**" (45)

    a. movement from one place to another

    b. change of wind direction

    c. settlement of farmland

    d. important event

_____ 6. "**indigenous** peoples" (46)

    a. persecuted

    b. born in a region

    c. weak

    d. unhappy

_____ 7. "**inconsistencies** between" (50)

    a. ideas that oppose one another

    b. logical connections

    c. hopeful dreams

    d. laws

_____ 8. "**dissenting** members" (55)

    a. approving

    b. pessimistic

    c. disagreeing

    d. illegal

_____ 9. "focus on **ethnicity**" (57)

    a. religion

    b. one's cultural or racial background

    c. skin color

    d. language

_____ 10. "will not **bolster** national unity" (58)

    a. destroy

    b. divide

    c. pillow

    d. encourage

Your instructor may choose to give a true-false vocabulary review.

VOCABULARY ENRICHMENT

A. Create your own analogies for each type of relationship. Think of a second word that establishes the indicated relationship, then finish the analogy with a similar comparison.

1. Degree: *Damp* is to _____ as _____ is to _____ .

2. Part to whole: *Toes* are to _____ as _____ is to _____ .

3. Cause and effect: *Careless* is to _____ as _____ is to _____ .

4. Classification: *Airplane* is to _____ as _____ is to _____ .

5. Function: *Oven* is to _____ as _____ is to _____ .

B. Choose one of the following transitional words or phrases to complete each sentence.

however	for instance	thus	in addition	in a like manner

6. Freud was the first to conceptualize a theory of personality; _____, he is considered the father of psychoanalysis.

7. Freud's theories were considered by many to be too sexual and caused some of his followers to create their own groups; _____, a group of his followers who broke away became known as neo-Freudians.

8. Karen Horney became a neo-Freudian who, _____, became the first American female psychologist.

9. Carl Jung began with Freud studying personality; _____, later in life he focused on learning theory.

10. Although the neo-Freudians discarded some of the negativity of Freud, they retained Freud's belief that the subconscious affects the personality and, _____, they popularized their own theories through research and publication.

ASSESS YOUR LEARNING

Review confusing questions, seek clarification, and make notes in your text to help you remember new information and vocabulary.

selection 3 🗝 Essay

"We must embrace pain and burn it as fuel for our journey."

—Kenji Miyazawa

On September 11, 2001, planes hijacked by terrorists hit the World Trade Center and the Pentagon, claiming the lives of more than 3,000 innocent people. In the aftermath, the country mourned the loss of life and commiserated about their fears. While almost every newspaper columnist wrote about these emotions, one opinion piece stood out. The following selection, "We'll Go Forward from This Moment," by Leonard Pitts of the Miami Herald, *was widely circulated on the Internet, generating over 30,000 e-mails. Since its publication the day after the attacks, the piece has been set to music, reprinted in poster form, read on television, and quoted by legislators.*

THINKING BEFORE READING

Preview for content and organizational clues. Activate your schema and anticipate what you will learn.

Where were you on September 11, 2001, when you heard of the attacks?

What surprising event happened at Pearl Harbor?

This selection will probably tell me _____.

VOCABULARY PREVIEW

Are you familiar with these words?

steeled	frivolous	minutiae	blithe	entitlement
grappling	recrimination	chastened	bickering	cherish

Are *frivolous* issues serious?

Is *minutiae* important?

Is *bickering* pleasant?

Your instructor may give a true-false vocabulary review before or after reading.

THINKING DURING READING

As you read, use the six thinking strategies of a good reader: predict, picture, relate, monitor, correct, and annotate.

WE'LL GO FORWARD FROM THIS MOMENT

Refer to the
Reader's *Tip*
for an **Essay** on
page 521.

September 12, 2001

It's my job to have something to say.

They pay me to provide words that help make sense of that which troubles the American soul. But in this moment of airless shock when hot tears sting disbelieving eyes, the only thing I can find to say, the only words that seem to fit, must be addressed to the

5   unknown author of this suffering.

You monster. You beast. You unspeakable bastard.

What lesson did you hope to teach us by your coward's attack on our World Trade Center, our Pentagon, us? What was it you hoped we would learn? Whatever it was, please know that you failed.

10   Did you want us to respect your cause? You just damned your cause.

Did you want to make us fear? You just steeled our resolve.

Did you want to tear us apart? You just brought us together.

Let me tell you about my people. We are a vast and quarrelsome family, a family rent by racial, social, political and class division, but a family nonetheless. We're frivolous, yes,

15   capable of expending tremendous emotional energy on pop cultural minutiae—a singer's revealing dress, a ball team's misfortune, a cartoon mouse. We're wealthy, too, spoiled by the ready availability of trinkets and material goods, and maybe because of that, we walk through life with a certain sense of blithe entitlement. We are fundamentally decent, though—peace-loving and compassionate. We struggle to know the right thing and to

20   do it. And we are, the overwhelming majority of us, people of faith, believers in a just and loving God.

Some people—you, perhaps—think that any or all of this makes us weak. You're mistaken. We are not weak. Indeed, we are strong in ways that cannot be measured by arsenals.

IN PAIN

Yes, we're in pain now. We are in mourning, and we are in shock. We're still grappling

25   with the unreality of the awful thing you did, still working to make ourselves understand that this isn't a special effect from some Hollywood blockbuster, isn't the plot development from a Tom Clancy novel. Both in terms of the awful scope of their ambition and

the probable final death toll, your attacks are likely to go down as the worst acts of terrorism in the history of the United States and, probably, the history of the world. You've
30 bloodied us as we have never been bloodied before.

But there's a gulf of difference between making us bloody and making us fall. This is
the lesson Japan was taught to its bitter sorrow the last time anyone hit us this hard, the
last time anyone brought us such abrupt and monumental pain. When roused, we are
righteous in our outrage, terrible in our force. When provoked by this level of barbarism,
35 we will bear any suffering, pay any cost, go to any length, in the pursuit of justice.

I tell you this without fear of contradiction. I know my people, as you, I think, do not.
What I know reassures me. It also causes me to tremble with dread of the future.

In the days to come, there will be recrimination and accusation, fingers pointing to
determine whose failure allowed this to happen and what can be done to prevent it from
40 happening again. There will be heightened security, misguided talk of revoking basic
freedoms. We'll go forward from this moment sobered, chastened, sad. But determined,
too. Unimaginably determined.

THE STEEL IN US

You see, the steel in us is not always readily apparent. That aspect of our character is seldom understood by people who don't know us well. On this day, the family's bickering is
45 put on hold.

As Americans we will weep, as Americans we will mourn, and as Americans, we will
rise in defense of all that we cherish.

So I ask again: What was it you hoped to teach us? It occurs to me that maybe you
just wanted us to know the depths of your hatred. If that's the case, consider the message
50 received. And take this message in exchange: You don't know my people. You don't
know what we're capable of. You don't know what you just started.

But you're about to learn.

(704 words)

—"We'll Go Forward from This Moment," by Leonard Pitts, *Miami Herald*

THINKING AND WRITING AFTER READING

RECALL Self-test your understanding.

Your instructor may choose to give you a true-false review.

REACT For what reasons do you think the author feels that "the steel in us is not
always readily apparent"? _____

_____

REFLECT How did Americans act like a family after the events of September 11,
2001? _____

_____

_____

THINKING CRITICALLY What does the author mean by "misguided talk of revoking
basic freedoms"? What would you assume are some of his biases on security
issues? _____

_____

THINK AND WRITE To whom is this column addressed? How does this perspective make the piece unique? Why do you think this column became so famous? __

_____

_____

CRITICAL READING

1. Why does the author begin the selection with "It's my job to have something to say"? _____

   _____

2. What is the author's purpose? _____

   _____

3. Who is the "cartoon mouse" to which the author refers? _____

   _____

4. How, unfortunately, would the terrorists differ with the author's reference to "your coward's attack"? _____

   _____

5. What does the author imply about a Tom Clancy novel? _____

   _____

Interpret the Quote

Now that you have finished reading the selection, "We'll Go Forward from This Moment," go back to the beginning of the selection and read the opening quote again. On a separate sheet of paper, list five ways that Americans used their pain as fuel in order to deal with the events of 9/11.

Name _____

Date _____

COMPREHENSION QUESTIONS

Answer the following with *a, b, c,* or *d,* or fill in the blank. In order to help you analyze your strengths and weaknesses, the question types are indicated.

Main Idea _____ 1. The best statement of the main idea of the selection is:

   a. The author appeals to Americans to rally against terrorism.
   b. The author condemns governments that harbor terrorists.
   c. The author condemns the terrorists and warns of American strength.
   d. The author condemns the cultural differences that created the hatred of the terrorists.

Inference _____ 2. The author's tone is

   a. compassionate.
   b. angry.
   c. sarcastic.
   d. melancholy.

Inference _____ 3. The author calls Americans a "family" because Americans

   a. are composed of racial, social, political, and class divisions.
   b. disagree with each other but come together to forget differences in a crisis.
   c. enjoy the same pop cultural minutiae.
   d. are people of faith.

Inference _____ 4. By using the phrase "we walk through life with a certain sense of blithe entitlement," the author suggests that Americans

   a. appreciate the trinkets and material goods that are readily available.
   b. are decent citizens who feel the suffering of others.
   c. casually act as if it is their right to have a grand array of goods.
   d. recognize the insecurity of the country's borders.

Inference   5. What does the author mean by Americans' being "capable of expending tremendous emotional energy on pop cultural minutiae"?

   _____

   _____

Inference _____ 6. By referring to the "special effects from some Hollywood blockbuster," the author suggests that Americans are

   a. addicted to violence in the movies.
   b. manipulated by Hollywood.
   c. suspicious that the idea for the attack came from a movie.
   d. still in some level of disbelief.

Inference _____ 7. The "lesson Japan was taught to its bitter sorrow" refers to

   a. the economic impact of tariffs on imported Japanese cars.
   b. the reduction of immigration quotas for Japan.
   c. the defeat of Japan in World War II.
   d. the sinking of American ships.

Answer the following with *T* (true), *F* (false), or *CT* (can't tell).

Inference _____ 8. By saying that "we are strong in ways that cannot be measured by arsenals," the author implies that the American military is not strong.

Inference _____ 9. The author implies that he trembles with dread of the future because he fears the terrorists.

Detail _____ 10. The author suggests that American investigators will seek answers to learn how the attacks were allowed to happen.

VOCABULARY

Answer the following with *a, b, c,* or *d* for the word or phrase that best defines the boldface word as used in the selection. The number in parentheses indicates the line of the passage in which the word appears.

_____ 1. "**steeled** our resolve" (11)

    a. stole
    b. strengthened
    c. lessened
    d. removed

_____ 2. "We're **frivolous**" (14)

    a. oblivious
    b. ignorant
    c. arrogant
    d. playful

_____ 3. "pop cultural **minutiae**" (15)

    a. trivia
    b. history
    c. questions
    d. arguments

_____ 4. "**blithe** entitlement" (18)

    a. equal
    b. carefree
    c. harsh
    d. dishonest

_____ 5. "blithe **entitlement**" (18)

    a. longing
    b. ownership right
    c. realism
    d. satisfaction

_____ 6. "**grappling** with the unreality" (24)

    a. sleeping
    b. struggling
    c. overreacting
    d. replying

_____ 7. "**recrimination** and accusation" (38)

    a. suggestions
    b. orders
    c. guesses
    d. blame

_____ 8. "sobered, **chastened**, sad" (41)

    a. punished
    b. hesitant
    c. afraid
    d. humiliated

_____ 9. "the family's **bickering**" (44)

    a. ethnic differences
    b. unity
    c. squabbling
    d. leadership

_____ 10. "all that we **cherish**" (47)

    a. value
    b. desire
    c. own
    d. lost

Your instructor may choose to give a true-false review.

VOCABULARY ENRICHMENT

Select the word from the list that best completes each sentence.

steeled	frivolous	minutiae	blithe	entitlement
grappling	recriminations	chastened	bickering	cherish

1. The new buildings at Ground Zero will have a memorial so that Americans can come to _____ the memory of those who were lost.

2. Families, _____ with the horror of missing relatives, posted pictures and pleas on the wall around Ground Zero.

3. The _____ spirited tourists enjoying Central Park froze in fear with the sounds and confusion of the disaster.

4. In the aftermath, _____ were hurled at the intelligence gathering of the FBI and the CIA.

5. The _____ of network sitcoms was replaced with 24-hour coverage of the disaster.

6. Unfortunately, agencies in charge of dispersing contributions engaged in some _____ with family members over the amounts.

7. Airline passengers _____ themselves for long delays and baggage checks.

8. In the September 11 attacks, Americans were _____ by the hatred of terrorists.

9. The feeling of a national _____ to security within American borders changed after September 11.

10. The _____ atmosphere of Times Square disappeared as people ran for protection.

ASSESS YOUR LEARNING

Review confusing questions, seek clarification, and make notes in your text to help you remember new information and vocabulary.

Vocabulary Lesson

Bend, Born, and Body

Study the roots, words, and sentences.

| **Roots** | *flex, flect*: bend | *nat, nasc*: born | *corp*: body |

Words with *flex* or *flect* = *bend*

Do dancers need to be <u>flexible</u>? Can you see your <u>reflection</u> in the pond?

- Flex: to bend

  Flex your muscles to show your strength.

- Deflect: bend away from

  The politician was able to *deflect* the vicious questions and move ahead.

- Genuflection: bending the knees, bowing

  My arrogant boss seems to expect total submission and *genuflection*.

- Inflection: the rise and fall of the voice

  The *inflection* in his voice revealed that his feelings had been hurt.

- Reflect: to think back to

  Reflect on literary readings through a discussion with others.

- Reflective: thoughtful

  Quiet, *reflective* moments can give a sense of inner peace.

- Reflector: that which sends back light

  Wear a *reflector* when you walk at night.

Words with *nat* or *nasc* = *born*

Does July 4th create a sense of <u>nationalism</u>? Is New York an <u>international</u> city?

- Native: belonging to by birth

  Are palm trees *native* to your area?

- Naïve: acting as one born yesterday

  The *naïve* respondent thought she had won a prize.

- Naturalize: to give citizenship to one foreign born

  Gisela has been a *naturalized* citizen of this country for two years.

- Innate: inborn

  Freud believed that mankind had an *innate* fear of spiders and snakes.

- Renaissance: a rebirth or revival

  The inner city is experiencing a *renaissance* with urban pioneers.

- Nationality: country of origin

  Her *nationality* is either Mexican or Costa Rican.

Words with *corp* or *corpor* = body

Are <u>corporate</u> headquarters lavish? Is any business <u>incorporable</u>?

- Corporal: relating to the body

  The scars indicated *corporal* punishment.

- Corporation: business people united legally

  The president of the *corporation* received stock bonuses.

- Incorporate: to unite legally, add

  You need to *incorporate* a visual display into the oral presentation.

- Corps: group organized for a common cause

  The Peace *Corps* members are sent to remote areas to help people.

- Corpuscle: a cell that flows in the blood

  A *corpuscle* can be a red or white blood cell.

- Corpse: a dead body

  An autopsy was performed on the *corpse* because of questions surrounding the death.

- Corpulent: excessively fat

  Santa Claus is *corpulent* and jolly.

Review

Part I

Answer the following with (*T*) true or (*F*) false.

_____ 1. A reflective thinker seldom recalls the past.

_____ 2. Flexible clay can still be molded.

_____ 3. A corpulent corpse will probably be difficult to move.

_____ 4. Spanking a child is corporal punishment.

_____ 5. Corpuscles are found in many plants.

_____ 6. If you look in a mirror, you can see your reflection.

_____ 7. An innate talent is a genetic gift.

_____ 8. Companies on the New York Stock Exchange are incorporated.

_____ 9. A deflected arrow is repelled from the target.

_____ 10. Immigrants must apply to become naturalized citizens.

Part II

Choose the best word from the list to complete the following sentences.

naïve	corps	reflectors	nationalism	inflection
flex	renaissance	genuflect	native	nationality

11. His final voice ——————— indicated that he was asking a question.

12. On Halloween night parents attach safety ——————— to costumes.

13. Some flowers ——————— to the swamp do not grow in the mountains.

14. The army called on the ——————— of engineers to replace the bridge.

15. Freshman are ——————— to think a late paper will not be penalized.

16. When the king entered, servants were to ——————— with respect.

17. The music of the military band heightened our feelings of ———————.

18. The ——————— of the speaker was Colombian, not Cuban.

19. When you lift weights, you ——————— your muscles.

20. New shops herald a ——————— of the downtrodden warehouse area.

Evaluating Internet Information

For researching anything from recent movie reviews to Shakespearean interpretations, the Internet offers easy access to up-to-date information. The disadvantage of Internet information, however, is that you must always question its reliability and credibility. Unlike the scholarly periodicals in libraries that are reviewed by experts, there are no gatekeepers on the Internet. Anyone from a Nobel Prize scientist to a paramilitary fanatic can purchase a Web site for approximately $100, self-publish, sound like an expert, and turn up in your search.

Be prepared to use your critical reading skills to evaluate Internet material. Question not only what is said, but also who wrote it and who paid for it.

Reader's *Tip* Critically Evaluating Electronic Material

Ask the following questions to evaluate:

- What are the author's credentials in the field? Is the author affiliated with a university? Check this by noting professional titles in the preface or introduction, finding a biographical reference in the library, or searching the Internet for additional references to the same author.
- Who paid for the Web page? Check the home page for an address. Does the electronic address end in *edu, gov, org,* or *com*? Depending on the material, this sponsor could lend credibility or raise further questions.
- What is the purpose of the Web page? Is the purpose to educate or to sell a product, a service, or an idea? Check the links to investigate any hidden agendas.
- How do the biases of the author and the sponsor affect the material? Is the reasoning sound? Check the tone, assumptions, and evidence. What opposing views have been left out?

Refer to the Web site on the following page to complete Exercise 1.

exercise 1

1. What is the purpose of this site? _____

2. What are the credentials of the author? _____

3. Who paid for the site? _____

4. Why are you inclined to believe or not believe the information in the letter?

_____

SanRafael.com

San Rafael
Nutrition Company, Inc.

Welcome to the new world of health and fitness, to the incredible benefits of looking great and feeling fantastic! Forget about sweating at the gym, tedious treadmills and crowded aerobic classes. What I have to offer is a no-hassle, easy way to drop unwanted pounds for a healthier, more energetic YOU!!

This is all made possible by the San Rafael Program™, my amazing combination of all natural ingredients, including Translite™ and ZX-12™. Until now, the patented formula in the San Rafael Program™ has been the secret of **Hollywood celebrities** and others whose careers depend on a youthful, healthy appearance. The **three simple steps** of the program have been clinically proven not only to help you lose weight fast and boost your energy level, but also to help rid your body of unhealthy toxins that upset your natural metabolic balance.

To find out more about the astounding results made possible by the San Rafael Program™, click on *Info*. To order samples or to get your own supply of this fantastic product, click on *Shopping*. To find out how you can enjoy the advantages of better health as well as the financial benefits of becoming a distributor of the San Rafael Program™, click on *Network*.

Whatever option you choose, I want to welcome you to a better, healthier life and to becoming a member of the San Rafael family!

Sincerely,

Marilyn Obado

Marilyn Obado
President
San Rafael Nutrition Co., Inc.

Info   **Shopping**   **Network**

exercise 2   Search the Internet for a Web site that sells antiaging products, such as creams that claim to prevent wrinkles or vitamin concoctions that claim to enhance vitality. Print the page, then make a list of the claims you feel are exaggerated and not supported by facts.

Appendix 1

Sample Textbook Chapter

As a further practice exercise, this appendix presents one complete textbook chapter, "Leadership and Management," which is Chapter 14 of John R. Walker's *Introduction to Hospitality*, Fifth Edition. No knowledge of the rest of that book is needed to fully understand this chapter. The superscript numbers in the text refer readers to the Endnotes, which appear on the last page of the chapter, page 490.

As you read, organize your study according to the strategies outlined in the previous chapters. Use the six thinking strategies of a good reader: predict, picture, relate, monitor, correct, and annotate as you read. Take notes on what you want to remember.

CHAPTER **14**

Leadership and Management

OBJECTIVES

After reading and studying this chapter, you should be able to:

- Identify the characteristics and practices of leaders and managers.

- Define *leadership* and *management*.

- Differentiate between leadership and management.

- Describe the key management functions.

467

Leadership

Our fascination with **leadership** goes back many centuries. Lately, however, it has come into prominence in the hospitality, tourism, and other industries as these industries strive for perfection in the delivery of services and products in an increasingly competitive environment. Leaders can and do make a difference when measuring a company's success.

One person working alone can accomplish few tasks or goals. You have probably already experienced being part of a group that had good leadership. It might have been with a school, social, sporting, church, or other group in which the leader made a difference. The reverse might also be true: You may have been in a group with ineffective leadership. Few groups can accomplish much without an individual who acts as an effective leader. The leader can and often does have a significant influence on the group and its direction.

Characteristics and Practices of Leaders

So, what are the ingredients that result in leadership excellence? If you look at the military for examples of leadership excellence, you see that leaders can be identified by certain characteristics. For example, the *U.S. Guidebook for Marines* lists the following leadership traits:

- Courage
- Decisiveness
- Dependability
- Endurance
- Enthusiasm
- Initiative
- Unselfishness

- Integrity
- Judgment
- Justice
- Knowledge
- Loyalty
- Tact

A Marine officer would likely choose integrity as the most important trait. Integrity has been defined as "doing something right even though no one may be aware of it."

In addition to these leadership traits, the following identifiable practices are common to leaders:

1. *Challenge the process* Be active, not passive; search for opportunities; experiment and take risks.
2. *Inspire a shared vision* Create a vision; envision the future; enlist others.
3. *Enable others to act* Do not act alone; foster collaboration; strengthen others.
4. *Model the way* Plan; set examples; strive for small wins.
5. *Encourage the heart* Share the passion; recognize individual contributions; celebrate accomplishments.

Definitions of Leadership

Because of the complexities of leadership, the different types of leadership, and individual perceptions of leaders, leadership has several definitions. Many definitions share commonalities, but there are also differences. In terms of hospitality leadership, the following definition is appropriate: "Leading is the process by which a person with vision is able to influence the activities and outcomes of others in a desired way."

Leaders know what they want and why they want it—and they are able to communicate those desires to others to gain their cooperation and support. Leadership theory and practice has evolved over time to a point where current industry practitioners may be identified as transactional or transformational leaders.[1]

INTRODUCING HERB KELLEHER

Former CEO of Southwest Airlines

Herb Kelleher, who recently gave up the titles of chairman and CEO to two other Southwest executives, is the living embodiment of the phrase "one of a kind." With his charismatic personality, he is a person who leaves a distinctive mark on whatever he does. Since the birth of Southwest Airlines in 1971 (actually, Rollin W. King, a banking client of Herb's at the time, conceived Southwest Airlines after he had drawn, on a cocktail napkin, a triangle connecting Texas's three major cities: Dallas, Houston, and San Antonio), Herb Kelleher—"Herb" to even his most distant acquaintances—nurtured Southwest Airlines into the seventh largest airline. The company has been profitable every year since 1973. When other carriers lost billions or were struggling with bankruptcy, Southwest was the only company that remained consistently profitable—a record unmatched in the U.S. airline industry—cheerfully pursuing its growth plans by buying more planes, expanding into new cities, and hiring personnel. Southwest is also a model of efficiency: It is a multiple-time winner of the U.S. Department of Transportation's Triple Crown, a monthly citation for the best on-time performance, fewest lost bags, and fewest overall complaints. Kelleher's operation, based on flights covering relatively short distances for prices that are sometimes shockingly low, is likely to experience rapid growth and become even more of a leading power.

One of the keys to this success lies in the company's mission. Southwest Airlines aims at providing cheap, simple, and focused airline service. Kelleher devoted enormous attention to thousands of small decisions, all designed to achieve simplicity. Among these small but tremendously strategic decisions were the removal of closets at the front of the planes to improve passengers' speed in boarding and departing and no onboard food, except snacks, which is justified by the number of short flights (those of about 400 miles). Southwest also refused full participation on computerized reservations systems used by travel agents. More than 80 percent of all Southwest tickets are sold directly to customers, saving the company millions annually. There is no assigned seating and no first-class seating. Planes have been

continued

INTRODUCING HERB KELLEHER (continued)

standardized: Southwest operates only one type of aircraft, the 737, which simplifies flight crew training and maintenance personnel training.

These relatively minor privations have their positive counterpart in the fact that Southwest ground crew can turn around a plane at the gate in about twenty minutes! The airline's customers especially appreciate its low fares and on-time schedules.

Who is behind all this? The airline's success is credited to Kelleher's unorthodox personality and entrepreneurial management style. Born and raised in New Jersey, he was the son of the general manager of Campbell Soups, Inc. He began to show leadership qualities as student body president both in high school and in college. From his original idea of becoming a journalist, Kelleher shifted his goal to the practice of law. By the mid-1960s, he was successfully practicing in San Antonio, Texas, his wife's hometown. However, he was always seeking the possibility of starting a venture of his own. The big chance came in 1966 when a banker client, Rollin King, suggested that Texas needed a short-haul commuter airline. That was the trigger: Southwest was born in 1971.

While CEO, Herb directly supervised his business, personally approving expenses over $1,000. His outstanding hands-on efforts also led to unusually good labor–management relations, on the basis of the motto "People are the most important of resources." In fact, he managed to establish a strong bond of loyalty between employees and their company that may have disappeared elsewhere in the American corporate environment.

He still represents some sort of a father figure to SWA, as well as the jester, and the "Lord of Ha-Ha." The effort that he was able to get out of his employees made the real difference. Unlike workers at most other carriers, Southwest employees are willing to pitch in no matter what the task. For example, a reservations sales clerk in Dallas took a call from an anxious customer who was putting his eighty eight-year-old mother aboard a flight to St. Louis. The woman was quite frail, the fellow explained, and he wasn't quite sure she could handle the change of planes in Tulsa. "No sweat!" replied the clerk. "I'll fly with her as far as Tulsa and make sure she gets safely on the St. Louis flight."

Kelleher's outstanding leadership ability is also demonstrated by his long-term thinking. He gathered a top-rank team of successors, which will guarantee the airline's future prosperity. Kelleher is the leader who inspires, the amiable uncle to consult, the cheerleader who motivates, and the clown who spreads cheer. There are many great stories about Herb Kelleher; this is one of the most popular: Southwest was being threatened by an aviation services company over the advertising slogan "Plane Smart." Instead of incurring huge attorneys' fees and dealing with months-long litigation, the two CEOs agreed to settle the matter with an arm-wrestling contest. Herb actually lost the contest, but the other CEO had so much fun that the lawsuit was dropped. Both companies saved a bundle in legal fees.

Transactional Leadership

Transactional leadership is viewed as a process by which a leader is able to bring about desired actions from others by using certain behaviors, rewards, or incentives. In essence, an exchange or transaction takes place between leader and follower. Figure 14–1 shows the transactional leadership model. This concept illustrates the coming together of the leader, the situation, and the followers. A hotel general manager who pressures the food and beverage director to achieve certain goals in exchange for a bonus is an example of someone practicing transactional leadership.

Figure 14–1 • Transactional Leadership Model.

Transformational Leadership

Leadership involves looking for ways to bring about longer-term, higher-order changes in follower behavior. This brings us to transformational leadership. The term **transformational leadership** is used to describe the process of eliciting performance above and beyond normal expectations. A transformational leader is one who inspires others to reach beyond themselves and do more than they originally thought possible; this is accomplished by raising their commitment to a shared vision of the future.

Transformational leaders practice a hands-on philosophy, not in terms of performing the day-to-day tasks of subordinates, but in developing and encouraging their followers individually. Transformational leadership involves three important factors:

1. Charisma
2. Individual consideration
3. Intellectual stimulation

Of course, it is also possible to be a charismatic transformational leader as well as a transactional leader. Although this does involve a measurable amount of effort, these leaders are guaranteed to rake in success throughout their careers.

Examples of Excellence in Leadership

Dr. Martin Luther King Jr. was one of the most charismatic transformational leaders in history. King dedicated his life to achieving rights for all citizens by nonviolent methods. His dream of how society could be was shared by millions of Americans. In 1964, Dr. King won the Nobel Peace Prize.

Another transformational leader is Herb Kelleher, former president, CEO, and current board

Martin Luther King Jr. One of the Most Charismatic Transformational Leaders of the Twentieth Century, Giving His Famous "I Have A Dream" Speech member of Southwest Airlines, who is profiled in this chapter. He was able to inspire his followers to pursue his corporate vision and reach beyond themselves to give Southwest Airlines that something extra that set it apart from its competitors.

Kelleher recognizes that the company does not exist merely for the gratification of its employees. He knows that Southwest Airlines must perform and must be profitable. However, he believes strongly that valuing individuals for themselves is the best way to attain exceptional performance. Passengers who fly Southwest Airlines may have seen Herb Kelleher because he travels frequently and previously was likely to be found serving drinks, fluffing pillows, or just wandering up and down the aisle, talking to passengers. The success of Southwest and the enthusiasm of its employees indicate that Herb Kelleher achieved his goal of weaving together individual and corporate interests so that all members of the Southwest family benefit. Kelleher is a great transformational leader who is able to lead by visioning, inspiring, empowering, and communicating.[2]

In their fascinating book *Lessons in Leadership: Perspectives for Hospitality Industry Success*, Bill Fisher, former president and CEO of the American Hotel & Lodging Association and currently Darden Eminent Scholar at the University of Central Florida, and Charles Bernstein, editor of *Nation's Restaurant News*, interviewed more than 100 industry leaders and asked each to give advice in an up-close-and-personal manner. Here is an example of the leaders' answers:

"Experience is a hard teacher. It gives the test first, and then you learn the lesson." Richard P. Mayer, former chairman and CEO of Kentucky Fried Chicken and president of General Foods Corporation, says that the key traits and factors that he looks for in assessing talent include the following:

- Established personal goals
- The drive and ambition to attain those goals, tempered and strengthened with integrity
- Proven analytical and communications skills
- Superior interpersonal capabilities
- A sense of humor
- An awareness and appreciation of the world beyond her or his business specialty
- Receptivity to ideas (no matter the source)
- A genuine, deep commitment to the growth and profitability of the business

The essence of success has as many meanings as there are people to ponder it. One concept of success is to couple one's personal and family interests, dreams, and aspirations with a business or professional career such that they complement and fortify each other. Another aspect of leadership is the ability to motivate others in a hospitality working environment; decision making is also essential. These are discussed later in the chapter.

FOCUS ON LEADERSHIP

Leadership—The Basis for Management

William Fisher, Darden Eminent Scholar in Restaurant Management, author and former executive vice president of the National Restaurant Association and the American Hotel & Lodging Association

The concept and practice of leadership as it applies to management carries a fascination and attraction for most people. We all like to think we have some leadership qualities and we strive to develop them. We look at leaders in all walks of life, seeking to identify which qualities, traits, and skills they possess so that we can emulate them. A fundamental question remains: What is the essence of leadership that results in successful management as opposed to failed management? At least part of the answer can be found within the word itself.

1. *Loyalty.* Leadership starts with a loyalty quadrant: loyalty to one's organization and its mission, loyalty to organizational superiors, loyalty to subordinates, and loyalty to oneself. Loyalty is multidirectional, running up and down in the organization. When everyone practices it, loyalty bonds occur, which drives high morale. Loyalty to oneself is based on maintaining a sound body, mind, and spirit so that one is always "riding the top of the wave" in service to others.

2. *Excellence.* Leaders know that excellence is a value, not an object. They strive for both excellence and success. Excellence is the measurement you make of yourself in assessing what you do and how well you do it; success is an external perception that others have of you.

3. *Assertiveness.* Leaders possess a mental and physical intensity that causes them to seek control, take command, assume the mantle of responsibility, and focus on the objective(s). Leaders do not evidence self-doubt as they are comfortable within themselves that what they are doing is right, which, in turn, gives them the courage to take action.

4. *Dedication.* Leaders are dedicated in mind, body, and spirit to their organization and to achievement. They are action oriented, not passive, and prefer purposeful activity to the status quo. They possess an aura or charisma that sets them apart from others with whom they interact, always working in the best interest of their organization.

5. *Enthusiasm.* Leaders are their own best cheerleaders on behalf of their organization and people. They exude enthusiasm and instill it in others to the point of contagion. Their style may be one of poise, stability, clear vision, and articulate speech, but their bristling enthusiasm undergirds their every waking moment.

6. *Risk management.* Leaders realize that risk taking is part of their management perch. They manage risk, rather than letting it manage them, knowing full well that there are no guaranteed outcomes, no foregone conclusions, no preordained results when one is dealing with the future. Nonetheless, they measure risk, adapt to it, control it, and surmount it.

7. *Strength.* Leaders possess an inner fiber of stamina, fortitude, and vibrancy that gives them a mental toughness, causing them to withstand interruption, crises, and unforeseen circumstances that would slow down or immobilize most people. Leaders become all the more energized in the face of surprises.

8. *Honor.* Leaders understand they will leave a legacy, be it good, bad, or indifferent. True leaders recognize that all their relationships and actions are based on the highest standard of honor and integrity. They do the right things correctly, shun short-term, improper expediency, and set the example for others with high-mindedness, professional bearing, and unassailable character.   *continued*

FOCUS ON LEADERSHIP (continued)

9. *Inspiration.* Leaders don't exist without followers. People will follow leaders who inspire them to reach beyond the normal and ordinary to new levels of accomplishment, new heights of well-being, and new platforms for individual, organizational, and societal good. Inspiration is what distinguishes a leader from a mere position holder, as the leader can touch the heart, mind, and soul of others.

10. *Performance.* At the end of the day, leader–managers rise or fall on the most critical of all measurements: their performance. Results come first, but the ways in which results are achieved are also crucial to sustaining a leader's role. Many dictators don't last despite results, and many charismatics don't last despite personal charm.

Putting the ten elements together spells LEADERSHIP! Always remember, if you want to develop a leadership quality, act as though you already possess it!

Demands Placed on Leaders

Demands on a leader in the hospitality industry include those made by owners, the corporate office, guests, employees, regulatory agencies, and competitors (Figure 14–2). In response to many demands, the leader must balance two additional forces: how much energy to expend on getting results and how much to expend on relationships (Figure 14–3).

Applied social scientists such as Peter Drucker, powerful industry leaders such as Bill Marriott, and public service leaders such as former New York mayor Rudolph Giuliani all seem to have common traits, among which are the following:

1. High ego strength
2. Ability to think strategically
3. Orientation toward the future

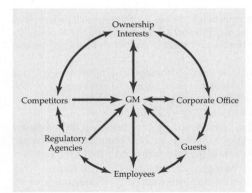

Figure 14–2 • Dynamics of Demands on General Managers in the Hospitality Industry.

Figure 14–3 • Amount of Energy the General Manager Needs to Spend on Getting Results and Maintaining Relationships.

4. A belief in certain fundamental principles of human behavior
5. Strong connections that they do not hesitate to display
6. Political astuteness
7. Ability to use power both for efficiency and for the larger good of the organization

Leaders vary in their values, managerial styles, and priorities. Peter Drucker, the renowned management scholar, author, and consultant of many years, has discussed with hundreds of leaders their roles, goals, and performance. These discussions took place with leaders of large and small organizations, with for-profit and volunteer organizations. Interestingly, Drucker observes:

> All the leaders I have encountered—both those I worked with and those I watched—realized:
>
> 1. The only definition of a leader is someone who has followers. Some people are thinkers. Some are prophets. Both roles are important and badly needed. But without followers, there can be no leaders.
> 2. An effective leader is not someone who is loved or admired. She or he is someone whose followers do the right things. Popularity is not leadership. Results are.
> 3. Leaders are highly visible. They therefore set examples.
> 4. Leadership is not about rank, privileges, titles, or money. It is about responsibility.[3]

Drucker adds that regardless of their enormous diversity with respect to personality, style, abilities, and interests, effective leaders all behave in much the same way:

1. They did not start out with the question "What do I want?" They started out asking, "What needs to be done?"
2. Then they asked, "What can and should I do to make a difference?" This has to be something that both needs to be done and fits the leader's strengths and the way she or he is most effective.
3. They constantly asked, "What are the organization's mission and goals? What constitutes performance and results in this organization?"
4. They were extremely tolerant of diversity in people and did not look for carbon copies of themselves. It rarely even occurred to them to ask, "Do I like or dislike this person?" But they were totally—fiendishly—intolerant when it came to a person's performance, standards, and values.
5. They were not afraid of strength in their associates. They gloried in it. Whether they had heard of it or not, their motto was the one Andrew Carnegie wanted to have put on his tombstone: "Here lies a man who attracted better people into his service than he was himself."
6. One way or another, they submitted themselves to the mirror test—that is, they made sure the person they saw in the mirror in the morning was the kind of person they wanted to be, respect, and believe in. This way they

fortified themselves against the leader's greatest temptations—to do things that are popular rather than right and to do petty, mean, sleazy things.[4]

Finally, these leaders were not preachers; they were doers.

The most effective leaders share a number of skills, and these skills are always related to dealing with employees. The following suggestions outline an approach to becoming a hotel leader rather than just a manager:

- *Be decisive.* Hotel managers are confronted with dozens of decisions every day. Obviously, you should use your best judgment to resolve the decisions that come to roost at your doorstep. As a boss, make the decisions that best meet both your objectives and your ethics and then make your decisions known.

- *Follow through.* Never promise what you can't deliver, and never build false hopes among your employees. Once expectations are dashed, respect for and the reputation of the boss are shot.

- *Select the best.* A boss, good or bad, is carried forward by the work of his or her subordinates. One key to being a good boss is to hire the people who have the best potential to do what you need them to do. Take the time and effort to screen, interview, and assess the people who have not only the skills that you require, but also the needed values.

- *Empower employees.* Give people the authority to interact with the customer. The more important people feel, the better they work.

- *Enhance career development.* Good bosses recognize that most of their people want to improve themselves. However, career development is a two-edged sword: If we take the initiative to train and develop our people properly, then the competition is likely to hire them. The only way a boss can prevent the loss of productive workers looking for career development is to provide opportunities for growth within the organization.

In recent years, the role of the hotel general manager has changed from that of being a congenial host, knowledgeable about the niceties of hotelmanship, to that of a multigroup pleaser. Guests, employees, owners, and community should all be not only satisfied but delighted with the operation's performance.

Many general managers (GMs) are so bogged down with meetings, reports, and "putting out fires" that they hardly have any time to spend with guests. One GM who makes time is Richard Riley, GM of the fabulous Shangri-La Hotel Makati in Manila, the Philippines. Richard extends an invitation for guests to visit with him in the hotel lobby between 5:00 and 7:00 P.M. every Thursday. As GM of a luxury Caribbean resort in Barbados, West Indies, the author personally greeted every guest to the property. Obviously, there is a difference between a small resort and a large city hotel. Resort guests stay for at least two, sometimes four, weeks in high season, so they need the individual attention.

▶ Check Your Knowledge

1. What three factors does transformational leadership involve?
2. Define *leadership*.
3. Describe some examples of leadership.
4. Explain the demands placed on leaders.

Hospitality Management

Managers plan, organize, make decisions, communicate, motivate, and control the efforts of a group to accomplish predetermined goals. Management also establishes the direction the organization will take. Sometimes this is done with the help of employees or outside consultants, such as marketing research specialists. Managers obtain the necessary resources for the goals to be accomplished, and then they supervise and monitor group and individual progress toward goal accomplishment.

Managers, such as presidents and chief executive officers, who are responsible for the entire company, tend to focus most of their time on strategic planning and the organization's mission. They also spend time organizing and controlling the activities of the corporation. Most top managers do not get involved in the day-to-day aspects of the operation. These duties and responsibilities fall to the middle and supervisory management. In hospitality lingo, one would not expect Bill Marriott to pull a shift behind the bar at the local Marriott hotel. Although capable, his time and expertise are used in shaping the company's future. Thus, although the head bartender and Bill Marriott may both be considered management, they require slightly different skills to be effective and efficient managers.

What Is Management?

Management is simply what managers do: plan, organize, make decisions, communicate, motivate, and control. *Management* is defined as "the process of working with and through others to accomplish organizational goals in an efficient and effective way." In looking at this statement, you can see that the functions of

INTRODUCING STEVE PINETTI

Senior VP Sales and Marketing, Kimpton Hotels and Restaurants

Steve Pinetti grew up in the San Francisco Bay area, worked for Hilton and Hyatt, taught at all the San Francisco Bay area colleges and universities, founded his own marketing company, and was one of Bill Kimpton's first partners in founding Kimpton Hotels and Restaurants. Steve now is the senior vice president of sales and marketing for Kimpton Hotels and Restaurants. Steve oversees branding efforts, sales, distribution, customer relationship management (CRM), Internet presence, public relations, strategic partnerships, and new hotel openings. Steve has an interesting challenge because both existing large hotel chains and new hotel companies claim to be the "boutique hotel" leader. In fact, Kimpton invented the concept in 1981: a unique, independent boutique hotel paired with a chef-driven/specialty restaurant. Says Steve, "The need to stay ahead of the growing competition as well as on top our own game is never ending. We stay tuned to our customers' behavior, needs, and purchasing process to better understand where consumer thinking, influences and spending are headed.

"Because word of mouth is the number one source of our business, we need to stay close to what our guests want, need, say, and do. We have developed a skill set around niche marketing. Since the advent of search on the Net, we have been able to get out from the shadow of the large bully brands and market to consumers who put value on personal preferences and individual style in all they do—especially travel. Since 9/11 we have found that there is a movement toward thinking about today versus the future. People are focusing their thinking on what's important to me today. What is that 'thing' I keep putting off—now is the time to do it. Wellness, pampering, learning nuggets of information (how to read a painting), and discovery skills (cooking classes) are what are becoming more important. These are the types of people looking for and staying at Kimpton Hotels". The biggest project on Steve's plate is the recent rollout of the new Kimpton brand. "Getting every employee to understand the Kimpton brand, its promise, and the guests' expectations around our promise is proving to be a very large, ongoing project. The other half of this proposition is making sure every guest in every hotel each day knows he or she is in a hotel that is part of a larger collection—Kimpton Hotels.

"You need to do the basics in order for your business to survive, but you also need to take calculated risks in order to outdistance and separate yourself from the competition as well as gain notice by the unchained shopper. Taking risks is not in one's human nature, but it is something we highly value at Kimpton. By taking risks we have come up with some of the firsts in our industry. They include social wine hour every night in every Kimpton hotel, tall rooms for tall travelers, complimentary goldfish, first company to offer complimentary high-speed access, celebrity suites (Jerry Garcia, Carlos Santana), specialty suites with workout equipment, and Eco Floors."

Advice

Anything that requires the understanding and implementation of employees needs to be fully communicated well before being instituted operationally. The communication process around understating why and how as well as the benefits to all involved is more important than the actual action. It creates buy-in and buy-off. It ensures that the people who are going to be responsible for implementing it or designing the process buy in versus inherit some program cooked up from the corporate offices.

Thoughts

Success comes from involving and harnessing all the technical and human resources available. It's vital to keep a balance in one's life between home, work, and self. You need to continue to maintain the basics yet reinvent yourself to keep up with trends and times.

management and working with and through the work of others are ongoing. Additionally, management involves getting efficient and effective results.

Efficiency is getting the most done with the fewest number of inputs. Managers work with scarce resources: money, people, time, and equipment. You can imagine the rush in the kitchen to be ready for a meal service. But it's not enough to just be efficient; management is also about being effective. **Effectiveness** is "doing the right thing." As an example, cooks do the right thing when they cook the food correctly according to the recipe and have it ready when needed.

Who Are Managers?

The changing nature of organizations and work has, in many hospitality organizations, blurred the lines of distinction between managers and nonmanagerial employees. Many traditional jobs now include managerial activities, especially when teams are used. For instance, team members often develop plans, make decisions, and monitor their own performance. This is the case with total quality management.

So, how do we define who managers are? A manager is someone who works with and manages others' activities to accomplish organizational goals in an efficient and effective way. Managers are often classified into three levels: **front-line managers** are the lowest-level managers; they manage the work of line employees. They may also be called supervisors. A front-office supervisor, for example, takes charge of a shift and supervises the guest service agents on the shift.

Middle managers are akin to department heads; they fall between front-line managers and top management. They are responsible for short- to medium-range plans, and they establish goals and objectives to meet these goals. They manage the work of front-line managers.

Top managers are responsible for making medium- to long-range plans and for establishing goals and strategies to meet those goals. Figure 14–4 shows the three levels of management plus nonmanagerial employees.

Key Management Functions

The key management functions are planning, organizing, decision making, communicating, human resources and motivating, and controlling. These management functions are not conducted in isolation; rather they are interdependent and frequently happen simultaneously or at least overlap. Figure 14–5 shows the key management functions leading to goal accomplishment.

Top Managers
Middle Managers
Front-line Managers
Nonmanagerial Associates

Figure 14–4 • Three Levels of Management Plus Nonmanagerial Associates.

Figure 14–5 • Key Management Functions Leading to Goal Accomplishment.

Hospitality companies exist to serve a particular purpose, and someone has to determine the vision, mission, goals, and strategies to reach or exceed the goals. That someone is management. The **planning** function involves setting the company's goals and developing plans to meet or exceed those goals. Once plans are complete, **organizing** is the process of deciding what needs to be done, who will do it, how the tasks will be grouped, who reports to whom, and who makes decisions.

Decision making is a key management function. The success of all hospitality companies, whether large, multinational corporations or sole proprietorships, depends on the quality of the decision making. Decision making includes determining the vision, mission, goals, and objectives of the company. Decision making also includes scheduling employees, determining what to put on the menu, and responding to guest needs.

Communication with and motivation of individuals and groups are required to get the job done. **Human resources and motivating** involves attracting and retaining the best employees and keeping morale high.

Controlling is the final management function that brings everything full circle. After the goals are set and the plans formulated, management then organizes, communicates, and motivates the resources required to complete the job. Controlling includes the setting of standards and comparing actual results with these standards. If significant deviations are seen, they are investigated and corrective action taken to get performance back on target. This scientific process of monitoring, comparing, and correcting is the controlling function and is necessary to ensure that there are no surprises and that no one is guessing.

Managerial Skills

In addition to the management functions of forecasting, planning, organizing, communicating, motivating, and controlling, managers also need other major skills: conceptual, interpersonal, and technical.

Conceptual skills enable top managers to view the corporation as a complete entity and yet understand how it is split into departments to achieve specific goals. Conceptual skills allow a top manager to view the entire corporation, especially the interdependence of the various departments.

Managers need to lead, influence, communicate, supervise, coach, and evaluate employees' performances. This necessitates a high level of interpersonal human skills. The abilities to build teams and work with others are human skills that successful managers need to cultivate.

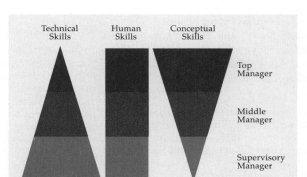

Figure 14–6 • Management Skill Areas.

Managers need to have the technical skills required to understand and use modern techniques, methods, equipment, and procedures. These skills are more important for lower levels of management. As a manager rises through the ranks, the need for technical skills decreases and the need for conceptual skills increases.

You next need to realize the critical importance of the corporate philosophy, culture, and values, and a corporation's mission, goals, and objectives. Figure 14–6 shows the degree of managerial skills required by top managers, middle managers, and supervisory managers.

The Manager's Changing Role

Managers may still have subordinates, but today's successful manager takes more of a team leader/coach approach. There are, of course, other ways to "slice and dice" what managers do. For example, managers don't just plan, organize, make decisions, communicate, motivate, and control. They wear a variety of hats, including the following:

- *Figurehead role.* Every manager spends some time performing ceremonial duties. For example, the president of a corporation might have to greet important business guests or clients or represent the corporation by attending dinners.

- *Leader role.* Every manager should be a leader, coaching, motivating, and encouraging employees.

- *Liaison role.* Managers spend a lot of time in contact with people in other departments both within the organization and externally. An example would be the sales manager liaising with the rooms division director.

- *Spokesperson role.* The manager is often the spokesperson for the organization. For example, a manager may host a college class visit to the property.

- *Negotiator role.* Managers spend a lot of time negotiating. For example, the head of a company along with qualified lawyers may negotiate with a union representative to establish wages and benefits for employees.

These roles, together with the management functions, encompass what managers do. Remember, managers need to be many things—often in quick succession—even to the point of wearing two or more hats at once.

Twenty-first-century managers face not only a more demanding and increasingly complex world, but also a more dynamic and interdependent one. The "global village" is a reality, and sociocultural traditions and values must be understood and diversity respected and encouraged by future managers. The two most important changes going on right now are the technological advances and the internationalization of hospitality and tourism. The extent to which you as a future **leader–manager** can master these events and functions will determine your future.

The manager's role is not only internal but also external. For instance, a manager must be responsive to market needs and income generation. Managers must continually strive to be innovative by realizing efficiencies in their respective areas of responsibility through process improvement—for example, by determining how to reduce long check-in lines at airports and hotels. Some companies use innovative and creative ways to streamline the check-in procedures to make the process a more worthwhile experience for the guests. Disney, for instance, uses the creative approach of sending Mickey and the gang to entertain the guests while they stand in line.

A General Manager's Survival Kit

Ali Kasiki is a top-level manager at the Peninsula Beverly Hills, California. He holds the title of managing director and is involved in creating and implementing broad and comprehensive changes that affect the entire organization. Ali offers his list:

- Know yourself, your own core competencies, and your values.
- Hire a seasoned management team.
- Build barriers of entry; that is, make yourself indispensable.
- Be very flexible.

You, Too, Are a Manager

Your classmates have just voted you to be the leader–manager of the summer study-abroad trip to France. None of you knows much about France or how to get there, what to do when you get there, and so on. Where would you start? (Resist the temptation to delegate the whole trip to a travel agent, please.)

You might start by thinking through what you need to do in terms of planning, organizing, deciding, communicating, motivating, and controlling. What sort of plans will you need? Among other things, you'll need to plan the dates your group is leaving and returning, the cities and towns you'll visit, the airline you'll take there and back, how the group will get around France, and where you'll stay when you're there. As you can imagine, plans like these are very important: You would not want to arrive at Orly Airport with a group of friends who are depending on you and not know what to do next.

Realizing how much work is involved—and that you cannot do it all and still maintain good grades——you get help. You divide up the work and create an organization by asking someone to check airline schedules and prices, another person to check hotel prices, and someone else the sights to see and the transportation needs. However, the job won't get done with the group members simply working by themselves. Each person requires guidance and coordination from you: The person making the airline bookings can't confirm the bookings unless she knows what city and airport the trip will originate in. Similarly, the person making the hotel arrangements can't make any firm bookings until he knows what cities are being visited. To improve communications, you could set up regular meetings with e-mail updates between meetings. Leadership and motivation could be a challenge because two of the group members do not get along well. So, ensuring that everyone stays focused and positive will be a challenge.

Of course, you'll have to make sure the whole project remains "in control." If something can go wrong, it often will, and that's certainly the case when groups of people are traveling together. Everything needs to be double-checked. In other words, managing is something managers do almost every day, often without even knowing it.

Source: Adapted from Gary Dessler, *A Framework for Management* (Upper Saddle River, NJ: Prentice Hall, 2002) 8.

- Get close to your guests and owners to define reality versus perception.
- Show leadership, from both the top and the bottom.
- Delegate. There is no way you can survive without delegation.
- Appeal to trends.
- Trust your instincts.
- Take risks and change the ground rules.
- Don't become overconfident.
- Look successful, or people will think you're not.
- Manage the future—it is the best thing you can do. Bring the future to the present.[5]

Distinction between Leadership and Management

Managing is the formal process in which organizational objectives are achieved through the efforts of subordinates. Leading is the process by which a person with vision is able to influence the behavior of others in some desired way. Although managers have power by virtue of the positions they hold, organizations seek managers who are leaders by virtue of their personalities, their experience, and so on. The differences between management and leadership can be illustrated as follows:

Managers
- Working in the system
- React
- Control risks
- Enforce organizational rules
- Seek and then follow direction
- Control people by pushing them in the right direction
- Coordinate effort

Leaders
- Working on the system
- Create opportunities
- Seek opportunities
- Change organizational rules
- Provide a vision to believe in and strategic alignment
- Motivate people by satisfying basic human needs
- Inspire achievement and energize people[6]

▶ Check Your Knowledge

1. What is management and what are the three management skill areas?
2. Explain levels of management.
3. Describe the key management functions.
4. What is the distinction between leadership and management?

Ethics

Ethics is a set of moral principles and values that people use to answer questions about right and wrong. Because ethics is also about our personal value system, there are people with value systems different from ours. Where did the value system originate? What happens if one value system is different from another? Fortunately, certain universal guiding principles are agreed on by virtually all religions, cultures, and societies. The foundation of all principles is that all people's rights are important and should not be violated. This belief is central to civilized societies; without it, chaos would reign.

Today, people have few moral absolutes; they decide situationally whether it is acceptable to steal, lie, or drink and drive. They seem to think that whatever is right is what works best for the individual. In a country blessed with so many diverse cultures, you might think it is impossible to identify common standards of ethical behavior. However, among sources from many different times and places, such as the Bible, Aristotle's *Ethics*, William Shakespeare's *King Lear*, the Koran, and the *Analects* of Confucius, you'll find the following basic moral values: integrity, respect for human life, self-control, honesty, and courage. Cruelty is wrong. All the world's major religions support a version of the Golden Rule: Do unto others as you would have them do to you.[7]

In the foreword to *Ethics in Hospitality Management*, edited by Stephen S. J. Hall,[8] Dean Emeritus of Cornell University, Robert A. Beck poses this question: "Is overbooking hotel rooms and airline seats ethical? How does one compare the legal responsibilities of the innkeeper and the airline manager to the moral obligation?" He also asks, What is a fair or reasonable wage? A fair or reasonable return on investment? Is it fair or ethical to underpay employees for the benefit of investors?

English Common Law, on which American law is based, left such decisions to the "reasonable man." A judge would ask the jury, "Was this the act of a reasonable man?" Interestingly, what is considered ethical in one country may not be in another. For instance, in some countries it is considered normal to bargain for room rates; in others, bargaining would be considered bad form.

Ethics and morals have become an integral part of hospitality decisions, from employment (equal opportunity and affirmative action) to truth in menus. Many corporations and businesses have developed a code of ethics that all employees use to make decisions. This became necessary because too many managers were making decisions without regard for the impact of such decisions on others.

Stephen Hall is one of the pioneers of ethics in hospitality; he has developed a code of ethics for the hospitality and tourism industry:

1. We acknowledge ethics and morality as inseparable elements of doing business and will test every decision against the highest standards of honesty, legality, fairness, impunity, and conscience.

2. We will conduct ourselves personally and collectively at all times so as to bring credit to the hospitality and tourism industry.

3. We will concentrate our time, energy, and resources on the improvement of our own products and services and we will not denigrate our competition in the pursuit of our success.

4. We will treat all guests equally regardless of race, religion, nationality, creed, or sex.

5. We will deliver all standards of service and product with total consistency to every guest.

6. We will provide a totally safe and sanitary environment at all times for every guest and employee.

7. We will strive constantly, in words, actions, and deeds, to develop and maintain the highest level of trust, honesty, and understanding among guests, clients, employees, employers, and the public at large.

8. We will provide every employee at every level all the knowledge, training, equipment, and motivation required to perform his or her tasks according to our published standards.

9. We will guarantee that every employee at every level will have the same opportunity to perform, advance, and be evaluated against the same standard as all employees engaged in the same or similar tasks.

10. We will actively and consciously work to protect and preserve our natural environment and natural resources in all that we do.

11. We will seek a fair and honest profit, no more, no less.[9]

As you can see, it is vitally important for future hospitality and tourism professionals to abide by this code. Here are some ethical dilemmas in hospitality. What do you think about them?

Ethical Dilemmas in Hospitality

Previously, certain actions may not have been considered ethical, but management often looked the other way. A few scenarios follow that are not seen as ethical today and are against most companies' ethical policies.

1. As catering manager of a large banquet operation, the flowers for the hotel are booked through your office. The account is worth $15,000 per month. The florist offers you a 10 percent kickback. Given that your colleague at a sister hotel in the same company receives a good bonus and you do not,

despite having a better financial result, do you accept the kickback? If so, whom do you share it with?

2. As purchasing agent for a major hospitality organization, you are responsible for purchasing $5 million worth of perishable and nonperishable items. To get your business, a supplier, whose quality and price are similar to others, offers you a new automobile. Do you accept?

3. An order has come from the corporate office that guests from a certain part of the world may only be accepted if the reservation is taken from the embassy of the countries. One Sunday afternoon, you are duty manager and several limos with people from "that part of the world" request rooms for several weeks. You decline, even though there are available rooms. They even offer you a personal envelope, which they say contains $1,000. How do you feel about declining their request?

Trends in Leadership and Management

- Leading a more diverse group of associates.
- Many entry-level employees do not have basic job skills.
- An increasing need for training.
- The need to create leaders out of line managers.
- Managing sales revenue all the way to the bottom line.
- Establishing independent business units to make their own profit, or subcontracting out that department.
- Instead of keeping a person on payroll for a function that is only needed occasionally, outsourcing that service to specialists.
- Cutting down on full-time employees and hiring more part-time employees to avoid paying benefits.
- An increasing challenge to keep up with technological advances and their benefits.
- Social and environmental issues continuing to increase in importance.
- A greater emphasis placed on ethics.

CASE STUDY

Performance Standards

Charles and Nancy both apply for the assistant front office manager position at a 300-room upscale hotel. Charles has worked for a total of eight years in three different hotels and has been with this hotel for three months as a front office associate. Initially, he had a lot of enthusiasm. Lately, however, he has been dressing a bit sloppily and his figures, cash, and reports have been inaccurate. In addition, he is occasionally "rattled" by demanding guests.

Nancy recently graduated from college, with honors, with a degree in hospitality management. While attending college, she worked part-time as a front desk associate at a budget motel. Nancy does not have a lot of experience working in a hotel or in customer service in general, but she is quite knowledgeable as a result of her studies and is eager to begin her career.

It appears that Charles would have been considered a prime candidate for the office manager position because of his extensive experience in other hotels and his knowledge of the hotel's culture. In view of his recent performance, however, the rooms division manager will need to sit down with Charles to review his future career development track.

Discussion Questions

1. What are the qualifications for the job that should be considered for both applicants?
2. How should the discussion between the rooms division manager and Charles be handled? Make specific recommendations for the rooms division manager.
3. Who would be the better person for the job? Why?

CASE STUDY

Reluctant to Change

You have just been appointed assistant manager at an old, established, but busy, New York restaurant. Your employees respond to your suggested changes with, "We have always done it this way." The employees really do not know any other way of doing things.

Discussion Question

1. How should you handle this situation?

Summary

1. Leadership is defined as the process by which a person is able to influence the activities and outcomes of others in a desired way.
2. Contemporary leadership includes transactional and transformational types of leadership.
3. Increased demands placed on hospitality leaders include ownership, corporate, regulatory, employee, environmental, and social interests. Leaders must balance results and relationships.
4. Managing is the process of coordinating work activities so that they are completed efficiently and effectively with and through other people.
5. Leaders, according to Drucker, realize four things and behave in much the same way.
   a. A leader is someone who has followers— some people are thinkers, and some are prophets.
   b. An effective leader is not someone who is loved or admired, but rather someone whose followers do the right things. Popularity is not leadership; results are.
   c. Leaders are highly visible. Leaders set examples.
   d. Leadership is not about rank, privileges, titles, or money. It is about responsibility.
6. There are six key management functions: planning, organizing, decision making, communicating, motivating, and controlling. However, in addition to these functions, managers occasionally have to fill roles such as figurehead, leader, spokesperson, or negotiator.
7. The difference between management and leadership is that the former is the formal process in which organization objectives are achieved through the efforts of subordinates, and the latter is the process by which a person with vision is able to influence the behavior of others in some desired way.

Key Words and Concepts

communication
controlling
decision making
effectiveness
efficiency
ethics
front-line managers
human resources and motivating
leader–manager

leadership
management
managing
middle managers
organizing
planning
top managers
transactional leadership
transformational leadership

Review Questions

1. From the DVD, what is the most fun thing that John Saputo has done in a leadership capacity?
2. What kind of leader–manager will you be?
3. Give examples of the management functions as they apply to the hospitality industry.

4. Discuss the changing role of managers.
5. Define leadership and name the essential qualities of a good leader.
6. Distinguish between transactional and transformational leadership.

Internet Exercises

1. Organization: **WetFeet.com**
   Web site: www.wetfeet.com
   Summary: WetFeet.com is an organization dedicated to helping you make smarter career decisions. WetFeet.com provides inside insight on jobs and careers for both job seekers and recruiters. By all means, take the time to check this one out!
   Click the "Careers" icon and scroll down to "General Management." Answer the following questions.

   (a) What are the requirements for becoming a GM, and what tips does WetFeet.com have to offer?
   (b) The "Career Overview" section illustrates several attributes that managers have in common. In groups, list these attributes and discuss their significance.

2. Organization: **American Management Association**
   Web site: www.amanett.org
   Summary: The American Management Association (AMA), a practitioner-based organization, offers a wide range of management development programs for managers and organizations.
   Find the section titled "AMA Research." Choose two current reports. Read through these and make a bullet list of the key information. Then, write a description of how this information might affect the way a hospitality manager plans, organizes, makes decisions, communicates, motivates, and controls.

Apply Your Knowledge

Your resort has management vacancies for the following positions: executive chef, executive housekeeper, and front office manager. List the traits and characteristics that you consider essential and desirable for these positions.

Suggested Activity

Think of someone you admire as a leader. Make a list of the qualities that make him or her a good leader.

Endnotes

1. For a more detailed review of the many leadership theories, consult one of the many texts on the topic.
2. Jay R. Schrock, presentation to University of South Florida students and faculty, May 2, 2005.
3. This draws on Peter F. Drucker, Foreword, in *The Leader of the Future,* ed. F. Hesselbein et al. (San Francisco: Josey-Bass, 1996), xii–xiii.
4. Drucker, Foreword, ix.
5. Personal correspondence with Ali Kasiki. August 4, 2005.
6. Vadim Kotelnikov, Ten3 Business e-Coach, version 2005a, www.1000ventures.com.
7. www.religioustolerance.org. nettme.htm
8. Stephen S. Hall, ed., *Ethics in Hospitality Management: A Book of Readings* (East Lansing, MI: Educational Institute, American Hotel & Lodging Association, 1992), 75.
9. Hall, *Ethics in Hospitality Management,* 23.

Appendix 2
Spelling Confusing Words

A president of the United States once said, "Damn a man who can't spell a word but one way." Nevertheless, college professors tend to expect one official spelling for a word. Unfortunately, no "golden rules" of spelling yield perfect results. There are a few spelling rules, but none is without exception. The following four rules may help you get through some rough spots.

RULE 1 Use *i* before *e* except after *c*.

believe	ceiling	receipt
grief	conceited	priest
cashier	yield	piece

Exceptions: height, either, leisure, efficient

RULE 2 Drop the final *e* when adding a suffix that begins with a vowel.

hope + ing = hoping

believe + ing = believing

nice + est = nicest

Keep the final *e* when adding a suffix that begins with a consonant.

use + ful = useful

retire + ment = retirement

lone + some = lonesome

RULE 3 When a word ends in a consonant plus *y*, change the *y* to *i* to add a suffix.

lazy + ness = laziness

penny + less = penniless

marry + age = marriage

RULE 4 Double the final consonant when all of the following apply.

a. The word is one syllable or is accented on the last syllable.
b. The word ends in a consonant preceded by a vowel.
c. The suffix begins with a vowel.

hop + ing = hopping

skip + ing = skipping

repel + ent = repellent

Appendix 3

Word Parts: Prefixes, Roots, and Suffixes

WORD PART	MEANING	EXAMPLE
Prefixes		
a-, an-	without, not	atypical, anarchy
ab-	away, from	absent, abnormal
ad-	toward	advance, administer
ambi-, amphi-	both, around	ambiguous, amphibious
anna-	year	annual
anti-, contra-, ob-	against	antisocial, contradict
bene-, eu-	well, good	benefactor, eulogy
bi-, du-, di-	two or twice	bicycle, duet, dichotomy
cata-, cath-	down, downward	catacombs
cent-, hecto-	hundred	centipede
con-, com-, syn-	with, together	congregate, synthesis
de-	down, from	depose, detract
dec-, deca-	ten	decade
demi-, hemi-, semi-	half	hemisphere, semicircle
dia-	through	diameter, diagram
dis-, un-	not, opposite of	dislike, unnatural
dys-	ill, hard	dystrophy
ex-	out, from	exhale, expel
extra-	beyond, outside	extralegal
hyper-	above, excessive	hyperactive
hypo-	under	hypodermic
il-, im, in-	not	illogical, impossible
in-	in, into	inside, insert, invade
infra-	lower	infrared
inter-	between	intercede, interrupt
intra-	within	intramural
juxta-	next to	juxtaposition
mal-, mis-	wrong, ill	malformed, mislead
mill-	thousand	milligram
nove-, non-	nine	novena, nonagon
oct-, octo-	eight	octopus
omni-, pan-	all	omnipotent, pantheist
per-	through	perennial, pervade
peri-, circum-	around	perimeter, circumvent
poly-, multi-	many	polygamy, multiply
post-	after	postscript
pre-, ante-	before	prepared, antebellum
pro-	before, for	promoter
proto-	first	prototype
quad-, quatra-, tetra-	four	quadrilateral, tetrad
quint-, penta-	five	quintuplet, pentagon

WORD PART	MEANING	EXAMPLE
re-	back, again	review, reply
retro-	backward	retrogress, retrospect
sequ-	follow	sequence
sex-, hexa-	six	sextet, hexagon
sub-	under	submarine, subway
super-	above, over	supervise
temp-, tempo-, chrono-	time	tempo, chronological
trans-	across	translate, transcontinental
tri-	three	triple, triangle
uni-, mono-	one	unicorn, monocle
vice-	in place of	viceroy

Roots

alter, hap	to change	alteration, mishap
ama, philo	to love	amiable, philosophy
anima	breath, spirit	animate
aqua	water	aquarium, aqualung
aster, astro	star	disaster, astronomy
aud	to hear	audible, auditory
auto, ego	self	autonomy, egotist
bio	life	biology
cap	head	caption, capitulate
cap, capt	to take	capture
card, cor, cord	heart	cardiac, core, cordial
cosmo	order, universe	cosmonaut
cresc	to grow, increase	crescendo
cryp	secret, hidden	cryptogram
dent	teeth	dental
derma	skin	dermatologist
duc, duct	to lead	reduce, conduct
equ, iso	equal	equivocal, isometric
err, errat	to wander	erratic
ethno	race, tribe	ethnic
fac, fact	to do, make	manufacture
fract	to break	fracture
frater	brother	fraternity
gene	race, kind, sex	genetics, gender
grad, gres	to go, take steps	graduation, digress
gyn	woman	gynecologist
hab, habi	to have, hold	inhabit, habitual
helio, photo	sun, light	heliotrope, photograph
homo	man	homo sapiens
lic, list, liqu	to leave behind	derelict, relinquish
lith	stone	monolith
loc	place	location, local
log	speech, science	logic, dialogue
loquor	to speak	loquacious, colloquial
lum	light	illuminate
macro	large	macrocosm
manu	hand	manual, manuscript
mater	mother	maternity
med	middle	mediate
meter	to measure	barometer

WORD PART	MEANING	EXAMPLE
micro	small	microscope
miss, mit	to send, let go	admit, permission
morph	form	morphology
mort	to die	immortalize
mut, mutat	to change	mutation
nat	to be born	natal, native
neg, negat	to say no, deny	negative, renege
nym, nomen	name	synonym, nomenclature
ocul	eye	oculist, monocle
ortho	right, straight	orthodox, orthodontist
osteo	bone	osteopath
pater	father	paternal
path	disease, feeling	pathology, antipathy
phag	to eat	esophagus, phagocyte
phobia	fear	claustrophobia
phon, phono	sound	symphony, phonics
plic	to fold	duplicate, implicate
pneuma	wind, air	pneumatic
pod, ped	foot	tripod, pedestrian
pon, pos	to place	depose, position
port	to carry	porter, portable
pseudo	false	pseudonym
psych	mind	psychology
pyr	fire	pyromaniac
quir	to ask	inquire, acquire
rog	to question	interrogate
scrib, graph	to write	prescribe, autograph
sect, seg	to cut	dissect, segment
sol	alone	solitude
soma	body	somatology, psychosomatic
somnia	sleep	insomnia
soph	wise	sophomore, philosophy
soror	sister	sorority
spect	to look at	inspect, spectacle
spir	to breathe	inspiration, conspire
tact, tang	to touch	tactile, tangible
tele	distant	telephone
ten, tent	to hold	tenant, intent
tend, tens	to stretch	extend, extension
the, theo	god	atheism, theology
therma	heat	thermometer
tort	twist	torture, extort
ven, vent	to go, arrive	convention, advent
verbum	word	verbosity, verbal

Suffixes

-able, -ible	capable of	durable, visible
-acy, -ance, -ency, -ity	quality or state of	privacy, competence, acidity
-age	act of, state of	breakage
-al	pertaining to	rental
-ana	saying, writing	Americana
-ant	quality of, one who	reliant, servant
-ard, -art	person who	wizard, braggart

WORD PART	MEANING	EXAMPLE
-arium, -orium	place for	auditorium
-ate	cause to be	activate
-ation	action, state of	creation, condition
-chrome	color	verichrome
-cide	killing	homicide
-er, -or	person who, thing which	generator
-esque	like in manner	picturesque
-fic	making, causing	scientific
-form	in the shape of	cuneiform
-ful, -ose, -ous	full of	careful, verbose
-fy, -ify, -ize	to make, cause to be	fortify, magnify, modify
-hood, -osis	condition or state of	childhood, hypnosis
-ics	art, science	mathematics
-ism	quality or doctrine of	conservatism
-itis	inflammation of	appendicitis
-ive	quality of, that which	creative
-latry	worship of	idolatry
-less	without	homeless
-oid	in the form of	tabloid
-tude	quality or degree of	solitude
-ward	in a direction	backward
-wise	way, position	clockwise

Appendix 4

ESL: Making Sense of Figurative Language and Idioms

- What is ESL?
- What is figurative language?
- What are common English idioms?

What Is ESL?

How many languages can you speak? Are you a native English speaker who has learned Spanish, or are you a native Farsi speaker who has learned English? If you have acquired skill in a second or third language, you know it takes many years and plenty of patience to master the intricacies of a language. Not only do you learn new words, but you must also learn new grammatical constructions. For example, the articles habitually used in English—*a, an,* and *the*—do not appear in Russian, Chinese, Japanese, Thai, or Farsi. In Spanish and Arabic, personal pronouns restate the subject, as in *My sister she goes to college.* In Spanish, Greek, French, Vietnamese, and Portuguese, "to" words are used rather than "ing" words, as in *I enjoy to play soccer.* These complexities, which are innately understood by native speakers, make direct translation difficult. The English language has many unusual phrases and grammatical constructions that defy direct translation.

To assist students with these complexities, most colleges offer courses in ESL (English as a Second Language) or ESOL (English for Speakers of Other Languages) designed to teach language skills to non-native speakers of English. If you are an ESL or ESOL student, you may have been recruited through an international exchange program with another college, you may be a newly arrived immigrant, or you may be a citizen with a bilingual background. You bring a multicultural perspective to classroom discussions and campus life that will broaden the insights of others. Not only are some of your holidays different from those of others, but your sense of family life, work, and responsibility may also be different. Share your thoughts and ideas with native English speakers as they share the irregularities of the language with you.

What Is Figurative Language?

One aspect of the English language that defies direct translation and confuses non-native speakers, and sometimes even native speakers, is **figurative language**. This is the manipulation of the language to create images, add interest, and draw comparisons by using figures of speech (see Chapter 10, "Inference"). The two most commonly used, *simile* and *metaphor*, are defined as follows:

Simile: a stated comparison using *like* or *as* (*example*: The baby swims like a duck.)

Metaphor: an implied comparison (*example*: The baby is a duck in water.)

Many figurative expressions have become commonplace in the English language. In the previous metaphor, the *baby* is not actually a *baby duck,* but the meaning is that *the baby swims very well.* However, neither direct translation nor a dictionary will unlock that meaning. When you encounter comparisons that seem out of the ordinary or ill chosen, ask yourself whether a figure of speech is being used, and look within the sentence for clues to help you guess the meaning.

The following practice exercises contain figurative language. Read each dialogue passage for meaning, and then use the context clues to match the number of the boldfaced figure of speech with the letter of the appropriate definition. To narrow your choices, the answers to 1–5 are listed within a–e, and the answers to 6–10 are listed within f–j.

practice 1

Maria: I am not going to be the one to stand in line for concert tickets this time. It is (1) **a pain in the neck**. Last time Fran left me (2) **holding the bag** on a $40 ticket for about a month.

Lynne: You did (3) **bend over backward** to organize the last outing. I would have (4) **jumped down Fran's throat** when she said she didn't have the cash to pay you. There is no reason (5) **to beat around the bush** with someone who doesn't pay promptly. Some people will (6) **walk all over you** if you let them.

Maria: I (7) **broke my neck** to get in line early. Those tickets were (8) **selling like hotcakes**. I think they (9) **jacked up** the price because they knew the demand would be high.

Lynne: I had to (10) **bite my tongue** not to say something to Fran about your efforts and her lack of gratitude.

_____ 1. a pain in the neck   a. owed money

_____ 2. holding the bag   b. avoid a clear answer

_____ 3. bend over backward   c. criticized angrily

_____ 4. jumped down Fran's throat   d. bothersome

_____ 5. to beat around the bush   e. make a great effort

_____ 6. walk all over you   f. being bought eagerly

_____ 7. broke my neck   g. raised

_____ 8. selling like hotcakes   h. keep from speaking

_____ 9. jacked up   i. take advantage of you

_____ 10. bite my tongue   j. tried hard

exercise 2

Ron: I've got (1) **to take my hat off to** the group that organized the charity drive for the children's hospital.

Eric: They started out with (2) **two strikes against them** because most people had just made a contribution to the American Red Cross drive.

Ron: The president of the organization is a real (3) **go-getter**. He tried to educate people before asking for a contribution.

Eric: Until he outlined the situation in the Friday meeting, I did not know the hospital was (4) **in a jam**. Purchasing equipment for the cancer unit had put them (5) **in the red**.

Ron: When the 15-year-old boy spoke at the meeting, I was ready to (6) **open my wallet**. He said he had come through the cancer treatment and (7) **passed with flying colors**.

Eric: I gave $5 and was happy to know that my money would help a good cause. Not all charitable solicitations are (8) **on the level**. I like to (9) **double-check** to make sure that the charity is not a (10) **fly-by-night** operation. Now I'm thinking about doing some volunteer work at the hospital.

_____ 1. to take my hat off to		a. in trouble
_____ 2. two strikes against them		b. losing money
_____ 3. go-getter		c. with little chance of success
_____ 4. in a jam		d. to admire
_____ 5. in the red		e. ambitious worker
_____ 6. open my wallet		f. investigate thoroughly
_____ 7. passed with flying colors		g. give money
_____ 8. on the level		h. untrustworthy
_____ 9. double-check		i. honest
_____ 10. fly-by-night		j. succeeded

practice 3

Ross: I heard (1) **through the grapevine** that you had a (2) **fender bender** and put a dent in your car.

Howard: Ross, please don't (3) **breathe a word** about that. My parents will not be happy. I was really (4) **out to lunch** at the time and have been (5) **kicking myself** for not being more alert. I want to keep it (6) **hush-hush** for a while.

Ross: Do you have a plan for getting it fixed, or should we (7) **put our heads together** to create one?

Howard: I am waiting for final grades to come out. If I have all A's, I will then (8) **put my cards on the table** with them.

Ross: Man, that is really (9) **using your noodle**.

Howard: If that doesn't work, I'll be (10) **back to the drawing board** and could use your help.

_____ 1. through the grapevine		a. regretting
_____ 2. fender bender		b. inattentive
_____ 3. breathe a word		c. by gossip from other people
_____ 4. out to lunch		d. tell, talk

_____ 5. kicking myself   e. minor accident

_____ 6. hush-hush   f. thinking

_____ 7. put our heads together   g. ready to start over

_____ 8. put my cards on the table   h. confer

_____ 9. using your noodle   i. secret

_____ 10. back to the drawing board   j. confess all

What Are Common English Idioms?

An idiom is an expression with a special meaning that cannot be understood by directly translating each individual word in the idiom. Because of years of exposure, the meaning is usually understood by native speakers, but it is confusing to those who are learning English as a second language.

Idioms are more common in spoken and informal language than in formal writing. In fact, most idiomatic expressions can usually be replaced by a single formal word. To add to the confusion, some idioms have dual meanings, and many idioms are grammatically irregular.

Reader's _Tip_ Categorizing Idioms

Idioms are sometimes categorized into the following groups:

- Word families: grouping around a similar individual word

  Down as in _step down, take down, pipe down, narrow down, nail down, run down, tear down, knock down, let down, die down, cut down_

- Verb + Preposition: action word plus a connecting word

  Hammer away means _persist_; _stand for_ means _represent_; and _roll back_ means _reduce_.

- Preposition + Noun: connecting word plus the name of a person, place, or thing

  On foot means _walking_; _by heart_ means _memorized_; and _off guard_ means _surprised_.

- Verb + Adjective: action word plus a, descriptive word

  Think, twice means _consider carefully_; _hang loose_ means _be calm_; and _play fair_ means _deal equally_.

- Pairs of Nouns: two words naming a person, place, or thing

  Flesh and blood means _kin_; _part and parcel_ means _total_; and _pins and needles_ means nervous.

- Pairs of Adjectives: two descriptive words

  Cut and dried means _obvious_; _fair and square_ means _honest_; _short and sweet_ means _brief_.

EXAMPLE What does the idiomatic expression *go over* mean in the following sentences?

(a) How did my speech *go over*?

(b) I want to *go over* the exam paper with the professor.

EXPLANATION In both sentences, the use of the idiom is informal. A more formal version of each would be as follows:

(a) *How was my speech* **received** *by the audience?*

(b) *I want to* **review** *the exam paper with the professor.*

Notice the grammatical irregularity in the first sentence. *Over* is not followed by a noun (name of a person, place, or thing), as a preposition (connecting words like *in*, *out*, and *at*) normally would be according to the rules of grammar; *over* becomes part of the verb phrase (words showing action). Thus the translation requires a change in wording, whereas the second use of the idiom is grammatically correct and can be directly translated by the single word *review*.

Nobody says that understanding idioms is easy. Books have been written about categorizing, recognizing, and translating thousands of them. To help clear up the confusion, some books group idioms according to families like root words, and others categorize them according to grammatical constructions. Either way, understanding idiomatic expressions depends more on using context clues to deduce meaning and familiarity with the informal, spoken language than with learning rules.

In the following practice exercises, idioms are grouped according to a common word. Use the context clues within each sentence to determine the meaning of the boldfaced idiom.

practice 4

up	down	around	across	over

1. Let's **nail down** a date for the next meeting before we leave today. _____

   _____

2. Close friends should **stand up for** what they know is right. _____

   _____

3. Children should not be allowed to **fool around** with matches. _____

4. With a quick example the student was able to **get across** the application of the theory. _____

5. They had a big **blowup** over who was responsible for the telephone bill.

   _____

6. Yesterday I **ran across** an old friend at the airport. _____

7. Because we are having a party, I asked a few friends in my psychology class to **drop over**. _____

8. The new grocery store is open **around the clock**. _____

9. If the class president would **step down** in March, we could get a more dynamic person for the position. _____

10. After winning the free concert tickets, she was **bubbling over** with excitement. _____

practice 5

| in | about | for | off | out |

1. Before school starts, we need to **see about** renting an apartment._____

2. The manager stayed late at work to **break in** the new employee. _____

3. If you need to shorten the paragraph, **leave out** the last sentence. _____

4. What do the school colors **stand for**? _____

5. Although the designer's name was displayed, the purse was actually a cheap **knockoff**. _____

6. As soon as class is over, we are going to **take off** for a weekend at the beach. _____

7. Because I have a car this semester, **getting about** is much easier. _____

8. This latest demand **calls for** immediate action from our coalition. _____

9. Let's all **chip in** to buy our professor a gift. _____

10. When cleaning, you do not want to **throw out** something that you may need later. _____

practice 6

free and easy	part and parcel	give-and-take	null and void
touch and go	spick-and-span	day in and day out	
little by little	high and low	sooner or later	

1. If you continue to drive with your gas gauge on empty, **sooner or later** you will be stuck on the side of the road. _____

2. By decreasing the medication **little by little**, the body can adjust without a painful reaction. _____

3. Overcooked food and slow service are complaints the restaurant managers hear **day in and day out**. _____

4. The peace negotiations were **touch and go** until the rebels accepted the compromise. _____

5. When I eat in a restaurant, I am more confident about cleanliness if the rest room is **spick-and-span**. _____

6. The opportunity to be with family is **part and parcel** of any holiday celebration. _____

7. After an appeal to a higher court, the previous decision to grant millions in damages could be declared **null and void**. _____

8. We will never decide which band to book for the party unless club members engage in a little **give-and-take**. _____

9. When she starts making her own money, she won't continue to spend with such a **free and easy** attitude. _____

10. After searching **high and low** for my keys, I found them under the computer. _____

Reader's *Tip* Internet Sites to Explore

Dave's ESL Café   www.eslcafe.com
Emphasis in this site is on English as it is spoken in the United States. It includes search tools for ESL books and a general discussion forum for ESL students and teachers.

EF Englishtown   www.englishtown.com
Englishtown is translated into eight languages and has learning games, bulletin boards where you can ask grammar and culture questions, a location for ESL/EFL teachers, a pen pal club, and a school where you can take classes online.

English Club   www.EnglishClub.com
This site has a 24-hour ESL Help Desk staffed with teachers to answer questions. Resources are available for both instructors and students in areas such as grammar, speech, and reading.

English Zone   www.English-Zone.com
This is a site for students who are learning English as a Second Language or studying English in general. It provides instruction and exercises on idioms, verbs, grammar, writing, spelling, vocabulary, and reading.

Tower of English   www.towerofenglish.com
Tower of English allows students to integrate lots of Web sources into their learning experience. It provides links to online ESL, exercises, search engines, reference tools, and news sources.

Appendix 5

The Reading Workshop: Additional Topics for Discussion and Journal Writing

Readers can find almost unlimited topics when talking or writing about books. The following list of topics offers some suggestions to supplement The Reading Workshops in *Breaking Through*, Ninth Edition.

The best book discussions, whether they are written or oral, go beyond the literal events and facts to consider broader concepts, truths, and elements of the author's style. Examples from the book are essential to illustrate your points, but interesting discussions do not dwell on a simple retelling of the story.

Topics to Consider: Fiction

(Several of these topics work for nonfiction books, too. This list includes some topics adapted from Richard Peck's "Ten Questions to Ask about a Novel," retrieved from www.booktalks.org.)

1. What do you think might happen next and what clues lead you to think so?
2. What do you think the author is like and why?
3. Other than the obvious, how would this story be different, or not, if the main character were of the opposite sex?
4. What confuses or especially intrigues you about the way the book is written?
5. If you were to make a movie or TV feature from this book, what characters and scenes would you leave out?
6. What would you have done differently if you were the author or the character?
7. What traits (not physical characteristics) does the main character have that are different from your own?
8. Would this story make a good TV series? Why or why not? Think about whether the central point of the book would be lost in separate TV episodes and whether the characters would still be interesting if they were placed in the first episode fully developed.
9. What makes the writing effective or ineffective?
10. How would you design a new cover that entices readers and also reflects the story?
11. If you have seen a movie based on the book, compare and contrast them. Which is better? Why?
12. What would you ask the author in an interview? Why? What responses would you expect? (Some authors and publishers offer readers this opportunity through online chats.)
13. Compare two or more books by the same author.

Topics to Consider: Nonfiction

Several of the previous topics for fiction books may be applied to nonfiction books; however, the following nonfiction topics will not work with fiction books.

1. How would the book be different if it had been written ten years earlier or later?
2. What illustrations would you add to the book? Why?

If you are writing in a Reading Workshop Journal, your professor may use some of the following items to evaluate your work:

- Amount of reading you have completed; time devoted to reading
- Did you avoid retelling the plot?
- Did you support points with examples from the book?
- Evidence of higher-level thinking

Glossary

abstract Short paragraph that summarizes an article, stating the author's premise, the subject or location of the project, and the conclusions.

acronym Abbreviation pronounced as a word and contrived to simplify a lengthy name and gain quick recognition for an organization or agency. For example, *UNICEF* is the abbreviation for the United Nations International Children's Emergency Fund.

addition pattern Pattern of paragraph organization that includes additional information.

analogies Comparisons that measure not only word knowledge, but also the ability to see relationships.

annotating Method of highlighting main ideas, significant supporting details, and key terms using a system of symbols and notations, so the markings indicate pertinent points to review for an exam.

applied level of reading This level calls for reaction, reflection, and critical thinking and involves analyzing, synthesizing, and evaluating.

argument Assertion or set of assertions that supports a conclusion and is intended to persuade.

bar graph Graph comprising a series of horizontal or vertical bars in which the length of each bar represents a particular amount. Often, time is represented by the vertical scale and quantity is measured by the horizontal scale.

bias Author's attitude, opinion, or position on a subject suggesting the facts have been slanted toward the author's personal beliefs. As commonly used, *bias* has a negative connotation suggesting narrow-mindedness and prejudice.

bibliography List of the sources consulted by the author of a scholarly article or paper.

biography The story of a person's life or a portion of it as told by another person.

bookmarking Save-the-site technique that allows the user to automatically return to the designated Web site with just one or two mouse clicks.

browser Software that searches to find the URL.

build meaning Good readers develop an understanding of what they read by using the following six thinking strategies: predict, picture, relate, monitor, correct, and annotate.

cause-and-effect pattern Pattern of paragraph organization showing one element as producing or causing a result or effect.

characters The main people in a story; they should be consistent in behavior and should grow and change according to their experiences.

citation In an index entry, a reference to an article that includes the title, author(s), name of the periodical, volume and page numbers, issue date, and descriptive notes or key search terms.

classification pattern Pattern of paragraph organization dividing items into groups or categories.

cliché Overworked phrase that should be avoided in formal writing (e.g., *working like a dog*).

climax In literature, the turning point near the end of a story in which conflict intensifies to a peak.

comparison pattern Pattern of paragraph organization listing similarities among items.

conclusion Logical deduction from both stated and unstated ideas, using the hints as well as the facts to interpret motives, actions, and outcomes. Conclusions are drawn on the basis of perceived evidence, and because perceptions differ, conclusions can vary from reader to reader.

conflict Clash of ideas, desires, or actions as incidents in a plot build progressively.

connotation Feeling or emotion associated with a word that goes beyond its dictionary definition.

context clues The words or phrases surrounding an unfamiliar word that help a reader identify its meaning.

contrast pattern Pattern of paragraph organization listing differences among items.

Cornell method System of notetaking in which you put questions on one side of a vertical line and notes that answer the questions on the other side.

creative thinking Ability to generate many possible solutions to a problem.

critical thinking Deliberating in a purposeful, organized manner in order to assess the value of old and new information.

critique Review that judges the merits of a work.

databases Computer-based indexes to assist research. A single article may be listed under several topics and may appear in several different indexes.

deductive reasoning Method by which one starts with a conclusion from a previous experience and then applies it to a new situation.

definition pattern Pattern of paragraph organization initially defining a concept and expanding with examples and restatements.

denotation Dictionary definition of a word.

description A form or pattern of writing that lists the characteristics of an object, event, person, place, etc.

details Specifics in a passage that develop, explain, and support the main idea, such as reasons, incidents, facts, examples, steps, and definitions.

diagram Outlined drawing or illustration of an object or a process.

directory path Particular location within the Web site's host computer.

domain name Name registered by the Web site owner.

domain type Category to which the site owner belongs.

download Method of saving or viewing an attachment by e-mail or importing programs from other sources.

editorials Subjective articles that express the opinion of a person or organization. A newspaper's editorial pages feature the views of its management and/or editors.

electronic mail (e-mail) Message sent from one person or organization to another person or group of people using the World Wide Web. These messages can be read, printed, saved, forwarded to someone else, and/or discarded.

encyclopedias Reference books that give comprehensive coverage of a subject. Many different encyclopedias, such as the *Encyclopedia of African American Religions*, *Encyclopedia of Earth Sciences*, and *The Cambridge Encyclopedia of Astronomy*, are available for specific topics.

essay Short work of nonfiction that discusses a specific topic. It does not develop as a story does, and it lacks characters and a plot.

etymology Study of word origins, involving the tracing of words back to their earliest recorded appearance.

fact Statement based on actual evidence or personal observation. It can be checked objectively with empirical data and proved to be either true or false.

fallacy Inference that appears to be reasonable at first, but closer inspection proves it to be unrelated, unreliable, or illogical. Tool used in constructing a weak argument.

feature stories In journalism, human interest stories that differ from typical news stories in their timeliness, style, and length.

fiction Writing invented by the imagination.

figurative language Words intentionally used in a different way—out of their literal context—so they take on new meaning.

file name Specific file within the host's directory.

fixations Stops lasting a fraction of a second that eyes make in order to read. On the average, 5 to 10 percent of reading time is spent on fixations.

generalization and example pattern Pattern of paragraph organization explaining a concept by illustrating with examples.

glossary A brief dictionary of terms relating to a particular field or topic; usually found at the back of a textbook.

graphic organizer A diagram that presents the major and minor details of a text passage in a visual form.

historical novel Story that blends both real and invented characters against a backdrop of documented historical events.

home page Main page for a Web site through which other areas of the site can be reached.

hypertext links In the World Wide Web, phrases that are often distinguished by a different color and are underlined. Clicking on them will not only move you from one page to another within the Web site, but can also send you to other related Web sites. The words chosen and underlined as the link describe the information likely to be found at that destination.

idioms Expressions that have taken on a generally accepted meaning over many years of use but do not make sense on a literal level. Idioms can be similes and metaphors. For example, *sleeping like a log* is both a simile and also an idiom, because it is an accepted and often used expression that is not literally true.

index Research tool that contains listings of articles organized by the topics within the articles. Most libraries have electronic periodical indexes.

inductive reasoning Method by which one gathers data and then, after considering all available material, formulates a conclusion.

inference Meaning that is not directly stated but suggested through clues that lead one to make assumptions and draw conclusions.

intent Reason or purpose for writing, which is usually to inform, persuade, or entertain.

Internet Electronic system of more than 25,000 worldwide computer networks. The Internet is the networked system that allows the World Wide Web to function.

interpretive level of reading At this level the reader makes assumptions and draws conclusions by considering the stated message, the implied meaning, the facts, and the author's attitude toward the subject.

inverted pyramid Format of news writing that begins with a summary paragraph and continues with paragraphs that explain details in a descending order of importance.

irony A figure of speech that states the opposite of the intended meaning.

issue An assertion or position statement in an argument. It is what the author is trying to convince you to believe or to do.

lateral thinking A way of thinking *around* a problem or even redefining the problem.

lead In a news story, the first paragraph that catches the reader's attention, establishes a focus, and summarizes the essential points of the story.

letter Formal communication appropriate for outside the company.

line graph Graph incorporating a continuous curve or *frequency distribution*. The horizontal scale (or *axis*) measures one aspect of the data (or *variable*), and the vertical scale measures another aspect, making it easy to see the relationship between the variables at a glance. As the data fluctuate, the line changes direction and, with extreme differences, becomes very jagged.

links See *hypertext links*.

LISTSERV Subscription service that sends out news, discussion, and research on particular topics by e-mail. You can post your own opinion as well as request assistance with specific questions related to the focus of the group.

literal level of reading At this level the reader might be able to answer detail questions asking *who, what, when,* and *where,* but not understand the overall purpose of the passage.

location or spatial order pattern Pattern of paragraph organization identifying the whereabouts of objects.

main idea Central message the author is trying to convey about the material.

map Visual representation of a geographic area.

mapping Visual system of condensing ideas or cognitive material through diagramming of major points and significant subpoints to show relationships and importance.

memo Short, informal business note usually for internal business purposes.

metacognition Knowledge of the processes involved in reading and the ability to regulate and direct them.

metaphor Direct comparison of two unlike things that does not use the word *like* or *as.* A metaphor and a simile can communicate the same idea and are differentiated only by the presence or absence of the word *like* or *as.*

minutes Official record of the business decisions for a meeting.

mnemonics Techniques to help the brain organize and recall information by incorporating the senses through pictures, sounds, rhythms, and other mental tricks to create extrasensory handles or hooks.

mood Overall feeling of the work, often conveyed by the author's emotional attitude toward the subject.

multiple meanings Some words are confusing because they have several different meanings. For example, the dictionary lists over thirty meanings for the word *run.*

newsgroup Topic-specific Web site where the user can review news on a particular subject and post and read one's own and others' opinions, discussions, and questions.

newsletter Mini-newspaper published within an organization to build group spirit.

news stories Newspaper articles that report the facts of events in descending order of importance.

nonfiction Writing that describes facts and reality.

notetaking Method of jotting down important ideas for future study from a lecture or text.

novel Extended fictional work that has all of the elements of a short story. Because of its length, a novel usually has more character development and more conflicts than a short story.

opinion Statement of personal feeling or a judgment. It reflects a belief or an interpretation rather than an accumulation of evidence, and it cannot be proved true or false.

outline Method of organizing major points and subordinating items of lesser importance with Roman numerals, letters, numbers, and indentations to show how one idea relates to another and how all aspects relate to the whole.

paragraph Group of sentences about a single topic that expresses a single main idea.

pattern of organization Organizational structure of a passage that can be a simple listing, time order, definition with examples, comparison-contrast, or cause and effect.

periodicals Publications that come out on a regular schedule, including popular magazines and scholarly journals.

personification Attributing human characteristics to nonhuman things.

pie chart Circle divided into wedge-shaped slices, with each slice representing a percentage of the whole. The complete pie or circle represents 100 percent.

plot Action in a story or a play. Sequence of incidents or events linked in a manner that suggests causes for the events.

point of view In writing, point of view is the author's attitude, opinion, or position on a subject. In literature, point of view describes who tells the story and is indicated most commonly by the third person (in which the author is the all-knowing observer). Alternatively, the first person (in which the main character tells the story by using the word *I*) or second person (in which the story is told through the use of the word *you*) may be used.

popular sources Newspapers and magazines aimed at the general public and written by professional journalists who are *reporters* rather than specialists in the field and thus focus on *who, what, where, when, why,* and *how*.

prefix Group of letters with a special meaning added to the beginning of a word.

premise Reasons provided in support of the thesis of an argument.

previewing First stage of reading: a method of reviewing material to guess what it is about, assess what you already know about the topic, decide what you will probably want to know after you read, and make a plan for reading.

previewing a textbook Examining the features and organization of a book before reading any of it in depth.

primary sources Public and private documents of a period, used by historians to research the times.

prior knowledge What is already known about a subject, which is the single best predictor of reading comprehension.

propaganda Information that is widely spread and that is intended to help or harm a person, group, movement, etc.

protocol Short for *hypertext transfer protocol (http)*, a type of language computers networked via the Internet use to communicate with each other.

purpose Reason or intent for writing, which is usually to inform, persuade, or entertain.

recalling Telling oneself what has been learned after reading, relating it to what is already known, and reacting to it to form an opinion.

reference bibliographies Book-length lists of research material related to a particular subject.

regression Rereading sentences or paragraphs because one's mind was wandering during the initial reading of the material.

root Stem or basic part of a word, derived primarily from Latin and Greek.

rubric A checklist by which students' work is graded.

scanning Process of searching for a single bit of information. Reader merely needs to pinpoint a specific detail, rather than comprehend the general meaning of the material.

schema Concept of a compartment similar to a computer chip in the brain that holds all that is known on a subject.

scholarly journals Regularly scheduled publications aimed at scholars, specialists, and students. They contain detailed research results written by specialists in the academic field of study and are frequently theoretical.

search engine Program that searches the Internet for information. Can be found at such Web sites as Google, Yahoo!, AltaVista, Excite, Go.com, or Lycos.

secondary sources Nonprimary sources, such as textbooks, that interpret or retell historical events.

server name Indicates the computer network over which the user travels to reach the desired location (in most cases, the World Wide Web).

setting Backdrop for a story and the playground for the characters. Setting may include the place, the time, and the culture.

short story Brief work of narrative fiction with a beginning, a middle, and an end that ranges from 500 to 15,000 words.

simile Comparison of two unlike things using the words *like* and *as* (e.g., "His words were like knives to my heart").

simple listing pattern Pattern of paragraph organization randomly listing items in a series.

situational irony Events occur contrary to what is expected, as if in a cruel twist of fate (e.g., Juliet awakens and finds that Romeo has killed himself because he thought she was dead).

skimming Technique of selectively reading for the main idea and quickly overviewing material. Involves skipping words, sentences, paragraphs, and even pages.

slant A bias or point of view.

subvocalization Inaudible voice in one's mind that reads.

suffix Group of letters with a special meaning added to the end of a word. Can alter the meaning of a word as well as the way the word can be used.

summary Brief, concise statement of the main idea of a piece of writing and its significant supporting details. The first sentence states the main idea or thesis, and subsequent sentences incorporate the significant details.

suspense As conflict builds in a plot, the reader's anxious concern about the characters' well-being.

symbolism Object, action, person, place, or idea that carries a condensed and recognizable meaning (e.g., an opened window might symbolize an opportunity for a new life).

table Organized listing of facts and figures in columns and rows to compare and classify information for quick and easy reference.

theme Heart, soul, or central insight of—or universal truth expressed by—a work. Message is never preached but revealed to the emotions, senses, and imagination through powerful shared experiences.

thesaurus A list of words and their synonyms.

thesis statement A sentence that states the main point; the topic sentence or main idea statement.

time order, sequence, or narration pattern Pattern of paragraph organization listing events in the order of occurrence.

tone Writer's attitude toward the subject or the audience. For example, an author's word choice may suggest humor, cutting remarks suggest sarcasm, and ironic remarks show the gap between the actual and the expected.

topic General rather than specific term that forms an umbrella under which the author can group the specific ideas or details in a passage.

topic sentence Sentence that condenses the thoughts and details of a passage into a general, all-inclusive statement of the author's message.

transitions Signal words that connect parts of sentences and lead readers to anticipate a continuation or a change in the writer's thoughts.

uniform resource locator (URL) On the Web, specific directions for finding your way to a specific site, just as an address and zip code are required to mail a letter. A URL is similar to an e-mail address, except that it routes the user to a source of information called a *Web page* or *Web site* rather than to the mailbox of an individual person.

verbal irony Use of words to express a meaning that is the opposite of what is literally said. In other words, it is saying one thing and suggesting another. If the intent is to ridicule, the irony can also be called *sarcasm*.

vertical thinking Straightforward and logical way of thinking that would typically result in a solution. It involves deeper exploration of the same idea for a problem solution (e.g., continuing to develop stronger poisons to kill insects).

vocalization moving one's lips as one reads.

Web directory Type of search engine that organizes hypertext links into categories like libraries organize books into categories.

Web pages Locations or "sites" of information provided by individual people, businesses, educational institutions, or other organizations on the Internet.

World Wide Web (WWW) Electronic information network that is similar to an enormous library, with Web sites like books and Web pages like the pages in the books.

Acknowledgments

Text Credits

Adams, James L. From *Conceptual Blockbusting* by James L. Adams. Copyright © 1974, 1976, 1979, 1986, 2001 by James L. Adams. Reprinted by permission of Da Capo Press, a member of Perseus Books Group.

Anzaldúa, Gloria. Selection of "How to Tame a Wild Tongue." From *Borderlands/La Frontera: The New Mestiza*. Copyright © 1987, 1999, 2007 by Gloria Anzaldúa. Reprinted by permission of Aunt Lute Books.

Armstrong, Gary and Philip Kotler. *Marketing: An Introduction*, 9th Edition. Upper Saddle River, NJ: Pearson Prentice-Hall, 2000.

Arrian. From *The Campaigns of Alexander* by Arrian, translated by Aubrey de Sélincourt, revised with an introduction and notes by J. R. Hamilton (Harmondsworth, England: Penguin Classics 1958, Revised edition 1971). Copyright © the Estate of Aubrey de Sélincourt, 1958. Introduction and Notes copyright © J. R. Hamilton, 1971. Reproduced by permission of Penguin Books Ltd.

Assael, Henry. *Consumer Behavior and Marketing Action*, 4th Edition. Boston: PWS-Kent, 1992.

Audesirk, Teresa et al. From *Biology: Life on Earth*, 6th Edition, by Audesirk/Audesirk/Byers. © 2002, 1999, 1996 Prentice-Hall, Inc. Reprinted by permission of Pearson Education, Inc., Upper Saddle River, NJ.

Bell, Arthur H. and Dayle M. Smith. *Interviewing for Success*, 1st Edition, © 2004. Adapted by permission of Pearson Education, Inc., Upper Saddle River, NJ.

Bittinger, Marvin L. and Judith A. Beecher. *Developmental Mathematics: College Mathematics and Introductory Algebra*, 7th Edition. Boston: Pearson Addison Wesley, 2008.

Burns, Edward McNall et al. *Western Civilizations*, 10th Edition. New York: W. W. Norton, 1984.

Cain, Herman. From Herman Cain, *CEO of Self: You're in Charge!* Irving, TX: Tapestry Press, pp. 7–13. Copyright © 2001 by Herman Cain. Reprinted by permission of the author.

Campbell, Neil. From *Biology*, 4th Edition, by Neil Campbell. Copyright © 1987, 1990, 1993, 1996 by The Benjamin/Cummings Publishing Company, Inc. Reprinted by permission of Pearson Education, Inc.

Chapman, Elwood N. and Sharon Lund O'Neil. From *Your Attitude Is Showing*, 9th Edition, by Chapman/O'Neil. © 1999. Adapted by permission of Pearson Education, Inc., Upper Saddle River, NJ.

Chapman, Elwood N. and Cliff Goodwin. *Supervisor's Survival Kit: Your First Step into Management*, 9th Edition. Upper Saddle River, NJ: Pearson Prentice Hall, 2002.

Chierici, Maurizio. "The Man from Hiroshima," *Granta*, #22, Autumn 1987.

Conlin, Joseph. *The American Past*, 5th Edition. Fort Worth, TX: Harcourt Brace, 1997.

Craig, Albert M., William A. Graham, Donald Kagan, Steven Ozment, and Frank M. Turner. *The Heritage of World Civilizations*, Combined Edition, 6th Edition. Pearson Prentice Hall, 2003.

DeVito, Joseph A. From *Human Communication*, 6th Edition, by Joseph A. DeVito. Copyright © 1994 by HarperCollins College Publishers. Reprinted by permission of Pearson Education, Inc.

DeVito, Joseph A. *Essentials of Human Communication*, 4th Edition. Boston: Allyn and Bacon, 2002.

DiBacco, Thomas V. From "Once Upon a September Day," *The Los Angeles Times*, September 28, 1983. Reprinted with the permission of Thomas V. DiBacco.

Donatelle, Rebecca J. From *Health: The Basics*, 5th Edition, by Rebecca J. Donatelle. Copyright © 2003 Pearson Education, Inc., publishing as Benjamin Cummings. Reprinted by permission.

Donatelle, Rebecca J. From *Health: The Basics*, 6th Edition, by Rebecca J. Donatelle. Copyright © 2005 Pearson Education, Inc., publishing as Benjamin Cummings. Reprinted by permission.

DuBrin, Andrew J. From Andrew J. DuBrin, *Human Relations: Interpersonal, Job-Oriented Skills*, 8th Edition, © 2004. Reprinted by permission of Pearson Education, Inc., Upper Saddle River, NJ.

Ebert, Ronald and Ricky Griffin. *Business Essentials*, 3rd Edition. Upper Saddle River, NJ: Prentice-Hall, 2000.

Fábrega, Marelisa. *5 Tips for Overcoming Failure*. © Marelisa Fábrega. Reprinted by permission of the author.

Fagin, James A. *Criminal Justice*, 2005 Update. Boston: Pearson Allyn and Bacon, 2005.

Feldman, Robert S. *Development Across the Life Span*, 4th Edition, © 2006. Adapted by permission of Pearson Education, Inc., Upper Saddle River, NJ.

Fobes, Richard. From *The Creative Problem Solver's Toolbox* by Richard Fobes. Copyright © 1993 by Richard Fobes. Reprinted by permission of Solutions Through Innovation.

Fritz, Susan, F. William Brown, Joyce Povlacs Lunde, and Elizabeth A. Banset. *Interpersonal Skills for Leadership*, 2nd Edition. Upper Saddle River, NJ: Prentice Hall, 2005.

Gardner, Martin. "Some Math Magic Tricks with Numbers," *Games Magazine*, May 1999. Reprinted by permission of Kappa Publishing Group, Inc.

Gardner, Mona. "The Dinner Party," *Saturday Review of Literature*, vol. 25, no. 5 (January 31, 1941).

Garraty, John and Mark Carnes. *The American Nation*, 10th Edition. New York: Longman, 2000.

Ginsberg, Benjamin, Theodore J. Lowi, and Margaret Weir. *We the People: An Introduction to American Politics*, 4th Edition. New York: W. W. Norton, 2003.

Gleick, James. "Life As Type A" from *Faster: The Acceleration of Just About Everything*. New York: Pantheon Books, 1999.

Gordon, Arthur. "The Alchemist's Secret" by Arthur Gordon. Copyright © 1952 by Arthur Gordon. Reprinted by permission.

Greenberg, Edward and Benjamin Page. From *The Struggle for Democracy*, 6th Edition, by Edward Greenberg and Benjamin Page. Copyright © 2003 by Addison-Wesley Educational Publishers, Inc. Reprinted by permission of Pearson Education, Inc.

Gregory, Paul. *Essentials of Economics*, 4th Edition. Reading, MA: Addison Wesley Longman, 1999.

Groff, David. "Taking the Test," *Wigwag*, June 19, 1990.

Hamblin, W. Kenneth and Eric H. Christiansen. *Earth's Dynamic Systems*, 9th Edition. Upper Saddle River, NJ: Prentice-Hall, 2001.

Harris, Fred R. *America's Democracy: The Ideal and the Reality*, 3rd Edition. Glenview, IL: Scott, Foresman, 1986.

Haviland, William A., Harald E. L. Prins, Dana Walrath, and Bunny McBride. *Cultural Anthropology: The Human Challenge*, 11th Edition. Belmont, CA: Thomson Wadsworth, 2005.

Henslin, James M. *Essentials of Sociology: A Down-to-Earth Approach*, 4th edition. Boston, MA: Pearson Allyn and Bacon, 2002.

Hoch, Edward D. (R. L. Stevens). "A Deal in Diamonds." Copyright © 1975 by R. L. Stevens. First published in *Ellery Queen's Mystery Magazine*. Reprinted by permission of Sternig & Byrne Literary Agency.

Ireland, Patricia. Quoted in Myra and David Sadker, *Failing at Fairness: How America's Schools Cheat Girls*. New York: Scribner's, 1994, p. 162.

Kassin, Saul. From *Psychology*, 2nd Edition, by Saul Kassin. Copyright © 1997. Reprinted by permission of Prentice-Hall, Upper Saddle River, NJ.

Kendler, Howard H. From Howard H. Kendler, *Basic Psychology*. Menlo Park: CA: Benjamin-Cummings, 1974. Reprinted by permission of Howard H. Kendler.

Kishlansky, Mark A., ed. *Sources of the West: Readings in Western Civilization*, 6th Edition. New York: Pearson Longman, 2006.

Kishlansky, Mark A., Patrick Geary, and Patricia O'Brien. *Civilization in the West*, 5th Edition. Addison-Wesley Educational Publishers, 2003.

Kishlansky, Mark A., Patrick Geary, and Patricia O'Brien. *A Brief History of Western Civilization: The Unfinished Legacy*, Volume II: Since 1555. New York: Pearson Longman, 2005.

Kosslyn, Stephen M. and Robin S. Rosenberg. *Psychology: The Brain, the Person, the World*, 2nd Edition. Boston, MA: Pearson Allyn and Bacon, 2004.

Kotler, Philip and Gary Armstrong. *Principles of Marketing*, 9th Edition. Upper Saddle River, NJ: Prentice-Hall, 2001.

Krauthammer, Charles. "Yes, Let's Pay for Organs," *Time*, May 17, 1999.

Kubey, Robert and Mihaly Csikszentmihalyi, "Television Addiction Is No Mere Metaphor," *Scientific American*, February 2002.

Lakein, Alan. From *How to Get Control of Your Time and Your Life* by Alan Lakein, copyright © 1973 by Alan Lakein. Used by permission of McKay, a division of Random House, Inc.

Lee, Li-Young. "The Gift" from *Rose*. Copyright © 1986 by Li-Young Lee. Reprinted with the permission of BOA Editions, Ltd., www.boaeditions.org.

Levin, Gerald. *Short Essays*, 7th Edition. Fort Worth, TX: Harcourt Brace College Publishers, 1995.

Lutgens, Frederick and Edward Tarbuck. From *The Atmosphere: An Introduction to Meteorology*, 7th Edition, by Lutgens/Tarbuck. © 1989. Reprinted by permission of Prentice-Hall, Inc., Upper Saddle River, NJ.

Macchiette, Barton and Abhijit Roy, eds. *Taking Sides: Clashing Views on Controversial Issues in Marketing*. Guilford, CT: McGraw-Hill/Dushkin, 2001.

Macionis, John J. From John J. Macionis, *Sociology*, 10th Edition, © 2005. Reprinted by permission of Pearson Education, Inc., Upper Saddle River, NJ.